LEARNING TO T[EACH] GEOGRAPHY IN THE SECONDARY SCHOOL

Praise for the first edition of *Learning to Teach Geography in the Secondary School*:

> 'This is a practical and visionary book, as well as being superbly optimistic. It has as much to offer the experienced teacher as the novice and could be used to reinvigorate geography departments everywhere. Practical activities and ideas are set within a carefully worked out, authoritative, conceptual framework.'
>
> *The Times Educational Supplement*

> 'This is a modern, powerful, relevant and comprehensive work that is likely to become a standard reference for many beginning teachers on geography initial teacher training courses in England and Wales.'
>
> *Educational Review*

Learning to Teach Geography in the Secondary School has become the widely recommended textbook for student and new teachers of geography. It helps them acquire a deeper understanding of the role, purpose and potential of geography within the secondary curriculum, and provides the practical skills needed to design, teach and evaluate stimulating and creative lessons.

This fully revised and updated second edition takes account of new legislation and important developments in geography education, including literacy, numeracy, citizenship and GIS. Brand new chapters in this edition provide essential guidance on fieldwork, and using ICT in the context of geography teaching and learning. Chapters on teaching strategies, learning styles and assessment place the learner at the centre stage, and direct advice and activities encourage successful practice.

Designed for use as a core textbook *Learning to Teach Geography in the Secondary School* is essential reading for all student teachers of geography who aspire to become effective, reflective teachers.

David Lambert is Professor of Geography Education at the Faculty of Culture and Pedagogy, Institute of Education, University of London and Chief Executive of the Geographical Association.

David Balderstone is Assistant Headteacher at Sharnbrook Upper School and Community College, Bedfordshire, and former lecturer in Geography Education at the Institute of Education, University of London.

Learning to Teach Subjects in the Secondary School Series
Series Editors: Susan Capel, Marilyn Leask and Tony Turner

Designed for all students learning to teach in secondary schools, and particularly those on school-based initial teacher training courses, the books in this series complement *Learning to Teach in the Secondary School* and its companion, *Starting to Teach in the Secondary School*. Each book in the series applies underpinning theory and addresses practical issues to support students in school and in the training institution in learning how to teach a particular subject.

Learning to Teach in the Secondary School, 5th edition
Edited by Susan Capel, Marilyn Leask and Tony Turner

Learning to Teach Art and Design in the Secondary School, 2nd edition
Edited by Nicholas Addison and Lesley Burgess

Learning to Teach Citizenship in the Secondary School
Edited by Liam Gearon

Learning to Teach Design and Technology in the Secondary School, 2nd edition
Edited by Gwyneth Owen-Jackson

Learning to Teach English in the Secondary School, 3rd edition
Edited by Jon Davison and Jane Dowson

Learning to Teach Geography in the Secondary School 2nd edition
David Lambert and David Balderstone

Learning to Teach History in the Secondary School, 3rd edition
Edited by Terry Haydn, James Arthur, Martin Hunt and Alison Stephen

Learning to Teach ICT in the Secondary School
Edited by Steve Kennewell, John Parkinson and Howard Tanner

Learning to Teach Mathematics in the Secondary School, 2nd edition
Edited by Sue Johnston-Wilder, Peter Johnston-Wilder, David Pimm and John Westwell

Learning to Teach Modern Foreign Languages in the Secondary School, 3rd edition
Norbert Pachler, Ann Barnes and Kit Field

Learning to Teach Music in the Secondary School, 2nd edition
Edited by Chris Philpott and Gary Spruce

Learning to Teach Physical Education in the Secondary School, 2nd edition
Edited by Susan Capel

Learning to Teach Religious Education in the Secondary School, 2nd edition
Edited by L. Philip Barnes, Andrew Wright and Ann-Marie Brandom

Learning to Teach Science in the Secondary School, 2nd edition
Edited by Jenny Frost and Tony Turner

Learning to Teach Using ICT in the Secondary School, 2nd edition
Edited by Marilyn Leask and Norbert Pachler

Starting to Teach in the Secondary School, 2nd edition
Edited by Susan Capel, Ruth Heilbronn, Marilyn Leask and Tony Turner

LEARNING TO TEACH GEOGRAPHY IN THE SECONDARY SCHOOL

A companion to school experience

2nd Edition

David Lambert and David Balderstone

Routledge
Taylor & Francis Group

LONDON AND NEW YORK

Second edition published 2010
by Routledge
2 Park Square, Milton Park, Abingdon, Oxon OX14 4RN

Simultaneously published in the USA and Canada
by Routledge
270 Madison Ave, New York, NY 10016

First published 2002 by RoutledgeFalmer
Reprinted 2002 (twice), 2003 (twice), 2004, 2005, 2006, 2007

Routledge is an imprint of the Taylor & Francis Group, an informa business

© 2010 David Lambert and David Balderstone

Typeset in Times New Roman by FiSH Books, Enfield
Printed and bound in Great Britain by TJ International Ltd., Padstow, Cornwall

British Library Cataloguing in Publication Data
A catalogue record for this book is available from the British Library

Library of Congress Cataloging in Publication Data
Balderstone, David.
Learning to teach geography in the secondary school : a companion to school experience /
    David Lambert and David Balderstone. – 2nd ed.
      p. cm. – (Learning to teach in the secondary school)
Includes bibliographical references and index.
1. Geography–Study and teaching (Secondary) I. Lambert, David. II. Title.
G73.L345 2009
910.71'2–dc22
                                                                    2009008743

ISBN10: 0–415–49909–7 (hbk)
ISBN10: 0–415–43786–5 (pbk)
ISBN10: 0–203–87168–5 (ebk)

ISBN13: 978–0–415–49909–5 (hbk)
ISBN13: 978–0–415–43786–8 (pbk)
ISBN13: 978–0–203–87168–3 (ebk)

CONTENTS

1 ROLE, PURPOSE AND PHILOSOPHY: SO WHY TEACH GEOGRAPHY?

■ advocating geography in your school ■ geography in the education system of England and Wales ■ the role of geography in education ■ the case for geography in the National Curriculum ■ the 'Queen of Sciences': daring to be a geograpy teacher ■ why subjects really matter ■ is geography a 'hard' subject?

2 PUPIL LEARNING: PLANNING FOR WHOLE CLASSES

■ pupils learn in different ways ■ intellectual development through geography ■ spatial cognition and graphicacy ■ language, literacy and learning in geography

3 PUPIL LEARNING: SUPPORTING PUPILS WITH SPECIAL EDUCATION NEEDS

■ meeting individual needs

4 TEACHING GEOGRAPHY

■ a matter of style and strategy ■ the craft of exposition ■ using questions in the classroom ■ collaborative strategies ■ using games and simulations ■ values education ■ problem-solving and decision-making strategies ■ teaching pupils to think

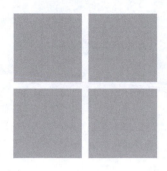

INTRODUCTION TO THE SERIES

Learning to Teach Geography in the Secondary School is one of a series of books entitled *Learning to Teach Subjects in the Secondary School* covering most subjects in the secondary school curriculum. The books in this series support and complement *Learning to Teach in the Secondary School: A Companion to School Experience*, 5th edition, (Capel, Leask and Turner, 2009), which addresses issues relevant to all secondary teachers. These books are designed for student teachers learning to teach on different types of initial teacher education courses and in different places. It is hoped that they are equally useful to tutors and mentors in their work with student teachers. In 2004, the second edition of a complementary book was published entitled *Starting to Teach in the Secondary School: A Companion for the Newly Qualified Teacher* (Capel, Heilbronn, Leask and Turner). This book is designed to support newly qualified teachers in their first post and covers aspects of teaching which are likely to be of concern in the first year of teaching.

The information in the subject books does not repeat that in *Learning to Teach*; rather, the content of that book is adapted and extended to address the needs of student teachers learning to teach a specific subject. In each of the subject books, therefore, reference is made to *Learning to Teach*, where appropriate. It is recommended that you have both books so that you can cross-reference when needed.

The positive feedback on *Learning to Teach*, particularly the way it has supported the learning of student teachers in their development into effective, reflective teachers, has encouraged us to retain the main features of that book in the subject series. Thus, the subject books are designed so that elements of appropriate theory introduce each element of the teaching and learning process. Recent research into teaching and learning is incorporated into the discussion. The material is interwoven with tasks designed to help you identify key features of the behaviour or issue and apply them to your practice.

Although the basic content of each subject book is shared, each book is designed to address the unique nature of each subject. Many different groups have an interest in geography education and so are interested in how to approach teaching geography and the contribution geography makes to the secondary school curriculum through its contents and methods of enquiry. In this book, for example, some of the controversies in education are addressed. Geography education has also developed new teaching approaches and these, too, are explored.

We hope that, whatever the type of initial teacher education course you are following and wherever you may be following that course, you find this book useful and supportive of your development into an effective, reflective teacher. Above all, we hope that you enjoy teaching geography.

Susan Capel, Marilyn Leask and Tony Turner
February 2009

ILLUSTRATIONS

FIGURES

TABLES

BOXES

ACTIVITIES

ACTIVITIES ■ ■ ■ ■

FOREWORD

Geography is a challenging subject. There are many reasons for this. Not least, it involves the study of multivariate people-environment interactions, which are by definition complex. Learning geography well is not an easy business.

It is therefore challenging for teachers of geography to find ways for young people to understand the subject matter without distorting or oversimplifying the actions of people and the character of places. Teaching geography well is not an easy business either.

The challenges facing geography teachers could be reduced to four broad areas:

1 What to teach – the curriculum changes and the discipline itself continues to evolve as society changes.
2 How to teach – the strategies and techniques that are available and appropriate to organise and maximise pupil learning, and these need careful selection.
3 How to judge success – the effectiveness of teaching and the level of pupils' achievements requires careful judgement, communication and interpretation.
4 The wider picture – individual success and professional development can only take place effectively in the context of teamworking, school policies and knowledge of the system at large.

These challenges relate very closely to the government's *Standards* for the award of Qualified Teacher Status. Student teachers need to develop a range of knowledge, understanding and skills under the four standards. This book takes up the challenge in a most comprehensive and direct way, offering a mix of idealism (e.g. stressing the importance of goals) and realism (e.g. giving practical advice on how to implement goals).

The authors are optimistic throughout. Geography, they seem to be suggesting, is able to challenge all young people in a way that can help them behave and operate more intelligently in the future. Learning to teach geography makes demands both on the intellect and on the emotional and practical capacities of those involved, and what the authors also seem to be saying is that once started, the process of learning to teach turns into a lifelong experience.

Professor Ashley Kent
former President of the Geographical Association (1996/7)
University of London Institute of Education

ACKNOWLEDGEMENTS

Acknowledgements are gratefully expressed for material from the following publications:

Bailey, P. and Fox, P. (eds) (1996) *Geography Teachers' Handbook,* Sheffield: The Geographical Association.

Bale, J. (1981) *The Location of Manufacturing Industry,* Harlow: Oliver and Boyd.

Bates, B. and Wolton, M. (1993) *Guidelines for Secondary Schools for Effective Differentiation in the Classroom,* Essex County Council Education Department.

Bell, D. (2005) *Teaching Geography* 30(1).

Boardman, D. (ed.) (1986) *Handbook for Geography Teachers,* Sheffield: The Geographical Association.

Butt, G. (1991) 'Have we got a video today?', *Teaching Geography* 16(2)

Butt, G., Lambert, D. and Telfer, S. (1995) *Assessment Works,* Sheffield: The Geographical Association.

Capel, S., Leask, M. and Turner, T. (1995) *Learning to Teach in the Secondary School: A Companion to School Experience,* Routledge.

Carpenter, B., Ashdown, R. and Bovair, K. (1996) *Enabling Access: Effective Teaching and Learning for Pupils with Learning Difficulties,* London: David Fulton.

Carter, R. (ed.) (1991) *Talking about Geography: The Work of Geography Teachers in the National Oracy Project,* Sheffield: The Geographical Association.

Corney, G. (1992) *Teaching Economic Understanding Through Geography,* Sheffield: The Geographical Association.

EXEL (1996) *Writing Frames,* Exeter University School of Education.

Fien, J. and Slater, F. (1981) 'Four Strategies for values education in Geography', Geographical Education 4 (1)

Fisher, T. (1998) *Developing as a Geography Teacher,* Cambridge: Chris Kington Publishing.

Hollingham, S. (1997) 'Using feature films in geography teaching', *Teaching Geography* 22(3)

Lambert, D. (1991) *Geography Assessment,* Cambridge: Cambridge University Press.

Lambert, D. (1996) 'Assessing pupils' attainment and supporting learning styles' in Kent, A. *et al.* (eds) *Geography in Education,* Cambridge: Cambridge University Press.

Leat, D. (1998) *Thinking Through Geography,* Cambridge: Chris Kington Publishing.

Leat, D. and Chandler, S. (1996) 'Using Concept Mapping in Geography Teaching', *Teaching Geography*

Lunzer, E. and Gardner, K. (1979) *The Effective Use of Reading project.*

Marsden, W. E. (1995) *Geography 11–16: Rekindling Good Practice,* London: David Fulton.

ACKNOWLEDGEMENTS ▨ ■ ■ ■

Matthews, H. (1998) 'Using the Internet for meaningful research'. First published in *Interaction, Journal of the Geography Teachers Association of Victoria* 26(1), 15–19.

Naish, M., Rawling, E. and Hart, C. (1987) *Geography 16–19: The Contribution of a Curriculum Project to 16–19 Education,* Harlow: Longman.

Natt, K. (1996) 'An example of pupil evaluation developed by a student teacher', in Kent, A. *et al.* (eds) *Geography in Education,* Cambridge: Cambridge University Press.

Nicholls, A. (1996) 'Who's to Blame for Sharpe Point Flats?', in the *Northumberland Thinking Skills in Humanities Project: A report on the First Year 1995–1996,* Northumberland Advisory/Inspection Division.

QCA (2007) *Geography in the National Curriculum.*

QCA (2007) *Key concepts underpinning the study of Geography.*

Rawling, E. (2008) 'Planning the Key Stage 3 Geography Curriculum', Sheffield: The Geographical Association.

Reid, A. (1996) 'Exploring values in sustainable development', *Teaching Geography* 21(4)

Roberts, M. (1996) 'Teaching Styles and Strategies', in Kent, A. *et al.* (eds) *Geography in Education,* Cambridge: Cambridge University Press.

Robinson, R. and Serf, J. (1997) 'Global Geography: Learning through Development Education at Key Stage 3', The Geographical Association: Birmingham Development Education Centre.

SCAA (1996) 'Consistency in Teacher Assessment: Exemplification of Standards', London: SCAA.

SCAA/NCVQ (1995) GNVQ Part One Leisure and Tourism Specifications: SCAA/NCVQ

Slater, F. (1993) *Learning Through Geography,* Washington: National Council for Geographic Education.

Stimpson, P. (1994) 'Making the most of discussion', *Teaching Geography* 19(4)

Tolley, H. and Reynolds, J. (1977) *Geography 14–18: A Handbook for School-based Curriculum Development,* Basingstoke: Macmillan Education. This was an outcome of the Schools Council Geography 14–18 Project, which was based at the University of Bristol 1970–75.

Waters, A. (1995) 'Differentiation and Classroom Practice', *Teaching Geography.*

Weeden, P., Winter, J. and Broadfoot, P. (2002) *Teaching, Learning and Assessment,* London: RoutledgeFalmer.

Also to:

ActionAid; British Film Institute, 2000; David Job; Joanne Clark, PGCE student, 1993; Lisa Shufflebotham, PGCE student teacher, Institute of Education, University of London, UK, 1995–96; Sunil Collett, Haverstock School; Anna Annavesian; Mary Biddulph (for the 'Fantastic Geographies' activity in Chapter 1); Susannah Osborne and Sharnbrook Upper School Geography Department

The material on page 359 from 'The Key Elements of Responsible Global Citizenship', p. 5 in 'The Challenge of Globalisation: A handbook for teachers of 11–16 year-olds', Oxfam 2003 is reproduced with the permission of Oxfam GB, Oxfam House, John Smith Drive, Cowley, Oxford, OX4 2JY, UK www.oxfam.org.uk. Oxfam GB does not necessarily endorse the text or activity that accompanies the materials.

Every effort has been made to contact the holders of copyright material. The publishers and authors would be pleased to hear from anyone whose rights have been inadvertently overlooked or infringed so that they can make the necessary arrangements at the earliest opportunity.

INTRODUCTION

This book has been written for men and women who are learning to teach geography in secondary schools. We work from the assumption that individuals opening this book are geographers: you probably have a geography degree, or if not, a degree in a closely related discipline. You also have an enthusiasm for the subject and are motivated by the thought of passing on your knowledge and enthusiasm to young people.

We make no further assumptions about your motives nor your subject knowledge. You may be a physical geographer, keen on the idea of taking off into the countryside and introducing children at first hand to the skills of landform interpretation. You may be a human geographer, excited by the subtleties and complexities of understanding the cultural worlds in which people live. You may be neither of these things exactly.

Perhaps the only definition of geography that covers the sheer breadth of the discipline is the one which runs: 'geography is what geographers do!' Of course, such breadth is one of the things that attracts us about the subject; it is also one of the strengths of geography in the school curriculum. But such is the breadth that an early realisation of student teachers of geography is they usually have significant gaps in their subject knowledge. These gaps have to be filled, for it is not an option to ignore aspects of the National Curriculum Programme of Study, or the GCSE syllabus, on the grounds that you did not study them at university. Thus we do assume that people wishing to become teachers of geography are themselves learners of geography. This book is not about the contents of geography but it is dedicated to a learning ethos: learning, in order to teach. Chapter 1 in particular encourages you, even cajoles you, to take such an approach seriously.

Part and parcel of the responsibility this implies takes you further than merely 'filling the gaps' in your subject knowledge. We assume you have knowledge and expertise of subject matters that may be in short supply in schools, for the discipline always moves on. Your degree contained material and ideas only recently hewn from the research frontier, and dynamic school geography departments, in which we hope you will undertake much of your training, will look to you to introduce such material, appropriately transformed for secondary pupils, into their schemes of work.

You will not find 'cultural geography' or 'medical geography', for example, named in the National Curriculum: but you will find plenty of scope within the National Curriculum to introduce such themes if you so wish – though not on the basis of whim. What we teach has to be justified. This point is raised in Chapter 1 (but also pursued in the later chapters, particularly Chapter 5), which examines the principles and practice of planning the geography curriculum with educational justification. 'Geography is what geographers do' is, on its own, an inadequate catchphrase for geography teachers therefore, for school teachers are accountable – particularly to those they teach.

There are further assumptions that have helped shape this book. These are not assumptions concerning you, the reader, but those which we, the authors, have tried to bring to the act of teaching. We believe in 'professional artistry', implying that all sorts of people from all ranges of background can learn the art and craft, and professional attitudes, of teaching. We do not believe that effective teachers are simply born to it. But we also recognise that, just as there are some naturally highly gifted teachers (who nevertheless still have much to learn), it is true that not everyone with a degree is able teach.

The key assumption to understand is our fundamental 'pupil-centredness' – our belief that good teachers develop a real feel for, and commitment to, the children they teach; it does not matter how good a geographer you are, if you cannot make a connection with the children in your class you will not be able to teach them effectively. Some commentators are apt to equate child-centredness with what are perceived to be discredited 'progressive' teaching techniques; this is done in such a narrow and polarised way that it mocks the seriousness with which most teachers approach their work. What follows from our understanding of pupil-centredness is that no techniques or approaches ('traditional' or 'progressive') can be excluded: the geography teacher will develop a wide repertoire of techniques and strategies, each appropriate for different purposes and which cater for the needs of different pupils.

Thus, in Chapter 5, the pupil lies at the heart of planning and decision making in relation to teaching: we do not believe that any particular approach to teaching x or y is superior to any other – it depends on who the learners are. We want to encourage teachers of geography to be pragmatic, imaginative and willing to try, try and try again if learning seems slow or even resisted by the pupils. Good teachers are usually relentless in this way.

So at the heart of this book, especially Chapters 2 to 9, the 'nuts and bolts' of teaching – that particularly complex mix of practical and intellectual activity in which teachers have to engage – are uncovered in detail. In studying and using the materials on lesson planning, resource selection, etc. you will gradually acquire more sophisticated ideas and understandings of how to teach geography effectively. We hope you will come to perceive technical issues in human terms rather than problems which lend themselves to a simple 'fix'; for example, 'differentiation' as the skill with which teachers set pupils personally appropriate pace and challenge, or 'progression' in terms of helping individuals grow their intelligence, rather than simply the design of another worksheet.

We do not like, and avoid using, the word 'ability' because of the tendency in this country to use the concept in a unidimensional way: the 'less able' and the 'more able' are shorthand, umbrella terms which mask individuals' different learning aptitudes, strengths and capacities (see Chapters 2 and 9 in particular). With the breadth of geography as a subject, including the range of learning styles that can be drawn upon at different times, it is therefore especially pertinent to teachers of geography to pay more than lip service to acquiring a wide repertoire of teaching approaches (Chapter 4) in order to tune in successfully to the full range of pupils' learning styles.

The structure of this book is fairly self evident. It has been arranged in such a manner that it makes sense to work through from the beginning. Although it is not necessary to do this, we do see the book as having value as a whole. Whilst it is not necessary to complete all the activities on offer (your period of training is too short), we hope you will select a range from throughout the book (appropriate to your experience and background) in order to help you engage with the whole story of learning to teach geography. We have also included a chapter on professional development at the end, designed partly to feed forward into your life as a 'newly qualified teacher' (NQT) and beyond, an explicit acknowledgement that your professional development has only just begun. Like my old driving instructor said: 'OK, you've passed your test, now you can learn to drive!' We want to help you conceptualise your initial training and subsequent emergence as a geography teacher as a process in which you are the principal agent.

We are both optimistic in believing that geography teachers can create a geography curriculum that excites pupils and stimulates relevant and worthwhile learning. To do so requires you to have a dynamic view of the subject and its pedagogy, to constantly and rigorously question what is worth teaching and how to approach it.

This book owes a lot to many people. We were both trained by Rex Walford whose influence is alive in us and probably still shows, years later. We have both been attached to the Institute of Education and will happily admit the deep and lasting guidance we have taken from the likes of Norman Graves, Michael Naish, Frances Slater and Ashley Kent over the years In more recent times Clare Brooks, Mary Fargher, Judy Hemingway, Sheila King, David Mitchell, John Morgan, Alun Morgan and Simon Scoones, have all contributed support and inspiration to us through their energy, enthusiasm and optimism, particularly in the context of our work with the Geography PGCE. We both readily acknowledge the impact and influence of former colleagues in the schools where we learned how to teach. But in many ways our biggest debt is to the several generations of student teachers we have known and who have successfully worked in the geography departments of over one hundred London partnership secondary schools. Evaluations, and subsequent contacts with these new teachers, suggest that geography education is in safe hands.

But be warned. Many found that preparing to become a geography teacher was the most challenging thing they had ever embarked upon: at times physically, emotionally and mentally exhausting, but also immensely satisfying.

ROLE, PURPOSE AND PHILOSOPHY

So why teach geography?

In our working lives as geography teachers we should never forget or abandon those ideals which draw us to the job in the first place. School geography has the potential to develop young people's understanding of their 'place' in the world and so help form their identity.

(Huckle, 1997: 241).

INTRODUCTION

This chapter aims to put contemporary geographical education in England and Wales into a broad context, and to examine, via two specially commissioned personal views, the place of geography in schools and, briefly, how this has evolved. It urges geographers who have chosen to teach to take a view on why geography should be taught and to be prepared to express this in terms of educational goals.

OBJECTIVES

By the end of this chapter you should be able to:

- describe recent historical events in the evolution of geography as a school subject
- contribute to the professional debates concerning the he nature of geography in the school curriculum
- understand the significance of what it means to be an advocate for geography – and geography as a medium of education
- explain the aims of geography in education
- present a personal view on the direction geography should take in its development within the education system
- clarify some distinctive contributions geography can make towards the achievement of educational goals.

ADVOCATING GEOGRAPHY IN YOUR SCHOOL

The study of geography as an academic discipline in Britain is a relatively recent phenomenon (since roughly the latter part of the nineteenth century). Although the grammar of geography (i.e. place names) had been present in schools since before that time, the study of geography in education (coupled to the systematic training of geography teachers) is an even more recent enterprise: Fairgrieve's 1926 book is a useful landmark. But it is also worth noting that some prestigious schools did not even teach it as recently as the 1960s, and occasionally geography is still openly attacked for somehow failing to box to the same intellectual 'weight' as related subjects such as history. The subjects are, of course, different, and we shall spend no time in this book 'defending' geography from its perceived deficiencies – we take it as read that you are as convinced as we are of the value of the study of geography, not least because you have chosen to teach it. However, it is important for those involved in teaching geography to be clear about its purpose and to be knowledgeable about its position in the education system. In this way, the practitioners of geography education (you) can become its effective and influential advocates. As this and the following chapter help to demonstrate, without effective advocacy, the pressures on the school curriculum are such that geography could easily disappear. It has no 'divine right' to be a part of the educational experience of young people; we need to be able to say why pupils' education would be impoverished without geography. Making the 'case for geography' needs, therefore, to be principled, knowledgeable and above all convincing (see Bailey and Binns, 1987).

New School Academy

'Striving To Succeed'

MEMORANDUM

From: Deputy Headteacher

To: Geography Department

As you know, we are revamping the way in which we handle 'options' during Y9.

I would like you and your department to give consideration to how 'geography' will be presented to the following:

■ parents (at the parents' evening in March)
■ pupils (during the weeks leading up to the parents' evening).

We want to ensure that all subjects address certain questions, but the particular spin you give geography is, of course, up to you. Essentially, your presentation of geography should be clear about what is distinctive about the subject, and what GCSE studies in Y10 and Y11 will involve.

We are considering the possibility of Heads of subjects making short presentations at the parents' evening. I assume you will be able to produce a visual display, but we also wish each subject to produce a <u>double-sided A4 leaflet</u>. Use the attached 'planner' to start your thinking.

I'll look forward to seeing what you produce.

■ **Box 1.1** Memo concerning open day preparation

As we will see from a later discussion ('The Case for Geography in the National Curriculum'), the geography community has, in the past, been challenged to justify its place in the curriculum. Today, there is a different challenge; to win the 'hearts and minds' of future generations of young people (Bell, 2005: 13). Over the last 10 years, geography has been falling in popularity with pupils. Despite still being one of the most popular non-core subjects, the numbers taking GCSE Geography have declined by a third since 1997. When he was Her Majesty's Chief Inspector of Schools, David Bell stressed the need for geography teachers to engage pupils more purposefully, help them realise the relevance and value of the subject and, 'most important of all, ensure that they enjoy it' (ibid: 13).

Of course, the most powerful advocacy of all is the positive encounter by pupils with relevant, worthwhile and significant experiences in geography, both inside and outside the classroom. The rest of the book is concerned with how to design, plan and implement such encounters. In the mean time, the following activity enables you to open up some of the arguments – and pitfalls – involved in the advocacy of geography in education.

Target group	What do they need to know (What is marketable about geography?)
Pupils	
Parents	
Local community	
Local employers	
Curriculum decision makers	
Others *(please specify)*	

Planning grid for selling geography.
Referring to the *Geographical Association's 2009 Manifesto* will help in completing this grid: www.geography.org.uk/adifferentview

Activity 1.1 **for groups of up to approximately five student teachers**

This activity is designed to simulate a secondary school geography department preparing for the annual 'open day'. This is the formal occasion during the year when the department can communicate its ethos and activities to future pupils and their parents. It is also a useful occasion to communicate to colleagues in other departments and to 'senior management'.

1 In your group, decide who is to play the role of (a) head of department (who will chair the discussion), and (b) observer (who will not take an active part in the discussion but look, listen and take a note of how things go).
2 Read the memo (Figure 1.1) and respond as a departmental team.
3 Reflect on the effectiveness of your response; to do this your 'observer' should lead a critical commentary on (a) the process of your discussion, and (b) the products of your work (mainly, but perhaps not only, your leaflet). Then, if you can, merge with one or more other groups and compare your efforts.

Discussion: When you were interviewed for a place on an initial teacher education course, you may well have been asked to 'justify' geography. The arguments should be fairly familiar to anyone who has studied for a geography degree. It is quite likely that your discussions uncovered many of the well-worn, yet useful, sound bites and catchphrases such as:

■ 'geography is everywhere'
■ 'geography makes sense of the world'
■ 'geography puts the knowing into seeing'.

We shall examine, and try to add some substance to, such viewpoints in the following chapter, in which we discuss the role of geography in the curriculum in terms of what distinctive learning outcomes we may be able to link to geography. What we wish to emphasise at this point is the need to do more than simply put forward a logical argument as to why all young people should study geography. As we noted previously, effective advocacy rests in 'doing' rather than 'do as I say'. If young people are enthused and motivated by geography, and also feel that they are learning (most likely when lessons are seen as not trivial, containing worthwhile content and activities which are deemed relevant by the pupils), then pupils, parents, colleagues and governors do not need 'arguments', no matter how ingenious.

The Geographical Association (GA) is the professional association for geography teachers in England and Wales. It supports geography teachers developing their practice in a variety of ways. Publications such as the *Careers Pack* (Palot, 1999) and *Promoting Geography* (Kent, 1999) supported the promotion of the subject with pupils in schools. The website www.geography.org.uk takes you to publications, posters and a range of digital resources that can be used to promote geography. Look out for *Worldwise*, and find out if your school participates in *Worldwise*. From 2006, 'Geography Action Week' became re-branded as 'Geography Awareness Week' (GAW) with a range of pupil-oriented activities aimed at promoting engaging geography in schools. Recent themes have included *Education for Sustainable Development* (2006) and *Geographic Futures* (2007), and the activities can be accessed from the Geographical Association's website (http://www.geography.org.uk). GAW activities are often picked up by the local press and there are few schools which do not like a positive press report about the achievements and activities of its pupils. GAW usually takes place in June. However, there may well be a school open evening near the start of your training that gives you the chance to mobilise your ideas and enthusiasm and to experience success at an early stage of your practical training.

GEOGRAPHY IN THE EDUCATION SYSTEM OF ENGLAND AND WALES

It was observed in the previous section that geography has no divine right to a place in the congested school curriculum. We argued that geography teachers are the guardians of the subject's development and are helped in this role by taking on the role of advocacy. This can be undertaken at many levels, from within the school's humanities faculty to the level of national discourse where geography teachers' representatives, in the form of the GA, engage civil servants and politicians with accurate and up-to-date information as to the functioning of the subject in the curriculum. There is no doubt that such advocacy is helped by some knowledge of how geography has become established in the curriculum.

To introduce the curriculum story for geography we have chosen to use a device which you may find useful to adapt to your own classroom. We are not going to tell you the story, but instead use an original source for you to interrogate (with our help). As a geography teacher you will, we hope, see the enormous scope in using the wide range of media text, photographs, videos, DVDs etc., which is available from textbooks, newspapers, television as 'evidence' which pupils can be taught to question, summarise, analyse or evaluate.

The text which follows was specially commissioned for this book. It is written by Michael Naish, who has been an influential voice in the field of geography education across the world, especially through his work on what was known as the '16–19 Geography Project' (see below) which transformed the study of geography at A-level in the early 1980s.

THE GEOGRAPHY CURRICULUM OF ENGLAND AND WALES FROM 1965: A PERSONAL VIEW

Introduction

The last quarter of the twentieth century saw dramatic changes in the nature and quality of school geography in England and Wales. The years from 1965 to the late 1980s saw rapid developments in the subject as a key element of the curriculum through the initiatives of curriculum development projects. This took place during what might be termed the *'laissez faire'* period of curriculum decision-making, when responsibility for the curriculum lay with the 113 Local Education Authorities. During the 1980s, the drive for centralisation of curriculum control gained pace and, as part of the Education Reform Act of 1988, a National Curriculum was set up. This was to lead to a period of turbulence for geography in schools, from which we are only just emerging.

The period of *laissez faire*, 1965–80

The year 1965 proved a significant starting point for a period of expansion and consolidation in the geography curriculum for several reasons. It marked the end of the first year of the Schools Council, which was to provide the stimulus for major curriculum development in the subject through the 1970s and 1980s. It was also the first year of the Certificate of Secondary Education (CSE), which offered the first real opportunity for the development of geography for 14 to 16 year olds for a very long time and led to important developments, for example, in the enhancement of fieldwork. In 1965 came the publication of *Locational Analysis in Human Geography* (Haggett, 1965) and *Frontiers in Geographical Teaching* (Chorley and Haggett, 1965), which heralded for British teachers the arrival of the so-called 'conceptual revolution'.

Geography was a popular subject *in* the mid-1960s, as is shown by the numbers selecting it at GCE O- and A-level and at CSE. Its characteristics are well summarised by Long and Roberson (1966) and by the UNESCO *Source Book* (1965). Although in theory there was a *laissez faire* approach to curriculum decision-making, in practice, the syllabuses of the Examination Boards exerted a strong influence on courses. The approach adopted for school geography was funda-mentally a regional one. In the best practice, this provided teachers with the opportunity to look for key features of regions, often problem features, to provide the focus for study, but at its worst study in geography was a catalogue of the characteristics of regions.

In addition there was a strong element of physical geography in courses, focusing mainly on geomorphology, meteorology and climate, with less attention being given to ecosystems and biogeography. Much emphasis was placed on enquiry learning, as is demonstrated by Long and Roberson (1966) and by other writers of the period (e.g. Bailey, 1974; IAAM, 1967). The teacher's role was to involve pupils in the investigation of key characteristics of regions or landforms and of processes in geomorphology. Much emphasis was placed on the importance of fieldwork. Teaching was in the hands of a largely specialist graduate teaching force, trained to teach the subject and supported by a considerable number of academics who took part in the work of the Geographical Association (GA) and the Examination Boards.

The conceptual revolution

The conceptual revolution can be traced back to Schaefer's paper of 1953, in which he calls for a move to more scientific approaches to research through the adoption of logical positivism. One important dimension was that the regional approach to human geography came under attack. Regional geography was seen to be largely descriptive, lacking explanatory and predictive potential. It was essentially idio-graphic, concerned with the unique. In an effort to improve explanation, researchers who were interested in developing a more nomothetic approach, concerned with the construction of general laws, adopted overtly scientific ways of working. The focus of interest was now spatial analysis, developed through the posing and testing of hypotheses. This often demanded that sampling should be undertaken and, with that, a powerful barrage of statistical checks and devices became part and parcel of geographical enquiry. A further element of this new positivistic approach involved the development and use of abstract, conceptual models. Many of the earlier models were borrowed from economics and were themselves dated. Others were created by the 'new geographers' of the 1960s and 1970s.

The ideas of the 'revolution' were made known to teachers in England and Wales in the mid-1960s, through publications such as Haggett's *Locational Analysis in Human Geography* (1965), and Chorley and Haggett's *Models in Geography* (1967). From the mid-1960s, individuals and groups of teachers began experimenting with the new ideas, some of them influenced by the American High School Geography Project (HSGP, 1971) (e.g. Chapallaz *et al.,* 1969; Cole and Beynon, 1969; Everson and Fitzgerald, 1969; Walford, 1969). But it was not until the late 1970s that aspects of the conceptual revolution were to be included in examination syllabuses, when the then London Board and the Joint Matriculation Board introduced new A-level syllabuses based on models and quantification.

Meanwhile geography at the research frontier was moving on. Spatial analysis was under attack from behaviourists, who argued that the study of human decision-making provided better answers to many questions about space. Humanists tended to move from the nomothetic back towards idiographic concerns in their study of actual lived space. At the same time, geographers with genuine concern about inequalities in the use of space and the issues that arise from the political nature of spatial decision-making were adopting radical or welfare approaches to the subject (Harvey, 1969, 1973; Smith, 1977). What was required in this situation of rapid development and change at the research frontier was the opportunity for a body of specialists to think through the nature of the discipline and its educational potential, in order to develop a system-wide curriculum approach to the subject. Such an opportunity was provided by the projects funded by the Schools Council.

The Schools Council Projects

Through the auspices of the Schools Council, curriculum development work in geography took place across the age range 5 to 19 between 1967 and 1984. The projects concerned were *Environmental Studies 5–13* (Schools Council, 1973), *History, Geography and Social Science 8–13* (Blyth *et al.,* 1976), *Geography for the Young School Leaver 14–16* (Boardman, 1988), *Geography 14–18* (Tolley and Reynolds, 1977) and *Geography 16–19* (Naish *et al.,* 1987).

There were certain characteristics which all the Schools Council Projects shared. All were initiated and directed by professional educators with a critical interest in the place of the subject in the school curriculum and with a desire to see it reach its full potential *as a medium the education of young people*. All the projects endeavoured to encourage an approach to learning geography that would help students to develop a range of skills and abilities in the process of gaining knowledge and understanding, They all tried to develop a particular view of the nature of geography and, in the case of the secondary and post-16 projects, it was increasingly the view that school geography has the potential to contribute towards the understanding and possible amelioration of environmental, spatial and social issues and problems. The secondary projects led to the establishment of examination courses at O-level, CSE and A-level.

CENTRALISATION OF CURRICULUM CONTROL, 1980–2008

The Schools Council Projects were working at a time when curriculum decision-making was decentralised, so part of their work was to disseminate ideas for teachers to consider and to offer alternative courses for them to take up if they wished to do so. The notion of *the teacher as school-based curriculum developer* was cherished. From the early 1980s, there was a systematic move to centralise control of education in England and Wales and vest ultimate decision-making in the hands of the Secretary of State. A series of events marked the progress towards centralisation, which began with the Labour Prime Minister James Callaghan's speech at Ruskin College, Oxford, in 1976. These events included the axing of the Schools Council in 1984, signalling a radical change of approach in the funding and management of curriculum development. There was public debate about the nature of the school curriculum, which focused on the issue of whether there should be a core curriculum and what form that curriculum should take.

Geography in the National Curriculum

The debate culminated in the establishment of the National Curriculum in 1988. Now, for the first time, teachers would have to conform to a statutory curriculum which would set out what was to be included in Programmes of Study and what was to be assessed in Attainment Targets and detailed Statements of Attainment. It is a tribute to the work of the Geographical Association that geography found a place in that curriculum, originally as a Foundation Subject to be studied by all pupils between the ages of 5 and 16. The quality of the geography curriculum that emerged as the first Statutory Order for Geography was a bitter disappointment for someone like me who had invested many years in curriculum development in an effort to demonstrate the educational potential of the subject.

The Geography Order of 1991 (DES, 1991) offered no clear view of the nature of geography that would provide any criteria for the selection of content. The Order listed five Attainment Targets, namely Geographical Skills, Knowledge and Understanding of Places, Physical Geography, Human Geography and Environmental Geography, and, spread across these, 183 Statements of Attainment. These statements acted, in effect, as 'behavioural objectives' and, as such, they caused a serious decline in curriculum thinking on the part of teachers. The statements also ensured that the geography curriculum, in common with all other subjects, would be assessment led, but attempts on the part of many teachers to create and implement a workable scheme of assessment proved unsuccessful and frustrating.

There was an overemphasis on knowledge content in the 1991 Order for Geography, at the expense of a balanced focus on skills development. The possible contribution of the subject to values education was also underplayed, apparently ignoring the fact that children are exposed daily in the media to a barrage of value-laden situations relating to environmental and spatial matters. The lack of emphasis on the necessity for enquiry into the factual and values dimensions of such matters threatened to deny students the opportunity to develop their political literacy which the study of geography can enhance.

The 1991 attempt at producing a National Curriculum was quickly shown by teachers, and particularly by those in the primary sector, to be flawed and unworkable. A rescue act was needed and Sir Ron Dearing was brought in to undertake a review and propose revisions. As a result of the review, a new Gecgraphy Order was published in January 1995 (DfEE, 1995). The new Order attempted to offer some form of curriculum framework which teachers can take forward through school-based planning. The content requirements now focused on broad topics and ideas rather than on specific items of content. The amount of content prescribed was substantially reduced. There was more emphasis on investigation and enquiry and it was expected that pupils would develop a range of skills and techniques used in geography. There was no overt mention of political literacy, values enquiry or values clarification, but, with flexibility now restored, there was every reason why teachers should build in such considerations appropriate for the age and experience of their pupils.

The most recent review of the National Curriculum carried out by QCA following the White Paper 14–19 Education and Skills (DfES, 2005) aims to ensure that the Key Stage 3 curriculum is less prescriptive, supports a smooth transition between the different pahses of education and provides greater flexibility to meet pupils' needs. The Programme of Study has been radically reconstructed into three key elements outlining the organising concepts of geography, the place and scale of study, and skills of critical analysis and investigation. This offers opportunities for geography teachers to recapture professional creativity and to make the curriculum relevant, worthwhile and enjoyable, responding to students' interests and topical events.

The launch of the government funded 'Action Plan for Geography' in spring 2006 was an ambitious and timely programme of support for the subject in schools. The Geographical Association (GA) and the Royal Geographical Society (RGS-IBG) worked closely to 'provide everyone – opinion formers, policy makers, schools, parents and students with a clear vision of geography as a relevant, powerful twenty-first century subject; and to equip teachers with the professional skills and support they need so that students enjoy and succeed in geography.' The programme provided further recognition of geography teachers' creative role in engaging with and teaching about the subject in schools.

Despite these encouraging developments, one major issue remains. Since September 1995, neither geography nor history have been obligatory Foundation Subjects at Key Stage 4 (that is, for 14 to 16 year olds). A student's study of geography or history may therefore come to an end at 14, before many students have developed their cognitive faculties beyond 'concrete operations' (see Naish, 1982 and Burton, 2005 in Capel, Leask and Turner, 2005.). What this means is that for many students their ability to think 'formally', for example, in hypothetical ways, in generalisations or 'for the sake of argument' is limited; their understanding of multivariate geographical issues and problems is, therefore, significantly truncated. Fortunately for those who do select the subject, GCSE courses have been retained as the basis of work for 14 to 16 year olds.

Though GCSE courses were developed in the 1990s to replace O-level and CSE, two key features of the accompanying 'national criteria' remain very significant to this day. One was the encouragement of learning through *enquiry* and the other was the focus on a *people-environment* approach, The criteria also ensure that examinations assess a balance of knowledge, understanding and skills, partly through the provision of *coursework assessment* which can test students' individual enquiry skills. However, the removal of coursework assessment from GCSE Geography courses following the revision of the national criteria in 2007 will pose new challenges for geography teachers. Controlled assessment may offer opportunities to maintain this balance in the assessment of knowledge, understanding and skills, particularly when assessing enquiry and fieldwork skills.

DEVELOPMENTS POST-16

The period of *laissez faire* for courses for 16 to 19 year olds lasted well into the early 1990s, when the government began to establish firmer control through the work of the School Curriculum and Assessment Agency (SCAA). SCAA (now known as the QCA) published its Principles for GCE A and AS Examinations in March 1992 and its Subject Core for Geography in December 1993. The main impact of the principles was to impose a 20 per cent limit on coursework in A and AS courses, which presented problems for the most popular of A-level courses, namely that based on the Schools Council Geography 16–19 Project, where coursework represented 35 per cent of the assessment. The core, on the other hand, strongly reflected two key elements of the Project, namely the people-environment approach and the enquiry approach to learning. These two elements were further strengthened in the revised core of 1996 (SCAA, 1996a), following a review of 16–19 qualifications led again by Sir Ron Dearing. The review led to further changes in post-16 qualifications, with a new Advanced Subsidiary examination forming the first year of the Advanced Level course. Reforms were delayed in the late 1990s. New AS courses were introduced in the year 2000. A further review and rationalisation of post-16 syllabuses led to the introduction of new AS and A-level courses since September 2008. One of the most significant features of this review was the removal of the coursework component of AS and A-level geography syllabuses. This has posed considerable challenges for the assessment of fieldwork which remains as a key feature of Advanced level geography courses.

THE CHARACTERISTICS OF SCHOOL GEOGRAPHY IN 2009

Geography is a Foundation Subject in the National Curriculum for 5 to 14 year olds, that is, Key Stages 1 to 3. It has ceased to be a compulsory subject for all pupils in maintained schools from the age of 14 and so is an option for GCSE. The new Statutory Order for Geography (from September 2008) offers a helpful framework from which teachers can construct and develop their schemes of work. The opportunity for school-based curriculum development is once again available after the darker years of the first Order.

Geography is now firmly in place as an element of the primary curriculum and this is encouraging positive developments in primary schools, well supported by the activities of the Geographical Association. The new National Curriculum requirements (2008) show a clear expectation that pupils will be given the opportunity to develop their information technology skills through geography, but many schools still have much to do to achieve this. New national criteria for GCSE published in 2007 form the basis of new GCSE syllabuses to be taught from September 2009.

For the post-16 age group, the subject core now has to be built into all A and

AS syllabuses. Courses redesigned to meet this requirement were introduced in September 1995 and, following the publication of the revised core, course development was once again rapidly undertaken to introduce revised courses in 1998, 2000 and 2008. Geography teachers are also being drawn into teaching some vocational courses, notably the Leisure and Tourism course. The character of geography at this level and for GCSE is influenced by ideas about people-environment relationships. This opens up the possibility that courses can focus on significant questions about the nature and quality of environments and the quality of life within these environments. Sustainability is an important concept in the more environmentally aware geography and now a compulsory element of school geography courses in the 21st century.[1]

The position of geography in the curriculum for 5 to 19 year olds is by no means secure in the early part of the twenty-first century and there is no room for complacency. The territorial war caused by the ever-increasing demands for space on the school curriculum continues. We have already witnessed geography lose its 'place in the sun' in the curriculum for 14 to 16 year olds and the development of vocational courses may present a further challenge.

The continuing debate about post-16 provision also needs careful consideration if an appropriate element of geographical education is to be offered in a broader curriculum for 16 to 19 year-olds (Dearing, 1995). In 2004, a report published by Sir Mike Tomlinson (a former Chief Inspector of Schools) recommended replacing A-levels and GCSE's with school-leaving qualifications that would combine vocational and academic elements. These proposals received widespread acceptance across the education community but were rejected by the government at the last minute. The debate about the need to reform the qualification and examination system has continued in recent years. New specialised vocational diplomas have been developed to run alongside A-levels (since September 2008) as part of a drive to promote the skills needed to enable Britain to compete in a global, knowledge-based economy. Geography can make a distinctive contribution to diplomas in 'Construction and the built environment' and in 'Land development'. It will also be an important part of a 'Humanities' diploma for which proposals are being developed.

The role of geography in the primary school curriculum needs further strengthening. Continuity and progression across phases and ages requires better planning and implementation. Geographers who believe that their subject can make a telling contribution to the education of our children must continue to ensure that the role of geography in the curriculum is publicly known and understood.

The importance of geographical ideas about the use or non-use of space and about people-environment interrelationships with respect to the world of work, for example, is a critical area for immediate consideration. Developments in this area should follow on from the earlier work of Corney and others in terms of industrial and economic understanding (Corney, 1985, 1991). It is important to ensure that pre-vocational and vocational courses do not ignore spatial and environmental impacts and that the key issue of sustainability is ever present.

---

1   The post-16 curriculum continues to undergo rapid change. Whatever the detail of new post-16 course structures, the role of geography will be shared by the perceived relevance of these fundamental ideas – and how well geography teachers are able to adapt to new structures and examinations.

Activity 1.2 **Geography in the curriculum: what's the story?**

1 Individually, you need to read Michael Naish's account. This will take you about ten minutes. You may want to jot down on paper points that seem significant to you; you may even try to draw a 'time line' to summarise the development of geography in the school curriculum since 1965. Can you think of other 'devices' that could help you structure a plain and useful summary?

2 With a partner, briefly compare your summaries of Naish's story. Have you picked out the same points? Have you selected different points?

3 In your pairs, discuss which two or three points in the story you feel that Naish himself thinks are the key ones. How does he 'value' the points you have identified? You may find it helpful to identify one negatively and one positively valued point. Can you suggest the basis, or foundation, for his value position?

4 Near the end of his piece, Naish writes that teachers must 'ensure that the role of geography in the curriculum is publicly known and understood'. Like us, he believes that geography teachers need to be advocates for the subject. On the basis of your reading of the text and subsequent discussions, identify (a) why he believes this to be important (and decide whether you agree?), and (b) the principal argument he uses in his advocacy.

Discussion: The dates and the facts of the geography curriculum story are useful to know because of the historical context they provide. That there is a story is worthwhile remembering: geography's presence in the curriculum, and the shape it takes, has not just happened, but has arrived through a human process which you are about to join (and which, of course, goes back further than 1965). Other individuals, working under different political, academic and educational conditions, may have created different curriculum solutions, as has happened in many countries in the world – including the USA, for example, where, in some States, geography barely exists in any recognisable form in the school curriculum.

Of equal interest to the dates and the facts is the particular 'spin' that the individual telling the story can provide. Michael Naish distinguishes two major periods: *'laissez faire'* and 'centralised control'. He places high value on the 'notion of the teacher as school-based curriculum developer' which, he argues, was cherished in the earlier period, only to be seriously weakened after 1988. He also implies that school-based curriculum development in fact flourished in the preceding period, supported by several influential Schools Council curriculum projects. Whether this was true can be contested. Teachers in primary and lower secondary schools used to have the freedom to teach what they wanted, but while this was freedom to innovate for some, for others it was freedom to stagnate; the quality of geography education that pupils experienced was entirely dependent upon the teacher.

It is also possible to contest, however, whether the introduction of a centralised National Curriculum can ensure that a high quality geography education will be experienced by all. As Michael Naish's analysis shows (supported by the 'fact' of the 1995 Dearing Review of the curriculum), the first attempt at laying down the law was mistaken.

He implies that the crucial reason for its failure was that it neglected to recognise the role of teachers in creating the curriculum – as if teachers can simply 'deliver' a body of knowledge, so long as it is spelt out in sufficient detail. It is highly significant to note that Naish finishes the story on an optimistic note; that the 2008 National Curriculum is nothing more, or less, than a framework in which teachers can once again develop geography's 'full potential' as a 'medium for the education of young people'. Further accounts of the development of the subject in school can be found in Butt (2002) and Rawling (2001).

It is in the last, deceptively simple phrase that we can find Michael Naish's key to the advocacy of geography in the curriculum: we agree that geography has to be seen as a means to an end; that is, serving the purpose of education. But for this to be convincing, for it to carry weight, teacher-advocates of geography need to have a vision of clear educational goals which geography is considered particularly well suited to serve. This is the business of the next section.

In the mean time, and since we have raised the question of goals, it is worth pondering another possible reason for the failure of the 1991 National Curriculum order, a point also raised in Michael Naish's version of events. Although it was clear enough what contents had been selected for the curriculum, what was missing from the legal documents was any sense of educational purpose, which could shed light on how and why certain contents had been selected (and others ignored). Thus, we knew from the documents *what* to teach, but there was confusion and uncertainty about what it was all *for*. With the reduced and more flexible framework of the later reforms of the National Curriculum (see Table 1.1), this serious problem was alleviated somewhat. Following subsequent revisions of the National Curriculum, the Programme of Study is, at last, stronger on aims and principles. The detailed selection of content is left to geography teams in schools. Thus, after several years of upheaval, significant aspects of curriculum development are being returned to teachers.

THE ROLE OF GEOGRAPHY IN EDUCATION

> The function of geography in school is to train future citizens to imagine accurately the conditions of the great world stage and so to help them to think sanely about political and social problems in the world around.
>
> (Fairgrieve, 1926)

This statement, published just eight years after the end of the First World War (and only seven years before Hitler came to power in Germany), still has contemporary significance. The only thing, arguably, that Fairgrieve might add today is the word environmental (and possibly 'economic') to the list of global issues. The statement expresses a goal – perhaps *the* overriding goal – for geography in education; it helps remind us why we are teaching geography and not something else. And the words chosen are significant: Fairgrieve could have used the word 'understand', but he preferred to write 'imagine'; why?

The purpose of this section is to examine the aims, or goals, of geography in education. A number of debates are explored which help identify the ways in which geography can be justified as a curriculum subject. In particular, we tackle the tension (picked up again elsewhere in this book) between school geography being tailored to serve the 'needs of pupils' on the one hand, and school geography being shaped by developments in 'the discipline' (i.e. in Higher Education) on the other.

■ Table 1.1 The Geography National Curriculum at Key Stage 3: a comparison

Source: Rawling, 2007: 6

Item	What it means for you	Section of the geography KS3 PoS in which it is found
Aims and purposes of geography at KS3 (What should we be aiming to achieve through geography at KS3?)	**Geography at KS3 should:** • Stimulate interest, enjoyment and a sense of wonder about the world's places and environments • Help students build on their own experiences and make sense of the dynamically changing world around them as they make progress in geography • Introduce and help explain places and landscapes, economies and societies, people/environment interactions • Incorporate an active enquiring approach to investigation such that students become confident learning inside and outside the classroom • Enable students to develop competence in a range of intellectual, practical and social skills • Include fieldwork as an essential element of geographical study that also makes a major contribution to helping students live safe, healthy lives • Involve students in using maps, visual images and new technologies as essential and creative tools for geographical study • Encourage students to develop confidence in their own abilities and pride in their contribution to society • Inspire students to become global citizens, with all the responsibility and commitment to people and the planet that this implies *Add any of own aims or objectives specific to the school*	Curriculum Aims Importance of Geography Statement
Key concepts (What big ideas must be addressed through the selection of geographical content and planning of work?)	Through studying the places, topics and issues in their geography course, students should move towards developing understanding of the following concepts fundamental to geography: • Place • Space • Scale • Environmental Interaction and Sustainable Development • Process (physical and human) • Interdependence • Cultural Understanding and Diversity	Key Concepts
Key processes (What important skills and approaches in geography must be addressed when selecting content and planning experiences?)	Through studying places, topics and issues in geography students should develop competence in: • Undertaking geographical enquiry activities, both individual activities (like asking questions, analysing evidence and applying critical thinking) and full sequences of planning and developing enquiry work themselves • Using a range of skills that are fundamental to geography, including using and constructing maps, plans and graphs, selecting and using fieldwork approaches and techniques • Communicating geographical knowledge, understanding and attitudes/values in both speech and writing (implied) using a full range of intellectual, social and study skills	Key Processes

■ **Table 1.1** The Geography National Curriculum at Key Stage 3: a comparison (continued)

Source: Rawling, 2007: 6

Minimum content (What must 11–14 year olds study at KS3? The initial required content to which your own selection can be added)	*At KS3 students must be taught through a combination of studies in overview and studies in depth. In order to give students a secure framework of people, place and environment, the choice of content should ensure that all students can understand the changing character and significance of their own community and of the UK in the wider world. They should also be aware of the major global, environmental, cultural and economic issues affecting the world's people, and of the broad location and significance of places and event in the news.* (This statement is my interpretation, based on the explanatory notes and importance of geography statement) Within these broad parameters, KS3 geography should include, for all students: • Key aspects of the UK, its changing human and physical geography, current issues and place in the world today • Physical geography, physical processes and natural landscapes • Human geography, built and managed environments and human processes • Interactions between people and their environments, including causes and consequences, and how to plan for and manage future impacts • Fieldwork investigations in different locations outside the classroom, individually and as part of a team • The location of places and environments (locational knowledge)	Range and Content
Criteria for curriculum planning (What are the criteria that should guide you when planning the curriculum and selecting further content?)	When selecting content and planning your curriculum you must ensure that the material chosen includes: • A variety of scales • Investigations focused on places, themes and issues • Reference to different parts of the world in their wider settings and contexts, including the EU and countries or regions in different states of development • Real and relevant contemporary contexts • Issues of relevance to the UK and globally *Add any of your own criteria*	Range and Content Curriculum Opportunities
Kinds of experience (What other opportunities and experiences must be addressed when planning the work?)	KS3 courses and schemes of work must provide opportunities for students to: • Build on their personal experiences of geography • Use a range of approaches to enquiry • Use varied resources, including maps, visual media and geographical information systems • Undertake fieldwork investigations in different locations outside the classroom, individually and as part of a team • Participate in informed responsible action in relation to geographical issues that affect them and those around them • Make links between geography and other subjects, including citizenship and ICT, and areas of the curriculum including sustainability and the global dimension *Add any of your own criteria*	Curriculum Opportunities
Level descriptions (What learning outcomes are expected? In what ways will students demonstrate their attainment in geographical knowledge, understanding and skills?)	Eight level descriptions (levels 1–E) outline the knowledge, understanding and skills that students will be expected to demonstrate as they make progress through geography from KS1 to KS3 and beyond. Each level description describes the type, and range of performance that students will normally exhibit and it should be used in a best-fit way in relation to many different items and aspects of students' work. At KS3 most students will be expected to demonstrate attainment somewhere between levels 3 and 7 (with the average performance being levels 5/6)	Level Descriptions

The Rt. Hon. Kenneth Baker, MP.,
Secretary of State for Education,
Department of Education and Science,
Elizabeth House,
York Road,
London SE1 7PH.

Dear Mr. Baker,

   We are writing to inform you about what we in The Geographical Association have been doing, in relation to curriculum reform and development, since your predecessor, Sir Keith Joseph addressed us at King's College, London on June 19th, 1985.

1   We would maintain that geography, which is the study of the earth and man's adaptation to its varied environments and resources, should be a fundamental element of every child's school education. We are concerned that in some schools, and particularly many primary schools, the geographical component is weak or perhaps totally absent.

2   Geographical study has its roots as much in the sciences as in the arts and social sciences. Therefore, geography should not be classified solely as a humanities subject, however convenient such a mistaken classification may be for some curriculum planners. We would emphasise the scientific, investigative and numerate aspects of geographical education at all levels, from primary school to university.

3   With its strong links with both the sciences and the arts, geography has powerful contributions to make to the better integration of the school curriculum. We do not advocate the complete integration of subjects, which is notoriously difficult to achieve, but we do advocate the systematic establishment of links between subjects, the distinctive or dominant contributions of which are clearly articulated.

4   Geographical investigation always begins with direct observation in some form. Ideally this should happen even in the primary school. We therefore attach great importance to fieldwork and direct experience, work which involves children discovering and handling information for themselves. Much of this work can be done within, or in close proximity to, the school, but we would draw attention to the considerable benefits, including social benefits, which can accrue from longer periods of properly planned fieldwork in contrasting areas which may be more distant from the school. We trust, therefore, that fieldwork will not be allowed to suffer from the economic stringencies which now beset us.

5   Geographical study at any level brings teacher and pupil face to face with issues and problems which have ethical, moral and sometimes spiritual dimensions. We believe that geography should expose, clarify and provide a sound balanced foundation for the study of such controversial topics. Perhaps such work is more easily done with older rather than with younger pupils. We would hope, therefore, that a geographical component which includes such matters would be included in the curriculum for all young people up to the age of sixteen.

   In his January 1986 address to the Institute of British Geographers, a body with which we have very close links, Sir David Hancock said of geography that it…'combines – possibly in a unique way – scientific thinking with the study of the behaviour of human beings and their values. It can be a vehicle for teaching scientific method and numerate techniques and also for assessing evidence which is not susceptible to this methodology. It provides plenty of scope for the study of problems'.

   We would agree with Sir David's observations. We are deeply convinced of the value of geography, in its modern form, as a vehicle for general education and believe that it should occupy a central place in the education of all young people in Britain, a country with long– established links with overseas countries and their people.

   Yours sincerely,

   Patrick Bailey, President 1985–86
   Elspeth M.Fyfe and Dr. J.A.Binns, Joint Hon. Secretaries.

■ **Box 1.2** An extract from The Geographical Association's letter to Mr Kenneth Baker, Secretary of State for Education, 4 August 1986

Source: Bailey and Binns, 1987: 79–80.

It is not difficult, when talking to a bunch of geographers, to draw up a list of good reasons to study geography. Try it for yourself by completing the following activity:

Activity 1.3 **For a group of approximately five**

1 Agree on someone to chair the following discussion and someone else to compile a list of the main points that emerge. The discussion topic is: 'In what ways can we justify the inclusion of geography in the secondary school curriculum?'

2 Now examine the paragraphs arranged in Box 1.2. These are quoted directly from a letter sent by the GA to the newly appointed Secretary of State for Education, Kenneth Baker. It was he who just two years later steered the Education Reform Act through Parliament, resulting in the National Curriculum. The letter was evidently part of a successful lobby, and the 'case' for geography apparently convincing. In your groups, try to match your list of main points with the GA's paragraphs; for example, did you identify geography as a 'bridging' subject, or 'synthesis', across the two cultures of 'arts' and 'science' (paragraph 2)? Did you manage to identify an argument that the GA letter missed?

Discussion: Though 'good reasons to study geography' are certainly indicative of the role of the subject, and therefore go some way to justify its place on the school curriculum, they are perhaps stated in too general a manner to specify geography in terms of its educational goals. In what ways do we expect young people to gain from the study of geography?

Discussion of goals often nudges us to use a travel metaphor (which you may think is particularly appropriate for geography in education), and we could usefully restate the above question in terms of where the study of geography is supposed to take us; where, and in what state, do we expect our pupils to end up? Refining the metaphor somewhat, the educationist R.S.Peters doubted whether the goal itself (i.e. the stated destination) was the thing to value, because this implies that goals can lie beyond the actual experience of education: 'to be educated is not to have arrived at a destination, it is to travel with a different view' (Peters, 1965; cited in Slater, 1992: 97). It is no accident that the GA's 2009 Manifesto is called 'A Different View' (www.geography.org.uk/adifferentview). Whether you favour the more 'instrumental' interpretation of goals (i.e. valuing achievable and measurable outcomes) or the classic 'liberal' stance which values educational experience for itself because it is this that changes people (i.e. valuing intrinsic rather than extrinsic motives), or a balance of both these interpretations, it is clearly very important indeed for the intended destinations to be identified. This is because, in instrumental terms, they show teachers and learners where achievement lies; they also give orientation and purpose to endeavour. In other words, the stating of goals helps us justify what we include in the curriculum in terms of the three criteria introduced earlier in this chapter: in what ways is the curriculum experience relevant, worthwhile and significant to the learner?

THE CASE FOR GEOGRAPHY IN THE NATIONAL CURRICULUM
(Bailey and Binns, 1987)

The distinctions made in the above paragraph can help us reflect on the way the GA chose to lobby the Secretary of State in the 1980s. If you look once more at Box 1.2, you might distinguish the two different kinds of goals we have identified being deployed in the GA's case for geography, though not necessarily explicitly. There was no doubting the politicians' views and the GA considered itself 'streetwise' to this: 'To politicians, geography was seen to have a useful role in the National Curriculum as a "general knowledge subject" (quoted from an interview with Prime Minister Margaret Thatcher (*Sunday Telegraph,* 15 April 1990)), with the expectation that pupils would get a good factual grounding about the world in which they live.' (Walford, 1991: 6). Official lobbying was willing to collude with a view of geography as an information rich subject, and although the special team appointed by the Secretary of State to write *Geography in the National Curriculum* (known as the Geography Working Group) was careful to state its aims, which suggest goals far broader than teaching general knowledge, in the end, what eventually passed through Parliament in 1991 was a very long list of undifferentiated factual knowledge. The Secretary of State (Kenneth Clarke by this time) struck out material he deemed inappropriate in the Order that was to come before Parliament, writing in his covering letter that geography: 'should emphasise more strongly knowledge and understanding of aspects of geography and put less emphasis . . . on skills . . . and less emphasis on . . . pupils' exploration of attitudes and values'.

The Secretary of State's view was extraordinarily narrow and unambitious, leading one commentator at the time to write that the geography curriculum had been 'mugged in the name of "traditional values" ' (Walford, 1991). It represented some kind of reaction to the perception that education was failing at the basics, leading to a response driven by political goals rather than educational ones. Though there were attempts by others to conduct a broader educational debate (see, for example, Box 1.3, which shows how 'values' are themselves part of the contents of geographical knowledge and understanding), the power of the State, of course, prevailed.

Some would say that despite claims of streetwiseness and the establishment of a new realism within the GA (see Bailey, 1991), the GA tried to play politics with the politicians in order to achieve geography's 'place in the sun' – and were beaten. True, geography had earned a place in the National Curriculum, but there was no clarity as to *what it was for*. This, together with strong messages that geography had been failing and that 'something new' was being put into place, had the net result of creating a decade which has exhibited a debilitating confusion or lack of professional self-confidence. In a telling phrase, Walford observed that with the introduction of the National Curriculum, geography teachers were 'uncertain of the terrain in immediate view, let alone the final destination' (Walford, 1991: 8).

Thus, we return to another use of the landscape/travel metaphor. The National Curriculum rhetoric was always that the precise details of what was to be taught and learned in geography classrooms, and how pupils and teachers should interact, was to be left for teachers to decide. But without the benefit of a clear sense of direction which teachers (and indeed pupils to some extent) feel they have played a part in forging, there is every chance that decisions concerning the precise whats and hows will be made by someone else (e.g. a textbook writer), and that geography lessons will become something of a chore.

The National Curriculum hiatus is now behind us. The revised curriculum for the year 2008 should invite a new wave of school-based curriculum development and innovation in teaching. We have seen that such activity needs to be guided by a clear sense of purpose which the new curriculum ought to provide.

The next section is devoted to stimulating thought on how to keep wider perspectives on geographical education on the agenda and under review.

Curriculum Aims

Learning and undertaking activities in geography contribute to achievement of the curriculum aims for all young people to become:

- successful learners – who progress and achieve
- confident individuals – who lead safe and healthy lives
- responsible citizens – who make a positive contribution to society.

The Importance of Geography

The study of geography stimulates an interest in and a sense of wonder about places. It helps young people make sense of a complex and dynamically changing world. It explains where places are, how places and landscapes are formed, how people and their environment interact, and how a diverse range of economies, societies and environments are interconnected. It builds on pupils' own experiences to investigate places at all scales, from the personal to the global.

Geographical enquiry encourages questioning, investigation and critical thinking about issues affecting the world and people's lives, now and in the future. Fieldwork is an essential element of this. Pupils learn to think spatially and use maps, visual images and new technologies, including geographical information systems (GIS), to obtain, present and analyse information. Geography inspires pupils to become global citizens by exploring their own place in the world, their values and their responsibilities to other people, to the environment and to the sustainability of the planet.

■ **Box 1.3** Curriculum Aims and 'The Importance of Geography'
Source: QCA, 2007, *Geography in the National Curriculum*

Activity 1.4 **Curriculum aims and educational goals**

Discuss the following questions informally for a few minutes with other student teachers of geography (ideally in a group of 3–4):

1. In what ways are the aims for Geography in the National Curriculum (Box 1.3) useful to teachers?
2. Can you identify any aims in Box 1.3 that you would prefer to delete? Are there any further aims you feel ought to be included in the list?
3. Can you perceive any substantial difference in the meanings given in this book to 'educational goals' and 'aims' for geography?

Discussion: This section has used the establishment of geography in the National Curriculum to help illustrate the principle that the curriculum is shaped at all levels

> by goals. If we accept educational goals which are 'traditional utilitarian' in a back-to-basics kind of way, then we can easily find a role for geography – geography as a general knowledge subject, with an emphasis on 'knowledge' aims. If, on the other hand, we aspire to educational goals which are more ambitious, we can find a greater role for geography – possibly expressed in terms of aims like those in Box 1.3. The problem with the National Curriculum, it turns out, was not the general concept; the idea of a National Curriculum always carried widespread support among teachers. The problem was that its value base, in terms of educational goals, was obscure; consequently, the curriculum aims of subjects like geography remained unclear.

THE 'QUEEN OF SCIENCES': DARING TO BE A GEOGRAPHY TEACHER (Richardson, 1983)

The previous section shows in a very direct way the ambition that geography teachers can hold for the contribution of their subject to the education of young people. And yet we implied earlier in this chapter that, since the onset of what Naish called 'centralisation' (see page 8), geography has played (perhaps inevitably given the government of the day) a rather restricted or conservative curriculum role. This was mainly because the aims were either confused or not evident. Remember that the splendid aims of the original Geography Working Group were not officially published, and in any case failed to match the politicians' perceptions of geography in the curriculum. But the argument 'Not just about maps', presented by Simon Jenkins, the then editor of the *Times* newspaper, at about the same time, is anything but conservative about geography. Geography, he writes,

> embraces *every fact* on Earth: every aspect of the composition, occupation and history of the planet. It is the monitor of our abuse of our environment and our guide to its preservation. As such, geography knows no intellectual boundaries. It deserves to sit at the centre of any liberal education...
>
> Without a clear grounding in the known characteristics of the Earth, the physical sciences are mere game playing, the social sciences mere ideology... Geography should be declared a core.
>
> (Jenkins, 1990)

In another article, published after the Dearing Review (DfEE, 1994), Jenkins declared even more forcefully his despair at the sheer lack of vision of the revised curriculum:

> Nothing, not even teenage sex, plumbs the depth of parental unreason like the school curriculum. At least sex is useful. The British curriculum is proud of its uselessness. 'Teach the blighters the rubbish I was taught, and they'll come to no harm' is the tone of the debate... The core curriculum [of English, mathematics and science] no more prepares children for the postindustrial society than Latin and Greek prepared them for the industrial one... Subjects that might expand the mind or imagination – the story of the Earth and its peoples, its ecology and economic and social history... are discouraged as promoting enquiry, argument and discovery, as questioning received wisdom. They are considered 'too difficult' for the young.
>
> (Jenkins, 1994)

These arguments about the value and importance of geography as a school subject were emphasised again more recently by David Bell who, when he was Chief Inspector for Schools, expressed the view that if schools aspire to develop pupils who are active citizens who can face their responsibilities and have a critical understanding of the rapidly changing world in which they live, 'there is no more relevant subject than geography' (Bell, 2005: 12). Drawing upon Ofsted inspection reports that highlighted the relative decline of the subject in many schools, Bell identified a number of challenges for geography teachers to make school geography more interesting, relevant and worthwhile for young people. The main thrust of his argument is that we need to ensure that geography is a subject which reflects the 'changing landscape and issues of the twenty-first century'. It is worth taking some time to reflect on Bell's views (see Box 1.4 on page 22) as they serve as a strong advocacy for the subject.

Activity 1.5

Read Box 1.4: The value and importance of geography

■ Identify the aims and goals for geography education in David Bell's discussion of the value and importance of geography in the school curriculum. In what ways do they add to or clarify the curriculum aims and goals you identified in Activity 1.4?

■ Carefully consider the questions David Bell asks about today's school geography. Imagine that you have been asked to respond to these questions on behalf of the Geographical Association. Discuss the questions with a small group of colleagues and, drawing upon your own experiences of geography education and what you have observed during your initial experience in schools, prepare a response to these questions on behalf of the subject association.

WHY SUBJECTS REALLY MATTER

The discussion of the value and importance of geography at the end of the previous section emphasises the importance of selecting worthwhile and interesting things to teach. There are ways to argue about what constitutes 'worthwhile learning', taking into account the kinds of *knowledge* that are thought to be worthwhile, the *ideas* that young people could be profitably exposed to, the *skills* which they will find useful in adult life and the *issues* about which they need to gain some understanding and learn how to face intelligently and confidently.

Richard Pring recently described the challenge in these terms:

Certainly, such 'worthwhile learning' goes beyond what is seen to be *useful* and embraces the capacity to think, to evaluate, to appreciate – indeed, to assess what counts as being useful within what is judged to be a valuable form of life. We have inherited a world of ideas through which we have come to understand the physical, social and moral worlds in a particular way. It is an inheritance, and it is the job of education to enable the next generation to gain access to that inheritance, to grasp and understand those ideas and to gain a deeper understanding of the world in

Listen to a news broadcast or open a newspaper and you cannot fail to be struck by the relevance of geography. This practical discipline enables us to understand change, conflict and key issues which impact on our lives today and which will affect our futures tomorrow. The floods in Cornwall and the destructive power of hurricanes in the Caribbean have highlighted changing climatic patterns and global warming. The devastation of the tsunami in the Indian Ocean and the world's reaction have further demonstrated the power of geography. Equally, war and conflict in the Middle East, water shortages, famine, migrations of peoples, disputes over oil, the complexities of world trade, interdependence, globalisation and debt are all major issues with which our world is grappling. All this is the geography of today and, in order to understand the intricacy of it, it is important that young people learn about the world they live in and on which they depend. It is important that the citizens of tomorrow understand the management of risk, appreciate diversity, are aware of environmental issues, promote sustainability and respect human rights and social inclusion. If the aspiration of schools is to create students who are active and well-rounded citizens there is no more relevant subject than geography.

Albert Einstein asserted that 'imagination is more important than knowledge'; he saw knowledge as being limiting, while imagination 'embraces the whole world'. Perhaps, questions about today's geography would include:

■ Should geographers put the focus less on the accumulation of knowledge and more on the application of concepts and the development of the skills to enable students to evaluate these critically?
■ Should students not just learn about issues, but be able to critically evaluate the impact that actions have on outcomes?
■ Have geographers focused on a too narrow range of experiences with repetition rather than progression turning students away from the subject?
■ Does a study of Kenya or rivers in each key stage stimulate interest, especially if the focus is on the factual?
■ Is the subject caught in a time warp where the curriculum is static and traditional? Is there an underlying reluctance to change and an unwillingness to make the curriculum more relevant to students in the twenty-first century?

So what can be done to enable geography to thrive? Geography is about places. It is not just knowing about places themselves, but understanding the interdependence and connectivity of places. It is about empowering tomorrow's adults to develop real global understanding and global citizenship so they have the intellectual understanding to participate individually and collectively in shaping the world around them. This knowledge and understanding of other places, cultures and societies underpins sensitivity and tolerance and contributes to good citizenship. Good geographers develop a range of skills which make them highly employable and which are relevant to any future workforce. They are able to understand the language of maps, which linked to a competency in ICT and the application of statistics provides a wealth of geographical information which is frequently used by both business and government. Such information is best interpreted by geographers who are used to problem-solving and decision-making and who have built up and developed their expertise through geographical enquiry.

■ **Box 1.4** The value and importance of geography, An edited extract from David Bell
Source: Bell, 2005: 12–13.

which they live. And there are pressing problems which beset us all and which need to be understood and grappled with – problems of the environment, of social and ethnic relations, of violence and injustice, of the exercise of power, of the prevalence of poverty. Such issues and problems need a grasp of the relevant scientific concepts and modes of analysis. They are also the very stuff of literature and the arts, of drama and of history, which did have and should retain a central place in the education of all young people.

(Pring, 2004)

However, in recent years, such has been the concern with the 'science of teaching' that it appears that the debate about what is worthwhile to teach has either been ignored or shelved for the moment. 'Student-centredness' is a fundamental principle driving our beliefs about the role, philosophy and purpose of geography education. Forming productive relationships with young people is crucially important. Our view is that this task is made more possible when the teacher is able to form a *productive and creative relationship with the subject matter*. Subjects therefore are *not* best seen as ends in themselves. This is often how subjects are caricatured, however, as refuges for nutty scientists, mad professors or (as with our subject) outdoor types with cords and stout boots. Here the teacher has to persuade the pupils of the subject's 'relevance' in terms governed by the subject.

Subjects are better understood as the distinctive means to desirable ends. They can be thought of as stimulating and useful *resources* which can be organised in such a way as to stir curiosity and motivate worthwhile learning. The learning is described and directed by carefully selected educational goals. The selection is based on what we think education is for, what kind of experiences and encounters students should have and where we think the subject resource can take us. Thus:

■ What concepts can be grown and developed within this subject?
■ What knowledge can be acquired and in what way is it known, and is useful to know?
■ Which skills can be developed and refined with this subject?
■ How can the subject help us make sense of the world and engage with it more intelligently?

If subjects are simply seen as the container or vehicle for 'delivering' authorised content, and they often are seen exactly in these terms, then it is not surprising that many pupils respond appropriately and sometimes with contempt.

Geography is a fantastic subject with extraordinary educational potential for informing future citizens. Geography not only helps pupils understand the savage power and differentiated impact of natural hazards but also the challenges in coping with the aftermath. It challenges pupils with 'real world' issues from the local and often nearby, to the global and sometimes distant. The subject is rich in multimodal information and communication skills, and can induct pupils into the £20 billion GIS industry that underpins almost all economic activity in the modern world. So *why* is geography experiencing something of a mini-crisis right now?

Like most subjects, geography is difficult to teach well if you are not sure about what it offers and where it can take you (Lambert, 2004 and 2005). Relatively few teachers have a meaningful relationship with the subject that involves a connection to what has been happening in the wider discipline during the last twenty years. And relatively few teachers have the space or time to engage creatively with the subject through asking fundamental questions about what is worth knowing. Relatively few would even recognise this as part of their job, and yet it is arguably the most significant element of being a teacher, to make an interesting, worthwhile and relevant school geography experience for young people. The purpose or value, therefore, of doing geography may indeed lie in the subject matter itself (Lambert, 2004: 82).

Centre-led initiatives and national strategies (perhaps unintentionally) suggest to teachers, curriculum managers and headteachers that teaching is a generic activity, a personalised set of skills that can be refined by application of the favoured formulae. This is unhelpful, especially to secondary teachers. So, some of the generic materials that flow into schools are augmented by subject specific exemplars. This also is flawed thinking and at worst can also be discouraging to the subject enthusiast. The subject is where good teachers *start* their work. *What* is worth teaching and why? Only when we have worked out an answer to this does the 'how shall I try to do this' make any sense. To treat the subject as the vehicle for a pedagogic adventure is, morally, education without a heart (Lambert, 2004).

The particular problem with geography is that its power as an educational resource is not fully realised. Its power has to be realised by teachers working in the company of others – geographers, teacher colleagues and pupils themselves – encouraged that they can create mind expanding experiences that can develop understanding of the threshold concepts of the discipline (Morgan and Lambert, 2005). These can literally change the way we see the world, for example, the meaning of *place*, the significance of *scale* (local, regional, national, international, global), *sustainable development, interdependence and diversity*.

In the following piece, Anna Avanessian, who recently became a geography teacher, reflects on her engagement with the subject discipline and how this has shaped her beliefs about the power of geography as an educational resource. These reflections show clearly how the *productive and creative relationship* she has formed with the subject matter influences the way she teaches geography. Read this piece as a stimulus for the subsequent activity (Activity 1.6: Fantastic Geographies).

Panel: Anna Avanessian

I love geography, but think that at the minute the subject has so much more to offer!

From the depths of the Amazon Rainforest, to the coal mines of South Wales, to the circulatory motions of the Hadley and Walker cells; geography has never ceased to amaze me! Apart from undoubtedly developing my colouring skills, in studying geography I came to realise just how relevant the subject is. It answered so many questions and formed the basis for my understanding of the modern world.

It is unsurprising perhaps that I chose to continue with a career in geography, not only developing my own personal knowledge and understanding of the subject, but attempting to instil my passion in hordes of unruly children! I remember during my degree course (at Manchester University) having to write an essay on the future of geography. I was dumbstruck to discover that there is current academic debate around the importance of geography in the school curriculum and controversy around the subject as a discrete entity. However, on my return to school as a teacher, it was not difficult to understand why such debates have arisen.

At school level, geography has so much more to offer. I have found a dated subject matter that skirts around or, more worryingly, fails to address key, current issues in the subject. For example, with the unparalleled growth of India and China why do our country studies still focus on Brazil and Kenya? Admittedly, the latter are still worthy of acknowledgement but why are we indeed constrained to individual countries (and topics) in isolation? Links must be made between topics to highlight how aspects of geography describe, explain and, to a certain extent, dictate our every-day lives. I would argue that there is a need to move away from discrete units of work to theme based studies. This is not to say that the accumulation of 'facts' and 'knowledge' should be discarded in favour solely of concept-based thought, but that the two should become more closely entwined and not restricted by the topic 'title'.

I challenge all of my pupils to come up with an object or issue that isn't in some way related to geography. Thus far I remain undefeated, though have received some interesting queries:

■ Duvet cover?
  I questioned where the pupils bought this duvet cover and linked this to geographies of consumption. Interestingly enough, here lies another area where I feel that we are teaching slightly outdated subject material. Yes, out-of-town retail centres marked a significant change on patterns of consumption, but more recently, city centres have fought back and undergone a huge facelift to turn around this trend. (Aware of the importance of using real examples, Manchester is an excellent candidate!)

■ Chips?
  I linked to issues around obesity and geographies of health – another key issue that we fail to look at. The 'fat map' of Britain (http://www.timesonline.co.uk/tol/news/uk/article624791.ece) shows that old mining and steel towns top the league for overweight people. Links can arguably then be made between socio-economic indicators and health patterns.

Geography can, and should, be used to explain everything! In fact, it could be possible to plan lessons using only a daily newspaper. I would argue that in some way, each story could be made geographical.

I don't wish to paint a picture of doom and gloom for the future of geography. A few small changes could help us to bring this fascinating subject to life, and perhaps more importantly, into the *real* lives of our students. Fieldwork has always been fundamental to the study of geography, though it isn't always feasible to take a Year 8 class to the shanty towns of Rio or the peaks of the Himalayas. We are fortunate enough to be in an age where technology can do almost anything, so why not use the increasing range of virtual-fieldwork on offer to aid learning. We have a wealth of resources at our fingertips that can bring the obscure and unknown into the classroom and into the lives of the students.

As already mentioned, there is also a need to question *what* it is that we are teaching students. Is our teaching up-to-date and relevant? Is it 'fantastic' and inspiring? Does it demonstrate how important geography is and justify it's place in the curriculum? Of course!

Activity 1.6 **Fantastic Geographies**

If geography is a diverse discipline and a powerful educational resource, then what other aspects of geography would you like to see included in the school geography curriculum? Are some of these geographies more appropriate for certain age groups?

■ What is your 'fantastic' geography?
■ Why is this fantastic geography for you?
■ What are the origins of this fantastic geography?
■ Why do you think it is important for pupils to study this fantastic geography?

In what ways is this fantastic geography different from the types of geographies you have seen in school to date?

Devise a short sequence of up to 5 lessons around your fantastic geography. Identify:

■ the geographical questions you might want pupils to explore
■ the geographical content
■ possible sources of information
■ possible teaching and learning strategies.

(Acknowledgement: We are grateful to Mary Biddulph and Dr Roger Firth of the University of Nottingham for permission to use this activity from their Geography PGCE course)

IS GEOGRAPHY A 'HARD' SUBJECT?

> For us, geography is a subject that can prompt reflection on the world in which we live, and can provide a resource for teachers who wish to fulfil their role as 'transformative intellectuals'. Part of this role means engaging with the intellectual debates that characterise the subjects we teach.
>
> (Morgan and Lambert, 2005: 23)

As the above quotation and the earlier discussion about the value and importance of the subject imply, geography is a 'hard' subject, if appropriate intellectual demands are made of the pupils who study it. If we teach geography to pupils in a way that discourages open questions, argument and discovery, and in so doing close the mind and imagination (by, for example, overloading lessons with the 'busy work' – colouring the map or shading the graph), then geography can be seen as a 'soft' subject. It possibly would not be seen as 'hard' in the sense that rigorous thinking is a requirement for progress, and, as is the case of any subject badly taught, such a soft geography would understandably be seen by many (including some pupils) as useless and a waste of time.

The need for teachers of geography to keep learning geography is perhaps one way of maintaining a keen intellectual edge in the geography classroom (Morgan and Lambert, 2005). John Morgan obtained a degree in geography, followed by a PGCE, taught for several years, mainly at sixth form level and is now a Reader in Geography Education both at the Institute of Education, University of London and the University of Bristol. He has views about the geography curriculum, particularly in relation to the tensions and contradictions which he argues geography teachers need to be aware of and address in some way. Read what he has to say here and respond to the questions in Activity 1.7.

THE FUTURE OF THE GEOGRAPHY CURRICULUM

INTRODUCTION

What I want to do here is consider different ways of conceptualising the geography curriculum. Then I shall look at how the work of geography teachers at present can be seen to be influenced by two contradictory codes (the *economic* and the *cultural*). Whilst these present problems for all teachers in terms of how they approach curriculum, pedagogy and assessment, I suggest that there still exists space for student teachers to influence the direction of change in geography education.

THE CURRICULUM AS...WHAT?

Traditionally, the school geography curriculum has operated on the assumption of mimesis, which means that it is assumed to be like a mirror, reflecting the real world as it is. This is true even though there have been shifts in emphasis over the years. In school geography the key shift has been from the 'capes and bays' approach, which sought to provide accurate descriptions of particular places and features, to a more scientific approach based on the positivist search for generalisation. In both cases, though, the concern was for the geographer to provide an accurate account of the world. This search for accurate description and explanation has provided the basis for the development of school geography, as it invites progression in curriculum planning. Thus, students may study the same topics or places at various stages of their school career, but they will be able to offer more detailed explanations, more complex accounts, and better understanding of geography's theories as they progress. In terms of the role of the geography teacher, these mimetic approaches suggest that there is a distinctive body of knowledge that makes up the geographic discipline, which operates as the 'curriculum-as-fact'. The geography teacher's role is to guide students through that curriculum. There may be space for innovation and individuality in the way the course is taught or planned, but the outcome is effectively the same for everyone.

I would suggest that this way of thinking about the geography curriculum is the dominant one. The curriculum is seen as an object, needing constant revision and updating. However, there are other ways of thinking about the curriculum, and these draw upon other theories of knowledge. In the 1970s, there emerged a phenomenological critique of the curriculum. The school curriculum, it was argued, was 'external to the knower', 'imposed' and had little connection to the common sense understandings of students. This argument was based on the idea that the curriculum was a social construction and could just as easily be constructed otherwise. According to this perspective, the geography curriculum was not a fixed, absolute reflection of reality, but was contingent and perspectival. This approach to the school curriculum was seized upon by geography educators who were interested in the humanistic geography that was developing in the 1970s, and by the early 1980s there were some clear arguments for a humanistic geography education.

Some of the key advocates of this phenomenological approach to curriculum quickly abandoned their original position on the grounds that to see all knowledge as a social construction led to a pluralist 'relativism' that offered little in the way of radical politics. If we all had different perspectives, then all were equally valid. What was important to understand was that some knowledge comes to be valued more than others. So, for instance, in the geography curriculum, the decision-making of industrialists is given greater attention than the views of industrial workers. This suggests that knowledge produced in the school geography classroom is ideological in that it represents the interests of certain groups and marginalises other perspectives. This type of thinking has been influenced by the idea of structuralism, which suggests that beneath the surface appearance of human activity there are underlying structures or causal processes that affect human behaviour and thought. In geography, Marxist-inspired theories of political economy have been most influential, and this has affected our understanding of the role of the geography curriculum. In this view, the geography curriculum operates as ideology, systematically representing the interests of capitalism.

So far we have outlined three approaches to the geography curriculum. In addition to 'curriculum-as-fact', we can identify 'curriculum-as-value' and 'curriculum-as-ideology', and each corresponds to a particular approach to knowledge; empiricism/positivism, phenomenology and structuralism. These categories are useful in helping us think about the way in which we teach geography. However, all three approaches can be said to be similar in that they are all striving to tell a better, more complete story about the world. They are all seeking mimesis, an accurate reflection of the world,

Since the late 1980s and early 1990s, geographers have become interested in the ways in which we represent the world. Whereas previous approaches had assumed that there existed a fixed real world, external to the observer, which could be accessed by the geographer using appropriate methods, in recent geographical theory there is a tendency to see the world as a 'text'. Thus the landscape can be read in exactly the same way as one might read a novel, or interpret a painting or film. The meanings of texts are not found in the text, but are produced in the act of reading. Thus different people, with different outlooks and experiences, will produce different meanings of the same text. In this situation, it is foolish to talk of the 'truth' or 'correct' interpretation. Our understanding is just one of many possible ways of understanding the text. This leads to the post-modern view that there is no privileged, superior way of looking at the world. A recent tendency is to regard the geography curriculum as text, in that there is no essential or fixed meaning to it, and teachers and students can interpret it in a creative way, devising their own routes through it, deconstructing its statements and reaching new understandings of it. In this way, the geography curriculum can be seen as 'ludicrous'. This term is useful because it suggests that the curriculum is 'absurd' in that there is no secure basis or (dare I say it) 'core' to the curriculum, and also suggests a degree of 'playfulness'.

I have taken time to highlight these different perspectives on the curriculum because I would suggest that in recent years geography teachers have forgotten these debates. This has been partly from necessity because the National Curriculum has been prescribed and teachers might as well get on with delivering it. One of the problems is that, when we look at how geography is being taught in schools, we see that it is not only geography that is being taught but the historiography of geography – implicitly at least. How often do our geography lessons suggest to students that it is not the 'real world' that we study in geography lessons but rather a discourse about the world – a representation of the world that is 'geographical' (as opposed to historical or sociological)? The answer is hardly ever, because the curriculum is based on an essentially 'realist' (empiricist) conception of knowledge and the world.

Regarding the curriculum as text is to suggest that geography teachers are not teaching knowledge, but preferred discourses. These are not necessarily chosen by the teacher, and he or she may not be aware of what is taking place. An example would be accounts of gentrification which are couched in terms of lifestyle choices and voluntarism, with no attention to the economic conditions that create low rents in certain parts of inner cities. We are all, always, involved in discourses frameworks for thinking about the world; the teacher's task is to de-naturalise (that is, to identify its ideological basis, or bias) these instead of endlessly validating them.

You can judge for yourself how useful is this typology of approaches to the geography curriculum. Currently, few geography educators would advocate a post-modern approach to curriculum, preferring to see the geography curriculum as a logical, rational and sensible 'selection' from the wider discipline. But at the same time, few would deny the basic truth of the analysis I have made!

THE IMPOSSIBILITY OF BEING A GEOGRAPHY TEACHER...?

We live, we are told, in changing times. In the economic sphere, globalisation has served to undermine the ability of governments to regulate an increasingly mobile capitalism. Things have 'speeded up'; capital, goods and people are on the move. Competition between firms means that those that employ flexible, efficient workers able to cope with the demands of the new economy win out at the expense of those that cannot adjust to the new conditions. All this has implications for education. Increasingly education is seen by national governments as essential in producing a labour force that has the skills and attitudes necessary for the economic new times. Workers have to be flexible, prepared to change their jobs, learn new skills ('lifelong learning' is the key phrase) and move on, recognising that the days of job security are gone. In the cultural sphere, post-modernism leads to the breakdown of distinctions between high and low culture, between the authentic and the inauthentic, and between reality and mediated experience, marked by the development of the 'three-minute culture', where events and images come thick and fast and appear to have no particular connection with each other. In addition, the institutions that once provided firm foundations for people's identity (organised religion, the job for life, the nuclear family, class) have seen their authority eroded, leaving people to cobble together their identities in a world without secure anchors. Knowledge is seen as provisional, contingent and relative, and society is made up of a 'semiotic glut' of different voices, images and signs, all floating without connection. Young people inhabit a media culture which is sceptical of authority, accepts relativity, and revels in the aestheticisation of everyday life at the expense of 'serious', organised politics. In changing times, the economic code (based on post-Fordism) and the cultural code (based on post-modernism) coexist uneasily, and schooling in the present era reflects this.

I have already commented on how the tensions implied here can influence our interpretation of the curriculum. For example, geographers increasingly recognise the ways in which the curriculum excludes certain voices and ways of looking at the world. Thus, in a post-modern culture where all knowledge is seen as uncertain and partial, and students are faced with a media culture that reflects these trends (mixing *cognitive* and *affective* aspects of understanding), geography teachers are faced with teaching a 'back-to-basics' curriculum that claims to provide a truthful reflection of the world.

In what follows, I outline two further contradictions, in pedagogy and assessment respectively.

Pedagogy

Pedagogy, like curriculum, is an area where geography teachers receive mixed messages: the unproblematic content of the curriculum is to be taught in a learner-centred manner. On the one hand, this type of learner-centred pedagogy can be seen to involve pupils in the regulation of the self, monitoring their own progress and identifying their own weaknesses to be rectified by action planning (rather than have these failings pointed out to them by teachers!), and moulding themselves into the types of workers required by a flexible capitalism. On the other hand, learner-centredness may aspire to the type of reflective, critical thinking required to breach conservative curriculum content and generate counter-discourses.

Further mixed messages are provided by the teacher accreditation system (run by the Training and Development Agency (TDA), which sets the standards for initial training) and the external school inspection system (Ofsted), both of which claim to have clear 'performance' or 'competence' based notions of what is meant by 'standards' and 'good teaching'. In such circumstances, how can teachers be encouraged to adopt innovatory or 'daring' approaches to teaching? Whilst the language is all about flexibility, empowerment and change, there are real difficulties in actually realising these ideas. Another example of the contradictions surrounding pedagogy is in the area of information technology. In theory, information technology has the potential to usher in new understandings of how knowledge is produced, and lead to more self-directed methods of learning. At the same time, however, there is the danger that information technology can lead to an increased packaging of knowledge, leading to a closing down of learning pathways. Again, there is a conflict between the economic and cultural aspects of schooling.

Assessment

Geography has been an area of the curriculum where moves towards 'authentic' assessment have been most developed. This can be seen as a reflection of the post-modern recognition that knowledge is constructed in the relation between teachers and learners, and that there are more elements to learning than can be examined by 'pen and paper' tests. Thus we see the increased use of pupil profiles, records of achievement and continuous assessment. These developments can be read as part of the new educational regime that seeks to provide flexible workers, but also reflects post-modern notions of playfulness and enjoyment, and a concern with the 'whole pupil'. However, these forms of assessment conflict with the need to generate simple measures of achievement which can be used to monitor school effectiveness and construct league tables to enable parental choice. As in the case of curriculum and pedagogy, teachers in schools are having to deal with two different messages about the purpose of schooling.

CONCLUSION

I am suggesting here that geography teachers are likely to experience contradictions in their work, and this is due to the fact that modern education systems are couched largely in terms of economic codes, whilst students and teachers increasingly live in a post-modern culture. A globalised economy dominated by large multinational corporations operating under a regime of 'flexible accumulation' has led to the rise of consumerism based on a radical individualism, and the ability of the nation-state to secure identity for its citizens has been challenged. This has led to a 'speed-up' of economic and cultural life, and the response of governments has been to attempt to suppress the diversity of post-modern culture, standardising and packaging the chaotic tendencies of everyday life into the certainties of a 'core' curriculum, going 'back to basics'. Occasionally, some geography teachers will have the opportunity to contribute to the process whereby these two codes (the economic and the cultural) are worked through at the levels of policy (e.g. in reviewing the National Curriculum). All geography teachers have the opportunity to contribute at the level of practice, however, not least by reflecting on their assessment, pedagogy and curriculum plans.

What I have tried to demonstrate in writing this piece is how my interpretation of geography in education has been shaped as much by my continuing education in *geography* (my growing understanding of the world) as by professional knowledge and skill as a *teacher* (in terms of curriculum pedagogy and assessment). I am not just a teacher I am a geography teacher.

For anyone wishing to take their thinking further and deeper on all this, I can recommend three books. John Huckle's (1983) *Geography Education: Reflection and Action* is probably the best introduction to alternative perspectives on the school geography curriculum, including essays on humanistic and radical approaches, Trevor Barnes and James Duncan (1992), in *Writing Worlds,* provide an introduction to the idea of 'geography-as-text'. The introduction and conclusion provide an overview of key ideas about text, discourse and representation. Finally, Usher and Edwards (1994), in a field dominated by North American writers, provide a readable and interesting account of the implications of post-modernism for education.

Activity 1.7 **For pairs or small groups**

1   Read John Morgan's text, *The Future of the Geography Curriculum*.
2   Clarify for yourself a number of key words used by Morgan:
   ■   cognitive
   ■   affective
   ■   curriculum
   ■   pedagogy
   ■   assessment
   ■   post-Fordism
   ■   post-modernism.
3   To what extent do you agree with his analysis? In your pair or group try to identify further examples of the basic contradiction he describes between the 'economic' and the 'cultural'.
4   To what extent is the geography teaching you have experienced or observed set within the frame of 'geography-as-fact'? In your group, identify the pros and cons of the geography curriculum interpreted and taught only in this manner (as 'fact').
5   What are the implications, for teachers, of accepting the notion of 'geography as text'?
6   Morgan describes the contemporary world as made up of a 'semiotic glut', 'without secure anchors' and 'floating without connection'. Other writers have described young people growing up in such relativist conditions as 'morally at sea'. To what extent should geography teachers go with the flow (accepting relativity) or attempt to resist it? Is there a third option?

Discussion: The ideas introduced by John Morgan are not particularly easy and it may be tempting, in the immediate and busy lives of teachers, to ignore them. But the alert and conscientious geography teacher knows that there is, at least, more to geography teaching than at first meets the eye.

A cursory glance at the rest of this book shows that the contents are dominated by the aspects that Morgan identifies: curriculum (Chapter 5), pedagogy (Chapters 2, 3, 4, 5, 6 and 7) and assessment (Chapter 10). Chapter 9 takes on the future orientation given to Morgan's piece explicitly and in detail, particularly the notion of critical thinking.

As a final word, it is worth emphasising that the discussion opened up here is not confined to a narrow subset of geography ('cultural' geography and 'economic' geography). In physical geography, how climatic change is represented in textbooks, TV programmes and newspapers is significant; can the topic be taught 'as fact' or is it more helpful to teach about the discourse? Another case is the use of the word 'natural', which is problematic in geography (e.g. 'natural vegetation', 'natural hazards'); for instance, it may be very instructive to follow how a supposedly 'natural' event like a major flood (such as the 2007 floods or the impacts of Hurricane Katrina on New Orleans in 2005) is represented in the media, as well as how short and longer term human responses are articulated and decided.

In their speculative article on 'Geography and Geography Education', Rex Walford and Peter Haggett (1995) look ahead to the twenty-first century with a discussion concerning changing world geography, the health of the subject at university level and the development of geography in schools. Merely to list the changes noted under the first of these headings (Box 1.5) serves to remind teachers to remain alert in their own role as learners – or else submit to teaching some kind of *morally careless* fictional geography of a world gone by (Lambert, 2005).

So far as geography in education is concerned, the authors identified three 'vital variables' that will determine its fate:

■ the extent to which legal structures enable or disable the subject within the future framework of the school curriculum
■ the extent to which the teaching of the subject continues to capture the interest of school pupils
■ the extent to which the subject exhibits intellectual coherence and a persuasive rationale within the whole curriculum.

Changes in world geography: speculations for the 21st century

1 Increases in world population
2 Increased resource consumption
3 Increased environmental pressures at local and global levels
4 Further collapse of long-distance space
5 Further switch of resource development into offshore areas
6 Trend away from hierarchically-organised structures
7 Instability in major geopolitical hegemonies

■ **Box 1.5** Changes in world geography: speculations for the 21st century
Source: Walford and Haggett, 1995: 3–5

Elsewhere, Castree, Fuller and Lambert (2007) have used the metaphor of a border to describe the very real divide between university and pre-university geography. They urge geographers to broaden the scope of 'cross-border' involvement in order to avert what they see as a potential crisis of geographical literacy in wider society (2007: 132).

SUMMARY AND KEY POINTS

This chapter has tried to encourage debate on each of these variables. For example, is the National Curriculum enabling or disabling? To what extent is geography education 'learner centred'? On what grounds do we advocate geography in education?

It is your responses to such questions that count. These are likely to be diverse and changing, but the wise teacher 'does not bid you enter the house of his [sic] wisdom, but rather leads you to the threshold of your own mind' (Gibran, 1926: 67; cited in Edwards, 1996: 222). Or, as one student teacher wrote, 'My teaching philosophy is based on the words of Proust: "the real voyage of discovery does not consist in seeking new landscapes, but in having new eyes"' (Walford and Haggett, 1995: 12). What you will find in this book is material to inform your response to these key questions. They are questions which you are well advised to return to from time to time.

FURTHER READING

Balderstone, D. (ed.) (2006) *'Secondary Geography Handbook'*, Sheffield: The Geographical Association.

Section One (chapters 1–8) explores important issues and debates about the role and purpose of geography education. These chapters explore the role of a geography teacher in shaping the geography curriculum in schools and providing relevant and meaningful learning experiences through geography for young people in the 21st century. The dynamic nature of geography as a subject discipline is emphasised and the implications of what it means to *'think geographically'* are explored.

Bale, J. and Speake J. (series editors) *Changing Geography*, Sheffield: The Geographical Association.

The *Changing Geography* series is aimed at A-level pupils but is a good way of maintaining your subject knowledge development. The series' publications introduce concepts and ideas from current research in higher education with themes for imaginative project work to provide pupils with more challenge and stimulating ares of the subject to investigate. The series includes publications on 'Disability, space and society', 'Everyday geographies', 'Citizen, state and nation', 'Sportscapes' and 'Glaciers and glacial landscapes'.

Morgan, J. and Lambert, D. (2005) *'Teaching school subjects 11–19: Geography'*, London: Routledge.

This book provides a more comprehensive discussion of the intellectual debates about the nature of geography and the ways in which school geography can interact with the wider subject discipline.

Rawling, E. (2001) 'Changing the Subject: The impact of national policy on school geography 1980–2000', Sheffield: The Geographical Association.

Eleanor Rawling was a member of the original Geography Working Group and later one of the Professional Officers for Geography at the Qualifications and Curriculum Authority until 2006. Her account of the impact of national policy-making on the development of school geography between 1980 and 2000 provides some illuminating insights into the politics of curriculum change and the factors influencing subject knowledge and identity (Rawling, 2001).

2 PUPIL LEARNING
Planning for whole classes

The distinctive aspect of a teacher's sense of purpose is that it is dominated by matters to do with children's learning.

(Lambert, 2004: 82)

Some pupils are better at geography than others. Some of this variation is accounted for by interest, motivation and quality of teaching, but much of it must be attributed to intellectual development.

(Leat, 1997: 151)

INTRODUCTION

The essence of being an effective teacher lies in knowing what to do to foster pupils' learning and being able to do it. Effective teaching is primarily concerned with setting up a learning activity for each pupil which is successful in bringing about the type of learning the teacher intends.

(Kyriacou, 1991: 1)

A recent OFSTED report stated that teaching and learning was outstanding or good in 52% of secondary schools; and a further 43% was classed as satisfactory. Successful lessons were characterised by high teacher expectation, good use of assessment data to plan further lessons for individual pupils, challenging tasks to ensure progress in learning (OFSTED 2006/07: para 65). In relation to pupils with learning difficulties, progress is good or better when tasks, resources and support are matched to the pupils' needs (OFSTED 2006/07: para 53). These findings applied generally to National Curriculum (NC) subjects. However, another report by OFSTED identifies weaknesses in the teaching of geography, particularly at Key Stage 3. One factor identified is the lack of challenge to pupils and a marked dissatisfaction by pupils of the curriculum and its presentation (OFSTED, 2008: 4).

Elsewhere, we have drawn your attention to a common failing identified in geography lessons, that of tasks not being matched to the differing abilities of pupils (Smith, 1997). In lessons reported as being unsatisfactory, this is frequently seen as a major source of the failings observed. While these observations may clearly reveal weaknesses in the planning of the lessons concerned, they may also reflect limitations in the teachers' understanding of pupil learning in geography and of the geographical abilities of their pupils.

There is certainly a close relationship between planning and the quality of teaching and learning in geography classrooms, but the quality of this planning will depend on your knowledge of how pupils learn geography as well as on knowledge of your pupils' learning in geography. The former may be based on some knowledge of theories about how pupils learn geography. Both will be informed by knowledge and understanding of learning derived from the assessments that you make of pupils' learning in geography. This knowledge and understanding about learning in geography cannot, therefore, just be acquired through reading or study. It is built up through practical experience: experience of planning teaching *for* learning, experience of observing pupils learning geography, listening to them talking about geography and making assessments of this learning (Chapter 10).

So planning involves knowing what to do to bring about successful learning. This is the 'essence' of being an 'effective teacher' referred to by Kyriacou. Knowing what is appropriate for pupils of different ages and abilities to learn in and through geography is essential if we are to plan for and achieve effective progression and differentiation in learning geography.

This chapter aims to provide you with some guidance about learning in and through geography in the belief that this will help you to do more to promote the intellectual development of your pupils. This requires us to give some attention to processes of learning, the development of learning skills and the fact that pupils learn in different ways. Your planning needs to take into account the range of abilities, aptitudes, interests, personalities, skills, cultural backgrounds and experiences of pupils within your geography classes.

Language plays an important role in the development of children's thought processes. Geography teachers need to explore ways in which work in geography can help to develop pupils' speaking, listening, writing and reading skills. We need to examine how pupils' understanding of geography can be enhanced by developing these skills. Geography has its own technical language which needs to be mastered if pupils are to progress to higher levels of understanding in the subject.

OBJECTIVES

By the end of this chapter, you should be able to:

■ describe different ways in which pupils learn in geography
■ understand how geography can promote the intellectual development of pupils and how to recognise progress in their learning in geography
■ identify ways in which geography can help to develop pupils' speaking, listening, writing and reading skills, and understand how their geographical abilities can be enhanced by developing these skills.

PUPILS LEARN IN DIFFERENT WAYS

Learning . . . that effective activity which enables the learner to draw upon previous experience to understand and evaluate the present, so as to shape future action and formulate new knowledge.

(Abbott, 1994)

In Chapter 5, we make a distinction between objectives-led and process models of curriculum planning in geography. We imply that geography teachers may use different models, or even elements of different models, depending on whether they wish to emphasise the outcomes of learning or the process of learning. Although we frequently use objectives (knowledge, understanding, skills, attitudes and values) to provide the teaching and learning that we are planning with a real sense of purpose, we indicate that the use of key questions can be helpful when planning lessons where it is difficult to predetermine precise learning outcomes or objectives. This enquiry-based approach developed from a belief in the intrinsic value of the learning process. Although it does not cover everything, the above definition contrasts with some of the more prevalent views, suggesting that learning is a passive process of knowledge acquisition, with predictable and measurable outcomes.

Abbott sees learning as an active process of relating new knowledge and meaning to existing knowledge and meaning. New ideas, thoughts and skills have to be accommodated and assimilated by the learner and connections made between past, present and future learning. This learning process is influenced by the way in which the learning is to be used, and whether this learning can be effectively retrieved and applied in future situations. We also need to acknowledge that some learning may be lost or undone as well as some relearning taking place. This is a person-centred view of learning that has important implications for us as geography teachers. Romey and Elberty see the task of the 'learner-centred' geography teacher as being to help pupils 'rediscover their "geographic antennae" and to bring the geographic dimensions of all their activities and all events into conscious awareness' (1984: 306).

This definition does not, however, take into account the wide variety of factors and conditions that influence this process of learning. For example, how do the characteristics of the teaching (style, skills, strategies, understanding of assessment and learning) influence the learner and the learning process? How do the characteristics of the learners (their expectations, abilities, personalities, preferred ways of learning, motivation, age, gender, social and cultural factors) influence their learning? What influence do the learning contexts (classroom, school and wider society) have on the ways in which the learning process varies for different learners? (See also Capel *et al.*, 2005: 151.) The model of learning shown in Figure 2.1 tries to summarise the different elements of the classroom system and to show the relationship between various influences on learning.

You should certainly give some further consideration to the importance of learner characteristics and how they influence learning processes and outcomes. Whole school and curriculum area policies have been developed to attempt to address the issues arising from these influences. Your initial training will seek to familiarise you with these issues and how they might be addressed in classroom, curriculum and school contexts. Your understanding of these issues and influences will, however, be developed through practical experience. More in-depth discussion of the importance of learner characteristics and pupil differences can be found in can be found in Capel *et al.*, 2005, Chapter 5 and Unit 6.1.

Clearly we do not all learn in the same way. We can all probably look back over our own experiences of geographical education and identify what we feel have for us been the most successful ways of learning geography: the types of lessons, teaching strategies and learning activities that we responded to most effectively. The significance of different learning styles is important for planning learning.

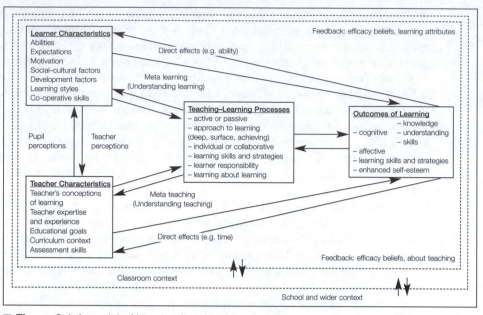

■ **Figure 2.1** A model of learning in school
Source: adapted from Biggs and More, 1993, and from Watkins *et al.*, 1996

Teachers use different strategies to achieve different learning outcomes, to facilitate different learning styles or processes, and to respond to the variety of ways in which different pupils learn and thus you need to develop a repertoire of teaching styles and strategies. Several researchers and education lists have tried to identify different learning styles to describe learners' preferences for particular ways of learning. David Kolb (1976) devised 'Learning Style Inventories' to describe learners' preferred ways of learning. This work has been adapted and developed by a number of others including Honey and Mumford (1986) (see Table 2.1). For further information on learning styles see Capel *et al.* (2005, Unit 5.1).

Did you teach each pupil today, this week, this month or even this term?

The idea of learning styles recognises that people learn best in different ways. The aim of learning style profiles is to describe the ways in which pupils learn and not to evaluate their learning ability. No single learning style has any overwhelming advantage over any other. They all have their own strengths and weaknesses. In reality, most people do not conform to just one of these learning styles, but learn in a combination of ways. Pupils will often adopt differing styles depending on the subject, the place or the time (see Box 2.1).

In theory, by helping pupils to develop their ability to operate in each of the different styles of learning they will become more 'effective' or better 'all-round' learners with a wide range of learning skills. Clearly, you cannot tailor every lesson that you teach to each learning style. However, it is worth reflecting whether, over a period of time, the geography lessons that you have been teaching have provided opportunities for all pupils to learn in ways that they are good at. Also, looking at the way in which individual pupils respond to different ways of learning geography will help you discover more about them as learners.

With older pupils (16–19) it can be useful to raise *their* awareness of different learning styles and of the ways in which they seem best able to learn. This enables them to reflect on their own learning, skills and particular strengths. They can then take more responsibility for their own learning, developing the skills needed to respond effectively to different information and situations. The overall aim should be to help pupils become good all-round learners capable of learning in a variety of different ways and of using a range of learning skills. The process of review of one's own learning, termed 'metacognition', is discussed in Capel *et al.*, 2005: 194–5 and 248–9.

■ **Table 2.1** Descriptions of learning styles

ACCOMMODATORS (DYNAMIC LEARNERS)	DIVERGERS (IMAGINATIVE LEARNERS)
■ independent and creative ■ likes taking risks and change ■ enjoys and adapts well to new situations ■ curious and investigative ■ inventive, experiments ■ shows initiative ■ problem solvers ■ involves other people ■ gets others' opinions, feelings ■ can be impulsive, 'rushes in' ■ uses 'trial and error' and gut reaction ■ relies on support network	■ imaginative and creative ■ flexible, sees lots of alternatives ■ colourful (uses fantasy) ■ uses insight ■ good at imagining oneself in new/different situations ■ unhurried, casual and friendly ■ avoids conflict ■ listens to others and shares ideas with a small number of people ■ uses all senses to interpret ■ listens, observes, asks questions ■ sensitive and emotional, deep feelings ■ cannot be rushed until ready
CONVERGERS (COMMON-SENSE LEARNERS)	**ASSIMILATORS (ANALYTIC LEARNERS)**
■ organised, ordered and structured ■ practical, 'hands-on'? ■ detailed and accurate ■ applies ideas to solving problems ■ learns by testing out new situations and assessing the result ■ makes theories useful ■ uses reasoning to meet goals ■ has good detective skills, 'search and solve' ■ likes to be in control of the situation ■ acts independently then gets feedback ■ uses factual data and theories	■ logical and structured ■ intellectual, academic ■ enjoys reading and researching ■ evaluative, good synthesiser ■ thinker and debater ■ precise, thorough, careful ■ organised, likes to follow a plan ■ likes to place experience in a theoretical context ■ looks for past experiences from which to extract learning ■ reacts slowly and wants facts ■ calculates probabilities ■ avoids becoming over-emotional ■ often analyses experience by writing it down

Source: developed from Fielding's (1992) adaptation of Kolb, 1976

Another useful way of looking at how pupils approach learning is to distinguish between surface and deep notions of learning (Marton and Saljo, 1976). This suggests that pupils adopt different approaches to learning depending on whether their intention is to remember specific information or to search for meaning. They use a surface-level approach to focus on the most important topics often using rote learning and memorisation so that they can reproduce them accurately. In contrast, pupils who adopt a deep-level approach are motivated by a desire to develop in-depth understanding and to solve problems. A third approach to learning has been identified as the achieving orientation where the motivation for pupils is to achieve high grades with or without understanding. This third style may therefore reflect both surface and deep approaches to learning.

This way of looking at how pupils approach learning suggests that some can effectively identify the most appropriate strategy for helping them make the most out of the situation or context in which they are learning. Biggs and Moore argue that this is a 'powerful' concept:

> Teachers need to realise that there is no one way in which students go about their learning; that some ways are more effective than others; and that, most important, there are things they as teachers can do to optimise the chances that students will go about learning in the most desirable ways.

(1993: 310)

Year 10 pupils

Sophie adopts a very logical approach to her work. She tends to be very objective and methodical, which explains why she regards researching information and writing effective notes as her learning strengths. She responds well to brainstorming activities and can generate new ideas. She does appreciate the opportunity for lateral thinking. Sophie does not regard herself as being a very practical person and she gets bored with routine tasks.

Rebecca is a cautious learner preferring to think through ideas and strategies before carrying out tasks. She does not grasp new ideas quickly and she prefers to use familiar methods that she is confident with. She feels more confident when carrying out practical tasks under clear instructions and discussing ideas in class to develop her understanding. One of Rebecca's strengths as a learner is her disciplined and thorough approach.

Matthew is a confident, enthusiastic and highly motivated pupil. His use of appropriate geographical language is highly developed. He is very interested in physical and environmental geography. He responds well to practical work and teacher directed work. He reflects on his learning experiences a great deal. Matthew regards himself as being an impulsive learner, being prepared to 'jump in' and take risks to develop new ideas. He enjoys practical demonstrations, discussion work and giving presentations, but does not feel that he is a very effective researcher.

Asif is an enthusiastic pupil who always tries to take a leading role in collaborative activities. He participates fully in discussions, asking questions and expressing his opinion confidently. He feels that he is good at researching information and relating theory to practice.

■ **Box 2.1** Learning style profiles: descriptions of learners

Activity 2.1 **Learning styles in geography**

This is intended as a discussion activity in a small group of student teachers 'brain-storming' ideas about the implications of different learning styles for teaching and learning in geography.

1 Carefully read through the descriptions of the four different learning styles shown in Table 2.1.
   a) Write down a list of different types of learning activity and teaching strategies in geography that you think each type of learner would respond to most effectively.
   b) Identify potential weaknesses associated with each learning style. For example, 'analytical learners' tend to be over cautious and wait for too much evidence before acting.
   c) Think of ways in which you could help learners to address such weaknesses.

2 Read the descriptions of the pupils' learning style profiles in Box 2.1.
   a) For each pupil, identify their 'preferred' learning styles in geography. (Remember that pupils can display elements of different learning styles and they can be stronger in some styles than in others.)
   b) Which areas of their learning does each pupil need to develop and how could you (or your teaching) help them to make these improvements?

As geography teachers, we need to give more attention to the processes of learning geography to set up activities which 'actively engage' pupils so that they can develop the use of deeper approaches to learning. The 'predictable pattern' of unsatisfactory lessons described by Gill Davidson suggests that pupils in these lessons are only likely to be using surface approaches to learning when tackling the 'fairly undemanding individual written task' that involves 'transferring or recording information' (1996: 13). According to OFSTED (1995) providing opportunities for pupils to use and develop the use of deeper approaches to learning through geography will help them to achieve high standards. At Key Stage 3, Peter Smith HMI observed best practice including occasions when:

pupils were regularly speaking and writing effectively to explain sometimes quite complex geographical processes and interrelationships.

And at post-16:

Many students can understand and handle complex and controversial matters involving both physical and human processes.
   Students show an ability to handle complex topics which require substantial knowledge as a pre-requisite to the development of understanding.

(1997: 125)

Activity 2.2 **Observing pupils' learning**

Following (or 'shadowing') a pupil or a class of pupils for a school day is a common task during your period of induction in your placement school. If possible, it would be helpful to use this 'shadowing' activity to focus on pupils' learning.

Pupils will often find themselves in different groupings for different lessons during the school day. If this is the case, choose one pupil or a small group of pupils that will be in the same class as each other for the whole day. During the day, try to construct a profile of each pupil as a learner. This profile could contain the following information:

■ age and personal characteristics
■ strengths and weaknesses as a learner
■ motivation and aptitude to learning
■ approaches to learning used in different subjects/lessons
■ opportunities to learn in different ways.

It would be helpful if you could observe the same pupil(s) in a geography lesson. Build up a profile of their learning in geography and contrast this with their learning in other areas of the school curriculum.

The information for these profiles will come from your own observations of the pupils' learning in different lessons and from talking to the pupils about their learning. During the lesson observations, you could devise a few simple questions to ask the pupil(s). Table 2.1 could be used to develop some questions to find out their 'preferred' ways of learning.

When completed, you need to find an opportunity to discuss these profiles with your geography mentor or a group of other teachers.

■ What opportunities do pupils have to learn in different ways in geography compared with other areas of the school curriculum? (i.e. learning styles)
■ What opportunities do pupils have to use different approaches to learning (surface, deep, achieving) in different areas of the school curriculum?
■ To what extent are pupils aware of the different ways in which they learn? Do they have opportunities to reflect on the ways in which they are learning in different subjects?
■ What factors appear to influence pupils' motivation to learn during a school day?

INTELLECTUAL DEVELOPMENT THROUGH GEOGRAPHY

At the start of this chapter, we argued that the 'essence' of being an effective geography teacher involves knowing what to do to promote the intellectual development of pupils through geography. This requires us to give some attention to the ways pupils learn through geography. Knowing what is appropriate for pupils of different ages and abilities to learn in geography will help us to match learning tasks to the differing abilities of pupils and to plan for progression in their learning. It should also help us to avoid delivering undemanding lessons consisting of 'busy work' in which pupils do little more than recording or transferring information.

Research into how children's thinking develops is well documented (see, for example Burton in Capel *et al.*, 2005). Although subject to some criticism and revision in recent times, Jean Piaget's studies in child development provide a general framework within which we can structure our understanding of children's mental development. These studies show that children's thinking develops as they mature and gain more experience of their environment. This framework, in relation to concept acquisition and logical thinking, suggests that mental development passes through a series of stages: sensori-motor, pre-operational, concrete operations and formal operations (a fully mature form of thinking).

David Leat points out that, in relation to school work, 'formal operational thinkers' have distinct advantages as they can deal with more complex relationships, formulate hypotheses and 'synthesize apparently unconnected information' (1997: 151). Leat suggests that this implies that pupils cannot successfully deal with some tasks because they are beyond their level of intellectual development. Pupils whose thinking is mainly at the concrete level tend to adopt rigid and over simplistic views, and descriptive accounts of issues. In short, they concentrate more on what happens rather than why it happens. These accounts may identify linkages between some factors but only at a basic level. Leat comments on how the explanations produced by concrete thinkers often reveal a 'black-and-white' view of the world:

> Having recently studied the work of a Year 7 (11–12 years of age) class on the removal of hedgerows, I was struck by the starkness of their views – this was a black-and-white issue. The common view was that it was bad for farmers to remove hedgerows because it affected wildlife, therefore it was unreasonable for farmers to do this. There was little room for compromise in their plans for the farm that they were studying.
>
> (1996: 253)

Concrete thinkers also find it difficult to hypothesise or to deal with a number of variables. This will limit their ability to develop explanations where they need to demonstrate an understanding of the relationships between several variables. These issues can have important implications for your work with Key Stage 3 pupils as this is the time when many pupils are making the transition between concrete and formal operational thinking.

Recently, one of our student teachers noted in her evaluation of work produced by Year 8 pupils in a unit of work about National Parks how most pupils were only able to describe some of the impacts of tourism on the Peak District. During this unit, pupils examined data showing the number of visitors to the National Park and the activities that they participated in. Photographic and video resources were used to study evidence of the impacts of tourism and the views of different interest groups were explored through a role play activity. Finally, a simple decision-making activity was developed to encourage pupils to consider possible solutions to the problems arising from tourism.

The solutions that pupils proposed tended to be simplistic; for example, ban cars and build large landscaped car parks. Some pupils provided explanations of problems arising from some of the impacts and their possible causes, but only at a very basic level. Very few showed any appreciation of interrelationships between factors such as landscape and environmental quality, access, amenity value, economic value, conservation and land use conflict.

Conversely, more able pupils might be expected to produce more detailed explanations showing greater understanding of relevant geographical processes. We recall observing an able Year 8 group making presentations about possible coastal protection measures for a stretch of coastline that they had been studying. The pupils displayed a number of geographical skills in the visual material that they had produced and they communicated their findings fluently. They also used appropriate vocabulary in a confident way and showed ability to recall knowledge about the places and processes studied. This included describing the way in which different coastal protection measures were designed to work.

Clearly, impressed by the pupils apparent grasp of relevant ideas and recall of detailed knowledge about the case studies, we shared the teacher's view that these pupils had displayed a high level of attainment. However, our joint evaluation of the lesson raised a number of issues which led us to consider the level of thinking displayed by the pupils.

It was clear that what we had observed was evidence of these pupils' ability to handle a lot of detailed information and to 'replay' explanations encountered during their study of this stretch of coastline. Their learning had been enhanced by a fieldwork visit to the coastline being studied. This provided a strong visual framework or experience with which to connect future learning. However, most of them were not demonstrating a clear understanding of relationships between various factors and processes. They could describe how coastal protection measures worked but could not evaluate their effectiveness in terms of how they influenced various processes.

Judgements about the ability of these younger pupils in terms of their capacity to recall more specific detail from their knowledge of certain places and processes are clearly valid. The depth and fluency of both written and oral work, and the use of appropriate vocabulary, are frequently used as indicators of pupil's level of attainment. However, developing pupils' capacity to think and their ability to use these powers of reasoning can produce more meaningful learning (Leat, 1998: 255). It therefore follows that in order to raise pupils' levels of attainment in geography, we need to consider how to accelerate their cognitive development using strategies that move them from concrete to more formal operational thinking. Strategies for teaching thinking and promoting such cognitive acceleration are discussed in Chapter 4 and at greater length in Leat (1998) and in Nicholls (2001), Ireson (in Capel *et al.*, 2005, Unit 4.3) and Burton (in Capel *et al.*, 2005, Unit 5.1).

In a discussion of 'worthwhile educational objectives' in geography education, Bill Marsden (1995) presents two dimensions of learning as a basis for considering how geography teachers can plan to promote the intellectual development of their pupils. *Abilities* refer to the intellectual skills that are being developed in the learner, while *principles, concepts and exemplars* provide the cognitive frameworks within which statements of learning objectives can be made.

Understanding the nature of concepts and how conceptual learning takes place should have an important influence on curriculum planning:

> If conceptual understanding is necessary for effective learning and problem-solving, then this suggests that our aim in teaching a subject will be to help children gain an understanding of those concepts which are fundamental to the field of study.
>
> (Naish, 1982: 47)

Marsden (1995) uses the common elements identified in the cognitive schemes of Bloom, Gagne, and Ausubel to propose a 'four-fold division' of the abilities dimension (see Box 2.2). This classification of objectives provides us with a helpful framework that can be used both to assist with curriculum planning (see Chapter 5) and to evaluate the way in which learning through geography can contribute to pupils' intellectual development. For more about Bloom, Gagne and Ausubel, see Capel *et al.*, 2005.

Principles, concepts and *exemplars* form what Marsden calls the 'raw materials' of the intellectual processes described above under the heading of 'abilities'. He argues that they represent higher levels of generality and thus provide 'the most convenient and cogent structures for curriculum planning' (Marsden, 1995: 67). They can help teachers to select content because, as Marsden points out, they are 'derived from the structure of knowledge itself' (Marsden, 1995: 67). Principles or *key ideas,* as defined earlier, involve the linking of two or more concepts. They are often used to provide a list of ideas which can be used to plan the objectives that form the basis of a curriculum unit.

Recall	the process of remembering which is assessed by asking questions requiring recall of memorised material
Comprehension	understanding or meaningful learning
Problem-solving	involves application, analysis and, to some extent, synthesis and evaluation. This ability is commonly associated with enquiry-based learning.
Creativity	is a very broad category emphasising the ability to use a range of principles, concepts and strategies to produce learning outcomes that may be unique and imaginative. The focus is therefore as much on the strategies used to facilitate this learning as on the content of the learning. Developing pupils' ability to use problem-solving skills and creativity are crucial if teachers are to help pupils to become autonomous learners.

■ **Box 2.2** The abilities dimension
Source: Marsden, 1995: 67

Learning concepts

Naish comments on how objectives in geographical education have moved away from explanatory descriptions of different parts of the world towards developing understanding of central concepts and principles. He defines a concept as 'an abstraction from events, situations, objects or ideas of the attributes which they have in common' (Naish,1982: 35). Concepts result from the way in which we classify these attributes, name them and put them into a 'growing filing system' to recall and use in future communication with others. Thus, conceptualising can be seen as a process of categorising.

In a similar way, Graves argues that a concept is 'basically a classificatory device which enables the mind to structure reality in a simplified manner by concentrating on the essential attributes of certain experiences' (Graves, 1975: 153). He moves on to suggest that geography teachers need to become much more aware of the cognitive hierarchy within the discipline. This is indeed a challenge as there is little authoritative guidance about how children develop their understanding of the wide range of concepts in geography. We will, however, try to provide some helpful advice based on evidence drawn from a variety of sources.

So what are these key concepts which form the core of geography? A number of studies have attempted to classify them. Catling (1976) suggested that there are three distinct but fundamentally interrelated organisational concepts in geography: spatial location, spatial distribution and spatial relations. He argued that the various ideas about the nature of geography could be reduced to these three basic concepts. Fundamental ideas about space and place continue to lie at the core of the wide variety of developments that have taken place in geography as a subject.

The attention given to the need to promote thinking through geography resulted in further consideration being given to the idea of concept elaboration. Leat (1997) argues that school geography revolves around a relatively small number of important concepts. Teaching programmes should aim, he contends, to make these concepts 'visible' and 'potentially transferable', thus elaborating their meaning to pupils over time. These prime concepts which underpin a sound understanding of geography include:

Classification	Cause
Conflict resolution	Effect
Location	Decision making
Planning	Systems
Inequality	

(Leat, 1997: 146)

Another way of classifying concepts would be to organise them into a hierarchy. The higher level concepts would be the more general organising concepts such as spatial interaction or inequality. These would be followed by more specific concepts. The implication is that the specific, higher level or abstract concepts can be understood. It would be worthwhile speculating what these higher level organising concepts in geography might be. How far do you agree with the 'prime concepts' identified by David Leat? Other organising concepts in geography might include distribution, interaction, distance, scale, region and spatial change (Naish, 1982: 37).

It is through this process of 'elaboration' that concepts become powerful and that higher cognitive skills such as explaining, analysing, synthesising and evaluating can be developed. Detailed subject knowledge also has a significant role to play in this process of concept elaboration, for without such knowledge these concepts mean little. The importance of this process of concept elaboration is illustrated in David Leat's discussion of 'cause' and 'conflict resolution':

> *Cause* becomes powerful when pupils know that there are causal factors, which can be classified as background (which predispose events, tend to be abstract and are ever present) or trigger (which are more time specific and visible). Explanations are often usefully structured by starting with background factors and proceeding to trigger factors. Explanations will often require branches to accommodate several factors. *Conflict resolution* becomes a powerful concept when pupils begin to discern through skilful debriefing, the recurring methods of resolving conflict that they have generated via the activities – through power, through zoning, through buying off, through amelioration, etc.

(Leat, 1998: 167)

The term 'concept' can be used in different ways. The majority of nouns, with the exception of particular people, places or events, are concepts. However, adding an adjective or combining two concepts forms what are termed 'compound concepts'. For example, river and pollution are concepts but river pollution is also a concept which is different from its component concepts.

Gagne (1965) distinguished between simple, descriptive 'concepts by observation' *(concrete concepts)* and the more complex organising 'concepts by definition' *(abstract concepts)*. The complexity of these concrete concepts depends upon how difficult they are to experience or whether understanding of other concepts is required. The complexity of abstract concepts is influenced by the number of variables involved in the defined relationships. This is an important distinction to make as it implies that the former may be learned through a process of discovery whereas the latter, expressing relationships of a more abstract nature, must be taught in some direct manner.

Key concepts provide the underlying structure for the subject in the revised National Curriculum (QCA, 2007). The Programme of Study (POS) has been reconstructed using the key organising concepts of geography, including the values dimensions of these ideas (see Figure 2.2). As they study geography, pupils will develop their understanding of these and other concepts that are central to the discipline. Curriculum design will involve planning for small steps of understanding and will need to make the purpose of learning explicit in relation to these concepts.

Understanding pupil learning in geography

Understanding pupil's learning is one of the key challenges facing us as teachers. Having examined how some of the theories about learning might be applied to geography, we shall now consider how geography teachers might develop their understanding of conceptual learning in geography. Developing this understanding might help us respond to Michael Naish's (1982) challenge that we should be aiming to provide 'appropriate experiences for conceptual learning' rather than 'factual information'. Frances Slater takes this further by suggesting that more could be done to 'engage the ability of the pupils to think abstractly and logically about their physical, economic, social and political environment' (1970).

Ghaye and Robinson (1989) argue that teachers need to develop ways of discovering and understanding pupils' 'structures of thought'. They suggest that concept maps can help us to learn something about the cognitive processes associated with the act of 'constructing meanings'. Leat and Chandler (1996) believe that concept maps have great potential to support pupils' cognitive development by providing 'powerful visual organisers of information' and encouraging them to 'access' their existing knowledge of a subject. In recommending the use of concept mapping in geography teaching they ask:

> If you were to be offered a teaching strategy that makes learning more meaningful for pupils, improves understanding, helps reveal misconceptions, reduces anxiety in pupils and helps teachers understand their subject matter, ought you to be interested?
> (Leat and Chandler: 108)

Key concepts that underpin the study of geography. Pupils need to understand these concepts in order to deepen and broaden their knowledge, skills and understanding.

1.1 Place
Understanding the physical and human characteristics of real places.
Developing 'geographical imaginations' of places.

1.2 Space
Understanding the interactions between places and the networks created by flows of information, people and goods.
Knowing where places and landscapes are located, why they are there, the patterns and distributions they create, how and why these are changing and the implications for people.

1.3 Scale
Appreciating different scales – from personal and local to national, international and global.
Making links between scales to develop understanding of geographical ideas.

1.4 Interdependence
Exploring the social, economic, environmental and political connections between places.
Understanding the significance of interdependence in change, at all scales.

1.5 Physical and human processes
Understanding how sequences of events and activities in the physical and human worlds lead to change in places, landscapes and societies.

1.6 Environmental interaction and sustainable development
Understanding that the physical and human dimensions of the environment are interrelated and together influence environmental change.
Exploring sustainable development and its impact on environmental interaction and climate change.

1.7 Cultural understanding and diversity
Appreciating the differences and similarities between people, places, environments and cultures to inform their understanding of societies and economies.
Appreciating how people's values and attitudes differ and may influence social, environmental, economic and political issues, and developing their own values and attitudes about such issues.

■ **Figure 2.2** Key concepts underpinning the study of geography (QCA, 2007)

CONCEPT MAPPING

1. Sort through the cards, discuss them and put aside any that you don't understand. You will be given an opportunity to check these out with me.
2. Put the cards on the piece of paper and arrange them in a way that makes sense to you. Discuss the possible links between the terms. Those with many links can be kept close together, but do not allow space between all cards, because more cards may be added later.
3. When you are satisfied stick them to the sheet.
4. Draw lines between the terms that seem to be connected.
5. Write on the line a short explanation of the link. Use arrows to show which way the link goes. Different links can go in both directions for any pair of terms and there can be more than one link in any direction. There does not have to be a link between all the terms.
6. On the blank card(s) add any missing terms that you think are important and add in the links.

■ **Box 2.3** Concept mapping: some instructions for pupils
Source: Leat and Chandler, 1996: 110

They outline the process of concept mapping, as conceived by Novak and Gowin (1984), and argue that as every concept depends on others for meaning 'the number and quality of connections made between disparate pieces of information' has potential to deepen understanding. They suggest that the concept of cause and effect, discussed earlier, provides a useful way of starting to explore the potential of concept mapping as it is possible to illustrate relationships between a variety of factors. Figure 2.3 shows an example of a concept map produced by an able Year 10 pupil to summarise her understanding of problems experienced by National Parks.

Concept mapping is a flexible teaching strategy that can be used to serve different purposes. Its potential to provide a good overview means that it can be used at the end of a unit of work to provide a summary or at the beginning to access pupils' existing knowledge and provide an advance organiser for the enquiry ahead. This is particularly useful at GCSE and A-level if pupils have encountered some of the concepts and processes at a younger age. It can also be an effective way of preparing pupils for written work, particularly when this work is to be used to reveal the depth of their understanding. See also Capel *et al.*, 2005: 264–5 and Frost and Turner 2005: 111–15 for further discussion and examples of concept maps.

So how can an understanding of concept acquisition help geography teachers? If we are aware of the level of difficulty of particular concepts for pupils' understanding, and how they come to acquire understanding of these concepts, we might be able to identify and prepare appropriate learning experiences for pupils of different ages and abilities more effectively.

'Practitioner knowledge', in other words the understanding developed by teachers through the practice of teaching, is of fundamental importance here due to the lack of conclusive research evidence. For example, Vass (1960) carried out research into concept

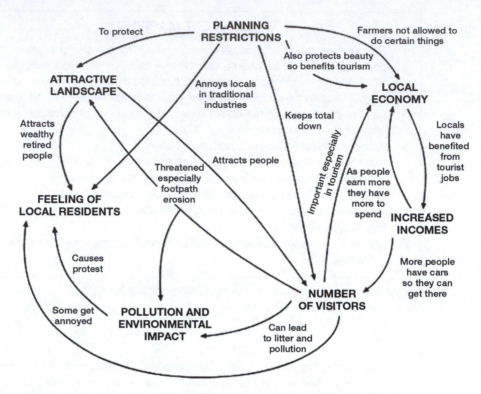

■ **Figure 2.3** A concept map produced by an able Year 10 pupil to show her understanding of problems in National Parks in England and Wales
Source: Leat and Chandler, 1996: 108

acquisition in physical geography. He observed a steady growth in children's under-standing of certain basic concepts in physical geography between the ages of 8 and 15, but found it impossible to determine an age at which physical geography might begin to be taught. A later study by Wilson investigated the extent to which certain basic geomorphological concepts can be taught to upper secondary children and found 'wide measurable differences in the level of understanding of the more fundamental concepts' (1971). More recent work identifying such common 'misconceptions' (Dove, 1999) can also provide valuable guidance for geography teachers.

However, it is not just in the work of pupils where geography teachers need to be aware of misconceptions. Throughout our discussion of 'Developing and using resources for teaching and learning in geography' (Chapter 6) we emphasise the need for geogra-phy teachers to evaluate critically the materials that they use with pupils.

The inference we are making here is not that you should throw out such textbook resources, but that you should help pupils to develop their critical skills so that they too can be aware of the limitations of how particular issues are presented. Encouraging pupils to identify 'hidden assumptions' and misconceptions in resources can aid conceptual learning.

Activity 2.3 **Conceptual learning in geography**

A) 1 To what extent do you agree with the assertion that school geography revolves around a small number of 'organising' or 'prime' concepts?

2 Write a list of what you feel these central organising or high level concepts might be.

Compare your list with the key concepts in the National Curriculum (Figure 2.2) and those suggested by David Leat, Michael Naish and Simon Catling.

B) Using concept maps in planning.

1 Choose one of the topics listed below:
■ The impacts of river flooding
■ Urban decline
■ Factors affecting coastal processes
■ Factors affecting agricultural land use
■ Inter-relationships between the different components of ecosystems.

2 Write a list of the concepts that you would expect pupils to learn about through a unit of work about this topic. (Decide on the age group of the pupils that would be studying this topic.)

3 Classify these concepts into abstract and concrete concepts and then attempt to arrange them hierarchically with the most general or abstract ones at the top to the most specific and concrete at the lowest level.

4 Now try to draw a concept map for your chosen topic.

5 When completed, carefully examine your concept map and consider how it might help you to plan a unit of work about this topic.

C) 1 Identify a topic that you are teaching where there would be an opportunity to explore pupils' conceptual learning through the use of concept maps.

2 Prepare a concept mapping activity for pupils studying this topic.

3 Carefully analyse the concept maps produced by the pupils. Is it possible to identify different levels of conceptual learning achieved by the pupils? You might try to use these concept maps to classify the degree to which particular concepts appear to have been understood by the pupils.

Try to write a brief description of these levels or categories of conceptual learning.

4 To what extent do these concept maps help you to evaluate the effectiveness of the teaching and learning activities in the unit of work for facilitating conceptual learning?

It would be particularly helpful to discuss the outcomes of activities B and C with other student teachers or with your mentor.

SPATIAL COGNITION AND GRAPHICACY

In Chapter 6, we emphasise the importance of maps as a way of storing and communicating information about people and places. Learning how to read and to use these maps contributes to the development of graphicacy in children. Rex Beddis (1983) described how pupils can be helped to understand the 'language' of maps just as they can be helped with any other language development.' OFSTED report that there is insufficient use of maps to progressively build up pupils' skills in data gathering, analysis and interpretation (OFSTED 2008: para 33). Helping pupils to understand the 'language' of maps is thus a central concern for geography teachers.

Spatial cognition (the development of map skills) forms a major part of graphicacy, which also includes the interpretation of photographs and other forms of graphic communication (Boardman, 1983). Pupils' spatial abilities are associated with their understanding of 'spatial location, spatial distribution and spatial relations' (Catling, 1976). These spatial abilities develop with the cognitive growth of children. For example, in the earlier stages of their development, children move from 'action in space' to 'perceptions of space' to 'conceptions about space' (Marsden, 1995: 78). Thus, spatial conceptualisation makes an important contribution to pupils' intellectual development.

Mental maps, in other words maps which people carry around in their minds, are often seen as a useful way of finding out about children's map drawing abilities and spatial cognition (Boardman, 1987, 1989). Pupils may be asked to draw from memory a spatial environment known to them such as that around their home or school, or perhaps the journey between the two. These mental or cognitive maps can then be compared with more formal maps or pupils encouraged to assess their accuracy on the journey home. Where several pupils follow the same route or live in the same area, they can be asked to compare their mental maps to identify similarities and differences.

Boardman (1987) comments on the way in which these mental maps can provide teachers with an understanding of pupils' perceptions of space and how they represent it. The nature of such maps and the detail shown on them indicate the pupils' ability to represent graphically their experience of environments. Boardman (ibid.) observes how the accuracy of pupils' mental maps is influenced by how familiar they are with their spatial environment and the distance of the route that they are trying to depict.

Research into the ability of children to represent their spatial environment by drawing mental maps has revealed that although they tend to show more information on their maps as they grow older, their learning process does not follow a simple linear progression (Matthews, 1984). Children learn about different environments in different ways. Consequently, although pupils' mapping ability and accuracy improve as they get older, they do not acquire these skills in a straightforward way. Boardman (1989) notes that a problem with such 'free-recall sketch mapping' is that children may actually know far more about their spatial environment than they are able to show on paper.

Cognitive mapping does not just have to be used to examine pupils' perceptions of familiar and proximal spatial environments. It can be applied effectively in problem-solving contexts to examine the impacts of people's perceptions of 'real space' or places. For example, Bale (1981), presents an activity using pupils' mental maps to explore the influence of spatial perception on decision-making in relation to economic activity (see Figure 2.4). Taking on the role of a 'potentially mobile industrialist', pupils assess the 'residential desirability' of fifty British towns. The scores allocated to each town are collated to produce a 'space preference map' of Britain for the class. The influences on pupils' perceptions can be considered and the outcomes compared with the result of economic surveys of industrialists' perceptions and the economic potential of different areas. It is possible to develop such activities into imaginative decision-making exercises to develop pupils' understanding of the complex interplay of factors influencing industrial location.

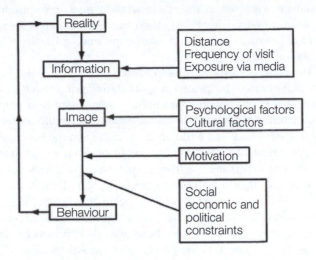

■ **Figure 2.4** Elements in behavioural geography
Source: Bale, 1981: 97

The Geography National Curriculum requires pupils to learn how to make, use and interpret maps and plans at a variety of scales. They should also be able to select and use appropriate techniques to present evidence on maps.

Paul Weeden defines these command words more precisely as:

■ using maps – relating features on a map directly to features in the landscape
■ making maps – encoding information in map form
■ reading maps – decoding successfully the element of map language
■ interpreting maps – being able to relate prior geographical knowledge to the features and patterns observed on the map

(Weeden, 1997: 169)

Gerber and Wilson (1984) proposed four essential properties of maps that should form the basis of any programme for developing mapwork skills:

■ Plan view (perspective and relief)
■ Arrangement (location, direction and orientation)
■ Proportion (scale, distance and selection)
■ Map language (signs, symbols, words and numbers)

Developing pupils' understanding of each of these properties poses different challenges for geography teachers. Often we need to focus on each one individually before integrating them with other map skills in learning activities that require pupils to apply these skills and their knowledge of geography. For example, until pupils have understood how contours are used to represent relief on a map, they are unlikely to be able to interpret landscape features. Indeed, it is usually the case that they reach higher levels of achievement when the different elements of maps are introduced to them separately (Boardman, 1989). Gerber (1981) also observes how pupils seem to be able to handle one element of a map at a time, but often experience difficulty when dealing with several elements together.

The concept of *location* is fundamental to all mapping. Mapping enables places, objects and events to be located in space. Using grid references to locate points on maps is a skill that builds on children's ability to draw and read graphs in mathematics. It is useful, therefore, with pupils who are experiencing difficulties with grid references to take a few steps back and build up their skills from the basic use of co-ordinates to four figure grid references. They can use one finger from one hand to follow on easting (east of the point of origin) and one from the other hand to follow a northing (north of the point of origin) until they meet at the reference point. This, and other techniques used by primary school teachers to help children learn about co-ordinates, can help us understand how to achieve a progressive development of the skills needed to use grid references. Only when these principles have been grasped is it possible to move on to using six-figure grid references to locate points more precisely within grid squares.

Being able to orientate a map and to describe *direction* are important skills. Pupils should learn how to describe direction using the points of the compass and encouraged to use the correct terminology throughout their geographical work (for example, when describing the direction in which rivers may be flowing and where places are in relation to each other). Marking the cardinal points on the walls of the classroom and giving pupils practical tasks requiring them to describe direction is helpful. It is important to avoid potential confusion by emphasising that wind direction refers to the direction from which winds blow, again with practical examples.

The concept of *scale* is challenging for some pupils as it requires them to not only measure distances accurately, but also to understand perspective and proportion. The basic principles underpinning the use of scale will have been taught in mathematics but, once again, when pupils are experiencing difficulties, it is helpful to go back a few steps and use strategies that may be used with younger children. Highly structured tasks requiring pupils to use different scales in small steps are needed. It is also very important to have maps of the same area at different scales for pupils to compare and to use to make similar measurements. Using scaled plans of the school and maps of the local area can be helpful as pupils are able to see the features that they are measuring.

Once pupils have learnt the skills needed to use grid references and scale, to describe direction and become familiar with the more common mapwork skills, they can tackle a variety of *route following* exercises. It is possible to devise some imaginative activities that require pupils to use these skills to follow routes or plan journeys. These could include treasure hunts, mystery tours and fugitive hunts. Grid references could be written in passages replacing the names of features or locations.

The use of *contours* to show height, slope and relief is another concept that pupils often experience difficulty with. If pupils are to be able to interpret the physical landscape shown on topographical maps, they must be able to identify and understand contour patterns. This is therefore a skill that needs to be introduced to them at an early stage in the secondary school and revisited several times to reinforce and progress their understanding and use of the skill.

Given the potential difficulties that pupils can experience, it is helpful to develop a range of visual resources with which to teach this particular skill. Clay or plasticine can be moulded into simple landscape features around which contours can be drawn

(Boardman, 1996). These models can then be cut into layers which the pupils can draw around and re-assemble. Relief models can be made to show particular landscape features using thick card or polystyrene tiles to build up layers representing the contours.

When pupils have grasped the basic principles relating the space of contours to the height and slope of land, it is possible to move on to examine common contour patterns and landforms. Pupils should learn how to identify specific landscape components (e.g. hills, valleys, ridges and spurs) before trying to interpret some of the larger scale features associated with particular types of scenery (e.g. limestone, glaciation).

Drawing *cross-sections* is a specific skill that can be used to interpret the relief of an area. Although it is a skill that builds on pupils' ability to draw graphs, you will often need to use a variety of strategies and supporting resources to help pupils develop this skill. For younger pupils it is usually a good idea to start with a simplified contour pattern with a line marked on it along which the cross-section will be drawn. The horizontal and vertical scales of the cross-section could be marked on graph paper and photocopied so that pupils can concentrate on the steps needed to transform the contours on to the section. You may also find it helpful to produce a resource sheet showing the different stages in the production of a cross-section.

When moving on to draw cross-sections directly from Ordnance Survey maps, it is a good idea to get pupils to first concentrate only on the bolder contours. When drawing their own axes for the cross-section on graph paper, pupils need to be shown how to avoid excessive vertical exaggeration in the scales. Boardman (1996) reminds us that a vertical:horizontal scale ratio of 5:1 is normally accepted as the maximum exaggeration to avoid turning a gently undulating landscape into one mountainous in appearance.

One very effective way of helping pupils to learn and practise map skills is through *orienteering* activities. Often described as a 'geographical sport', orienteering has the advantage of providing an active way of learning map skills and being a strategy that can be adapted for use in a wide variety of environments to focus on particular skills. Short exercises can be developed for use in and around the school and its local area. Boardman points to other advantages:

> Orienteering not only provides practice in using map reading skills but also helps to develop an eye for terrain, slope and accessibility, as well as an appreciation of map scale. The sport is essentially concerned with navigation and involves making decisions about map interpretation, and taking aid using compass bearings. Orienteering helps to develop confidence with maps and self-reliance out of doors, giving participants responsibility for making their own decisions.
>
> (Boardman, 1989: 329)

Activity 2.4 **Learning mapwork skills**

Arrange to observe a lesson (or lessons) in which pupils are being taught how to use one specific mapwork skill (e.g. the use of grid references).

In consultation with the class teacher, identify a small number of pupils (maximum of five) across the range of ability in the class that you will focus on for the purpose of this activity. If pupils are grouped according to ability, it would be helpful to observe different classes learning the same skill.

During the lesson(s) find opportunities to observe each of the pupils working on the tasks set by the teacher. Make a note of which aspects of the tasks each pupil succeeded with, and any with which they experienced difficulties.

■ Outline the strategies used by the teacher.
■ Summarise the problems and successes experienced by the pupils.
■ From your observations during the lesson and by studying the work produced by the pupils, evaluate the effectiveness of the resources and strategies used to teach this particular mapwork skill.
■ How were the resources and strategies adapted for pupils of different abilities? In what ways could these resources and strategies have been developed further?

If possible, you will find it helpful to discuss your findings with those of other student teachers who have observed other mapwork skills being taught.

There is now an increasing range of computer software available that can be used to enable pupils to learn as well as to practise mapwork skills. Some include simple activities that pupils can use to test their knowledge and understanding of map symbols or their ability to use grid references. Some programs demonstrate how cross-sections can be drawn and particular contour patterns interpreted, while others produce three-dimensional representations of relief patterns. Others provide a wide variety of maps and aerial photographs that can be used to develop imaginative activities. Digitised map data are now available for use with appropriate GIS (Geographical Information Systems) software. Such software can produce three-dimensional representations of the relief of areas shown on the maps.

Using *Google Earth* (www.earth.google.com), pupils can explore the physical and human features of a place at a range of scales, in plan, profile and oblique views. Whilst the technological advances continue, it remains to be seen whether they will actually enhance pupils' skills of graphicacy and in particular, their ability to recognise and interpret landscape features. Martin (2006) shows how ICT can be used effectively to improve pupils' use of maps and contribute to the development of their visual literacy and skills of graphicacy.

Although it is possible to develop pupils skills of graphicacy in a progressive way, the learning of these skills is 'seldom linear', and there is 'no one way of setting out the objectives of map learning' (Bailey and Fox, 1986: 114). It is important that you are aware of the different aspects of map understanding and use so that you can identify opportunities to introduce and develop them in your teaching. For example, in relation to scale, between the ages of 11 and 14 pupils should learn how to measure distances and convert measurements using scale. They should have opportunities to draw plans to scale, to compare maps at different scales and to describe routes giving distances and directions using information shown on maps. Between 14 and 16 years of age, pupils might learn how to carry out a range of calculations using scale including gradients, the vertical exaggeration of cross-sections and the approximate areas of landscape features shown on maps. Post-16, scale might be used to carry out more complex calculations such as drainage densities and bifurcation ratios or to delimit areas such as that of a drainage basin.

Activity 2.5 **Applying mapwork skills**

1　Select examples of Ordnance Survey (OS) map extracts available in your school.

How could these map extracts be used to investigate aspects of particular geographical themes?

2　Devise tasks for Year 9 pupils that require them to use specific mapwork skills to investigate aspects of one geographical theme on each of the map extracts provided.

You will also find it helpful to look through examples of examination papers to see how maps are used in questions. Find examples of questions that fit into each of these categories:

■ reading and calculation
■ transformation
■ interpretation.

If available, read through the examiners' reports and mark schemes to find out what the examiners were looking for in the answers, and the common mistakes and misconceptions of the candidates. With colleagues, identify what you could do to help pupils to avoid mistakes.

At some time during their geographical education, pupils will encounter assessment tasks where they will need to use and apply their mapwork skills. Questions using Ordnance Survey maps are included in most GCSE examinations. These questions usually fall into three categories. First, there are questions where pupils need to use specific skills to identify features at particular grid references, measure distances, state directions and estimate heights of gradients. Second, there are questions requiring pupils to transfer or 'transform' information shown on a map into another form, for example, onto a sketch map or cross-section. This includes questions where features identified on aerial photographs have to be matched with corresponding features shown on a map. Finally, there are questions where pupils need to apply their mapwork skills to describe and interpret features of both physical and human environments. This will require them to combine these skills with their knowledge and understanding of geography. For example, they may be asked to describe and explain patterns of relief, drainage, settlement or communications shown on a map.

LANGUAGE, LITERACY AND LEARNING IN GEOGRAPHY

Language provides the medium for learning geography in every classroom and should therefore be a major consideration in the planning and preparation of lessons.

(Butt, 1997: 154)

All teachers are now required to consider ways of developing their pupils' use of language. The National Curriculum orders for every subject to make it clear that the development of language skills is an entitlement for all pupils:

> Pupils should be taught to express themselves clearly in both speech and writing and to develop their reading skills. They should be taught to use grammatically correct sentences and to spell and punctuate in order to communicate effectively in written English.

This statement reflects the government's concern with the importance of spelling, punctuation and grammar. However, though clearly important, this is a somewhat narrow view of the role of language in learning. Graham Butt reminds us that the 'action of learning is closely associated with that of comprehending and using different forms of language' (Butt, 1997: 154). Frances Slater (1989) describes the two distinct functions of language use in geography lessons as being to communicate what has been learnt and is known as well as being part of the activity of learning. The latter emphasises the importance of 'talking, reading and writing to learn' (Roberts, 1986; Hewlett, 2006).

A great deal has been written about the relationship between language and learning and the role played by language in the development of children's thought. This role becomes more and more important away from the acquisition of concrete concepts to those representing more abstract ideas (Graves, 1975). Within geography, research reported by Williams (1981), Slater (1989), Carter (1991), and Butt (1993) has made a significant contribution to our understanding of the role of language in the process of learning.

The lack of conclusive evidence means that many questions relating to the role of language in cognitive development remain unanswered. In particular, more research is needed into the processes by which children use language both to learn and to develop their understanding of concepts through talking and writing. The difficulty in collecting and interpreting such evidence is one reason for this lack of evidence. There are also problems isolating specific learning associated with language development from other learning processes in the classroom.

You need to develop an understanding of how the use of language can influence learning. Guidance on geography and the use of language suggests that to be successful learners, pupils need to be given opportunities to:

■ **speak** clearly and effectively to convey information and ideas to a variety of audiences
■ **listen** attentively to others to take in meanings, intentions and feelings
■ **read** confidently to gain ideas, information and stimulus from written text
■ **write** accurately and appropriately to express understanding and present information and imaginative ideas.

(See http://www.nc.uk.net/nc-resources/html/language.shtml)

Developing pupils' literacy skills helps their learning in geography in a number of ways (DfES, 2002: 1):

■ Pupils need vocabulary, expression and organisational control to cope with the cognitive demands of the subject.
■ Reading enables pupils to learn from sources beyond their immediate experience.
■ Writing helps to sustain order and thought.

■ Language enables pupils to reflect, revise and evaluate the things they do, and the things that others have said, written or done.

■ Responding to higher order questions encourages the development of thinking skills and enquiry.

■ Improving literacy and learning can have an impact on pupils' self-esteem, motivation and behaviour. It allows them to learn independently. It is empowering.

Geography can provide a wide range of experiences, both in the classroom and through fieldwork, in which pupils can develop their language skills. Giving attention to the use of appropriate skills can also help to enrich pupils' extensive and wide-ranging vocabulary, which needs to be developed if pupils are to gain a sound understanding of the subject. Enabling pupils to write effectively and talk confidently about their work helps them to understand ideas and make connections. Reading and listening are necessary for access to information and ideas from a range of sources, and can thus extend and consolidate their knowledge and understanding. In 2001, the Literacy Strategy was introduced in all maintained schools in England as part of the National Key Stage 3 Strategy (now known as the Secondary National Strategy). This strategy has sought to address concerns about weaknesses in literacy preventing pupils from accessing the curriculum and making progress that reflects their ability as well as preparing them for life beyond school.

The Literacy Strategy is based on a framework of 'word', 'sentence' and 'text' level objectives (see the Framework for literacy on the DCSF website). 'Word' level development focuses on improving spelling and vocabulary, whereas 'sentence' level objectives focus on sentence construction and development of paragraphs. 'Text' level objectives are divided between reading, writing, speaking and listening. Geography teaching can help to raise pupils' standards of literacy using the National Literacy Framework (Thompson *et al.*, 2001). The authors emphasise the need to use classroom approaches that embed literacy developments into the routines of teaching and learning; and that pupils to take some responsibility for, and recognise the value of, developing their own literacy skills (Thompson *et al.*, 2001: 174)

Achieving these objectives requires you not only to be aware of the opportunities for developing pupils' language skills but also to plan specific activities which develop pupils' use of language in geography. Hewlett (2006) suggests a range of stimulating strategies for developing pupils' literacy skills through geography.

Providing appropriate opportunities for pupils to talk about geography is important for developing both their language skills and their understanding of the subject. In talk, you use language to organise your thoughts and give shape to your ideas. Pupils should be given opportunities to talk in a range of contexts and for a variety of purposes in geography including describing and explaining, negotiating and persuading, exploring and hypothesising, challenging and arguing. Carter describes the ways in which children use talk in learning to:

■ engage – relate new information to existing experience and knowledge
■ explore – investigate, hypothesise, speculate, question, negotiate
■ transform/restructure – argue, reason, justify, consider, compare, evaluate, confirm, reassure, clarify, select, modify, plan
■ present – demonstrate and convey understanding, narrate, describe
■ reflect – consider and evaluate new understanding.

(Carter, 1991: 2)

Activity 2.6 **Language, literacy and learning in geography**

These tasks explore 'talking, listening, reading and writing' in geography. They should be carried out during your induction period in school when you are undertaking a broad programme of classroom observation. Discuss your findings with other student teachers and with your geography mentor.

A) Speaking and listening
   1   What opportunities are there for pupils to talk about geography? Briefly describe examples from the lessons that you observe where pupils are given opportunities to talk about geography. What evidence is there that the pupils are learning about geography through speaking and listening? What do teachers do and say to 'shape' or to 'guide' this learning?
   2   Reflection: What type of learning activities and teaching strategies promote learning through speaking and listening in geography?
   3   Summarise the factors that 'encourage' and 'discourage' teachers from giving pupils opportunities to talk about geography.
B) Reading
   1   What types of text do pupils use in geography?
   2   What kinds of reading take place in geography lessons? What is the purpose of this reading?
   3   What difficulties do pupils experience when reading in geography? How can or could some of these difficulties be overcome?
C) Writing
   1   What different kinds of written work do pupils undertake in geography? It may help to consider three different forms of writing:
      ■   transactional (to inform others and record information)
      ■   poetic (for aesthetic purposes)
      ■   expressive (for thinking and exploring ideas).
   2   Collect examples of two or three different pieces of writing in geography. These pieces of writing can either illustrate:
      ■   different forms of writing
      ■   writing by pupils of different abilities
      ■   problems that pupils experience when writing in geography.

Be prepared to talk about these pieces of writing.
   Make a note of any specific strategies that you observe teachers using to support pupils' writing in geography.

Teacher talk dominates geography classrooms and controls the process by which communication takes place, by deciding what kind of talk is permissible, by whom and for how long (Roberts (1986), Butt (1997). Thus, teachers exert a strong influence on how talk is used to help pupils learn. They also convey messages about what they think is important. Roberts reminds us that 'some teacher talk is highly desirable':

> It is a means of conveying excitement in the subject, of motivating pupils and of introducing pupils to the specialist language of geography which is best done in talk where meanings can be fully explored.
>
> (Roberts,1986: 68)

Anxieties about classroom management lead many teachers to control pupil talk tightly and pupils are rarely given opportunities to 'negotiate' what is talked about (Butt, 1997). Specific strategies are needed to promote more focused pupil talk and thus alleviate some of these anxieties. There are a range of appropriate collaborative strategies (discussed in Chapter 4) and ways of using resources that can provide the focus for pupil talk. As well as being stimulating and motivating, evidence shows that discussing issues, questions or problems helps pupils to engage in higher level thinking (Slater, 1989). Butt argues that:

> If the discussion tasks are clearly set, the duration of the group work firmly established, reporting back procedures clarified, and teacher interventions timed correctly, the results can be impressive.
>
> (Butt,1997: 159)

It is a good idea to start with simple strategies requiring pupils to talk in pairs. One such strategy involves pupils describing the distribution of a geographical feature shown on a map, for example, the global distribution of population. Two pupils sit back to back, one with a blank outline map of the world, one with a map showing global distribution of population. The latter pupil describes the distribution of population shown on her map to the former, who marks it on to the outline map with appropriate shading and labels. This activity provides opportunities for pupils to develop their use of appropriate geographical terminology as well as their understanding of particular ideas. It can also be adapted for use with a wide range of geographical maps and diagrams. Its main advantage is that it provides a clear focus for pupil talk within a manageable period of time (approximately ten minutes).

Pupils need to use a wide range of reading skills in their work in geography. Enquiry-based approaches to learning geography require pupils to read widely from a variety of texts and other sources of information. As well as following written instructions, they need to select, compare, synthesise and evaluate information from different sources. They will also need to use other skills to distinguish fact and opinion, and to recognise bias and objectivity in sources. Add to this the fact that geography has its own extensive vocabulary which needs to be mastered if pupils are to be able to understand and interpret what they are reading.

Opportunities for pupils to read material from a variety of cultures and traditions are often not fully exploited by geography teachers. Development Education Centres have a wide range of such material including poetry, short stories, fiction and drama, as well as first-hand or eye-witness accounts. Using such material can provide stimulating and challenging ways of studying geographical issues and questions through the eyes of people from other cultures.

The development of reading skills is often neglected in geography lessons. Evidence shows that most of the reading that takes place in social studies lessons (including geography) is in short bursts of less than thirty seconds, which does not provide adequate opportunity for critical evaluation of or engagement with text (Roberts, 1986). This contrasts with the continuous reading that is frequently required for homework when pupils are less likely to have any support available. Roberts argues that geography teachers can:

help the development of reading skills firstly by being aware of the difficulties pupils have, secondly by providing a variety of reading materials, and thirdly by devising activities which enable pupils to read intensively and grapple with the meaning of what they read.

(Roberts, 1986: 72)

'Reading around the class' is a strategy frequently used that illustrates many of the problems highlighted by Margaret Roberts and which gives us cause for concern. Too often it is used as a control strategy rather than a lead into particular learning activities. Pupils are usually asked to read a short section of text in turn. Sometimes the teacher asks questions to check understanding, but usually there is no intervention to improve reading skills, evaluate content or to explain meaning. Other pupils are passive listeners and gain little, particularly if the reading is poor. We should give reading the attention that it deserves as a vital aspect of language and literacy development within the subject.

Butt (1997) quotes research which showed that sixth form pupils often do not have the 'competence expected of the "implied reader"' and reported frustration caused by an inability to link together text and the range of illustrative material (maps, diagrams, photographs and statistics) in geography text books. Butt also comments on how:

The length and complexity of sentences in texts and worksheets, together with unfamiliar and technical works, density of text, font size and abstraction of concepts can also make pupil understanding a problem.

(Butt, 1997:163)

Directed Activities Related to Text (DARTs)

Directed Activities Related to Text (DARTs) can be used to help pupils understand texts they are reading and thereby to develop their reading skills (see Roberts, 2003 for examples in relation to enquiry learning). These activities are designed to focus pupils' attention on the structure and meaning of part of a text (see Box 2.4). On a copy of the text, pupils could be required to underline different categories when classifying information, different arguments or the advantages and disadvantages of schemes. Diagrams could be labelled with important information and key terms to develop understanding of the text. Reorganising or reassembling information into a diagram, table or list is a frequently used DART strategy. Comparing different texts can help pupils to develop skills needed for critical evaluation. Butt also advocates encouraging pupils to discuss the outcomes of such activities and present their interpretations of texts to the rest of the class (Butt 1997: 164). Hewlett suggests a creative 'trash it or treasure it' activity for developing pupils' ability to analyse and synthesise material they read (Hewlett 2006:128). Pupils identify information that is relevant to the purpose of the task and what should be left out.

The bulk of the writing that children undertake in school is transactional involving copying, reorganising, reporting and perhaps translating information. The nature of geography as a subject *demands* that a great deal of writing in the subject is transactional. However, as Butt points out this 'may not help the pupil learn from the writing experience' (Butt 1997: 160). The need to learn through the writing experience is elaborated by Slater:

Directed Activities Related to Text (DARTs)

Devised by the 'Effective Use of Reading' project

■ **Reconstruction DARTs** – text is altered in some way so that pupils can reconstruct it perhaps by printing it in sections on card. *Sequencing* and *diagram completion* are useful in geographical enquiry (Roberts, 2003: 130-132)

■ **Analysis and reconstruction** – the text is presented as a whole with activities designed to enable pupils to analyse the components of the text (through underlining, highlighting or labeling) and then reconstruct these components into a simpler form (in lists, tables, flow diagrams, and annotated maps and diagrams).

■ **Box 2.4** Directed Activities Related to Text

Source: Lunzer and Gardner, 1979, *The Effective Use of Reading project*

> The demand for impersonal, unexpressive writing can actively inhibit learning because it isolates that which is to be learned from the vital learning process – that of making links between what is already known and the new information. It is through the tentative, inarticulate, hesitant, backward- and forward-moving, expressive mode that connections and links between old and new knowledge can be made. Then a student may be ready to set the understanding down in a formal transactional mode.
>
> (Slater, 1993: 113)

Research by Hamilton-Wieler (1989) noted the importance placed by A-level students on writing in geography. Writing was seen as an opportunity to develop ideas further and to 'argue things better'. Students felt that there were opportunities to speculate as there was a feeling that there was 'no certainty about anything in geomorphology' so 'you can't really be wrong' (Hamilton-Wieler 1989: 60). Her research highlights a fundamental dilemma facing us as teachers whereby writing that encourages language development and understanding is significantly different from that required to demonstrate to 'an unknown examiner acquired information and knowledge' (Hamilton-Wieler 1989: 60). In other words, the emphasis is on language as an assessment tool rather than a vehicle for learning. Roberts (2003, Chapter 7) discusses how pupils' writing can be developed throughout the process of geographical enquiry to promote understanding. She provides a range of examples of practical activities to show how writing can contribute to learning.

There are plenty of opportunities for aesthetic and imaginative writing in geography. Pupils can be offered opportunities to write poems about places they have visited, perhaps as part of a fieldwork activity. David Job (1998) describes how pupils can construct Haiku poems to express their feelings about places. To generate writing for aesthetic purposes in geography requires us to be imaginative when designing motivating learning experiences that will stimulate pupils and encourage them to use all of their senses.

Research by Butt (1993) has explored how expressive language can be encouraged in geography by getting pupils to write for different audiences from those which they normally encounter. The aim is to reduce the 'immediacy of the teacher's assessing role' by getting pupils to write for more 'realistic audiences' (Butt 1993: 24). Butt envisaged that using such audiences would encourage more original and creative writing in geography:

The Rainforest

The rainforest : a lush canopy of moist green leaves,
An animal paridise, full of tender new shoots,
And fruits fell of delicious flavours.
A parrot screeches, fluffing up it's vividly couloured feathers,
As it sits high up in the trees, almost completely camourflaged,
by hanging leaves from the branches above.
All kinds of animals scamp along the floor of the jungle,
But the most spectacular are the ones which patgrol the airways.
Birds are only the beginning of these magnificent airborne creatures.
The paradise tree snake slithers up an almost vertical tree,
It then drops off in to the air and spreading out it's body,
It flattens itself and glides effortlessly to the ground.
A gliding squirrel has flaps of extra skin stretching from head to toe,
It stretches out it's limbs and drops from a great height,
The wind catches this skin like a sail and it swoops to safety,
There are all sorts of nasty creepy-crawlies in the Rain Forest,
Such as terrantulars and scorpions,
But they all serve their purpose as food or to eat others as food.
Marmosets swing easily from one tree to another,
Collecting tasty tit-bits along the way to feed on.
These small furry animals are strong even though they are
small. An arrow poison frog is a very concientious parent,
After dipositing each tadpole in a separate pool in a plant it
returns every few days to lay unfertilised eggs for the young
tadpole to eat.
There is more to the rain forest than you see at first and it
is sad that it is dissapearing so fast.

Tropical Rain forests

Tropical rainforests are found in warm, wet parts of the world, such as Brazil, Indonesia and West Africa. Life is abundant here in many forms because of the ideal conditions.

The first thing that would strike you if you entered a tropical rainforest would be the sound. You would hear howling monkeys, screaming and chirping birds and all kinds of other animal noises. You may also see the creatures, but many of them would be camouflaged or hidden in the tops of the trees (the canopy). The tallest tree in a tropical rain forest is the Capoc. Compared with the other layers of the forest not much lives here, only birds of prey like eagles which would kill and eat anything that dares to venture above the canopy. The Capoc grows to a height of 200 ft and the air around it is considerably more breezy than in or below the canopy. The canopy is sometimes known as the pastures of the jungle. Insects, parrots, monkeys and many more animals live here. Nearer the ground there is comparatively little vegetation or animal life, because of the amount of shade provided by the canopy. Only in less dense areas is there a shrub layer which will in turn support it's own variety of creatures.

In the rainforest there are no seasons, it is warm and wet all the year round, like an eternal summer. Consequently plants flower and animals breed at different intervals for each species, anything from every ten months to every ten years. This ensures there is food for everything at all times.

■ **Figure 2.5** Writing by 14-year-old pupils

Source: Lambert, *Geography Assessment* © Cambridge University Press, 1991. Reproduced with permission.

It was postulated that changing the audiences that pupils wrote for might change their thought, learning and understanding processes and ultimately improve their writing and talking in geography lessons.

(Butt, 1997: 161)

Setting up audience-centred writing requires careful preparation. The original audience needs to be established so that pupils understand that this audience is the main focus for their work. A variety of resources and strategies, including pupil-centred discussion, will need to be used to create this (Butt, 2001).

Through his research, Graham Butt found that changing the audience has 'some effect on the learning process' (Butt 1993: 24). Pupils frequently demonstrated 'a deeper understanding of the geography being studied and a greater appreciation of values and attitudes' in their writing. There were also other benefits including an improvement in the quality of discussion and questioning as well as the development of the teacher's role as a 'geographical consultant'.

Audience-centred writing is certainly worth exploring as a strategy for developing pupils' language skills. However to use this strategy effectively some attention should be given to establishing the following necessary pre-conditions:

■ that a sense of trust and purpose needs to be established before good audience-centred writing will appear – boys did not reveal this sense of trust as readily as girls

■ that removing the idea of teacher as assessor in pupils' minds is important, but also extremely difficult

■ that audience-centred writing should be integrated into schemes of work, but not over-used; that audiences should be realistic and plausible

■ that if levels of pupil involvement, discussion and enquiry are allowed to increase through audience-centred work, geographical attainment may also rise.

(Butt, 1993: 22)

- pupil to self
- pupil to trusted adult
- pupil to teacher, as partner in dialogue
- pupil to teacher, as examiner or assessor
- pupil to pupil, or peer group
- pupil to younger child

■ **Box 2.5** Audiences that pupils can write for
Source: Slater, 1993; Butt, 1993

As well as providing opportunities for pupils to write for different purposes in geography, we need to look for strategies that can help them improve the quality of their written work. Too often assumptions are made about pupils' ability to write in different forms and not enough attention is given to helping pupils develop the skills needed to write effectively in geography. No, this is not just the task of the English department or the Special Needs' team, it is the responsibility of all teachers.

Pupils frequently have the opportunity to draft work in English yet this is not a strategy in common use in geography lessons. Increasingly, we are seeing our student teachers making effective use of writing frames to help pupils who experience difficulties with their writing in geography. This is a strategy which is now widely advocated by Special Needs Co-ordinators so there is likely to be support and expertise available to help you in schools.

The use of writing frames to support pupils with writing difficulties was developed by the Extending Literacy Project team at Exeter University (Box 2.6). The frames are a strategy which help children use their 'generic structures of recount, report, procedure, explanation, exposition (arguing a point of view) and discussion until they become familiar enough with these written structures to have assimilated them into their writing repertoire' (EXEL, 1995). A writing frame consists of various key words and phrases in a basic skeleton framework which is used to 'scaffold' pupils' writing. Table 2.2 shows an example of one writing frame that could be used in geography.

The intention is that by using different writing frames, pupils will become increasingly familiar with their generic structure:

The template of starters, connectives and sentence modifiers which constitute a writing frame gives children a structure within which they can concentrate on communicating what they want to say, rather than getting lost in the form.

(EXEL, 1995)

Writing frames can help children by:

■ providing experience of a range of generic structures
■ offering a structure in which the given connectives maintain the cohesive ties of the text thus helping pupils maintain the 'sense' of what they are writing
■ offering a varied vocabulary of connectives and sentence beginnings thus extending pupil's experience beyond the familiar 'and then'
■ encouraging pupils to give a personal interpretation of the information they have gathered by the careful use of personal pronouns. It is tempting to talk about this process in terms of giving pupils ownership of the information they are working with
■ asking the pupils to select, and think about what they have learnt, by encouraging pupils to re-order information and demonstrate their understanding rather than just copying out text
■ enabling pupils to achieve some success at writing, a vital ingredient in improving self-esteem and motivation
■ preventing pupils from being presented with a blank sheet of paper – a particularly daunting experience for some children especially those for whom sustained writing is difficult
■ giving pupils an overview of the writing task.

■ **Box 2.6** Writing frames
Source: EXEL, 1996

The EXEL team developed a model for teaching using writing frames (Figure 2.6). The process should always begin with discussion and teacher modelling before moving on to a joint (teacher and pupil/group) learning activity followed by the pupil undertaking some writing supported by the frame (scaffold activity). It should be made clear that the frame is just a draft which pupils can amend and add to. The aim is to improve the quality of pupils' 'independent' writing at the end of the process. The National Strategy materials on 'Literacy in Geography' (DfES, 2002, Unit 4) provide guidance on how different text types can be used in geography. Extended writing provides opportunities for pupils to present the outcomes of geographical enquiry. It helps them to make sense of information they have collected, to make connections between different bits of information and present their analysis of geographical questions, issues or problems. Further helpful guidance on strategies for developing pupils' extended writing skills can be found in Butt (2001) and Roberts (2003). George *et al.* (2002) outline approaches for helping pupils to develop their understanding of the characteristics of 'better descriptions' and 'better explanations' in geography.

■ **Table 2.2** Examples of writing frames in geography

(a) Comparing and contrasting places

Although the UK and Italy are different, they are similar in some interesting ways.
For example, they both ....
....

They are also similar in ....
....

They also have the same ....
....

Finally, they both ....
....

(b) Sometimes it can be helpful to use a grid to organise information about places and features before pupils use 'comparison and contrast' frames.

Characteristics	UK	Bangladesh
Climate		
Farming		
Population Growth		
Health Care		
Industry		
Average Wealth (GNP per person)		
Education/literacy		

(c) Using a writing frame to explain a process in geography.

I want to explain how the process of frost-shattering (freeze-thaw action) works......................................
....

It starts by ....
.... and ....

This causes ....
....

After that ....
....

and as a result ....
....

Then ....
....

The final result is that ....

(d) Writing about an issue in geography. Using a writing frame to present arguments and information about different viewpoints.

The issue that we discussed was about whether more new housing should be built in rural areas.
Some people think that ....
....

because ....
....

They argue that ....
....

Another group who agree with this point of view are ....
They say that ....
....

On the other hand ....disagree with the idea that ....
....

They claim that ....
....

They also say that ....
....

My opinion is ....
....

because ....
....

Source: EXEL, 1995

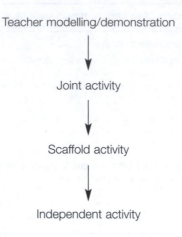

Teacher modelling/demonstration

Joint activity

Scaffold activity

Independent activity

■ **Figure 2.6** Using writing frames – a teaching model

Activity 2.7 **Developing writing frames – for use in geography**

Writing frames should not be used as rigid generic structures. They provide one strategy for extending pupils' experience of writing in a range of genres and contexts. It should also be remembered that not all pupils in a class will need to use a writing frame.

1   Identify a range of situations in your teaching in which writing frames may help some pupils to improve their writing skills in geography.
2   Design some writing frames to help these pupils.
3   When you have used these writing frames, collect examples of the written work produced by pupils.

Use these examples to report back to your geography mentor or a group of other student teachers about the effectiveness of the writing frames used. Discuss the contexts in which they were used and the principles influencing their design (i.e. generic structure, purpose of the writing, etc.).

SUMMARY AND KEY POINTS

This chapter has been about learning – specifically, about learning in geography. The key concepts in geography have been identified and their importance in structuring the curriculum. The ways in which pupils acquire concepts has been raised by recognising the stages pupils pass though in their cognitive development. Concept development and concept mapping have been addressed. The different ways in which pupils learn was raised under the topic of 'learning styles'. The importance of teachers using a range of teaching strategies acknowledged these different styles. The unit was completed by a section on language, its role in teaching, learning and cognitive development and the development of literacy.

You should check your course requirements against the standards for QTS for the topics raised in this chapter.

FURTHER READING

Balderstone, D. (2006) *What's the point of learning geography?* Chapter 1 in Balderstone, D. (ed.) *Secondary Geography Handbook*, Sheffield: The Geographical Association.

What sense do pupils make of learning geography? This chapter explores ways of connecting with the personal geographies and lived experiences of young people to help them to 'think geographically' and develop their 'geographical imaginations'.

Battersby, J. and Hornby, N. (2006) *Inspiring disaffected students*, Chapter 31 in Balderstone, D. (ed.) *Secondary Geography Handbook*, Sheffield: The Geographical Association.

The authors explore ways of developing learning through geography which engages pupils and have the potential to reduce disaffection as well as reducing underachievement. They emphasise the value of 'real world' learning and practical activities in geography.

Brooks, C. (2006) *Cracking the code – numeracy and geography*, Chapter 12 in Balderstone, D. (ed.) *Secondary Geography Handbook*, Sheffield: The Geographical Association.

This chapter explores opportunities for developing and extending pupils' numeracy skills within geography and explains strategies for developing these skills.

Hewlett, N. (2006) *Using literacy productively*, Chapter 11 in Balderstone, D. (ed.) *Secondary Geography Handbook*, Sheffield: The Geographical Association.

The author explores the role of geography in enhancing pupils' literacy skills. There are several examples of strategies and activities for developing reading, writing, speaking and listening skills in geography classrooms.

Roberts, M. (2003) *Learning through enquiry: Making Sense of Geography in the Key Stage 3 Classroom,* Sheffield: The Geographical Association.

Part One of this excellent book explores the relationships between geographical enquiry and literacy and numeracy. There are practical examples of a range of useful strategies.

PUPIL LEARNING
Supporting pupils with special educational needs

All children have the right to a good education and the opportunity to fulfil their potential. All teachers should expect to teach children special educational needs (SEN) and all schools should play their part in educating children from the local community, whatever their background or ability.

(Removing the Barriers to Achievement, DfES 2004)

INTRODUCTION

The revised National Curriculum reinforces a commitment to the inclusion of all pupils (QCA, 2007). Inclusion emphasises the right of all pupils to feel they belong and can achieve in school. This Inclusion Statement is based on the following principles:

- The need to establish a culture of high expectations for all and set learning challenges matched to pupils' abilities
- Responding to students' diverse learning needs (including adapting the physical teaching and learning environments)
- Overcoming potential barriers to learning and assessment.

(Peacey, 2005: 229)

Understanding approaches to meeting the diverse needs of all students is an essential responsibility of all teachers and is outlined in the professional standards for Qualified Teacher Status. Meeting the special educational needs of pupils is only one aspect of inclusion and it implies that something 'additional' or 'different from' what is provided for other pupils is required. A revised SEN Code of Practice (DfEE, 2000) has been implemented from January 2002 identifying four main categories of special educational need:

- communication and interaction
- cognition and learning
- behaviour, emotional and social development
- sensory and/or physical.

Special needs includes gifted pupils. Educating the most able children in appropriate ways is a challenge that society must take seriously. We cannot afford to foster underachievement, disaffection and alienation amongst these children (George, 1997: 111). Addressing these needs is the challenge for all teachers.

OBJECTIVES

By the end of this chapter, you should be able to:

■ describe the legislative framework for the identification and support for pupils with special educational needs (SEN)

■ identify your role in supporting pupils with special needs and with SEN

■ identify pupils with special educational needs in geography and the range of strategies that can be used to meet these needs

■ recognise that gifted pupils with exceptional ability in geography also have special needs and how they can be addressed.

MEETING INDIVIDUAL NEEDS

Every child is special. Every child has individual educational needs.

(Warnock Report)

Meeting the diverse range of individual learning needs within geography classes is frequently quoted by student teachers as being one of the greatest challenges facing them during their initial training. For some it can be a frustration. How can I involve pupils who can hardly speak any English in my geography lessons? What can I find for Martin to do when he cannot really write anything that makes any sense? Do I have to produce differentiated worksheets to support the less able pupils in all my lessons? What do you do if the pupils cannot read any of the material in the textbooks? The learning support budget has been cut so there are not enough learning support assistants or community language teachers to go round all the classes where they are needed!

These are familiar stories and ones that are not only experienced by student teachers, so the first thing to realise is that you are not alone in having to face up to such challenges. The second thing to realise is that there are issues that you cannot resolve on your own. These issues are often part of a wider problem and we have noted that OFSTED has reported how matching tasks to the differing abilities of pupils continues to be a problem in geography (Smith, 1997). The provision in geography for lower ability pupils is often poor in schools where pupils are organised into ability groupings, such as broad bands or sets, with Peter Smith HMI reporting that: 'Poorest quality teaching is in lower ability classes in Years 7 and 8 where one quarter of lessons are unsatisfactory' (ibid.: 126).

The above comment stating that 'every child is special' and has 'individual educational needs' reflects a belief that you can 'make a difference', particularly in the attitude that you adopt towards all the pupils that you teach. The 'sensitive teacher', to which we refer, seeks to develop pupils' self-esteem and create a classroom climate in which all pupils can succeed. Broad generalisations, though frequently used in education, are not always helpful. It is perhaps easy to understand why teachers use terms such as 'less able', 'slow learner', and 'lower ability' but this categorisation is a mere convenience and does not help you meet the needs of these learners. Labelling also runs the risk of creating an 'underclass' or 'sink group' which is characterised by low expectations and aspirations and which often leads to a spiral of decline in pupils' achievements. The focus is on the pupils with the assumption that their learning difficulties are the result of some deficiency on their part (Ainscow and Tweedle, 1988).

It is important for you to be aware of the legal requirements and your professional responsibilities as a teacher in relation to provision for special educational needs. A more detailed discussion of these legal requirements can be found in initial teacher education texts such as Capel *et al.,* (2005, Units 1.2 and 8.3).

It is important to remember that most of us will probably have experienced some form of learning difficulty at some time in our lives. Most of us are able to cope with these difficulties without any special assistance. In school, however, some pupils need additional support while others will be identified as having special educational needs.

The Warnock Report, published in 1978, brought about a fundamental shift in our thinking on special educational needs. Previously, children with learning difficulties were viewed as being different from 'normal' children and were therefore educated separately. The Warnock Report encouraged teachers to take a broader view of special education with educational provision being based on an assessment of an individual's needs. Although the Report recognised that pupils with the most complex needs would still need access to special units or schools, it established the responsibility of all schools and their teachers in meeting the full range of pupil needs.

The 1994 Code of Practice extended this responsibility with schools now being required to publish a policy describing how they intend to meet pupils' special educational needs. Every school is required to appoint a Special Educational Needs Coordinator (SENCO) to oversee the implementation of this policy. The Revised Code of Practice replaced the original five stages involved in the identification and assessment of special educational needs with two levels of provision:

▪ **School Action** – where the school acts within its own resources (placing the emphasis on the need for a 'whole school' approach)
▪ **School Action Plus** – where the pupils have additional access to external support.

This Code of Practice emphasises the role of the class teacher in supporting individual pupils who have learning or behavioural difficulties.

It requires Individual Education Plans (IEP) to be produced outlining the explicit learning needs of each pupil with special educational needs. These plans should identify targets for each pupil which are linked to the knowledge, understanding, skills and attitudes that can be developed through the subjects in the curriculum. These targets will thus reflect the learning that the pupils will experience through the school's curriculum. Clearly, you have a responsibility to familiarise yourself with the Individual Education Plans for pupils that you will be teaching. You should find out how it is intended that these pupils might achieve the targets in their IEP's through their work in geography.

Emotional difficulties may be temporary because of circumstances outside school which can eventually be resolved. Specific learning difficulties can be deep-seated requiring more long-term support. Physical and sensory impairments should not necessarily prevent pupils from participating in the mainstream school curriculum. Appropriate provision, such as wheelchair access, can help to ensure that the impact of these difficulties on pupils is minimised. For a fuller description of special educational needs, including disability see Peacey, 2005 (in Capel *et al.*, 2005, Unit 4.6).

Who has special educational needs?

Although identifying that a pupil has special educational needs is an important first step, it does not in itself help you address the challenges presented by these 'needs'. Indeed giving 'labels' to particular pupils can have negative consequences for both pupil and teacher. In the case of the latter, teachers can become anxious and feel 'deskilled' if they are not confident about their ability to respond to the needs in question. Telling a teacher that a pupil is 'dyslexic' for example, does not help anyone as 'dyslexia' covers a very broad range of specific learning difficulties that can affect different children in different ways. It is also possible that some very able pupils can suffer from learning difficulties that mask their real ability. What is important is that you know the specific nature of the difficulties experienced by particular pupils, how these difficulties manifest themselves and affect those pupils' learning in geography, and what strategies might help them to limit the impact of these difficulties on their work in geography.

Where do you get this information from? As a student teacher, it is right to expect the normal class teacher to provide you with background information about the pupils that you will be teaching, including advice about pupils with special educational needs and the implications of these needs for their work in geography. Each school is required to keep a register of pupils' specific needs and outlining the strategies that are being used to address these needs. The geography department should also have its own policy outlining how special educational needs are being addressed within the subject. Your geography mentor and the school's Special Educational Needs Coordinator (SENCO) are the people to approach for advice and support in this area.

Description of pupil's individual needs	Pupil's strengths and weaknesses	Adaptations to classroom work in geography	School-based support: role of SENCO and learning support assistants	External support: LEA, Education Psychologists, Welfare Officers, etc.	Comments on progress

■ **Box 3.1** Analysing and meeting the needs of individual pupils in geography
Source: adapted from Capel *et al.*, 1995: 210

Adopting a differentiated approach to lesson planning will help you to address the needs of some pupils with SEN; see also Chapter 4. Differentiation can be described in many ways; one such is 'a planned process of intervention by the teacher in the pupil's learning' (Capel *et al.*, 2005: 159). This reference also provides an in-depth discussion of differentiated approaches to lesson planning.

Some years ago OFSTED noted that:

> There is some evidence that when there is no differentiation, pupils identified as having learning difficulties do not achieve all they might. This was illustrated vividly in two contrasting lessons in Key Stage 3: in one, pupils with special needs were struggling too long over recording information and not reaching the real focus of the lesson, which involved looking at the geographical settlement pattern and accounting for it; in the other, they were working hard and successfully on well-chosen differentiated tasks which provided appropriate challenge.
>
> (OFSTED, 1995: 21)

More recently, OFSTED have reported that where geography teaching is poor there is little action to identify underachievement or set development priorities (OFSTED 2008: para 46); in the same report by contrast, good practice was illustrated by the use of a differentiated (formative) assessment approaches which led to improved pupil participation and enjoyment (OFSTED 2008: para 62). The same report criticised lesson planning in geography as 'too often teaching is directed at pupils of average ability so limiting the opportunities for independent inquiry and extended writing' (OFSTED 2008: para 42). Such an approach does not address the needs of pupils with special needs, especially those with SEN.

Low expectations can result in pupils with SEN being presented with inappropriate tasks providing them with inadequate challenges. Some unsatisfactory lessons with 'lower ability' classes often involves pupils in undemanding tasks such as recording or transferring information. Such tasks may not provide any intellectual stimulus or challenge. Pupils with special educational needs may also find them to be time-consuming and frustrating because their specific learning difficulties limit their ability to complete such routine tasks.

The following example of addressing the needs of a pupil may be helpful.

The situation was a Year 9 lesson about climatic zones and ecosystems with pupils with a range of abilities, including SEN. The pupils had been given clear large outline maps of the world and asked to transfer information about climate and vegetation from thematic maps in an atlas to appropriate zones shown on their outline maps. The classroom had that buzz of activity as all pupils, including those with special educational needs, tackled this apparently simple task. However, one pupil, Paul, appeared to be struggling and was making a right mess of his map. Questioning Paul revealed that he actually understood a great deal about the relationship between climate and vegetation, and could describe where different ecosystems might be found. Reassured, the teacher moved on only to notice Paul becoming increasingly frustrated within a matter of minutes.

The teacher sought the advice of the Learning Support Assistant who accompanied Paul in his other geography lesson that week. Paul's learning difficulties were that he could not always link 'thinking' and 'doing'; that is, his 'motor sensory skills' did not link with his 'cognitive skills'. Asking him to transfer this information without any supporting structure resulted in some of the information being confused or lost in the process of being transferred from the atlas map to the outline map, through Paul's mind to his pencil and onto the map.

In future, Paul was provided with maps and diagrams labelled with arrows against which he would record information or his interpretation. Tracing or transparency overlays were used to help Paul (and pupils with similar difficulties) to focus on particular areas of photographs.

(Personal communication, DB)

The strategies above illustrate examples of scaffolding pupils writing. The example above illustrates, too the importance of consulting the Special Needs Register, the SENCO and the Learning Support Assistants. Simple information about individual pupils, their learning strengths as much as their weaknesses, and adaptations made to the classroom experience in other subjects helps to build up a body of knowledge and expertise. An important strategy developed from the above experience was the use of a personal notebook to record observations and reflections about pupils with special needs, using one page per pupil. Recording the information about one pupil during a lesson is a manageable task.

This anecdote reveals another vitally important message – the need to communicate and work with support teachers. OFSTED regularly report a mixed situation on the ground, ranging from the support teacher who always has to go into a lesson 'cold', not even knowing the topic in advance, to the other end of the scale in which the support teacher is even able to offer the subject teacher advice and suggestions in planning the whole lesson.

Schools are very busy places and there will certainly not be enough time to involve support teachers fully in the planning of your lessons. Find time to provide the support teachers working in your lessons with an overview of work planned for a sequence of lessons and to seek their advice about individual pupils' needs. In each lesson, share your objectives, plans and resources with the support teacher. Support teachers are unlikely to be able to use their skills to the full if they do not know what was planned. Learning support assistants are a valuable resource for your planning, so utilise their knowledge and skills to the full.

Activity 3.1 **Analysing the needs of individual pupils**

During your initial teacher education course, you will be developing your knowledge of teaching strategies which can be used for pupils with different special educational needs. The aim of this activity is to help you identify the range of pupils who may have additional needs and to consider ways of addressing these individual needs.

You should record your observations and reflections, together with other information obtained about the individual pupils studied, on a table like the one in Box 3.1.

It will be helpful to compare what you find in your placement school with student teachers working in other schools. Share your observations and reflections about the work of pupils with different special educational needs in geography. To do this, it is important that you use fictional names to preserve confidentiality.

You can add information to this table about other pupils with special educational needs that you work with during your initial training. This record becomes a resource for future teaching and planning and part of your Career Entry and Development Profile.

Task 1

Identify a pupil with special educational needs. If possible this should be a pupil with whom you have or will have contact. (Use fictional names to preserve confidentiality.)

Try to find out the following information about this pupil:

■ Describe this pupil's special educational needs.
■ What are the pupil's strengths and weaknesses?
■ What adaptations are made to classroom work for this pupil in geography? (i.e. what support is provided?)

Draw upon the expertise of different staff as necessary (e.g. subject co-tutor, support teachers, SEN co-ordinator). Obtain and refer to a copy of the pupil's Individual Education Plan (IEP).

If possible, observe this pupil during a geography lesson and identify:

■ whether the pupil responds well to any particular teaching approaches or activities
■ whether, and how often, the pupil seeks help from other pupils and/or the teacher
■ how the pupil relates to others in the group.

Make a note of your observations/reflections.

Task 2

Find an opportunity to talk to the pupil and discuss his or her attitude towards their work in geography. Which aspects of the work does he or she experience problems with? Which aspects do they enjoy and where are they successful?

If possible, examine some of this pupil's work in geography and try to identify whether there are any common errors or problems. How much work is finished by the pupil? What is the nature of the feedback that the pupil receives from teachers?

Task 3

If possible, obtain a copy of the department's SEN policy. You may also want to talk to your geography mentor or other teachers in the department to find out about the strategies that are used to support pupils with SEN in geography.

Pupils with special educational needs require learning activities matched to their needs and abilities; guidelines are given in Box 3.2. Lesson planning must take account of these needs if learning is to take place. In some cases, individualised approaches may be necessary. However, in other situations it may be possible to plan resources and strategies that can support a group of pupils with similar needs. Sometimes it is necessary to adapt the task, i.e. to differentiate or provide help with recording and writing, e.g. scaffolding as described earlier. Further guidance can be found in Chapter 6 (designing resource sheets), Chapter 4 (differentiating teaching) and in Unit 2.1, the section on language and literacy.

During the planning process, the following points should be considered:

■ any particular requirements of a pupil's individual education plan or statement of special educational need
■ the current interests, attitudes and achievements of pupils
■ the level of work appropriate to each pupil's needs
■ whether it will be necessary to draw upon work from the programmes of study for Key Stages 1 and 2 and how this can be presented in age-appropriate contexts
■ how activities can be adapted to allow access by all pupils
■ the range of alternative activities which may be necessary to allow individual pupils to participate and to demonstrate progress in most aspects of the programme of study
■ the variety of resources necessary to support the range of work being covered and the range of teaching and learning styles which may be used
■ the way in which work will be presented to accommodate any difficulties which pupils may have with reading and writing
■ how use will be made of specialist equipment and any additional staff available to support learning
■ the way in which pupils' progress will be monitored and recorded so that small advances are not missed
■ the most suitable pace of teaching and quantity of work to allow pupils to complete tasks, to retain concentration and motivation and to be sufficiently challenged
■ the way in which pupils' personal skills, such as independence and cooperating with others can be developed.

Varying the teaching approach according to need by:

■ employing different teaching styles and methods, such as:
 □ whole class instruction, small group or individual help
 □ use written, taped or visual materials
 □ use of resources, artefacts and visits.
■ setting tasks which allow pupils to respond in different ways
■ planning to make varied use of the time available to allow pupils opportunities to complete tasks satisfactorily whilst maintaining acceptable levels of concentration and behaviour
■ planning to use the time of any support staff effectively and flexibly
■ monitoring the success of the lesson and responding to any difficulties as they arise
■ reflecting or using the work undertaken by pupils in regular sessions with therapists or other specialist staff.

Enabling all pupils to participate and to work effectively by:

■ setting clear objectives and instructions that are understood by all pupils
■ using appropriate levels of spoken and written language
■ providing an appropriate range of support materials
■ making appropriate and effective use of any specialist equipment provided to support particular difficulties
■ providing adult intervention as necessary
■ encouraging and supporting independent learning
■ encouraging and teaching the skills of group work
■ providing opportunities for pupils to achieve success, including the use of non-writing activities
■ creating an atmosphere of encouragement and success.

■ **Box 3.2** Matching the learning opportunities provided for pupils with special educational needs to their needs and abilities

Source: SCAA, 1996b

The professional standards for QTS require teachers to be able to identify the levels of attainment for pupils with EAL, to analyse the language demands of learning activities, and to provide support to help them to meet the cognitive challenges of these activities. For EAL pupils to acquire sufficient linguistic competence to enable them to understand concepts and processes in geography, they need support to extend their speaking and writing repertoires and to practise using new words and phrases in relevant contexts. More resources can be found in the Further Reading section at the end of this chapter.

■ **Table 3.1** Stages of English learning in the secondary phase indicating pupils' prior experience of learning English

Stage 1: Beginner Bilingual
Beginner bilingual learners of English will have minimal or no literacy skills in English. They are likely to have only been living in England for a very short period of time. They may well remain completely silent in the classroom or use just a little (supported) English because their speaking and listening skills will be at a very early stage of development. However, they will be competent and fluent speakers of their first language. They may engage in learning activities, in groups, using their mother tongue but will need considerable support to do so in English.

Stage 2: Developing Bilingual – becoming familiar with English
Students at this stage will often have increased their fluency in spoken English and will be able to understand instructions and conversations. They can participate in learning activities where the context is clear. Although they may be able to express themselves orally in English quite successfully, their reading and writing will require considerable support. Their 'social talk' may suggest that they are more competent with oral language, but the development of English for academic purposes can take much longer and needs to be planned for, explicitly taught and learning reinforced in meaningful contexts.

Stage 3: Developing Bilingual – growing in confidence as users of English
Bilingual students whose oral and written English is developing well, enabling them to engage successfully in all learning activities. They will need continuing support to develop their reading and writing skills. Their written English will tend to lack complexity and show evidence of structures and errors associated with the student's level of language acquisition. Errors in writing often result from different syntaxes of English and their first language. Help is needed particularly with extended writing about academic and abstract concepts.

Stage 4: Fluently Bilingual
These students will be competent and fluent users of English, as well as other languages, in most social contexts and learning activities. They write as native speakers and do not make errors that are influenced by their mother tongue. Being literate in other languages, they will understand how more than one language is structured. They will often high attainers capable of being very successful learners in geography.

If pupils have difficulties in cognition and learning, it might be necessary to take a step back and refer to the QCA Geography P scales that have been designed for work with pupils who are not yet working at national curriculum level one.

Challenging pupils with exceptional ability in geography

> 'Bright' or 'gifted' pupils show a high level of general intellectual ability or specific academic aptitude which may be accompanied by creative thinking.
>
> (Grenyer, 1986: 171)

Grenyer's definition of 'gifted' pupils may not be accepted by all; and therein lies half the problem. Teachers seem to have greater difficulty in agreeing on a way of identifying pupils within this category of special educational needs than they do with other categories. Some prefer not to talk about 'gifted' pupils because they associate the term with elitist ideas while others assume that such pupils can look after themselves. 'Yes, but someone who is brilliant at English, mathematics, science or design technology does not necessarily have exceptional ability in geography!', we hear you say. Well, whatever the problems of definition, it is certain that we will be doing our able pupils a grave disservice if we do not give some consideration to their special educational needs in geography.

David George argues that 'definitions abound and create much confusion' (George 1992: 1). He urges us to get away from 'pseudo-scientific labelling' of children and suggests that the term 'intellectually underserved' may have some value when describing pupils with exceptional ability. It is clear that the 'gifted' and 'talented' are not a homogeneous group; they come in all shapes and sizes! Consider, for example, the contrasting needs of the following pupils in an A-level class taught by one of the authors. Each had exceptional ability in geography and went on to attain the highest levels of achievement in the subject.

Danielle enjoyed practical work and fieldwork. Watching geographical videos and reading articles were amongst her favoured methods of learning. Observed during a lesson she would often appear to be withdrawn and did not get actively involved in discussion activities. Danielle did not feel that lectures were an effective way of learning for her. She was, however, prepared to take risks with new ideas and responded well to questions that encouraged speculative thinking. She was very methodical, planning work thoroughly and practised different skills.

Nick enjoyed the study of economic issues in geography. Although he enjoyed studying environmental issues he did not like the factual and theoretical emphasis in many of the lessons about landform systems. Fieldwork, small group work and 'stimulating' lectures were amongst his most favoured methods of learning. Sometimes impatient, he responded well to the opportunity to debate ideas and develop discussions to a higher level.

Tom was a pupil with all-round ability and displayed characteristics of all four learning styles. He was adaptable and flexible in his approach to study. He regarded himself as a practical and logical thinker. Although Tom had good listening and memorising skills, he did not feel that he responded well to more didactic styles of teaching. With excellent communication skills, he always took an active role in group discussion and practical activities. He enjoyed fieldwork and reading articles in geographical journals but commented on his dislike of what he called 'textbook learning'.

All three pupils would have appeared to be making good progress with their A-level studies and had shown no evidence of frustration. But fed on a monotonous diet of overlong exposition, taking notes from and copying diagrams in textbooks, it is likely that their intellectual abilities would have gone unchallenged for long periods of time.

It is often mistakenly believed that such pupils can be 'stretched' just by providing them with more information to process. Once again this passive transmission-reception process is unlikely to provide these pupils with adequate intellectual challenge.

Understanding the ways in which pupils with exceptional ability learn and how they can be challenged is important. But recognising pupils with exceptional ability is not always a straightforward process. Nick, Tom and Danielle would always have appeared to be able because they were high achievers. However, their exceptional ability would not necessarily have been revealed in many learning tasks. Nick's written work was often rushed and superficial until it came to examination time. Danielle rarely participated actively in lessons in the first part of the course. Only Tom overtly demonstrated signs of exceptional ability on a regular basis.

Fieldwork provided some of the critical experiences that revealed signs of particular abilities and perhaps, more significantly, it helped these pupils develop a rapport with their peers and their teachers that gave them confidence and recognition. A lack of 'acceptance' and recognition can lead many 'gifted' pupils to become frustrated and bored, sometimes resulting in low motivation and a tendency to withdraw even more.

Fortunately, the early part of the A-level geography course experienced by Nick, Tom and Danielle involved a wide variety of learning activities that required them to use a range of learning styles and skills. The emphasis on developing practical, critical and decision-making skills created opportunities for pupils to demonstrate a range of intellectual skills and abilities. The geography teachers also used strategies designed to encourage pupils to reflect on the learning skills that they were developing as well as on the geographical content of what they were learning. The importance of creating positive social contexts in which this learning could take place should also not be underestimated.

Box 3.3 shows some of the characteristics that *may* help you to recognise pupils with exceptional ability. The emphasis is on the *'may'* because such behavioural check-lists present characteristics as 'symptoms' which can be interpreted in different ways. A further set of characteristics of pupils with high levels of ability or potential in geography are given in Table 3.2 (Enright, Flook and Habgood 2006: 370).

But what happens if 'gifted' pupils are not naturally active, curious or easily motivated? If they do not use their abilities, such pupils may react in one of two ways. Low motivation can result in 'acting out behaviour' in the form of disruptiveness where pupils may be inclined to show off, display aggressive behaviour or temper tantrums, and even destroy their own work. They may appear to be lazy, apathetic, unco-operative and unenthusiastic about classwork. Some may be hypercritical, particularly in their assessment of situations and other people.

Alternatively, gifted pupils may 'withdraw' from active participation in lessons, being obstinate and refusing to work, sometimes to the extent of truancy and absenteeism. It is not easy to determine whether these behaviours are masking ability for such pupils will rarely display much evidence of their real abilities and they frequently under-achieve. They can be very articulate, but unable to write well. Einstein's school report described him as 'mentally slow, unsociable and adrift forever in his foolish dreams' (George 1997: 10).

Low self-esteem often appears to be at the root of under-achievement problems. Pupils with exceptional ability are often 'at high psychological risk in that their unique intellectual and creative abilities make them vulnerable to pressures at home and at school which may initiate under-achievement' (George 1997: 11). This can lead to 'academic avoidance behaviour' and consequently to poor study habits and skills, a lack of concentration and problems in obtaining the acceptance of their peers.

■ **Table 3.2** Possible characteristics of high levels of ability or potential in geography

Possible aspects	Possible student responses
Curiosity	Students will seek information and understanding beyond that which is immediately presented to them. They raise questions and are motivated to find the answers.
Scope of general knowledge	Students will want to discuss topical issues relating them to the work being covered in class. They will have a wide range of interests and an excellent memory for detail.
Conceptual understanding and application	Students quickly and easily grasp new ideas and theories and are able to apply them to real situations. It will sometimes feel as though full explanations from the teacher are unnecessary.
Perceptiveness	Students appreciate the complexity of the world around them. They can identify and justify other people's viewpoints. They have acute observation skills.
Well developed thinking skills	Students demonstrate originality and divergent thinking when they approach problems. They can see many different routes for getting to the same end point. They are capable of metacognition (thinking about thinking) and can help to raise the roof off the classroom.
High levels of geographical literacy	They are accomplished at matching style of communication (whether oral or written) to the task and audience. They are also likely to have an advanced vocabulary. They will be excited by and sensitive to the fact that geography has its own language for learning and will enjoy technical terms and precise definitions.
High levels of geographical numeracy	Students very quickly pick up on sequences and patterns. They are confident in applying mathematical principles such as area and shape. They enjoy looking for spatial patterns in map work tasks and will be excited by learning situations involving statistical testing or geographical information systems.
Attitude towards less formal learning experiences	Some students will come into their own in situations where they are asked to take part in a role play or simulation. They will display innate confidence and adopt a leadership role. They will tend to be very enthusiastic about fieldwork and relish the challenge of setting and testing hypotheses.
Interaction with peers	Gifted students have no consistent manner of interaction with their peers. Some may display a preference to work alone or with older students. Others will relate very well with their peers and be keen to help those who are not as quick to grasp new ideas. Some will look to hide their ability from the rest of their classmates.
Teacher perceptions	This list does not profess to be exhaustive but students may be considered to be one or more of the following: aloof, arrogant, eccentric, impatient, insensitive, intolerant, intuitive, lazy, non-conformist, obstinate, opinionated, perfectionist, persistent, precocious, preoccupied, rude, sensitive, underachieving, withdrawn.

Source: Enright, Flook and Habgood, 2006: 370

The exceptionally able child may show some of the following:

1 *Great intellectual curiosity:*
   wanting to know why and how
   provocative questions cannot be
   fobbed off with simple explanations.

2 *Superior reasoning ability:*
   can handle abstract concepts; can
   generalise from specific fact; can see
   connections between events.

3 *Unusual persistence:*
   to complete tasks to own satisfaction;
   can concentrate for a long time.

4 *Exceptional speed of thought:*
   rapid response to new ideas.

5 *Ability to learn fast and easily:*
   understands before full explanation is
   given; needs little practice to acquire
   competence.

6 *Good memory:*
   apparently effortless.

7 *Extensive vocabulary:*
   sensitivity to language; likes precise
   meanings; enjoys technical terms.

8 *Acute powers of observation:*
   in great detail.

9 *Vivid imagination:*
   verbal and other forms.

10 *Divergent thinking:*
    finds unusual ways of solving
    problems.

11 *Great initiative:*
    preference for independent work.

12 *Highly developed sense of humour:*
    loves verbal puns.

13 *Unusually high personal standards:*
    perfectionist demands high
    standards of self and others.

14 *Impatience:*
    intolerance of less able, and of own
    limitations.

15 *Sensitivity:*
    highly strung behaviour; easily
    frustrated; highly perceptive

16 *Wide range of interests, hobbies:*
    often a collector.

17 Specialist knowledge and expertise
    in one subject.

18 Prefers to be with older children or
    adults.

19 Desire to lead and direct.

20 Pre-occupied with deeper matters.

■ **Box 3.3** Behavioural checklist that may help in recognising exceptional ability
Source: Bates and Wolton, 1993

When considering how to 'stretch' your more able pupils, it is worth thinking in terms of *challenging* their ability and *enriching* or *enhancing* their learning. The approach you adopt should not encourage these pupils to be passive receivers of information. Activities should challenge them to analyse, interpret and evaluate information, to search for meaning and derive theories and generalisations. For example, presenting land use data can be a fairly undemanding task unless pupils are required to make decisions about appropriate forms of presentation before looking for patterns and suggesting reasons for these patterns. Thus, open-ended tasks and questions are more likely to provide challenge than closed ones. It is also important to challenge pupils to learn for themselves and to develop their capability to do so. Pupils with exceptional ability do not necessarily have the skills needed for effective independent learning. These pupils may need to be taught how to learn if they are to become successful autonomous learners. For instance, a very able pupil may spend an excessive amount of time searching out information rather than analysing it and applying it to particular problems if she has not developed appropriate information handling skills. See Enright *et al.*, 2006 for suggestions about practical ways of meeting the needs of pupils with exceptional ability.

Above all, you must be flexible in the way you respond to the needs of these pupils. You will find that many of the strategies you use to support pupils with learning difficulties can be applied in different ways to challenge those with exceptional ability in geography. Games and simulations, for example, can be used with pupils across a wide range of abilities – that is their strength. The way pupils are grouped and the activities used to debrief them can be adapted to provide different levels of challenge. Decision-making during games and simulations can operate at different levels of complexity. Designing their own games challenges able pupils to apply their knowledge and understanding as well as using their creative skills.

Strategies used to promote values education can be used to challenge pupils with exceptional ability, particularly when they are required to go beyond the stage of giving opinions to analysing the values underpinning different viewpoints, as well as identifying and explaining bias in different sources of information. Media and multimedia technology can provide opportunities for pupils to harness technical and creative skills to present work for different audiences. There is also an evolving pedagogy in relation to the development of thinking through geography that can be exploited.

Activity 3.2 **Working with pupils with exceptional ability in geography**

Educating the most able children in appropriate ways is a challenge that society must take seriously. We cannot afford to foster under-achievement, disaffection and alienation amongst these children.

(George, 1997: 111)

The following activities are more appropriate for the latter part of your initial teacher education course, after you have carried out a substantial period of practical teaching.

A) A brainstorming activity in a small group of student teachers.

1 How might you be able to recognise 'exceptional ability' in geography? (i.e. what characteristics might a pupil who is an 'exceptional geographer' display?)

2 Which aspects of geography (activities, content, skills, etc.) appear to motivate pupils with 'exceptional ability' in the broadest sense of the term? Which aspects of learning geography provide appropriate challenge for these pupils?

B) Here is a list of general aspects of learning in which pupils may display 'exceptional ability'. For each of these aspects of learning, suggest examples of skills and activities in geography that could provide appropriate challenge for these pupils.

Abilities	Examples of skills and activities in geography
■ expressive	
■ logical thinking and analysis	
■ oral/communication skills	
■ mathematical	
■ artistic/creative	
■ scientific	
■ design/craft skills	

Bates and Woolton provide some useful advice about how teachers can help pupils to overcome what they call the 'handicap of high achievement' where they find themselves on a 'treadmill of success'. The following suggestions might help them to 'accept reality and relax about their personal performance'. You might reflect on their particular relevance within teaching geography:

■ Award grades for individual effort as well as for achievement.
■ Develop co-operative, negotiated assessment where teacher and pupil share opinions and judgements about a piece of work. Differences of opinion become a basis for learning.
■ Encourage real exploration of learning – investigate experiential learning.
■ Send them on a 'quest for understanding' where they ask lots of questions and search for the answers in different resources and through discussion, etc.
■ Help them to recognise the relative nature of information, its links and its transferability (rather than for its own sake).
■ Stress that outcomes do not have to be right or wrong; they will be interesting and formative, providing the next step forward. There is no success or failure.

(Bates and Woolton, 1993: 49)

Activity 3.3 **Working with other student teachers**

Towards the end of your course or after you have read Chapter 4 (Teaching Geography), suggest how particular teaching strategies might be adapted to:

1   provide support for pupils with specific learning difficulties
2   provide appropriate challenge for pupils with exceptional ability.

It is suggested that each student teacher should take one of the strategies in Chapter 4 and consider the adaptations that may be helpful for pupils with different special educational needs. This may include examples that you have seen or used yourself. The suggestions should then be shared and discussed as a group.

SUMMARY AND KEY POINTS

This chapter has discussed the way in which you can teach pupils with individual learning needs, including pupils with Special Educational Needs (SEN). The last group of pupils have Statements and, as a result, bring with them an Individual Educational Plan (IEP) specifically addressing how their needs may be met. Schools have a responsibility under the Code of Practice to teach pupils with special needs, including Statemented pupils.

Your school experience school has a policy for special needs and SEN; you should inquire about the resources available to meet those requirements. The SENCO and Learning Support Assistants are important staff to whom you may turn for advice.

Planning for individual needs is important as some pupils may require different resources and strategies to help them achieve the learning outcomes expected of them. To do this, you will need to identify the range of pupils who may have additional needs and then consider approaches to meet these individual needs. This chapter gives advice on how to work with special needs pupils in your classroom, including gifted pupils. The chapter identifies some features of gifted pupils including their social, behavioural and academic characteristics together with ways in which you can begin to address the needs of such pupils.

You should check your course requirements for special needs against the standards for obtaining Qualified Teacher Status.

There are perhaps two points to make in conclusion. The first is that, we know that we have done little more than scratch the surface of an enormous topic. In doing so, we hope that your appetite is whetted sufficiently to persuade you into a long-term commitment to learn more about how your pupils learn. So use the contents of this chapter as a platform on which to conduct experiment after experiment to maximise the potential of your pupils.

This naturally leads to the second point which is perhaps equally self-evident: in discussing learning, we cannot avoid interacting with teaching – teaching for learning. There are techniques and strategies which teachers can acquire and develop (as the following chapter shows) but the discussion here gives credence to the notion that good teachers carry on learning by trial and error: 'Let's see' could be our motto, and in geography, we have an enormous canvas of possibilities from which to choose.

FURTHER READING

Balderstone, D., Dow, M. and Henn, V. (2006) *Geography and students with EAL*, **Chapter 27 in Balderstone, D. (ed.)** *Secondary Geography Handbook*, **Sheffield: The Geographical Association.**

This chapter considers some of the challenges that face bilingual pupils in geography. The authors provide guidance for ways of working with bilingual pupils and a range of strategies that can help to raise their achievement in geography.

Enright, N., Flook, A. and Habgood, C. (2006) *Gifted young geographers*, **Chapter 28 in Balderstone, D. (ed.)** *Secondary Geography Handbook*, **Sheffield: The Geographical Association.**

The authors examine the identification of exceptional ability in geography and suggest an extensive range of ideas and strategies for providing appropriate challenge and enabling 'gifted' pupils to achieve their potential.

Evans, L. and Smith, D. (2006) *Inclusive geography*, **Chapter 26 in Balderstone, D. (ed.)** *Secondary Geography Handbook*, **Sheffield: The Geographical Association.**

The authors explore the challenges involved in developing effective inclusive practices that will enable pupils with individual educational needs to make progress in geography. They provide a wealth of practical ideas and strategies for promoting inclusion and meeting the individual learning needs of pupils in geography.

Peacey (2005) *An introduction to Inclusion, Special Educational Needs and Disability*, **Unit 4.6 in Capel, S., Leask, M. and Turner, T. (eds)** *Learning to Teach in the Secondary School: A Companion to School Experience*, **London: Routledge.**

This text provides some more generic advice about the statutory requirements and different special educational needs.

Swift, D. (2005) *Meeting SEN in the curriculum: Geography*, London: David Fulton/The Geographical Association.

This book provides a wealth of practical suggestions about how to respond positively and productively to pupils' different learning needs in geography. It covers a wide range of aspects of inclusion including meeting statutory responsibilities, types of SEN, monitoring and assessment, working with support staff and reducing barriers to outdoor learning for pupils with SEN.

TEACHING GEOGRAPHY

The passionate teacher will not only recognize the need for, but will also want to employ a range of teaching approaches that take account of the most up-to-date knowledge of teaching and learning. Such approaches will most effectively stimulate and support students' learning, are fit for purpose and relate to teachers' moral imperatives.

(Day, 2004: 82)

Geography can make a significant contribution to the moral education of young people. If ethics can be defined as the systematic reflection on moral questions or specific moral concerns, within geographical contexts, then all geography teachers are engaged in an ethical endeavour.

(McPartland, 2006: 179)

There is sometimes a narrowness in the range of teaching methods characterised by over-long expositions, over-directed styles inhibiting curiosity and initiative and discussions mediated by and through the teacher, all of which reduce opportunities for developing thinking...Also some teachers intervene too quickly and then provide an answer in their own words.

(Smith, 1997: 126)

INTRODUCTION

Successful teaching involves knowing what to do to bring about the desired pupil learning and being able to do it. In our initial remarks, we asserted that this book is dedicated to a learning ethos: *learning* in order to teach geography. Your main concern as a teacher will be to learn how to set up learning activities that will be successful in bringing about the aspect of learning in geography that you intend for each pupil.

Even though recent years have seen the increasing standardisation of the *aims* and *content* of geographical education, teaching geography remains a very personal activity. It will be for you to choose which teaching strategies and learning activities you intend to use. This chapter seeks to introduce you to a range of teaching styles and strategies that can be used to bring about learning through geography. It will begin what we hope will be a process of learning about teaching geography that will sustain and stimulate you throughout your career as a geography teacher.

We cannot tell you 'how' to teach geography but we will endeavour to help you understand some of the principles that underpin the effective use of particular teaching skills and strategies. Teaching methods are often described using narrow and polarised terminology such as 'traditional' and 'progressive'. We aim to go beyond this popular mythology so that you can learn how to make informed decisions about which strategies might be appropriate in particular situations. Exploring different teaching strategies requires us to consider the role of the learner as well as the actions of the teacher.

Our principal aim is, through discussion, to encourage you to develop a wide repertoire of teaching strategies that you can use successfully to bring about appropriate pupil learning. But this is not a 'manual' of techniques for teaching geography. There are principles to be interpreted and applied as you learn the *art* and *craft* of teaching geography.

OBJECTIVES

By the end of this chapter, you should be able to:

■ understand the importance of using a range of teaching styles
■ understand the principles that underpin the effective use of different teaching strategies
■ develop a repertoire of teaching styles and strategies that you can use successfully to bring about pupil learning in geography.

A MATTER OF STYLE AND STRATEGY

With education currently being the focus of much discussion and debate, we could be forgiven for believing that teaching is anything but a personal activity. Attention has now moved from a desire to specify and standardise what is taught in schools towards attempts to influence how it should be taught. In searching for ways of raising 'standards' it is often suggested that certain methods of teaching are more appropriate than others. However, these methods of teaching are usually presented as a narrow range of over-generalised alternatives ignoring important considerations such as learners' needs and teaching contexts.

Despite these pressures, Margaret Roberts rightly asserts that teachers still have considerable freedom to decide 'how they are going to teach and how their pupils are going to learn' (Roberts, 1996: 232). To exercise such professional judgement we need to understand how and when we can use different teaching styles and strategies effectively. Such decisions also require us to consider the diversity of ways in which pupils learn geography (Chapter 2).

The study of what teachers do to ensure that pupils learn, i.e. the *craft* of teaching, is often referred to as *pedagogy*. The approach tends to be one of 'advice based on experience'. Indeed, much of your early development as a teacher will be guided by 'experienced practitioners' who provide advice based on their professional teaching experience. However, you need to develop a framework within which to interpret this advice as you learn to think about your own teaching.

The term 'teaching style' is used to describe the way in which geography is taught. It has a very important influence on the educational experience of pupils in geography because it affects how they learn geography. Your teaching style is determined by your 'behaviour' (demeanour and the way in which you relate to pupils) and the 'strategy' that you choose to bring about the learning intended (McCormick and Leask, 2005).

Although you may feel that certain teaching styles and strategies might be more appropriate for you, given your personality and philosophy about teaching, it is important that you develop a repertoire of different styles and strategies. This is because you need to consider the characteristics and needs of the pupils (their attitudes, abilities and preferred learning styles) and the intended learning outcomes, as well as your own preferred ways of teaching. You should draw upon your pedagogic knowledge about how teachers teach and how pupils learn. You can consider how your personal qualities and approach to classroom management influence the way that you teach. The nature of the learning environment (classroom appearance and layout), the size of the class and the availability of appropriate learning resources also have a significant influence on the decisions that you make.

Some of the terms that are used to describe different ways of teaching are not always helpful. Terms such as didactic, teacher directed, whole-class, experiential and practical are at best only general descriptions. At worst they are vague and open to misinterpretation.

For example, terms like 'progressive' and 'traditional' teaching styles are value laden and stereotypical extremes. One view of progressive teaching might be that it is enquiry based, child-centred, concerned with problem-solving and as such is forward looking and good. Another might be that it is trendy and lacking intellectual substance. Traditional teaching may be seen as being old-fashioned, autocratic, didactic and lacking creative opportunities or as being reliable and effective at maintaining academic standards. Opinions about the strengths and weaknesses of different styles vary and in reality, such descriptions give only a partial view of how a teacher may be teaching.

In the past, research has focused on the relationship between different styles of teaching and the effectiveness of pupil learning. This often tends to lead to more value being placed on one style than another because it is believed to be more effective or, as Roberts also suggests, because it relates more to the researchers' 'particular educational aims and philosophy' (Roberts, 1996: 235). This can be seen in the work of the Schools Council geography projects, which from the 1970s advocated and valued particular styles of teaching. Roberts illustrates this point by quoting Renwick (1985) who suggests that the Geography for the Young School Leaver Project:

> encouraged the move away from didactic methods of teaching to experiential learning...the project particularly encourages the move towards a discovery/investigative approach in situations well structured by the teacher. The teacher is encouraged to be a guide and stimulus, and to abandon the traditional expository approach in favour of more 'open learning'.
>
> (Roberts, 1996: 235)

The 14–18 Bristol Project (a 1970s Schools Council project to influence geography for high achieving pupils) identified three styles of classroom interaction (Figure 4.1) but indicated a strong preference for an interactionist style of teaching geography. One of the main aims of this project was to influence teaching styles through a process of school-based curriculum development. The weaknesses of the transmission and structured learning approaches were highlighted while greater emphasis was placed on the significance of values in decision-making and on the deeper learning processes inherent in the interactionist model.

Another influential curriculum development project, the Schools Council 16–19 Geography Project, advocated an 'enquiry based' approach to teaching and learning that 'encourages students to enquire actively into questions, issues and problems, rather than merely to accept passively the conclusions, research and opinions of others' (Naish *et al.,* 1987: 45). The project envisaged a continuum of approaches to teaching and learning (Figure 4.2). Although this provided 'scope for an effective balance of both teacher-directed work and more independent enquiry' (Naish *et al.,* 1987: 46), the project's view of 'enquiry-based learning' focused predominantly on 'structured problem-solving' and 'open-ended discovery' (Naish *et al.,* 1987: 45).

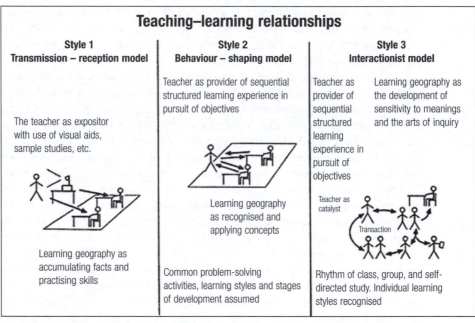

Teaching–learning relationships

Style 1 Transmission – reception model	Style 2 Behaviour – shaping model	Style 3 Interactionist model

Style 2 – Teacher as provider of sequential structured learning experience in pursuit of objectives

Style 1 – The teacher as expositor with use of visual aids, sample studies, etc.

Learning geography as recognised and applying concepts

Teacher as catalyst

Transaction

Style 1 – Learning geography as accumulating facts and practising skills

Style 2 – Common problem-solving activities, learning styles and stages of development assumed

Style 3 – Teacher as provider of sequential structured learning experience in pursuit of objectives. Learning geography as the development of sensitivity to meanings and the arts of inquiry. Rhythm of class, group, and self-directed study. Individual learning styles recognised

■ **Figure 4.1** Alternative styles of teaching and learning in geography

Source: Tolley and Reynolds, 1977: 27. This was the an outcome of the Schools Council Geography 14–18 Project, which was based at the University of Bristol 1970–75.

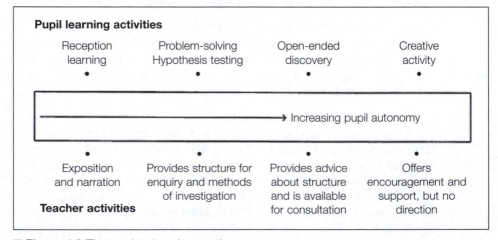

Pupil learning activities

Reception learning	Problem-solving Hypothesis testing	Open-ended discovery	Creative activity

→ Increasing pupil autonomy

Exposition and narration	Provides structure for enquiry and methods of investigation	Provides advice about structure and is available for consultation	Offers encouragement and support, but no direction

Teacher activities

■ **Figure 4.2** The teacher-learning continuum

Source: Naish *et al.,* 1987: 45

It will not take you long to realise that there is often a gap between the rhetoric or ideals espoused about teaching styles and what actually happens in the classroom. Pragmatism and an understanding of particular school contexts and cultures lead teachers to adapt their teaching styles and strategies. This should not, however, be taken to its extreme, leading to the false belief that you cannot use a particular style or strategy with the pupils in a particular school.

To learn about teaching styles and strategies it is important for you to analyse and engage critically with your own practice. To do this, Roberts (1996 and 2006) has introduced a different framework for looking at style and strategy. The 'participation dimension' (Table 4.1) can be used as 'an analytical tool to identify "styles" of teaching' and 'to show how teachers can adapt their strategies operating across different styles according to the context in which they are working' (Roberts, 2006: 96). Margaret Roberts has adapted this framework so that it can be used to analyse and interpret different styles of teaching and learning in geography (Table 4.2). By carefully studying this framework it is possible to imagine what geography lessons consistent with particular styles of teaching and learning might be like.

■ **Table 4.1** The participation dimension

	← ——— **Closed** ——— **Framed** ——— **Negotiated** →		
Content	Tightly controlled by teacher. Not negotiable	Teacher controls topic, frames of reference and tasks; criteria made explicit	Discussed at each point; joint decisions
Focus	Authoritative knowledge and skills; simplified, monolithic	Stress on empirical testing; processes chosen by teacher; some legitimation of student ideas	Search for justifications and principles; strong legitimation of student ideas
Pupils' role	Acceptance; routine performance; little access to principles	Join in teacher's thinking; make hypotheses, set up tests; operate teacher's frame	Discuss goals and methods critically; share responsibility for frame and criteria
Key concepts	'Authority': the proper procedures and the right answers	'Access': to skills processes, criteria	'Relevance': critical discussion of students' priorities
Methods	Exposition; worksheets (closed); note-giving; individual exercises; routine practical work. Teacher evaluates	Exposition, with discussion eliciting suggestions; individual/group problem-solving; lists of tasks given; discussion of outcomes, but teacher adjudicates	Group and class discussion and decision-making about goals and criteria. Students plan and carry out work, make presentations, evaluate success

Source: Barnes *et al.,* 1987

■ **Table 4.2** A framework for looking at styles of teaching and learning in geography

Stage of teaching and learning	Closed	Framed	Negotiated
Questions	Questions not explicit or questions remain the teacher's questions	Questions explicit, activities planned to make pupils ask questions	Pupils decide what they want to investigate under guidance from teacher
Data	Data selected by teacher, presented as authoritative, not to be challenged	Variety of data selected by teacher, presented as evidence to be interpreted	Pupils are helped to find their own data from sources in and out of school
Interpretation	Teacher decides what is to be done with data, pupils follow instructions	Methods of interpretation are open to discussion and choice	Pupils choose methods of analysis and interpretation in consultation with teacher
Conclusions	Key ideas presented, generalisations are predicted, not open to debate	Pupils reach conclusions from data, different interpretations are expected	Pupils reach own conclusions and evaluate them
Summary	The teacher controls the knowledge by making all decisions about data, activities, conclusions. Pupils are not expected to challenge what is presented	The teacher inducts pupils into ways in which geographical knowledge is constructed, so that they are enabled to use these ways to construct knowledge themselves. Pupils are made aware of choices and are encouraged to be critical	Pupils are enabled by the teacher to investigate questions of concern and interest to themselves

Source: Roberts, 1996: 240 (and 2006: 96)

In the closed style of teaching, the learners are passive as the teacher controls the selection of content and the way it is presented to the learners. This content is presented as 'authoritative knowledge' to be learnt by the pupils. The teacher also decides how this content or 'data' is to be investigated and analysed by prescribing the procedures to be followed. The pupils follow instructions presented in textbooks and worksheets or through whole-class teaching. The learning outcomes or key ideas and generalisations are predetermined by the teacher to be accepted by the pupils as valid conclusions.

A framed style is guided by more explicit geographical questions. Even though the teacher still decides the focus of the geographical study or enquiry, pupils are encouraged to generate their own questions. Presenting pupils with questions or problems to be solved, or decisions to be made creates what Roberts describes as a 'need to know' among these pupils. The resources and content are still selected by the teacher but they are more usually presented as 'evidence' to be interpreted and evaluated.

In the framed style, the teacher helps the pupils understand the processes and techniques involved in geographical enquiry. Evaluation is important as pupils need to understand the strengths and limitations of different sources of information and techniques for presenting or analysing these data. Conflicting information or viewpoints will need to be explored and it will be possible for pupils to come to different conclusions when examining this information.

In a negotiated style of teaching and learning, the teacher will identify the general theme to be studied but the pupils will generate the questions that will guide their enquiry either individually or in groups. These questions will be negotiated with the teacher, who will also provide guidance about the methods and sequence of enquiry as well as about the suitability of the sources of information to be used.

The information will be collected independently by the pupils and they are responsible for selecting appropriate methods for presenting, analysing and interpreting these data. The outcomes or conclusions of these enquiries are not always predictable. The processes of learning involved are often as important as the outcomes themselves. It is therefore helpful to consider the limitations of the sources of data selected and to review the methods used.

How teachers teach does not just depend on their educational philosophy. Much of the content of the geography curriculum in schools is prescribed by examination syllabuses and the National Curriculum, even though there is some flexibility in how this content may be interpreted. Teachers often regard the time available to deliver this content and the way this time is structured as a major constraint. The nature of the school and department contexts, the characteristics of their pupils, and the resources available for teaching geography have a significant influence on how the subject is taught.

In Chapter 6, we describe how a 'single textbook resource' influenced the geography curriculum in many schools during the 1990s. We explain how the breadth and depth of geographical enquiry can be limited by the nature of the activities in some textbooks. You might find it helpful to use the framework described here to analyse some of the activities provided in textbooks. Many textbooks operate at the 'closed end' of the participation dimension. Look for examples of activities that encourage pupils to speculate and to generate their own questions. In her discussion of the influence of textbooks on teaching and learning style, she asks some pertinent questions.

> To what extent are they controlling pupils' geographical knowledge, to what extent are they framing knowledge, giving access to principles of constructing knowledge, and offering support for pupils to carry out their own investigations?
>
> (Roberts, 1996: 249)

Activity 4.1 **Alternative styles of teaching and learning in geography**

Carefully study the frameworks for looking at teaching styles shown in Tables 4.1 and 4.2.

Use Margaret Robert's framework to analyse teaching styles and levels of pupil participation in the geography lessons that you are observing. Use an outline of the framework to record your observations. Table 4.3 provides an example of how this framework can be used in an observation of a geography lesson.

> When using this framework, it is important to examine the resources being used and the instructions being given to the pupils to guide their studies. Are they closed, framed or negotiated? What are the pupils doing? How do they use the information and resources provided?
>
> It might be helpful to use this framework to analyse some of the examples of geography lessons outlined in Chapter 5 before you use it during a lesson observation. Later, during your own practical teaching experience, you may wish to ask your tutor or another teacher to observe some of your lessons using this framework. The feedback will help you reflect critically on your own practice. If other student teachers have also engaged in these activities, you will gain a great deal from a group discussion about teaching styles and levels of pupil participation in geography lessons.

■ **Table 4.3** Using the participation dimension as a framework for analysing 'style' and 'strategy' in a Year 10 lesson about indices of development

Teaching and learning activities	Closed	Framed	Negotiated
Questions The teacher selects the overall focus: indices of development. The class is presented with a list of indices for which there are data on the ICT database in a file on development. Pairs of pupils are asked to produce their own hypotheses about which indices will show positive correlations, which will show negative correlations and which will not correlate at all. This stage of the scheme of work is negotiated in that the pupils can set up their own hypotheses to explore during the lesson. It is within the broad frame set up by the teacher, however.		✓	✓
Data The class is given details of what types of information are in the database and what units of measurement are used. The sources of information are not discussed, nor the validity of data questioned. The data are given as authoritative data.	✓		
Interpretation Pupils are given precise instructions on how to select two variables and draw scattergraphs on the computer. They are expected to follow instructions to use this technique for correlating data. To this extent the interpretation is closed in that there is no choice of methods for correlation. The pupils have to decide, however, from the scattergraph whether they think there is a correlation, and so at this stage are involved in making their own interpretations of the data.	✓		
Conclusions There is a class discussion on the findings of pairs of students and lists are made of indices which correlate positively, those which correlate negatively, and those where there is no correlation. Pupils are invited to speculate on the reasons for their findings.			✓

Source: Roberts, 1996: 231–259

THE CRAFT OF EXPOSITION

Exposition is one of the most fundamental and frequently used strategies in teaching. It performs a number of functions and purposes with pupils learning by listening, thinking and responding to what the teacher has to say. There are three main uses of teacher exposition:

■   making clear the structure and purpose of the learning experience
■   informing, describing and explaining (or demonstrating)
■   using questions and discussion to facilitate and explore pupil learning.

(Kyriacou, 1997: 40)

In the early days of learning to teach, being able to 'inform, describe and explain' effectively is, alongside managing discipline, one of the most highly valued skills by student teachers. Good exposition is also highly regarded by pupils who feel that enthusiasm for the subject and 'clarity of explanation' make a significant contribution to educational attainment. Indeed, there is a great deal of research evidence to support this view.

Student teachers usually over prepare for this first experience of exposition. It is not uncommon to find them spending a few hours preparing for a short presentation. These presentations are often supported by too many visual aids with Power Point slides crammed with text that would take the audience several minutes to read and distract them from listening to the exposition. Such practice is clearly not sustainable.

The 'learning about teaching' that results from this first experience of exposition is usually significant. It takes us forward from thinking just about the geographical content to be covered to a consideration of how to provide a stimulus to elicit audience attention and a framework to support the development of understanding. You are more likely to achieve your objectives if your exposition has a clear structure that the audience can follow.

It is also worth remembering that exposition in a geography classroom is fundamentally different from the lecture style that we may have experienced as adult learners. It can still motivate and inspire pupils, and hopefully stimulate their intellectual curiosity. However, exposition in school tends to be shorter often lasting little more than ten minutes, particularly with younger pupils. It is often more informal and spontaneous, responding to the learners' needs that have been identified by the teacher. It is usually interspersed with other classroom activities such as dialogue or academic tasks carried out by the pupils.

One of the most important functions of teacher exposition is to provide what Ausubel (1968) described as 'advance organisers'. In other words, briefing the pupils about the learning tasks that are to be undertaken and the intended learning that takes place during the lesson. Ausubel described expository learning as 'meaningful verbal learning', which should not be confused with rote learning where the aim is for the learner to be able to recall information, but not necessarily to understand it. Learning is considered to be expository where the subject matter to be learnt is presented to pupils, either orally or in writing, in its final form (Jones, 1984). 'Meaningful verbal learning' requires pupils to relate new ideas to knowledge and understanding that they already possess.

Activity 4.2 **Microteaching – making a short presentation**

Learn through experience! This is an obvious but vital activity for the earliest days of your course – your first experience (possibly) of teaching.

Prepare a short presentation (no longer than five minutes) about an aspect of geography that interests you.

An audience is essential. A group of student teachers guarantees a receptive or supportive audience! You can prepare and use visual aids, but remember not to over do this as you only have five minutes.

Suggested time schedules
Presentation five minutes, followed by:

■ Written evaluation
■ Praise
■ Questions and/or suggestions for improvement.

What makes an effective presentation?

■ There is no formula for this, no 'right way'.
■ However, more effective presentations tend to include some of the following:

1 Rehearse your presentation – organisation, sequence and timing.
2 Tell your audience your objective. Smile. Look committed. Mean it!
3 List your procedures, so they can follow your progress during the presentation.
4 Involve your audience in an activity or use a good visual aid.
5 Be conscious of your audience – their disciplines, experience, needs.
6 Discuss the presentation. Invite audience reaction, e.g.
   a) things they like and why
   b) questions about your content and methods
   c) their suggestions for improving your presentations.

Do not:

■ describe anything in prolonged detail
■ read your presentation or parts of it
■ assume knowledge of specific issues, local features, etc.

Videoing this microteaching provides an added dimension to this activity. Seeing yourself on film for the first time can be a revealing experience. However, try not to be too analytical or over-anxious about personal traits!

Joyce and Weil (1980) used Ausubel's ideas to develop a three-phase model of expository learning (Figure 4.3). In phase 1, the advance organiser is presented to clarify the objectives of the lesson and raise awareness of the learner's prior knowledge and understanding. This is followed by the presentation of the material to be learned or task to be undertaken in a structured and logical way in phase 2. The purpose of phase 3 is to reinforce and strengthen cognitive development by relating this new material to the learner's existing cognitive structures.

Phase 1: Presentation of advance organiser

Clarify the aims of the lesson
Present organiser

- Identify defining attributes
- Give examples
- Provide control
- Repeat

Prompt awareness of learner's knowledge and experience

Phase 2: Presentation of learning task or material

Make organisation explicit
Make logical order of learning material explicit
Maintain attention
Present material

Phase 3: Strengthening cognitive organisation

Use principles of integrative reconciliation
Promote active reception learning
Elicit critical approach to subject matter
Clarify

■ **Figure 4.3** The three phases in Ausubel's advance organiser model
Source: Jones, 1984; adapted from Joyce and Weil, 1980

Ausubel's advance organiser concept can be applied to the geography classroom in a variety of ways. In briefing pupils about the objectives of the lesson ahead, it is often an opportunity to introduce geographical concepts and terminology or to reinforce the use of appropriate geographical language:

Teacher:

'We are going to try to find out some of the reasons why big foreign companies are investing in building new factories in Britain. One example of such a company is Lucky Goldstar (LG), a very large company based in Korea that built two factories near Newport in South Wales.'

Learning activity:

Pupils watch a short video extract of two news reports about the construction of Lucky Goldstar's plants near Newport in South Wales.

Information from these reports and from resource sheets produced by the teacher are used to produce annotated sketch maps explaining the location of plants.

The pupils then produce a flow diagram summarising investment on the Newport area and South Wales. In the final phase of the lesson, the teacher uses questions to explore pupils understanding, constructing a table on the blackboard which summarises the positive and negative impacts of inward investment by transnational companies like Lucky Goldstar.

At the end of the lesson the teacher provides a summary:

'Companies like Lucky Goldstar are often referred to as transnational companies because they operate in more than one country. The investment that they make in other countries like Britain is sometimes called "inward investment" because most of the profits from this investment go to the transnational company, and therefore out of the country.

This is the result of an important economic process that we call globalisation. Much of today's economic activity is global with production, organisation and distribution taking place in several countries.

In the next lesson, we will investigate the problems that can arise when these companies experience difficulties. This happened to Lucky Goldstar leading the company to decide to close one of its factories in South Wales with serious consequences for the economy of the region.'

The design of this lesson can perhaps be summarised in Table 4.4.

The lesson described in Table 4.4 illustrates the role of teacher exposition in briefing and debriefing pupils about the learning taking place. In your early experiences of practical teaching, tutors are likely to place a great deal of emphasis on the need for effective and efficiently managed 'starts' and 'ends' to lessons. Providing 'advance organisers' and 'end of lesson reviews' is an important part of good whole-class teaching.

It is usually a good idea to make the structure of your exposition clear to pupils. The advice frequently given to student teachers goes something like:

'Tell them what you are going to say; then say it; then tell them what you have said'.

■ **Table 4.4** The three main phases of whole-class teaching

The Advance Organiser	The Development phase	The Consolidation phase
Whole-class teaching • teacher exposition to introduce new case study and concepts • emphasise appropriate vocabulary • link with previous learning about the location of industry • explain learning tasks and activities Video extract 1 to introduce new case study.	Video extract 2 – impacts of LG factories Pupils work on main tasks producing an annotated sketch map showing reasons for the location of the factories, and a flow diagram.	Teacher exposition • using questions to explore understanding of inward investment • summary table to consolidate learning (understanding of impacts) • 'end of lesson review' emphasising key concepts and vocabulary (inward investment, globalisation, transnational companies).

Sometimes the main elements of an exposition can be summarised as enquiry questions or sub headings printed on a resource sheet or written on the board. This helps to provide a framework for new learning and to consolidate pupils' understanding of concepts and other information. Waterhouse (1990) describes some of the more common structures used in teacher expositions as:

■ The sequential structure – explaining a sequence of events, steps in a process or a chain of causes and effects.
■ The deductive structure – explaining and justifying a set of rules or principles followed by a description of examples or consequences derived from these principles.
■ The inductive structure – presenting a number of examples or case studies from which the pupils are helped to derive generalisations or rules.
■ The problem-solving structure – encouraging pupils to find a solution or make a decision by evaluating evidence and, the strengths and weaknesses of alternative solutions.
■ The compare and contrast structure – identifying similarities and differences between various situations or events.
■ The subject heading structure – organising the presentation of large amounts of information.

During these early experiences, whole-class teaching presents two fundamental challenges, both of which require a high level of expertise to be developed. First, your exposition must gain and sustain the interest and attention of pupils. Second, the style and content of the exposition must be 'pitched' at an appropriate level for all the pupils in the class. Gaining and sustaining attention requires stimulating, clear and perhaps even charismatic or inspiring presentation as well as good classroom management skills. In the latter aspect of their work, experienced teachers often make effective use of non-verbal behaviour such as facial expression, eye contact and 'conductor-like' hand movements in what could be described as the teaching 'performance' (Slater, 1988).

We cannot all be charismatic orators, but as geography teachers we can utilise a range of strategies to develop or support our styles of exposition. To illustrate this point we can draw upon some examples of approaches used by our own student teachers. Introducing a lesson about the impacts of the Aswan Dam with a Year 10 class, Sarah used a slide of a large dam to help her pupils understand what a multipurpose scheme might involve, and an atlas map of Egypt to help them locate the places encountered during the lesson.

The lesson about the features of a tropical rainforest ecosystem described in Chapter 2 used poetry, video and a tape of rainforest sounds in an attempt to stimulate pupils' imagination and create a sense of place. This might be an example of a 'lead lesson' being used to provide a different form of 'advance organiser' developing and consolidating understanding over a sequence of lessons.

In another lesson about tropical rainforests, Richard drew upon his extensive travels as well as his own creative instincts. Bringing in some of the contents of his bathroom cabinet, he tried to establish some links between distant environments that he had visited and the more immediate world of his pupils. Slides from his travels showed plants from which medicines have been derived, including alcheloids from which chemotherapy drugs have been developed. A variety of specimens, each with its own story, was circulated around the class. The slides and the stories of his travels helped Richard demonstrate the diversity of rainforest environments that exist in the world, indicating their location on the large wall map in the classroom. His exposition drew skillfully on his own unique experiences and provided a source of genuine fascination for the pupils. For them, the textbook descriptions had certainly been brought alive.

Our final example comes from a lesson about pollution of the natural environment. Even though we often claim that geography involves the 'study of issues of current relevance and concern', it is not always easy to respond to issues in the news or to find space in a curriculum with prescriptive schemes of work. When an oil tanker ran aground off the coast of South Wales, Lisa saw an opportunity to produce a stimulating lesson about the pollution of natural environment for her Year 8 class.

Her video was ready to record short clips from television news bulletins as the disaster unfolded over the week. A plethora of articles from national newspapers provided lively headlines, useful maps and photographs with which to produce resource sheets. But how could the resources be used in a stimulating way and how should the learning activity be structured? How could she 'gain and sustain' the pupils interest?

With props at the ready, the lesson began. A large clear plastic bowl containing some water was presented to the class and the pupils challenged to work out what today's lesson was about. An air of excitement was generated as, unsurprisingly, the initial guesses fell short of the mark. A can containing some motor oil was brought out. Some pupils at the front of the room were asked to describe to the rest of the class what happened to the contents of the can as they were poured into the bowl. As the oil floated as a sticky layer over the water, a couple of small plastic birds were dropped into the bowl. This imaginative strategy captured the pupils' attention and generated a wonderfully positive atmosphere in the room. The pupils were, to coin a phrase, 'eating out of the teacher's hands'.

A 'newsroom simulation' was used to provide a context for the lesson and Lisa had devised some appropriate enquiry questions to focus the data collection in the learning activity (Box 4.1). Pupils followed the sequence of news bulletins shown in the video. As the events unfolded, they were recorded on a sheet set out as a diary for the week in question and as annotations on a blank outline map of South Wales. Atlas maps were used to locate the places and events shown in the video.

Instructions for pupils

You have been asked to write a script for a TV presenter's report about the *Sea Empress* disaster. This report will be shown in a programme that provides a summary of the week's main news items. Make sure that your report includes information to answer the following enquiry questions.

■ When and where did the Sea *Empress* run aground and what cargo was it carrying?
■ What impacts has the disaster had on the environment so far?
■ Why has the disaster been worse than people first thought?
■ What have people been doing to try to minimise the impacts of the disaster?
■ What effects do you think the disaster will have on the area in the short-term and in the long-term?

■ **Box 4.1** The *Sea Empress* disaster: a Key Stage 3 enquiry

The lesson concluded with a discussion about the enquiry questions and about the need for pupils' news programme scripts to analyse the geographical issues and events as well as 'telling the story'. Lisa was rewarded with some excellent writing from pupils across a wide range of abilities. Her creative approach was matched by some imaginative learning outcomes including a couple of 'role played' radio interviews and reports produced on cassette by some inspired pupils.

Another common use of exposition in geography teaching is the demonstration of some technique or skill such as the drawing of a graph, map or diagram. It is a strategy that is frequently used when teaching mapwork skills. In all these situations, the teacher demonstrates the different stages with pupils observing and copying the techniques used. Sometimes pupils are challenged to work out these stages and techniques from the teacher's explanation.

Such demonstrations are usually followed by learning activities and tasks where pupils are required to repeat or apply the techniques in the belief that 'practice makes perfect'. This form of teacher exposition geography requires careful planning as well as clarity in delivery. Preparation may involve producing graph or sketch outlines and resource sheets or overhead transparencies to support the demonstration.

Figure 4.4 shows some of the resources used to demonstrate how to draw an annotated sketch map to summarise the impacts of the Volta Dam scheme in Ghana. Pupils could be provided with a blank sketch outline map to use with an atlas map to save time so that the focus can be on the selection and presentation of information on the map. The teacher would also have a copy of this map on an overhead transparency for the demonstration. Relevant information about the impacts is extracted from the article and from a video about the scheme. Providing the pupils with information from different sources means that the teacher can demonstrate the technique in a more interactive way using questions to guide the selection and presentation of information.

This example aims to show the impacts of a large dam scheme

Step 1 – Draw a simple outline map showing the main features of the area in the case study

■ **Figure 4.4** Demonstrating the technique of drawing an annotated sketch map to show the main features of a case study

Step 2 – Mark on important locational information physical geography (rivers, lakes, seas) and human geography (towns, cities, economic activity). Add a title, approximate scale and a north sign.

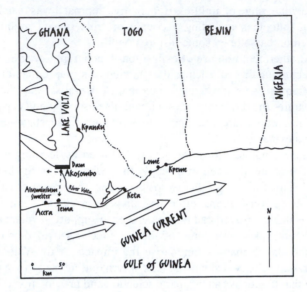

Step 3 – Add important information about the case study using labels and annotations. These should be relevant to the question which the case study is being used to answer.

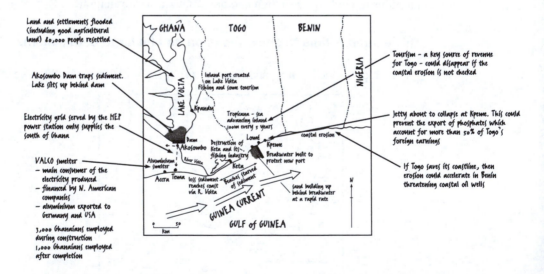

A sketch map showing the impact of the Akosombo Dam/Volta River project on surrounding countries

■ **Figure 4.4** Demonstrating the technique of drawing an annotated sketch map to show the main features of a case study (continued)

By now it should be clear that teacher exposition demands more than just good presentational skills. Being able to explain something effectively requires us to take account of our pupils' existing level of knowledge and understanding, as well as ensuring that the explanation is meaningful by providing an appropriate structure to help them follow and understand its content. As a strategy, exposition can do more than simply relay information to pupils. It can help us to introduce pupils to new or more challenging ideas, explanations and generalisations.

Activity 4.2 includes opportunities to plan some geographical expositions as part of discrete lesson episodes. Some require skills and techniques to be demonstrated. Others require effective explanation of geographical ideas and processes. Practising the delivery of teacher exposition in geography is a logical way of following up Activity 4.2. Undertaken as a group activity, Kyriacou's (1997) summary of the key features of 'effective explaining' could be used to evaluate your expositions providing some helpful feedback about the skills that you need to develop for whole-class teaching (Box 4.2).

Clarity	It is clear and pitched at the appropriate level.
Structure	The major ideas are broken down into meaningful segments and linked together in a logical order.
Length	It is fairly brief and may be interspersed with questions and other activities.
Attention	The delivery makes good use of voice and body language to sustain attention and interest.
Language	It avoids use of over-complex language and explains new terms.
Exemplars	It uses examples, particularly ones relating to pupils' experience and interests.

■ **Box 4.2** Key features of effective explaining
Source: Kyriacou, 1997: 42-3

USING QUESTIONS IN THE CLASSROOM

Questioning is another vital teaching skill. Using questioning to develop a class dialogue is an important aspect of whole-class teaching. By asking questions and building on pupils' responses, teachers can skilfully lead or 'shape' pupils' thinking and learning (cognitive development). It is a skill that can be used in a variety of different ways. Simple questions can focus pupils and quickly check on understanding. These lower order questions require the recall and reporting of information and usually have answers that are clearly right or wrong. More complex and intellectually challenging questions can encourage speculation and deeper thinking. Such higher order questions require pupils to think about, evaluate or apply information.

Another common distinction is made between 'closed' questions, which usually have only one right answer, and 'open' questions, where a range of answers are possible. The style of questioning used is influenced by the teacher's intention (Butt, 1997). Most questions asked in geography lessons are closed. The teacher's purpose is to structure and control how geographical knowledge and understanding is developed by taking pupils through a particular line of reasoning. The pupils are being asked to tell the teacher what is already known.

Such questioning can actually restrict the learning process as the dialogue between teacher and pupils becomes:

> a guessing game whereby the teacher has the knowledge, and tries through questioning to extract the right answers from the pupil. They in turn reach towards the preferred response, the correct answer. Alternatively they adopt a variety of strategies to keep their heads below the parapet.
>
> (Carter, 1991: 1)

Where the intention is to facilitate 'new learning', more open questions can encourage pupils to explore concepts and thinking. The answers given by pupils to these questions are often tentative and can be more challenging for teachers to manage as pupils' responses move away from the 'known' and 'expected'. In these situations, the teacher has to be more flexible and responsive, listening to and making sense of pupils' contributions before asking further questions or providing a coherent summary to extend or consolidate learning.

Roberts explains the function of open questions which:

> allow pupils to put into words what is in their minds rather than guess what is in their teacher's minds. They enable pupils to make their own sense of new knowledge and to interpret it in the light of what they already know. Open questioning assumes that what pupils have to say, what they understand or misunderstand is important even if it does not fit the teacher's line of thinking. It leads to exploratory talk, to much better class discussion and to greater willingness on the part of pupils to participate.
>
> (Roberts, 1986: 70)

She also offers an analytical framework that can be used to describe the questions teachers ask (Figure 4.5). This framework considers two dimensions of questioning. One dimension shows how more open questions can encourage pupils to consider a range of answers. The other shows the increasing cognitive demands made upon pupils of questions that promote higher order thinking. If the majority of questions asked in geography lessons require factual recall or limited comprehension, we may be giving pupils the impression that remembering facts is more important than working things out.

Roberts does remind us, however, that the difference between open and closed questions is not always evident in the words used by a teacher. For example, asking pupils 'what did the programme show you about the impact tourism has had on Thailand?' could be a closed question where the pupils are required to identify the things that the teacher thinks are important. Alternatively, it can be an open question if it is being used to explore pupils' thinking about tourism and its impacts. It depends on whether the teacher is trying to understand or control the pupils' understanding.

Carter (1991) takes this idea further identifying a range of question types from closed recall questions to more evaluative and problem-solving ones (Table 4.5). It is important to remember that each method of questioning has its place in the geography classroom. Closed questioning can be particularly useful when you are trying to check pupils' ability to recall geographical terms and information. When you are trying to probe understanding of specific ideas more open questions beginning 'why do you think that...' or 'what do you think about...' will usually have greater success in eliciting a more extensive personal response.

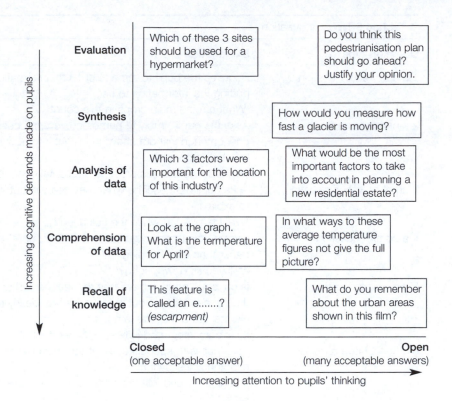

■ **Figure 4.5** Two dimensions of questioning
Source: Roberts, 1986: 68–78

As well as the style of question, the timing of questions and decisions about when or when not to intervene may all influence pupils' learning opportunities. At the start of this chapter we quoted Peter Smith's observation that 'some teachers intervene too quickly and then provide an answer in their own words' (Smith 1997: 126). Allowing time for reflection, introducing further areas for consideration or broadening discussion from the specific to the general can help to encourage deeper thinking and maintain pupils' interest.

Activity 4.3 **What kind of questions do geography teachers ask?**

When you are observing some geography lessons, try to use the framework provided in Table 4.5 to analyse the questions being asked by the teachers. Write down some examples of the different geographical questions.

■ **Table 4.5** Types of question

Question type	Explanation
1 a data recall question	Requires the pupil to remember facts, information without putting the information to use. 'What are the main crops in this country?'
2 a naming question	Asks the pupil simply to name an event, process, phenomenon without showing insight into how it is linked to other factors. 'What do we call this process of coastal deposition?'
3 an observation question	Asks pupils to describe what they see without attempting to explain it. 'What happened when the soil dried?'
4 a control question	Involves the use of questions to modify pupils' behaviour rather than their learning. 'Will you sit down, John?'
5 a pseudo-question	Is constructed to appear that the teacher will accept more than one response, but in fact s/he has clearly made up his/ her mind that this is not so. 'Is this an integrated railway network, then?'
6 a speculative question	Asks pupils to speculate about the outcome of a hypothetical situation. 'Imagine a world without trees, how would this affect our lives?'
7 a reasoning question	Asks pupils to give reasons why certain things do or do not happen. 'What motivates these people to live so near a volcano?'
8 an evaluation question	Is one which makes a pupil weigh up the pros and cons of a situation or argument. 'How strong is the case for a bypass round this village?'
9 a problem-solving question	Asks pupils to construct ways of finding out answers to questions. 'How can we measure the speed of the river here and compare it with lower down?'

Source: Carter, 1991: 4

Marsden sees questions as forming the basis of enquiry learning. He identifies the following attributes of good questioning:

■ asking questions fluently and precisely
■ gearing questions to the student's state of readiness
■ involving a wide range of students in the question-answer process
■ focusing questions on a wide range of intellectual skills, and not just on recall
■ asking probing questions
■ not accepting each answer as of equal validity, though sensitively
■ redirecting questioning to allow accurate and relevant answers to emerge

■   using open-ended as well as closed questions, so that creative thought and value judgements are invited.

(Marsden, 1995: 94)

To use questioning effectively, you need to develop a number of skills. Being able to identify appropriate questions and to present them clearly are of fundamental importance. This depends on your ability to take account of pupils' existing knowledge and understanding as well as to manage the selection of pupils to answer. Targeting is needed to involve as many pupils as possible and to match the questions to the pupils selected. It is important to use these questions to show the connections between previous and new learning. It is also helpful to use questions to provide a framework within which pupils can make sense of ideas and new learning.

Sequencing questions is an appropriate way which helps teachers develop classroom dialogue. 'Staging' questions can be used to increase the level of challenge as the lesson proceeds. This is an important skill when you are trying to develop or explore pupils' understanding. You can either start with a narrow focus and broaden outwards, or start with a broad focus and narrow down into more detail. It helps you both to monitor and to facilitate pupil learning. In these contexts, the quality of feedback provided by the teacher is vital. Every effort needs to be made to create a positive classroom atmosphere in which pupils' contributions are valued and respected. Well-judged praise and encouragement helps to protect pupils' self-esteem and to develop their self-confidence. How questions are used can therefore have a profound influence on both the classroom atmosphere and the rapport which develops between pupils and teachers.

COLLABORATIVE STRATEGIES

Earlier in this chapter, we suggested that some of the terms used to describe different teaching strategies can be value-laden, stereotypical and open to misinterpretation. The use of group work has been the subject of some controversy, partly because it has usually been discussed in the context of the debate over the relative effectiveness of 'traditional' and 'progressive teaching'. It is usually associated with more open-ended investigational tasks carried out by pupils working in small groups.

We prefer to use the term 'collaborative learning' to describe the academic tasks and activities undertaken by groups of pupils, and which involve some degree of discussion, reflection and collaboration (Kyriacou, 1997). There are some educational goals, such as learning to co-operate and learning to work in a team, that can only be attained through group work (Desforges, 1995).

Bennett and Dunne (1992) argue that well planned and managed group work can also increase levels of academic attainment and pupils' self-esteem. Learning for understanding is essentially a social process, collaborative learning can enhance comprehension by creating situations in which intellectual exchanges take place. The broader educational value of collaborative activity is also stressed by Whitaker (1995) who suggests that it:

■   creates a climate in which pupils can work with a sense of security and self confidence
■   facilitates the growth of understanding by offering the optimum opportunity for pupils to talk reflectively with each other
■   promotes a spirit of co-operation and mutual respect.

Learning is often seen as an individual process. Although it is certainly true to say that pupils need to internalise learning on an individual basis, it is important to provide opportunities for pupils to work together. Working in groups can promote more effective learning, particularly when it encourages creativity or the clarification of understanding. This notion reflects some of the shifts in conceptions of the learner that have taken place in recent years. These conceptions place far more emphasis on the social nature of learning. Bruner and Haste (1987) argue that '"making sense" is a social process' and stress the importance of the social setting in classroom learning. Bruner was influenced by the work of Vygotsky (1978) who argued that social interaction plays a central role in facilitating learning.

When managed effectively, working in groups can promote the development of a range of valuable learning and interpersonal skills. If the pupils are 'active' for a large part of the time, working in groups can increase their enthusiasm and motivation to learn. It can also help to build-up their self confidence to share ideas and opinions. Talking through ideas helps pupils to test out their thoughts and improve their understanding. Where open-ended tasks are used as the focus for work in groups there are likely to be more opportunities for pupils to explore areas and ideas they are interested in at their own levels (Robinson and Serf, 1997). In the longer term, this enables pupils to take more responsibility for their own learning. It helps them use and value their own experiences as well as those of other pupils. Freeman and Hare (2006: 309) provide a helpful summary of the benefits of collaborative learning.

As well as helping pupils to develop their ability to co-operate, collaborative activities provide opportunities for them to practise and improve their communication skills. Encouraging pupils to discuss geographical ideas in a purposeful way helps facilitate learning in geography. The process of selecting, organising and presenting ideas during discussion reinforces and enhances conceptualisation (Stimpson, 1994: 154; Freeman and Hare, 2006). Discussion involves a search for correct explanations with concepts being retrieved from long-term memory to be 'reviewed and re-established' (Stimpson 1994: 154). As pupils talk through their interpretations, so their understanding increases. Jacobson and colleagues (1981) suggest that discussion helps pupils learn how to:

- summarise group opinion
- handle controversy
- search for consensus
- use self-directed learning skills
- use higher order thinking skills such as those of analysis, synthesis and evaluation.

To be effective, learning in groups must involve genuine collaboration and purposeful activity. Pupils may sit in groups in many classrooms but most of the time they are working independently and only occasionally are they involved in any collaborative learning activity or required to share answers. This is usually because the tasks that are given to the groups do not require collaboration or co-operation. The main advantages of learning in groups are therefore lost.

Organising and managing learning in groups can be demanding. Once the focus of the activity has been identified appropriate strategies need to be planned with thought given to how these strategies are to be structured to produce the desired learning outcomes. This may sometimes just require the planning of a sequence of discussion questions but often supporting resources need to be designed and prepared. Decisions have to be made about pupil groupings. During the lesson itself, a range of classroom management skills need to be employed to ensure that the planned learning takes place. These include briefing and debriefing skills as well as management skills to keep pupils actively engaged in the tasks. You should also actively monitor and assess pupils' contributions and the learning taking place. Freeman and Hare (2006) identify six key features of collaboration and provide very helpful guidance about how to plan, launch and manage collaborative activity successfully (see Figure 4.6).

Given these challenges, using collaborative strategies can require a 'leap of faith' for many teachers who feel more confident when using other teaching strategies. Sometimes small group work fails to achieve its potential leading to a reluctance to use similar strategies again. Typical concerns relate to the breakdown of groups, the difficulty of keeping all pupils actively engaged in the task and worries about time being wasted. Others are uncertain about the value of some pupil comments or lack confidence in their ability to assess these contributions and shape the understanding that is developing through the discussion that is taking place.

To be successful, small group work requires careful planning. Bennett (1995) has reviewed evidence from research showing that a number of factors can influence the effectiveness of group work including:

■ group size and composition
■ the nature of the tasks assigned
■ whether the pupils have been given any training in the use of social and co-operative skills.

The size and composition of pupil groupings is a particularly important issue influencing the success of collaborative learning activities. Teachers often use groups of between four and six pupils. However, it is generally accepted that the ideal group size when working with pupils aged between 11 and 16 is two, three and four pupils. Such groups are large enough to participate. Larger groups can inhibit learning if pupils have to wait a long time to give their views or if certain pupils dominate the discussion leaving others as peripheral non-participants.

The gender and ability composition of groups is another important issue. Lower secondary pupils often appear to be more comfortable in single-sex groups and so developing the use of mixed groups can play an important role in breaking down gender barriers and enhancing social relationships (Stimpson, 1994). Some teachers feel that work in smaller groups can counteract the dominance of boys in whole-class situations where they can be more aggressive. However, Bennett and Dunne (1992) found that where there were equal numbers of boys and girls, or where girls outnumbered boys, both had similar learning experiences. Girls were disadvantaged when outnumbered by boys. Often ignored by the boys, girls tended to speak less and at a lower level of reasoning. Interaction in such groups has been found to be detrimental to girls' achievement (Webb and Kenderski, 1985).

Studies comparing ability and mixed-ability co-operative groups have raised substantial doubts about some aspects of ability grouping (Bennett, 1995). High ability pupils appear to perform well irrespective of the type of group they are placed in. They often talk more, and more of this talk is academic in content. In low-ability groups, substantially less time is devoted to interactions concerning academic content and few relevant explanations are offered. This is usually because the pupils in these groups have

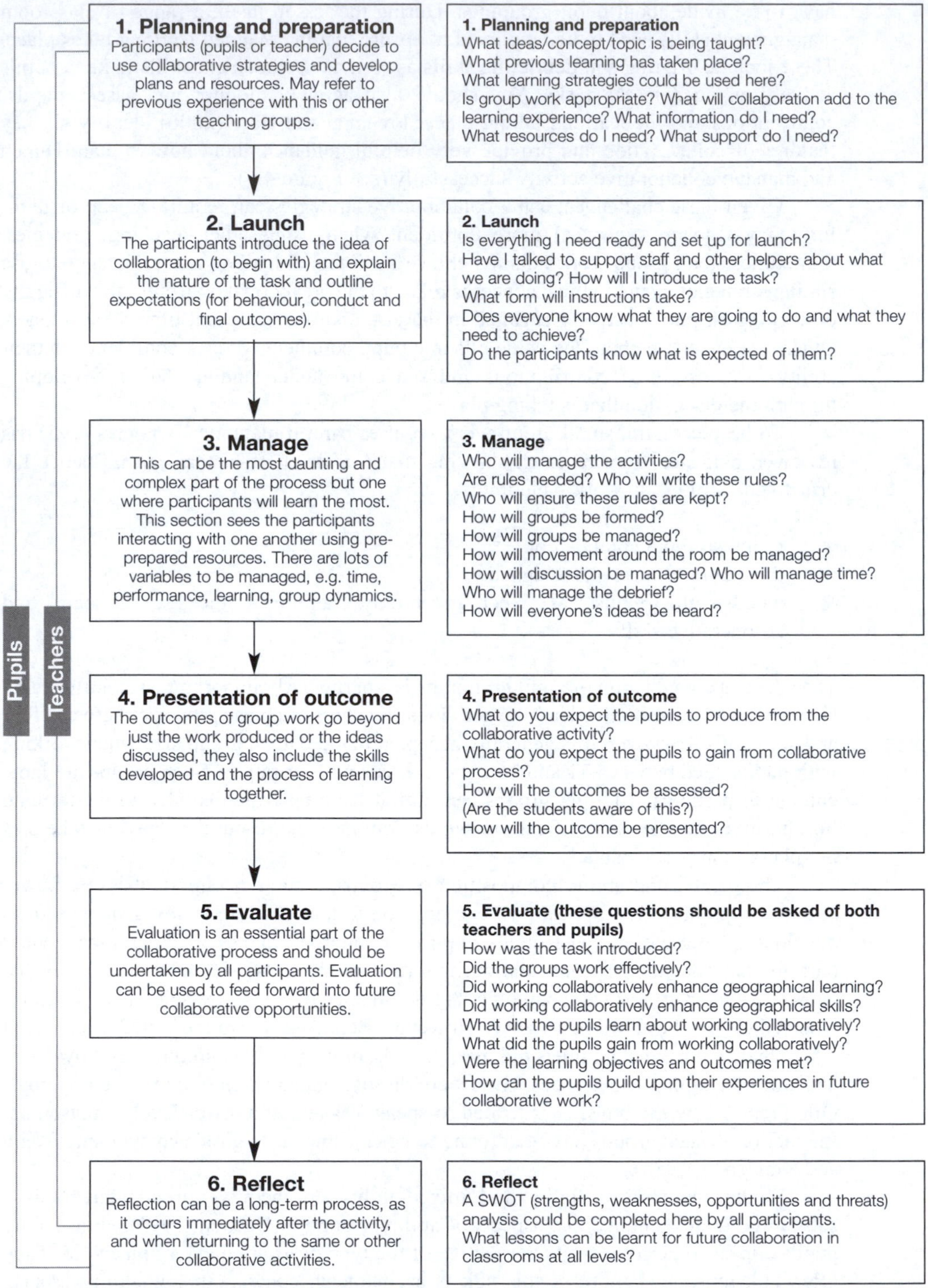

1. Planning and preparation
Participants (pupils or teacher) decide to use collaborative strategies and develop plans and resources. May refer to previous experience with this or other teaching groups.

1. Planning and preparation
What ideas/concept/topic is being taught?
What previous learning has taken place?
What learning strategies could be used here?
Is group work appropriate? What will collaboration add to the learning experience? What information do I need?
What resources do I need? What support do I need?

2. Launch
The participants introduce the idea of collaboration (to begin with) and explain the nature of the task and outline expectations (for behaviour, conduct and final outcomes).

2. Launch
Is everything I need ready and set up for launch?
Have I talked to support staff and other helpers about what we are doing? How will I introduce the task?
What form will instructions take?
Does everyone know what they are going to do and what they need to achieve?
Do the participants know what is expected of them?

3. Manage
This can be the most daunting and complex part of the process but one where participants will learn the most. This section sees the participants interacting with one another using pre-prepared resources. There are lots of variables to be managed, e.g. time, performance, learning, group dynamics.

3. Manage
Who will manage the activities?
Are rules needed? Who will write these rules?
Who will ensure these rules are kept?
How will groups be formed?
How will groups be managed?
How will movement around the room be managed?
How will discussion be managed? Who will manage time?
Who will manage the debrief?
How will everyone's ideas be heard?

4. Presentation of outcome
The outcomes of group work go beyond just the work produced or the ideas discussed, they also include the skills developed and the process of learning together.

4. Presentation of outcome
What do you expect the pupils to produce from the collaborative activity?
What do you expect the pupils to gain from collaborative process?
How will the outcomes be assessed?
(Are the students aware of this?)
How will the outcome be presented?

5. Evaluate
Evaluation is an essential part of the collaborative process and should be undertaken by all participants. Evaluation can be used to feed forward into future collaborative opportunities.

5. Evaluate (these questions should be asked of both teachers and pupils)
How was the task introduced?
Did the groups work effectively?
Did working collaboratively enhance geographical learning?
Did working collaboratively enhance geographical skills?
What did the pupils learn about working collaboratively?
What did the pupils gain from working collaboratively?
Were the learning objectives and outcomes met?
How can the pupils build upon their experiences in future collaborative work?

6. Reflect
Reflection can be a long-term process, as it occurs immediately after the activity, and when returning to the same or other collaborative activities.

6. Reflect
A SWOT (strengths, weaknesses, opportunities and threats) analysis could be completed here by all participants.
What lessons can be learnt for future collaboration in classrooms at all levels?

Pupils

Teachers

■ **Figure 4.6** Managing collaborative learning
Source: Freeman and Hare, 2006: 308–329

a poor understanding of the task or because they do not have the skills or knowledge of the subject matter needed to offer such explanations. These factors lead most advocates of co-operative or collaborative learning to favour mixed ability grouping. Webb (1989) argues that high-attaining children gain, both academically and socially, from the opportunity to work with and tutor lower-achieving colleagues.

Designing and presenting appropriate tasks is one of the biggest challenges facing teachers when using collaborative strategies. Two important issues need to be considered when planning these tasks: the cognitive demand and the social demand.

There are two main types of co-operative group work with different demands for co-operation. In the first, pupils may be given a specific task to achieve such as the preparation of a presentation or production of a newspaper report. The focus is on the production of a group outcome. Each pupil works on one aspect of the task, which is divided in such a way that the group outcome cannot be achieved until every pupil has completed his or her element of the 'jigsaw'. The pupils plan together, but work individually before fitting the elements of the jigsaw together to produce a coherent group outcome.

In the second type of co-operative task, pupils are required to share their knowledge, understanding and skills to achieve a common objective through some form of problem-solving or open-ended investigation. Barnes and Todd (1977) observed how teachers distinguished between 'loose' and 'tight' tasks used for group work. This distinction reflects the difference between activities that have 'correct' or 'predictable' solutions and those where the responses can be more wide ranging. Freeman and Hare (2006: 312) suggest a variety of ways in which collaborative activity can be organised in geography. A comprehensive range of ideas for collaborative, active and student-centred learning activities can also be found in 'The Teacher's Toolkit' (Ginnis, 2002).

A further distinction can be made between tasks demanding action talk and abstract talk (Bennett and Dunne, 1992). This distinction is derived from Piaget's (1959) ideas about the development of children's conversations whereby tasks which demand no more than talk related to the 'ongoing action of the moment' are distinguished from those which demand explanations or reconstruction.

One of the most common ways of organising co-operative and collaborative learning in geography is through the use of various types of card sorting activities. Such activities are an effective and flexible way of providing a focus and structure for small group work. They can help you overcome some of the anxieties that we identified earlier in this section. In particular, they provide a focus for discussion between pupils as well as a focus for teacher intervention and monitoring of learning during activity. Nash (1997) identifies a range of benefits from using card sorting activities as a focus for small group work (see Box 4.3).

Cards can be used effectively to support observational activities where pupils are identifying geographical features and describing landscapes or land use patterns. This could involve matching terms or descriptions on cards to features shown in resources like photographs, maps and diagrams. Sometimes these resources and cards can be temporarily fixed to display paper and arrows drawn using marker pens to label these features. Pupils could then write further information onto the display paper, for example, to suggest explanations for particular features or to suggest geographical questions that could be used to stimulate enquiry.

Card sorting activities can be used effectively to develop pupils' knowledge and understanding of geographical terms. For example, various indicators of development are written on some of the cards and the pupils match these with definitions written on other cards. Writing the terms and definitions on different coloured card can help with the organisation of such activities. An extension to this activity could require pupils to then select and justify their choice of four or five indicators that they feel would provide a good measure of quality of people's life in different countries (i.e. as part of a quality of life index).

■ It is a relatively quick and simple method of enabling pupils to work in groups.

■ It provides pupils with a clear and focused task – opportunities for them to move off – tasks are limited.

■ It can be used very flexibly across the full age and ability range.

■ It can allow for differentiation even when the same resource is being used in a mixed ability or streamed situation.

■ It can be used to impart information to pupils in an interesting and motivating way.

■ It allows pupils to develop skills of communication and co-operation.

■ It involves pupils actively in their own learning.

■ It enables more meaningful teacher-pupil contacts in the classroom.

Card sorting activities can be used in geography lessons in a variety of ways including:

■ labelling features

■ matching words and definitions

■ classifying features and factors

■ ranking and identifying priorities

■ looking for relationships and explanations.

■ **Box 4.3** The benefits of using card sorting activities
Source: Nash, 1997: 22

One of the most common uses of card sorting activities helps pupils understand how various geographical features, factors or processes might be classified. These activities may require them to decide which groups different cards may fall into. For example, they could be asked to distinguish between benefits and problems resulting from the construction of a large multi-purpose dam, or between the arguments for and against the building of a new road, housing development or out-of-town retail park.

In sorting out statements into two categories, pupils are undertaking a simple form of evaluation. A different form of classification whereby factors that can influence the decisions that farmers make about activities and land use on their farms could be sorted into groups distinguishing between the physical, economic, social/personal and technical influences. Different types of employment or economic activity could be written on cards which pupils then sort into primary, secondary, tertiary and quaternary sectors. In this latter example, pictures cut from magazines could be used in conjunction with vocabulary cards to help pupils with special educational needs such as bilingual learners. Further development of these classification activities would involve pupils looking for and determining their own categories for grouping cards.

Another purposeful discussion task based around the use of a card sorting activity requires pupils to identify priorities from a variety of alternatives. Diamond ranking is a technique that is frequently used when asking pupils to distinguish between the 'most important' and the 'least important' ideas, factors, problems or solutions. Working in pairs or small groups, pupils are asked to organise their cards in the shape of a diamond, with the idea they agree most with at the top and the one they least agree with at the bottom (see Figure 4.7).

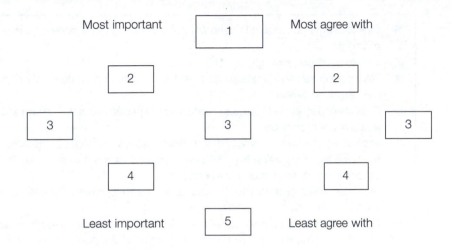

■ **Figure 4.7** Identifying priorities using diamond ranking

Using information cards to identify priorities, as in the above example, is an effective strategy for developing pupils' critical thinking and problem-solving skills through more open-ended discussion activities. They can also be used in a purposeful way to provide opportunities for pupils to search for relationships in geographical data, and to suggest explanations and generalisations. Information about particular geographical processes or events can be written on cards which pupils have to organise into some sort of order; for example, into a flow diagram explaining these processes or events.

Above all, getting the most out of discussion activities requires you to know your pupils. This is important both during the planning stage, when you are preparing appropriate resources and organising effective pupil groupings, and when you are managing the activities in the classroom. Other teaching skills, such as questioning (discussed earlier), have an important role to play in ensuring that co-operative learning and discussion are successful. Questioning at individual, group and whole-class levels helps the teacher to monitor and explore the learning that is taking place. Ideas that emerge through discussion need to be clarified and links between different ideas established to take pupils' thinking and learning forward.

Managing classroom discussion and co-operative learning activities can therefore be very demanding as you need to monitor a multitude of exchanges as well as maintaining an overview of the progress of the whole class towards achieving the intended learning objectives. This requires the 'flexible and responsive' approach that we described in our earlier discussion of questioning skills. You also need to develop your ability to observe, listen to and make sense of the learning that is taking place. This 'active assessment' of learning helps you to summarise and consolidate the learning that has taken place through these activities. It therefore follows that adequate time must be made available to 'debrief' the activities we have described in this section. Box 4.4 provides some helpful suggestions about how teachers can improve the quality of classroom discussion.

■ Plan carefully: discussion is generally not something to be done on the spur of the moment.

■ Create small cohesive groups of 2 to 4 pupils.

■ Take care in setting up groups so that they contain neither dominant minorities nor 'shrinking violets'.

■ Establish open-ended topics to discuss and specific tasks which can act as a focus and a framework.

■ Provide information to stimulate and direct discussion. Pupils are generally quick to realise that discussion is getting nowhere and thus not worthwhile. The outcome is only frustration for all concerned.

■ Produce varied resources for the pupils with as much visual material as possible so as to minimise the time taken up in reading.

■ Provide a focus of guiding questions or instructions to give shape to what pupils have to say. The younger and more inexperienced the pupils, the more explicit should be the instructions.

■ As the teacher, avoid giving answers or judgements; neutrality is needed whilst discussion proceeds. More direct intervention on the part of the teacher may be needed if pupil discussions start to go off track, and it becomes necessary to refocus what is being talked about.

■ Think carefully about how much time should be allocated for the activity. In general, the time given to pupils should be short so as to concentrate minds and prevent a tendency to drift away from the task.

■ Provide a clear idea of the outcomes expected from the discussion, e.g. a solution to the problem given. The discussion should result in a specific product such as a summary, list or series of conclusions.

■ Follow-up is crucial if the most is to be made out of discussion. The key geographical points intended need to be summarised and ordered in follow-up exercises.

■ **Box 4.4** Improving the quality of classroom discussion
Source: Stimpson, 1994: 156

USING GAMES AND SIMULATIONS

The essence of simulation is to provide learning through experience (and through subsequent reflection on experience) rather than by the processing of information through more dialectic means. Pupils involved in a game or role play are likely to come to grapple with ideas based on their own experience and on discussion with their peers, rather than being told about the ideas.

(Walford, 1987: 79)

Games and simulations are another way of providing active learning experiences for pupils in geography classrooms. As such, they are an important part of a geography teacher's repertoire of teaching strategies. The games and simulations used in geography lessons can range from simple to quite sophisticated activities. However, what they all have in common is that they 'invite pupils to imaginatively "put themselves in other people's shoes" and exercise thought and reflection in making a decision of some kind' (Walford, 1987).

Using games and simulations can certainly improve most pupils' levels of motivation. However, they have a number of other important attributes that make them effective strategies to use when teaching geography. They can improve pupils' understanding of geographical processes and provide intellectual stimulation through a variety of more demanding skills such as analysing, synthesising and evaluating, which may need to be used in the process of making decisions or solving problems. They also provide further opportunities for purposeful classroom discussion, negotiation and other collaborative activities that help develop pupils' social, co-operative and communication skills.

Another significant attribute of many simulation activities is how they simplify aspects of reality so that pupils can more readily understand the 'dynamics of a rapidly changing world' (Walford, 1987: 79). Simulations can also help pupils to 'recognise the "interdisciplinary" nature of real life situations' (Bale, 1987: 125). Bale and Walford both comment on the role of classroom simulation in helping pupils to develop empathy, however partial, with people from other places, environment, cultures and occupations. (*Empathy* is used here to refer to the ability to identify with other people's situation or circumstances. It does not suggest that their view(s) should be accepted uncritically.)

Through experience, we have also found that games and simulations can be used effectively with classes where there is a wide range of ability to involve the whole class in the same learning activity at the same time. As well as providing valuable 'social training' in co-operative activity, games and simulations can be understood at different levels by pupils across the range of ability. They often present a variety of problem-solving or decision-making situations that can be interpreted at differing levels of complexity. What pupils learn from these activities depends on 'their own aptitudes and intelligence' (Grenyer, 1985: 25).

Grenyer makes a clear distinction between a game and a simulation. He argues that a geographical simulation involves 'a testing of a model against reality in an attempt to predict how a pattern will develop or to analyse the reasons for the development of that pattern' (Grenyer, 1985). A geographical game is seen as a form of simulation with 'an element of competition added'. The intention is to simplify reality so that in the process of attempting to win the game, pupils will increase their understanding of that reality.

What is clear, however, is that teachers need to consider a number of important issues when planning to use a game or simulation in the classroom. These issues relate to the preparation and management of the activity. There is also a need to consider how the outcomes of the activity will be assessed and evaluated.

The preparation stage includes the selection and preparation of appropriate material. Initially you will probably find it helpful to use examples from the extensive range of published games and simulations. Resources produced by the Development

Education Centres and agencies can be a rich source of ideas and activities covering a wide range of geographical issues and locations. Much of this development education material is carefully designed to facilitate collaborative activity in the classroom and to develop pupils' understanding of real issues, places and relevant geographical processes. Using such materials will help you to understand how to design and organise appropriate simulation materials and activities. You will also be able to focus your attention on learning how to use appropriate teaching strategies to manage these games and simulations successfully in the classroom. As your understanding of the principles underpinning the effective use of games and simulations improves, you can begin to develop your own material and adapt existing ones to produce more complex or more simple activities.

Choosing when to use particular games and simulations with your classes is another important aspect of the planning phase. Sometimes using a simple game or simulation in the early days of teaching particular classes can do wonders for pupil motivation as well as for beginning to establish a rapport with these pupils. It was for these reasons that we used the Trading Game (Christian Aid) with our classes within their first three weeks at the school. Not only did it help to establish positive teacher-pupil rapport and the role of collaboration in learning, it also sent out clear messages about the active nature of learning in geography. However, this would not be a wise strategy in your early days as a student teacher when you are learning to appreciate and master the fundamentals of classroom management. You need to be confident in your classroom management skills and your ability to be flexible in your use of these skills.

Your management of games and simulations also needs to be sensitive and responsive. This follows on logically from being confident in your classroom management skills and knowing your classes. Although games and simulations can be very enjoyable and stimulating, different pupils respond in different ways. Some pupils become so 'submerged' in their role or the activity that they react instinctively. Your observation skills help you monitor the actions of pupils and the learning that is taking place. This is one of the most demanding aspects of managing games and simulations.

You need to monitor a multitude of different exchanges and actions in different parts of the classroom. Decisions have to be made about when and how to intervene. Interventions can be to review events or the learning that has taken place during simulations. Alternatively, the purpose of interventions can be to introduce new factors and situations or to change the direction of particular activities.

In making these interventions you should try to be flexible and not 'pull the reins in' too tightly. Providing too many interpretations along the way can reduce the pace and flow of the activity which inhibit some of the learning opportunities. With some simulations it is possible to plan the interventions perhaps through the introduction of chance factors. A good example of this can be seen in the Oxfam Farming game that was widely used during our early years as teachers. In trying to simulate the experience of a West African subsistence farmer, pupils make decisions about which crops to plant year by year. A variety of factors can be introduced through the use of 'chance' cards (disease and disasters) creating a changing situation with which the farmers have to cope. As the game develops, they can become caught up in a cycle of poverty which provides opportunities to explore the precarious nature of decision-making in such situations and the relationship between aspects of this downward cycle, such as between malnutrition and disease.

It should be remembered, however, that pupils receive what Walford calls a kind of 'shadow-reality':

It is a mistake to see simulation as a replica of reality. It can never go that far. It is better seen as a vehicle for teaching about reality and a help in bringing pupils into an empathetic frame of mind in order to better understand it.

(Walford, 1987: 83)

As well as planning when and how to intervene, you should give some consideration to the strategies to be used to debrief and follow-up simulation activities. Pupils need to have opportunities to explore and consolidate the learning that has taken place. Timing and preparation are crucial in this respect. You should plan to allow enough time for discussion and reflection immediately after the end of the game or simulation. Enabling pupils to reflect on their actions, on the way in which the game or simulation operates, and how this mirrors the dynamics of the real world, makes a significant contribution to pupils' learning.

A debriefing session might consist of a number of different elements where the teacher works with the pupils to assess the learning outcomes from a game or simulation. Walford recommends that this should include 'some element of action replay (to recognise key moments and interventions in retrospect)' (Walford, 1996: 143). This strategy is often not effectively utilised and consequently an opportunity to help pupils gain a valuable insight into the learning that has taken place is missed.

It is helpful to organise some analysis of the views presented during a role play as well as the evidence used in support of these views. A table or matrix could be drawn to provide a structure for this analysis, summarising the views and highlighting the conflicts between different interest groups. Contrasts could also be made between views presented during the role-play and those that might be expressed when pupils are out of role.

A variety of strategies can be used to explore pupils' understanding of the concepts and generalisations developed through simulations. Explanations can be sought for particular events or actions with concept maps (see Chapter 2) used to identify links between different factors and processes. Introducing data and case studies from the real world provides opportunities for pupils to apply their conceptual understanding and test the models on which the simulations are based. This is certainly possible with most of the published simulations, which include examples to illustrate their underlying principles in their guidance for teachers.

Attention should also be given to the affective outcomes of simulations as well as the cognitive ones. As we suggested earlier in this discussion, pupils can become 'submerged' in a role and so their feelings about the learning experience can be used to explore ideas and issues. This is certainly the case in the farming and trading games described earlier. The main outcomes of the Trading Game might include an understanding of how the process of trade can affect the prosperity of a country. However, this game usually arouses feelings of unfairness so it is worth asking groups to comment on how they felt about being poor or rich. Pupils can be encouraged to recall particular incidents in a game and to describe their reactions to what happened.

Box 4.5 suggests some generic questions 'informed by a variety of geographical perspectives at a variety of levels' that can be used to help pupils to reflect on their learning experiences during the Trading Game. In Reid's discussion of the Trading Game, the pupils' experiences and reflections on these experiences are used as a context for exploring issues related to sustainable development (Reid, 1996).

Skilful debriefing could therefore interweave the affective and cognitive dimensions of pupils' learning experiences. The game's own 'guidelines for discussion'

> ■ What is going on in the game and what is it simulating?
> ■ How do you feel about your actions arising from your role in the game? What about the real world parallels?
> ■ Some of the resources in the game will eventually run out. What would happen if the game had continued uninterrupted? What are the consequences of depleting resources?
> ■ What alternative strategies could be pursued in the game? With what consequences?
> ■ Who gains and who loses through participating in the real world version?
> ■ What values and actions are implicit within and/or fostered in such a simulation? How may they be challenged? Should they be challenged?
>
> (NB. These questions would be modified for use with different age groups and ranges of ability.)

■ **Box 4.5** Some generic questions used in debriefing pupils after the Trading Game
Source: Resources 1, 3 and 6, Reid, 1996: 168–172

suggest that 'injustices in the structures of the world's trade' should be examined with 'players' own experiences of helplessness and anger' reflecting the 'sentiments felt on a world-wide scale' by the poorer nations. Examples of exploitation might be introduced:

> how does an Indian tea-worker feel, for instance, when the decisions affecting her livelihood are made mainly by western commercial interests?
>
> (Christian Aid, 1986: 4)

The teacher could 'dig' a little deeper and explore more challenging issues. The Trading Game can raise some difficult questions about concepts such as ownership and control:

> If the world is an unfair place, and if we admit that its structures need changing, what sort of attitude should we have towards the world's resources and the use we make of them?
>
> (Christian Aid, 1986)

Some may feel that such issues and questions are beyond the scope of geography education in the secondary school. However, we share Rex Walford's view that:

> the essence of many simulations involves feelings as well as minds. Thus some simulations have, as their major objective, the revelation of a particular process in order to have participants re-assess their attitudes towards it.
>
> (Walford, 1996: 143)

There is wider potential for experiential learning in the Trading Game which can be limited when the focus of discussion is solely on the process of trade:

> Once one broadens the horizon of the exercise with a view to exploring economic awareness, values, inter-group and personal behaviour and the workings of the groups themselves the possibilities become apparent.
>
> (Dennison, 1990: 103)

When reviewing the learning outcomes of many games and simulations it is therefore worth giving some consideration to the contribution that these learning experiences make to pupils' personal and social education. We can recall many instances where pupils have produced enlightening insights into their feelings and behaviour when describing their reactions to particular experiences during games and simulations. The group representing the USA recognised how the Trading Game was set up and refused to exploit the poorer countries, deciding instead to share their equipment rather than maximising their own gains at these countries' expense. The pupils who recognised the importance of raw materials tried to strike a balance between their exploitation of resources and the need for conservation so that they would be able to continue being involved in the game at a later stage.

Many simulations that involve pupils working co-operatively provide opportunities for them to learn about how groups work and to reflect on their own interpersonal skills. Leadership and individual roles, communication skills, sharing and supporting, the organisation and structure of groups, can all be explored. Through such experiential learning pupils are certain to learn more about themselves. They may gain a greater insight into their own strengths or weaknesses in such skills as leadership, communication and negotiation. The experiential learning that takes place through simulation activities in geography can contribute much to pupils' personal development and their ability to reflect on this development.

Role plays

Role-play activities require pupils to take on the role of another person and take part in a simulated meeting or enquiry of some kind where negotiations take place and decisions have to be made. Examples of the contexts used for such activities might include government or council meetings, public enquiries or even global conventions (e.g. conferences about environmental, economic, trade or development issues). Pupils present or argue viewpoints which may not be ones they hold personally.

The quality of the role-play simulation can vary considerably depending on the aptitude and ability of the pupils, the quality of their preparation and communication skills, and the skill of the teacher in managing the activity. In order to get the best out of such activities, pupils need to be given time to prepare adequately. It is often helpful to assign roles to pupils in pairs or small groups so they can discuss the attitudes that might be held by the people they represent and prepare the views that they present.

Sometimes these simulations have little structure with the teacher just setting the scene, describing the issue to be debated and assigning roles to particular pupils or groups of pupils. Also, role-play activities do not have to lead to whole-class debate or presentation. A visual stimulus (short video sequence, slide or textbook photograph) can be presented, an issue or question established and pupils asked, in pairs, to act out a scene or take on particular roles to debate this issue or question. In each of these scenarios pupils need to empathise with the people they represent and consider their likely attitudes and values. These forms of role play are challenging for both teacher and pupils as the activity is more open-ended and the outcomes less predictable.

Alternatively, the teacher may issue role cards which describe the role and provide information about people or groups' likely attitudes. Sometimes prompts or questions are used to guide pupils in their preparation of views and arguments to be presented. The cards contain questions which act as prompts to help pupils consider the implications of one possible solution for different groups of people. In such situations it is interesting to note how some pupils stick closely to the points outlined on their role cards while other more inventive and articulate pupils contribute their own ideas and consider other possibilities.

As well as providing information on role cards to help pupils 'get into role', it is a good idea to provide some guidance to structure their discussions. Box 4.6 shows the pupils' instructions which gives them specific tasks to undertake during a role-playing activity. These tasks provide a clear focus for their discussions and therefore help you manage the activity effectively.

It is also possible to devise simulations where pupils take on similar roles but respond in different ways to the task or problem presented to them. For example, in ActionAid's case study of sustainable development on the Altiplano in Bolivia ('Picking up the threads') one activity simulates a year in the life of a Puca Pampa textiles group. Pupils make decisions about how to respond to different situations, design and produce publicity materials for their textiles project and prepare a business plan for their group for the coming year. The activity aims to help pupils gain an understanding of some of the challenges facing people living on the Altiplano and how development projects in the area try to respond to these challenges in a sustainable way.

Sometimes you may want pupils to do more than just present different viewpoints and arguments. Information from a variety of sources can be made available and pupils required to select appropriate evidence to support these viewpoints and arguments. To ensure that there is a realistic debate, it is worth encouraging pupils to consider questions that they might be asked by other interest groups and how they could respond to these questions using the evidence available.

The presentation phase of a role-play activity is usually very enjoyable, stimulating and, if there has been adequate preparation, it contains much worthwhile learning. We can recall numerous occasions where well-motivated pupils have used preparation time between lessons to produce appropriate visual aids to support their presentations and even arrived 'dressed in role'.

The next challenge for the teacher is to ensure that, without diminishing the enjoyment of the occasion, pupils are able to digest, make sense of and internalise some of the worthwhile learning that takes place in this phase of the activity. If exhorted to 'make notes', they are more likely to try to write down everything that their colleagues say. Make sure that the purpose of any note-taking is made clear and provide some guidance about what should be noted. This could be done using some general questions such as:

- What is the group? Who do they represent?
- What are their views?
- Why do they hold these views?
- What evidence do they use to support these views?
- What was or could be argued to counter these views?

Sometimes the pupils could think of questions that they could ask other groups to challenge or seek clarification of the views presented. Each of these strategies promotes more 'active listening' as pupils are being asked not just to record but to analyse what is being argued. Another way of analysing what is happening during a role play is to use some pupils as observers recording what is happening in different groups while they prepare or act out their role. This is a particularly useful strategy if you want to analyse

Role-play scenario

This role play asks pupils to take on the roles of members of the community and to discuss the problems people face. The roles include those of the village leader, a settler, a Quichua farmer and a local development worker. Each pupil is given a role card outlining the likely attitudes and interests of the person that they represent.

The pupils are presented with three options for action.

1 Do nothing. Many people are concerned about chance. They do not have many resources, so cannot invest in a risky scheme which could be of questionable benefit. Everyone is busy working on their farms so it is difficult to take on any extra work.

2 Cash crops. Selling cash crops, such as cocoa beans, would earn everyone money. It is mainly settlers, with large farms and more money, who grow cash crops. Also the soils are unsuited to cash cropping. This option is less favourable to the Quichua people.

3 Eco-tourism. People can make money, using their knowledge to guide the tourists, while still preserving the forest. The community will have to work together to provide the tourists with meals and accommodation. However, tourists can bring problems, such as crime, and a lack of respect for local people.

Preparation (Pupils)

Each pupil should take one card and spend some time reading through their information. Ask the pupils to answer these questions in their roles:
Who are you? What do you do? What do you want for the future?

Pupils then follow the instruction card.

Instruction card

Rules
■ Do not interrupt people when they are speaking.
■ Allow everyone to discuss their point of view.
■ The village leader should make sure everyone has had a fair chance to speak.

Stages
■ Read the information in the following order: village leader, settler, Quicha farmer, local development worker.
■ Make a list of the different options you have.
■ Write down what you have all chosen to do.
■ If you cannot decide as a group, write down the reasons why you could not agree.

These questions can be used to structure the discussion:

■ What are the advantages and disadvantages of each option?
■ What has to take place to make each option a success?
■ Who would gain and lose from each option?

Possible questions to structure pupils' follow-up work (e.g. homework write-up)

■ Who are you?
■ What problems did you face?
■ What did you want for the area?
■ What did other people want for the area?
■ What decisions did you agree on?
■ Did they feel the group made the right decision?

■ **Box 4.6** What do people want for their future in Napo, Ecuador?
Source: ActionAid

the stages that groups go through in reaching a decision or solving a problem, or to reflect on collaborative processes and interpersonal skills during your debrief of the activity.

It is often necessary for the teacher to intervene at different stages during a role-play simulation. Sometimes pupils who are relatively unskilled in the 'art' of rational discussion may benefit from guidance to help them to re-focus on appropriate lines of thought and argument when they are losing their way. At some point you could stop the action and use the break to discuss what has been happening or what particular people or groups are feeling. More information could be introduced, perhaps selectively, in some cases, to benefit particular groups. This information might come in the form of 'chance factors' presenting news of changing conditions or unexpected events. But as Walford reminds us:

> the teacher will need to intervene judiciously here and there – guiding thought or argument away from blind alleys, helping a team understand the deeper implications of an issue that they are discussing, or enlivening a declining discussion with fresh insights or information at an appropriate moment. The teacher mixes administration, management and education for the most part, but the latter may be more effective for not being presented in an obvious expositional mode.
>
> (Walford, 1996: 143)

It is disappointing to see a role-play simulation that has been so diligently prepared failing to achieve its potential, either because the teacher has given insufficient thought to how the events and learning taking place will be processed and followed up, or because the teacher is not actively assessing what is happening and 'intervening judiciously'. The exercise investigating eco-tourism in Napo, Ecuador (Box 4.6) includes some follow-up questions that require pupils to explore what happened during the role play and comment on the decisions made.

Using games to foster collaboration

There is an extensive range of games available for use in the geography classroom. These games can be obtained from a wide variety of published sources including textbooks and their accompanying resource packs. Most textbook series today include examples of different types of geographical games and simulation activities reflecting the recognition that these are an essential part of a geography teacher's repertoire of teaching strategies.

What all these geographical games have in common is the fact that they have sets of rules and a predetermined structure that influence how the participants plan and make decisions. There is also often a competitive element to the game driving the decision-making. The decision-making may be complicated by unpredictable chance events simulated by the throw of a dice or by a randomly drawn chance card (e.g. to determine the influence of weather and other environmental processes). This is the format taken by many games, particularly those used to simulate decision-making in farming. The role adopted by the teacher in these situations is one of the 'game master' controlling the pace and direction of activity, probing pupils' understanding and helping them to make sense of what is happening.

There are many games that successfully combine elements of gaming, simulation and role-play. Walford notes how pupils 'often pick up the role-play element within games quite unconsciously in their desire to make the game work', and how 'this can be an advantage where the more conscious ascription and adoption of roles might be viewed with fear or suspicion' (Walford, 1996: 141).

Walford also refers to the 'simplicity of simulation' (Walford, 1996: 139) which makes it attractive to pupils. One of the major attractions of the Trading Game (described earlier) is the simplicity of its structure and rules. Careful preparation is needed by the teacher but a long introductory explanation of the rules is not required. Our experience shows that the benefit of providing a 'short and snappy' outline of the aims and rules is effective with pupils across the range of ability (and age). It is rewarding for the teacher to observe the learning place as the game unfolds and the participants become more conscious of the implications of the game's rules and structure. Pupils' understanding of the concepts and processes underpinning the game gets broader and deeper as the teacher introduces different factors representing real-life events, like changes in prices, technology, resources and terms of trade.

The Trading Trainers Game (CAFOD) is another imaginative simulation game that successfully mirrors real world situations and processes. The game is set in an imaginary Latin American shanty town where small family businesses are making training shoes to sell to pay the rent, buy food and send their children to school. Other roles include those of money lenders and rent collectors. The families work hard to produce the training shoes (with their familiar trademarks) but are vulnerable to changes in supply and demand, fashion, the competitiveness of rival producers and other economic factors like inflation. Not only does the experiential learning through the use of this game present opportunities to explore attitudes and values in relation to economy and society, but it can also be a stimulating way of introducing the study of global economic processes and systems with examples drawn from pupils' immediate lives.

There are also numerous examples of geographical 'board' games. The boards usually have a simple framework with participants moving from the start to the finish and responding to different instructions or questions when they land on particular squares. Cards taken randomly may be used to introduce chance factors with a dice being used to determine the rate of movement. In some board games, for example those of the 'snakes and ladders' variety, the participants have a fairly passive role just responding to and logging the events determined by the passage of the game. Sometimes decisions have to be made about how to respond to the factors introduced by the chance cards.

This then raises the question about how the learning that has taken place during a game should be 'processed'. We feel that the experiential learning cycle proposed by Dennison and Kirk (1990) provides an appropriate framework with which to address this issue (see Figure 4.8). The activity involved in the game or simulation represents the 'do' stage of the learning cycle with the all-important 'review' of both the cognitive and the affective learning that has occurred taking place during the debrief of the activity. Any follow-up work must, as part of the 'learning' stage, seek to reinforce the conceptual understanding, attitudes and values developed through the activity. It would be important to bring in more case study material to reinforce pupils' knowledge and understanding of place-specific examples. The opportunities for creative follow-up are endless – stories, newspaper reports, TV/radio reports and so on.

But what of the 'apply' stage? Old examination questions (particularly as tiered questions target different ability levels) provide resources and tasks that can be used to assess whether pupils can use the knowledge and understanding derived from the activity and its follow-up work. These tasks might involve the analysis of data (statistics or choropleth maps) about other geographical contexts. What is clear is that, whichever framework you adopt, simulations need to be integrated within a coherent sequence of work.

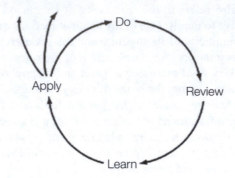

■ **Figure 4.8** The experiential learning style
Source: Dennison and Kirk, 1990

Designing your own card games can be a quick and imaginative way of bringing variety into classroom activity. Draw or stick pictures of symbols on some cards and write words on the others (e.g. OS map symbols, synoptic weather symbols). Pupils shuffle the pack and distribute some cards then take it in turns to return a card and collect a new one until they can make up a hand of matching symbols. The variations are endless (snap, rummy, etc.) showing that there is no limit to the imaginative geography teacher's repertoire! Walford (1991) shows such imagination in designing a game of Metrummy for an A-level group studying meteorology (see Table 4.6). Geography is a subject rife with classifications of one kind or another so take up the challenge and produce a card game of your own!

Other simulation activities

It is not always possible to classify simulation activities within discrete categories. As you can imagine there are a vast range of geographical ideas and processes that could be explored through simulation. It is also possible for geography teachers to use basic simulation ideas and structures to create their own activities. For example, there are numerous ways of using simulation to develop pupils' understanding of factors influencing industrial location.

The transnational electronics or car company looking for a suitable location for a new manufacturing plant has provided a popular focus for industrial location exercises in recent years. Such exercises would be able to develop the use of a variety of geographical enquiry skills and draw on a range of geographical resources and data:

- atlases
- employment and other census data
- company/product brochures
- maps showing transport and communication networks
- the availability of government assistance/regional aid and the location of other plants
- publicity material (newspaper adverts, brochures and even video/DVD) designed to attract companies to different locations (towns, business and science parks, industrial estates).

■ **Table 4.6** Metrummy – an A-level card game

Metrummy – The Game

1   Consider the elements of meteorology (or another topic) and list the basic vocabulary words. Refine these down to 13 sets of 4 words (see below).

2   Take a set of small plain file cards and label them on one side only with the 52 words chosen. (Label the centre of the card in large letters and repeat this on the top left corner in smaller lettering so that it can be seen when being held in a 'playing-card hand' fashion.)

3   Divide the class into groups of players, with not more than 6 in a group. Replicate the sets of cards if necessary so that two or three games can be played at the same time.

4   Have the players sit at tables. A dealer deals 4 cards to each of the players and leaves the rest of the pack on the table face downwards, with the exception of the top card which is turned face upwards and placed next to the pack.

5   Players begin the game. The person next to the dealer has the choice of picking up the upturned card or one from the pack and discarding one from his/her hand on to the face-upwards pile. The object of the game is for players to collect a SET of cards (as in rummy). However – unlike rummy – the cards offer no indication as to which set they belong to. *The players themselves have to decide what might constitute a set as they play.* This can be done co-operatively or individually, as they choose.

6   When a player considers that he or she has a SET it is laid down on the table for inspection (and possibly challenge). Players have to give a NAME to the set in order to win the game.

7   Repeat the sequence 4–6 two or three times so that players come to have increasing familiarity with the cards (and hopefully discuss their linkages).

8   After about 20–30 minutes of play suggest that the players stop the game and spread out the 52 cards on the table in front of them. Invite each group to sort the 52 cards into 13 sets.

9   Discuss possible alternatives or disputes which arise and explain words if required.

10 Invite the groups to give NAMES to each of the 13 sets, and then duly record names of sets and the component words in their notebooks for future use.

Names for the Meteorology Game

Absorption	Anti-cyclone	Barograph
Depression	Equinox	Global Warming
Isohels	Kuro Siwo	Nimbus
Perihelion	Roaring Forties	Stratosphere
Acid Rain	Aphelion	Benguela
Diffusion	Ferrel Cell	Gulf Stream
Isohyets	Labrador	Nitrogen
Radiation	Rossby Waves	Stratus
Anemometer	Argon	Carbon dioxide
Doldrums	Front	Hadley Cell
Isotherms	Monsoonal	North-East trades
Reflection	Solstice	Subtropical Jetstream

■ **Table 4.6** Metrummy – an A-level card game (continued)

Cirrus	Cumulus
Horse Latitudes	Ionosphere
Occlusion	Oxygen
Thermometer	Troposphere
Convectional	Cyclonic
Hygrometer	Isobars
Orographic	Ozone Hole
Tropopause	Use of CFCS

It is satisfying to work out and NAME the classification for yourself – but just in case you haven't the time:

Classification of the Names
Ocean currents
Elements of the atmosphere
Threats to the planet
Weather instruments
Wind systems
Elements of the weather
Types of contour on weather maps
Cloud types
Elements of the global weather machine
Layers of the atmosphere
Positions of the sun
Types of heating
Types of rainfall

Source: Walford, 1991: 174

Structured exercises could be designed to help pupils interrogate these data as part of a decision-making process. The analysis of the data, evaluation of alternative locations and decision about which location to recommend could be presented in a written or poster report. Enquiry skills developed through location simulation exercises like these are becoming increasingly important when preparing pupils for the decision-making and problem-solving exercises that are now more common forms of assessment in public examinations.

Newsroom simulations provide another flexible simulation strategy with a structure that can be easily adapted for the study of a wide range of geographical issues. This strategy can also facilitate the integrated use of ICT in geography lessons. Initially it is worth using a 'ready-made' version of this type of activity so that you can familiarise yourself with its structure and the strategies employed when using it.

There are many other interesting aspects of geography that do not lend themselves to the types of games and simulations described so far. It is difficult, for example, to devise games that simulate the processes responsible for the movement or diffusion of phenomena. Geographers have long been interested in the processes by which diseases are diffused across areas. Mathematical procedures incorporating probability factors, for example, Monte Carlo simulations, have been used to simulate the spread of disease.

Realistic diffusion simulations are more likely to be developed in the form of ICT software. There are already numerous examples of computerised simulations dating back to the early days of ICT use in geography classrooms. Some of these software simulations gave pupils opportunities to study the impact of different factors on coastal or hydrological processes by changing different variables, whilst others focused on location decisions, planning journeys and transport routes as well as evaluating the impacts of motorway or bypass construction. Some computerised simulations provide opportunities to integrate the use of other geographical skills and resources, such as OS map skills, within the simulation. Sim City, a computerised simulation about urban change, can be addictive, particularly for older pupils, and has a wide range of classroom applications.

Activity 4.4 **Geographical games and simulations**

The following activities will be worthwhile preparation to undertake before embarking on your first experience of using games and simulation activities in the geography classroom.

1 Evaluating games and simulations

Collect together a variety of different geographical games and simulations covering a range of topics. Use the following questions to help you to review these games and simulations.

The content

What is the central problem presented in the game or simulation?
What is its relationship to real-world situations?
Which geographical concepts will be developed through the game or simulation?
Which geographical processes are simulated?

The activities

What moves and choices are available to the players?
What strategies might be used by the players?
Which geographical skills might be developed through the simulation or game?
Will the activities encourage co-operative learning and how will the groups work together?
What is the teacher's role in the game or simulation?
How can the teacher influence the way in which the game or simulation develops?

The learning sequence

How can the game or simulation be integrated within a coherent sequence of learning activities?
What prior learning is needed by the pupils?
Which resources can be used with the game or simulation?

The review

What questions can be used to debrief the pupils and help them to review the
learning that has taken place during the game or simulation?

How can the pupils be helped to relate the game or simulation to real-world
situations? (What case studies might be useful?)

What types of follow-up activities could be used? (interesting, imaginative and
relevant?)

(Source: adapted from Elliott, 1975) 'Evaluating classroom games and simulations'

2 Observing games and simulations in action

Try to arrange an opportunity early in your practical teaching experience to observe
an 'experienced' practitioner using a game or simulation in the classroom. Consider
the following questions before and during the observation:

■ What planning and preparation did the teacher undertake before using the
game or simulation?

■ How was the game or simulation integrated within a scheme of work (i.e. where
does it come in the learning sequence)?

■ How is the classroom organised for the activity? How are the pupils organised?
(And how were any groupings determined?)

■ How does the teacher introduce the activity and set the scene?

■ What strategies does the teacher use to manage the activity? Make a note of
the type, purpose and frequency of the teacher's interventions. How does the
teacher draw pupils' attention to important geographical concepts and
processes during the activity?

■ How does the teacher brief the activity? Make a note of the questions that are
used to review the learning that has taken place (cognitive and affective). How
is the game or simulation (its rules, processes and outcomes) related to the real
world? Are any real case studies or data used? Is any attention given to
attitudes and values?

What follow-up activities are used and how do these activities use or build upon the
learning outcomes of the game or simulation? Are pupils given opportunities to
apply any understanding or skills developed through the game or simulation?

VALUES EDUCATION

When considering the role and purpose of values enquiry in geography education, one of
the authors recalls a defining moment in his PGCE geography course when he was introduced to the work of the Schools' Council's Geography 16–19 Project, in particular to its
contribution to the development of an enquiry-based approach to learning geography.
This approach stressed that geographical enquiry had to incorporate reference to values
and attitudes. Values enquiry was seen as a 'fundamental element of credible explanation
in the subject' (Naish *et al.,* 1987: 173). Values enquiry, it was argued, helps to explain
what people do and why they do it. The characteristics of the Geography 16–19 Project's
approach to values enquiry are shown in Box 4.7.

The Project stated:

Credible explanation in geography demands that value positions are examined and that their role in environmental decision-making is revealed. Explanation which ignores attitudes and values is likely to be arid and meaningless. More important from an educational point of view, failure to provide for consideration of attitudes and values represents a missed opportunity for geographic education and a narrowing of the curriculum for the individual pupil. Unless issues involving a range of viewpoints and values positions are opened up in the classroom, students may find few chances to clarify their own values, to develop their own convictions and commitments, and to have confidence in the actions they take in society. With this potential for values education in mind, Geography 16–19 recommends that the examination of values should take place through enquiry with students actively engaged in the process of investigation.

(Naish *et al.*, 1987: 174)

In its quest for a 'place in the sun' (referred to in Chapter 1), the Geographical Association was addressed in 1985 by the then Secretary of State of Education, Sir Keith Joseph. In his address, Sir Keith Joseph asked some important questions about the role of geography in developing political literacy:

And how adequate is the political understanding achieved through geographical studies? Do teachers take full advantage of their opportunity to give attention to a wide range of political processes and activities at local, national and international level? Cannot a deeper understanding of economic and political processes be linked to teaching the analysis of the way in which decisions are made about the use of environments, a matter which I know is of increasing interest to geography teachers?

(From 'Geography in the School Curriculum' – a speech given by Sir Keith Joseph, Secretary for Education, to the GA, 19 June 1985)

Politics are a means of promoting values. By political literacy we mean the ability to recognise the value basis of opinions and the effect of values on decisions. At one level it can be seen as a knowledge of political systems and how they work in practice. But political literacy is also acquired through contact with, and recognition of, the politics of everyday life. This requires an understanding of (political) issues, an ability to explore the beliefs and values of the major participants, and a grasp of how these issues are likely to affect people (Butt, 1990; McPartland, 2006).

Involvement is a critical factor in political literacy. McElroy argues that 'literacy means that participants are aware of how they are involved' (McElroy, 1988). Participation is essential in any democracy. Some of the teaching strategies that we have described earlier in this chapter (e.g. role play, discussion and debate) help us to show pupils why people hold particular views and whether the decisions made are welcomed or rejected by particular individuals or groups. Helping pupils to understand the process by which decisions are made is extremely important. We need to involve pupils in realistic decision-making as a step towards their future roles in life (see Chapter 9). Once the realisation occurs that the established political system can, at a variety of scales, affect what decisions are made (by whom and for whom), pupils begin to see their position within this decision-making process and can perhaps start to assess it (Butt, 1990). Thus,

This influential curriculum development project made a clear statement about the role and purpose of values enquiry in geography education:

- The initiation of learning experiences by means of stimulus resource material related to questions, problems and issues about the interactions of people with their environments.
- The active involvement of pupils in exercises and activities aimed at exploring and analysing the values positions implicit in a given people-environment issue.
- The intention that pupils be assisted to clarify and develop their own attitudes and values.
- Active encouragement to pupils to see the link between their attitudes and values and the actions they take in their own lives.
- The importance of providing the opportunity to develop skills of values enquiry, which can be transferred and used in their own personal lives.

In order to develop skills in values enquiry, pupils should be exposed to a wide variety of experiences including:

- analysing and discussing conflict situations
- examining resultant impacts upon the lives and environments of people when decisions are taken
- empathising with the opinions and viewpoints of others
- listening to arguments and opinions from a wide spectrum
- meeting (or reading the views of) people with strong viewpoints
- expressing in a range of ways their own feelings for a situation or environment
- reaching a negotiated agreement with those who hold views different from their own.

Values enquiry aims to make pupils aware of their own values through the consideration of attitudes and values held by others in the situation under study. This may help pupils to develop:

- an awareness of the feelings and opinions of others
- an awareness of the nature of attitudes, values and prejudice
- the ability to analyse the influence and effect of values in particular environmental and spatial situations
- a willingness to give consideration to all viewpoints and all available evidence within the scope of geography
- the realisation that their own values influence the way in which they evaluate evidence
- the ability to make a personal decision about an environmental question, issue or problem and to justify this in terms of evidence and values
- the confidence to base commitment and action upon the choices and decisions they have made.

■ **Box 4.7** The characteristics of a 'values enquiry'
Source: Naish *et al.,* 1987: 174 and 177–8

increasing the political literacy of pupils should enable them to make real-life decisions in a more reasoned and confident way. Geography 'has a duty to foster political literacy in societies where life is becoming more complex and demanding', in order to encourage 'competent participation' (Naish *et al.*, 1987: 177).

Values education and environmental literacy

School geography has at various times been accused of 'green washing' and some newspaper headlines should lead us to reflect further on the importance of values education and the need for geography teachers to become conversant with strategies for values enquiry. For example,

> School children are 'victims of green conspiracy'
>
> > (*Times*, 6 October 1997)

> Backlash challenges green 'nonsense'
>
> > (*TES*, 10 October, 1997)

The articles to which these headlines belong reported the publication of *Environmental Education* (Aldrich-Moodie and Kwong, 1997) by a London-based 'rightwing think tank' the Institute of Economic Affairs (IEA), which analysed school textbooks in the USA and UK. The report claimed that pupils are being 'indoctrinated with environmental nonsense', controversial theories being presented as fact, specious 'issues' getting in the way of sound reasoning and popular misconception taking hold rather than being challenged. The report concluded by arguing that 'Doomsday scenarios and indoctrination should be replaced with scientific reasoning: how to collect data, how to develop theories and how to test such theories against the data' (see also Standish, 2009).

This reveals a particular viewpoint concerning educational value: a belief in the scientific method. But in a *supercomplex* world in which 'all is challengeable and there are no durable frameworks, there is no such pool of security; such a belief is no longer feasible. Teaching has to reflect this and adopt as one of its goals the creation of disturbance in the minds of learners, and the ability to live with disjunction' (Barnett, 1997, cited in Lambert, 1998). Through writing about higher education, we believe Barnett's point is of great relevance to all teachers.

We return to this question of *supercomplexity* in a later discussion (Chapter 9) but the point that we wish to make here is in relation to *teaching and learning processes* in geography classrooms and in particular values education.

We are suggesting through these personal reflections that geography teachers need to rediscover the procedures and processes of values education. Geography teachers can do so in a particular way, by using distinctive subject matter, such as people-environment processes or the significance of place and location in people's lives, and by emphasising special skills, such as mapwork (the language of space) and direct observation through fieldwork. When the content of geography lessons consistently fails to incorporate a values education dimension, it may be accused of *moral carelessness,* because it fails to prepare pupils mentally and emotionally for an uncertain and unpredictable future in which their (and their teachers'!) grasp of change may at best be described as 'fragile'. Values education sessions therefore provide a formal vehicle that enables moral development to take place (see Chapter 9).

Values education approaches

Values education is a planned activity, meaning that teachers need to have the conscious intention to do it. One of the main challenges for geography teachers is that of selecting an appropriate approach to values education through geography. There are a variety of different approaches to values education depending on whether the purpose is to explore some specific values or to help pupils in analysing and clarifying values as part of a process of making decisions. In the route for geographical enquiry (Figure 5.3 on page 200) values enquiry may encompass a range of approaches (values analysis, moral reasoning, values clarification and action learning) as appropriate to the issue or question being studied.

It is perhaps important at this point to consider what distinguishes values and attitudes. Slater uses Rokeach's (1973) definition of a value being 'an enduring belief that a specific mode of conduct or end state of existence is personally or socially preferable to an opposite mode of conduct or end state of existence' (Slater, 1982: 90). Some of these values are central to what we consider to be important in life, whereas others may be more peripheral and therefore receive less personal commitment.

Attitudes can be defined as 'packages of beliefs which influence us in decisions' (Slater, 1982: 91); in other words, when we focus on a particular situation they 'predispose' us to act in a particular way. Slater summarises the distinction by suggesting that 'attitudes are value expressive', whereas 'values are strongly held attitudes'. Michael McPartland (2006: 172–3) classifies the values which underpin the study of geography into:

■ *Social values* [e.g. the need to respect human rights]
■ *Economic values* [e.g. the need for wealth creation]
■ *Environmental values* [e.g. the need to maintain biodiversity]
■ *Aesthetic values* [e.g. the need to conserve forested landscapes]
■ *Political values* [e.g. the need to participate in the life of the local community]
■ *Moral values* [e.g. the need to act in accordance with a moral code]

He suggests that all values, in whatever arena they are located, may take on an ethical dimension and become, therefore, moral values. Thus, if you regard an issue as a moral issue, then social, economic, environmental, aesthetic and political values related to the study of this issue can become subsumed within the category of moral values (McPartland, 2006: 173).

Activity 4.5 **Values education in geography lessons**

To what extent can geography lessons become 'morally careless'?
We envisage this as a discussion activity in a small group of student teachers or with your geography tutor. The discussion has two components (A and B below).

Part A
■ Identify and describe examples of geography lessons that you have observed, encountered or even taught yourself which have developed pupils' skills in values enquiry and/or contributed to the development of political literacy.
■ Identify examples of values enquiry in geography textbooks and resource materials with which you are familiar. Describe the teaching and learning strategies involved in these activities.

In what ways might these lessons and activities that you have identified above help to prepare children for 'life in a changing world?'

How effectively do they respond to the challenges posed by the late Sir Keith Joseph in the quotation on page 129?

Part B

Here is a summary of some of the main arguments presented by Aldrich-Moodie and Kwong (1997) in their report *Environmental Education*:

1   In both the USA and the UK, children are being presented with biased information about the environment.
2   Popular UK textbooks frequently present controversial theories, such as human-induced global warming, as fact.
3   Recent scientific evidence is often omitted. For example, children are presented with outdated studies citing acid rain as a major factor in lake acidification and forest decline, while more recent studies contradicting that view are ignored.
4   In the UK, some textbooks aim for a more balanced discussion but are constrained by National Curriculum requirements to address specious issues such as 'desertification'.
5   The popular misconception of an environmental problem often becomes the basis for classroom presentations, thereby perpetuating inaccuracy.
6   Basic economic reasoning is lacking in many discussions. For example, children are taught there is a finite bundle of natural resources we must conserve lest we use it all up, without regard to the role of pricing, supply and demand, or economic trade-offs.
7   In the USA, children are taught the prevailing view of issues before they can understand the underlying science and economics. For example, they are told that 'recycling is good' before they even know what a resource is or what recycling means.
8   This 'issues' teaching precludes rational debate and stymies the development of an enquiring mind.
9   The prevailing tone of most textbooks is negative. Rarely is there any mention of the significant improvements in environmental quality which have occurred in the last twenty years in developed countries.
10 Environmental education in both the USA and the UK is in need of significant reform. Doomsday scenarios and indoctrination should be replaced with scientific reasoning: how to collect data, how to develop theories and how to test such theories against the data.

The claims made in the report are based on a partial analysis of school textbooks in the USA and UK. The researchers did not observe lessons, nor did they interview teachers. Nevertheless, the points summarised above represent a critique of environmental education.

■   To what extent does the classroom practice identified and described in part A of this discussion:
  a)   support, or
  b)   counter
  the claims made by Aldrich-Moodie and Kwong?

■ How would you, as a geography teacher, defend the way you teach environmental topics as being 'morally careful' in the light of Aldrich-Moodie and Kwong's attack?

Each of the different teaching approaches to values education have been designed with different 'valuing objectives' in mind. To be effective, the approaches selected by geography teachers should therefore reflect the objectives of their teaching programmes (Fien and Slater, 1981; Huckle, 1981). The teaching strategies that can be used in values education range from individual reflection and writing to group discussion, role playing and structured analysis of situations where there is conflict (Rawling, 1986).

Values analysis emphasises that judgements are based on facts and values. Structured rational discussion and the logical analysis of evidence is used to investigate issues. Marsden describes the objective of values analysis as being to equip pupils with the 'capacity and inclination to make rational and defensible value judgements' (Marsden 1995: 6). Fien and Slater (1981) outline a sequence of procedures for achieving this which involves:

■ identifying the decisions to be made to resolve the value issue
■ assembling the purported facts on the issue
■ establishing the veracity of the purported facts so that decisions will be based on objective evidence
■ establishing the relevance of the facts and removing distracting information
■ arriving at tentative decisions
■ testing the value principles involved in the decision.

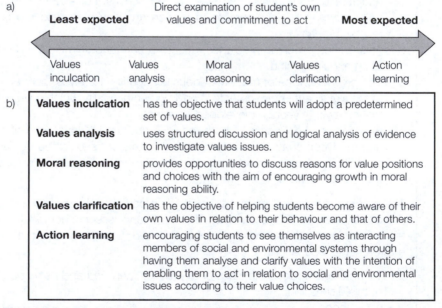

■ **Figure 4.9** Approaches to values education
    a) The degree of student involvement in examining own values and actions
    b) A brief description of approaches to values education
Source: Fien and Slater, 1981

The role of the teacher is to help pupils understand the decision-making process while leaving them free to make their own independent judgements. The intention is that by studying relevant factual evidence, and clarifying appropriate policies pupils will engage, at their own level, in the type of decision-making carried out by planners and others (Huckle, 1981). Thus pupils use a process of rational analysis to conceptualise and interrogate their own values.

Teaching strategies used for *values analysis* frequently include role play and the simulation of public inquiries. The aim is usually to help pupils appreciate the value positions of people involved in the planning and decision-making process. The issues used for these enquiries often include the construction of major new roads, the siting of new economic activities or other significant changes in land use. The issues chosen are often local ones that will engage pupils because they are immediate and of current relevance and concern.

The content of the role cards provides pupils with an insight into the value positions of the people involved in and affected by the proposed scheme, as well as guidelines to help them prepare their presentations. Pupils working at this level could be expected to use materials produced by groups involved in the issue to search for relevant evidence and find out how evidence is used to support particular viewpoints.

As a strategy for values education, values analysis does have its limitations. Huckle points to its 'readiness to cling to what some consider a debased form of rationality' (Huckle, 1981: 156) and the continued promotion of ideas and cognitive skills at the expense of values and feelings. He suggests that the desire for balance and consensus can dominate approaches to rational decision-making in the classroom resulting in pupils gaining 'a view of society in which fundamental change and conflict are denied' (Huckle, 1981: 156). Thus, Huckle believes, values analysis may 'merely reinforce the status quo' and create a 'false confidence in democratic society which is likely to be frustrated later in life' (Huckle, 1981: 158).

Moral reasoning has similar objectives to values analysis but pursues them in a less structured way using small-group discussion and debate (McPartland, 2006; Marsden, 1995). Case studies are presented to pupils as moral dilemmas to be resolved. These moral dilemmas provide pupils with opportunities to discuss reasons for value positions and choices with the aim of encouraging growth in their moral reasoning ability.

The moral reasoning strategy is based on Kohlberg's (1976) theory which suggests that an individual's ability in moral reasoning passes through a series of stages (now questioned) before attaining moral autonomy. As they pass through these successive stages, pupils can take account of an increasing amount of evidence about a particular situation and be able to empathise with different groups. Kohlberg developed the use of the 'moral dilemma', a story in which there is a conflict over what is right or wrong.

The role of a teacher when using a moral reasoning strategy is to try to expose pupils to moral reasoning typical of a higher level. This can usually done by discussing moral dilemmas in small groups (McPartland, 2001 and 2006). When a person is faced with a moral dilemma, they are obliged to make a choice between different courses of action, and for each of these there are moral arguments which might suggest that course of action (i.e. a moral argument) (McPartland, 2006: 175). When pupils have adopted a position, questions should be used to introduce arguments appropriate to higher levels of reasoning than the pupils appear to be at. This should encourage the pupils to examine their reasoning and the assumptions behind this reasoning.

Slater reminds us that 'it is the type of argument and not the content or position that indicates the stage of moral reasoning' (Slater, 1982: 98). Box 4.8 is an example of a moral dilemma based on an imaginary character. McPartland (2001 and 2006) provides helpful guidance for geography teachers about how to create and use moral dilemmas successfully.

Nestor is a graduate student living in England, studying for an M.Sc. in Chemistry. He is from Benin. He came to the university on a scholarship financed by the Benin government. His father, Desire, is a cotton farmer in the Borgou province in the north of Benin trying to earn a living from his three hectares of land. The cotton he produces is exported to Italy to make jeans. The lack of urban centres, the undeveloped infrastructure and high transport costs all make it difficult to grow crops so cotton is the main cash crop. But the soil is degraded. Cotton cultivation robs the soil of nutrients. Crop rotation and use of fallow periods are not used, and so artificial chemical pesticides and fertilisers are used to maintain yields. There is some concern that the use of pesticides is having a negative impact on river quality, biodiversity and the health of workers in the ginning mills. Last year, one of Nestor's cousins was poisoned eating corn which was growing near his father's cotton field.

Nestor is in the final stages of his M.Sc. He is an excellent student, hard working and committed to his research. Last week, a well-known international French Chemical Company offered him a well-paid job based in Paris. Nestor is fluent in French, the official language of Benin. His job will be to develop a new range of pesticides.

He has to make a decision by next week.

What are the moral reasons and, therefore, moral requirements underpinning his decision: to take or not to take the job. How finely balanced are they?

■ **Box 4.8** An example of a moral dilemma
Source: McPartland, 2006: 175

Values clarification encourages pupils to become aware of review and express their own values as well as examining those of others. The aim is to help pupils use both rational thinking and emotional awareness to examine their personal feelings, values and behaviour patterns (Huckle, 1981). According to Frances Slater this process of 'articulating and understanding the basic values which underlie and inform one's attitudes towards people, places, object or issues' is important for two reasons. First, because it helps pupils to recognise the 'processes underlying preferences and judge-ments'. Second, pupils can use a variety of issues to provide the context through which the 'implications and consequences' of holding particular values can be explored (Slater, 1981: 85).

Activity 4.6 **Using moral dilemmas in geography**

Brainstorm a list of current or recent geographical issues which, because they do not exhibit clear cut solutions, could be presented as moral dilemmas. If you have the opportunity to discuss these ideas with other geography teachers, consider how they might be presented to pupils in different age groups. It would also be helpful to consider what types of argument might be used at different levels of moral reasoning for some of these dilemmas. A variety of teaching strategies, including role playing, games and simulations, can be used to explore real or imaginary situations. However, as Slater suggests:

> Perhaps students need to be given opportunities to sort out their own positions on an issue and to argue this rather than always being asked to adopt a role.

> (Slater, 1981)

Figure 4.10 shows some extracts from a values clarification activity. The activity 'valuing the forest' enables teachers and pupils to explore some aspects of rainforest politics and to develop an understanding of some basic concepts relating to environmental economics.

The activity would be introduced by asking pupils why people may wish to conserve the rainforests. Their responses would be summarised and grouped into different categories which reflect different reasons for conservation. (The difference between conservation and preservation would need to be made clear.) Pupils would then be asked to consider who is involved in conserving rainforests. They would associate rainforest conservation only with groups like the World Wide Fund for Nature and Friends of the Earth, so this is an opportunity to remind them about the role of other agencies – governments and non-governmental agencies as well as the indigenous people themselves.

Figure 4.10 shows some of the many reasons why Amazonia is valuable. In valuing the rainforest, people usually draw on one or more of these values:

> Environmental economists suggest that it has direct use value (timber, rubber, medicines and education); indirect use value (environmental services like watershed protection and climatic regulation); option value (the amount which people would be willing to pay to conserve the forest for future use) and non-use or existence value (as a unique cultural and heritage asset).

> (WWF, 1991: 30)

Pupils have their own ways of expressing some of these values, many of which they will have encountered in a variety of sources, particularly in the media. They can use these ideas about ways of valuing the rainforest to help them interpret the views expressed by different people in some of the extensive material available about this issue. Who values the rainforest as a source of economic wealth? As an environmental regulator? As a source of livelihood? As a political safety valve?

'Personal values clarification scales', or 'Values continua' as they are sometimes called, provide another useful tool for helping pupils clarify their own personal values. Fien (1985) uses this strategy in an activity that asks pupils to consider statements about

Amazonia is valuable because it is...

a) An Environmental Regulator
    It is an important regulator of the local and global environment. The forest recycles rainfall, protects soils, cycles nutrients, and prevents extremes of climate. It also produces oxygen and acts as a huge carbon store which slows down global warming.

b) A Source of Scientific Knowledge
    It is a giant scientific laboratory containing one of the earth's oldest most complex forest ecosystems. The Amazon contains valuable knowledge and still has a lot to teach us about evolution and ecology.

■ **Figure 4.10** Extracts from 'Valuing the Forest' activity sheet
Source: WWF, 1991

moral values for world citizenship. To clarify their own viewpoints and value positions, pupils indicate their level of agreement with each statement on a 'personal values clarification scale'. Such a strategy could be readily adapted for use with pupils across a range of age and ability to help them to consider their position in relation to different values statements.

Figure 4.11 shows an example of an activity in which 'values continua' are used to investigate the values underpinning statements about sustainable development. After discussing which aspects of sustainability and development appear to be favoured by the author of each statement, pupils mark where they think the statements should be on the values continua scales. When the points for each statement are joined up (using different coloured lines) the values underlying each statement can be explored. The aim of this strategy is to promote a critical analysis of the relationship between ecological and economic principles which relate to sustainable development (Reid, 1996: 171).

Marsden reminds us that 'Values clarification' does have its limitations as a strategy for values education as it 'suggests that values are subjective and all a matter for individual choice: that everybody's opinion is as good as everybody else's' (Marsden, 1995: 6). He warns that it could 'tend to foster the primacy of self-interest'. However, in reality, values clarification is likely to be one of a range of strategies used to explore values, particularly when the route for geographical enquiry is used to provide a broad framework around which teaching programmes are organised.

The aim of *action learning* is to provide pupils with opportunities for personal and social action based on their values (Figure 4.12). Though not yet fully autonomous, they are encouraged to see themselves as 'interacting members of social and environmental systems'. Action learning incorporates the range of strategies used to clarify and analyse values but also enables pupils to act on their value choices. There is often scope for action in relation to social and environmental issues within the school community. This might result in environmental improvements on or around the school site or changes in practices within the school community, such as the implementation of recycling schemes co-ordinated by pupils as part of eco-school initiatives promoted by some of the environmental agencies like WWF (http://www.wwflearning.org.uk/oneplanetschools/).

Action strategies might also lead to involvement in the wider community or environment. There are examples of schools, their teachers and pupils, taking leading roles in small-scale conservation projects or Agenda 21 activities within their localities. This can also lead to pupils lobbying for action on local issues and the involvement of adults other than teachers in teaching programmes within the geography curriculum (see also Chapter 6). Thus, action learning approaches to values education can be seen to support pupils' development of citizenship skills.

It is not uncommon for teachers and pupils to initiate fundraising activities that represent the outcomes of action learning through the geography curriculum and lead to engagement with environments and communities on a wider scale. Letter writing is a common outcome of teaching programmes with human rights dimensions. There is a multitude of fund-raising activities promoted by non-government agencies that provide links with wider communities and environments through such indirect action. Schools and their pupils have been known to take on a commitment to school-linking and to sponsoring children (and even schools!) in economically developing countries.

Many of the issues explored through values education are by their nature contro-versial. Almost any issue can become controversial if individuals or groups hold differing views or offer differing explanations about events, what should happen and how issues

Values continua

| Supports the preservation of the natural environment | | | | | | Encourages the exploitation of the natural environment for human needs |

| Supports zero economic growth | | | | | | Supports high economic growth |

| Supports fairness between all species for the present generation (intragenerational equity | | | | | | Does not support intragenerational equity |

| Support fairness for future generations (intergenerational equity) | | | | | | Does not support intergenerational equity |

Statements about sustainable development

1. Sustainable development can be briefly described as working for economic growth without cheating on our children.

Taken from the Department of the Environment's pamphlet (1994) *Sustainable Development* (p. 1).

2. Sustainability means the capacity to satisfy current needs without jeopardising the prospects of future generations . . . [This entails] protecting the ozone layer, stabilising climate, conserving soils, stabilising forests and population.

Attributed to Lester Brown of the Worldwatch Institute.

3. Sustainable development is development that meets the needs of the present without compromising the ability of the future generations to meet their own needs . . . and extending to all the opportunity to fulfil their aspirations for a better life.

From the World Commission on Environment and Development (1987) in *Our Common Future* (p. 8).

4. Sustainable development means more than seeking a compromise between the natural environment and the pursuit of economic growth. It means a definition of development which recognises that the limits of sustainability have structural as well as natural origins.

Made by Michael Redclift (1987) in *Sustainable Development: Exploring the Contradictions* (p. 199).

■ **Figure 4.11** Using values clarification scales to explore values in statements about sustainable development

Source: The full version of this activity can be found in Reid, 1996: 168–172. It was designed for use with post-16 pupils and is drawn from a workshop developed by Macleod (1993)

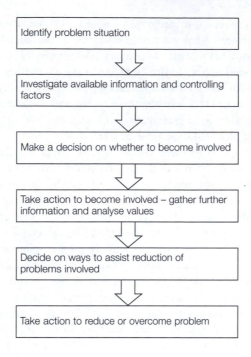

■ **Figure 4.12** A general action strategy

should be resolved (Oxfam, 2006). They can also be controversial if these views and explanations are presented in a way that raises an emotional response from those who might disagree. Controversial issues can be personal, local or global and they are often complex with no easy answers with people holding strong views based on their different experiences, interests and values:

> Issues that are likely to be sensitive or controversial are those that have a political, social or personal impact and arouse feeling and/or deal with questions of value or belief

(QCA, 2001)

Until the 1980s, most school geography textbooks avoided controversial issues, but by the early 1980s, different 'intensities of issues-pervasion' became identifiable in the geography curriculum (Marsden, 1995: 141). Marsden identified these as being *issues-permeated, issues-based* and *issues-dominated* geography. His concern was that if the main focus were on the issue, as in issues-dominated and issues-based geography, then the process of enquiry would not be approached in a 'distinctively geographical way'. He made the case for a 'global geography' into which issues are permeated. In other words, issues-permeated teaching programmes would be implemented through distinctively geographical frameworks.

The case is well argued and worth some consideration at this point. It connects with our earlier concerns about the dangers of geography teachers being 'morally careless' if they fail to adopt appropriate values education strategies when investigating issues which are often controversial in geography lessons. Bill Marsden's argument is that there is a difference between what we would all agree to be 'laudable educational aims' and the possibility that what we teach becomes so dominated by issues that the 'self-evident good causes embraced appear to justify indoctrination'. Further dangers can be seen in some of the issues-dominated texts and teaching materials at Key Stage 3 in which superficial enquiry approaches lack any cognitive rigour and adequate engagement with geographical data. Over simplistic presentation of issues can lead to 'little more than an incitement to offer an opinion' (Marsden, 1995: 143).

So to respond to these concerns it is important that not only should the issue selected for study be relevant, but it should also have a strong and geographically distinctive conceptual structure. Consideration should be given to how pupils are able to recognise the distinctive contribution that geography can make to an understanding of this and similar issues. Appropriate geographical concepts should be identified and attention given to how they are developed through enquiry.

Using challenging material and discussing controversial issues can encourage pupils to develop a range of thinking skills including information-processing, reasoning, enquiry, creative thinking and evaluation skills. Oxfam (2006) provides examples of approaches that can be used to explore controversial issues including 'community of enquiry' drawn from the 'Philosophy for Children' approach to exploring big ideas. Students are encouraged to listen to the ideas of others, reflect on their own views and to modify their views in response to what they hear. Activities used for media literacy and photographic interpretation (see Chapter 6 and Durbin, 2006) also develop pupils' skills for thinking critically about issues. Thinking skills' activities (see later in this chapter) and drama (see Chapter 6 and Biddulph and Clarke, 2006) can also be helpful when exploring controversial issues. McPartland (2006: 177) provides suggestions for activities that can promote effective discussion about issues such as those raised by the moral dilemma outlined in Box 4.8 including role play, a 'court of enquiry', 'badge of allegiance' (pupils wear a badge which represents the degree of agreement or disagreement they feel), hot seating and concentric circles.

Box 4.9 shows the procedure developed by the Geography Schools and Industry Project (GSIP) for studying a controversial issue (Corney, 1992). This procedure aims to provide pupils with opportunities to develop skills for analysing and clarifying values. The emphasis is on helping them to learn *how* to evaluate rather than *what* to value. The use of this procedure may help pupils to appreciate that controversial issues can be resolved in different ways reflecting the values of those making the decisions. Studies following this procedure can contribute to pupils' political education as they are involved in considering various ways of responding to the issues and the possible consequences of these actions. The GSIP team also argued that this approach 'ensures an open, enquiring classroom where indoctrination is less likely' (Corney, 1992: 51).

There are teachers who are unwilling to tackle controversial issues through concerns about bias and possible accusations of indoctrination. Even with the developing concern for values and relevance in geographical education through the 1980s there were teachers who believed (and some who still believe) that values should be kept out of school education. Slater reminds us that 'the content and procedure of geography has never been, and cannot be, value free' (Slater, 1993: 130). To help us to consider the role of the teacher when dealing with controversial issues in the classroom, Slater (Slater, 1993: 114) draws our attention to the strengths and weaknesses of four approaches suggested by Stradling (1984). You may wish to consider where you would stand in relation to these approaches (see Table 4.7) although in reality, as Slater suggests, we are likely to use a mix of approaches.

With all the different approaches to values education, the teacher has a key role to play in the successful implementation of the teaching strategies that we have outlined. The generation of an atmosphere of mutual trust and respect in the classroom is as important as the selection of appropriate strategies and resources. Such an atmosphere is not only a reflection of positive teacher-pupil relationships but also of pupils' respect for each other. You need to work at this as much as at developing a rapport between yourself and the pupils. The content of many values activities and the strategies used often need sensitive handling. Pupils should not be pressurised into answering or participating and your evaluation of their learning should be based on their ability to apply skills related to valuing rather than on the values themselves (Maye, 1984). Skilful and flexible questioning is a crucial element of this, enabling you to help pupils reflect on the skills of values enquiry that they are developing. Your ability to make sense of the variety of classroom conversations and interactions during values activities helps you to actively assess the learning taking place.

---

1   Teachers (and sometimes students) select an issue…which should interest and involve students.

2   Students introduced to the issue: initial perception
- What values does each student have at the outset?
- What different values are held on this issue?

3   Students identify and clarify different values underlying the issue: definition and description
- Who is involved?
- What values do they hold?
  - ☐ at the cognitive level: the reasons people give to justify their views
  - ☐ at the affective level: the underlying beliefs people hold which affect their views.

4   Students analyse and evaluate different values underlying the issue
- Are the values supported by facts?
- Can the values be grouped?
- Which values have priority/power?
- Which values does each student identify with?

5   Students simulate and/or predict how the issue might be resolved
- What procedures can be used for resolving the issue?
- What are the possible solutions to this issue, and the likely consequences for the people involved?
- What is the likely solution, and consequences?

6   Students clarify their own values and response to the issue
- How might each student try to resolve the issue, and why?
- What views does each student hold at this stage, and why?
- Does any student wish to enquire further, or to become involved outside the school?

■ **Box 4.9** Studying a controversial issue
Source: Corney, 1992: 50

■ **Table 4.7** Four teaching approaches for dealing with controversial issues in the classroom

Potential strengths		Potential weaknesses
Minimises undue influence of teacher's own bias. Gives everyone a chance to take part in free discussion. Scope for open-ended discussion, i.e. the class may move on to consider issues and questions which the teacher hasn't thought of. Presents a good opportunity for pupils to exercise communication skills. Works well if you have a lot of background material.	***Procedural Neutrality*** **In which the teacher** **adopts the role of an** **impartial chairperson** **of a discussion** **group.**	Pupils find it artificial. Can damage the rapport between teacher and class if it doesn't work. Depends on pupils being familiar with the method elsewhere in the school or it will take a long time to acclimatise them. May only reinforce pupils' existing attitudes and prejudices. Very difficult with the less able. *Neutral chair* doesn't suit my personality.
Pupils will try to guess what the teacher thinks anyway. Stating your own position makes everything above board. If pupils know where the teacher stands on the issue they can discount his or her prejudices and biases. It's better to state your preferences after discussion rather than before. It should only be used if pupils' dissenting opinions are treated with respect. It can be an excellent way of maintaining credibility with pupils since they do not expect us to be neutral.	***Stated Commitment*** **In which the teacher** **always makes known** **his or her views** **during discussion.**	It can stifle classroom discussion, inhibiting pupils from arguing a line against that of the teacher's. It may encourage some pupils to argue strongly for something they don't believe in simply because it's different from the teacher. Pupils often find it difficult to distinguish facts from values. It's even more difficult if the purveyor of facts and values is the same person, i.e. the teacher.
Essential: I think one of the main functions of a humanities or social studies teacher is to show that issues are hardly ever black and white. Necessary when the class is polarised on an issue. Most useful when dealing with issues about which there is a great deal of conflicting information.	***A Balanced*** ***Approach*** **In which the teacher** **presents pupils with** **a wide range of** **alternative views.**	Is there such a thing as a balanced range of opinions? As a strategy it has limited use. It avoids the main point by conveying the impression that 'truth' is a grey area that exists between two alternative sets of opinions. Balance means very different things to different people. The media's view of balance is not mine. Teaching is rarely value-free. This approach can lead to very teacher-directed lessons. Like media interviews, you are always interrupting to maintain the so-called balance.
Frequently used by me. Great fun, and can be very effective in stimulating the pupils to contribute to discussion. Essential when faced by a group who all seem to share the same opinion. Most classes which I have taught seem to have a majority line. Then I use this strategy and parody, exaggeration, and role reversal. I often use this as a device to liven things up when the discussion is beginning to dry up.	***The Devil's Advocate*** ***Strategy*** **In which the teacher** **consciously takes up** **the opposite position** **to the one expressed** **by pupils or in** **teaching materials.**	I have run into all sorts of problems with this approach. Children identifying me with the *views* I was putting forward as devil's advocate; parents worried about my alleged views, etc. It may reinforce pupils' prejudices. Only to be used when discussion dries up and there are still 25 minutes left.

Source: Slater, 1993: 114 (after Stradling *et al.*, 1984)

PROBLEM-SOLVING AND DECISION-MAKING STRATEGIES

Problem-solving and decision-making activities are frequently used by geography teachers to provide contexts in which pupils can apply and develop skills related to valuing. Pupils are expected to become involved in issues, carrying out both factual and values enquiry in relation to them, seeking solutions and considering the possible consequences of these solutions. These issues can have economic, political and social dimension as well as a focus on people and their interrelationships with their environments.

Strictly speaking, decision-making is not the same as problem-solving. *Decision-making* is the systematic process of identifying an issue, question or problem, investigating the evidence, evaluating the alternatives and choosing a course of action. In geographical enquiry, this involves a meaningful sequence of learning activities designed to provide opportunities for pupils to practise and develop a range of geographical skills and techniques. Decision-making ends with the decision and recommendations for action. However, *problem-solving* involves two further stages putting the decisions into effect (action) and evaluating the consequences of these actions. Whereas the decision-maker attempts to predict the consequences of decisions, the problem solver actually follows the progress of these consequences.

The difference between issues and problems is also worth noting. Viewing issues as problems to be solved implies that there is a gap between reality and the ideal (Maye, 1984). A problem is more specific and may be symptomatic of a wider issue. For example, the suburbanisation of rural settlements is a broad issue relating to the physical growth and resulting change in the character of rural settlements. A specific problem to be investigated through a geographical enquiry might be the impact of recent or proposed housing developments on a particular village. The former can be seen as the wider implications of the latter. Decision-making in geography can be seen as the systematic process of making sense of and resolving issues, questions and problems which can arise from people-environment relationships.

Decision-making exercises are designed to involve pupils in the application of skills of geographical enquiry to a particular issue, question or problem arising from the interaction of people with their environments. They are now a well established part of the assessment process with several GCSE and A-level examinations including decision-making, problem-solving or issues-enquiry papers. These papers assess pupils' abilities in undertaking a structured sequence of enquiry, carrying out both factual and values enquiry about a real situation (Naish *et al.,* 1987). More specifically they are assessed on:

■ the ability to follow a logical and well-reasoned sequence of enquiry in the process of reaching a decision

■ the use of appropriate methods and techniques to identify and analyse different resource, data and evidence

■ the appreciation of different values positions in the data provided and the steps involved in clarifying their own values

■ the ability to assess and evaluate alternative solutions and their likely consequences

■ the ability to make logical reasoned decisions and to justify recommendations

■ the quality of reporting.

Decision-making exercises often require pupils to take on a role. They have to examine the evidence and data provided to reach a justifiable and defensible decision from the point of view of the person whose role they are adopting. These exercises use a wide range of resources including maps, diagrams, photographs, statistics, newspaper or journal articles and statements of views. Sometimes pupils are required to analyse and interpret views presented. On other occasions they may need to indicate or consider the likely views of individuals and groups involved in the issue.

These are demanding exercises as pupils are required to use their knowledge and understanding of geographical concepts and processes in the interpretation of data which may be complex and wide ranging. They are also expected to utilise a wide variety of geographical skills and techniques. The task of the teacher therefore is also demanding, helping pupils to develop their understanding of the process of geographical enquiry, their competency in a wide range of skills and their ability to apply in-depth knowledge and understanding of geography. Familiarity with the decision-making process should be developed throughout the whole course of study rather that just in the preparation for examinations.

Activity 4.7 **Decision-making exercises in geography**

Obtain an example of a decision-making exercise in geography. Some GCSE and GCE A-level examinations have decision-making or problem-solving papers that would be appropriate for this activity.

A)
1   Carefully read through the exercise and the resources provided.
2   Write down a list of the geographical skills and techniques that pupils need to be successful in this exercise.
3   Identify the geographical knowledge and understanding that are needed by the pupils.
4   How can pupils use their skills in values enquiry in this exercise?

B)
Examination awarding bodies usually provide pupils with copies of resource materials that can be used fourteen days before the examination. The intention is to provide pupils with the opportunity to familiarise themselves with the large amount of data and to focus their knowledge and understanding in preparation for the examination. Teachers are encouraged to organise preparation activities and sessions.

1   What would you do to prepare your pupils for this examination?
2   Describe the preparation activities that you would use.

Pupils must be encouraged to use data from all the resources provided somewhere in their final report. Your preparation activities should therefore get them to use the resources and data in an active way – to do something with them to practise relevant skills and to understand what they show!

Decision-making exercises used in examinations also provide excellent resources that can be used in your lessons in an imaginative way. Not only does this help pupils practise the skills needed in the examination, but it also provides some creative and stimulating learning activities.

TEACHING PUPILS TO THINK

In some people's eyes, geography is not seen as an intellectually challenging subject. While this may not be based on informed opinion about what a geographical education can contribute to the education of young people, there may be some justification for this view if we examine the evidence about what is happening in many geography class-rooms. Notwithstanding any doubts that we may have about the current school inspection process, some of OFSTED's conclusions in recent years have drawn attention to some fundamental weaknesses: challenge, pace and motivation often being unsatisfactory, undemanding activities, insufficient attention to 'real places' and over-reliance on a limited range of textbooks (OFSTED, 2007).

David Leat suggests that there is a particularly serious problem in some geography teaching: 'too much concern with teaching and not enough with learning, too much empha-sis on substantive aspects of geography and not enough on the intellectual development of pupils' (Leat, 1997: 143). As our later discussion about the development of an 'answer culture' in geography education and the re-establishment of geography as a content-rich subject after the introduction of the National Curriculum shows, this is a view that we feel has credibility. Furthermore, Peter Smith, when reviewing the earlier OFSTED inspection findings, reports that where standards in geographical education are low, 'teachers often use unsuitable activities or geographical contexts to promote thinking' (Smith, 1997: 125).

The implications of these and other findings should rightly give us some cause for concern and reflection about the effectiveness of the teaching strategies that we are using. Leat (1997) draws our attention to some of the possible impacts on pupil attainment. An analysis of pupils' examination papers in one GCSE Geography examination revealed that almost 40 per cent of these pupils gained no marks on the case study element of questions in the structured questions paper (Battersby *et al.,* 1995). Clearly there could be a variety of reasons for this lack of achievement: some may not have attempted these questions, others may not have been able to explain their answers or have made an incor-rect interpretation. Whatever interpretation we may care to place on this evidence, it is perhaps a further reflection of the problems arising from a content-driven curriculum.

If raising attainment is one of our major educational goals, something must clearly be done to address such problems. It is our belief that unless we can change pupils as learners we are not likely to raise their levels of achievement. David Leat argues that adopting this 'changing the pupil' approach requires us to change our view of teaching and learning from one that assumes that intelligence is fixed to one that assumes that it is not fixed and can therefore be developed:

> In my twelve years as a school teacher I worked largely on the assumption… that intelligence is fixed! One adapted the curriculum to fit the pupils so that they could cope easily with it.
>
> (Leat, 1997: 144)

To respond to this challenge the 'Thinking Through Geography Project' (TTGP) was developed to help geography teachers design activities that raise levels of pupil achieve-ment in geography:

> Rather than 'water down' the curriculum to improve the student's chance of success, the aim is to develop the student's ability to cope with intellectually challenging tasks, leading to improved self-esteem through genuine achievement.
>
> (University of Newcastle School of Education, 1995: 3)

This project drew its inspiration from some of the cognitive acceleration projects such as Cognitive Acceleration in Science Education (CASE), as well as the more generic Somerset Thinking Skills. There is a growing body of evidence that when implemented successfully these thinking skills programmes can bring about significant gains in achievement and motivation (see Adey and Shayer, 1994). The CASE project found that not only did pupils who had experienced the cognitive acceleration programme in Years 7–9 do better at GCSE in science, but they also did better in English and mathematics. There also appeared to be a 'gender effect' with the experience of cognitive acceleration having a stronger impact on boys' achievement.

The broad aims of the Thinking Through Geography Project were defined as being:

■ to devise adaptable strategies and curriculum materials that make geography lessons more stimulating and challenging
■ to help pupils understand some fundamental concepts in geography in an explicit way so that these can be transferred to new contexts
■ to aid the intellectual development of pupils so that they can handle more complex information and achieve greater academic success.

(Leat, 1997: 145)

Figure 4.13 shows the main elements of the process of cognitive acceleration and clarifies the main principles that underpin the Thinking Through Geography (TTG) group's approach to curriculum design and teaching. *Concrete preparation* occurs in the introductory lessons which provide pupils with new technical vocabulary and help them to become confident in its use. *Constructivism* provides a framework through which pupils learn how to access their existing knowledge and understanding. Pupils are encouraged to go beyond their present thinking by interpreting new information through existing 'knowledge structures':

It is well understood that pupils are assisted in their understanding of, for example, condensation by reference to breathing on cold window-panes, but it is less well appreciated that their understanding of conflict in National Parks can be assisted by reference to conflict and its resolution within families.

(Leat, 1997)

The nature of activity within the *construction zone* is crucial to pupils' intellectual development. Their thinking needs to be challenged by new experience or evidence. This may take the form of cognitive conflict in which pupils' existing understanding is established and then challenged (Leat, 1997:146). There is a variety of strategies that can be used to provide this challenge. There may be some ambiguity in the tasks used to challenge pupils' thinking with the process of clarifying the task and resolving the challenge resulting in cognitive development. The role of the teacher changes during this phase of construction zone activity.

Whereas the teacher is involved in helping pupils to establish and explore the use of technical vocabulary during the concrete preparation stage, there is a need to adopt a more 'hands off' approach during the phase of construction zone activity. The teacher becomes more of a classroom observer carefully studying the actions of the pupils, listening to conversations about the tasks and trying to make sense of their reasoning and the strategies being used to resolve the cognitive conflict. During the debriefing, the teacher takes on more direct control using questioning to explore pupils' thinking, clarify understanding and establish patterns in the reasoning used.

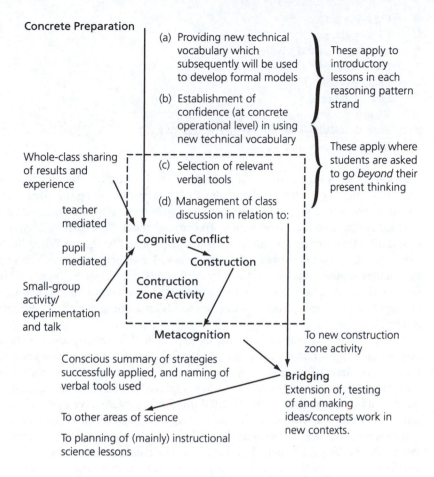

Concrete Preparation

(a) Providing new technical vocabulary which subsequently will be used to develop formal models

(b) Establishment of confidence (at concrete operational level) in using new technical vocabulary

These apply to introductory lessons in each reasoning pattern strand

These apply where students are asked to go *beyond* their present thinking

Whole-class sharing of results and experience

(c) Selection of relevant verbal tools

(d) Management of class discussion in relation to:

teacher mediated

Cognitive Conflict

pupil mediated

Construction

Small-group activity/ experimentation and talk

Contruction Zone Activity

Metacognition

To new construction zone activity

Conscious summary of strategies successfully applied, and naming of verbal tools used

Bridging
Extension of, testing of and making ideas/concepts work in new contexts.

To other areas of science

To planning of (mainly) instructional science lessons

■ **Figure 4.13** Summary of the features of a cognitive acceleration programme
Source: Leat, 1998

The purpose of this debriefing activity is to help pupils 'understand the significance of what they have done' (Leat, 1997). Knowledge and concepts that have been developed are organised (or 'filed') so that they can be used again. *Metacognition* and *bridging* are two important principles underpinning this debriefing. Developing an understanding of their own thinking *(metacognition)* helps pupils interpret different patterns of reasoning so that they can be applied to appropriate problems and situations. *Bridging* is the transfer of these concepts and reasoning patterns to other contexts in geography in order to generalise and consolidate learning. Further discussion of cognitive development can be found in Capel *et al.*, (2005, Unit 4.3).

Designing appropriate activities and strategies to facilitate cognitive conflict during the construction zone is an important part of a teacher's planning and preparation in cognitive acceleration programmes. A variety of strategies have been developed that can be used or adapted to provide appropriate challenge. Examples and a fuller discussion of these strategies can be found in Leat (1998) and Nicholls (2001).

These strategies include:

- Odd one out
- Living graphs
- Mind movies and Mysteries
- Story-telling
- Fact or opinion?
- Classification
- Reading photographs.
- Five W's (What? Where? Who? When? Why?)
- Maps from memory

Figure 4.14 shows an example of a 'Living Graph' activity. The aim is to personalise ideas that might be abstract and complex to pupils by describing the effects on people of changes shown on a graph. In this example, pupils have to match prepared statements to appropriate parts of the Demographic Transition Model. This activity encourages pupils to question their understanding of what the graph actually shows. When the statements have been matched to the graph, they can be asked to indicate which of them are 'causes' of changes on the graph and which are 'effects' (some might be both!). This provides opportunities to debate the differences between cause and effect, which are important concepts in geography, and to examine pupils' reasoning for their placement of the statements.

The debrief exploring how pupils approach this activity usually reveals some interesting insights into their reasoning. Clearly if they have some prior knowledge about how a population changes, they are able to make connections with this existing knowledge. Pupils often describe how they 'replayed the story' in the statements and how their thinking was influenced by 'mental images' that were developing (in other words, how they translated words into pictures). The latter observation perhaps leads one to question whether we undervalue the role of children's visual and mental images in learning. The way in which they take out and then add detail in their explanations provides an interesting insight into the role of abstraction in cognitive development.

Teachers using 'Living Graphs' have found this to be a very flexible and effective strategy to promote thinking in pupils across the age and ability range. Graphs and their accompanying statements can be adapted to support differentiation. They are accessible to low achievers as statements can be simplified and the use of 'stories' or characters aids interpretation. Higher achievers can be extended by asking them to devise and justify the use of additional statements or even getting them to produce similar activities for other graphs. Once teachers have been introduced to this strategy, they appear, instinctively, to find other opportunities to use it in geography lessons: to interpret climate graphs generated by spreadsheets, to simplify interpretation of flood hydrographs and so on.

Earlier in this chapter we examined the use of card-sorting activities to promote classroom discussion in geography. Table 4.8 shows an example of a card-sorting activity used to develop pupils' thinking skills. 'Who is to blame for Sharpe Point Flats?' can be used to investigate the role of political, social, economic and environmental influences in bringing about change in a residential environment. Once again, experience has shown how pupils across a broad ability range at GCSE can have meaningful access to it. This is the 'essence of good differentiation' and that a 'pupil's output reflects his or her level of understanding of the issues involved' (Nicholls, 1996). Thus you would expect some pupils to be able to identify and explain more sophisticated relationships in the information provided.

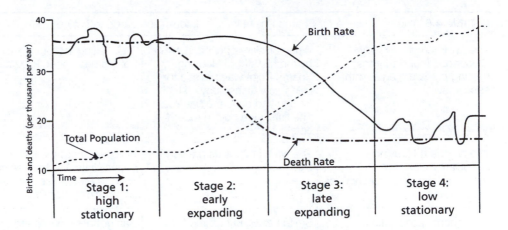

LIVING GRAPHS

Demographic Transition Model

Place these statements on the graph of birth rates, death rates, Population and Stages.

1   Billy White loses his job as a gravedigger.
2   Parents start to think more about family planning.
3   Children are warmer in bed at night because they have more brothers and sisters.
4   There are more Golden Weddings.
5   A mother sobs over the grave of the last of six children who died in a typhoid epidemic.
6   A lot more houses are being built.
7   The Public Health Inspector smiles as the building of the sewers is completed.
8   Fewer children share a bedroom.
9   Grandparents are very rare.
10 People are encouraged to emigrate to the colonies.

■ **Figure 4.14** Living graphs – the demographic transition model
Source: Fisher, 1998

An easier way into classification is perhaps provided by 'Odd one out' activities such as the one about river basins shown in Table 4.9. In the first task, pupils identify which one of the words in each set is the odd one out and explain what connects the other two words. Further challenge is provided through tasks requiring pupils to make up their own combinations, which can then be tried out with other pupils. Appropriate differentiation is thus built into the activities. Once again this type of activity provides opportunities for pupils to respond to a cognitive challenge, clarify their thinking and understanding through discussion, and make decisions which have to be justified.

Tony Fisher describes cognitive acceleration as a 'simple process demanding sophisticated teaching skills' (Fisher, 1998: 76). Confidence in your own classroom management skills may appear to be of paramount importance but the real challenge is more likely to come when you are observing and assessing the learning taking place, and when you are debriefing the pupils after the activities:

■ **Table 4.8** Who is to blame for Sharpe Point Flats? a) Information cards to cut up

The Environmental Health Officer has found that the heating pipes are aged with asbestos.	When officially opened in 1969 by the Minister of Housing, Sharpe Point was praised for using new technology – steel frames and concrete panels. The flats were built in record time.	The waiting list for council homes has about 1500 names.
The Northern Housing Association has recently renovated 100 Victorian houses near the river.	The walls in the flats are very thin.	Proceeds from the sale of council flats and houses can be used to modernise and repair its remaining homes
The tenants association members refuse to pay any rent unless the building is repaired and a security guard is put in the entrance at night.	Smith Fastbuild Ltd, the builders, went bankrupt in 1978 after a major scandal over the faulty workmanship in pre-fabricated buildings.	Baz got a second-hand drum kit for his birthday. He practises with his mates when his mum is out at work behind the bar at the Boilermaker's Arms.
A group of 'new age' travellers are squatting in Flat 38, one of 22 empty flats (out of 182).	Over half of the residents of the block are retired or unemployed.	The Boilermaker's Arms and St Justin's church are all that remains of the old days.
Steve and Claire McLean with their baby daughter were on the TV news when they camped outside the council offices in protest at being offered a flat in the block.	There are fantastic views over the city and along the river from the top floors.	Safebury's have been looking for a large inner city site for a new supermarket and are prepared to contribute to the costs of site clearance.
Asbestos is known to cause cancer if it gets into people's lungs.	Mr and Mrs Walker have to replace their mouldy wallpaper every year.	Mr Walker has a pigeon loft on his allotment, half a mile away.
The Walkers are the only people in the block who have bought their flat.	Cyril Beecham, 72, spends his evenings watching TV in his overcoat with an eiderdown over his legs to keep warm.	When the old terraces were pulled down in 1968, the community was scattered to new houses on several different outer city council estates.
When old Mr Clark died, he had been dead for 8 days before anyone noticed. They could not get his coffin in the lift.	Spike (12) and Baz (14) enjoy playing in the lifts.	Gary Payne, Chairman of the Sharpe Point Tenants' Association, was elected to the Council last May.
Janet Dalton won't let Diane (8) and Richie (10) play outside after police found them sniffing glue at the bottom of the stair-well with older kids.	All council tenants have the right to buy their home from the council at a discount price.	
Many people have been mugged and cars stolen and vandalised on the estate.	The estate, in which the block is located, has the worst health statistics in the city.	

Source: Nicholls, 1996

Main activity (Construction Zone): Instructions

The flats have been surrounded by controversy ever since they were built in 1969 and the Council has decided that *something must be done!*

Sort out the information cards into three groups

- ■ Background problems.
- ■ Recent events that may have caused the council to make this decision (trigger factors).
- ■ Information that you feel is not relevant, i.e. that does not help to explain the decision.

(The number of information cards can be reduced according to the age and ability range of the pupils. GCSE groups of average ability can usually handle up to 30 pieces of information. Other descriptive information, e.g. about the inner city environment before comprehensive redevelopment and about the construction of the flats, can be added to the photo cards.)

Optional activity 1

There are perhaps five 'core factors' involved, although this may be open to debate!

- ■ Structural/design problems
- ■ Insecurity/fear
- ■ Health
- ■ Empty flats
- ■ Council finances

These factors are interrelated in many ways. Perhaps by using a concept web, pupils can try to explain the relationships between any pairs of factors.

Optional activity 2

To facilitate a structured analysis of the issues, pupils could be asked to classify each piece of information into social/political, economic or environmental categories. This could be written up in a summary table. Who is to blame for Sharpe Point Flats having to be demolished?
Pupils regroup the information into categories which relate to:

1 The Council
2 The residents
3 The architects and builders.

They then discuss and write down why each group is partly responsible for the demolition of the flats.

Additional resources to set the scene

- ■ 1:10,000 OS map extract of an old inner city area (showing terraced housing, mixed industry, etc.).
- ■ Aerial photograph of the same/similar area.
- ■ Video clip about inner city redevelopment.
- ■ Newspaper articles to provide 'real life stories' about life in high-rise redevelopment blocks.
- ■ Photographs of high-rise redevelopment blocks.

Introduction (concrete preparation)

1 Explore pupils existing knowledge – including experiences of living or visiting high-rise blocks of flats.
2 Using the photographs as a stimulus, discuss the meaning of important technical vocabulary such as highrise blocks, inner city, terraced/back-to-back housing, inner city, comprehensive redevelopment.
3 *Speculate:* What do you think it is like to live in a block of flats like these?
4 Show the video clips about inner city redevelopment and the demolition of high-rise blocks.
5 Each pair of pupils looks through the information cards to find any that help to *describe* the environment in which the Sharpe Point Flats are situated.

Pupils could then write down their own description.

■ **Box 4.10** Who is to blame for Sharpe Point Flats? b) Strategy
Source: Nicholls, 1996

■ **Table 4.9** 'Odd one out' worksheet

Wordsheet – River basins and flooding

1	evaporation	18	drought
2	tarmac	19	stores
3	grass	20	tidal waves
4	planting trees	21	slope
5	watershed	22	lake
6	heavy rain	23	precipitation
7	transfers	24	sand
8	high tides	25	deforestation
9	monsoons	26	typhoons
10	vegetation	27	mouth
11	drainage basin	28	channel
12	condensation	29	groundwater
13	concrete	30	surface water
14	urbanisation	31	snowmelt
15	dam building	32	raising river banks
16	source	33	throughflow
17	tributary		

Source: Leat, 1998

Teaching thinking is hard and it demands some changes in teaching style. That can be very disconcerting. You have to be able to tolerate ambiguity and students talking. You have to know your subject very well conceptually. You have to wean yourself off asking too may closed and pseudo-open questions, and you have to learn to debrief (mediate).

(Leat, 1997, cited in Thomas and McGahan, 1997: 117)

The purpose of debriefing ('mediation') is to help pupils identify what they have learnt and to think about how they might use this in other situations (Nicholls, 2006). The process of cognitive acceleration shown in Figure 4.13 implies that there are distinct stages in this debriefing. When *briefing* the pupils, you tried to ensure that they understood the task and the main concepts associated with it. Your debriefing therefore depends to some extent on this initial briefing, which has established a context and meaning for the task. It also depends on what you have discovered from observing and eavesdropping on the groups as they tackled the task.

During the first part of the debriefing your aim is to get the pupils to present and explain their ideas and solutions to the task. You then need to encourage them to talk about how they approached the task. This should involve an element of 'collective' evaluation so that pupils can identify and clarify useful strategies (metacognition). Different ways of organising information cards (linear, diamond ranking, flow charts) and links between statements can be explored. Nicholls (2001: 157–162 and 2006) provides some detailed guidance on how to debrief thinking skills' activities effectively.

Cause, effect, consequences and solutions are important concepts in geography which are not always readily understood. Time needs to be taken to explore the

■ **Table 4.10** 'Odd one out' instructions – river basins and flooding

Instructions

You have been given a list of words which you might have come across during your work on *Rivers and Flooding*. You are going to use these words to complete the following tasks.

Task 1

Working with a partner, look at the sets of numbers below, which match to a word from the list on the wordsheet. Pick out the words and write them in your book. Then try to decide which word from each set is the *Odd One Out*. Underline this word in your book and explain why it is the *Odd One Out* and what the other two have in common.

Set A	*Set F*
2	30
13	11
3	29
Set B	*Set G*
4	14
15	20
6	32
Set C	*Set H*
8	31
27	20
31	8
Set D	*Set I*
22	23
10	28
25	17
Set E	*Set J*
1	5
12	16
14	19

Task 2

Now that you have started to see a pattern, add an extra word to each group, but keep the same *Odd One Out*.

Task 3

Now try to put together your own group of words with an *Odd One Out,* and you must have a good and obvious reason. Swap your group of words with your partner and see if they can work yours out and vice versa.

Task 4

Now try to sort out all the words from the list on the wordsheet into 4 to 6 groups.

Source: Leat, 1998

relationships between different concepts like these. A simple way of managing this is to print some of the information onto overhead transparencies which are then cut up so that the information can be moved about the screen (Leat *et al.*, 1998). When cause – effect relationships have been established, individual bits of transparency can be removed to explore possible solutions (i.e. Can we remove the cause? What is the impact of removing the cause?)

Helping pupils to see how their thinking and learning can be applied to other contexts ('bridging') requires careful planning. Pupils could be presented with case studies about other issues and geographical contexts, and asked to consider whether they could use the strategies or classifications that they developed through the earlier activity. For example, after examining factors affecting the impact of earthquakes can pupils apply the groups of factors they have identified to other hazards like flooding? Do these categories fit or do they need to be amended? In what ways would the concept map in Figure 4.15 be different for a less economically developed country?

Getting pupils to think and talk about thinking and learning does not happen just because you have planned to use some of the strategies described above: it is a cumulative process. Both you and your pupils need time to 'acclimatise' and gain confidence in using different strategies.

Creating an appropriate classroom climate is of vital importance in this respect. You need to be patient in establishing an atmosphere in which all pupils feel that their contributions are valued. Getting pupils to build on each other's contributions is a feature of high-quality classroom interaction but achieving such reciprocity in pupil conversation requires skilful teaching and takes time. This means using open questions, reinforcing positively and helping pupils to develop the use of appropriate language for these geographical conversations. Pupils need to be encouraged to listen carefully to what others have to say, to develop and reinterpret their ideas, and to offer alternatives. You need to draw out some of the key ideas and make connections between different contributions, but be careful not to impose your own interpretation. You also need to be sensitive about how much listening a particular class is prepared to do!

Activity 4.8 **Thinking through geography**

Arrange to observe a lesson in which one of the strategies described in this section is used to promote thinking through geography.

Either (a) During this observation record the following:

■ The strategies, tasks and questioning used by the teacher during the stage of concrete preparation to establish what the pupils already know and understand.

■ Pupils' existing knowledge, concepts and technical vocabulary identified.

■ The nature of the activity used to provide 'cognitive conflict' during the 'construction zone'.
  ☐ What planning and preparation had been necessary?
  ☐ How was the activity introduced?

■ Strategies used by different groups of pupils to carry out these tasks or solve the problems posed.

■ Strategies and questions used by the teacher during the debrief to help pupils review their thinking and learning (metacognition), and to provide opportunities for them to apply what they had learnt to other geographical contexts (bridging). You will probably find it helpful to refer back to our earlier discussion of debriefing to clarify your understanding of the issues involved.

Or (b) An alternative observation activity would be to focus on one group of pupils during the lesson. Record:

- Their comments and contributions during different activities and phases of the lesson:
  - □ evidence of existing knowledge and understanding, and use of concepts/ technical vocabulary (concrete preparation)
  - □ strategies used to tackle tasks and evidence of 'cognitive conflict'/ challenge during the 'construction phase'
  - □ comments and contributions during the debrief (evidence of 'metacognition' and 'bridging').
- It is sometimes helpful to draw a seating plan indicating the location of different pupils. Draw lines to record the links between different pupils' contributions and conversations. These links can be annotated to record the nature of the interactions between different pupils within the group, with the teacher and with pupils in other groups.

Leat and McAleavy argue that promoting critical thinking enables pupils to become more reflective and to develop their reasoning abilities. It also provides them with greater challenge as they engage with more complex subject knowledge. It is their belief 'not so much that history and geography can contribute to critical thinking, but rather that they are nothing without it' (Leat and McAleavy, 1998: 112). Critical enquiry in geography encourages pupils to assess the validity of different value positions, resolve the differences between these and their own positions, and consider the limitations of stereotypical views. It can therefore make a significant contribution to education for citizenship.

Differentiating teaching to achieve pace and challenge

We began our earlier discussion about the potential of strategies for developing thinking through geography by drawing your attention to concerns expressed about some fundamental weaknesses identified in many geography lessons where challenge, pace and motivation has often been unsatisfactory. Clearly many of the issues relating to differentiation are addressed through appropriate planning and preparation. Differentiation is based on an understanding of individual learners, their needs and their strengths as much as their weaknesses. We should select a variety of strategies to provide a range of learning opportunities for all pupils to make progress.

However, achieving differentiation in learning is not just dependent on our ability to design appropriated 'targeted' or open-ended tasks to meet the needs of various ability groups. Diversity also applies to teaching strategies which have to be used flexibly and implemented successfully.

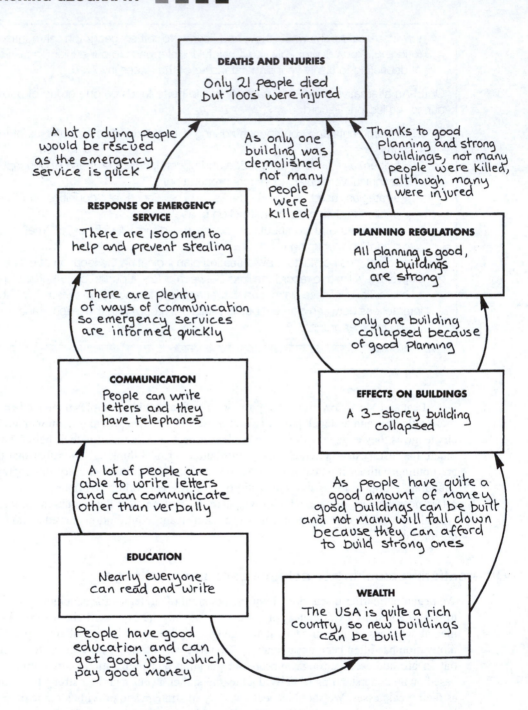

■ **Figure 4.15** Connections between factors affecting the impact of an earthquake in the USA – a concept map

Source: Fisher, 1998

From her own experience as an OFSTED inspector, Gill Davidson reveals how the weaknesses mentioned above manifest themselves in some geography lessons:

> Lessons which are unsatisfactory often follow a predictable pattern of teacher talk, some limited question and answer, followed by a fairly undemanding individual written task involving transferring or recording information. In such lessons pupils are passive; they are not actively engaged in activities which facilitate learning and the development of learning skills.

> (Davidson, 1996: 13)

Breaking this predictable pattern evident in poor lessons requires us to raise our awareness of how we can influence the pace and direction of learning, and how we can provide appropriate challenges for all learners. The pace and flow of a lesson refers to both the teaching and the learning taking place. It is important to maintain an appropriate pace in a lesson as this can influence pupils' interest and motivation levels. Try to avoid slipping into overlong monotone expositions which can create tensions within lessons as pupils' concentration levels fall. Effective explanations are often fairly brief and may be interspersed with questions or short activities (Kyriacou, 1991).

How you intervene in classroom activity has a major influence on the flow of a lesson. Dwelling for too long on particular situations and interruptions, for example, when dealing with discipline or individual needs, affects the momentum of a lesson. Try to avoid talking for longer than is necessary to clarify pupils' understanding.

Skilful teachers appear to attend to a variety of things at one time. This is due to what is sometimes called 'withitness', which describes teachers' awareness of what is going on in all parts of the classroom. Constantly monitoring classroom activity helps you recognise and react to different needs in relation to both learning and discipline. Eye contact and body language can be used effectively to communicate this awareness to pupils and often makes it possible for you to refrain from interrupting the whole class and slowing progress.

To be able to differentiate our teaching we need to develop these monitoring skills and this is an essential part of what we described earlier as the 'active assessment' of learning. Frequently, teachers use questioning and whole-class discussion to explore and check pupils' learning. A teacher's questioning skills have a significant influence on the quality of whole-class interactive teaching described earlier in this chapter. Remember that simple, closed questions are only likely to check pupils' ability to recall information, whereas open and more intellectually challenging questions are likely to be more helpful when it comes to exploring thinking and learning.

During a lesson you will make numerous observations and ask many questions (both individually and collectively) that help you to make judgements about pupils' progress and competence in learning. This process challenges your powers of analysis, as you have your own ideas about what constitutes knowledge and understanding of particular subject matter and what level of competence in the use of different geographical skills is needed by pupils of varying age and ability.

Initially you are very much be guided by your plans and preparation for the lesson. However, avoid becoming a 'slave to the plan'. Your active assessment of the learning taking place will lead you to modify your original objectives, breaking them down into smaller targets for individuals, groups and even the class as a whole. Thus, the process of setting different targets and refining objectives is an effective way in which you can influence the pace and depth of learning during a lesson.

This process of active assessment during lessons is an important part of formative assessment (discussed in Chapter 10). Observing pupils working, looking at their work, listening to their conversations about tasks and asking them questions about this work helps you analyse the outcomes of the learning activities that you have devised and the teaching strategies that you are using. You can then make decisions about how and when to intervene and at what level (individual, group or whole class). One of the principles guiding these interventions will be that of 'consequential validity' in other words, they have a positive impact on pupils' learning. These impacts might include the successful completion of a task, improvements in knowledge and understanding, or the promotion of thinking or critical analysis in response to greater intellectual challenge.

Whether they have these desirable consequences depends on the quality of feedback provided by the teacher. Such feedback should aim to reinforce positively, consolidate and extend learning. Once again flexibility is needed in the way that you approach these issues. Sometimes it is necessary to adopt a very 'hands on' approach taking careful control of each phase of activity to ensure a smooth transition between activities, and thus maintaining the momentum in a lesson. On other occasions a 'hands off' approach might be preferrable as too much intervention will break up any continuity in the learning taking place. Care has to be taken to try to build on pupils' own knowledge and understanding rather than imposing your own version (echoes here of Peter Smith's observation quoted at the start of this chapter).

As well as mastering these 'techniques', we have to work hard to establish a climate for learning in our geography lessons. If the main goal of education is to promote the social and intellectual development of pupils, then we need to create the conditions in which this can take place. Throughout this chapter, we make frequent reference to the need to create a positive classroom atmosphere in which pupils' contributions are valued and respected. Appropriate praise and encouragement develops pupils' self-confidence and enhances their self-esteem. A phrase used elsewhere is that the 'best resource is a sensitive teacher'. It takes time and effort as well as sensitivity to build a positive rapport with pupils and develop effective working relationships. These are also the conditions needed for developing a teacher's self-confidence, the feeling that you can 'make a difference'!

If we are to 'make this difference' and help all pupils to maximise their achievements in geography, we need to establish a 'culture of success' in our lessons, a 'culture' that is based on high expectations for all pupils and that is closely associated with learning geography. This means establishing an effective classroom presence and a positive working atmosphere. Our own experience of teaching geography and of working with many student teachers is that all these skills help us to differentiate our teaching successfully. They all interact to create something that is difficult to define or describe. Rather it is something that you feel when you have been part of a successful lesson. This is the real 'stuff' of differentiating teaching and why it is of crucial importance in facilitating intellectual development and the raising of pupil attainment.

An important part of 'learning to teach geography' involves developing your pedagogic knowledge, in other words, your knowledge and understanding of processes of teaching and learning in geography. This does not imply a simple 'this is how you do it' approach to learning to teach. There are no short cuts to acquiring this pedagogic knowledge. Initially this knowledge will be developed from your observation of experienced classroom practitioners at work, advice from mentors and other teachers, and reflections on your own experiences of practical teaching. Part of this will involve acquiring a language for talking about geography teaching. However, once the initial frameworks have been established and you become more autonomous, you will, as a reflective practitioner, make more sense of your own teaching and increase your pedagogic knowledge in a more independent way.

Learning to teach involves personal professional growth. There is a growing awareness of the complexity of classroom processes and of the ways of interpreting and influencing these processes. There is also usually a significant shift in focus from a concern with your own performance towards greater consideration of what Tony Fisher describes as a 'complex interplay of three specific types of knowledge' (1998: 32): knowledge about learners, knowledge about geography and pedagogic knowledge (Figure 4.16).

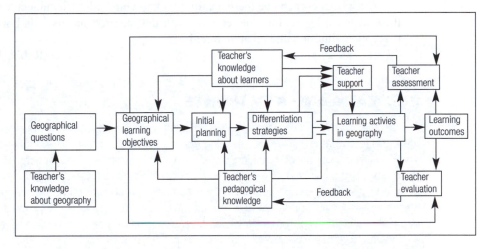

■ **Figure 4.16** The 'teaching and learning complex' – a model of teaching for learning in geography

Source: Fisher, 1998

This is a useful dynamic model for thinking about the interrelationships between teaching and learning in geography as teaching is 'seen as both a causal and an enabling activity' (Fisher, 1998: 32).

Central to the development of a geography teacher's pedagogic knowledge is the need to build up a broad repertoire of teaching styles and strategies. David Leat describes geography as 'an enormously eclectic borrower' with geographers being 'inclined to play fast and loose in applying ideas and techniques' (Leat and McAleavy, 1998: 113). Receptiveness to ideas about different approaches and a willingness to be flexible, imaginative and take risks can only enhance one's pedagogic knowledge. It also puts us in a better position to promote the intellectual development of pupils and respond to recent concerns about the lack of challenge in many geography lessons. In this context we feel that the development of strategies to promote 'thinking through geography' is making a significant contribution to pedagogy in geography. We share David Leat's optimism and belief that:

> Teaching thinking strategies and pedagogy can add substantially to the repertoire of teachers and schools to make changes in the classroom without which raising attainment becomes an end without a means.

> (Leat and McAleavy, 1998: 113)

There is also that certain something about teaching that is difficult to put your finger on, the atmosphere in those successful geography lessons. You can feel it, but cannot find the words to describe it – you had to be there! The interplay between effective teaching and successful learning has sometimes been referred as 'artistry'. The idea of artistry recognises that teaching is a highly creative and personal activity. We often return to Rubin's words to describe that feeling:

> There is a striking quality to fine classrooms. Pupils are caught up in learning; excitement abounds; and playfulness and seriousness blend easily because the purposes are clear, the goals sensible and an unmistakable feeling of well being prevails.
>
> Artist teachers achieve these qualities by knowing both their subject matter and their students; by guiding the learning with deft control that itself is born out of perception, intuition and creative impulse.
>
> (Rubin, 1985: v)

SUMMARY AND KEY POINTS

For us, this extensive overview of teaching strategies has provided an opportunity to reflect on just what is involved in teaching geography. We began by drawing you away from simplistic notions of teaching styles and warning about the dangers of being influenced by dogma. What we share with Margaret Roberts (1997) is a belief not that geography teachers should operate within one particular style but that they should use a variety of styles and understand when and how particular styles are appropriate for a particular educational purpose. However, as she also acknowledges, how they teach is 'not simply a matter of efficiency or philosophy' (Roberts, 1997: 247). Teachers are influenced by the contexts in which they work, the pupils that they work with and the resources available to them.

This does not mean to imply that there are strategies that cannot be used in particular school contexts. In our work as teacher educators we rightly ban the use of the phrase 'you can't do that with the pupils in this school'. This is not to deny the influence of particular contexts on how we teach or the autonomy of teachers to decide what happens in their classrooms. Rather it is a recognition that using such a phrase conveys low expectations of what these pupils can achieve and as such is likely to reinforce a climate of underachievement. It should also be clear from this chapter that not using particular teaching strategies results in opportunities being missed for worthwhile learning to achieve certain educational goals.

FURTHER READING

Biddulph, M. and Bright, G. (2003) *Theory into Practice: Dramatically Good Geography*, **Sheffield: The Geographical Association.**

This text examines the role of creative talk and drama in helping pupils to explore their own values, beliefs and opinions and those of other people. It also considers how such strategies can help pupils develop their understanding of complex people-environment relationships so that they can develop informed arguments and critically evaluate different perspectives. The authors suggest a framework for planning to use drama in geography lessons and provide examples of a variety of strategies.

Biddulph, M. and Clarke, J. (2006) *Theatrical geography*, **Chapter 24 in Balderstone, D. (ed.) Secondary Geography Handbook, Sheffield: The Geographical Association.**

The authors examine the potential for using drama to explore the 'affective' dimensions of geography. They suggest a wide range of strategies and explain how drama can be used effectively in geography.

Ferretti, J. (2007) *Meeting the Needs of your Most Able Students; Geography*, **London: Routledge/GA.**

The book is an essential resource for secondary geography teachers, it features comprehensive appendices with linked resources available online that feature:

- lesson plans and examples of activities
- departmental procedures and action plans
- identification strategies
- guidance on auditing provision for more able pupils.

Both Swift's and Ferretti's specialised handbooks can be obtained via the geography shop on www.geography.org.uk

Freeman, D. and Hare, C. (2006) *Collaboration, collaboration, collaboration*, **Chapter 25 in Balderstone, D. (ed.) Secondary Geography Handbook, Sheffield: The Geographical Association.**

The authors explain the processes involved in facilitating successful collaborative learning in geography. They show how this can promote greater engagement and encourage pupils to take more responsibility for their own learning. They provide a wide range of creative ideas and strategies for developing collaborative learning.

Ginnis, P. (2002) *The Teacher's Toolkit: Raise achievement with strategies for every learner*, **Carmarthen: Crown House Publishing.**

This book is packed with creative ideas and practical classroom strategies for developing stimulating learning activities that respond to the needs of different learning styles. Links are made to relevant theories about learning. The ideas and strategies can be applied across a range of subjects and contexts.

Heilbronn, R. and Turner, T. (2005) *Moral Development and Values*, **Unit 4.5 in Capel, S., Leask, M. and Turner, T. (eds)** *Learning to Teach in the Secondary School: A companion to school experience*, **London: Routledge.**

This text explains your legal responsibilities in relation to the spiritual, moral, social and cultural development. It explores opportunities to develop pupils' values and moral judgement in school contexts including citizenship education.

Leat, D. (ed.) (1998) *Thinking through Geography*, **Cambridge: Chris Kington Publishing.**

This book explains a range of different strategies for developing thinking skills in geography and provides an extensive variety of resources and activities.

McPartland, M. (2001) *Theory into Practice: Moral Dilemmas*, **Sheffield: The Geographical Association.**

This text explores ways of getting young people engaged in the process of moral reasoning through the medium of moral dilemmas. It shows how geography can contribute to a number of wider educational agendas relating to values education, citizenship education and pupils' spiritual, moral, social and cultural development.

McPartland, M. (2006) *Strategies for approaching values education*, **Chapter 15 in Balderstone, D. (ed.) Secondary Geography Handbook, Sheffield: The Geographical Association.**

This chapter explores the significant contribution geography can make to the moral education of young people. It explains different approaches to values education and provides stimulating ideas for strategies that promote values' enquiry.

Nicholls, A. (2006) *Thinking skills and the role of debriefing*, Chapter 16 in Balderstone, D. (ed.) Secondary Geography Handbook, Sheffield: The Geographical Association.

This text explores the relationship between thinking skills, thinking skills' strategies and teaching thinking. There is thorough guidance about debriefing strategies and their role in scaffolding learning and in promoting metacognition.

Nicholls, A. with Kinninment, D. (2001) *More Thinking Through Geography*, Cambridge: Chris Kington Publishing.

This book provides more activities and resources for promoting thinking through geography. There is guidance about how to launch activities and debrief learning as well as advice on how to use concept mapping effectively.

PLANNING FOR TEACHING AND LEARNING IN GEOGRAPHY CLASSROOMS

Our lesson observations revealed that in classes run by effective teachers, students are clear about what they are doing and why they are doing it. They can see links with their earlier learning and have some ideas about how it could be developed further. The students want to know more.

(Hay McBer, 2000: para 1.2.4)

An enquiry approach to learning is consistent with a widely held theory of learning. Enquiry can be justified because of the emphasis it places on thinking and understanding, rather than on memorisation. Enquiry can also be justified because it can be used to achieve broader educational purposes.

(Roberts, 2003: 36)

The quality of teaching and learning in geography in survey schools was generally satisfactory, often good, but rarely outstanding. Limitations to the quality of teaching include:

- a focus on content rather than learning
- insufficient development of geographical skills
- insufficient use of maps and fieldwork to progressively build up pupils' skills in data gathering, analysis and interpretation.

(OFSTED, 2008: 20)

INTRODUCTION

This chapter explores the fundamental aspects of lesson planning and provides some guidance to help you start developing some of the skills needed to plan lessons effectively. Before you start to teach a lesson, you need to have some idea of the learning you would like to take place and how the lesson will facilitate this learning. This involves more than just a consideration of how to structure the time available within a lesson.

You need to take into account the requirements of the curriculum and how pupils learn in geography. Decisions need to be made about the resources to be used or prepared. Consideration should also be given to how the lesson will build upon previous learning and how it will contribute to future learning in subsequent lessons.

Another level of planning involves the development of lesson sequences, or schemes of work, which provide learning experiences for pupils over a longer period of time.

As a result, the planning process described in this chapter draws upon the understanding that you develop the issues addressed in other chapters in this book.

The experience that you gain of planning lessons and schemes of work during your school experience will help develop your ability to plan for successful teaching and learning in geography.

OBJECTIVES

By the end of this chapter, you should be able to:

- understand the relationship between planning and the quality of teaching and learning in geography classrooms
- produce effective lesson plans
- construct schemes of work.

THE PURPOSE OF PLANNING

There is plenty of evidence to suggest that there is a close relationship between the quality of what happens in a classroom and the thoroughness of planning by teachers (Hay McBer, 2000). As teachers, our main task is to design learning activities that will help our pupils achieve the learning outcomes we have intended. Reviews of geography in secondary schools have provided further evidence of the crucial role of planning in promoting effective learning in geography.

> Where the standards are low, teachers often use unsuitable activities or geographical contexts to promote thinking. Unclear lesson objectives, resulting from inadequately detailed planning, lead to students being unsure of what they are doing and why, and as a consequence they are unable to build on previous work.
>
> (Smith, 1997: 125)

Initially, lesson planning might feel like a problem-solving process with the challenge being how to structure time available and organise activities and resources. In this sense, planning helps reduce the amount of thinking that we have to do during lessons so we can concentrate on managing the lesson, directing pupils' learning and responding to their learning needs.

Effective planning involves making decisions about the *purpose* of the lesson (aims and objectives), *what* is to be taught (content) and *how* you are going to teach it (teaching methods or strategies). Your lesson plans will be particularly useful as a record of the teaching and learning that has taken place and also help you plan future work as you seek to build upon and extend pupils' learning in subsequent lessons.

FEATURES OF A LESSON PLAN

> Teaching as much as dramatising is a planned performance and presentation. Teaching is both planning and a performed presentation with learning often taking place for individuals in distinct episodes within that planned performance.
>
> (Slater, 1986: 42)

This frequently used analogy sees a lesson as a play with a number of scenes that follow a clear structure and develop a plot (relating to the objectives). The process of deciding about teaching and learning activities, their order and timing is the selection and scripting of a lesson (Kyriacou, 1991). The props are the resources and equipment that have been identified and prepared, and the arrangement of the classroom layout can be thought of as the set. Your first encounters of teaching may even involve some rehearsal!

Many experienced teachers have a mental framework for their lesson plans which often become internalised as a result of being used several times. As a student teacher, you are required to produce explicit written plans for your lessons. Over time, you will develop a format for your plans that reflects and best suits your approach to lesson planning. Alternatively, Table 5.1 provides a basic framework within which to record your lesson plans.

Whatever framework you adopt, there are certain basic features of a lesson plan as shown in the example in Table 5.1. There should be a clear statement of the purpose of the lesson (aims) and the intended learning outcomes (learning objectives). Initially, student teachers often find it difficult to distinguish between aims and objectives. Defining these learning objectives as clear statements of what it is expected that the pupils will know, understand and be able to do by the end of the lesson is often a challenging activity. However, establishing these specific targets is an essential first step in planning for learning. If you are clear in your own mind about what you expect the pupils to be able to achieve, it will help you direct and guide their learning during the lesson and evaluate the effectiveness of the lesson afterwards. Activity 5.1 will help develop your ability to specify such learning objectives.

Sharing these objectives with pupils can help facilitate a more 'student-centred' approach to teaching and learning. For teaching and learning to be 'student-centred' pupils need to be aware of these learning targets and how they represent the criteria for success in a lesson:

> In order to foster motivation, interest and responsibility, pupils need to know what they are required to do, why they are required to do it and how they can succeed.
>
> (Davidson, 1996: 11)

Evidence from OFSTED inspections shows that in some schools, the development of knowledge, understanding and skills in geography is not sufficiently integrated (Davidson, 1996 and 2006). This means that the full range of educational opportunities which geography can offer is not being exploited. In the example shown in Table 5.3 the skill of using the maps to describe the location and layout of housing, together with the use of photographs/slides and selected census data to extract information about housing quality, helps develop pupils' knowledge and understanding about the characteristics of different residential areas. Similarly, in the lesson outlined in Table 5.2, the pupils are required to extract information about climate and vegetation from an atlas and other sources to develop their knowledge and understanding about different global environ- ments or ecosystems.

■ **Table 5.1** The features of a lesson plan

Date_____ Lesson_____ Time_____ Class_____ Room_____

Title of Lesson

Lesson's Aims
State clearly the overall purpose of the lesson – what you are hoping to achieve.

Learning Objectives and Enquiry Questions
These represent your specific targets for pupils' learning. Write clear statements of what you expect pupils will know, understand and be able to do as a result of the activities in this lesson.

Subject Content: National Curriculum/ Syllabus Links Indicate which aspects of the National Curriculum Programme of Study or the examination syllabus are being covered in this lesson.	**Cross-Curricular Links/Themes/Competences** Indicate any links that there may be with the content of other subjects. What other aspects of learning may be evident? Could the lesson contribute to the delivery of any cross-curriculum themes such as citizenship or SMSC dimensions (see Chapter 9)?
Resources What resources will be needed for this lesson – materials and equipment? Use this as a checklist for your preparation.	**Advance Preparation (Room and Equipment)** Does the room need to be prepared for the activities that you have planned (grouping and seating arrangements)? Does any equipment need to be set up?
Differentiation How do you plan to address particular pupils' learning needs – specific adaptations of resources and strategies, extension/enrichment activities? How will learning support assistants be used?	**Action Points** What are the links with learning that has taken place in previous lessons? Also indicate any issues that you need to follow up from previous lessons with this group (pupils, learning, or classroom management).

Learning Activities/Tasks	**Time**	**Teaching Strategies/Actions**
Describe the nature of the learning activities. What will the pupils be required to do? How will the resources be used? What learning skills will be used? What learning processes will be evident?	Indicate how much time you are planning to allow for each activity. This will help you to monitor the pace of activities in the lesson.	How will activities be introduced? Use key words as prompts for explanations, demonstrations or for any exposition. You can also indicate any specific questions that you may wish to use. Avoid too much detail as this is a working document. How will you monitor, manage and conclude activities?

Assessment Opportunities, Objectives and Evidence
Consider the potential outcomes from the learning activities and tasks. What evidence of attainment might be provided by these tasks? Where relevant this could be related to aspects of NC level descriptions or examination syllabus assessment objectives. You can add to this section after the lesson as a result of monitoring the learning that has taken place during the lesson.

Evaluation of Learning	**Evaluation of Teaching**
Comment on the learning that has taken place. Refer back to the learning objectives. How successful were the learning activities in achieving these aims and objectives? Comment on pupils' progress, competence, motivation and interest in learning. How appropriate were the activities in meeting the learning needs of particular pupils?	Your reflections on the effectiveness of the teaching strategies used in the lesson. Focus on the clarity of your explanations and exposition. What strategies, actions or interventions were effective when managing activities or monitoring pupils' learning? How successful were particular classroom management strategies? Be objective and realistic. Try not to be too self-critical.

Action Points
What issues need to be followed up? This might include concepts or generalisations that need to be reinforced, skill or viewpoints that need to be clarified. It could also include issues relating to your own professional development such as classroom management or ways in which you monitor or support learning.

Activity 5.1 **Writing learning objectives**

The aim of this activity is to provide you with an opportunity to practise writing 'learning objectives'. Read the following descriptions of geography lessons and then write appropriate 'learning objectives' for these lessons.

Lesson 1

This is a Year 7 lesson during the pupils' first term at the school. The teacher is aiming to build upon the pupils' knowledge and understanding about different types of rock and the ways in which they can be classified from Key Stage 2. The pupils are working in groups of four (mainly due to the resources available). Each group has a box containing samples of about five different types of rock.

The introduction to the lesson involves the pupils suggesting the ways that the different properties of rocks might be assessed. There is also a brief recap of the ways in which rock types are classified (igneous, sedimentary and metamorphic).

The main tasks in the lesson, involve the pupils assessing and describing the main properties of their rock samples. Individually, they record this information on a printed rock identification/classification sheet and include an annotated sketch of each sample. The teacher monitors the pupils' progress checking the outcomes.

In the final third of the lesson, the teacher shows some slides of different land-scapes in Britain associated with each rock type and distributes an activity sheet 'Rock around Britain'. The pupils have a list of well-known landscape features and rock types. Using atlases (physical geography and geology maps) the pupils have to match the labels of the rock type and landscape to the correct location on the map.

Lesson 2

This is a Year 9 lesson in which pupils are investigating the influence of distance from the sea on temperatures. It builds on earlier work in Key Stage 3 where pupils learnt to draw and interpret climate graphs.

The pupils plot the average monthly temperatures for Berlin (Germany) and Falmouth (UK) on the same graph. The differences between the two temperature curves are described identifying the highest and lowest monthly temperatures for both places and then calculating the annual temperature ranges.

The teacher explains how land and sea heat up and cool down at different rates, drawing on pupils understanding of these principles from their work in science. The pupils summarise these ideas and use them to explain the reasons for the different annual temperature ranges in Berlin and Falmouth. The teacher introduces the terms 'Continental' and 'Maritime' climates.

The pupils are then given the average monthly temperatures for ten other places, asked to work out the temperature ranges and describe whether these places have 'Continental' or 'Maritime' climates. They use atlases to check the location of these places.

Lesson 3

Year 10 pupils have been studying Changing Economic Activities and are examining the changing location of industry in Britain. The lesson begins with the teacher questioning the pupils to develop a brief recap of factors influencing the location of particular industries that they have studied.

Working in pairs, the pupils are given copies of a wide range of adverts and promotional literature designed to attract new businesses or industries to different places in Britain. The pupils are initially encouraged to find the location of these places in an atlas. The teacher uses a couple of examples to draw pupils' attention to the locational factors that are emphasised in the adverts and the image of the places that are promoted in the adverts (through both the illustrations and the written information). The pupils record the relevant information that they have identified for each place in a table under appropriate headings such as accessibility, environmental factors, available services, proximity to markets, government aid/grants, etc.

The lesson concludes with a discussion about the relative importance of the factors identified and about the images that each of the places are trying to promote. A homework exercise requires the pupils to design and produce a similar promotional advert for a local industrial estate/business park that they surveyed as part of a fieldwork visit.

Lesson 4

A Year 8 lesson is examining ways in which land use and environments have changed in towns and cities. The lesson begins with the teacher showing 8–10 images of urban environments in different parts of the world that have been changed for a variety of reasons (e.g. a tourist resort in Spain, old warehouses in a British city, bomb damage in Beirut, the commercial centre of Hong Kong, Kobe and San Francisco after earthquakes, new flats in a Russian city, urban freeways in a West African city, etc). Some background music about city life is played to help the pupils to focus on the task.

The pupils have been given three questions to answer for each slide:

■ How has the urban environment been changed?
■ What do you think this scene might have looked like before the change?
■ What has caused this change to take place?

This is followed by a feedback discussion on the nature and causes of change in urban environments with the teacher directing questioning to classify these changes (i.e. natural hazards, commercial, transport, tourism, economic/industrial decline, planning, etc.).

In the second part of the lesson the pupils, working in pairs, are given an OS Map (1:25,000 scale) and two aerial photographs of an area in the city where they live (one taken in the early 1960s and the other in 2005). The teacher uses questioning to recap briefly some of the skills needed to interpret aerial photographs and OS Maps. The pupils are required to describe the location of areas where changes have taken place and to describe the nature of the changes that can be interpreted from the evidence available. Possible reasons for some of these changes are discussed.

Lesson 5

An A-level group are studying natural hazards. The lesson begins with the pupils watching a six-minute video extract showing a simulation of the potential primary impacts of an earthquake in Tokyo on a Japanese house and inside an office on the upper floor of a skyscraper. The pupils write a list of the earthquake's effects and the issues that arise from these.

The pupils are then given a set of cards listing some of the factors influencing the effects of earthquakes. In pairs, they use a diamond ranking exercise to prioritise the importance of these factors in relation to different earthquakes that they have been researching.

The teacher leads a feedback discussion in which the pupils justify their selection of factors for each earthquake studied. The pupils are then shown two more video extracts of other earthquakes in California. A follow-up (homework) activity requires the pupils to draw concept map diagrams to explain how people respond to earthquake hazards.

Lesson 6
A GCSE group have been investigating the distribution of crime in their local town. They have collected data from a variety of sources and are using this lesson to study any patterns that are emerging and analysing any relationships in an attempt to identify any factors that may account for the patterns that they find.

Secondary data on the number of different types of offence in each area of the town have been obtained from the local police force. Census data have been collected on the residential, demographic, employment and ethnicity characteristics of these areas. Fieldwork visits have been made to different parts of the town to survey the housing and environment quality of the area. Pupils have also used questionnaires to survey people's perception of the crime hazard. Data on house prices have also been collected from local estate agents and newspaper advertisements.

Information Technology has been used to record the data collected and to speed up the processing of these data. A GIS programme has been used to map the distribution of the data collected. Spreadsheets and databases have been set up to record the data so that any relationships can be analysed.

The teacher begins the lesson by recapping the enquiry questions that had been identified at the start of the study unit and reminding the pupils about the data that had been collected. The pupils are provided with a prompt sheet containing questions to guide their interrogation of the maps and databases.

Working in groups of three, the pupils use the GIS programme to map the distribution of two different offences and up to four sets of data on factors that may help to explain these patterns. IT is used to interrogate the data in the spreadsheets and databases, and to graph relationships between sets of data.

The maps are annotated (using the prompts as guidance) and displayed together with the graphs, and the descriptions and possible explanations of the patterns and relationships.

Lesson 7 (adapted from Digby, 1997)
This is the first lesson in an A-level Global Futures module on Health and Welfare which aims to establish the nature of the enquiry. The teacher has photocopied a range of articles from newspapers and geographical magazines/journals about health-related issues that are linked to geographical patterns at a range of scales

(local, regional, national and global). A sequence of relevant enquiry questions have been identified to structure the pupils' examination of the issues involved. These have been listed in a data collection table.

Each pupil chooses an article and uses the enquiry questions to summarise the main geographical features of the issue. Each pupil then prepares a short presentation about the issue to make to the rest of the group. This presentation focuses on the nature of the issue, who is affected, the different viewpoints that are likely to arise from this issue and how they might be resolved, if at all.

These presentations are made in the next lesson. The teacher encourages the rest of the group to ask each pupil further questions about the issue that they have studied. The lesson concludes with a discussion about the geographical aspects of health-related issues – the patterns, range of scales, impacts (social, economic, environmental) and possible causes, as well as the implications (management of and response to) and future possibilities or alternatives.

Lesson 8

A Year 11 group are producing a case study of the impacts of a large multipurpose dam scheme in an Economically Developing Country. This is part of a GCSE study unit on Ghana which is examining alternative approaches to development.

The teacher begins the lesson by showing slides of some large-scale dam schemes and establishing an understanding of the purpose of such schemes. The River Volta is located on an atlas map of Ghana together with the location of Accra, Akosombo and other places studied previously. The pupils are reminded about the situation of Ghana in relation to West Africa and possible links between this topic and some of the pupils' earlier studies of river processes.

A video is shown about the Volta Dam (Ghana's Big Project) with the pupils being asked to make brief notes about the positive and negative impacts of the scheme in a table. After the video, the teacher distributes base maps of Ghana (within West Africa) and reminds the pupils of the benefits of displaying information about case studies on annotated sketch maps. A couple of examples of impacts shown in the video are discussed and then labelled on the sketch maps. The pupils then use their notes and atlases to add more annotations to the sketch map.

In the last part of the lesson, the teacher distributes copies of a short article that outlines some of the other impacts of the Volta Dam scheme along the coast of West Africa. This information is added to the sketch map.

For homework, the pupils are given an example of a GCSE question to answer. This question requires them to compare the relative advantages and disadvantages of different approaches to development using examples that they have studied.

When planning your lessons, you should consider some of their broader educational purposes as well as the more specific aspects of learning in geography (knowledge, understanding, skills, attitudes and values). These broader objectives might relate to the development of key skills such as literacy, oracy and numeracy. They might also indicate some of the processes of learning involved in the lesson (i.e. if the pupils will be working independently or collaboratively).

■ **Table 5.2** Lesson planning framework: Year 10, the characteristics of different natural ecosystems

Date_____ Lesson_____ Time_____ Class ____Yr 10_____ Room_____

Title of Lesson The characteristics of different natural ecosystems

Lesson's Aims
To examine the characteristic features of different natural ecosystems in the world.
To examine relationships between climate and vegetation.

Learning Objectives
• To know the main global climatic zones.
• To know the characteristic features of the main natural ecosystems in the world.
• To understand how climate influences vegetation.
• To interpret climatic data and thematic atlas maps (climate and vegetation).
• To produce displays to reinforce learning of global ecosystems.

Subject Content: National Curriculum/Syllabus Links	**Cross-Curricular Links/Themes/ Competences**
GCSE Unit 1 Simple recognition of the existence and variety of major world biomes (global scale ecosystems) related to climate graphs and vegetation zones.	Environmental education **(about** the environment – nature of ecosystems) Science/biology – global vegetation zones

Resources	**Advance Preparation (Room and Equipment)**
Atlases	Television and video
Sheets with summary of natural ecosystems table and Disney video clips, Pictures from wildlife and geographical magazines, World map outlines.	

Differentiation	**Action Points**
Mainly by support. John and Liz have problems identifying information from thematic maps. The summary table should provide a suitable structure.	Make links with Key Stage 3 study of the characteristics and distribution of one type of vegetation (tropical rainforest) and its relationship with climate, soil and human activities.

Learning Activities/Tasks	**Time**	**Teaching Strategies/Actions**
Identifying links with previous learning. Recap KS3 study of tropical rainforests.	5	**Introduction** What are the differences between the amount and types of vegetation in the Arctic, in a tropical rainforest and a desert? What are the reasons for these differences?

Learning Activities/Tasks	**Time**	**Teaching Strategies/Actions**
Use atlas maps to mark the following lines of latitude on to a world map outline: Equator (0) Arctic Circle (66.5 N) Antarctic Circle (66.5 S) Tropic of Cancer (23.5 N) Tropic of Capricorn (23.5 S) Then label the climatic zones – Tropical, Temperature, Polar. Identify characteristics of natural ecosystems shown in Disney clips.	15	Explain activity 1 – Identifying global climatic zones (monitor the pace of the activity and check atlas skills).

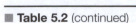

■ **Table 5.2** (continued)

Learning Activities/Tasks	Time	Teaching Strategies/Actions
Find the 20 E longitude meridian and mark it on the map. Also mark the following points along this line – 5 N, 10 N, 23.5 N, 40 N, 52 N, 65 N, 70 N. Use climate and vegetation maps to complete the summary table.	10	Show video clips from Disney films and ask pupils to identify the characteristic features of the characteristics shown: • Jungle Book • Tropical rainforest • Aladdin • Desert • Lion King • Savanna grassland • Bambi • Temperate woodland Check the location of the longitude meridian and places marked.
	25	Use one example to illustrate how the table should be completed. Ask pupils to search out and collect pictures of different ecosystems (and vegetation) for the display in the next lesson. Debrief the lesson's objectives using 'Assessment for Learning' matching activity in groups.

Assessment Opportunities, Objectives and Evidence

Use of atlas skills and interpretation of thematic maps. Written homework after next lesson to assess pupils' understanding of the relationship between climate and vegetation and their recall of knowledge about the characteristic features of global ecosystems.

Evaluation of Learning	Evaluation of Teaching
Good recall of previous learning from KS3 about climate and vegetation in tropical rainforests. All the pupils managed to identify the climatic zones successfully. Most of the weaker pupils experienced difficulties in interpreting the thematic atlas maps when completing the summary table. The table helped to structure learning successfully.	Timing of the initial activities was about right but the table took longer to complete mainly because of the difficulties in interpreting climatic maps. The use of the Disney clips was extremely effective – interesting and motivating – the characteristics were clear. Perhaps use Powerpoint slides of the world map and ecosystems table to demonstrate and support explanation of tasks.

Action Points

Complete the Global Ecosystems table and name the ecosystems. Examine the influence of climate upon vegetation using examples from the table. Begin work on displays of global ecosystems showing climatic data, vegetation and world distributions.

The learning objectives are related to specific subject content, determined by the department's scheme of work. This subject content should be indicated in the lesson plan. The lesson may also include cross-curricular themes (discussed elsewhere in this book), or other subjects; see Table 5.2.

Your plan should contain information about the context of the lesson. If you are to be observed teaching this lesson, such information will be particularly useful to the observer, especially if they are unfamiliar with the school or with this class. It may include details about the composition of the group (its size, gender balance and ability range) as well as background information about prior learning and action points brought forward from previous lessons.

Many teachers include a section in their lesson plans where they identify specific issues relating to differentiation. This may contain information about certain pupils and their learning needs as well as an indication of the strategies to be used to support these pupils. For example, when there are particularly able pupils in a class, 'enrichment' or 'extension' activities may be needed to provide them with appropriate challenges in their learning. Where Learning Support Assistants or teachers are available, you should give some consideration to their role in the lesson so that the valuable support they provide can be used effectively.

Planning and preparation are closely related. Resources should be identified and how they are to be organised. Consideration should be given to the preparation of the room (layout, location of equipment, diagrams/information/questions on the black/white board) and resources organised. Sometimes you will need to prepare your own resources to support the activities that you have planned for the lesson. There is an extensive range of resources that geography teachers can use or develop to provide a rich variety of stimulating learning experiences for their pupils (see Chapter 6).

Although the subject content to be covered with particular age groups is determined by the National Curriculum Programme of Study or an examination syllabus, how it is taught still rests with the teacher. When planning for learning, teachers can select from a wide variety of activities and strategies (see Chapters 2 and 4).

The activities selected for a lesson depend upon the teacher's beliefs about and understanding of the relative effectiveness of different activities for the type of pupil learning intended (Kyriacou, 1991). Responding to the learning needs of particular pupils and groups of pupils is a major consideration. Your ability to do this will improve with time and experience as you develop your understanding of pupils' learning and of the relative effectiveness of different teaching strategies and learning activities. The development of this 'professional' knowledge and understanding is a fundamental requirement of the 'student-centred' approach to teaching and learning that we are advocating in this book. Activity 5.2 is designed to help you plan learning activities to achieve particular learning objectives or outcomes.

As well as helping pupils to achieve the learning objectives that we have intended, another concern is the desire to elicit and sustain pupils' attention, interest and motivation. It is desirable for lessons to include a variety of activities. For example, in the lesson shown in Table 5.2 the teacher could just describe the location and features of the different global environments. However, even if they were highly motivated, the pupils would find it hard to concentrate and to retain information from the teacher's exposition for a long period.

This variety will also be evident in the different phases of the lesson. In the lessons shown in Tables 5.2 and 5.3, the teacher uses different strategies in the initial phase to set the scene. In the lesson in Table 5.3, the aim is to recap briefly the ideas about land use in towns and thus to establish links with learning in previous lessons. The images of different types of houses and associated questioning helps the teacher assess what the pupils already know and establish the descriptive vocabulary to be used in the main activity of the lesson.

The initial phase of the lesson in Table 5.2 is designed to elicit pupils' interest in a stimulating way. The teacher uses questioning to draw pupils' attention to the key features of the environments and highlight links with previous learning about one of the ecosystems studied in Key Stage 3. This also helps the teacher emphasise the relevant vocabulary used to describe the ecosystems being investigated in the main activity of the lesson. During or towards the end of this initial 'scene setting' phase would probably be an appropriate time for the teacher to share the objectives of the lesson with the pupils.

▪ **Table 5.3** Lesson planning framework: Year 9, Investigating housing areas in towns and cities

Date_____ Lesson_____ Time_____ Class____Yr 9____ Room_____

Title of Lesson Investigating housing areas in towns and cities

Lesson's Aims
To examine the characteristics of different housing areas within a city using a variety of different sources of data.

Learning Objectives
- To understand how different residential areas can be compared in terms of the age, design/type, density, quality, cost and revenue of housing.
- To know the main differences between the housing characteristics of a range of contrasting residential areas in a city.
- To interpret and record data from a range of different sources including maps, photographs, graphs and census information.
- To develop an awareness of different housing conditions and appreciate what it may be like to live in different residential environments.

Subject Content: National Curriculum/Syllabus Links	**Cross-Curricular Links/Themes/Competences**
The pattern of land use in a city (Space and Place, Diversity). Knowing where things are located, why they are there, the patterns and distributions created, how and why these are changing. Enquiry – present and analyse information; interpret place and space. Graphicacy – construct maps, use graphical techniques to present evidence.	Reinforcement of work in maths – drawing graphs and pie charts. Interpretation of data. (Handling data – Maths PoS)

Resources	**Advance Preparation (Room and Equipment)**
Resource packs containing information about different housing areas in the city (map extracts, census data, photos, house price adverts), Powerpoint presentation (housing types and residential areas). Data record sheets. Sheet with table for recording housing characteristics. Music – Madness 'Our House'.	Powerpoint presentation, data projector and sound/CD player.

Differentiation	**Action Points**
Sheets with graph and chart outlines, pie chart dividers (%) and use of ICT. Pupil groupings.	Establish link with previous lessons about land use in towns and cities and later fieldwork visits.

Learning Activities/Tasks	**Time**	**Teaching Strategies/Actions**
Look at slides and note contrasts between different types of housing in different residential environments.	10	Introduce the focus of the lesson: How can we describe contrasts between different residential environments? Show slides of different houses and residential areas with background music to focus. Outline the learning objectives for the lesson.

■ **Table 5.3** (continued)

Learning Activities/Tasks	Time	Teaching Strategies/Actions
Pupils work in groups of 4. Each pupil studies a different residential environment and completes a summary sheet for that area.	25	Distribute resource materials and sheets. Explain tasks and materials. • Interpretation of maps and photos • Use of data to draw graphs and pie charts. Define terms: • tenure • amenities • density and layout. Monitor progress and check understanding through questioning. Explain summary table and map.
Each pupil summarises the characteristics of the residential area of the rest of their group. Pupils use this information to complete a summary table listing the characteristics of different residential areas in the city.	15	Introduce house price data.
	10	Issue base maps and explain homework activity: • locate the different residential areas • add labels to summarise the characteristic of these areas. Outline links with next lesson (who lives where and why?) and with fieldwork investigation.

Assessment Opportunities, Objectives and Evidence
Skills – Focus on pupils' ability to use Census data and to use appropriate graphical techniques to present data.
Knowledge and understanding – patterns of residential location will contribute to assessment activity on settlement.

Evaluation of Learning	Evaluation of Teaching
The main ideas did not appear to be difficult for any of the pupils to grasp. They were able to relate these to their own knowledge and experience. The pupils did not appear to have any problems interpreting the maps and photographic evidence. The census data did not reveal particularly significant differences in household space and amenities.	The timing was about right. Most pupils were able to complete their summary of one area in 20 mins. The summary table took longer. The introduction with the presentation got the lesson off to a 'sharper' start and the music did help to focus pupils' concentration. The differentiated sheets with graph outlines were effective and reduced the time needed to present the data. My conclusion was a bit rushed but I did manage to ensure that the key points of the lesson were emphasised.

Action Points
Recap/check understanding of key terms particularly tenure, amenities and density/layout. Next lesson will examine the reasons for patterns of residential location 'who lives where and why?' – social class, family status, ethnic origin.

Activity 5.2 **Planning learning activities and teaching strategies**

When you have identified the learning objectives for a lesson you need to make decisions about *how* you are going to teach and *how* the pupils are going to learn. The nature of the teaching strategy and the learning activity, and the relationship between these two components of a lesson, need to be planned carefully.

A lesson contains discrete 'episodes' or 'scenes' based around individual activities and strategies. The aim of this activity is to help you to plan coherent 'episodes'. The following structure should help you with this planning activity and illustrate the links between these components of a lesson plan.

Learning Objectives
Learning Activity
Timing
Teaching Strategy
Learning Outcome/ Assessment Opportunity
Resources

Indicate what you want the pupils to 'know, understand and/or be able to do (skills)'. Write objectives as 'can do' statements.
Describe what the pupils will do to achieve the planned learning objectives.
Include learning objectives.
Indicate how long this 'episode'/ 'scene' will take. Monitor the pace of the activity.
What will you do to introduce or guide the activity?
What will you need to explain or demonstrate?
How will you manage, monitor and conclude the activity? Key words can be used as prompts to guide you.
What are the likely outcomes of the activity (written, oral, etc.)?
These will help you to judge whether the learning objectives have been achieved.
What materials will be needed for this activity?

Use a similar framework to plan individual activities that would form coherent 'episodes' in a lesson to achieve the following objectives.

1   To help pupils to understand the relationship between the global distribution of earthquakes and the location of the boundaries of crustal plates.
2   To introduce pupils to images about lifestyles and culture in Japan to help to develop a 'sense of place'.
3   To show variations in the 'quality of life' in a local town or city.
4   To help pupils to understand the relationship between relief and rainfall in Britain.
5   To show pupils how to draw a climate graph.
6   To help pupils to understand and be able to use a 6–figure grid reference.
7   To help pupils to understand how to devise enquiry questions in geography (for example, about a place).
8   To challenge common misconceptions about 'developments' and/or 'aid'.
9   To show pupils how to draw an annotated field sketch or photo sketch of a landform or landscape feature.

Discussion: Where possible you could negotiate with your mentor/tutor for an opportunity to use one of these activities with a group of pupils within a class. Alternatively you could plan another activity selected by your mentor/tutor. This could be a valuable first step in your induction as a teacher as it would provide you with an opportunity to plan, teach and evaluate an activity. Focus your evaluation on the relationship between learning objectives, teaching strategies and learning activities.

■ Did the activity help the pupils to achieve the objectives that you had planned?
■ Were there any 'unintended' learning outcomes?
■ How did the pupils tackle the activity (i.e. what learning processes were evident)?
■ How effective was the 'teaching strategy' (i.e. your explanations, demonstration and other interventions)?
■ How did you manage, monitor and conclude the activity?
■ Were the resources that you used appropriate for the activity, and for all the pupils?
■ How long did the activity take? What did you notice about the pace of the learning that took place?

These questions help you to evaluate your teaching, one aspect of becoming an effective, reflective teacher.

In both lessons (Tables 5.2 and 5.3) the teacher moves on to introduce the main learning activity by familiarising the pupils with the resources that they will be using and helping them to understand the task. This involves working through an example with the pupils to show how to extract relevant information from the different sources.

The lesson about urban residential areas (Table 5.3) has probably required more preparation for the teacher, as relevant census data and other information has been selected and presented on resource cards for use by the pupils. In both cases, the teachers prepared frameworks within which the pupils would record the relevant information that they have extracted. This helps the teacher provide a structure for the pupils' learning and a summary record of the outcomes.

In the final phase, the teacher planned to review the learning that has taken place during the lesson. This may involve some reinforcement of the key ideas and vocabulary as well as comments about the skills that have been developed. Links with future learning (i.e. why and how the learning in this lesson may contribute to learning in subsequent lessons) can be established. It is also useful to allow some flexibility in the timing for each phase to enable problems that arise to be addressed.

Although it is not essential that every lesson follows this general pattern, it may be helpful to have it clearly in mind when planning lessons in the early part of your practical teaching experience. Sometimes it is necessary for pupils to work over extended periods of time to develop knowledge, understanding and skills in greater depth. However, what is certain is that in order to plan successful geography lessons, you need to identify and plan distinct phases in these lessons. These phases are sometimes referred to as lesson 'episodes' or 'scenes' and they should outline both what you, the teacher, will be doing (teaching strategy) and the nature of the learning activity for the pupils.

It is also important for these different 'episodes' to be in a coherent order. For a lesson to be effective it needs to be well structured to maintain its challenge, pace and motivation:

> Pupils usually respond well and learn best in lessons which have clear targets and a carefully defined structure which enables them to achieve the targets at a pace and depth appropriate to their abilities.

> (Davidson, 1996: 13)

Although located towards the end of our lesson planning framework, *assessment* should not be an afterthought. It is an integral part of the process of successful teaching and learning. While planning your lessons, you will become aware of opportunities to monitor pupils' progress in their learning. The work produced as outcomes of the learning activities could be used to assess the development of pupils' knowledge, understanding, skills and values. However, there will be a number of informal opportunities during lessons to monitor their progress. Sometimes this may be through your questioning. You will also gain a lot of information about pupils' progress through observation of their learning experiences.

It is helpful to indicate where these opportunities might arise when you are planning a lesson. Alternatively, you may become aware of such opportunities during a lesson. As you are learning to teach, it would be useful to record these ideas in your plan which, as mentioned earlier, is a record of the learning that has taken place as well as what has been planned.

In this sense, lesson plans are also a record of your learning as a teacher of geography. The lesson *evaluation* is therefore a vital component of any lesson plan. It will be based largely upon your reflections on the lesson and as such it will be rather subjective, as these reflections depend on your perception of what happened during the session. Sometimes this evaluation can be informed by a discussion with a mentor or observer after the lesson.

During your early experiences of teaching, your reflections will focus largely on issues relating to classroom management. However, if you are to develop as a geography teacher, you will need to focus your evaluation on the teaching strategies and learning activities. How effective were the strategies used? Did the activities planned help the pupils to achieve the intended learning outcomes or objectives? What showed me that this was the case? How clear and effective was my exposition, presentation or demonstration of a skill? What improvements could I make to the planning, preparation or delivery of this lesson or activities and strategies within the lesson? These considerations could help you to establish targets for your future teaching and as such they form a crucial part of your professional development as a teacher.

So far we have considered each of the different aspects of planning a geography lesson in some depth. It should be clear from this discussion that there are important links between the different aspects of the planning process. For example, there should be a close relationship between the learning activities, the intended learning objectives and the learning needs of the pupils. These will in turn influence the preparation of resources, although in many cases, the available resources will determine what is possible in terms of teaching strategies and learning activities.

Activity 5.3 Observing lessons and identifying planning issues

This activity examines the relationship between planning and what happens in a classroom. The assumption is, as stated earlier, that effective planning brings about successful learning. To this end, one of our principal tasks as a teacher is to design learning activities and teaching strategies that help pupils to achieve various intended learning outcomes.

A useful task to undertake when observing an experienced teacher teaching a lesson is to try to develop a written plan for the lesson that you are observing. Familiarise yourself with the main features of a lesson plan that are described earlier in this chapter and then use a copy of the lesson planning framework (Figure 5.1) to record the features of the lesson that you are observing.

Try to focus on the following aspects:

■ Is it possible to identify distinctive episodes in the lesson? How long do they last?

■ What are the learning activities and teaching strategies that comprise these episodes?

■ How does the teacher manage, monitor and conclude these lesson episodes? (Where appropriate, write down any key words that would help you as prompts if you were to teach this lesson.)

■ Is it possible to identify a coherent structure to the sequence of these lesson episodes?

■ What learning processes are evident in the lesson (i.e. what skills will the pupils be missing)? Do you focus on what they learn or what they did not learn?

■ What are the learning objectives for this lesson? How are they revealed? (These learning objectives may be shared with the pupils at the start of the lesson, during activities, or by way of conclusion. Alternatively, they may be self-evident in the activities and strategies that you observe.)

■ How does the teacher know whether these learning objectives have been achieved during the lesson?

■ Are any links made with previous or future learning?

What strategies are used to support differentiation in the lesson? (These may include specific resources, tasks or activities, the use of a learning support assistant, feedback or support from the teacher, and variations in the pace and depth of learning.)

Discussion: Discuss this plan and what you have observed with the teacher of the lesson or your tutor. The discussion should focus on the relationship between planning and what happens in the classroom (teaching and learning). The questions indicated above may be helpful to this discussion. Record any reflections the teacher shares with you on the success of the lesson in the lesson evaluation section of the plan!

Boardman (1986) represented these interrelationships and interactions between different elements in the planning process in an interactive planning model (Figure 5.1). This objectives-led approach has had a significant influence on planning in geography education for over thirty years. The use of objectives in planning can help to provide teaching and learning with a real sense of purpose as assessment can be used to find out whether these objectives have been achieved. However, such an approach can be criticised for focusing too much attention on the final and predetermined outcomes of learning (Roberts, 1997).

It is unlikely that all the outcomes of learning can be predetermined. There is often learning taking place in a classroom which is unpredictable and unintended. Also, if we recognise that individual pupils have different abilities and learning needs, it is difficult to determine common objectives for all pupils.

These criticisms and a belief in the interest value of the learning process led to the development of an alternative model of planning. The influence of this process model in geography can be seen in the development of the enquiry approach to learning. The enquiry approach emphasises the importance of both teachers and pupils asking questions. The pupils then need to be actively involved in the learning processes necessary to answer these questions (Rawling, 2007; Naish *et al.,* 1987).

This has led to the use of key questions at an early stage in planning in geography. Slater (1982) identified the important role of key questions in guiding the direction and selection of teaching and learning strategies and resources. An enquiry-based approach to learning in geography involves following a meaningful sequence of enquiry questions when investigating any geographical issue or problem (Table 5.4). This route for enquiry provides a framework within which teachers can organise learning 'pathways' in geography.

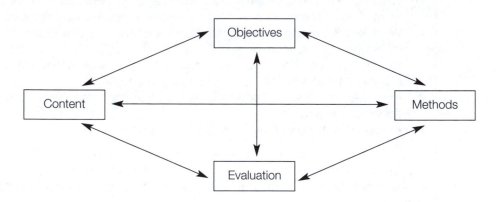

■ **Figure 5.1** An interactive planning model
Source: Boardman, 1986: 27–40

Key questions can be particularly useful when planning lessons where it is difficult to predetermine precise learning outcomes or objectives. For example, in the lesson shown in Table 5.5, the nature of the learning experience is as important as any knowledge and understanding gained about tropical rainforest environments. Key questions can also help to relate individual lessons to particular stages of the enquiry process. The example of the A-level lesson about 'urban futures' (Table 5.6) involves prediction as well as 'personal evaluation and judgement'.

■ **Table 5.4** The Enquiry Sequence: Key questions and key concepts

Example route for enquiry	Same enquiry questions	Key concepts (examples from PoS and others)	Key processes/skills (examples from PoS)
What? (observation and perception)	What's happening? What is the topic or place? What do I observe? How do I see it? How do others see it? What is the main question, problem or issue?	**Space, Place, Cultural Diversity** Image, identity, perception, conflict	Ask geographical questions; identify bias and opinion; undertake fieldwork; topical relevant issues, geography in the news
What and where? (definition and description)	What's it all about? What is the background? What is taking place? How can the issue/ question or place be defined, categorised and described? What is an appropriate sequence of enquiry for this investigation?	**Place, Space, Scale, Cultural Diversity** People, environment, ecosystem, region, nation, location, distribution, pattern	Ask geographical questions; identify bias and opinion; plan geographical enquiries; collect, record and display evidence via fieldwork and secondary sources; construct maps and plans; communicate in talk and writing
How and why? (analysis and explanation)	How did it happen? What gave rise to this situation? Why is this place like it is? What processes are involved? What people/ environment interactions are occurring? How are features/events interdependent? What theories/models might help explain this?	**Process (physical and human) Environmental Interaction, Scale, Interdependence** Time, change, cause/effect, development, globalisation	Analyse and evaluate evidence; present findings and draw conclusions; think creatively, find new ways of applying geographical skills and understandings to create new interpretations; fieldwork, GIS, using a range of resources including ICT; make link between geography and other subjects; solve problems and make decisions; develop analytical skills/ creativity; communicate in talk and writing
What might happen? What impact? What decision? (evaluation, prediction and decision-making)	What are the impacts and consequences? Who will gain? Who will lose? What might happen in the future? Which human and physical processes will be in operation? What trends can be identified? What will be the effect? What are the alternative viewpoints and solutions? What decision is likely to be made – with what consequences and impacts?	**Environmental Interaction and Sustainable Development, Interdependence, Cultural Diversity, Place** Environmental impact, environmental quality, quality of life, social justice, equality, futures, welfare	
What do I think? Why? What will I do next? (personal evaluation evaluation and response)	How do I weigh up the alternatives? What is my view? Who do I think this and how do I justify my decision? How should I respond? Should I take some action? How will I go about this? What will I do next?	**Sustainable Development, Cultural Diversity, Interdependence, Scale** Judgement, commitment, empathy, morality, quality of life, futures	Analyse and evaluate; ask questions; think constructively and creatively; make decisions; communicate in talk and writing; participate in informed, responsible action

Source: Rawling, 2007: 44

■ **Table 5.5** Lesson planning framework: Investigating tropical rainforest environments

Date_____ Lesson_____ Time_____ Class_____ Room_____

Title of Lesson Tropical Rainforest Environments

Lesson's Aims
To develop pupils' understanding and appreciation of the nature of tropical rainforest environments. To provide a stimulus for creative writing in geography.

Learning Objectives
- To know some of the main features of the ecology of tropical rainforests (identifying some of the plants and animals).
- To understand some of the inter-relationships between different components of rainforest ecosystems.
- To develop a 'feel' for rainforest environments using a range of senses.
- To value the ecological wealth of rainforest environments.
- To write creatively.

Subject Content: National Curriculum/Syllabus Links	Cross-Curricular Links/Themes/Competences
The characteristics of one type of vegetation and its relationship with climate and soil. Key concepts. Place and Space, Environmental Interaction, Physical processes, Geographical imaginations.	Environmental education (**about** the environment). Development of language and literacy. English – creative writing, speaking and listening.

Resources	Advance Preparation (Room and Equipment)
Video clips – life in a rainforest, CD player and data projector; CD – sounds of the rainforest; Powerpoint presentation – Tropical rainforests. Extracts from texts about tropical rainforest environments (poetry and stories).	Set up TV/video, Powerpoint presentation and CD player. Pull down blinds to darken room. Perhaps boil a couple of kettles for a few minutes before the lesson to create a damp feeling in the room.

Differentiation		Action Points
Learning Activities/Tasks	**Time**	**Teaching Strategies/Actions**
(Timings need to be flexible for these activities)	5	Tight management at the start of the lesson – control entrance of pupils into the room and get them settled quickly.
Pupils listen to the sounds of a rainforest.	5	'What would it feel like in a tropical rainforest environment?' Explain the need for pupils to use their imagination to respond creatively to a range of stimuli. Ask pupils to close their eyes and settle. Play an extract from the 'Sounds of the rainforest' tape.
Listen to the commentary describing the features and components of rainforest environments (vegetation, wildlife and climate).	7	Play the first part of the 'Life in the rainforest' video with commentary about the features and components/layers of tropical rainforest environments.
	5	Read extracts (poetry and narrative) about rainforest environments.
Brainstorm – pupils identify key terms and descriptive words from various stimuli.	10–15	Divide blackboard into 3 sections (climate, wildlife, vegetation). Initiate 'brainstorm' – key terms and words used to describe features of the ecology.

■ **Table 5.5** (continued)

Learning Activities/Tasks	Time	Teaching Strategies/Actions
What would it feel like in a rainforest environment (visual images in . presentation) If time, pupils can watch the first part of the video 'Life in the rainforest' to reinforce learning.	10	Use questioning to explore pupils' feelings about rainforest environments (also use slides). Check understanding of relationship between climate and vegetation. Explain and plan homework task – a piece of writing about the ecological wealth of tropical rainforests – poetry or narrative.

Assessment Opportunities, Objectives and Evidence
Attitudes and values – awareness/appreciation of rainforest ecology. Understanding of rainforest ecology. Creative writing (poetry or narrative) from the homework could be used for English NC assessment.

Evaluation of Learning	Evaluation of Teaching
The pupils responded very positively and concentrated hard throughout (I had anticipated potential for silly behaviour). The activity seemed to be very effective for developing the use of language (vocabulary/descriptive words) – I was surprised how much they could remember.	This seemed to be a very successful lesson – particularly for generating interest and motivation. The variety of resources used was a key factor. The brainstorm was very lively and enjoyable. Dividing up the board into climate, vegetation and wildlife certainly helped to structure the responses.

Action Points
Inform the English Department about the activity. Next lesson – check understanding of key terms, share some of the homework outcomes. Develop understanding of rainforest ecology further – structure components and interrelationships.

The impact of the enquiry process can be seen in the revised Geography National Curriculum (QCA, 2007; Rawling, 2007) with the requirement that 'Pupils should be given opportunities to undertake studies that focus on geographical questions such as What/where is it? What is it like? How did it get like this? How and why is it changing? What are the implications?' There is also the implication that pupils should be involved in the processes needed to answer these questions rather than being provided with the answers by the teacher.

Activity 5.4 **Devising key questions in geography**

For this activity, you need to find a small number of articles about geography issues from newspapers or geographical journals.

■ Identify the geographical issues that are reported in these articles.
■ Write a series of key questions that could be used to help pupils to investigate these geographical issues. Try to put these questions into a logical sequence so that they could be used to structure an enquiry for pupils.
■ Identify some key ideas and geographical concepts that could be linked to these key questions. These ideas and concepts could be the likely learning outcomes of a geographical enquiry that focuses on the questions that you have devised.

▪ **Table 5.6** Lesson planning framework: Year 13, Urban features and sustainable cities

Date_____ Lesson_____ Time_____ Class_____ Room_____

Title of Lesson Urban futures and sustainable cities

Lesson's Aims
To examine possible futures for large urban areas. To consider whether ideas about 'sustainable development' can be applied to urban planning.

Learning Objectives
• How can ideas about 'sustainability' be applied to the study of urban areas and urban planning?
• What scenarios have been identified for the future development of cities?
• What consequences could these 'urban futures' have for the environment and for the quality of life?

Subject Content: National Curriculum/Syllabus Links	Cross-Curricular Links/Themes/Competences
Sustainable cities – urban planning for sustainable futures.	Environmental education (**about** and **for** the environment). Development of critical thinking skills.

Resources	Advance Preparation (Room and Equipment)
Video. Resource sheet: Sustainable Urban Futures. Extracts from – The Gaia Atlas of Cities: New Directions for Sustainable urban living.	Resource packs – extracts from different sources. Materials. Television/Video.

Differentiation	Action Points
	Pupils have previously watched a video discussion about possible futures for British cities – The Regeneration Game.

Learning Activities/Tasks	Time	Teaching Strategies/Actions
Summarise the possible futures discussed in previous lesson.	10	Establish links with previous learning about possible urban futures. Check understanding of 'sustainable development'.
Watch extracts of the video 'Metropolis' about the 'metabolism' of London.	25	How can ideas about 'Sustainable development' be applied to urban planning? Discuss ideas in relation to London. Emphasise different aspects: • environmental • economic • social • cultural.
Pupils begin work on a 'charter' of principles to guide planning for 'Sustainable' cities in Britain. Working in pairs to produce a poster display, written report and short presentation.	15	

Assessment Opportunities, Objectives and Evidence
Understanding of concepts relating to sustainability. Development and application of critical thinking skills. Ability to evaluate evidence and present a coherent argument.

■ **Table 5.6** (continued)

Evaluation of Learning	Evaluation of Teaching
The pupils were able to apply ideas about urban futures from the previous lesson surprisingly well. They were able to apply ideas about environmental and economic sustainability but several struggled to grasp ideas about social and cultural sustainability.	Initially I thought that the nature of the two videos might be too heavy (i.e. the amount of commentary/discussion). However, the pupils appeared to be stimulated by the discussion of future scenarios and the open nature of the enquiry. Managing the discussion – choosing appropriate questions and responding to pupils' contributions was challenging.

Action Points
Poster displays and written report to be presented in two weeks. Perhaps invite Mrs Rees (local planning department) to hear and respond to presentations. Follow up by relating outcomes to exam questions.

Further evidence of this can be seen in relation to the development of geographical enquiry outlined in the Programme of Study below.

Pupils should be able to:

- ask geographical questions, thinking critically, constructively and creatively collect, record and display information
- identify bias, opinion and abuse of evidence in sources when investigating issues
- analyse and evaluate evidence, presenting findings to draw and justify conclusions
- find creative ways of using and applying geographical skills and understanding to create new interpretations of place and space
- plan geographical enquiries suggesting appropriate sequences of investigation
- solve problems and make decisions to develop analytical skills and creative thinking about geographical issues.

(QCA, 2007)

The enquiry process is also reflected in Level Descriptions used to describe pupils' attainment in geography (see Chapter 10). For example, at Level 4 pupils 'suggest suitable geographical questions, and use a range of geographical skills to help them investigate places and envrironments' whereas at Level 6 they are able to draw upon their 'knowledge and understanding to suggest relevant geographical questions and issues and appropriate sequences of investigation'.

The enquiry process has also influenced the development of a number of GCSE and GCE AS/A2–level examination syllabuses. Enquiry questions are often used to provide a structure for the content of such syllabuses. Different examination styles, such as the use of decision-making papers, can further encourage the development of enquiry approaches. Such papers assess pupils' ability to apply their geographical knowledge and understanding to the analysis of particular geographical issues and questions. Pupils can also be actively engaged in the enquiry process through the individual coursework investigations required by some external examinations.

The influence of the enquiry process does, therefore, have important implications for the planning of teaching and learning in geography. Roberts (1997) suggests that there are a number of important questions that need to be considered by teachers when applying a process model of planning (Box 5.1). It is useful to reflect on these issues and questions when using enquiry approaches to plan lessons.

■ What key questions need to be asked to enable pupils to engage with this area of subject-matter?

■ Which questions need to be asked initially by the teacher?

■ How can teaching and learning activities be devised to encourage pupils to ask their own questions?

■ What resources are needed to enable pupils to answer these questions?

■ How are these resources collected and selected?

■ What geographical techniques and procedures could be used to answer these questions?

■ How can these techniques and procedures be incorporated into pupil activities?

■ Which parts of the enquiry process will pupils be engaged in during the course unit and which during individual lessons?

■ How can the processes in which the pupils are engaged be evaluated during and after lessons?

■ How can what has been learned from the evaluation be built into subsequent lessons and units of work?

■ **Box 5.1** Applying the process model of curriculum planning: some questions to answer
Source: Roberts, 1997: 45-6

PLANNING SCHEMES OF WORK

> The first target is clearly to become proficient at leading a successful lesson. However, in time it becomes clear that the real problem is not the individual session but the run of lessons over a month or half a term. This is what creates the pupils' learning experiences.
>
> (Marland, 1993: 141)

Planning successful geography lessons is in itself a demanding activity given the wide range of considerations to be taken into account. However, pupils' knowledge, understanding, skills, attitudes and values in relation to geography will need to be developed over a longer period of time. It is, therefore, *the scheme of work* which provides the rationale and framework for developing pupils' educational experiences in geography.

The term *scheme of work* identifies the educational goals of a course and a strategy for achieving them. It outlines the subject content to be covered, the resources available, and the teaching strategies and learning activities that determine the nature of this educational experience for the pupils. Schemes of work have a key role to play in ensuring *continuity* and *progression* in pupils' learning in geography. As such, they represent longer term plans for pupils' learning (see Boxes 5.2 and 5.3).

Above all, a scheme of work should be a planning tool. It should be a working document summarising teachers' thinking about a course, providing a structure and offering guidelines for more detailed lesson planning. It should be a flexible plan and not one that is followed rigidly. All schemes of work should be reviewed and evaluated so that improvements can be made where necessary.

How should schemes of work be planned?

Returning to the earlier discussion about the use of objectives and questions in planning for learning in geography, it is clear that both have a role to play in the design of schemes of work:

> This may mean using different models for different units of work, having some units emphasising questioning and the enquiry process, and others concentrating on the product of learning. It may mean modifying the process model so that enquiry is rarely open-ended but is to a large extent controlled by the teacher. It may mean attempting to define objectives which would assess, formatively, a pupil's ability to engage in the enquiry process.
>
> (Roberts, 1997: 47)

A useful way of planning a scheme of work is to develop a planning grid or chart which identifies all the elements that need to be considered (Box 5.2). The goals will provide a clear indication of the overall educational purposes of the course including the aims, which are general statements about the direction of learning intended and the priorities within a course. The learning objectives will show the more specific goals of the course indicating the geographical knowledge, understanding, skills and attitudes through which the aims are realised.

The content should be stated in terms of the places, themes, topics and issues which have been selected for study (Box 5.3). The selection of this content will be influenced by the requirements of the National Curriculum Programme of Study or examination syllabus. The content of specific lessons is indicated in the statement of key ideas or concepts. Key questions arising from these ideas can then be used as a structure for the learning in the lessons. The sequence of these key ideas and questions needs to be planned carefully as it will have a significant influence on the development of progression in learning through this course of study.

Decisions can then be made about the most appropriate learning activities and teaching strategies for the learning intended. A scheme of work should include a range of learning activities and teaching strategies so that the variety of styles of teaching and learning is catered for (see Chapters 2 and 4). It should also take into account the range of pupils' learning needs and abilities, providing an indication of how objectives, strategies, activities and resources will be differentiated. Such differentiation will be influenced by the organisation of teaching groups.

The planning of learning activities and teaching strategies will reveal opportunities for assessing pupils' achievements and progress in geography. Again, the aim is to use a variety of assessment methods so that all pupils have the chance to show what they 'know, understand and can do'. You should try to balance the assessment of knowledge, understanding and skills and match the assessment tasks to the learning objectives. It is also useful to consider the potential outcomes from the learning activities and assessment tasks.

Although a scheme of work may often be produced by an individual teacher, a collaborative approach to planning can be of great value to a geography department. The discussion which accompanies planning can bring assumptions to the surface to be

Year Group _____ Time/Number of lessons _____

TITLE OF UNIT/THEME

SYLLABUS/SUBJECT CONTENT/ PROGRAMME OF STUDY COVERAGE

Indicate the broad areas of subject content that will be covered – places, themes, issues. Identify specific aspects of the syllabus or National Curriculum Programme of Study.

CROSS-CURRICULAR ELEMENTS

Indicate how the unit may contribute to any cross-curricular themes, dimensions or competences. Are there any links with work in other subjects?

KEY QUESTIONS	LEARNING OBJECTIVES Key ideas and generalisations	LEARNING ACTIVITIES TEACHING STRATEGIES	SKILLS	RESOURCES	ASSESSMENT OPPORTUNITIES OBJECTIVES and EVIDENCE
Use key questions to structure the learning objectives and to provide a sequence to the learning through an enquiry approach.	Identify specific learning objectives which relate to syllabus generalisations or the National Curriculum Programme of Study. Aim for a balanced coverage of knowledge, understanding and attitudes/ values.	Use a variety of learning activites and teaching strategies. Activities should be designed to investigate the key questions and develop the learning objectives identified.	Which geographical skills will be developed or used in the learning activities? Also indicate any other general learning skills that may be developed.	Use a variety of resources to support learning and to provide interesting and motivating learning experiences.	Indicate possible learning outcomes that could provide evidence of pupils' attainment in geography. How do these relate to syllabus assessment objectives or National Curriculum level descriptions? Match assessment tasks to learning objectives. Try to balance the assessment of knowledge, understanding, skills and attitudes/values. Be selective – you don't have to assess everything!

■ **Box 5.2** The features of a scheme of work

Themes	This approach uses specific geographical themes (such as settlement, landforms, economic activities, weather and climate) to provide a structure for organising content. Concepts are used to link the content of the curriculum.
Places	Using areas/regions as the focus for the systematic study of geographical themes.
Issues	Often involves the study of people-environment questions and themes. For example: how do human activities modify the atmosphere, both in the short term and in the long term, and with what consequences? These issues usually involve political, economic, social and environmental dimensions.

■ **Box 5.3** The organisation of geographical content in schemes of work

questioned and reflected upon. It can encourage teachers to focus on important curricular issues with consideration being given to criteria for the selection of content, learning activities and teaching strategies. Agreement can be reached about the ways in which pupils' progress and achievements will be monitored, assessed and recorded.

A scheme of work can provide support for other staff who have not been involved in this planning process. This may include non-specialist teachers, learning support teachers and staff responsible for broader curricular policies and decisions within a school. Schemes of work will provide information about the geography curriculum in a school for senior staff and governors as well as advisers and inspectors. They can also facilitate valuable dialogue with teaching colleagues in other schools, for example, as part of the process of cross-phase liaison.

It should be remembered that geography courses make an important contribution to the whole curriculum experience of pupils in a school. Learning and undertaking activities in geography should contribute to achievement of the overall curriculum aims for all young people to become successful learners who progress and achieve, confident individuals who lead safe and healthy lives and responsible citizens who make a positive contribution to society (QCA, 2007). Schemes of work are therefore helpful when reviewing the overall breadth and balance of the curriculum. You should give some attention to cross-curricular links by considering how the work that pupils will be doing in this course of geographical study may fit in with work that pupils may do in other subjects. These can be indicated in your plan together with a recognition of the contribution that the scheme of work could make to the delivery of cross-curricular themes and dimensions (see Table 5.8). Some schools also place particular importance on the development of whole-school curricular issues such as language across the curriculum (see Chapters 2 and 3) and learning skills.

The review of the secondary curriculum has stressed the importance of meeting the Every Child Matters agenda and the need to develop personal, learning and thinking skills. Many new terms, such as curriculum lenses, cross-curricular dimensions, personal learning, thinking skills and functional skills have been introduced. There are also messages from other initiatives such as the National Strategies and bodies such as the Specialist Schools Trust to take into account (see Capel *et al.*, 2005: Unit 7.4 – Pedagogy and practice: The Key Stage 3 and Secondary National Strategy in England). Each of

■ **Table 5.7** Example of a scheme of work about food

Module Title: The Geography of Food	Year 7	
Aims To understand the global distribution of food production To understand the inequalities in trade To understand how climate influences where food is grown To evaluate arguments for and against importing food from other countries To consider food and trade issues from different perspectives	**Language for Learning** Food Miles MEDC LEDC Multicultural Import Export	Trade Climate Distribution

Key understandings learners will develop (key concepts)

Place – Explore different perceptions of places associated with different food (Geographical imaginations). Understand the physical and human characteristics of these places.

Space – Know and understand the global distribution of food production and the implications for people. Understand the interactions between places through trade in food.

Scale – Understand the links between personal decisions about food consumption and the impact on people and places at different scales (local, national, international and global).

Interdependence – Understand the significance of trade (including fair trade) and its impacts on people and places.

Environmental interaction and sustainable development – Consider the sustainability of food production and trade, and the tensions between economic prosperity, social fairness and reducing environmental impacts (food miles).

Cultural understanding and diversity – Explore what food can tell us about the social and cultural diversity of different places.

Key processes learners will draw upon and develop (enquiry skills):

Investigation, through primary and secondary information, of the different ways in which people perceive the links between places and food.

Fieldwork survey of local food outlets.

Graphicacy – Using Google Earth to investigate the location of food production and food miles.

Geographical enquiry – Creative thinking, analysis, evaluation and decision-making about geographical issues (food production and trade).

■ **Table 5.7** Example of a scheme of work about food (continued)

Enquiry	Lesson Objectives	Teaching Activities		Skills	Resources
What?	To understand the links between geography and food To be able to describe what food can tell us about different places and cultures To be able to explain how the social diversity of place is reflected in its food	S	Watch YouTube video of rat eaters. What can you see/hear? How does this make you feel? What are the similarities and differences with our lives? What questions could we ask to get a better understanding of this situation?	**Ask questions** **Draw on own experience** **Work collaboratively** **Collect evidence**	Lesson 1 Flipchart Food questionnaire sheet Writing frame Level criteria Exit cards ***Homework:*** *Survey of local takeaways*
		M	Students complete questionnaire about food they eat/food related to their culture Students move around room to compare answers Complete paragraph about what food can tell us about people and where they live Self-assessment against criteria Students join answers together to develop best composite answer and present to rest of class		
		P	Exit card – Identify as many links between geography and food as you can		

Table 5.7 Example of a scheme of work about food (continued)

Enquiry	Lesson Objectives	Teaching Activities		Skills	Resources
What/ Where?	To be able to describe the global distribution of different crops To be able to explain the distribution of different crops around the world	**S**	K, W, L grid: Students fill out first two columns – Things they already know about the distribution of crops around the world (e.g. what are good growing conditions for crops? Where are these areas found? Where does all our fruit come from?) Feedback and compare answers.	**Use maps, images and text** **Explore real and contemporary contexts**	K, W, L grid (to be handed in as students leave room to review learning) Food Fact/Climate graph cards
		M	**Mapping exercise – 1: Match food fact cards to climate graph cards, Use info from food fact cards and atlases to mark foods to production areas on maps** **Complete Tesco consultant worksheet –** students suggest where in world Mr Tesco should get various foodstuffs from based on growing characteristics		Tesco consultant sheet A3 maps
		P	Select students using lollipop sticks to come and place food card onto correct part of map on board		

■ **Table 5.7** Example of a scheme of work about food (continued)

Enquiry	Lesson Objectives		Teaching Activities	Skills	Resources
How and why?	To be able to describe the different stages of a product's journey	S	Students read statements from slide and guess which food we will be learning about (bananas)	**Use geographical imagination and creativity**	Lesson 3 Flipchart Role cards
	To understand who benefits most from the trade	M	In pairs order cards to describe journey from plantation to plate. Group work – Students allocated role cards. Read and decide how much of 30p they think they deserve through group negotiation. Feedback using mini-whiteboards. Reveal true results. Discuss which stages involve LEDC/MEDC. Who gains most?	**Explore real and contemporary contexts** **Work collaboratively**	Mini whiteboards Red, Amber, Green cards (student diaries) **Homework:** *Diary of a banana worker worksheet*
		P	Odd one out statements. Whole class feedback using Red, Amber, Green cards	**Communicate in talk and writing** **Make a personal response**	
What are the options?	To understand what is meant by fair-trade products	S	Talking heads – Students fill out speech bubbles for two characters to review last lesson. What would this person feel/say/think?	**Make a personal response**	*Fair-trade poster/rap homework sheet*
What do I think	To understand how your actions can affect others around the world	M	Look at cartoon. What is the message? Watch fair-trade video. As students watch they must put the video summary cards into the correct column of table. In groups students golden rules for fair-trade		
		P	As teacher reads statements, students move to agree/disagree corner of room		

■ **Table 5.7** Example of a scheme of work about food (continued)

Enquiry	Lesson Objectives		Teaching Activities	Skills	Resources
What impact/ decision?	To describe and understand what food miles are	S	Global or Local? Students identify which foods from slides are sourced locally and globally	Evaluate quality of information and bias	Lesson 4 Flipchart ICT room
	To evaluate the impacts of importing foods from different countries	M	Using worksheet and Google Earth students investigate location of different products, food miles, views of different groups of people	Use the internet Use GIS (Google Earth)	Food Miles worksheet Post it notes
		P	Opinion Line – should we import our food from abroad		
What do I think? (Assess-ment Task)	To evaluate the arguments for and against importing food from other countries	S	Students identify arguments	Communicate through writing	Passage on A3
	To be able to summarise arguments and express opinions	M	Read through passage of text and highlight arguments for and against importing food from other countries	Explore conventions of text	A3 For and against cards
			Students given either for or against card on A3. As teacher reads through passage, student stands up if they identify argument for or against.		Essay plan worksheet
			Pick out connectives, WOW words and other features that make it a good piece of writing – pairs to fours		
			Talk through essay plan proforma with students. Students fill out before beginning essay		
			Peer assessment		
		P	Self-assessment: Two stars and a wish		

■ Table 5.8 Cross-curricular dimensions

CROSS-CURRICULAR DIMENSIONS (CCD)

'some of the major themes that young people need to explore in order to develop a broad understanding of the world in which they live'

Continuum of capabilities to apply knowledge, skills and understanding in relation to one's self, own community and the wider world

CCD focused on self/immediate → CCD focused beyond self to wider world

	CCD	Geography contribution (some aspects)
	Healthy lifestyle: *How can I make safe and healthy choices about the way I live?*	**Interdependence, Place, Process** Personal geographies; home/school locality; fieldwork/outdoor activity; inequalities in health/wealth
	Community participation: *How can I participate and make a difference?*	**Place, Cultural Diversity, Interdependence** Locality, community, region, cultural diversity and change; UK geography, migration, urban and rural change, EU context, comparisons with other countries in different states of development; fieldwork, outdoor education and work experience, participation in environmental and community projects
	Identity/culture: *What are we? What kind of society do we want to live in?*	
	Creativity/critical understanding: *How can I generate ideas and innovation to improve the quality of life?*	**Interdependence, Scale, Process** Geographical enquiry especially problem-solving, decision-making and creatively applying geographical ideas to places and environments
	Enterprise and entrepreneurship: *How can I make a positive contribution to the economy?*	**Space, Place, Process, Environmental Interaction** Industry and economic activity, consumer/producer; work and leisure activities; trade/aid; decision-making; creative application of geographical ideas
	Technology and media: *Can I believe what I read/see? How does the media affect me and public opinion?*	**Process, Scale, Interdependence** Geographical enquiry with range of resources including ICT and internet; media; Geography in the News; people/environment conflicts; economic, social, political issues
	Sustainable futures: *How can we achieve a more sustainable future? How can I contribute?*	**Environmental Interaction, Sustainable Development, Scale, Process** Society/nature links; climate change; resource use; studies of countries with different development issues
	Global dimension: *How do I make sense of the big issues? How do we share the planet?*	**Interdependence, Scale, Process, Place** Local–global connections and enquiries; causes and consequences of environmental/social change; personal geographies; internet/GIS/maps

Source: Rawling, 2007: 44

these has important messages and geography can, potentially, make a significant contribution to many of these initiatives. Rawling (2007) provides some sensible advice here distinguishing between:

■ Those things which you must address because they are statutory and immediately and directly relevant to you.
■ Those things which are only advisory but represent relevant official advice and so should certainly be considered and checked.
■ Those things which are non-official advice and guidance, some of which may be very helpful and some of which may not, but which can all be used at your own discretion.

Using the enquiry process in planning schemes of work

> Geographical enquiry is about having an inquisitive attitude towards the world and to what we know and understand.
>
> (Roberts, 2006: 97)

Although geographical enquiry is given a prominent place in the geography national curriculum, there is nothing particularly new or geographical about the use of 'enquiry' (Roberts, 2006: 90). It is used in other national curriculum subjects, notably in history, science, mathematics, ICT, design and technology, and in citizenship. What makes an enquiry 'geographical' is *what* is being investigated and *the kinds of questions* being asked (Roberts, 2003 and 2007). For us, its importance as an approach to learning geography can be justified in relation to the purposes of education and in relation to how knowledge is constructed. It emphasises a student-centred approach to learning that involves students in making sense of new information for themselves, in constructing geographical knowledge and thus having the potential to give them more control over their own learning.

Roberts (2003 and 2007) suggests four essential aspects of geographical enquiry that need to be considered when planning both individual lessons and schemes of work: creating a 'need to know'; using data as evidence; making sense of data; and reflecting on learning (see Figure 5.2). Even when the enquiry questions are identified by teachers or by the programme of study, it is important that students can take ownership of these questions to create a 'need to know'. Any geographical enquiry needs data that can be used as evidence in the investigation providing students with opportunities to use and develop a range of enquiry skills. It involves using information collected from this data to develop understanding and construct geographical knowledge. Pupils need to make sense of what they are learning, to see relationships between different bits of information, to make connections and relate it to what they already know. Roberts (2007: 101) also argues that geography teachers need to adopt an approach that encourages critical reflective thinking throughout the enquiry process that enables students to 'go meta' (Bruner, 1996) by helping them to become more aware of their own thought processes.

When investigating an issue, question or problem in geography, a sequence of questions can be used to guide pupil learning through a series of stages, often referred to as the 'route to enquiry' (see Table 5.4, Figures 5.2 and 5.3). This process can be used as a structure when planning a sequence of lessons. Enquiry learning usually refers to situations where pupils are actively enquiring into issues, questions or problems rather than passively receiving information from teachers and other sources. When using the

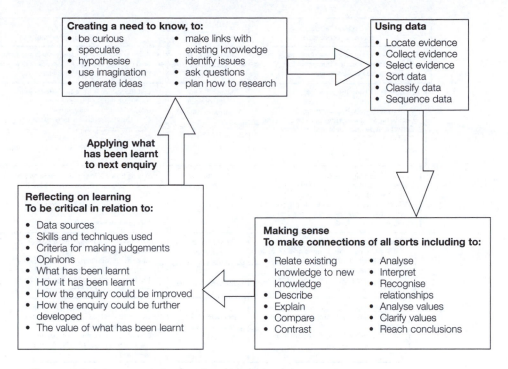

■ **Figure 5.2** A framework for learning through enquiry
Source: Roberts, 2003: 44

enquiry process to plan a scheme of work, key questions and learning activities need to be developed which relate to the different stages of this process.

Any study of people-environment issues, questions or problems will inevitably involve some consideration of the significance of attitudes and values in influencing decisions taken about the environment and in giving rise to conflict between groups and individuals (Naish *et al.,* 1987). The route for geographical enquiry therefore incorporates values enquiry (Figure 5.3). This provides opportunities for values analysis and values clarification. It should also provide a framework within which pupils can develop and justify their own values and responses. Strategies for dealing with values enquiry in the classroom are discussed in Chapter 4.

The Geography National Curriculum PoS is clear that knowledge, understanding and skills should be developed through involving pupils in a process of geographical enquiry so it is important to focus scheme of work planning around enquiry. The PoS also requires that pupils are given opportunities to undertake a range of enquiries from more structured teacher-directed enquiries through to more open-ended and active learning situations so that they can develop a variety of enquiry skills:

> If you want (pupils) to plan their own enquiries and be capable of 'creating new interpretations of place', then they must be given opportunities to plan their own sequences of work and to reflect on existing interpretations of places rather than relying on the teacher for these.

> (Rawling, 2007)

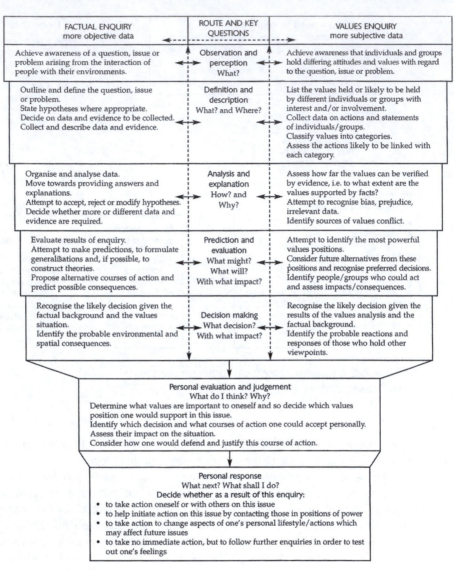

FACTUAL ENQUIRY more objective data	ROUTE AND KEY QUESTIONS	VALUES ENQUIRY more subjective data
Achieve awareness of a question, issue or problem arising from the interaction of people with their environments.	Observation and perception What?	Achieve awareness that individuals and groups hold differing attitudes and values with regard to the question, issue or problem.
Outline and define the question, issue or problem. State hypotheses where appropriate. Decide on data and evidence to be collected. Collect and describe data and evidence.	Definition and description What? and Where?	List the values held or likely to be held by different individuals or groups with interest and/or involvement. Collect data on actions and statements of individuals/groups. Classify values into categories. Assess the actions likely to be linked with each category.
Organise and analyse data. Move towards providing answers and explanations. Attempt to accept, reject or modify hypotheses. Decide whether more or different data and evidence are required.	Analysis and explanation How? and Why?	Assess how far the values can be verified by evidence, i.e. to what extent are the values supported by facts? Attempt to recognise bias, prejudice, irrelevant data. Identify sources of values conflict.
Evaluate results of enquiry. Attempt to make predictions, to formulate generalisations and, if possible, to construct theories. Propose alternative courses of action and predict possible consequences.	Prediction and evaluation What might? What will? With what impact?	Attempt to identify the most powerful values positions. Consider future alternatives from these positions and recognise preferred decisions. Identify people/groups who could act and assess impacts/consequences.
Recognise the likely decision given the factual background and the values situation. Identify the probable environmental and spatial consequences.	Decision making What decision? With what impact?	Recognise the likely decision given the results of the values analysis and the factual background. Identify the probable reactions and responses of those who hold other viewpoints.

Personal evaluation and judgement
What do I think? Why?
Determine what values are important to oneself and so decide which values position one would support in this issue.
Identify which decision and what courses of action one could accept personally.
Assess their impact on the situation.
Consider how one would defend and justify this course of action.

Personal response
What next? What shall I do?
Decide whether as a result of this enquiry:
- to take action oneself or with others on this issue
- to help initiate action on this issue by contacting those in positions of power
- to take action to change aspects of one's personal lifestyle/actions which may affect future issues
- to take no immediate action, but to follow further enquiries in order to test out one's feelings

■ **Figure 5.3** The route for geographical enquiry
Source: Rawling, 2007

Developing a 'sense of place'

Enquiry can provide the most appropriate vehicle through which to develop a sense of place for pupils:

> Through enquiry, pupils can contextualise issues and begin to see the interrelationships of places. They can start to make sense of some of the processes involved in both the human and physical elements of the subject, thereby increasing their knowledge and understanding of geography.
>
> (Battersby, 1995: 21)

An enquiry-based approach to the study of places would consider the following fundamental questions:

- What is this place?
- Where is it?
- What is this place like?
- How did it get like this?
- How is this place linked to other places?
- How is this place changing?
- What do local people feel about the changes?
- What would it be like to live in or to visit this place?

Place is one of geography's fundamental key concepts and pupils' understanding of 'place' will develop progressively through their study of a range of simpler ideas in a variety of contexts. Every place has a particular location and a unique set of physical and human characteristics. Furthermore, the same place can be represented differently. Places are dynamic and subject to constant change. What we think about places is both shaped by, and shapes, our 'geographical imagination' (Lambert, 2007: 9).

There are a number of smaller concepts that sit beneath the big idea of place. These include, for example, settlement, population, location, landscape, site. There are some even smaller, more concrete, concepts that lie underneath these, such as house type, shop, street. In addition, there are some fairly generic, but useful concepts that can be used, such as comparison, change and futures.

When designing a scheme of work, teachers select from a range of geographical content – expressed by a range of smaller concepts – deemed to be worthwhile, relevant or enjoyable to study. In studying these things, the geographical understanding of the big organising concepts such as place can be deepened. Ideally, a deepening understanding of place will be enhanced by the study of real places – occasionally first-hand, through fieldwork. Pupils have a natural curiosity about places, and this should be nurtured through geographical enquiry. Ideally, this should encompass a variety of scales, and a range of contexts. One challenge for geography teachers is to teach about places in a way that provides both breadth (e.g. pupils acquire a vocabulary and locational knowledge of Africa, Europe, United Kingdom) and depth (e.g. pupils study the real daily lives experienced by people in particular places).

Here is a useful checklist of questions to consider when choosing place coverage at Key Stage 3 (Ranger, 1995):

- How can I link the place to the pupils' own local area?
- How can I best capitalise on the pupils' own experiences?
- Which geographical themes can I best develop through this unit?
- How can this progress from pupils' previous learning about places? Do I know what they have covered at Key Stage 2, for instance?
- How will I reflect the cultures, the religion, the history?
- Is my emphasis on the people or the location?
- How will I contextualise this place study in a changing world geography?
- How can I foster a questioning attitude?
- How can I explore geographical issues from a variety of perspectives?
- How can I make links to other places, where they are relevant?

■ How can I best make use of enquiry-based approaches to learning?
■ And what do I leave out?
■ How do I resource what I put in?

The importance of study at different scales is emphasised in the Geography National Curriculum and most examination syllabuses. If geography courses and schemes of work do not include a range of scales of enquiry from small and local scale, through regional and national scales to the global scale, then the range of opportunities for developing enquiry skills may be limited (Naish *et al.*, 1987; Robinson, 1995). It is also likely that an inadequate range of 'reinforcing' case studies will restrict pupils' acquisition of important concepts. A 'matrix' of scales is therefore a useful format for planning studies to ensure that pupils are able to develop an *informed world view* (see Box 5.4).

Scale \ Themes or Places			
Local and Small scale			
Regional			
National			
International			
Global			

■ **Box 5.4** Curriculum matrix for identifying the coverage of scales

The 'local' scale can refer to any small-scale study anywhere in the world; for example, the study of a favela in Rio de Janeiro. Counter-urbanisation in south-east England might be an example of a regional issue or case study. Urbanisation in Brazil would provide a study of urban processes at a national scale, whereas the international scale would involve the study of activities or patterns in two or more countries such as urban change in European cities or trade and aid between Britain and Bangladesh. World patterns and processes that affect all countries would be classified as 'global' studies. This may include examples such as global climatic processes or the globalisation of economic activities.

One of the limitations of using a matrix like this as a planning tool is that a place may be chosen for study to fill in a box at a particular scale. This may lead to inter-relationships with other 'scales' in the study of that place or issue being ignored. For example, at a 'local' scale a study of urban regeneration in the Docklands area of London could examine population movements, changes in employment and the local economy, as well as the impacts on social and environmental change in the area. However, any real understanding of the changes that have taken place in the Docklands area would need to consider the role of economic processes at the regional, national and international scales as well as the influence of national, political and planning policies.

Brooks and Morgan (2006) warn of the dangers resulting from using case studies to present a 'bite-sized take on the world'. They argue that pupils need to have opportunities to explore the 'messiness and complexity of places' if they are to develop a more sophisticated understanding of the world and their place in it, what Massey (1993: 146) describes as a 'global sense of place'. Brooks and Morgan (2006: 13) believe that limited and partial case studies can lead to an 'impoverished geographical imagination' that is potentially damaging when they involve oversimplification and overgeneralisation about the real world. They provide a range of activities that can encourage pupils to generate a sense of place and explore representations of places. Rawding (2007) also explores ways in which recent developments in geographical thinking can be used to enhance pupils' understanding of place in geography.

In order to understand studies of distant places, pupils need to have small scale examples of people and places to relate to (Robinson, 1995). For example, in order to develop an understanding of the 'reality' of contrasting regions of Brazil, pupils need to have the opportunity to find out about specific places and learn about the lives of people in these areas. Wellsted (2006) suggests a variety of creative strategies for studying distant places that help to promote the development of critical thinking skills as well as positive attitudes towards different cultures, places and environments.

The Development Compass Rose is another useful planning tool when thinking about the different scales of processes important in a local case study (see Figure 5.4). The points of the compass are replaced by four major dimensions or processes affecting the geography of places. The interaction between social, political and environmental elements is essential to the understanding of people and places. In this sense the Development Compass Rose helps to embed the study of places within an enquiry-based approach to learning in geography.

PLANNING FOR DIFFERENTIATION IN TEACHING AND LEARNING

In a good lesson pupils with differing abilities are able to make progress in learning, and tasks and activities are within the extended grasp of all pupils.

(Davidson, 1996: 13)

Natural

These are questions about the environment – energy, air, water, soil, living things, and their relationships to each other. These questions are about the 'built' as well as the 'natural' environment.

Who decides?

These are questions about power, who makes choices and decides what is to happen; who benefits and loses as a result of these decisions and at what cost.

Economic

These are questions about money, trading, aid and ownership.

Social

These are questions about people: their relationships, traditions and culture, and the way they live. They include questions about how, for example, gender, race, disability, class and age affect social relationships.

■ **Figure 5.4** The Development Compass Rose
Source: Robinson and Serf, 1997: 12

There is some evidence that when there is no differentiation pupils identified as having learning difficulties do not achieve all they might. This was illustrated vividly in two contrasting lessons in Key Stage 3: in one, pupils with special needs were struggling too long with recording information and not reaching the real focus of the lesson, which involved looking at the geographical settlement pattern and accounting for it; in the other they were working hard and successfully on well-chosen differentiated tasks which provided appropriate challenge.

(OFSTED, 1995: 21–22)

These quotations indicate one of the fundamental challenges facing teachers when setting out to plan for successful learning. The need to improve differentiation has been a key issue in the drive to raise standards in education for a long time. Within geography education it has been identified as a key issue in OFSTED's review of its inspection findings with the recognition that tasks were not being matched to the ability of individual pupils in many of the lessons reported as unsatisfactory (Smith, 1997). OFSTED has also reported on the need for more challenge in geography for higher attaining pupils, particularly in Key Stages 3 and 4:

Too often, teaching is directed at pupils of average ability. Lessons which are highly structured or too teacher-directed limit the opportunities for independent enquiry and extended writing. Yet higher attainers and others can flourish in an environment of research, discussion, collaboration and initiative.

(OFSTED, 2008: 22)

Differentiation is a planned process of intervention in the classroom designed to maximise learning potential based on individual needs. There are differences in all classes. These differences may be in the amount of work that pupils complete, in their ability to work independently or collaboratively, or in specific learning skills such as reading, writing or listening, etc. Differentiation is not about simply allowing these differences to show themselves. It involves intervention to make a difference for all pupils. The aim of this intervention is to help all pupils to maximise their potential.

A planned process suggests that differentiation does not just happen and that teachers need to do something intentionally. In other words, it needs to be planned for. However, it is a process – not an event. This process will often take the form of a dialogue between teachers and individual learners about progress.

There are a wide range of considerations influencing successful differentiated classroom practice. It is not simply about the design of tasks. Figure 5.5 outlines the principles which underpin successful classroom practice and subsequent geographical learning and suggests a range of strategies for achieving effective differentiation (Figure 5.5).

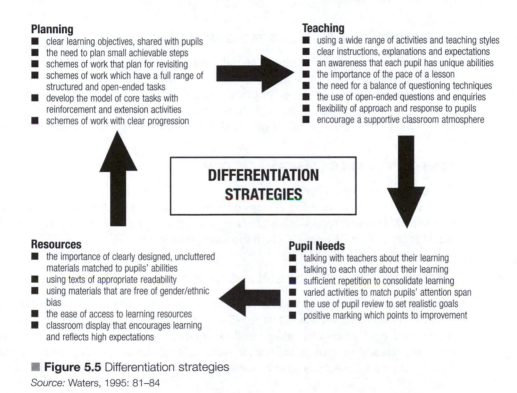

Planning
- clear learning objectives, shared with pupils
- the need to plan small achievable steps
- schemes of work that plan for revisiting
- schemes of work which have a full range of structured and open-ended tasks
- develop the model of core tasks with reinforcement and extension activities
- schemes of work with clear progression

Teaching
- using a wide range of activities and teaching styles
- clear instructions, explanations and expectations
- an awareness that each pupil has unique abilities
- the importance of the pace of a lesson
- the need for a balance of questioning techniques
- the use of open-ended questions and enquiries
- flexibility of approach and response to pupils
- encourage a supportive classroom atmosphere

DIFFERENTIATION STRATEGIES

Resources
- the importance of clearly designed, uncluttered materials matched to pupils' abilities
- using texts of appropriate readability
- using materials that are free of gender/ethnic bias
- the ease of access to learning resources
- classroom display that encourages learning and reflects high expectations

Pupil Needs
- talking with teachers about their learning
- talking to each other about their learning
- sufficient repetition to consolidate learning
- varied activities to match pupils' attention span
- the use of pupil review to set realistic goals
- positive marking which points to improvement

■ **Figure 5.5** Differentiation strategies
Source: Waters, 1995: 81–84

Curriculum planning provides teachers with a great deal of scope for responding to differentiation issues. Teachers can make decisions about learning objectives, content, teaching strategies and learning activities, learning materials and assessment strategies for different pupils.

Here is some practical advice about a range of strategies that can facilitate differentiated learning opportunities in the classroom.

1 DIFFERENTIATION BY OUTCOME

This is the result of pupils following common tasks developed around the use of common resources. Differentiation is represented by the different responses that pupils make to the task. The Year 9 lesson about rainforest environments described earlier (Table 5.5) is an example of a lesson where differentiation is achieved by outcome. The criteria that would be used to assess the creative writing would reflect the different levels of achievement possible.

2 DIFFERENTIATION BY RESOURCES AND BY OUTCOME

All the pupils could be working on the same task but with a range of different resources. These resources would be targeted at specific pupils taking into account their ability to read, understand or interpret material provided. It represents quite a breakthrough for many student teachers to accept that the pupils need not all do the same work – and that it may be better for them that they do not. It requires very careful and decisive planning by the teacher, however.

3 DIFFERENTIATION BY GRADED TASKS AND OUTCOMES

Pupils may use the same stimulus, materials and resources but they will follow a series of tasks or questions which become increasingly difficult and demanding. All the pupils may begin with the same 'starter' but then move on to tasks beyond which some pupils may not be able to progress. Next, in theory, such 'stepped tasks' are very difficult to design. Many GCSE questions are designed in this way and would be useful to analyse.

4 DIFFERENTIATION BY TASK AND OUTCOME

This category openly recognises the difficulties noted in 3. In other words, just because a pupil 'gets to' the more difficult steps does not guarantee high-level achievement (and vice versa). This is a reminder for teachers to keep an open mind about the work their pupils produce (see Chapter 10 which discusses assessment).

5 DIFFERENTIATION BY STIMULUS AND BY TASK

In this category, the teacher takes a very early decision, attempting to tailor the initial stimulus (presumably including text to be read) to meet pupils' needs. This can only be done on the basis of detailed and accurate knowledge of the pupils. The diagram has a linear appearance: to what extent does it show 'self-fulfilling prophecy' and is it, therefore, a danger (and obstruction) to maximising pupil achievement? Always keep an open mind.

What is 'hidden' in these theoretical representations of differentiation strategies is, arguably, the real key: that the teacher differentially *supports* individual learners, trying to stretch each one to their most impressive achievement. We should use such approaches in a flexible way as unplanned and unexpected outcomes can have benefits for the learner. For example, pupils might do better than expected or alternatively, just fail to reach a target as it is just beyond their scope at this particular stage in their development. As teachers, we are continually adjusting our expectations of what pupils can achieve as we monitor and assess their progress in learning.

PLANNING FOR CONTINUITY AND PROGRESSION IN PUPILS' LEARNING IN GEOGRAPHY

> Progression in pupils' geographical understanding is closely associated with the development of their ability to describe and explain geographical conditions, patterns, relationships and changes. This is often dependent on them developing general geographical ideas (concepts, generalisations and models) and being able to apply these to new situations. Understanding is revealed by the ability of pupils to interpret, analyse, synthesise and evaluate information. There is, therefore, a close relationship between the development of understanding and more intellectual capabilities.
>
> (Bennetts, 1995: 18)

As pupils mature intellectually, the geography curriculum they experience should reflect this development (Bennetts, 2005). Schemes of work represent longer-term plans for pupils' learning. As such, they have an important role to play in ensuring continuity and progression in pupils' learning in geography. Continuity refers to the way the curriculum is structured to ensure that breadth and depth is developed in the subject and to provide opportunities to widen the pupil's understanding. This often involves revisiting ideas, knowledge and skills in different contexts to reinforce learning through a 'spiral curriculum' (Bruner, 1960).

To ensure 'continuity' of learning a scheme of work should be designed to build upon pupils' previous learning in geography. This suggests that there are certain significant features of geographical education that will be evident throughout a pupil's experience of geography in school. These might include aspects of content or particular types of learning activity. Can we be sure that what we have planned will actually 'take the pupils somewhere' and allow them to 'go further' in geography? (Rawling, 2007)

Where continuity is strong, pupils will be able to build upon their previous experience and learning. This will help them acquire knowledge and develop understanding, skills, attitudes and values in a structured way. Geography courses in secondary schools should build on pupils' experience of and learning in geography from Key Stage 2 in primary schools. We should also be able to identify continuity between courses within a school, i.e. between Key Stage 3 and GCSE. Prominent aspects of continuity across the key stages include:

- ■ the emphasis on the study of places
- ■ the attention given to location, spatial patterns and the links between places
- ■ the concern with physical and human geography, and with the relationships between people and their environments
- ■ the use of maps; and
- ■ the investigation of places and themes

(Bennetts, 1995: 76)

The term 'progression' can be used in two senses: to refer to the way in which pupils' learning advances; and to the planned development of pupils' knowledge, understanding, skills, attitudes and values in geography in a structured way over a period of time. The idea of progression is, therefore, complementary to that of continuity. As geography teachers, we want pupils to improve their skills and abilities through geography, but we also want them to become better in geography itself.

It should also be remembered that progress in geography is not just an accumulation of facts and information; geographical learning requires a greater understanding, and an increased ability to interpret and make sense of complex issues which shape the world.

(Davidson, 2006: 106)

This development is influenced by the ways in which pupils mature as well as by their educational experiences. Progression in geography for 5–16 year olds should involve the following:

■ An increase in the breadth of studies. There should be a gradual extension of content to include different places, new landscapes, a variety of geographical conditions and a range of human activities.

■ An increasing depth of study associated with pupils' growing capacity to deal with complexities and abstractions. As pupils mature intellectually, they are able to make sense of more complex situations, to cope with more demanding information, to take account of more intricate webs of inter-relationships and to undertake more complicated tasks.

■ An increase in the spatial scale of what is studied. The growth in pupils' abilities to take account of greater complexities and to make use of general ideas enables them to undertake successful geographical studies of larger areas.

■ A continuing development of skills to include the use of specific techniques and more general strategies of enquiry matched to pupils' developing cognitive abilities.

■ Increasing opportunity for pupils to examine social, economic, political and environmental issues. Older pupils should not only be more skilled at evaluating evidence and the consequences of alternative causes of action, but should develop greater appreciation and understanding of the influence of people's beliefs, attitudes and values.

(Bennetts, 1995 and 2005)

As they progress through Key Stage 3, pupils will increasingly:

■ broaden and deepen their knowledge and understanding of places and themes
■ make use of a wide and precise geographical vocabulary
■ analyse, rather than describe, geographical patterns processes and change
■ appreciate the interactions within and between physical and human processes that operate in any environment
■ appreciate the interdependence of places
■ become proficient at conducting and comparing studies at a widening range of scales and in contrasting places and environments
■ apply their geographical knowledge and understanding to unfamiliar contexts
■ select and make effective use of skills and techniques to support their geographical investigations
■ appreciate the limitations of geographical evidence and the tentative and incomplete nature of some explanations.

(cited in Bennetts, 1996: 85)

When planning for progression, try to ensure that your teaching builds upon pupils' existing knowledge and previous experience, and that tasks that are carefully matched to pupils' capabilities. You should also give attention to ensuring progression in those aspects of a subject which are likely to be important to pupils' future learning, for example, ideas and skills which have wide application and which underpin more advanced learning in that subject (Bennetts, 1996: 82).

Your own subject knowledge of geography as an academic discipline will be a major source of ideas and understanding when planning for progression. It helps you identify aspects of a theme that are worthy of study and select geographical concepts, theories and models that are relevant to the study of this theme. It will help you analyse what is involved in understanding particular ideas and relationships in geography.

At the start of this section, we suggested that your 'working knowledge' or 'practical experience' of teaching geography informs your understanding of continuity and progression. This 'practical experience' will be derived from using a wide range of teaching strategies, learning activities and resources with pupils of different ages and abilities (Chapters 2, 3, 4 and 6). Your understanding will also develop as you gain more experience of monitoring and assessing pupils' learning in geography (Chapter 10).

Weather is a theme which features in key stages 2 and 3, and in most GCSE and AS/A2–level courses. In Key Stage 2, pupils might study how weather varies between places and over time, by examining the influence of site conditions, seasonal weather patterns and weather conditions in different parts of the world. In Key Stage 3, the focus is on the differences between weather and climate and on reasons for the spatial variations in aspects of weather and climate.

At GCSE, pupils would be expected to develop a broader geographical perspective and to examine the processes in greater depth. A GCSE course might therefore examine:

■　The measurement of weather conditions and the use of these measurements to identify variations in weather patterns and distinctive climatic regions.

■　The influence of different types of atmospheric systems on weather and climate in different parts of the world.

■　The ways in which weather and climate affect people's activities.

■　The ways in which human activity can indirectly change weather and climate.

At A-level, there is likely to be some continuity in these ideas and sub-themes. The challenge for the teacher therefore would be to introduce pupils to new content and to extend them more intellectually. For example, factors influencing atmospheric circulation (the Earth's heat budget, global surface and upper wind circulation, including cells, Rosby waves, jet streams and fronts) and the resulting global patterns of pressure precipitation and temperature could be studied. More complex ideas about the causes of condensation and precipitation would be considered, including the importance of lapse rates and different conditions of atmospheric stability.

Pupils might be expected to develop a more detailed understanding of atmospheric systems and the characteristics of the weather associated with these systems. This would probably include the ability to interpret synoptic charts and satellite photographs. The concept of microclimates could be studied, including the formation of fogs and local winds as well as the development of urban microclimates. A more detailed interpretation of theories about the impact of human activity on global weather and long-term climatic change would be expected.

Table 5.9 Geography in the 5–16 curriculum: a summary of its characteristics and content

	Key Stage 1: 5–7 (NC)	Key Stage 2: 7–11 (NC)	Key Stage 3: 11–14 (NC)	14–16 years (GCSE)	16–19 years (A/AS)
Character and purpose of geography	• building on own experience and skills to reach better understanding of own local surroundings and some knowledge and awareness of the wider world	• widening the range of scales and contrasting environments studied, to gain deeper understanding of places and to investigate aspects of physical and human geography	• broadening and depending geographical understanding and skills, through study of a wide range of places and themes at a full range of scales. Increasing ability to recognise processes, patterns and trends in geography	• growing ability to understand the character of places and environments, to be aware of geography's contribution to understanding issues, and to form own views on environmental and spatial matters	• deeper understanding of particular aspects of geography, and growing competence in applying wide range of knowledge, skills and understanding to real world issue and problems • greater stress on global issues, interrelationships and interdependence
Geographical enquiry and investigative work	[Understanding my own place and becoming aware of the wider world] focus on asking: • what/where is it? • what is it like? • how did it get like this? opportunities to: • observe, question, record • communicate ideas and information	[growing awareness of how my place compares with other places and how geography helps me understand the world around me] focus on asking: • what/where is it? • what is it like? • how did it get like this? • how/why is it changing? opportunities to: • observe, ask questions • collect and record evidence • analyse evidence, draw conclusions, communicate findings	[greater awareness of the value of geography in explaining features and places, and in giving a wider national and global context] focus on asking: • what/where is it? what is it like? • how did it get like this? • how/why is it changing? • what are the implications? opportunities to: • identify geographical questions • establish appropriate sequence of investigation • identify evidence and collect, record and present it • analyse/evaluate • draw conclusions and communicate findings	[using geography to make sense of the world and to form views and opinions based on evidence and understanding] focus on: a range of geographical enquiry skills including: • identification of questions/issues • establishing appropriate sequence of enquiry • identifying, collecting evidence • recording and presenting it • describing, analysing and interpreting evidence • drawing conclusions and communicating findings • evaluating methods and evaluating evidence/conclusions	[competence as a geographer and ability to use and apply this to real world] focus on: ability to produce a complete enquiry, including: • collect, record, interpret evidence • select from enquiry methodologies • organise, present, communicate information • analyse, synthesise, critically evaluate • use quantitative and qualitative investigate techniques

Source: adapted from Rawling,, 1996

This is perhaps a useful example of one of the ways in which teachers can plan for progression. *Routes* or *threads* are planned so that pupils' learning advances in a systematic way as they return to different elements of their geographical education. The progressive development of concepts (revisiting, reinforcing and refining, rather than repeating) conforms with Bruner's idea of a spiral curriculum. Table 5.10 provides a helpful summary of some key issues that need to be considered when planning for progression in pupils' learning in geography. Teachers can also draw upon evidence from educational research about the development of pupils' capabilities (both general and geographical) to inform their planning.

Activity 5.5 **Reviewing schemes of work: identifying evidence of continuity and progression in planning for teaching and learning**

Progression is the planned development of pupils' knowledge, understanding, skills, attitudes and values over a period of time.

For this task, investigating continuity and progression you need a range of schemes of work covering Years 7–11 from one school, ideally your teaching placement school.

Task 1: Progress in geography within Key Stage 3
Familiarise yourself with the view of progression outlined on pages 210 and 212. Review the Key Stage 3 schemes of work for Years 7–9 to find out the extent to which this view of progression is reflected in one school's planning. Which issues have and have not been overtly addressed in this planning?

Task 2: Features of progression in planning for Years 7–11
Use Table 5.9 on page 210 and the summary of the main features of progression in geographical learning on page 212 to help you to review the evidence of progression in the schemes of work for Years 7–11. Make a list of the main features of progression (with examples, if possible) in geographical learning in your school's planning under the following headings:

- Increasing the breadth of study
- Increasing the depth of study
- Increasing the spatial scale of study
- Developing geographical skills
- Developing enquiry skills and strategies (and pupils' understanding of enquiry)
- Increasing opportunity to examine geographical issues and relevant attitudes and values.

Identify aspects of progression that could benefit from further development. Your tutor might be able to suggest some of the aspects that could be considered. It should be remembered that schemes of work benefit from review and are not intended to be 'tablets of stone'.

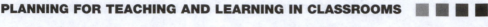

■ Table 5.10 Planning for progression in geography

Breadth of geographical knowledge	Depth of geographical understanding	Use of geographical skills	Attitudes and values
Strongly influenced by the content of the curriculum, including the requirements of the National Curriculum or examination syllabuses. To plan for breadth of knowledge: • Identify the degree of choice that is available (topics and case studies) • Identify previous learning (i.e. case studies, topics, places, themes, issues studied in previous key stage/level) • identify previously acquired knowledge which is relevant to new learning • consider which information is to be used primarily as part of the learning process, and which information needs to be memorised for future recall. *Key Principles* • Breadth of knowledge is fostered by ensuring that pupils study a variety of places at a range of environmental and social conditions and processes. • The sequence in which knowledge should be acquired depends on context and use. • There should be a balance between breadth and continuity.	To plan for progression in understanding within a current theme: • identify the ideas to be introduced • analyse these ideas to clarify the meaning of each, the links between them, and the scope of their application • consider the level of understanding appropriate for the age, ability and experience of the pupils • explore pupils' pre-conceptions which inhibit their acceptance and development of new ideas • take account of the various dimensions which can create barriers or difficulties for learning e.g. remoteness from experience; levels of complexity and abstraction; the degree of precision required; and the extent to which values are embedded in an idea relevant to a particular situation • prepare learning materials and design learning tasks that are suitably matched to pupils' capabilities (differentiation) • devise an overall structure for the theme, which enables pupils to progressively develop their understanding.	Distinguish between: 1 *Specific techniques* – such as mapwork, fieldwork, statistical techniques, use of diagrams, IT and remote sensing. 2 *General categories of cognitive activity* – such as describing, analysing, explaining, evaluating. 3 *Enquiry strategies* – ways of carrying out investigations in order to arrive at valid and substantiated conclusions. Repeated use improves quality. Plan sequences of learning activities which enable pupils to improve the quality of what they do. Progression in skills involves: • building on previous learning • matching tasks to pupils' responsibilities • increasing complexity • increasing the level of precision required in their use. Do not divorce the application of skills from context. The link with knowledge and understanding is important in the development and use of the higher order skills of analysis, synthesis and evaluation, and in the carrying out of investigations.	Values and attitudes usually appear in relation to issues arising from people's interactions with the environment. You should provide opportunities for pupils to: • explore their own attitudes and values on a wide range of issues and themes • recognise those attitudes and values held by other people and how they influence their decisions and behaviour • explore the impacts of these decisions and behaviour • explore how decisions are made. Progression is determined by the extent to which pupils can demonstrate an increasingly detailed and reasoned response to particular issues and situations. Strategies that can help pupils to develop their understanding of different attitudes and values held by different individuals and groups include role play, simulation and decision-making exercises.

Source: Extracts from Bennetts, 1996 in Bailey and Fox: 81–94

Task 3: Continuity in pupils' learning in geography
This task would be a logical follow-up to task 2. When you have reviewed aspects of progression, consider what evidence there is of 'continuity' in aspects of learning in geography between Key Stage 3 and GCSE courses in the school. Bennetts' (1995) list of the most prominent aspects of continuity across the key stages may be helpful (see page 212). Where you are able to identify specific aspects of continuity (for example, in a particular place or theme, the use of particular types of learning activity or the development of a particular skill), try to assess the extent to which the schemes of work are designed to build upon pupils' previous learning in geography.

Discuss your responses with other student teachers or your tutor.

CURRICULUM THINKING IN GEOGRAPHY

The starting point for curriculum design in geography should be a rigorous and defensible version of the subject matter to be taught in the light of teachers' knowledge and understanding of the pupils they teach.

(Morgan and Lambert, 2005: 95)

More than ever, teachers need to bear in mind that the curriculum is a means to an end and not an end in itself.

(Graves, 1997: 30)

In putting the above quotes together in this way, we want to make a point. The first is unambiguous in urging teachers to be 'curriculum developers', indeed that they *need* to be in order to safeguard geography's educational role. The second quote seems less assertive but makes a similar, telling point: the curriculum is a servant, something to be controlled and deployed by teachers. The broad aim of this chapter as a whole has been to show how and why, even when we have a national geography 'curriculum' laid down in law, teachers need to take on the responsibility of curriculum developer.

'Curriculum' is a much used word. In some ways it gives expression to a simple idea: for example, 'the curriculum is often referred to as...those planned events on the timetable that occur during school hours' (Dowson, 1995). But, as with many apparently straightforward ideas, simplicity is only skin deep. Scratch below the surface and engage the concept at a deeper level and we encounter questions and issues which do not yield easily to simple or common-sense solutions. Thus, writers such as Dowson distinguish the whole curriculum from the subject curriculum, the pastoral curriculum from the academic curriculum, the hidden curriculum from the visible curriculum – and add to this list cross-curricular themes, issues and dimensions, and the 'extra-curricular' curriculum!

What we also wish to emphasise in this section is that an absence of *curriculum thinking* within the subject can result in the pupils' actual experience of geography (the contents and activities geography lessons) being left deficient in a number of ways. We seek to engage you in curriculum thinking which takes you beyond the level of the competently planned lesson. To be able to plan a good lesson is certainly necessary, but alone it is not sufficient to implement an effective and purposeful geography education. For example, as we know the content of geography is potentially infinite ('making sense of the world'), how can we be assured that our content selection is appropriate? What do we have to cover, in what depth, and how? We need some kind of *mechanism,* or mechanisms, to help us tackle such issues. We are looking ahead to when you are competent and have developed some skills, gained some experience and start to question the content and appraoach to your subject. The degree to which the principles of curriculum development are understood and can be applied is one indicator of a teacher's graduation from basic practical competence to become a reflective and proficient teacher.

'I know what this about, but what is it for?': the role of curriculum thinking

You can probably bring to mind a lesson which you (or your tutor) found difficult to specify in terms of its purpose. Sometimes it is the pupils who articulate this kind of difficulty, either explicitly ('why are we doing this?') or implicitly by turning off or refusing to co-operate fully. But when the tutor expresses the concern, often in writing during a lesson which is being observed, the comment can be along the lines of the quote which heads this section: I can see that the lesson is about climate graphs (or population change or whatever), but *why* are we doing what we're doing? Where does it 'fit in' (in relation to what the pupils did last week, last term or last year, or what they are going on to do)? What is it for? What do we expect the pupils to gain from doing this? What do they need to know? Such questions invite response – but where to begin?

For you, the question 'why' may have arisen at the planning stage, that is before the lesson was taught. But it could equally first arise *during* the lesson (i.e. when you first sense that perhaps things are not going as well as they might, or according to plan), or *after* the lesson during your evaluation or a challenging debrief with your tutor. 'Curriculum development' is a process which encompasses all three components – before, during and after the lesson(s) – and the question (why?) is quintessentially one requiring response based on what we have called curriculum thinking. What this implies, above all, is that a full response cannot be left in terms of a single lesson; though you may have felt that the lesson was justifiable in its own right, it is unlikely that you can always, or even often, justify a lesson without referring to your analysis of a bigger picture. Generally speaking, we can identify three levels of resolution in such analysis:

- the individual lesson – what I want to accomplish today
- the medium term – what I want to accomplish with my pupils over the term/year/key stage
- the longer term – what I hope my pupils will have gained of lasting value. This is what has been called the 'residuals' of a geography education

(Haggett in Lambert and Matthews, 1996)

These levels of resolution in thinking are not dissimilar to the levels of curriculum planning discussed elsewhere in this chapter, incorporating such technical devices as the lesson plan, scheme of work and syllabus or programme of study. Table 5.11 summarises the idea of levels of planning (Rawling, 1996 and 2007).

'Level 1', or the general (macro) level, is, to all practical intents and purposes, beyond our control and laid down by statute or Awarding bodies, they provide a summary of medium-term aims, broad principles and rough guidance over content selection and

■ **Table 5.11** Levels of curriculum planning for geography

Level	Who does it?	What questions are asked?	What does it provide?
LEVEL 1 General level	National bodies – QCA, the national agency for curriculum and assessment acting on behalf of the government. Consultation with the subject community. (In the 1970s, curriculum projects funded by the Schools' Council.)	*What* contribution can/should the subject make to the education of young people? *What* broad areas of geographic knowledge and skill development are essential for pupils to acquire at school? *How* can the subject's contribution be best outlined so that schools can develop this potential? *What* targets might be set for pupil achievement and how might this be monitored?	■ Broad aims for the subject ■ A framework of themes, concepts and skills fundamental to the subject ■ Procedures/guidance on interpreting and implementing the framework ■ Assessment requirements and arrangements
LEVEL 2 School level	The school geography department (using the stimulus of interdepartmental and teacher group discussions).	*How* do we translate the broad aims? What is the general purpose and character of geographical education appropriate to our pupils? *What* particular content emphases, key ideas, skills and learning experiences will we offer to particular age groups of pupils? *How* and *when* will we assess pupil progress and achievements? *How* will we evaluate the success of programmes offered?	■ Specific objectives for geographic education in the school and for each age group ■ Course outlines and teaching programmes ■ Departmental assessment strategy and agreed policy on monitoring/reviewing courses
LEVEL 3 Classroom level	The individual geography teacher in discussion with colleagues.	*What* particular sequences of activities and experiences do I provide for each element of the geography course? *What* teaching/learning approaches and resources shall I use in particular lessons? *How/When* shall I assess pupils' progress and achievements? *How* will I know how successful my lessons are?	■ Detailed schemes of work ■ Detailed lesson plans and decisions about resources ■ Plans for preparing/ administering assessment tasks and recording/ reporting results ■ Commitment to collect evidence/review lessons

Source: Rawling, 1996: 102

without a curriculum plan. Therefore, we need to focus on the two remaining levels, the school/departmental (meso) level ('level 2') and classroom (micro) level ('level 3'). Level 2 curriculum planning is usually the scheme of work, and at level 3 the lesson plan. Each of these levels has been considered fully in earlier sections of this chapter.

In developing the notion of curriculum *thinking* (which is an essential component of planning), the emphasis is on the language of goals, aims and objectives. Thus:

■ *the short term (the individual lesson)* – requires specific objectives, often identified in terms of the 'elements of learning', i.e. knowledge, understanding, skills and values. Specifying objectives is not meant to cover all the learning possible in the lesson, but to show where the emphasis or priorities lie.

■ *the medium term* requires medium-term aims, which are less specific (more open ended) than objectives but which express the sense of learning outcomes. For example, an aim may be 'to enhance an awareness of the potential and limits of forms of graphical communication in geography'. This would be one of several aims that would remain constant in the medium term, whilst individual lessons would build with pupils a range of specified skills associated with cartography and graphicacy. It is worth noting that medium-term aims can often be taken directly from syllabus documents or from the National Curriculum Programme of Study.

■ *the longer term* is described by broad *educational goals* which articulate something beyond geography as an end in itself. When a writer such as Naish (1997) refers to geography as a 'medium of education', and Slater (1982) entitles her influential book *Learning Through Geography,* it is the longer term goals that they have in mind. In this sense, longer term aims are to do with questions of moral purpose – the worthwhileness of teaching geography.

If we imagine these levels of resolution as a nested hierarchy, then we can see immediately that goals, aims and objectives are linked. In other words, the lesson objectives are influenced by the aims of the course, and the aims of the course are guided by the educational goals of the subject matter.

The distinction between aims and objectives is fuzzy: as a philosopher wrote 'nothing is gained by attempting to legislate *particular* uses for these terms (Hirst, 1974: 16) [our emphasis]. Thus, our distinctions are not set in stone but a useful starting point. One student teacher has made sense of this 'big picture' using the appropriately geographical metaphor of the map; see Box 5.5.

When is a curriculum not a curriculum?

To illustrate the significance of the riddle, we can quote Norman Graves at length (see Figure 5.6). Graves was responsible for important clarifications in curriculum thinking in geography, most notably establishing the idea of the curriculum as an interactive process rather than the more mechanistic linear, 'objectives led' system that perhaps common sense would favour (and which influenced the first version of geography in the National Curriculum). Hence the riddle cited at the head of this section. The original National Curriculum was not 'a curriculum' in the sense that the National Curriculum Orders neither stated goals and aims, nor made decisions about how we should teach.

Understanding the role of aims and objectives: a student teacher talking near the end of her PGCE. She does not mention 'goals': in her travel metaphor, goals are to do with the reasons to go to Manchester in the first place – is it a worthwhile journey to make? For what reason?

'You must state your aims and objectives,' said my tutor. 'You must state your aims and objectives,' said my tutor. 'Where are your aims and objectives?' both of them asked.

Despite the consistency of their position I must admit I had trouble getting to grips with the message. Did they really think that my agreeing to fill in a lesson plan sheet would make me a better teacher (or a better bureaucrat)? And then, breakthrough! I realised that 'aims 'n' objectives' were not meant to create for me some kind of a bureaucratic diversion; and that if I couldn't (or wouldn't) identify where I was going in my teaching, I would probably have limited effectiveness. Worse, if I didn't say where I was going with the kids, how could I possibly expect them to come with me? Worse, if I didn't know where I was going, how could I possibly claim success in getting there?

I found the idea of a map really useful. By 'aims' I understand intended destination as in, for example, 'I intend to travel to Manchester' (I'm in London). By 'objectives' I understand what it is that I have to accomplish (the intermediate steps) in order to get to Manchester (and I eventually accomplish my aim). One helpful point this travel metaphor also brings out is that precisely which objectives require to be met depends entirely on the point of departure (including the existing knowledge and skill) of the travellers concerned – the objectives may vary from group to group and between individual pupils.

■ **Box 5.5** Stating your aims and objectives

Figure 5.6 shows the elements of the interactive process which Graves went on to develop in the context of the geography curriculum. It is natural for you, as a student teacher, to focus first on elements 5 and 6 (or in some cases perhaps 2 if you have a strong affiliation to a particular version of the spirit and purpose of geography). The Graves model strongly implies that the process of curriculum planning starts with the 'aims' (we would say 'goals') of education. Without a view on the purpose of education in general, the model implies, our conception of the aims of *geography* in education must remain relatively rudderless.

Activity 5.6 **Understanding the role of aims and objectives**

1 Read Box 5.5 'Stating your aims and objectives'.
2 Can you add to the list of difficulties that may result from teaching and learning in which aims and objectives remained unstated?
3 Either develop further the travel metaphor (in which ways is it helpful to your

understanding of the language of aims and objectives?) or, in discussion with others, is it possible to identify other metaphors that manage to illustrate 'curriculum thinking'?

4   Identify and discuss any weaknesses or deficiencies in the travel metaphor.

When you have completed this task, read the section below.

Discussion: The travel metaphor is a strong one. It is closely related to the idea of a map, which is also a useful potential line of reflective thought. Where it falls down, perhaps, is the implication that aims have to be identified as specifically as points on a map – and indeed that the journey is of no interest other than in its function in ultimately helping us get from A to B. Neither of these points necessarily result from the travel model, and recognising such points of discussion demonstrates the model's strength: it is flexible and provocative. Indeed, it invites response. An educational philosopher R.S. Peters wrote: 'to be educated is not to have arrived at a destination, it is to travel with a different view' (Peters, 1965; cited in Slater, 1992). As a result of taking part in educational endeavour, we are able to see things differently, gain new, wider perspectives and share new understandings.

These thoughts take us into the realms of what we value in geography, and arguably to a component of 'curriculum thinking' that the student teacher's writing failed to address: the issue of goals which we tackled to some extent in Chapter 1 under the guise of the role of geography in education. In the present context, we can simply note once more that the goals for geography in the curriculum need expression every now and then, for they guide what we settle on as worthwhile and legitimate course aims. Goals express our educational values, principally the balance we strike between the intrinsic and the instrumental purposes of education (see Box 5.6). Intrinsic purposes state that geography education is worthwhile in its own right because it broadens and deepens the mind, whilst the instrumental (usually extrinsic) purposes state the value of learning geography in terms of its 'value added' function for society – what skills, knowledge and understandings does geography provide for our collective social, political, environmental and economic well being?

The current National Curriculum Orders are the result of a review of the Key Stage 3 curriculum undertaken by the Qualifications and Curriculum Authority (QCA). A principal aim of this review was to ensure that the Key Stage 3 curriculum is less prescriptive and provides teachers with the flexibility needed to better meet pupils' needs. However, it also addressed the need to be clearer about the aims, purposes and values of the curriculum. Geography teachers are encouraged to consider how learning in geography can contribute to achievement of the curriculum aims for all young people to become:

■   successful learners who enjoy learning, make progress and achieve
■   confident individuals who are able to live safe, healthy and fulfilling lives
■   responsible citizens who make a positive contribution to society.

(QCA, 2007)

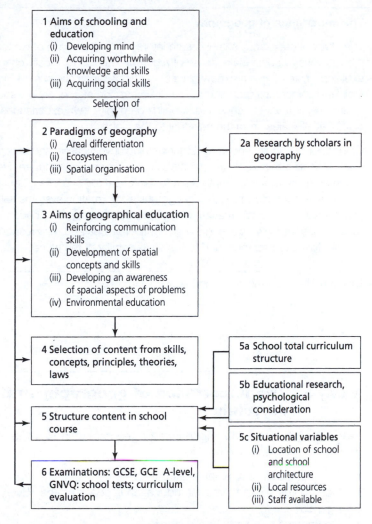

■ Figure 5.6 Graves' model for curriculum planning in geography
Source: Graves, 1979

After the initial statement of these broad educational goals, there is a statement of the 'Importance of geography' which attempts to provide a clear statement of the aims, purposes and values of a geographical education, something the earlier versions of the National Curriculum neglected (see Box 5.6). You might consider whether this statement could be added to. Which parts should be emphasised? Which help develop geography's contribution to your school's ethos? How does geography contribute to the broader educational goals of the 'Every Child Matters' agenda? How could the statement be adapted to share and promote the subject with pupils, parents, non-specialist teachers, senior school leaders and governors?

The importance of geography

The study of geography stimulates an interest in and a sense of wonder about places. It helps young people make sense of a complex and dynamically changing world. It explains where places are, how places and landscapes are formed, how people and their environment interact, and how a diverse range of economies, societies and environments are interconnected. It builds on pupils' own experiences to investigate places at all scales, from the personal to the global.

Geographical enquiry encourages questioning, investigation and critical thinking about issues affecting the world and people's lives, now and in the future. Fieldwork is an essential element of this. Pupils learn to think spatially and use maps, visual images and new technologies, including geographical information systems (GIS), to obtain, present and analyse information. Geography inspires pupils to become global citizens by exploring their own place in the world, their values and their responsibilities to other people, to the environment and to the sustainability of the planet.

■ **Box 5.6** The importance of geography

Activty 5.7 **The importance of geography in the currciulum**

Read the statement 'The importance of geography' in Box 5.6. Respond to this statement by considering how it:

- Can be added to it; what is left out?
- Contributes to the broader educational goals of the 'Every Child Matters' agenda?
- Contributes to your school's ethos.
- Might help promote geography in your school in talking to parents, pupils, governors, etc.

'Concept-led' curriculum design in geography

So how will this understanding of curriculum aims and the significance attached to the subject's key concepts influence our planning? In the context of these statutory educational goals, the view we are emphasising is that more operational, medium-term aims have to be created and recreated by teachers. No one apart from teachers can do this, and thus operationalise the worthwhile educational goals. What is clear is that the new curriculum (2007) offers fantastic opportunities for geography teachers to recapture professional creativity and to make the curriculum relevant, worthwhile and enjoyable for our pupils.

USING AIMS

Geography schemes of work could address the overall aims of the Key Stage 3 curriculum in the following ways:

Successful Learners Some ideas could include:

■ Geography develops young peoples' natural curiosity about places and encourages them to seek possible answers to geographical questions.

■ Geography is a subject that develops young peoples' abilities to think about inter-connections, for example by linking knowledge and understanding of human and physical phenomena though geographical investigations.

■ Geography supports young learners in using spatial data and geographic information that now underpin so many decisions about places and how they are represented.

■ Geography gives pupils a disciplined framework through which to share and develop their personal experiences and sense of place.

Confident Individuals Some ideas could include:

■ Being able to find out about places, and where they are using a variety of media, including maps, atlases, globes and geographical information helps young citizens to move around their world and look beyond their horizons more confidently.

■ Geography helps pupils to think about and represent spatial phenomena by using maps, charts, plans, photographs, images, diagrams, graphs and other visual representations. The spatial and visual skills of graphicacy are essential in this 'information rich' 21st century.

■ Geography's key concepts provide an excellent structure to help us think about complex people-environment issues.

■ A concept-led curriculum in geography enables teachers to support learners to look out beyond themselves, seeing things from a range of perspectives. This is a key aim for the discipline.

Responsible Citizens Some ideas could include:

■ In relation to sharpening young people's perceptions of themselves and to developing their knowledge and understanding about the world, geography offers a means for young people to connect their local experience to regional, national and international scales.

■ Geography education empowers young people to use the subject as a resource to make and articulate reasonable and informed judgements. These should be informed by the geographical knowledge, skills and understanding that they develop.

■ Geography empowers learners to know more about why phenomena are located where they are and the implications of these locations for people and the environment. This helps them to be confident, informed, participative citizens.

■ Geography enables pupils to think about the potential of places to be different in the future and the implications of this for both people and the environment. The networks, processes and interconnections that link places also have the potential to be different. This would create different global patterns and distributions. Careful thinking about the future informs the decisions and choioces that young people will make about how to live their lives.

Using the key concepts

We should also think about what it means to plan with concepts. The revised Key Stage 3 PoS offers teachers an opportunity to develop stimulating new schemes of work in geography. Many concepts are inter-disciplinary. Some concepts in Key Stage 3 may offer opportunities for curriculum collaborations that draw on the specialist knowledge understanding and skills from a small number of disciplines. The key concepts in geography are meant to show the essence of the subject, enabling teachers to develop their pupils to 'think geographically' – a disposition to think critically and creatively about people and places using geographic information. The key concepts provide the underlying structure for the subject – they are central to its understanding. As they study the subject, pupils will develop their understanding of these and other concepts that are central to the discipline. Growing familiarity with these concepts will help pupils to understand what it means to think geographically – literally to see the point of geography.

The use of concepts in curriculum planning enables us to be more selective about what we teach. The breadth of study (coverage) is important. Locational knowledge, places, spatial and graphical information need to be accessed when developing understanding. The depth of study is also significant. The use of concepts enables us to link essential geographical knowledge to the development of progressively deeper understanding.

We are continually developing our understanding of the discipline's key concepts. The definitions of concepts in the Key Stage 3 programme of study represent but one articulation of these key concepts. A helpful and thorough discussion of these key concepts and their implications for planning teaching and learning can be found in Rawling, 2007. They are not immutable or fixed. But they are meant to suggest a shared view of geography's essence – to enable us to plan a relevant, motivating and meaningful curriculum. This curriculum may take *many* forms, but must be recognisable geography.

Designing and making a curriculum: planning using concepts

The Key Stage 3 key concept definitions are for teachers to use to aid curriculum design. It is not intended that these definitions be taught directly to pupils. The nouns may be used a lot, for example, when we talk about the concept of 'place'. The activities, information and selected content will enable the pupils to develop their conceptual understanding through enquiry about places, people and environments in today's world and the potential of these places to be different in the future.

Curriculum design will involve planning for small steps of understanding and providing learning experiences in relation to selected content and activities. You will plan a balanced scheme of work, using the frameworks and checklists in the Key Processes, Range and Content and Curriculum Opportunities sections. This gives you a profoundly creative and significant role in 'curriculum making' (see Box 5.7).

Box 5.8 provides an example to show how this approach to planning using concepts might be applied to an enquiry into the concept of a 'park' (Lambert, 2007). Substantive concepts such as space and place are very broad and are open to many different

1. Decide on the purpose of the learning. Make these aims explicit, particularly in relation to the key concepts.

2. Select the places, themes, and issues you are going to use and show how these relate to the key concepts and aims. Check that you have taken in the Range and Content specified in the PoS. Typically, this forms the skeletal scheme of work divided into Units.

3. Build in the key processes across the Key Stage. If possible, create activities that enable the pupils to draw on prior and new knowledge to explore key questions (see below). They should also be 'fit for purpose'.

4. It may be helpful, therefore, to list the 'understandings' that you would expect the pupils to derive from scheme of work.

5. Consider key questions that could relate to these understandings, so that these can be used to support pupil enquiry. The use of questions is significant: 'When the curriculum is formed around questions rather than objectives the clear message to the pupils is that you are probing with them.' (Lyn Erickson, 2003: 91)

6. Enable the pupils to access a range of information from a variety of sources and perspectives.

7. Leave space for and create an assessment activity for each unit – that enables pupils to demonstrate what they know, understand and can do. Typically this is designed so that pupils need to apply their understanding to new data, places or examples. It need not be seen as a test but a classroom activity to reinforce learning.

8. Planning for progression is essential. Review your draft scheme of work specifically from the point of view of progression. In what ways is this scheme of work leading the pupils forward?

9. It may therefore be useful to finally reflect on the scheme of work and write a curriculum statement that shows, in relation to the selected content:
   - ■ what we want pupils to know (statements of essential knowledge)
   - ■ what we want pupils to understand (conceptual understanding)
   - ■ what we want pupils to be able to do (geographical skills and enquiry).

10. Topicality is vital in geography. Curriculum time should be set aside to tackle significant events that occur during the year and to feature places or topics in the news.

■ **Box 5.7** Designing and making a curriculum: Planning using concepts
Source: Kinder, 2007: 131–134

geographical interpretations. To make use of them in curriculum planning you must be clear about the focus you wish to develop. Is the sequence of work designed to develop an understanding that places are contested, that places are connected, or that people belong or not belong to places? (Taylor, 2007)

Overall purpose of the learning

For learners to understand competing demands on space; to appreciate the value of the local park or green space; to express informed opinions about its current state and future development.

The place, theme or issue to be used (the content focus)

The local park or green space in the context of the concept of a 'park'.

Key understandings learners will develop (drawn from the key concepts)

■ The concept of a 'park' is wide-ranging and includes wild landscapes, tended gardenscapes and modern retail and industrial zones.

■ The concept of a park is often used to conjure images of naturalness and peacefulness. This concept does not always bear close scrutiny.

■ People can perceive and use the same space in very different ways.

■ The interactions between different groups of people, and between people and environment, can be challenging to manage and resolve.

■ The successful resolution of these challenges is worthwhile in order to sustain valuable landscape resources and balance the needs of recreation and conservation.

Key processes learners will draw upon and develop

■ Investigation, through primary and secondary information, of the different ways people perceive and use the same environment/landscape resource.

■ Fieldwork investigation of the location, use, conflict and management of a local park/green space.

■ Internet research and interviews to establish the Green Flag status of a local park.

■ Use of ICT to communicate findings and recommend future actions about the use of a local park.

Key questions that relate to key understandings

■ Enquiry question: A Green Flag for our local park?

■ What are 'parks' and what are they for?

■ Where is our local park or green space?

■ What do we think about this park?

■ What do we use it for?

■ Who else uses the park and what else is it for?

■ Who owns and manages the park?

■ How do people affect the park?

■ How are conflicts between different users resolved?

■ How can the needs of recreation and conservation be met in the same space?

■ What makes a 'successful' park?

■ Does our local park have a Green Flag Award?

■ Does it deserve one and how can we help get it?

■ **Box 5.8** Using concepts to plan a scheme of work on a local park

Source: Lambert, 2007, in Kinder 2007:133

Range of sources of information

- Photographs of national, retail, industrial, country, science and other 'parks'
- Map information about local and other parks
- Fieldwork data on local park environment, facilities, users and management
- Interview with Parks Department representative
- Interviews with members of local community
- Green Flag Award website

Assessment activity

Management plan and accompanying letter to Parks Department to attain Green Flag status for local park.

Curriculum statement (what learners know, understand and are able to do)

- Know a range of examples of types of park
- Know the location of the local park and its facilities, uses, ownership and Green Flag status
- Understand why different groups perceive and use parks in different ways
- Understand how the local park is managed to resolve competing aims and sustain its use, landscape and environment
- Understand the role they can play in maintaining the park and sustaining it in future
- Be able to pose relevant questions about the park, and identify and use suitable sources of information
- Be able to communicate their feelings and recommendations clearly, using ICT where appropriate.

■ **Box 5.8** (continued)
Source: Lambert, 2007, In Kinder 2007:133

SUMMARY AND KEY POINTS

You should now have developed an understanding of some of the key issues involved in planning lessons and schemes of work in geography. As well as being able to recognise the main features of lesson plans and schemes of work, you should also understand the relationships between learning objectives, teaching strategies, learning activities and assessment in planning for learning in geography. This chapter has introduced you to some frameworks and processes that will help you to plan geography lessons. As you gain more experience of planning lessons, you will develop your own approach and adapt these frameworks to reflect your own needs.

This chapter has also introduced you to the role of the enquiry process and key questions in planning for learning in geography. The route for geographical enquiry provides a framework within which teachers can organise what Slater (1982) calls 'learning pathways'.

The importance of continuity, progression and differentiation has been highlighted in relation to planning. Practical experience of teaching and helping pupils to learn through geography will help develop your understanding of these complex issues. The discussion of these issues is developed further in other parts of this book where we examine teaching strategies, resources for learning, pupil learning and assessing (valuing) pupils' learning in geography.

FURTHER READING

Capel, S., Leask, M. and Turner, T. (eds) (2005) *Learning to Teach in the Secondary School: A companion to school experience*, London: Routledge.

Unit 2.2 provides generic guidance on planning lessons and schemes of work. Unit 4.1 explores pupil grouping, progression and differentiation. Unit 7 explores different aspects of the school curriculum, in particular Unit 7.1 (Aims of Education), Unit 7.3 (The National Curriculum for England and Wales) and Unit 7.4 (Pedagogy and Practice: The Key Stage 3 and Secondary National Strategy).

Kinder, A. and Widdowson, J. (eds) (2008) *The KS3 Geography Teachers' Toolkit*, Sheffield: The Geographical Association.

This is a series of schemes of work with supporting resources for delivering aspects of the new Geography National Curriculum at Key Stage 3. The series shows how to use the Key Concepts, Key Processes and Curriculum Opportunities in the new PoS in short and medium term planning. There are ready-to-use resources and lesson plans on a CD accompanying each book which can be personalised for use in different contexts. The titles include:

Moving Stories: Why is the population of the UK changing?
Into Africa: How are our lives connected with Africa?
Faster, Higher, Stronger: Is the Olympics the best way to regenerate East London?
The Rise and Rise of China
Water Works: Sustainable use of water resources
A Thorny Issue: Should I buy a Valentine's rose?
Look at it this way: What are your views of landscapes?
Future Floods: How can geography make a difference?
Changing my World: What difference can we make to climate change?

Rawling, E. (2007) *Planning your Key Stage 3 Geography Curriculum*, Sheffield: The Geographical Association.

This text provides practical guidance for planning using concepts in the revised Geography National Curriculum and explores ways of designing creative schemes of work to provide stimulating learning experiences for pupils at Key Stage 3.

Roberts, M. (2006) *Geographical Enquiry*, Chapter 9 in Balderstone, D. (ed.) Secondary Geography Handbook, Sheffield: The Geographical Association.

The author advocates a crucial role for teachers in stimulating pupils' curiosity and promoting a critical, questioning attitude towards data. Examples of geographical enquiry are used to show how pupils can be involved in making sense of new information.

Roberts, M. (2003) *Learning through Enquiry: making sense of geography in the Key Stage 3 classroom*, Sheffield: The Geographical Association.

This text provides many interesting and innovative ideas for developing enquiry with over 50 examples, all tried and tested in the classroom. Enquiry is presented as a process in which pupils are actively engaged in constructing geographical knowledge.

Taylor, E. (2004) *Re-presenting Geography*, Cambridge: Chris Kington Publishing.

This text draws upon many ideas from cultural geography to provide creative ideas and approaches for geographical enquiry. The enquiry sequences explain how these ideas and resources can be used in the classroom to explore how different people see the world and how pupils represent the world through constructing their own written texts.

Wellsted, E. (2006) *Understanding 'distant places'*, Chapter 14 in Balderstone, D. (ed.) **Secondary Geography Handbook, Sheffield: The Geographical Association.**

The author provides creative ideas and strategies for teaching about 'distant places' in meaningful ways that develop pupils' 'sense of place'. She provides helpful suggestions for resources and activities that can develop pupils' critical thinking skills when studying 'distant places'.

DEVELOPING AND USING RESOURCES FOR TEACHING AND LEARNING IN GEOGRAPHY

Poor teaching may result from inadequate resources.

(Smith, 1997: 126)

A major part of school geography is about what can be seen in the world, and geography teachers rely heavily on visual material to bring some reality into their classrooms.

(Robinson, 1987: 103)

As geography teachers, it is important for us to help young people to understand media constructs of reality so that they can be critical watchers, and aware of what is absent as well as what is present.

(Durbin, 2006: 229)

INTRODUCTION

As teachers of geography, we are able to draw upon a very rich variety of resources. The resources that we use and the ways in which we use them help us to bring what we teach alive. As such, they have an important influence on pupils' interest and motivation to learn. The quality and suitability of the resources that we select and the ways in which they are used by pupils are critical factors influencing whether learning is successful or not.

Our decisions about which resources to use and how to use them are influenced by a wide range of considerations, not least what is available in the school where we teach. The accessibility of resources to pupils of different abilities is a key factor influencing these decisions. The readability of text and the level of complexity of its content need to be considered together with the suitability of accompanying activities.

As geographers, we should be concerned with the topicality, relevance and accuracy of material that we use in the classroom. Often the topicality and current relevance of what we study in geography means that we engage young people in enquiries about controversial issues and questions. It is therefore important that the materials we use convey a realistic view of such issues and events, giving consideration to relevant attitudes and values as well as issues relating to power and agency in decision-making.

The resources that pupils use in their learning can significantly influence the images they develop about people and places. In selecting these resources we need to be aware of the images they portray, both implicit and explicit, about these people and places.

Teaching materials should be analysed to identify bias of any kind. When 'biased' materials are used by pupils we need to develop teaching and learning strategies that help them to identify, challenge and address any bias.

OBJECTIVES

By the end of this chapter, you should be able to:

- ■ identify a whole range of resources that can be used to support and facilitate learning in geography
- ■ produce some of your own resources for teaching and learning in geography
- ■ critically evaluate resources available to support teaching and learning in geography.

SELECTING RESOURCES

> The care and effort that teachers take over preparation can have a major positive impact on pupils' sense that the teacher cares about their learning and that the activities to be undertaken are worthwhile and important.
>
> (Kyriacou, 1991: 27)

We are using the term 'resources' in its general sense to describe anything that you use to support your teaching and to help pupils' learning in geography. This includes: published material such as textbooks, journals, activity packs and photocopiable resource sheets; audio-visual materials such as DVD, video and television programmes, photographic images and music; models, artefacts and materials that you have collected; resource sheets, activity sheets and illustrative material that you have produced. The range of resources that we can draw upon as geography teachers is extensive, particularly with the rapidly growing availability of e-Learning resources via the Internet.

This is seen by many pupils as one of the major attractions of the subject. However, if we recognise some of the notions of what geography is about (as discussed in Chapter 1), the nature and quality of the resources that we use are of more fundamental importance. Echoing Roger Robinson's earlier quote we rely, as geography teachers, on the quality of the materials that we use as well as the quality of our teaching to bring the subject alive in the classroom.

Creative use of resources can be very important in this respect. The quality, variety and use of resources will have a significant influence on pupils' interest and motivation to learn. Evidence from inspections of geography lessons frequently reveals a link between poor quality, poor use of resources and ineffective teaching and learning in geography (Smith, 1997). It therefore follows that resources and how they are used have an important role to play in pupils' intellectual development.

With these considerations in mind, we need to be able to give a critical evaluation of the geographical resources we encounter for their potential to engage pupils' interest and motivation, and to facilitate successful teaching and learning in geography. These principles, together with those relating to equal opportunities, should guide our decisions about the selection and development of resources for teaching and learning in geography.

The questions in Table 6.1 may provide some useful general criteria for the evaluation of teaching and learning resources.

Clearly teachers and learners can themselves be valuable resources for learning in geography. Often the knowledge and experiences that they bring into the geography classroom are rarely used or exploited. Teachers (and pupils) have often travelled extensively, gathering images, visual resources and experiences of people and places in the process. These can be used to bring some 'reality' into the classroom in a stimulating way, either physical or even perhaps through the use of a narrative.

Kyriacou's point about the positive impact of teachers' careful preparation of resources on pupils' attitudes to learning is a very valid one. Such resources provide an example of the standards expected and an indication of the value that teachers place on their pupils' learning. After all, how can we expect pupils to produce work of a high quality if the resources that we prepare for them are of a poor quality?

PREPARING RESOURCES

There should be a very close relationship between the planning processes described in Chapter 5 and the preparation of resources. When identifying and selecting resources or designing and preparing new resource materials, you should have a clear idea of their purpose. In other words, the resources needed are determined by the nature of the teaching strategies and learning activities that have been planned to achieve particular learning outcomes or to investigate particular enquiry questions. However, the discovery of a particular resource or activity may in itself provide the source of inspiration for a lesson.

In recent years, the rapid development of new technologies and their applications in education has made it possible for teachers to improve the quality and design of resource materials that they produce for use in the classroom. The 'ubiquitous' worksheet can serve a number of purposes:

- Providing information that is not found in textbooks or other whole class resources. This may include additional data, case study material or information about a local example. This information is often accompanied by relevant questions.
- Additional or alternative activities making use of resource material in textbooks.
- Introducing other resource material such as cartoons, diagrams and topical newspaper articles.
- Providing resource material and activities for homework.
- To support differentiation by adapting text, illustrations and tasks to the needs of pupils within one class.
- Providing instructions and guidance for an enquiry or activity.
- Providing a base sheet for pupils to write or draw on, e.g. to complete a graph, label a diagram or perhaps draw a valley cross-section. This minimises the time spent copying out and maximise the mental processes involved in learning.
- Providing pupils with step-by-step guidance about how to use a resource such as a computer program, CD-Rom or an audio-visual aid.
- Introducing fun activities such as word-searches, quizzes, or puzzles.

■ **Table 6.1** Some general criteria for the evaluation of teaching and learning resources in geography

Content

Is the geographical content relevant, accurate and up to date?
How will the geographical content contribute to the intellectual development of pupils:

■ knowledge to be acquired?
■ concepts to be developed?
■ skills to be used or developed?

Design

Is the resource well-presented and clear?
How original or creative is the content, presentation or approach?
Would pupils find the presentation and approach to be interesting and motivating?
Are the images and text clear, and do they support each other?

Pupils' learning needs

Are the images, text and activities used accessible to pupils with different learning needs?
Is the resource appropriate for pupils of a particular ability or range of abilities?

Language

Is the language level/readability appropriate?
Will the resource develop pupils' understanding and use of language in geography?
Will the resource enhance pupils' literacy skills?

Equal opportunities

Are the images, text and activities free of bias?
Will the resource challenge or reinforce stereotypical images and views about people and places?
Is there a gender and racial/cultural balance in the images and examples used in the resource?

Pupil involvement

Will the pupils enjoy using this resource?
Will the pupils be able to use the resource in an active way?
Will the resource, and how it is used, promote pupils' development and understanding of enquiry skills?

The key question is:

Will the resource make a significant contribution to the geographical education of pupils?

Activity 6.1 **Evaluating geographical resource sheets**

For this activity, you need to gather a variety of different worksheets that have been or are being used to support teaching and learning in geography. Evaluate the strengths and weaknesses of each worksheet.

It would be helpful to discuss your findings with a small group of student teachers. Try to prepare a spider diagram summarising your ideas about the principles that should guide the production of effective worksheets in geography.

The preparation of worksheets and other resource sheets is an important part of your lesson planning. Producing such resources to a high quality is frequently a time-consuming and demanding task. However, it gives you an opportunity to be creative and imaginative in your attempts to provide interesting and stimulating learning in the classroom. It is also one of the most frequently used strategies for differentiating learning in the classroom. As with all resources, a cautionary note is to avoid over-production and not to rely too heavily on worksheets. 'Worksheet fatigue' can have a damaging effect on pupil motivation, so try to ensure that there is a clear purpose for the worksheets you produce and that they are carefully planned and well presented.

Design often refers to the way in which material is organised and presented. In most cases, worksheets in geography include a combination of text, illustrations and learning activities for pupils. There is now a wide range of educational technology available to help geography teachers to produce high quality resource sheets.

The introduction of the Geography National Curriculum was accompanied by a large-scale expansion in the production and publication of resource materials, particularly for the lower secondary age range. Many of the textbooks produced have been accompanied by the ubiquitous teachers' resource pack of photocopiable resources. In addition to this, the publication of resource sheets and electronic resources offer information and activities on a wide range of topics for flexible use by teachers. More recently, several publishers have offered photocopiable and electronic resource material aiming to support work with pupils with learning difficulties. Consequently, there is an extensive range of published resource sheets that can be used 'off the shelf' or be adapted for use in different learning contexts. A browse through these may not only reveal some useful and relatively up-to-date information, interesting activities and diagrams, but also provide you with ideas about the design and layout of worksheets. Most, and particularly those designed for use with pupils with special educational needs, follow a common format.

Figure 6.1 shows the process of planning and preparation of resources as a series of stages. Many of the questions relate to practical issues, and the role of evaluation in developing your understanding of factors influencing the production and use of resources is emphasised. In Box 6.1, Dilkes and Nicholls (1988) provide a summary of some of the main factors that need to be considered when designing resource sheets. This also acts as a useful checklist to guide the preparation of text in geography worksheets that are to be used with pupils with learning difficulties.

USING TEXTBOOKS

As mentioned earlier, the introduction of the Geography National Curriculum, followed by changes in A-level and GCSE examination syllabuses led to a massive expansion in the publication of resources for geography teaching and stimulated 'a resurgence of the influence of the geography textbook' (Butt and Lambert, 1996: 202). They suggest further that the educational outcomes of geography courses, 'what pupils learn, how effectively they learn it and how well they perform in examinations is probably tied up in some way with the provision of textbooks'.

It is certainly true to say that in the past, the majority of schools spent a large proportion of any extra financial resources provided to support the implementation of Geography National Curriculum on textbooks. This, in many ways, compensated for inadequate resourcing of Key Stage 3 (KS 3) geography curriculum in the past. Although

Stage 1: Deciding to develop your own resource
■ What am I trying to achieve?
■ Who do I need the resource for?
■ Is there a resource already available which would be appropriate to use?

Stage 2: Practical implications
■ How do my ideas relate to the scheme of work and relevant National Curriculum programme(s) of study?
■ How do my ideas relate to the learning needs of the pupils?
■ Have I the practical skills, e.g. desktop publishing skills, to develop a resource which is of a high quality?
■ Has the school got the resources to reproduce my resource in sufficient quantity?
■ Is there another teacher or group who could also benefit from using my resource?

Stage 3: Planning the detail
■ What is to be the subject of my resource?
■ What skills and concepts do I want the pupils to develop/enhance?
■ What are the generic skills (numeracy/literacy) I want the pupils to use?
■ How will I cater for the different abilities within the class?
■ When will I discuss my ideas with my mentor?

Stage 4: Presentation issues
■ What title will I give to my resource?
■ What font size and style shall I use to make it: (a) accessible to pupils; (b) interesting to look at?
■ What visual images, e.g. diagrams, do I want to include?
■ How will I present the information/tasks I want the pupils to access?
■ How will I differentiate between pupils who have different learning needs?

Stage 5: Using the resource
■ What are the time scales I need to consider when creating my resource? i.e. can I get it copied in time?
■ How and where will I build it into my lesson plan?
■ Where will I store it to make it accessible to myself and others?
■ How will I introduce it to the pupils?

Stage 6: Evaluation
■ Did the resource help me to achieve my objectives?
■ Were pupils of different abilities able to use it?
■ Do I think the pupils enjoyed using it?
■ Was the outcome relevant to the demands of the scheme of work?
■ Would I use this resource again?
■ If I were to change it, what changes would I make?
■ What have I learnt about the planning and use of resources?

■ **Figure 6.1** Stages in the planning, preparation and use of resources

Style: Single sheet or resource booklet

portrait
(vertical)

or landscape
(horizontal)

Layout

■ The organisation of text, illustrations and activities.

■ Pupils should be able to follow the sequence of text and illustrations easily.

■ Try to achieve a balance between text and illustrations. Avoid large blocks of text and try not to cram too much on to one sheet.

■ Use illustrations and borders to stimulate interest and to create visual variety.

■ Activities and tasks should be clearly identified.

■ Wherever possible, try to ensure that each sheet is self-contained.

Text

■ Avoid the use of text continuously from one side of a page to another. A grid can be used to provide a structure to work to (i.e. using columns to determine width and depth.

■ Hand-written text can be used if it is neat and clear. In some cases, handwriting can be effective as it introduces variety into the presentation of worksheets.

■ Identify key words and headings in a separate typeface or in bold type.

Illustrations (maps and diagrams)

■ Clear black line drawings reproduce more effectively when printed.

■ Where possible, use borders to frame and highlight maps and diagrams.

■ All maps should have a title, scale north direction arrow and where appropriate, a key.

■ Photographs do not always reproduce clearly. Sometimes a master copy needs to be made using specialist equipment or a scanner can be used to incorporate photographs and other illustrations within a document being produced on a computer. It can also be helpful to add clear, black outlines or shading to enhance photographic images.

Graphics

■ Computer word-processing and desk-top publishing software packages now contain a vast range of graphics and illustrations.

■ These graphics can be used to present information effectively or to highlight activities or areas of text.

■ **Figure 6.2** Designing resource sheets

a wide variety of geography textbooks were produced for KS 3, the market for textbooks became extremely competitive, increasingly resembling a 'winner takes all scenario'. Lambert (1996) attributes this partly to 'network externalities', a process which explains

1   Make the text personal wherever possible (pupils gain access to some difficult concepts if they can relate to people).
2   Have a principle of organisation for each paragraph so that sentences follow each other in a necessary sequence. (If the sentences could be rearranged with no loss of meaning then the paragraph is not as helpfully structured as it could be!)
3   Make the link between ideas explicit but avoid difficult connectives: *consequently, furthermore, hence, likewise, moreover, similarly, that is, thus*.
4   Avoid long subjects, interruptions and some kinds of ellipses.
5   Use technical and foreign vocabulary only where strictly necessary.
6   Be particularly careful about technical terms that also have a different everyday meaning (e.g. bank of a river).
7   Avoid unnecessary formality in general vocabulary.
8   Be sparing with brackets and inverted commas, making sure they do not carry a weight of implicit meaning.
9   Overall, the best test of readability is to read the passage aloud. It should be pleasant and as easy to read as a story.

■ **Box 6.1** Checklist for writing geography worksheets
Source: Dilkes and Nicholls, 1988

the ability of the first product on the market to command an increasing share of the market simply because it gets known. This discussion is not included by way of a diversion from the main purpose of this section, but to explain why you may find that the geography curriculum in many of the schools that you may encounter as a teacher is dominated by the use of a single textbook resource. It also explains why resource decisions are not always influenced by educational criteria such as fitness for purpose, such as we are advocating in our advice about planning and preparation.

Activity 6.2 **Evaluating published resources**

This activity aims to help you start thinking about the evaluation of published resources such as textbooks. For this activity you need a range of textbooks (preferably for Key Stage 3) and it would be helpful to work with a small group of other student teachers to discuss your findings.

Using a copy of Box 6.2 to provide a framework, evaluate one or more geography textbooks. Share your findings with other student teachers.

■   What are the fundamental differences between the textbooks you have evaluated?
■   Are there any significant similarities between books that you have evaluated?
■   Which textbooks would you prefer to use and why?

Clearly your thinking about textbook resources will develop further when you have gained more practical experience of planning lessons and using textbooks in your teaching. However, it is helpful to raise your awareness of the design and presentation of resources and activities for teaching and learning that are to be found in geography textbooks.

The level of investment in a single textbook series that we described earlier often means that these books become the principle resource used by pupils. The danger is that the belief that these books 'cover' the curriculum can lead to a textbook series actually 'becoming' the curriculum (Widdowson and Lambert, 2006). The introduction of the National Curriculum may have established the importance of enquiry learning in geography and helped to specify a common content for the subject at Key Stage 3. However, in the past these requirements have been interpreted in different ways by different authors and publishers.

Building schemes of work around a particular textbook series may certainly help heads of department to ensure a fairly common curriculum experience for pupils, especially where non-specialist teachers need to be supported. However, curriculum delivery involves far more than just the coverage of specific subject content. Our advocacy for a more pupil-centred approach implies that we need to give more thought to the ways in which particular resources and learning activities such as those found in textbooks engage pupils in enquiry-based approaches to learning in geography (Widdowson and Lambert, 2006). This means that we should be striving to enhance the quality of pupils' thinking and other outcomes from learning geography, rather than just occupying them with activities and tasks.

The dangers of geography teachers relying too heavily on textbooks has been recognised by OFSTED, who have repeatedly commented on how 'many schools relied on a limited, and sometimes limiting single textbook series' (OFSTED, 1995: 14; Smith, 1997). A further concern may come from Walford's (1995) research into changes in the balance between text, illustration and activities in geography textbooks. In discussing the 'strange case of the disappearing text', Walford provides further evidence of the changing role of textbooks in geography over the last twenty years. The greater range of resources for learning to be found in geography textbooks is to be welcomed. However, the dominance of the 'double-page spread', the variable quality of often repetitive activities and the lack of genuine problem-solving or decision-making tasks can limit the breadth and depth of geographical enquiry. As a consequence, there may be insufficient challenge for pupils who are capable of working at higher levels, thereby placing a ceiling on their achievements. A reductionist view about the amount of text that pupils are capable of dealing with can also restrict the potential of geography for developing pupils' literacy and use of language.

An analysis of eight geography textbook series being used with pupils at Key Stage 3 raised a number of important issues about the suitability of these resources (SCAA, 1997). Particular concerns were expressed about the uneven provision of opportunities to meet common requirements regarding the use of language and information technology. Although most textbooks contain a good range of different types of resource material, a shortage of text limits opportunities for pupils to undertake extended reading. There were also worries about the overuse of graphical devices such as talking heads and cartoon sketches, rather than photographs, which it was felt could lead to over simplification and stereotyping.

A simple sheet to help organise initial thinking on textbook resources

Title...

Author...

Publisher...

Category	Positive	Negative
Claims made by publisher		
How are the contents organised and expressed?		
How is text presented and organised?		
How clearly are key concepts, themes or ideas signposted?		
How successfully are photos and artwork used?		
What forms of exercises and activities have been designed?		
What appears to be the 'ethos' of the book?		
How attractive is the book to young readers?		
Other?		

■ **Box 6.2** Evaluation of published resources

Source: Boardman, 1996, in Bailey and Fox

This scrutiny added further weight to OFSTED's concern about over-reliance on a single textbook series. Although the textbooks analysed contained a wide range of activities, the limited number of challenging tasks requiring pupils to use higher order skills was not considered satisfactory. Many of the tasks involved the simple transfer or re-organisation of information; for example, copying or filling in gaps in sentences and tables. Fed on a diet of such tasks, pupils are only likely to develop the use of comprehension skills rather than those required to analyse, synthesise and evaluate information. Questions have also been raised about the ability of the materials provided to sustain higher order tasks (Lambert, 2000; Widdowson and Lambert, 2006).

Many of these limitations are easy to comprehend. Textbooks have to meet a huge range of often conflicting needs from different potential users (including non-specialist teachers). We have long been sceptical of publishers' claims that their textbook series successfully deliver all the requirements of the National Curriculum for pupils across the range of ability. As the SCAA analysis found, most of these textbooks appear to be generally successful at meeting the needs of pupils working at levels 4–6. To differentiate effectively, geography teachers need to develop appropriate activities and often produce additional resource materials to supplement the textbooks available to them. It is also difficult to identify any clear evidence of progression in many textbooks so this is a further consideration in your planning.

Publishers are increasingly giving more consideration to issues relating to equal opportunities in the production of textbook resources. Greater attention is being given to the reduction of bias in the use of language and illustrations. If language is misused, it can distort reality and reinforce stereotypical images and prejudice. A frequently used example in geography is the ambiguous use of 'man' as a generic term in the study of 'man and the environment'. The use of 'people-environment' conveys a more appropriate and non-sexist image.

The introduction of the revised National Curriculum for Geography in 2008 with its emphasis on the subject's important concepts and absence of prescribed content should bring a fresh approach to production of textbook resources. Widdowson and Lambert (2006) raise questions about the role of textbooks in an 'information age' and the balance between the teacher, students and the learning resources in generating the 'learning energy' of a classroom. They conclude that textbooks do still have a role in geography classrooms, but that it is unlikely to be the same role they had in the past (Widdowson and Lambert, 2006: 157). They draw attention to research evidence showing that textbooks can lead to healthy curriculum change and renewal (Chambliss and Calfree, 1998; Lambert, 2000). They provide examples of different approaches to using textbooks depending on the extent to which the lesson depends on the textbook or uses textbooks as part of a 'framed enquiry'.

Gender bias in geography textbooks has been a concern, and although progress has been made there is still work to be done to address some of the issues. Several authors have warned about the dangers of ethnocentric bias in geography textbooks. Hicks draws our attention to how the way in which people and places are represented reveals evidence of European bias in teaching materials:

> All teaching materials that deal in any way with images of the world bring with them a set of attitudes and assumptions, explicit or implicit, conscious or unconscious, which are based on broader cultural perspectives. These perspectives tend to the ethnocentric, i.e. they generally measure other cultures and groups against the norms of one's own, or racist in that one's own culture is considered to be superior and thus, by definition, others are inferior.
>
> (Hicks, 1980: 3)

Christine Winter provides a significant contribution to the debate about these issues in her account of an attempt to 'raise pupils' awareness of the subjectivity involved in representing knowledge about people and places in geography' (Winter, 1997: 180). She argues that geography teachers need to review textbooks critically in order to identify and reject those which show evidence of ethnocentric bias. She also urges teachers to enquire into the 'values implicitly underpinning textbook interpretations of the curriculum'.

Winter uses principles taken from McDowell's (1994) new cultural geography perspective as a basis for analysing a case study of the Maasai way of life in the *'Key Geography: Connections'* textbook (Waugh and Bushell, 1992: 78–9). This analysis aims to deconstruct the authors' interpretation of the Geography National Curriculum in relation to the Maasai people of Kenya. The following extract from this analysis illustrates how ethnocentric bias can manifest itself in a geography textbook:

In spite of the frequent reference to the idea of change in the National Curriculum policy document, the authors make no reference in the textbook pages to the Maasai places and people as undergoing change; instead, a picture of a static way of life is presented. There is no mention of the reduction in Maasai grazing ground as a result of the appropriation of land by the European settlers; soil erosion caused by the overgrazing of pasture on reduced amounts of land; the employment of Maasai people as cattle-herders by European ranch-owners and employment in the tourist trade. Neither are the development of fixed villages with wooden homes, more sedentary lifestyles, tanked water supplies, schools and community health-care projects mentioned.

The representation shows no evidence of a range of voices involved in the place being studied. The text is dominated by a white, male, western voice, with no views of the Maasai people about their places, history, stories and lives. If Maasai authors had written the two pages, what would they have looked like? How would they have represented themselves and their land? What do the Maasai women say about their places? And what about the other voices to be heard in a study of this place; the voices of the Kenyan government, the tourists, the cattle ranchers and the safari travel firms?

(Winter, 1997: 183)

Activity 6.3 **Identifying bias in published resources**

Select a number of case studies about people and places from a small range of textbooks. Carefully study the text, illustrations and activities in these examples.

■ Examine the way in which these case studies portray people and places.
■ Describe any examples of gender or ethnocentric bias that you have identified. Suggest alternative ways in which these people and places could have been portrayed. Could the resources in the textbook be used with pupils in different ways so as to avoid the development of ethnocentric or gender-biased views?

Develop an activity to be used with pupils to find out how aware they are of bias in the textbook resources that they use in geography.

Winter's deconstruction of this case study shows how one textbook's interpretation of the National Curriculum can present an ethnocentric view through a 'one-dimensional, static, unproblematical representation' of Kenyan people and place (Winter, 1997: 184). She then uses the same principles to reconstruct the case study providing alternative suggestions about how more appropriate teaching materials and activities could be developed. In doing so, Winter demonstrates the crucial role of geography teachers in developing in pupils 'the ability to think for themselves, to ask questions, to make decisions and judgements on the basis of their own rational reflections, supported by materials and teaching which uphold a notion of social justice' (Winter, 1997: 187).

We have not engaged in such a lengthy analysis of issues relating to the *use* of textbooks because we are in any way paranoid about them being used by geography teachers. However, in acknowledging that textbooks are one of the principal resources used in geography classrooms, we recognise the influence that they can have on the nature and outcome of pupils' geographical education (see also Widdowson and Lambert, 2006).

As teachers, we need to be aware of the messages that they give about people and places. As with all resources used for teaching and learning, we should critically review their contents and approach to learning in geography as well as considering the potential learning outcomes (knowledge, understanding, skills, attitudes and values) from using them. We should not let the attractive presentation of teaching materials distract us from being critical of an over-simplified treatment of important issues based on unquestioned assumptions or outdated theories. As well as trying to ensure that pupils do not develop or reinforce negative stereotypes of people and places, we need to look out for misconceptions about issues and questions that can be found in some textbooks.

USING MAPS AND ATLASES

Maps are one of the geographer's most important tools, providing useful ways of storing and communicating information about people and places. If geography involves the study of the relationships between people and places, then maps help geographers to present, describe and explain the spatial information, patterns and processes that they observe in the world around them.

Learning to read and to use maps makes an important contribution to the development of graphicacy in pupils. During their geographical education, pupils should encounter a wide variety of maps drawn for different purposes and at different scales. As geography teachers, we need to help our pupils develop and learn how to use the essential map skills. A structured approach involving practice in reading and using a variety of maps can certainly help pupils develop these skills and apply them in different contexts.

Maps have four main functions:

■ location, enabling the user to find a place (e.g. in an atlas, on a street map)
■ route-displaying, allowing the user to get from A to B (e.g. a road atlas, underground map or street map)
■ storing and displaying information, allowing the user to isolate and sort information from a wide range of different items (e.g. OS maps), or to consider patterns and relationships of selected information (e.g. distribution maps)
■ problem-solving, helping the user to solve problems by interpreting or inferring from the information provided (e.g. why a road does not take the most direct route or where to locate a factory). Skilled map-users have learnt to 'see' the landscape from the information on the map.

(Weeden, 1997: 173)

Start collecting a wide variety of examples of such maps for use in your lessons. Interesting classroom displays can be created classifying the examples that you collect under the headings identified above. Alternatively, you could devise an interesting activity for pupils where they are required to identify the main functions of a variety of maps together with their strengths and limitations (in relation to their properties).

Activity 6.4 **Teaching and learning with maps**

Collect a variety of different types of map that pupils might encounter during their geographical education, perhaps in textbooks or even in examinations.
   For each example:

■   identify the properties of a map that could be demonstrated
■   identify any potential learning difficulties that pupils might experience when using this map. Try to think of ways in which you could help them overcome these difficulties
■   suggest possible learning activities that could be developed using this map.

Ordnance Survey maps

During their secondary school education in geography, pupils are required to use and interpret Ordnance Survey maps and plans at a variety of scales (the OS has for several years offered all Y7 pupils a free 1:50000 map, delivered via the school. Most schools now take advantage of this offer. By 2008, over 5 million maps had been distributed in this way. Research shows that many children love to have their very own map). To use and interpret maps successfully pupils need to develop a range of essential skills so that they can use these maps in their studies of different places and geographical themes. Most schools have a good range of Ordnance Survey maps including ones of the local area as well as a collection of map extracts of other areas from previous examinations. Table 6.2 summarises the main features of Ordnance Survey maps at different scales.

   Once again, a display of these maps, preferably of the local area, at different scales for comparative purposes can be an effective strategy. The ways in which similar features (i.e. the language of the maps) are represented on maps at different scales can be compared. It is particularly helpful if pupils are familiar with these features because they are to be found in their local area. They can also gain a feel for the purposes of the different Ordnance Survey maps, i.e. how they might be used. Wherever possible, pupils should be given experience of using these maps for different purposes.

Weather maps

Weather maps or synoptic charts are another type of map that are used in geography. They provide a summary of the weather conditions being experienced in particular places at a particular point in time. A synoptic chart gives an indication of air pressure, temperature, wind strength and direction, and the amount of rainfall received. From this, judgements or forecasts can be made about probable future weather conditions.

   As with other types of map, pupils need to understand the essential elements and features of synoptic charts before they are able to interpret weather patterns. These skills can be developed systematically and progressively so that able pupils can be challenged by the need to interpret more complex patterns and relationships. It should also be remembered that pupils can encounter synoptic charts alongside other resources in tasks (such as those in examination questions) that require them to describe and explain ways in which weather and climate can affect people's lives and activities. Pupils should,

■ **Table 6.2** Comparison of Ordnance Survey maps at different scales

Title	Scale	Equivalent	Feature
Superplan	1:1250	1 cm to 12.5 m or 50 in to 1 mile	Site-centred plots in urban areas
Superplan	1:2 500	1 cm to 25 m or 25 in to 1 mile	Site-centred plots in rural areas
	1:10 000	1 cm to 1 00 m or 6 in to 1 mile	Contours at 5 m vertical interval (10 m in mountain and moorland areas)
Pathfinder Explorer Outdoor Leisure	1:25000	4 cm to 1 km or 2.5 in to 1 mile	Maps for walking: contours at 5 m vertical interval
Landranger	1:50000	2 cm to 1 km or 1.25 in to 1 mile	Maps for motoring and walking: contours at 10 m vertical interval
Travelmaster	1:250000	1 cm to 2.5 km or 1 in to 4 miles	Maps for motoring: contours with hill shading

Source: Boardman, 1996 in Bailey and Fox: 118

therefore, have opportunities to apply their understanding and skills. For example, an A-level student might be asked to use the synoptic chart in Figure 6.3 to explain why the Meteorological Office might have issued a severe weather warning for midnight for the London area. Sometimes synoptic charts are used with satellite photographs: for example, to examine a weather system such as a depression or a tropical cyclone. This can help pupils visualise features like weather fronts and the cloud patterns associated with different weather systems.

Atlases

There is now a great range of atlases (including electronic atlases) available to support and enhance pupils' learning in geography. Notwithstanding the changing nature of the world around us, the atlas still has an important role to play in helping pupils to both locate places within their regional, national and global contexts and study a wide range of geographical phenomena. The range of opportunities for using atlases to support different learning activities has been extended by the development of electronic atlases (on disk, CD-Rom or the Internet). The data in such atlases can be interrogated, manipulated and presented cartographically, giving pupils the potential to use the geographical information that they contain in a more active way.

Atlas maps only show a limited amount of information and 'abstract thinking' is often required in the interpretation of this information. A number of interpretation problems can be associated with the use of these maps including:

■ Complex patterns of colours and symbols
■ A wide variety of type faces and type styles
■ High density of information which can make the maps difficult to read
■ The inter cutting of map labels and labels with lines and colour

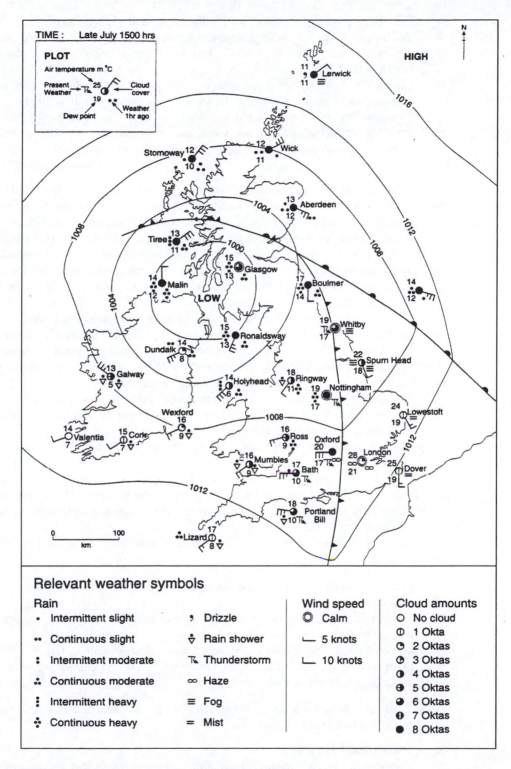

Relevant weather symbols

Rain

• Intermittent slight	, Drizzle	
•• Continuous slight	⩫ Rain shower	
: Intermittent moderate	T⩘ Thunderstorm	
∴ Continuous moderate	∞ Haze	
⦙ Intermittent heavy	≡ Fog	
⦂ Continuous heavy	= Mist	

Wind speed

◎ Calm	
— 5 knots	
∟ 10 knots	

Cloud amounts

○ No cloud	
◐ 1 Okta	
◑ 2 Oktas	
◑ 3 Oktas	
◑ 4 Oktas	
◕ 5 Oktas	
◕ 6 Oktas	
◕ 7 Oktas	
● 8 Oktas	

■ **Figure 6.3** Synoptic chart for the British Isles in late July

- Foreign place names that can be difficult to spell and to pronounce
- The use of colours with ambiguous meanings (e.g. green areas on topographic maps can be read as 'grassy' or 'fertile' when the colour is being used to indicate the height of the land)
- Choropleth and isopleth maps can mislead pupils into believing that sudden changes occur at the zone boundaries when in reality there is likely to be a transition from one zone to another
- Standard world map projections, when used in isolation from alternatives, or a globe, can distort pupils' understanding of spatial relationships.

(Wiegand, 1996: 125–6)

These problems are not always readily evident to a teacher and they can often be overlooked. We should be aware of the fact that, like any other reference book, an atlas presents only a 'partial and selective view of the world' (Wiegand, 1996: 126).

Another issue that is often neglected is the importance of the type of projection that is used for different maps. Pupils need to be familiar with a variety of different projections and to understand that the selection of a projection is determined by the purpose for which the map is used. It is not possible to have a map that accurately shows both the relative shape and the area of land masses.

It is worth developing some activities to help pupils understand some of these issues and principles. At the very least, raising your awareness encourages you to look out for potential problems that could hinder pupil learning. Spending some time examining the differences between projections could perhaps remove a possible cause of misinterpretation when pupils are using atlas maps in the future.

To explore the way in which different projections distort the size and shape of land masses, pupils could be asked to colour in and then compare the appearance of different continents like Africa and Antarctica on different projections. Another common task is to get pupils to compare the direct route between two places shown to be a straight line on a map with the shortest route between these places on a globe (i.e. the 'great circle' route), which can be measured using a piece of string. Pupils' thinking could be further developed by suggesting various tasks (i.e. different information to be displayed) and asking the pupils to select and justify their choice of the most appropriate projection for this task (Wiegand, 1996).

In order to make effective use of atlases, pupils need to develop a range of interrelated skills:

- Locational skills – using the index and system of co-ordinates; understanding latitude and longitude.
- Symbol skills – learning about the different uses of colour and point symbols; using the key to interpret symbols.
- Sense of scale – using scale to compare areas and to estimate distances.
- Interpretation of data – describing, retrieving, using and comparing information about places shown on thematic maps.

A 'progressive teaching sequence' for developing pupils' understanding of longitude (meridians) and latitude (parallels) could be:

- The earth has two poles.
- There are two sets of imaginary lines circling the earth (lines that go round the earth at its maximum extent).

■   Parallels do not join and only one of them (the equator) is a 'great circle'.

■   Meridians and parallels are numbered in degrees.

■   Some parallels have special names – the equator, the tropics and the polar circles.

■   Meridians are numbered east and west from the prime meridian.

■   The prime meridian is not 'natural'. It is only fixed by international agreement.

■   Parallels are numbered north and south from the equator.

■   The equator divides the world into north and south hemispheres.

(Wiegand, 1996: 130)

Electronic atlases offer a vast amount of information in a range of formats including maps, text, statistics and both photographic and video material. Where these electronic atlases can be used flexibly and interactively by pupils, there is a great deal of potential to enhance pupil learning. There is also an increasing range of atlas material available on the Internet. As with all ICT resources, the presentation of these and the applications provided need to be carefully evaluated. If pupils do not understand the purpose of the applications and if they lack the skills needed to identify, select and use appropriate information, they cannot be able to make effective use of these resources. The quality of the support material available with these interactive atlases can be an important factor determining whether they are used effectively by teachers.

USING IMAGES

Aerial photographs

Aerial photographs are often used in conjunction with Ordnance Survey maps to help pupils visualise landscapes shown on the maps. Photographs, however, have completely different characteristics. This may help to explain why some pupils can find it difficult to correlate features on aerial photographs with corresponding features on Ordnance Survey maps (Boardman and Towner, 1980). This is because the processes involved in 'reading' and 'interpreting' photographs are different from those used in map reading and interpretation (Boardman, 1987).

Pupils should be helped to understand the important elements of aerial photographs if they are to be able to use these resources effectively. The effect of perspective will influence the shape and spatial arrangement of features viewed in a photograph. The effect of scale means that as the scale of a photograph becomes smaller it becomes more difficult to identify the detail of features. Whereas the scale of a map is consistent over the whole of the map, the scale of a photograph varies with distance from the camera. Pupils often overestimate the size of areas shown on a photograph when they are comparing it with a map, so it is useful to get them to measure the distances across the various components of the area shown on the photograph using the scale on the map.

For pupils who are unfamiliar with aerial photographs, a useful strategy to illustrate the effect of perspective is to start with ordinary ground level photographs before moving on to investigate the different perspectives shown in oblique and vertical aerial photographs. Ground level photographs show features in the foreground more prominently than those in the background and the variations in scale mean that distances cannot be measured. The transition between this view and that shown by a vertical aerial photograph is provided by an oblique aerial photograph. As such, it forms an intermediate stage in the mental processes involved in transforming the three-dimensional landscape of the real world to the vertical representation on the map (Boardman, 1987: 133). The effect of perspective in an oblique aerial view is greater due to the distances and variation in scale between the foreground and the background. This means that the area shown on an oblique aerial photograph is not rectangular when represented on a map. It is therefore helpful to pupils to mark the edges of the area shown on the photograph on to the map.

Once pupils comprehend these elements of aerial photographs, they should be given a variety of opportunities to practise and to develop their skills in interpreting these photographs progressively. Figure 6.4 attempts to summarise a possible approach to the progressive development of these skills. As with all geographical skills, the aim is to move from an awareness of the important characteristics of a resource, through an understanding of how to identify features and interpret evidence, towards the ability to select and use appropriate skills in the study of particular geographical themes and places.

Aerial photographs taken of the same area at different dates are a particularly helpful and interesting resource when pupils are investigating changes in land use that have occurred in a settlement. It is possible to identify specific buildings on aerial photographs at an appropriate scale (e.g. 1:5,000). Shapes, patterns and relationships can also be studied and other skills, such as drawing sketch maps, developed and utilised to help pupils in the interpretation of these photographs.

Oblique aerial photographs at an appropriate scale can help pupils to visualise the shape, scale and appearance of landforms and landscape components. Patterns in physical systems (e.g. drainage patterns) and relationships between physical features (e.g. between a meandering river, its floodplain and valley) can also be examined. In all of these examples, the enquiry is enhanced if the aerial photographs are supported by Ordnance Survey maps of the same area and the pupils are encouraged to correlate the features on these different sources.

Box 6.3 has been included as an example of a geographical enquiry that makes use of a variety of resources and learning activities using aerial photographs to develop a range of geographical skills in investigating an issue. Google Earth and the recent BBC series 'Britain from Above' (BBC 2008) provide further excellent resources for developing stimulating geographical enquiries using aerial views.

Activity 6.5 **Using aerial photographs in geographical enquiries at GCSE**

Design a sequence of tasks to develop pupils' skills in interpreting aerial photographs. You might find it helpful to use the approach suggested in Figure 6.4 to develop some progression in this sequence of tasks. This sequence could build up to a more substantial enquiry that requires pupils to apply these skills in investigating a particular geographical issue or theme.

The final enquiry could provide an appropriate means of assessing pupils' understanding of particular concepts, issues or themes as well as their ability to use and apply specific geographical skills associated with the interpretation of maps and aerial photographs. If the opportunity arises, you could try out these tasks with a range of pupils to help you evaluate their effectiveness as well as develop your understanding of pupil learning using these resources. Tracing overlays can be used to help pupils draw sketch maps and grids and can be photocopied onto overhead transparencies to assist with the identification of features and descriptions of their location.

Stage One: Familiarity with aerial photographs
■ Understanding the effects of 'perspective' and 'scale'.
■ Differences between ground level, oblique and vertical views.

Stage Two: Recognition and identification
■ Identifying specific features starting with familiar local features of those with shapes that are easy to recognise.
■ Human features such as type of building and housing, transport routes and other land use.
■ Physical features such as large coastal landforms, valleys, montain ranges and drainage patterns.

State Three: Interpretation
■ Identifying less obvious features.
■ Describing patterns and simple relationships.
■ Using evidence from the images to investigate patterns and relationships between places.

Stage four: Advanced interpretation
■ Using evidence from the images to suggest reasons for patterns and relationships.
■ Using this evidence with information from other sources, selecting and using appropriate skills in geographical enquiries.

■ **Figure 6.4** Progression in the development of skills used to interpret aerial photographs

Satellite (remote-sensing) images

'Remote-sensing' is a term used for a method of obtaining information about a place or an area from a distance. This information is collected by cameras and scanners that are carried by aeroplanes and satellites, and it is presented in the form of photographs and images. As described earlier, aerial photographs usually show this information in much the same form as the human eye would see it (Barnett *et al.*, 1995). However, the information that is shown in satellite images has been processed by a computer.

Remote-sensing images often motivate pupils as they can show more detail and depth of information than can usually be found on a map. The information collected by the scanners carried by satellites goes beyond what the human eye can see. We can only see 'visible light' (red to violet), which is only part of the much wider spectrum of electromagnetic spectrum of radiation which includes microwaves, radio waves, X-rays and infra-red waves. The types of electromagnetic energy that are most commonly detected by satellite scanners are light and radiant heat. Some satellites can now detect radio waves.

The information collected by the scanners is recorded as a series of electronic signals which are then transmitted back to earth where they are processed by computers. The human eye would not be able to see many of the things shown on a satellite image so the images are often presented in 'false-colour' (unnatural colour) schemes that highlight interesting features.

A unit of work was developed to investigate the location of a new football stadium. The aim of this curriculum unit was to introduce Year 8 pupils to a decision-making exercise about location and conflicts over land use. This focus provided an opportunity for the pupils to use some 1:5,000 scale, colour aerial photographs.

With the local football club having just been promoted to the Premier League, an introductory activity examined where supporters would have to travel to when they visited other clubs. The main activity started with an evaluation of the club's existing ground, concentrating on:

■ its limited size
■ its lack of scope for expansion
■ the need for parking facilities.

Once this background to the issue had been established, a proposal was made suggesting that the directors of the club would like to build a new multi-purpose stadium if a suitable site, with enough space and adequate access, could be found. Four possible sites were identified and the pupils were given information about each of these sites. The pupils were required to evaluate each site considering the arguments for and against its development. To do this they used a 1:10,000 scale map and 1:5,000 scale vertical aerial photographs to identify evidence of what was on or around each site. A 1:50,000 scale map was used to investigate access to major transport routes and the rest of the urban area.

A matrix was provided to help the pupils to structure their evaluation and guidance given about how the photographs could be used to determine:

■ the type of land use
■ the effect of noise and other factors on the surrounding area
■ the effect of traffic on the road system.

To complete the matrix, scores were allocated to each site for a variety of factors including:

■ access for cars
■ access to public transport
■ distance from large populations
■ least opposition from supporters
■ least traffic congestion
■ cheapest site
■ access for away supporters.

After completing the matrix, the pupils produced a written report justifying the selection of the site with the lowest score and commenting on any problems that it presented. The final part of the activity involved the pupils using the resources to identify evidence to support a particular pressure group's case. This was followed by a debate in which each group presented its arguments. The enquiry was concluded with each pupil coming out of role to vote for their preferred choice of location for the stadium.

■ **Box 6.3** Using aerial photographs: a case study – home and away
Source: Barnett *et al.*, 1995: 108

There are two main types of satellites providing images which can be used in teaching:

■   weather satellites such as METEOSAT
■   land observation satellites such as the American LANDSAT and the French SPOT.

Some schools have computers that can obtain, store and display images from these satellites. There is also software available to enable pupils to process data and create their own remotely-sensed images. Most schools now have examples of satellite images either from published resource packs, examination questions or textbooks.

Using satellite images is an important 'application of information technology' and can therefore make a useful contribution to the development of pupils' IT capabilities. Many schools are teaching pupils how to 'read' and interpret satellite images and some are teaching pupils how to use image-processing software to investigate a sequence of weather images; for example, to study the passage of a depression. However, there is little evidence yet of pupils using satellite images as learning resources for their own enquiries (Barnett and Milton, 1995).

As with aerial photographs, there is no strict progression in the way which pupils' skills for interpreting satellite images should be developed. However, as a general rule, the sequence suggested for aerial photographs in Box 6.3 may be helpful to follow. To stimulate their interest it is helpful not to provide a key for the image at the outset and encourage pupils to think about:

■   what the different colours might show
■   what aspects of geography might be studied using this image?

The pupils could also be asked to generate a series of enquiry questions that could be used as a basis for investigating the image. An open-ended approach, where the teacher does not prescribe what pupils should be looking for too tightly, can be more motivating. It can also stimulate more independent thinking and enquiry. A sketch outline of the area shown on the image can then be used to record pupils' findings.

Photographs and slides

Photographs and slides are important sources of visual material that help geography teachers bring some reality into their classrooms. They also make an important contribution to the development of pupils' vocabulary through picture and word association. Textbooks and other published resources make use of a wide range of photographic material and pupils' skills of photographic interpretation are frequently assessed in examinations.

The key role that visual images play in helping pupils to acquire knowledge about and perceptions of people and places means that, as teachers, we need to give careful attention to the strategies we employ when using these images with pupils. Often photographic images are just used to illustrate what a feature being studied actually looks like. However, too often the potential for pupils to learn from photographs can be hindered by teachers using closed learning strategies. As a result, opportunities for pupils to share ideas and to explore values and attitudes in relation to issues are not exploited. Visual images can also create or reinforce generalisations and stereotypes about people and places. Robinson (1987: 130) reminds us that photographs can be used to provide a

■ Making careful visual observations and verbal comments.
■ Acquiring information from a visual source.
■ Analysing and evaluating information.
■ Relating one's own views to the image.
■ Recognising the value of different interpretations.
■ Producing a written or oral interpretation of an image.
■ Empathising with the people or situations portrayed.
■ Forming links between photographs.

■ **Box 6.4** Learning skills that can be developed using photographic material
Source: Robinson and Serf, 1997: 58

resource for building images that involve alternative viewpoints and develop empathy and to encourage discursive learning based in the 'real' world of the pupils and involving their own attitudes and values.

The use of photographic material can help pupils to develop a variety of learning skills. Skills of photographic interpretation should be developed gradually and it is important to focus on some basic skills before challenging pupils to make more detailed analyses. For example, pupils should be encouraged to look carefully at and assimilate the content of a photograph before attempting any interpretation. They should also be given the opportunity to relate what they see to their own experiences.

Robinson and Serf (1997) have suggested a common framework of questions to use when introducing a photographic image (see Figure 6.5). The key questions in this frame should help pupils to focus their thinking about the image in different ways. It should therefore encourage deeper observations of the view shown in the photographic image.

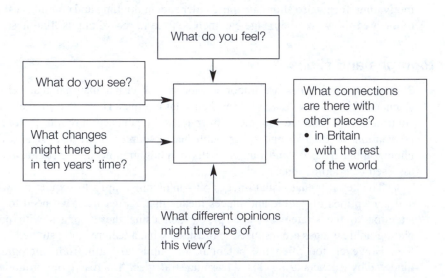

■ **Figure 6.5** Framing an image
Source: Robinson and Serf, 1997: 58

Robinson and Serf (1997) have provided suggestions for a range of interesting activities designed to develop pupils' observational skills when using photographic images in development education. These activities can be adapted and applied in a variety of other contexts. Pupils can be encouraged to identify their own enquiry questions for investigating issues raised in photographic images. When there are a limited number of photographs, one effective way of showing the outcomes of pupils' discussions is for them to write their enquiry questions or thoughts on sugar paper around their photograph.

When pupils have learnt how to explore their own perceptions about the content of a photograph image, they should have opportunities to engage in deeper enquiry to develop their skills of interpretation and analysis. Frameworks like the Development Compass Rose (shown on page 204) can be useful in this respect. Activities drawn from media education, like story-boarding and scripting a documentary using a selection of photographs, provide creative and motivating strategies for promoting discovery learning (see Durbin, 2006: 234–5).

When studying photographs of physical landscapes, pupils should be encouraged to adopt a structured approach examining different parts of the photograph and identifying the significant components of the landscape shown. This would involve observing the foreground, middle ground and background before dividing the landscape into its natural components (such as hills, valleys, beaches, cliff face and cliff top) and then describing the appearance of specific natural features. Patterns of land use, relief, drainage and vegetation can also be interpreted. Evidence of people – environment interactions and interrelationships should also be identified:

■ What influence do natural elements of the landscape have on people's use of the area?

■ How have people changed the natural (physical) environment of the area shown in the photograph?

Drawing a photo-sketch of the landscape shown can help with the identification of features and landscape components. Using tracing paper or providing a sketch outline can be a useful first stage in this process. Strategies for helping pupils to develop the skills needed to draw annotated sketches and sketch maps are discussed in Chapter 4. Higher level interpretation would involve pupils using evidence from the photograph, together with their own knowledge and understanding, to suggest reasons for the patterns shown or to explain how particular landforms might have been formed.

Given the experiences that many geography teachers have of different places, landscapes and cultures, it is perhaps surprising that relatively few make use of their own photographic resources. A personal experience or story can bring such images to life! One of our teaching colleagues has developed an interesting collection of slides showing different coastal landforms and coastal protection measures gathered on the annual family holiday. The clarity of these images enables pupils to look for evidence of coastal processes. Another colleague has used photographs from his climbing and pot-holing expeditions to develop photo-packs for pupils to use in studies of glaciated landscapes and limestone scenery. So exploit your experiences of visiting different places to extend the range of visual resources available for you to use in the classroom.

Photographic images can be used with pupils in a great number of imaginative ways. Pupils can learn through discovery by taking photographs to record their own observations in fieldwork activities. This can be particularly useful when analysing attitudes and values involved in issues. For example, when investigating the impacts of recreation in an area within a National Park, pupils could be asked to take photographs to show evidence of particular recreational activities and their impacts. The effectiveness of different management strategies could also be analysed. A poster display could be used to present the pupils' findings with appropriate photographs being selected and annotated with analytical comments. This display should incorporate a sketch map identifying the locations featured and using appropriate cartographic techniques to show relevant patterns. The outcome would represent pupils' interpretation of a case study, an interpretation developed through enquiry learning and one which is therefore more likely to be internalised.

A variation on this approach would be to get pupils investigating the regeneration of an urban area and to take photographs to support a particular viewpoint. For example, one group would take appropriate photographs to construct a display to show that the regeneration had been successful while another group would attempt to show evidence of failure, concentrating on the negative impacts. An interesting discussion could be developed if pupils chose similar views for different purposes. Alternatively, images can be selected to support the views of different interest groups.

Our experience has shown that older pupils (15–19) are particularly motivated by such strategies for using photographic images. They help to promote more student-centred approaches to learning and are effective in reinforcing knowledge and understanding of case studies.

Younger pupils could be presented with a number of photographs and asked to select appropriate ones for various purposes. For example, photographs of different river features could be provided and the pupils required to identify where they might be found in the course of a river. An interesting fieldwork investigation could be set up by providing groups of pupils with different sets of photographs of geographical features and locations in an area to be visited. During the visit, the pupils would have to match the photographs to particular locations which would then be identified on an Ordnance Survey map of the area. To develop pupils' skills of interpretation and encourage more in-depth enquiry, they could be asked to devise their own enquiry questions about each site or feature.

Televisual resources

> Because so much of our geographical source material is derived from television, it is vital that in a secondary school geography curriculum we take account of the distortions that can result from this particular source of images and ideas. Many television genres are constructions of reality and can bias our views, albeit unintentionally.
>
> (Durbin, 2006: 229)

Televisual resources make a significant contribution to teaching and learning in geography. As with photographic images, televisual resources help us to bring some 'reality' into our classrooms. The images that pupils see in videos influence the sense of place that they develop as well as their perceptions of other cultural groups. These visual impressions can 'become very strongly rooted and may need to be questioned if pupils are not to go through school carrying partially accurate impressions of an issue' (Butt, 1991: 53; Durbin, 2006: 229). GCSE and A-level examiners have also warned of these dangers when commenting on the amount of 'television geography' that is evident in many pupils' answers.

We should not lose sight of the educational potential of televisual material as a motivating resource for teaching and learning. However, we should be aware of its limitations and the dangers of being dominated by the medium. If we do not give some thought to imaginative and active ways of using televisual resources, they can become demotivating and ineffective resources for teaching and learning. If televisual resources are to fulfil their educational potential, we need to adopt active strategies that encourage pupils to 'use and analyse' the televisual material provided rather than just looking and seeing'. The old 'watch and make notes' strategy encourages pupils to adopt a very passive role. An experiment carried out with PGCE teachers illustrates the limited educational benefits of the narrow transactional writing involved in taking notes on the content of a television programme:

> A group of student teachers were shown a television programme and asked to take notes on what they learned from it. The programme was stopped after five minutes and the transcript of the commentary was read out. The students were asked to delete from their notes anything which they had written down during the programme that was in the transcript. Not a single student had anything left! They had made no record of what they had just seen.
>
> This revealed that the students were not interpreting the pictures; they had behaved as if it was a simple dictation exercise. Visual information was not recorded.
>
> (Roberts, 1987: 116)

At the outset, it is important to consider what video can do well for teaching and learning in geography as well as what it does not do well! From his own research, Chris Durbin (1995) suggests that television and video resources are helpful because they:

■ bring distant places to the classroom
■ enable people's views to be heard, although they are often short sound bites
■ can explain a difficult concept or process using a combination of images, graphics and commentary
■ can relate the location of a place to a wider region or even the world, through a series of 'nested' maps
■ can give a visual impression of change over time in relation to various geographical phenomena.

Our attention should then be drawn to the limitations and constraints of these resources so that we provide appropriate support materials. Durbin reminds us that it is difficult for television to:

■ convey detail on maps and also specific locational knowledge
■ convey complex geographical data
■ give subtle and complex viewpoints about an issue
■ allow enough time to dwell on images to enable the viewer to absorb complex information.

As geography teachers, we can do much to develop pupils' media literacy and we can learn a great deal from media studies when looking for strategies to enhance the value of using televisual resources (Durbin, 2006). For a start we should ensure that pupils do not assume that what they see in a televisual resource represents the objective truth. Media literacy is a vital part of geographical education and that as geography teachers, we must ensure that pupils are aware of how their views of the world are shaped by the images and messages they receive from the media:

> When young people study geography they are in fact studying many geographies – of rich and poor, young and old, rural and urban, and so on. They are also studying the world as it is perceived and experienced – both by themselves directly, and indirectly through various media. Thoughts, attitudes and values do not develop in isolation.'
>
> (Durbin, 2006: 226)

Just taking notes requires transactional writing and does not challenge pupils to interpret critically what they see. Pupils should be encouraged to look for 'bias, omissions, stated values and impressions created' (Butt, 1991: 51). Durbin (2006) suggests a range of strategies that can develop critical literacy about media sources and make creative use of various media as sources of information and stimuli for learning. These strategies approach the development of geographical knowledge and understanding as 'tentative enquiry':

> As geography teachers we have a particular responsibility because our subject is full of partial truths, is in many ways an uncertain science, and involves issues in which there are vested interests and about which there are varying opinions.
>
> (Durbin, 2006: 236)

Although it can be time-consuming, we should find time to preview and evaluate televisual materials that we intend to use in the classroom. Here are some criteria for evaluating televisual resources:

- ■ Images
  - – clarity
  - – appropriateness
- ■ Narration
  - – language level
  - – clarity of speech
  - – clarity of explanation
- ■ Graphics
  - – explanation of
- ■ Content
  - – geographical content
  - – value position (bias)

(Durbin, 1996: 262)

The potential of the programme to motivate pupils and stimulate their interest in its content should also be considered.

As with other resources, you should analyse the content of televisual resources for gender and ethno-centric bias (Butt, 1991). Examine the roles in which different groups are portrayed and encourage pupils to question images that are stereotypical or that only present certain groups of people in 'problematic' situations. Geography teachers can draw upon a variety of strategies to address bias in visual material.

Occasionally it is worth involving pupils in an evaluation activity of this nature. This encourages them to question and challenge visual images that they are presented with. It can also enable them to express their own value position on an issue or theme. This could lead to a written activity with pupils writing a letter to a programme like *Right to Reply* or *Points of View* about the programme that they have been watching and analysing.

Watching television in the classroom must be developed into an 'active learning experience'. Chris Durbin suggests that four qualities are needed to promote such active watching:

- *an inspiring lead in,* to give pupils a clear idea of what they have to do
- *a high quality environment* in which to watch (bigger screen, darker room, etc.)
- *an active watching strategy* which requires pupils to interpret the pictures, not just the commentary
- *a clear understanding* that they must *watch* the programme, as well as *listen* (the pause button might be used for personal reflection or paired discussion to help pupils process the information in some way).

He provides suggestions for a wide range of learning activities that can help develop pupils' sense of place (see Box 6.5). These activities are based on the assumption that three interrelated elements help pupils to develop this sense of place:

- An awareness that the knowledge and understanding of all places is a *perception,* and that the nature of this perception depends on personal knowledge of values and attitudes towards those places.
- A sense of what makes a place unique and different from all others is built up through a knowledge of its landscape, climate, landuse, economic activity and other aspects of its human and physical geography.
- Recognition that the lives and the priorities of the people who live in a particular place help to determine its unique character.

(Durbin, 1996: 118)

Butt has also provided a set of questions linked to enquiry processes that could be used by pupils as they watch a video (Table 6.3). He suggests that these questions could either be 'applied to the geographical content' of the video, or used to 'focus on the way the video chose to present images' (Butt, 1991: 54).

Using clips from television programmes can serve a number of purposes. They can be very effective in 'capturing' pupils' interest or providing an 'inspiring lead into' an activity. For instance, the opening sequence of 'The Disappearing Sea' (from the BBC series *The Geography Programme*), about the Aral Sea disaster, shows a ship left high and dry in a desert-like landscape. This could be shown without the commentary, then stopped and the question posed 'What has happened here?' There are numerous examples of clips that could be used in a similar way.

As well as being used to 'capture interest', video clips can be interspersed with key questions and activities to enable pupils to follow an enquiry sequence. The same approach can also be applied when using whole programmes. Alternatively, brief video sequences can be recorded from news programmes and accompanied by enquiry questions to bring in topical items with geographical relevance. Some recently developed series have done this for us, providing clips from news and current affairs programmes about the impact of economic change on environmental issues, as well as the cause and effect of environmental hazards. The late-night weather reports can also provide another useful source of up-to-date material.

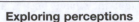

Exploring perceptions

Visual images have an important influence on how pupils perceive distant places. 'Brainstorming' activities can help to identify the words that pupils associate with particular places. Try to be imaginative, for example by showing part of a video without the sound and asking pupils to try to identify the place, or to write down adjectives that describe the visual images. The BBC has produced 'Flightpath' sequences of different places that can be used for the same purpose.

'Where is this place?'
'When did you know that it was this place?'

Positive (+) negative (–) and neutral (0) perceptions could also be indicated and discussed.

Another approach would be to supply pupils with an envelope containing a range of adjectives from which they would select words to describe what they have seen. Alternatively, pupils could write down their perceptions about a place before watching a programme and then examine the extent to which the programme reinforced or changed their perceptions.

Building descriptions

There are some interesting ways of developing pupils' geographical vocabulary through picture and word association. The pause button on a video can be used to freeze an image of a particular landscape. The pupils could then be given an outline sketch of this landscape and asked to annotate it with appropriate adjectives to describe its appearance, creating a 'wordscape'.

This activity could be developed further by asking the pupils to identify words describing the 'shapes, textures, colours and patterns' before labelling the sketch. Shape poems are another creative way of developing geographical vocabulary.

These strategies can also help to develop pupils' appreciation of the aesthetic aspects of geography.

Explaining geographical phenomena

Geography programmes often use graphic presentations to explain the processes responsible for the development of particular landforms or for the location of particular features. These presentations are helpful because they 'shrink' the time scales involved in processes that are difficult to observe in operation. For example, in the BBC programme *Earthquakes* (The Geography Collection) there is a graphic sequence showing the movement of continents with an explanation of plate tectonic theory. One way of helping pupils to use these sequences would be to produce a worksheet with a 'storyboard' structure showing the different stages in the formation of a feature. The pupils would write a summary of each stage in the space provided alongside a diagram. In some cases they could also draw the diagram themselves.

■ **Box 6.5** Developing pupils' 'sense of place' using televisual resources: some possible activities

Source: Durbin, C., 1995, 'Using televisual resources in geography', *Teaching Geography* 20(3) 118–121 1996 and 2006

Exploring issues

Geography programmes often show real people expressing their views about an issue. For example, in one programme about coastal management along the north Norfolk coast, people representing different interest groups express their views about the issue. An engineer justifies the defences under construction while a geomorphologist argues that the coastline should be allowed to find its natural equillibrium with landowners being compensated for the consequent loss of land. Pupils could be asked to summarise the viewpoints of different interest groups and then make a note of any supporting evidence shown in the rest of the programme. This could initiate an enquiry into the viability of coastal protection strategies with pupils researching further evidence.

Valuing people's views

Pupils usually interpret what they see and hear from their own cultural perspective. Some 'cultural interpretation' is therefore needed to help pupils to make sense of what is shown in programmes about 'distant places'. Durbin (1995: 120) describes the example of Japan where the 'Confucian philosophy, which underpins parts of the Shinto and Buddhist religions, makes controversial issues difficult to identify. Both sides of an argument (known as Ying and Yang) can be articulated by the same person.'

'Active listening' strategies should therefore be employed and adequate time provided to help pupils to absorb complex viewpoints. Support materials accompanying the Japan 2000 series include profiles of some of the people featured to help pupils to 'get to know individuals better and to emphathise with people in cultures different from their own.' Transcripts of the views expressed by some of the people featured in programmes can also be helpful. Asking pupils to devise an interview with people featured is an example of a strategy that can be used to encourage 'active watching and listening'.

■ **Box 6.5** (continued)

Source: Durbin, 1995, 'Using televisual resources in geography', *Teaching Geography* 20(3): 118–121, 1996 and 2006

Geography teachers make use of a wide variety of documentary and other programmes. Over the years, programmes like *Horizon* and *Panorama* have provided interesting material about an extensive range of environmental, social, economic and political issues and themes. Sometimes it is not appropriate to view these programmes in their entirety but once again relevant clips and sequences can be selected. They can also help to update your own subject knowledge.

Other non-educational television programmes can be exploited by geography teachers. For example, Rachel Edwards demonstrates the potential of television soaps as a 'valuable geographical resource' (1995: 176). Sequences would need to be carefully selected and strategies devised to avoid the danger of reinforcing narrow stereotypical images of places. However, Edwards provides a rich analysis of how programmes like *Eastenders, Neighbours* and *Home and Away* could be used to introduce pupils to various geographical concepts as well as considering how they might contribute to the development of their sense of place.

■ **Table 6.3** Enquiry processes and the use of video

	Geographical Enquiry	Values and Attitudes Enquiry
1. Observation and Perception	1. What is the point of focus for enquiry in the video? What is the question, issue or problem that the video addresses?	1. What are the values and attitudes of different individuals or groups in the video (or implied by the video makers)?
2. Definition and Description	2. What geographical questions can pupils suggest (or formulate) to give definition and direction to the enquiry? How can the questions 'where?', 'what?', 'how?', 'why?' and 'how ought?', be incorporated? What information needs to be collected from the video?	2. Can the values and attitudes of different individuals or groups in the video be 'classified' into categories? Can the actions of each individual or group be assessed? (Can the values and attitudes of the video makers be assessed)?
3. Interpretation and Analysis	3. How can we organise, interpret and analyse the information collected from the video? Is more data needed from the video (or other sources)? What explanations can be produced?	3. How far can the values and attitudes be verified by evidence? Are these values and attitudes supported by factual evidence in the video, or from other sources?
4. Evaluation and Conclusions	4. What conclusions can be drawn? Are explanations possible? Are predictions, proposed actions, future alternatives and evaluations possible from the results of the enquiry process?	4. Are there a set of preferred values and attitudes (in the video)? What are the implications of the findings and the conclusions drawn for the personal assumptions, understandings, values and attitudes of the pupils?
5. Decision-Making	5. Presentation of results and findings, and possible decision making.	5. Can the enquiry process be used to create a decision concerning the values and attitudes held by the people in the video, the video makers or the pupils themselves?

Source: Butt, 1991: 51–55

The British Film Institute's 'Moving Images in the classroom' (bfi, 2000) provides a rich collection of strategies for using moving images (televisual, film and digital media) and developing media literacy. Table 6.4 suggests how some basic techniques used to develop media literacy could be applied in some geographical enquiries. 'Images and Reality' is another useful resource for geography teachers produced by the British Film Institute. It explores ways of teaching about moving image representations of the developing world.

Activity 6.6 **Reviewing your use of televisual resources**

The most appropriate time to carry out this activity would be towards the end of your 'practical teaching experience'. There could also be great value in sharing your ideas and examples with other student teachers.

1. Reflect on how you have used televisual resources during your practical teaching experience.
2. List examples of how you have used video clips, sequences or whole programmes for the following purposes
   - ■ as a stimulus to 'capture interest'
   - ■ to introduce a theme or raise an issue
   - ■ to explain a process
   - ■ to illustrate a case study or key idea
   - ■ to compare two places
   - ■ to provide a summary at the end of a unit of work.
3. Which strategies have you found useful for:
   - ■ exploring perceptions
   - ■ building descriptions
   - ■ explaining geographical phenomena
   - ■ exploring issues and view points
   - ■ valuing people's views?

From our own experience we would advise you to build up your own collection of geographical videos. Not all geography departments have copies of the educational geography programmes that you might expect to find in schools. There is not always adequate technical support for geography departments so do not expect the programme or sequence required to be immediately available. Unfortunately, the only way to ensure this might be to invest in your recording equipment.

USING NEWSPAPER RESOURCES

Newspapers provide us with opportunities to bring up-to-date information about the geography of the world in which we live into the classroom. They can help us develop case studies about people and places, as well as about global trends and issues that are of current relevance and concern. They often provide us with information about the opinions and views of different people or interest groups involved in or affected by geographical issues.

The style in which most newspaper articles are written makes them a lively and informative geographical resource. Articles are sometimes accompanied by maps showing the location of places referred to in the article or displaying relevant spatial information. These are particularly useful when they show spatial patterns or distributions revealed in recently published statistics; for example, in social, economic, health or crime

■ **Table 6.4** Using media literacy techniques creatively in geography

Basic Technique	Possible Teaching Activities	Learning Objectives
Freeze Frame	While watching a film clip which has strong landscape scenery (e.g. *Thelma and Louise* to illustrate the landscapes of south west USA) the pupils write down adjectives which will support written description, classifying them into colours, shapes, patterns and textures.	Pupils should learn that: ■ Film-makers choose camera position, framing, angle and movement to create a particular impression of landscape, weather and human activity. ■ Films can be shot in different ways to portray a place.
Sound and Image	■ While watching a film sequence, without sound, set in a specific location, pupils hypothesise the sounds suggested by the visuals. ■ With another piece of video and three or four pieces of music or sound effects, pupils work in pairs to evaluate the effects of music on the image of the place.	■ Sound is as influential as pictures in creating an image of place. ■ The image of the place conveyed in a film is influenced by the nature of the sound tracks. ■ The atmosphere of the place is conveyed by the choice of music.
Top and Tail	Pupils are given a printout of some of the credits from a diverse range of films about the rainforest or another issue of human impact on the environment (e.g. natural history documentary, adventure fiction, charity appeal, etc). They are shown the tops of the programmes including the first few minutes of the film and they have to match them with the credits, justifying their choices.	■ The values and attitudes of film-makers, sponsors and production companies can differ and these differences can often be evident in their programmes or films. ■ Moving image texts targeted at different audiences can have different perspectives on their subject.
Cross-Media Comparisons	Pupils evaluate the portrayal of an earthquake or volcanic eruption, comparing a fictional film interpretation such as *Dante's Peak* (Roger Donaldson 1997) with a BBC Horizon documentary and/or the ITV *Savage Earth* on the Mount St Helen's eruption.	Fact and fiction provide different kinds of evidence about natural phenomena: fiction may provide emotional involvement but be unreliable as evidence; documentary may fail to communicate the immediacy of the experience.

Source: British Film Institute, 2000, p. 25 'Moving Images in the Classroom'

statistics. They can also update some atlas maps showing the impact of recent political developments such as regional and national boundary changes. However, we should be aware of the fact that these maps are not always accurate and there are numerous examples of distorted patterns or incorrect locations being shown on newspaper maps.

It is useful to start collecting newspaper articles about a range of geographical issues. The Royal Geographical Society's 'Gegraphy in the News' website (www.geographyinthenews.rgs.org) is also a useful resource for busy geography teachers looking for information about topical geographical issues and events. Pupils are often impressed when teachers respond to issues of current relevance and concern, providing opportunities to analyse and interpret the geographical aspects and processes. Using such material also helps to support our claim that geography is a dynamic subject relevant to young people growing up in the world today.

While acknowledging the benefits of using information and images about current issues, we also need to be aware of the limitations of newspaper material. Articles are usually, by their nature, concise (one of their advantages) and can therefore oversimplify information and explanations. The bias of the writer (and sometimes of the newspaper itself) also needs to be recognised as this influences the selection of information to be included as well as the interpretation of information and viewpoints. This can lead to pupils developing a partial or superficial understanding of some case studies.

Even with these limitations, the use of newspaper articles can actually have a valuable role to play in helping to promote and develop pupils' critical thinking. Articles can be used to stimulate interest and debate. Pupils should be encouraged to identify which information is critical and relevant. Key ideas, facts and geographical terms should be considered as well as any conflicting evidence or viewpoints not included in the article.

Articles about environment issues and natural hazards seem to appear fairly regularly in the 'broadsheet' newspapers. An early way to exploit this is to create a wall display around a world map indicating the location of places and events referred to in the articles. Such a display could be used actively later in lessons analysing the distribution of particular issues or hazardous events. Reports about social, economic and planning issues can also be useful. Geography teachers need to help pupils understand the geography involved in the issue or event. The following framework helps pupils to not only learn about the events and their impacts but also to examine them critically:

- Why did they happen?
- Why did they happen here?
- What are the possible consequences going to be in both the short term and long term?
- What do the pupils themselves wish to understand about the issue?
- What are the social, political, economic and environmental causes of the event?
- What can geography contribute to the analysis of this event?
- What are the opportunities for bridging to other examples or case studies?
- What predictions can we make about the long- and short-term effects of this event?

(Brooks, 2003: 70)

A note of caution should perhaps be considered at this stage, however. There is a danger that if we focus solely on problems, we might engender a view of geography as a 'doom-laden' subject with pupils developing a pessimistic view of a future dominated by prospects of 'eco-catastrophes' – therefore be on the look-out for good news. For example, the sports pages can provide opportunities for creative work that will interest pupils (boys and girls!). Features on countries participating in major sporting events can be supported by studies of the 'geography' of these countries; relationships between wealth, demographic features and sporting success analysed ('who won the Olympics?'). Colourful previews of new sporting seasons can be exploited by finding the location of participating clubs and atlas work using scale to calculate distances that supporters may have to travel to watch their team.

Activity 6.7 **Geography in the news!**

Find some examples of newspaper articles about geographical issues and themes.

■ Identify the key ideas, facts and geographical works in each article.
■ Is there any other information or evidence that could or should have been included?
■ Identify any opinions or viewpoints expressed about the issue or theme. Are there any other views, or other interest groups with views, about this issue?
■ Devise some appropriate enquiry questions that would help pupils to use this article.

Once pupils have developed the skills needed to use newspaper articles effectively, newspapers can become a useful source of information for meaningful homework activities. On a regular basis, pupils could select a relevant article about a geographical issue, note the key facts and summarise the key ideas covered in the article.

USING CARTOONS

Cartoons have become an increasingly used resource in geography teaching. They are to be found in published resources such as textbooks and have featured in GCSE and A-level examination questions. Some notable publications such as *Thin Black Lines* (Birmingham DEC) recognise the potential use of cartoons in political and development education. As teachers, we are also likely to come across cartoons about a wide variety of geographical issues in newspapers and magazines, usually when these issues are topical.

Clearly the apparent simplicity of cartoons and their potential to generate humour makes them appealing resources to use with pupils. As well as being motivating to use for many pupils, cartoons are flexible resources which, like other visual material, can be used in a wide variety of ways. They can be particularly useful for helping pupils to recognise and evaluate different viewpoints about an issue. However, as with all resources, we must be aware of their limitations when selecting cartoons for use in the classroom. We should also be careful to devise appropriate strategies for using cartoons that challenge rather than reinforce bias and stereotypes.

Marsden has raised concerns that cartoons could become the 'new stereotyping' in geography. He urges us to balance the advantages and disadvantages of the various types of cartoon material. He is particularly concerned about the use of comic-type caricatures which he regards as 'the most dangerous manifestation of the "new stereotyping"' Marsden reminds us that the process of 'caricaturing' is the 'art of pictorial ridicule which, through grotesque exaggerations of human features into debased likenesses, implicitly dehumanised' (Marsden, 1992: 128). In doing so, he argues that such material can be 'educationally and socially damaging in that while complex reality has to be made more clear-cut than it really is, the crass over simplification sometimes presented can reduce important issues to triviality' (Marsden, 1992: 129).

A general perusal of the geography textbooks being used in schools today is likely to reveal a number of what might be described as 'narrative *talking-head* depictions' of people presenting different viewpoints. These are often used to simplify the attitudes and values of different individuals or groups involved in an issue. However, they can sometimes reveal more about the humour or creativity of the graphic designer than the real-life people that they are supposed to represent. The absence of real places in most cartoons can also be an issue of concern. Fortunately, as we mentioned earlier, most publishers are becoming more aware of these dangers.

The perceived advantages of using cartoon material in geography texts include:

■ Motivational – providing 'entertainment value'.
■ Pedagogical – a way of simplifying the complexities of reality.
■ Presentational – adding to the variety of stimulus materials.
■ Logistical – a convenient way of providing generalised impressions of life in other places (in the absence of 'real photographs').
■ Cognitive – using cartoons as teaching material requires the 'application of often high level interpretational skills'

(Marsden, 1992)

Marsden's final point about the potential 'cognitive value' of using cartoons highlights the importance of the teaching and learning strategies employed. The apparent simplicity of the cartoon and its captions may conceal more complex messages. The interpretation of these hidden messages and agendas could provide the focus for many worthwhile learning activities.

Activity 6.8 **Using cartoons in geography lessons**

Select a range of cartoons from sources of teaching materials commonly used in geography teaching. Evaluate the potential of these cartoons as a resource for teaching and learning in geography. Referring to our earlier discussion, consider whether the advantages of using each cartoon would outweigh its disadvantages.

Select one of these cartoons and devise a range of strategies for using this cartoon. Identify a relevant geographical theme or context and an appropriate level (Key Stage 3, GCSE or post-16) for using this cartoon.

Discussion: A good starting point would be for pupils to identify enquiry questions relevant to the cartoons being studied. Alternatively, you could pose some appropriate enquiry questions and ask pupils to suggest a range of possible answers. The questions could focus on alternative interpretations of the cartoons. They could also encourage pupils to think of different viewpoints from the ones expressed by the cartoons. The values of any people shown in a cartoon might be explored and other relevant interest groups identified. These activities could lead to some creative writing with pupils devising appropriate captions or the cartoon acting as a stimulus for an article based on its message or theme. Used in this way, cartoons are less likely to generate stereotypical views of people and places, and more likely to provide opportunities to promote critical thinking.

DIAGRAMMATIC REPRESENTATIONS

In addition to the range of visual material that we have described so far, geography makes use of a very wide variety of diagrams. Whilst photographic and televisual resources can help to bring real people and places into the classroom, diagrams are extremely effective when we are trying to show the main features of landscapes or trying to illustrate particular geographical processes. Geographers also use diagrams to summarise the features of models and theories that seek to explain or account for geographical phenomena or processes.

Block diagrams are three-dimensional drawings of landscapes that are used to illustrate the features of these landscapes (usually in a simplified form). Annotation helps pupils to associate relevant vocabulary or terminology with the appearance of these features. Such diagrams are particularly useful when combined with photographic images of landforms and landscapes. They can also be very effective when a sequence of these diagrams is used to show different stages in the development of a landform or landscapes (e.g. glaciated landscapes and coastal landforms).

Simplified or idealised maps are effective when used to show the main features of geographical patterns or the typical spatial impacts of processes involved in a geographical model. Flow diagrams are also frequently used to show the impacts and consequences of different geographical processes. Graphical representations of models are used to show changes in geographical phenomena over time.

It is important that pupils gain experience of using a very wide range of diagrams, not least because they are sure to encounter such resources in assessment tasks and examination questions. As geographers, we are familiar with such diagrams as a method of communicating geographical ideas and we are experienced at interpreting them. But do our pupils see things in the same way? How do they interpret diagrammatic representations of reality, especially if they are not able to draw upon a similar level of experience or understanding?

Whenever you use different forms of diagram it would be helpful to consider what pupils need to know and to understand in order to use or interpret these diagrams. Consider whether there are any potential barriers to understanding or whether there is any potential for misunderstanding or misinterpretation.

You might find it helpful to explore this issue by selecting a range of different diagrams and presenting them to a variety of pupils. Ask them to describe to you what they think that these diagrams show and to identify any aspects of the diagrams that they do not understand. Record and try to analyse any misunderstanding.

THE 'ARTS' AS IMAGINATIVE RESOURCES FOR GEOGRAPHY

We hope that the National Curriculum in geography will stimulate the use of painting, photography, music, prose, poetry, dance and drama as well as radio, film and video. They are of value in the evocation of a sense of place and can stimulate hearts and minds. They also add immensely to the enjoyment of geography.

(DES, 1990, para 7.20)

We would like to draw your attention to a rich source of stimulus materials that is underused by geography teachers and which can provide the inspiration for some imaginative geography lessons. The following scene from Bernstein and Sondheim's *West Side Story* can provide a stimulating introduction to a study of migration and the distribution of immigrant ethnic concentrations in New York. Anita and Rosalia are both Puerto Rican migrants in New York. In the song 'America', they compare their feelings about their former home, in Puerto Rico's capital city San Juan, with their present home in New York City. The lyrics can be used to illustrate migration stories.

Relevant scenes from the film of *West Side Story* can be used as the stimulus for a discussion about the reasons why Puerto Rican migrants like Anita decided to leave San Juan to move to New York. The reality of life in New York for the migrants can also be explored using scenes from the film. Even better if *West Side Story* is to be the school production. The geographical background to some of the issues and themes developed in this musical would merit investigation: the waves of immigration from different areas that have given rise to a mosaic of ethnic neighbourhoods and to a complex process of 'succession' from one group to another; the process of filtering which resulted in the high concentrations of immigrant groups in the inner areas of New York; the progressive replacement of these immigrant groups by more affluent residents as a result of gentrification in the 1970s.

There are probably a great number of feature films that have potential as learning resources in geography. Sarah Hollingham (1997) has outlined ways in which a number of feature films such as *Lawrence of Arabia, The Italian Job* and *Medicine Man* can be used creatively in geography lessons. As with the earlier example of *West Side Story,* it is important that pupils are clearly briefed about the purpose of viewing parts of the film, such as what to look out for and what tasks they may be required to do after viewing. It is also important to ensure that enough time is provided afterwards for pupils to respond to and discuss the geographical issues and themes highlighted in the film.

Hollingham describes the value of the film *Medicine Man* in setting the scene for an investigation of issues relating to the medicinal properties of plants found in tropical rainforests and the impact of logging on both the environment and the indigenous populations. The quality of the visual images of the Amazon rainforest, supported by some dramatic music, can help to develop pupils' sense of place by showing the scale of the rainforest environment and the diversity of its plant life. The role and impact of these images and the music are in themselves issues that could be explored. However, Hollingham feels that the main advantage of using *Medicine Man* is that pupils can identify with the characters in the film, thereby giving them 'a personal perspective on rainforest issues which is sometimes lacking in other resources' (Hollingham, 1997: 133). Box 6.6 shows the enquiry questions that Hollingham identified and the strategies she used with this film.

If school geography is to connect with the experiences of young people, it must provide them with opportunities to question cultural representations (Morgan, 2003; Balderstone, 2006). This, Morgan suggests, can perhaps best be done by using advertisements, television programmes, films, music and travel guides to help students explore how particular views of the world are constructed. He describes how the film 'The Full Monty' can provide significant opportunities for teaching geography in ways that reflect developments in the subject discipline, particularly drawing upon cultural geography. Geography teachers have used this film successfully, exploring themes about the gendered nature of work, the separation of private and public spheres and the gendered use of space to enrich geographical enquiries about economic change.

In exploring the everyday landscapes of national identities, Winchester, Kong and Dunn (2003) recognise the influence of films as a form of text or cultural product in the social construction of such identities. They observe how Australians increasingly

Relevant enquiry questions:

1   What is the rainforest like?
2   How do people use the tropical rainforest?
3   How do indigenous people live?
4   How do people exploit the tropical rainforest and with what impact?
5   How can rainforests be managed?
6   What are the implications for the future

Some possible learning activities:

■   Pupils produce a time line showing the sequence of events from the discovery of the cancer cure to deforestation.

■   Pupils describe the scene which best depicts a given concept, for example, the scale of the forest, natural beauty, suffering, disaster, hope.

■   Switch off the sound for the logging sequence. Pupils suggest the types of music which should be used here. What mood does the music need to portray and why?

■   Pupils watch the relevant sections of this film in order to identify all the information needed to make a particular case. One way of doing this is to ask one group to take the statement 'Deforestation can benefit the inhabitants of a country' and another group, 'Deforestation is a problem for people who live in the forest and elsewhere'. The second statement draws on the concept that important medicines can be made from rainforest plants.

■ **Box 6.6** Using the film *Medicine Man* to explore rainforest issues
Source: Hollingham, 1997: 133

identified with the 'red centre' (Uluru) and areas of wilderness such as Kakadu in films like *Priscilla: Queen of the Desert* and *Crocodile Dundee*. Such films were also seen as an attempt to counter Australia's perceived vulnerability to the cultural dominance of the United States with early reviews of *Crocodile Dundee* commenting on how the main character (Mick Dundee played by Paul Hogan) 'oozed Australian-ness' (Winchester, Kong and Dunn, 2003: 45). They observed how urban landscapes were often portrayed as a 'site of problems and injustice', whereas rural and wilderness areas are portrayed as 'harsh, but communal and level playing fields' (Winchester, Kong and Dunn, 2003: 47). More recently, films such as *Rabbit proof fence* provide opportunities to explore challenging questions of race, identity and multiculturalism.

Literature and poetry

Literature and poetry can be exploited in imaginative ways by geography teachers. They can provide many interesting opportunities for developing a 'humanistic' approach to the study of places (see the Autumn 2008 issue of *Geography* [Vol 93, 3] which features place and poetry as a theme). There are many novels which provide what Rex Walford has called a 'regional comprehension'. Appropriate extracts from novels by authors like

Thomas Hardy could be read and interpreted to consider the sense of place that they develop. There are also novels that focus on geographical themes and issues. For example, Steinbeck's *Grapes of Wrath* explores the impact of the motor car on transport in America, while *Paradise News* by David Lodge describes the impacts of tourism.

Landscapes have often provided the inspiration for poetry. The landscapes of the Lake District can be explored through the poetry of John Ruskin, Walter Scott and William Wordsworth amongst others. This poetry could be used when visiting such landscapes or when viewing photographic images of them. John Betjeman's poems about 'metro-land' can be used to support studies of the growth of London. Can pupils identify the elements of these landscapes that have so inspired these poets? What feelings does the poetry generate?

Yearning for the Lakes

I weary for the fountain foaming,
For shady holm and hill,
My mind is on the mountain roaming
My spirit's voice is still.

I weary for the woodland brook
That wanders through the vale,
I weary for the heights that look
Adown upon the vale.

The crags are lone on Coniston
And Glaramara's dell,
And dreary on the mighty one
The cloud enwreathed Sca-fell.

Oh, what although the crags are stern
Their mighty peaks that sever,
Fresh flies the breeze on mountain fern
And free on mountain heather.

I long to tread the mountain head
Above the valley swelling,
I long to feel the breezes sped
From grey and gaunt Helvellyn.

There is a thrill of strange delight
That passes quivering o'er me,
When blue hills rise upon the sight
Like summer clouds before me.

John Ruskin

Pupils' learning experiences in geography can also inspire them to express their reactions, feelings and understanding through poetry. The lesson about rainforest environments outlined in Chapter 5 could lead to some creative writing with pupils using poetry to describe the nature of these environments. Fieldwork provides many opportunities for different sensory learning experiences. Pupils could, for instance, write 'Haiku' poems to express their feelings about an environment.

Haiku is a Japanese term describing a simple three line poem consisting of seventeen syllables. Such poems arise from personal experiences of environments. Using Haiku writing as a way of raising pupils' awareness of their surroundings would require them to find a suitable place to sit and to relax. They should be encouraged to clear their minds so that they can then become aware of stimuli (visual, sounds, smells) from their surroundings. A blindfold could even be used to help them concentrate on sounds and smells for a few minutes.

After about ten minutes they should write down some words to describe the sights, sounds, smells and feelings. These words can then be arranged in a Haiku structure. This can be done individually or collectively. By having five syllables in the first and last line, and seven in the middle line, the Haiku has a balanced form. The examples shown below are not quite as they should be!

Haiku poems about the environment

Swirling green water
Flows endlessly on to the
Limitless ocean

Your time here is short
Thinks the round golden pebble
In rhythmical waves

Fumes from a taxi
Swirl round the face of the child
As she sleeps unaware

Acknowledgement: These examples were provided by David Job in a workshop for geography teachers at the Institute of Education, University of London.

Art and aesthetics

The way in which we use our senses to perceive the world around us and the development of these senses might be referred to as 'aesthetic awareness' or 'aesthetic education'. It forms an essential part of our development as human beings and geography can make a significant contribution to this aspect of pupils' learning by developing their sense of place through an emotional and intellectual response to places. Pupils should have opportunities to appreciate the beauty of landscapes and scenery, and the qualities of built environments.

Eric Brough describes the valuable contribution that geography teachers can make to pupils' aesthetic education. He urges us to:

> preserve and intensify the vividness of sensory experience and help pupils to relate action to feeling, and reality to ideals. Idealism would then become not an escape from reality but a background determining a response to it. Education's task is to help children to develop aesthetic sensitivity which will enable them to evaluate their experiences and make intelligent choices and judgements, a task more pressing than ever in the present world.
>
> (Brough, 1983: 58)

And what about art itself? What 'sense of place' do artists communicate in their paintings and drawings? It is now possible to obtain posters and postcards of many famous landscape paintings. These lend themselves to a number of interesting tasks, not least to consider the impression of a landscape that an artist is trying to convey. In what ways do the artists use the weather to evoke a mood? What images do Lowry's paintings present of industrial north-west England? There are, therefore, several opportunities for meaningful co-operation with art teachers including the development of pupils' field sketching skills.

Music

There are several different ways in which music can be used in geography lessons. Short sections of instrumental music can help to focus pupils on a task such as watching a slide sequence. In the lesson about different housing areas described on page 176 the song 'Our House' by Madness is used as background music while the pupils look at slides of different types of house in contrasting residential areas.

Playing music can also help to evoke images and develop a 'sense of place'. Classical music can be particularly useful. For example, slides showing views of coastal landforms could be accompanied by Debussy's *La Mer* whilst Wagner's *Flying Dutchman Overture* provides more dramatic sound to use with some slides from a holiday in Australia, showing stormy seas around the 'Seven Apostles' on the coast of Victoria. Film of volcanic eruptions is often accompanied by dramatic music from Holst's *The Planets*. Similarly Dove and Owen (1991) describe how a peaceful rural scene can be invoked by music from Beethoven's 'Pastoral Symphony' or Grieg's 'Morning'.

The role of music in creating moods and evoking a sense of place suggests possibilities for more direct use of music in learning activities. Music is often used to emphasise the impact of visual images in documentaries and other television programmes. Pupils could be shown the visual sequences without the sound and asked to write down words to describe their feelings about what they are looking at. They could also describe the type of music that they might use as background for these sequences. The sequence could then be replayed with the sound and the role of the music in influencing the impact of these images discussed. For example, Michael Jackson's 'Earth Song' has often been used as the soundtrack to back film about environmental issues such as the exploitation of tropical rainforests. The producer of the film has clearly selected this music to enhance the impact of the film's message. There are, therefore, plenty of opportunities to consider the influence of music on our perceptions about issues.

Music is a powerful source of images and symbolism. It is possible to identify references to geographical terms, places and issues in the lyrics of contemporary music. Through these lyrics, songwriters impart images of popular culture. How these images are perceived and interpreted depends on the listener. However, the use of geographic symbolism in contemporary music is extensive and, as most cultural geographers would argue, the dynamic nature of culture puts it at the heart of human geography.

The selection of appropriate contemporary songs to use in the classroom immediately raises a potential problem. Will pupils relate to or be motivated by the music that we select? Most of us would not want to impart the image of an ageing rocker and surely we cannot be expected to keep up with all the changing trends in popular music.

It is usually not a problem if we set the context for using a particular song and do not make wild claims that pupils will necessarily enjoy it. Try providing some of the lyrics for examination and devise an interesting or challenging activity that requires the pupils to analyse these lyrics and interpret the song's message.

Songs about issues are useful for this purpose. From different eras 'Streets of London' (Ralph McTell), 'Another Day In Paradise' (Phil Collins), 'Living In A Box' (Living In A Box) present images and views of the homeless. 'Mandela Day' (Simple Minds), Nelson Mandela (The Special AKA) and 'Don't Want To Play' (Sun City) could be used in a study of South Africa to consider the legacy of apartheid. The Levellers have written many songs about popular protest in Britain (e.g. by the 'tree people'/Eco-Warriors against new road building). 'Something Inside So Strong' (Labi Sifri) is a powerful song about human rights issues, which themselves can have a geographical perspective.

It would also be interesting to explore the impact that songs and their lyrics might have on pupils' images and perceptions of different places. Find some songs about a number of different places and give pupils a list of these places (see Box 6.7 for examples). Ask the pupils to write down their impressions of what these places might be like. Then play them extracts from the songs asking them to write down the impression of each place that is portrayed in the song (is it positive, negative or neutral?). They can then compare these with their original impressions and consider whether the songs have influenced their views of these places. Alternatively, you can develop a fun activity for the end of term quiz by recording sections of songs that name places. Pupils have to locate these places on a map as they listen to the music. Although video is not used as much as it used to be to promote records, there are some examples that can be used creatively to provide stimulating learning activities in geography. The video for the Faithless song 'I want more' is a favourite, including a range of images from North Korea that can be used to analyse and challenge pupils' perceptions of places. The Asian Dub Foundation's 'Flyover' has some great images for analysing urban environments.

Orinocoflow	– Enya
Kingston Town	– UB40
New York, New York	– Frank Sinatra
(or *An Englishman in New York*	– Sting)
Belfast Child	– Simple Minds
The Lebanon	– Human League
Ferry Cross the Mersey	– Gerry and the Pacemakers
Barcelona	– Montserrat Caballe and Freddie Mercury
Streets of Philadelphia	– Bruce Springstein
Oh Carolina	– Shaggy
Going Loco Down in Acapulco	– The Four Tops
London Calling	– The Clash

■ **Box 6.7** Songs about places

USING MODELS

Models can be of value in helping pupils to learn a range of ideas and concepts in geography. Even when considering the constraints imposed by the limited time available for geography in the curriculum of many secondary schools, it is possible to find opportunities to use resources like models in a creative way. The impacts of learning experiences using models on both pupils' motivation to learn and their understanding of concepts and processes can justify the time devoted to using them. As Yoxall argued in relation to the use of hardware models in earth science instruction: 'Often an hour of relatively simple experimentation can teach more than pages of book reading or hours of classroom talking' (Yoxall, 1989: 169)

Although Yoxall is referring to the use of larger scale hardware models that only tend to be found in the earth science laboratories of some universities, his justifications can be applied to the use of a range of models. Scaled models, whether they are relief models or models of coastal landforms in a wave tank, can help pupils to gain a more 'holistic perspective' of landscape systems than they could get from a groundlevel view in the field. Where the models are dynamic, as in the case of wave tanks and flumes, they can help pupils to conceptualise links between form and process by 'collapsing' time scales (Job and Buck, 1994: 106). The process of discussing the limitations of these models as closed systems representing what are actually open systems in the natural environment is in itself a valuable learning activity.

You do not, however, need access to an earth science laboratory to create opportunities for using models. Geography teachers have often been creative in building simplified stream tables and models of the hydrological cycle.

Helping pupils to understand the role of contours in depicting the relief of an area on a flat topographical map can present a challenge. Until pupils have grasped this concept they find it difficult to interpret relief on a map and to transform contours into a cross-section of a landscape. Relief models of an area can be built using thick corrugated card or polystyrene tiles. Contour patterns can either be enlarged or projected onto paper using an overhead transparency of an area shown on a map. Larger scale maps (i.e. 1:10,000) are usually the most appropriate maps for this task. Each contour pattern can be traced onto the card or tile and then cut out. Each tile is then stuck in its place to form a layer model with its edges representing the contours. A plaster filler can then be used to smooth over the layers and complete the relief model. The 'landscape' and its features can then be painted and labelled.

If there is insufficient time for every pupil to build their own model, you might find it helpful to build your own examples for demonstration purposes. You can either leave some of the layers showing or have two models, with one displaying just the layers of tiles to show the method of construction (Rhodes, 1994). If models are made of a variety of landscapes, they can be displayed with relevant map extracts to help pupils identify significant landscape features that might be shown on maps.

Search the depths of your imagination and you will probably come up with some stimulating ways of using models in your geography lessons. Some of our most memorable experiences of using models come from our own days as student teachers. The blancmange glacier was created by pouring some thick blancmange along an elevated length of plastic guttering (see Figure 6.6). Placing matchsticks across the width of the blancmange glacier simulated that famous experiment demonstrating that a glacier moves forwards at different rates, with the faster movement in the centre and at the surface where there is less friction. Some icing sugar can be sprinkled over the surface to reveal the crevasses that are formed when the blancmange glacier moves over any rock barriers (used tea bags!). Inman (2006) includes examples of pupils' responses to this experiment and suggests a range of other creative approaches to what he calls 'classroom fieldwork' to bring alive the study of environmental processes in the geography classroom. These include the use of analogies, or 'models of the mind' to aid 'visualisation' and learning about processes and landforms (Inman, 2006: 273–4).

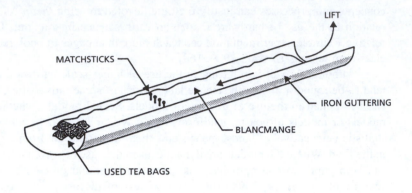

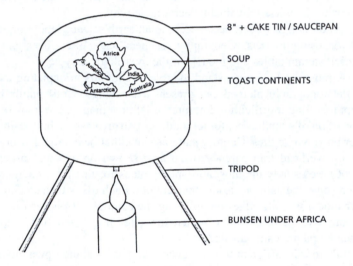

■ **Figure 6.6** Imaginative use of simple models

Continental drift can be demonstrated using a can of tomato soup and some toast (the thin crispy variety). A focused heat source is needed and the Bunsen burner found in the school's science laboratory is appropriate for this purpose. The soup is poured into a large saucepan and pieces of toast, cut approximately to match the outlines of the continents of Gondwanaland, placed on the surface of the soup. Bloomfield (1993) recommends heating the soup first so that skin forms on to which the continents can be placed. Heat from the Bunsen burner is directed under the saucepan, roughly between Africa and South America – do not worry too much about the accuracy of the continents' movements. The principles of convection currents and continental drift can be demonstrated and you can clearly build on this activity using other resources to develop pupils' understanding of the important concepts and processes involved.

One of our most successful and stimulating model building activities involved a simulation of the development of a squatter settlement (Balderstone and Payne, 1992). The stimulus for the activity was provided by using photographic images of different squatter settlements and video clips to develop a 'sense of place'. Profiles of families involved in building homes in squatter settlements were presented in video clips and study cards to help pupils develop some empathy with the people involved.

Over a few weeks a large collection of simple materials had been assembled to provide the resources for this activity. These included scraps of paper and card, matchsticks, match boxes, lolly sticks, paper clips, twigs, blutack, clay, string and plastic. These materials formed a city dump on a separate table. The pupils were organised into small groups (2–4 pupils) and a short period of time allocated for planning and the collection of materials. Each group was given a piece of card on which to build their house. Once the context for the activity had been established, the pupils were given the remaining thirty minutes of the lesson to construct a basic shelter. The fact that many of these initial land invasions take place at night can be stimulated by using blinds to darken the room and providing only small torches for light.

In the subsequent lesson, further stages in the development of the squatter settlement were simulated. Various issues can be introduced and the impacts on the development of the squatter settlements evaluated. New materials can be provided to help pupils improve the construction of their houses (stronger card, glue and scissors for some). Some pupils can be given difficult sloping sites on which to build their homes. The teacher can represent the city authorities and adopt different approaches to the squatters which either help or hinder their efforts. Co-operation and access to suitable materials results in more rapid progress in improving the model settlements.

Pupils are certainly motivated by learning experiences like this simulation activity. However, the teacher's skill in debriefing the pupils, helping them to make sense of what has been happening and how it relates to reality is *crucial* if the intended conceptual understanding is to be achieved. Tom Inman (2006: 272) warns that the 'realism' and strong visual quality of the model itself can sometimes inhibit pupils' ability to transfer their understanding from the simulation to reality. This is why careful debriefing is vital to develop conceptual understanding. Linking the above activity with appropriate visual images and information about real case studies helps to maximise the potential of this learning experience. It can also be integrated effectively with role-play or decision-making exercises about ways of addressing housing problems in a large city in a less economically developed country.

USING OTHER RESOURCES

'Adults other than teachers'

At best, outside speakers can enhance lessons by stimulating interest, transmitting enthusiasm for a place, increasing motivation, providing expertise and challenging stereotypes. At worst, they can send whole classes to sleep, talk over everyone's head, drivel on about irrelevant facts and figures, lose themselves in personal anecdotes of the 'you had to be there' kind and confuse and prejudice important issues.

(Pomeroy, 1991: 56)

In recent years, adults other than teachers have become an increasingly familiar sight in schools. Educational partnerships and links are being formed between schools and their wider communities. People from the community are often involved in making a direct contribution to areas of the school curriculum like Careers Education and Personal, Health and Social Education. There are also numerous opportunities for a wide range of subjects to draw upon the contribution of professional and other people from the community. The development of the vocational aspects of the School Curriculum in recent years has broadened and enhanced this contribution.

This involvement of adults other than teachers is not new to geography. Geography teachers have been able to involve people from the wider community for many years. Visiting speakers from development agencies and charitable organisations have often been used to share their experiences of different countries, cultures and a wide range of geographical issues. Planners often find themselves being approached for information about local issues by both geography teachers and pupils carrying out their geographical enquiries. Our own experiences have shown that planners can provide a valuable perspective when evaluating the outcomes of decision-making exercises and role plays of planning enquiries.

However, as Joseph Pomeroy's comment above illustrates, the involvement of outside speakers is not always a guarantee of a motivating, meaningful and active learning experience for pupils. After exploring the potential problems that could be experienced, Pomeroy describes how he used a 'press conference' framework for a visit by a black South African woman to talk about apartheid. The key to the success of this visit was the active involvement of the pupils who were required to prepare a range of relevant questions. Pomeroy also noted how the speaker's thought provoking questions led to a 'fascinating discussion on the nature of stereotypes' (Pomeroy, 1991: 57).

Careful planning and preparation is essential when involving people from the community. For people who do not have our experience of working with school pupils, a visit to a classroom can be a daunting experience, so they need to be reassured and clearly briefed about their role in any learning activities. Involving these people in the planning of the learning activities will certainly help to clarify their role and contribution. It is also helpful to involve them in the evaluation of the outcomes of the activities as this will develop their understanding of classroom processes and pupil learning.

One of the crucial elements of the Geography Schools and Industry Project (GSIP) in the 1980s was the involvement of people from the community. The large number of geography teachers involved in this project were able to share and evaluate their experiences. GSIP has therefore been able to provide geography teachers with some practical advice and guidelines about how to involve people from the community in effective ways (Corney, 1992). The project identified four main types of involvement (see Table 6.5) and provided examples of the variety of people from the community who had worked with geography teachers involved in GSIP.

■ **Table 6.5** Involving people from the community

Type of Involvement	Description
1 Communiction	Teachers contact people from the community for resources/information for a planned lesson or unit of work
2 Consultation	Teachers ask people from the community to comment on a draft lesson or unit of work
3 Collaboration	Teachers collaborate with people from the community to plan a lesson or unit of work
4 Participation	Teachers and people from the community work with pupils in the classroom or elsewhere, and help with evaluation

Source: Corney, 1992: 85

STATISTICAL DATA AND OTHER INFORMATION

The nature of geographical enquiry means that geography teachers are able to draw upon an increasingly extensive range of sources of statistical data and other information. This includes data such as census returns, health and welfare statistics, social and regional statistics and other official data from government departments, national and international organisations. Many of these sources can be found in reference libraries and some are available on the Internet.

A number of large businesses and public organisations publish statistics relating to their activities as well as educational and public relations material. National Park authorities, regional tourist boards, oil, electricity, gas and water companies, amongst others, produce materials that could be used by geography teachers. The bias evident in most of these materials should not necessarily preclude their use. Indeed, such material could provide the focus for worthwhile and stimulating values enquiry with pupils analysing evidence of bias (see Chapter 4).

You may well come across some surprising sources of material. The local Records Office is one of these sources that is rarely exploited by geography teachers. It can provide a range of interesting materials for studying the ways in which places have changed, including old maps, photographs and accounts about people and events. These can help you to add real characters and events to the study of changes in localities. Kelly's Directories are a useful source of information about places listing the names of residents and their occupations at different times in the past. These can be used to study the changing function of settlements in rural areas, including those from an agricultural base to those with dormitory status. They provide a useful contrast to the collective totals shown in census data and pupils are fascinated by the persistence of local family names as well as the changing nature of their occupations.

Collaboration with history teachers could produce an interesting local study incorporating fieldwork studies of the changing physical structure of a settlement and drawing upon the skills of the historian in evaluating sources of information. It is also possible to purchase old Ordnance Survey maps of some areas to support such studies. Walford (1995) demonstrates how fieldwork surveys of a local parade of shops could be enhanced and supported by the use of historic material from local archives.

Aid agencies and development organisations (Non-governmental organisations or NGO's) are another major source of information and materials for geography teachers. Their work in different global locations provides a rich source of case studies about geographical issues and localities. Most of these organisations have education officers and produce a wide range of materials for classroom use. A big advantage of many of these materials is that they are designed to involve pupils in active and collaborative styles of learning. They are also usually excellent value for money.

Classroom display

The quality of the learning environment, in other words the appearance of classrooms, can have a significant influence on pupils' attitudes towards learning. As well as making the classroom an attractive place to work in, the context and visual impact of a classroom display helps to establish the 'ethos' of the geography department. It reflects the teacher's or the department's view of geography and the value that is placed on pupils' work.

A classroom display is more than just 'educational wallpaper'. It acknowledges the efforts and achievements of pupils in their geographical studies. It can also perform a number of other functions. Earlier in this chapter we described an example of a display using a variety of maps to illustrate the different forms and purposes of maps. This display would be a source of information and illustration for teaching and learning. The display about global ecosystems developed in the lessons about the characteristics of different natural ecosystems (described in Chapter 5) would also help to reinforce pupils' learning about the concepts and places that they have studied. The pupils actively and collectively contributed to the production of this display.

Producing a poster display can be a stimulating and valuable learning activity for pupils. In Chapter 5 (pages 186–7) the A-level lesson about 'urban futures and sustainable cities' involves the pupils producing poster displays to show their ideas about principles that could guide planning for 'sustainable cities' in Britain. Earlier in this chapter, we described other activities where pupils could produce poster displays using photographs from fieldwork to show the impacts of recreation on an area and the effectiveness of appropriate management strategies. Another involved pupils taking photographs and collecting evidence to support a particular view about an issue, showing that a regeneration scheme had either been a success or a failure.

These are challenging activities designed to assess pupils' understanding of particular geographical concepts and processes, as well as their analytical skills and ability to communicate this understanding effectively. Appropriate assessment criteria reflecting these objectives would be developed for the tasks and shared with the pupils. Clear guidelines, including the criteria used to assess the outcomes, should be given to pupils. To ensure that the activity is manageable and achievable, you can specify the dimensions of the display and impose time constraints. You can get some useful advice about display techniques from colleagues teaching art and design. However, it is likely that the pupils themselves will have plenty of imaginative ideas about how to use these techniques. For large wall displays, it is worth planning the general layout, first giving some thought to the balance between different aspects of the display (i.e. maps, headings, illustrations and pupils' work). Also think about the visual impact of the display including the colours to be used. Mounting and double-mounting using contrasting colours can enhance a display and draw attention to specific aspects (i.e. headings, texts, commentary and pupils' work). Matchboxes and corrugated card can be used to give displays more depth, especially where a three-dimensional element would be helpful, for example, to show the structure of a Central Business District (Dove and Tinney, 1992).

Wherever possible and relevant, include a map to help remind pupils about the location of places featured in the display. It is also useful to highlight key geographical terms and place names in bold type to reinforce pupils' learning of geographical vocabulary. You can take this a step further by including definitions of these key terms within the display. Relevant enquiry questions could also be indicated.

You will not always be able to produce the displays that you would like to, no matter how creative you are. The classrooms in which you teach may be shared with other subjects and corridor displays are vulnerable to wear and tear. But do not let these constraints deter you from experimenting. Displays are not just for parents' evenings and open days. You will benefit from making a classroom an attractive environment in which to learn geography. Use your imagination to find stimulating ways in which pupils can learn geography through the production and use of displays.

SUMMARY AND KEY POINTS

This chapter has introduced you to some of the many resources that are available to geography teachers. Most of your pupils have not had any direct experiences of many of the places and issues that they study in geography, so the range and quality of the visual materials that you use has a significant influence on their geographical education. Hopefully, you are now aware of some of the important considerations that should influence your decisions about which resources to use and how to use them. In particular, you should be concerned to identify and, where possible, to avoid using resources that show evidence of gender or ethnocentric bias. Where this is not possible, you may be able to devise strategies for using those resources that seek to address issues of bias.

We hope that you look for opportunities to be creative in the way that you develop and use resources to support teaching and learning in geography. Make use of your own interests and experiences as well as those of your pupils. Put the pupils at the centre of your decisions about which resources are used in your lessons. Will these resources stimulate your pupils' interest and motivate them to learn? How will these resources be used by pupils? Which skills will they develop through using these resources? What knowledge, understanding, attitudes and values will pupils develop? Will all pupils be able to learn successfully using these resources?

Remember that the care and effort that you put into the preparation and selection of resources has a positive impact on pupils' interest in and motivation to learn geography!

Given the breadth and diversity of resources available to geography teachers it has not been possible for us to discuss every geographical resource and its applications. We would urge you to raise your awareness of what is available by joining The Geographical Association and attending its annual conference, which has the largest exhibition of published resources for geography in Britain. The conference workshops also provide you with new ideas about how to develop and use resources.

FURTHER READING

Durbin, C. (2006) *Media literacy and geographical imaginations*, Chapter 19 in Balderstone, D. (ed.) *Secondary Geography Handbook*, Sheffield: The Geographical Association.

> The author argues that geography teachers should employ the techniques and strategies of media literacy and provides a wide range of examples and activities to show how this can be done creatively. This text provides stimulating ideas for developing pupils' critical thinking skills to help them understand how media constructs reality.

Inman, T. (2006) *Let's get physical*, Chapter 22 in Balderstone, D. (ed.) *Secondary Geography Handbook*, Sheffield: The Geographical Association.

> This text provides a variety of stimulating ideas about ways of using models creatively to simulate physical processes.

Martin, F. (2006) *Using ICT to create better maps*, Chapter 10 in Balderstone, D. (ed.) *Secondary Geography Handbook*, Sheffield: The Geographical Association.

> The author argues that understanding maps and how they are drawn forms an important aspect of visual literacy. Pupils need to understand how maps are drawn if they are to make effective use of them in their geographical enquiries. He provides an extensive range of ideas for using ICT to help pupils to create maps.

Widdowson, J. and Lambert, D. (2006) *Using geography textbooks*, Chapter 13 in Balderstone, D. (ed.) *Secondary Geography Handbook*, Sheffield: The Geographical Association.

This chapter explores the important and changing role of textbook resources in teaching and learning geography. It provides criteria for selecting textbook resources and a wide variety of strategies for using these resources effectively to develop different learning skills through geography and provide worthwhile learning experiences.

FIELDWORK AND OUTDOOR LEARNING

Fieldwork is central to the ethos, culture and pedagogy of geography.

(Holmes and Walker, 2006: 210)

To me, fieldwork is the heart of geography...It renews and deepens our direct experience of the planet and its diversity of lands, life and cultures, immeasurably enriching the understanding of the world that is geography's core pursuit and responsibility...Without fieldwork, geography is secondhand reporting and armchair analysis, losing much of its involvement with the world, and its original insight, its authority, its contributions for addressing local and global issues, and its reason for being.

(Stevens, 2001: 66)

One lesson outdoors is worth seven inside.

(Professor Tim Brighouse)

INTRODUCTION

Most initial teacher education courses provide a period of school induction, a period of time when you may observe teachers, shadow pupils, take part in lessons and take other opportunities to get to know and understand classrooms and pupils. If, during this time, you get the chance to talk to a small group of pupils an obvious question to pursue would concern the role and purpose of geography, or at least what the pupils consider to be distinctive about it. Though dependent to some extent on the age of the pupils you ask and on your school's traditions and practices, a very common answer is 'fieldwork'.

Fieldwork tends to be highly valued by pupils: it transports them out of the class-room; it allows them to work collaboratively, often on tasks that last for several hours or even a whole day (in contrast to the bitty school day of possibly as many as eight single lessons); it is often very much 'hands on' kind of work; it is sometimes very 'learner centred' in the sense that pupils are involved in formulating questions to investigate and identifying the possible routes of enquiry; and residential work in particular often provides intense group feelings of achievement and togetherness. Fieldwork can also open up access to, and engagement with, the spiritual aspects of personality, stimulating interest in the environment and passion for outdoor education (May and Richardson, 2005: 6). For many young people, the impacts of fieldwork and outdoor learning are life-long and life-changing:

> Certainly, when we look back on our own experiences of geography we frequently remember the trek across some windswept moorland or standing at some street corner asking passers-by to complete a questionnaire about their journey to work. Equally, there are often fond memories of the geographical residential visit complete with hostel accommodation, packed lunches eaten in the rain, the camaraderie and the realisation that geography teachers are human after all.
>
> (Bell, 2005: 12)

Indeed, fieldwork *is* one of the distinctive attributes of geography and, in Britain, has a long tradition as an established component of geography education. There is substantial evidence indicating that when planned rigorously, well-taught and effectively followed up, fieldwork provides learners with opportunities to develop their knowledge, understanding and skills in ways that add value to their everyday classroom experiences (FSC, 2004). HMI have also frequently commented on the contribution fieldwork has made to achievement in geography. The recent manifesto for outdoor education has provided further endorsement of the contribution fieldwork makes to a young person's education (DfES, 2006).

OBJECTIVES

By the end of this chapter, you should be able to:

■ identify the different purposes of and approaches to fieldwork in geography
■ understand how to use a range of fieldwork strategies
■ plan and prepare geographical fieldwork that is of a high quality, safe, successful and sustainable
■ understand how to ensure that pupils can make progress in developing their skills and in extending their conceptual learning through geographical fieldwork.

THE PURPOSES OF FIELDWORK

Fieldwork is expensive, however, and not always fully understood by colleagues and senior management. For these reasons, fieldwork cannot be taken for granted. It is often under threat because it is mistakenly considered to be an unnecessary luxury which disrupts pupils' progress in other subjects whose lessons they miss when they are out of school. Residential work in particular can also result in supply teachers having to be brought in to cover geography lessons, which may be considered disruptive to the pupils not on fieldwork. It is therefore important for geography teachers to be clear about fieldwork:

■ What is fieldwork?
■ How is fieldwork justified?

In addressing these questions in what follows, we provide a framework to help you include fieldwork within your own advocacy for geography in education.

At one level, the purpose of fieldwork is self-evident: it is to engage pupils in learning directly, in a manner similar to the notion of 'experiential learning', which can be very motivating. Aspects of the environment are observed directly rather than via some form of mediated image or secondary source (although additional data of these kinds are certainly not excluded from field study, and information technology now allows considerably enhanced possibilities of merging and manipulating large quantities of data of all kinds). But we cannot leave our definition here, for such loose statements of purpose lack robustness. To be sure, learning in the field is enjoyable, even desirable, but is it essential? And if we are to argue that it is essential, in what manner can we do so, because we certainly need some kind of caveat in order to escape ridicule. Is it really 'essential' to visit Rio de Janeiro if we are to understand it adequately?

To reach a satisfactory position on fieldwork, we need to focus on it as embodying a range of *skills:* fieldwork as a mode of 'learning to learn' rather than an opportunity to learn about a particular unique place or feature. By focusing on skills we do not mean to be exclusive of knowledge and understanding – indeed the aim of fieldwork will often be to gain knowledge and deepen understanding. But we do wish to show that the strength of fieldwork is that it requires pupils to project a range of practical, organisational and intellectual skills onto a 'real world' question or issue. What characterises the real world is that it is complex and messy rather than simplified and neat (or archetypal). Because geography is concerned with making sense of physical and human environments and their interactions, it follows that pupils must have the chance to 'have a go' at the interpretation of the world at first hand, or else their instruction in geography (and how geographers make sense of the world) will be deficient.

There is a long tradition of fieldworking in British geography and it is now possible to make a number of useful distinctions in the ways it has been undertaken (see Figure 7.1). These different approaches help illustrate the definition of fieldwork we have suggested above, and take it forward, for it is apparent that fieldwork focused too heavily on skills (and driven exclusively by 'cognitive' aims, based on empiricist assumptions) may literally cut off the pupil from his or her feelings for the environment. Indeed, David Job (1996: 42) has noted that there is a common tension in planning fieldwork between those more tangible (and overt) aims to do with knowledge and understanding, and less concrete (more implicit) intentions summed up in phrases like 'an appreciation of a sense of place', 'a sense of wonder' and 'sensitivity to the environment'. The former are given emphasis, especially for older pupils, because they ensure that fieldwork is being seen to serve the needs of the examination. But the latter are, arguably, at the very heart of individuals 'interpreting the world'.

Introducing pupils to fieldworking is a particularly demanding challenge for geography teachers and is therefore best done in teams. It is not quite the same as planning and organising classroom learning. Apart from the particular organisational demands (including health and safety considerations) of working in potentially hazardous situations such as a high street or a coastline, the geography teacher usually has to apply considerable high-level geographical skills of interpretation, before even starting to address the question of how to arrange things so that young and inexperienced pupil geographers can learn to do the same. Traditional field teaching, often associated with the field excursion in Figure 7.1, is sometimes limited because the *geographer,* having made the links and understood the landscape palimpsest, has not considered (as a *teacher*) how inexperienced observers may gain access to the inescapable complexity and subtlety of landscape interpretation.

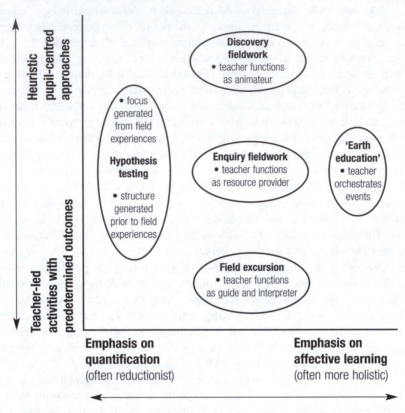

Heuristic pupil-centred approaches

Teacher-led activities with predetermined outcomes

Discovery fieldwork
• teacher functions as animateur

• focus generated from field experiences

Hypothesis testing

• structure generated prior to field experiences

Enquiry fieldwork
• teacher functions as resource provider

'Earth education'
• teacher orchestrates events

Field excursion
• teacher functions as guide and interpreter

Emphasis on quantification
(often reductionist)

Emphasis on affective learning
(often more holistic)

■ **Figure 7.1** Some fieldwork approaches
Source: Job, 1996, in Kent, Lambert, Naish and Slater (eds)

There is a requirement, therefore, to design something for the pupils to do or, if circumstances permit, design *with* pupils what they are to do. The point of issue here is the design of a route for enquiry. The dominance of more quantitative fieldwork since the 1970s can be explained by this felt need to engage children in 'doing': and if we can measure something, so much the better, for the doing also generates numerical data which readily submit to statistical and graphical description and analysis, and the inevitable production of data for processing. One challenge in this genre of field investigation is to keep the geography whole. Although pupils may learn a lot about techniques in relation to specific elements of geography, they may find it difficult to see the 'bigger picture'.

But even when we have the geography straight, and have worked out a route for enquiry, there remains a third challenge: how are we to encourage and enable pupils to respond, individually, to the field experience in a way that allows feelings to be expressed – towards nature, places, landscapes? Sketching, poetry, photography and other creative activities are all possible to embroider into the field experience.

Figure 7.2 summarises in a slightly different, but useful way the teaching – learning processes outlined here – except that it appears wholly pupil-centred: the additional point we have made is that the geography teacher needs to begin with a personal heightening of awareness, sharpening of perceptions and critical analysis before they can reasonably hope to support pupils attempting to do the same. This point is of course wholly consistent with the Training and Development Agency's (TDA's) insistence that secondary school teachers should be able to demonstrate and continue to develop specialist subject knowledge and expertise.

What also remains implicit in Figure 7.2, perhaps, is the full significance of the third box, 'concern and action'. David Job's (1996) analysis of fieldwork is set within the context of environmental education. He repeatedly makes the point that fieldwork often stops short of asking critical questions concerning alternatives; for example, whilst a common field activity might be to examine the arguments surrounding the siting of a new reservoir, less common is the consideration of whether rising demand of a finite resource such as water should simply always be met, or whether demand could be managed more effectively by introducing conservation measures. He draws on what for geography teachers is an extremely helpful distinction between fieldwork *about* the environment (knowledge and understanding), fieldwork *through* the environment (experiential, activity-based learning)

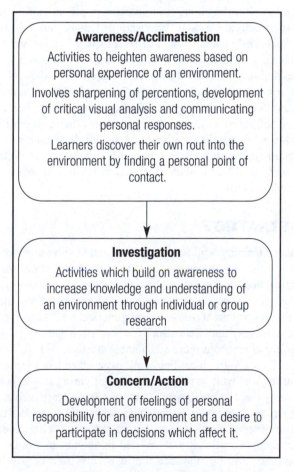

Figure 7.2 A process teaching–learning model for outdoor experience
Source: Derived from Hawkins, 1987

and fieldwork *for* the environment. The latter is viewed as having a more explicit agenda of values education and social change, driven by educational goals formulated to promote lifestyles compatible with a sustainable future. John Fien expressed the distinction thus:

> Education *about* and *through* the environment are valuable only in so far as they are used to provide skills and knowledge to support the transformative intentions of education *for* the environment.
>
> (Fien, 1993)

Futures education is taken up in more detail in Chapter 9.

The choice of approach will clearly influence the direction of learning through geographical fieldwork (see Table 7.1). Field research (or hypothesis testing) uses a scientific approach to test models or expected trends providing pupils with a clear structure and purpose as they work through a series of stages to find the answers. Pupils develop a range of skills in collecting, presenting and analysing data. However, questions have been raised about levels of engagement and conceptual learning achieved through field research (Caton, 2006). Research by Harvey (1991) also suggests that the transfer of conceptual understanding from quantitative fieldwork to examinations can be limited.

Enquiry fieldwork (Figure 7.3) involves pupils in exploring a range of geographical factors to investigate an issue or question. This requires them to draw upon different aspects of the discipline and work at different spatial scales, with subsequent benefits for their conceptual learning. Through values analysis, pupils are likely to develop their decision-making skills and ability to identify geographical questions. However, Job identifies a number of limitations to enquiry fieldwork (Job,1996 and 1999). He argues that pupils may not feel personally involved in or motivated by their research if the fieldwork enquiries are not based on questions about issues that concern them. He also points out that pupils are often asked to predict outcomes of decisions, which can be difficult to do with any accuracy. Job also argues that pupils should not be limited to considering where a development should take place, but should be able to consider critically whether it should take place at all.

FIELDWORK STRATEGY

Perspectives on teaching and learning styles can also be used to make sense of different approaches to fieldwork in geography. In the previous section, we considered the role and purpose of fieldwork in the geography curriculum. This discussion focused on the role of fieldwork 'about' the environment (developing knowledge and understanding), fieldwork 'through' the environment (developing practical skills and providing activity-based learning experiences) and fieldwork 'for' the environment (with its agenda for social change, aiming to promote more sustainable lifestyles). It follows that the purpose you have in mind for a geographical fieldwork experience has an important influence on your choice of strategy as well as on your role in delivering this experience.

You may, for example, want your pupils to learn about how the characteristic features of a river change as you move downstream. A number of fieldwork tasks could be devised to observe, measure and record features such as the channel characteristics (width, depth, cross-sectional area, wetted perimeter, hydraulic radius), the velocity of the river and the nature of the load that it is carrying. As you have particular learning outcomes in mind, you might adopt a hypothesis testing approach to the design of this fieldwork.

■ **Table 7.1** Fieldwork strategies and purposes

Strategy	Purposes	Characteristic activites
The traditional field excursion	• Developing skills in geographical recording and intervention • Showing relationships between physical and human landscape features • Developing an appreciation of landscape and nurturing a sense of place	Pupils guided through a landscape by teacher with local knowledge, often following a route on a large-scale map. Sites grid-referenced and sketch maps to explore the underlying geology, topographical features, the mantle of soil and vegetation and the landscape history in terms of human activity.
Field research based on hypothesis testing	• Applying geographical theory or generalised models to real world situations • Generating and applying hypotheses based on theory to be tested through collections of appropriate field data	The conventional deductive approach involves initial consideration of geographical theory, leading to the formulation of hypotheses which are then tested against field situations through the collection of qualitative data and testing against expected patterns and relationships.
Geographical enquiry	• Encouraging pupils to identify, construct and ask geographical questions • Enabling pupils to identify and gather relevant information to answer geographical questions and offer explanations and interpretations of their findings • Enabling pupils to apply their findings to the wider world and personal decisions	A geographical question, issue or problem is identified, ideally from pupil's own experiences in the field. Pupils are then supported in the gathering of appropriate data (quantitative or qualitative) to answer their key question. Findings are evaluated and the implications applied to the wider world and personal decisions where appropriate.
Discovery fieldwork	• Allowing pupils to develop their own focus of study and methods of investigation • Encouraging self-confidence and self-motivation by putting pupils in control of their learning	Teacher assumes the role of animateur, allowing the group to follow its own route through the landscape. When pupils ask questions these are countered with further questions to encourage deeper thinking. A discussion and recording session then identifies themes for further investigation in small groups.
Sensory fieldwork	• Encouraging new sensitivities to environments through using all the senses • Acknowledging that sensory experience is as valid as intellectual activity in understanding our surroundings	Structured activities designed to stimulate the senses in order to promote awareness of environments. Sensory walks, the use of blindfolds, sound maps, poetry and artwork are characteristic activities. Can be used to develop a sense of place, aesthetic appreciation or critical appraisal of environmental change.

Source: Job *et al.,* 1999, 'New Directions in Geographical Fieldwork' Cambridge: Cambridge University Press/Queen Mary Westfield College

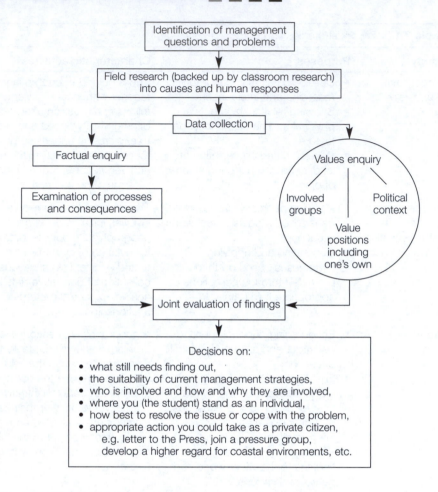

■ **Figure 7.3** Enquiry fieldwork

Source: Naish, Rawling, and Hart, 1987, *Geography 16–19:* 185 (figure 67). The Contribution of a Curriculum Project to 16–19 Education, Harlow, Longman. National Oracy Project (1990)

You present hypotheses about how these characteristic features might change between different sites along a river, select the sites for study and the techniques to be used to measure these characteristics. The pupils follow your instructions in collecting these data and in using various graphical and statistical techniques to present and analyse the data. The findings are more or less what is expected with possible reasons suggested for any that do not fit the predicted patterns.

This is an example of fieldwork designed and carried out in a closed style. Pupils across the range of abilities should be able to achieve success as they are following instructions to complete the various tasks. Differentiation is likely to be by outcome and reflected in the accuracy of data presentation as well as the depth of analysis of the results. The pupils learn how to carry out an enquiry, including fieldwork techniques for collecting the data and graphical techniques for presenting and analysing the results.

Pupils are usually motivated by their involvement in the physical act of collecting data. There is a sense of achievement and satisfaction when the results fit the predicted patterns, thus supporting the initial hypothesis. There are, however, a number of limitations to such an approach. Job argues that the process of hypothesis formation can be reductionist and narrow, leading us away from a sense of the uniqueness of place. Focusing on particular physical or human subsystems can also fail to 'deliver a holistic and integrated landscape view in which interactions between subsystems [are] vital to an understanding of the functioning of the whole' (Job, 1996: 37).

In a framed style of working, a teacher could create a decision-making exercise to provide the structure for a fieldwork investigation. The main aim is to investigate the impacts that recreation can have on the countryside and to consider ways in which these impacts can be reduced or alleviated. The teacher has chosen this issue because it provides a good example of people-environment interactions which are central to the examination syllabus being followed and because there are opportunities for pupils to use a range of data collection techniques in a fieldwork enquiry. Also, by presenting the pupils with a problem to solve there are opportunities for them to establish priorities, interpret data in different ways, consider viewpoints about the issue and show their ability to apply their understanding of geographical ideas relating to this issue.

Preparation for the fieldwork involves the teacher creating 'a need to know' among the pupils (Roberts, 1996: 243). Sites are identified around a popular attraction in a nearby National Park. The pupils consider the different types of recreational activity in the area and how the impacts of these activities might manifest themselves around this honeypot site. The teacher suggests a variety of relevant enquiry questions that guides the fieldwork and encourages the pupils to suggest some other questions that might be worth investigating.

The pupils then decide what information can be collected to investigate these enquiry questions and what fieldwork methods could be used for this data collection. The teacher guides this preparation by drawing pupils' attention to sampling issues and by helping them plan techniques for assessing visual quality, footpath erosion, vegetation trampling and other environmental impacts. The pupils have been organised in groups for these tasks and for the fieldwork itself as the teacher believes that this collaborative effort will help the pupils understand the relevance of the enquiry questions as well as the principles guiding the planning of methods of fieldwork data collection. It is also of value when the data collected is analysed as these data will be presented as evidence to be interpreted and evaluated.

Each group is provided with equipment needed to measure footpath erosion (tape measures, quadrants, etc.) and large-scale plans of the sites visited to record information about some of the impacts of recreation observed. In addition, each group is provided with a film to take photographs of these impacts and any management strategies observed.

The pupils' findings are presented in poster reports illustrating the evidence collected about the impacts of recreation and suggesting possible strategies for reducing these impacts. The pupils are encouraged to use a range of different techniques to present their findings graphically and cartographically. Appropriate photographs are selected and annotated to illustrate the impacts observed and to justify the group's management plan for the area. In the final follow-up lesson, each group makes a short presentation describing the problems observed, the methods of data collection used and explaining their choice of management strategies. The teacher uses the frameworks illustrated in Figures 7.4 and 7.5 to summarise the impacts of recreation identified through the fieldwork and to explore the rationale for the different management strategies selected by the pupils. In

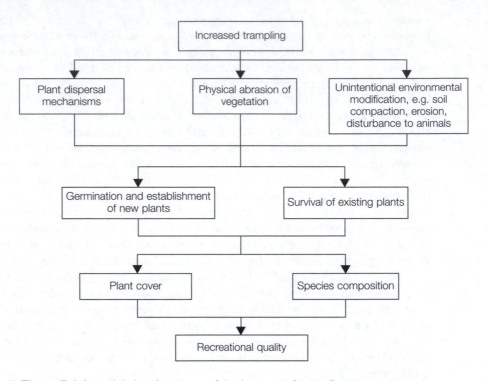

■ **Figure 7.4** A model showing some of the impacts of trampling on an ecosystem

Source: Harrison, 1986, 'Managing recreational areas; the effects of trampling on an ecosystem', in Slater (ed.), *People and Environments: Issues and Enquiries*, London: Collins Educational.

this way, the outcomes of the fieldwork are related to the key ideas and generalisations in the examination syllabus.

The benefits of this framed style of working are not only the knowledge and understanding of geographical ideas and issues, or the skills of data collection and analysis developed by the pupils. By controlling the development of the 'frame' the teacher is able to 'induct the pupils into the techniques and principles of geography' (Roberts, 1996: 245). The teacher is able to help pupils understand these principles and to make choices between different ways of collecting, representing and analysing data. In this way, pupils can become aware of the strengths and limitations of these different methods.

What the pupils learn may be less predictable than in the 'closed style' but the data collected and skills developed are still largely controlled by the teacher. The data are, however, presented as 'evidence' to be interpreted and there are opportunities for conflicting information or opinions to be explored. It is also possible for pupils to reach different conclusions which can be debated and challenged. A framed style of working in fieldwork can thus create opportunities to use a wide range of teaching and learning strategies leading to 'deeper' understanding as well as enhancing pupils' problem-solving skills.

Individual studies, particularly at GCE A-level, provide opportunities for 'negotiated' styles of fieldwork enquiry. The requirements of an examination syllabus and its approach to the study of geography may influence the choice of topic, issue or

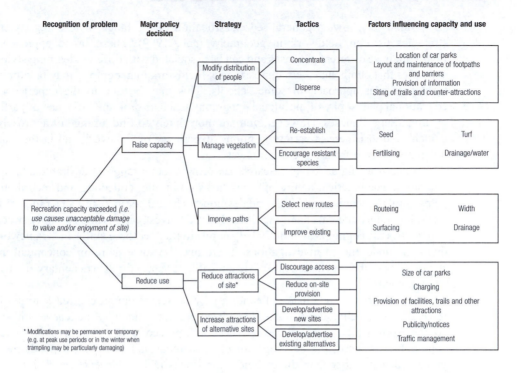

■ **Figure 7.5** Recreation management strategies: balancing the usage and capacity of a site
Source: Countryside Commission, Tarn Haws, in Harrison, 1986: 404

question to be investigated. However, the 'essence of the start of the negotiated sequence is that the questions which form the basis of subsequent enquiry come from the learners' (Roberts, 1996: 245).

It is the learner who makes the choices about which sources of primary and secondary data are appropriate to answer the questions to be investigated in the enquiry. The learner also chooses the methods to be used to analyse the data collected and is responsible for the interpretation of these data. The role of the teacher in this 'negotiated' style is as a 'consultant' advising and supporting the pupil. This advisory role is particularly important when the pupils are selecting appropriate enquiry questions and methods, and when they are evaluating the outcomes.

Such a study in many ways represents the 'pinnacle' of pupils' achievement in relation to geographical enquiry, it provides an opportunity to demonstrate knowledge and understanding of geographical ideas and skills as well as an ability to apply these successfully when investigating an issue or question.

What should be clear from this consideration of the participation dimension in relation to fieldwork is that in order to carry out an individual enquiry successfully, pupils need to have experienced a range of fieldwork styles and strategies. You will need to develop an understanding of how different strategies can be employed to help pupils develop appropriate enquiry skills and to learn how to apply them independently.

Table 7.1 shows a generalised classification of the range of teaching styles and strategies used in fieldwork in geography (Job, 1999). These broad approaches to fieldwork have different purposes and can be associated with different learning styles and strategies that pupils may be required to use. Fieldwork in geography may be dominated by a particular approach in some schools. This may be due to the experience and educational philosophy of individual geography teachers or to the influence of particular examination syllabuses. However, you are more likely to find a range of approaches in evidence so that there is variety in pupils' experience of fieldwork and in the learning outcomes derived from these experiences.

Field teaching and field research can bring about a range of desirable educational outcomes. The practical nature of many tasks observing, collecting and recording data helps pupils to acquire new skills and develop 'technical competency' in a range of fieldwork, laboratory and data handling skills. Focused investigations and carefully structured approaches to geographical enquiry help pupils to transfer these skills and frameworks to their own independent investigations. There may be some gains in conceptual understanding and the development of technical and specialised vocabulary is usually strengthened.

However, can such data collection really be seen as pupil-centred learning if the focus of study, techniques and sites have been pre-determined by the teacher rather than arising from pupils' own field experiences and perceptions? When hypothesis-testing approaches are used, the development of conceptual understanding depends more on processed data rather than direct field experiences (Job, 1996). Research into pupils' experiences of fieldwork at GCE A-level suggests that the quest for generalisations dominating the more heavily quantitative approaches to fieldwork can result in a neglect of 'sense of place' (Harvey, 1991; reviewed in Job, 1995).

Job (1996) suggests a variety of less structured fieldwork activities that can be used to encourage deeper thinking about landscapes and environmental issues. These qualitative activities are derived from the work of Steve Van Matre (1979) and others involved in earth education, which aims to promote love and respect for nature. Steering cards, like the ones shown in Table 7.2, and other sensory activities (Figure 7.6) can be used as starting points for fieldwork investigations raising pupils' awareness of an environment based on their own personal experiences and perceptions. Job emphasises the importance of this *'engagement with places at an emotional or sensory level'* in developing pupils' *'sense of care and concern about places and landscapes'* (Job, 1997: 156), which is a key element of any deeper environmental perspective. The role of art, poetry and literature in providing sensory experiences and helping pupils develop a 'sense of place' is also discussed in Chapter 6.

Caton (2006) suggests how trails can be used to encourage pupils to look closely at and experience the place they are visiting on fieldwork. An effective approach is to ask the pupils to devise a trail for users with particular needs (for example, elderly people or people with visual impairment or physical disability). Mapsticks can also be a stimulating way of giving pupils personal ownership of their fieldwork and encouraging them to *'see what's in between'* places. Pupils are given lengths of coloured wool and explore a place in small groups collecting small 'momentoes' of their journeys and an attractive stick. They use the wool to bind the objects to their stick which forms the base of their map. After completing the personal record of their journey they should simply share their stories with other groups. This is an effective strategy for awareness raising and acclimatisation in an investigation.

What should be clear from this discussion is that planning fieldwork in geography should involve more than just organising the collection and processing of data. As well as developing pupils' practical skills, producing case studies and coursework for use in examinations, fieldwork in geography can provide valuable qualitative and affective learning experiences which may encourage deeper thinking about the environment.

■ **Table 7.2** 'Steering cards' as an introductory activity for fieldwork in a rural area

The following cards (cut up and pasted) have been used to stimulate thinking and observation as an introductory activity in a rural environment.	What three features of this landscape would you most like to see conserved and why?
What changes might you see in this landscape in six months' time?	What three features of this landscape would you most like to remove or change and why?
Face North, then East, then South, then West. In which direction would you take a photograph if you wanted to show someone who had not been here what this place is like?	Would you describe the present human use of this landscape as mainly sustainable or unsustainable?
	What natural hazards (if any) can you identify in this landscape?
How might the view in front of you have looked: 10,000 years ago? 100 years ago? 10 years ago	What features in this landscape might be the result of past processes?
What clues can you see in the landscape which might tell you what rock type you are on?	Find two processes in the landscape (physical, ecological or human) which might be contributing to global environmental change.
	Observe the landscape around you over the next five minutes. What events take place?
Imagine you have been kidnapped, transported blindfold and dumped at this spot. On removing your blindfold, what clues in the landscape would tell you: i) Which country you were in? ii) Which country/region you were in?	Close your eyes and listen carefully. What is the first sound you notice? What are the second and third sounds you notice? Which are a result of human activity and which arise from nature?
Suggest two ways in which people have enhanced this landscape and two ways in which people have degraded the landscape.	Choose three words which epitomise (sum up) this locality.

Source: Used in a session led by David Job on the PGCE Geography course at the Institute of Education, University of London

Encounters with pebbles

from sensory exploration to key questions and geographical investigation
(and deep ecology if you want it!)

1 Choose a pebble *(aesthetic judgement/ownership established)*
2 Close eyes. Describe feel of pebble (one or two words). *(sensory experience)*
3 Open eyes. Describe shape and colour in your own words. *(perception/observation)*
4 Give pebble a name *(personalisation)*
5 Ask pebble two questions – a personal question *(confidential)* and a more
   geographical question.

Follow-up:

Brainstorm geographical questions as a source for the refinement of key questions as a basis for
further investigative work. Any subsequent geographical investigation is then rooted in personal
sensory experience contributing to a collective endeavour.

What we might do with our chosen pebbles can also open up valuable discussion – should we
keep them as a memento or, are there reasons why we should leave them on the beach and just
remember them occasionally, perhaps reflecting on the personal question we asked and seeking
our own answer *(environmental values and attitudes, reflection on possession/letting go)*

■ **Figure 7.6** An example of a sensory fieldwork activity
Source: Job, 1996, in Kent *et al.*

Activity 7.1 **Analysing provision in geography fieldwork**

This activity can either be carried out independently with you examining the nature
of fieldwork provision in your placement school or collaboratively with a group of
pupil teachers examining a range of examples from different schools.

■ Collect examples of different fieldwork activities from one or more schools.
  These should be from a variety of age groups. You can use resource sheets to
  explain the fieldwork activities or to record the data collected. Examples of work

produced by pupils as a result of fieldwork can also be used. If you have participated in any of these fieldwork activities, describe the role of the teacher and the strategies used by the teacher.

■ Try to classify these examples of geography fieldwork using the approaches identified in Table 7.1.
■ Discuss the role of the teacher in relation to the 'participation dimension' considered earlier in Chapter 4.
■ List the positive learning outcomes from the fieldwork activities and summarise these positive outcomes for each approach.
■ Consider the limitations of each approach to fieldwork in relation to the learning outcomes.

PLANNING FIELDWORK

Fieldwork is an entitlement for all pupils. The Geography National Curriculum states that pupils should be given opportunities to 'undertake studies that focus on geographical questions and that involve fieldwork'. Resourcing issues and the constraints imposed by a school's timetable may well limit these opportunities so it is vital for fieldwork activities to be well planned in order to maximise the wide-ranging educational benefits from such activities. It is also an area in which your legal responsibilities and obligations as a teacher, particularly in relation to health and safety, demand that your planning and preparation are of the highest standards possible. The planning issues that need to be addressed include:

■ the learning framework
■ the fieldwork style and strategy (see Table 7.1)
■ resource preparation
■ organisation (including health and safety)

Hart and Thomas recognise the importance of pre-fieldwork preparation and post-fieldwork follow-up in achieving the desired learning outcomes. You should identify what the pupils need to do to prepare for the fieldwork activity. This preparation should focus on what they need to know, understand and are able to do if they are to derive the maximum benefit from the fieldwork. This may in part be driven by the assessment objectives of an examination syllabus or relevant aspects of the Geography National Curriculum. But it may also be influenced by wider curricular and cross-curricular objectives.

Identifying relevant geographical ideas, processes and, where appropriate, people – environment interactions helps you decide what data need to be collected before planning the techniques to be used in the field enquiry. These considerations will in turn influence decisions about learning objectives and enquiry processes. Although fieldwork provides pupils with experiences that are intrinsically valuable, you should plan follow-up that uses the findings and experiences to consolidate and extend learning. This involves more than just writing up and presenting data collected. Try to be imaginative and creative with this follow-up phase.

There is a wide range of fieldwork styles and strategies that can be used. It is common to classify these into three broad categories or approaches to fieldwork (see Table 7.1). In reality, geography teachers draw upon a range of styles and strategies, particularly when devising fieldwork courses lasting a few days. It should also be remembered that interesting fieldwork investigations can be carried out around the sites of a school or its local area in a single lesson or part of a day (e.g. the micro climate of a school, land use in the local area). The variety of opportunities for geographical field-work are summarised in Figure 7.7.

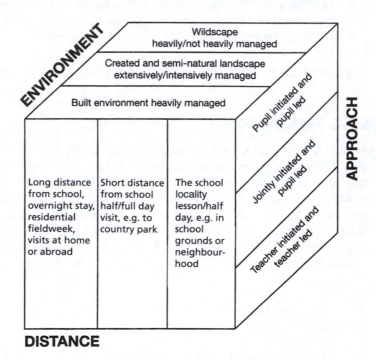

■ **Figure 7.7** Decisions to be made: choices for fieldwork
Source: Bland, Chambers, Donert and Thomas, 1996, in Bailey and Fox (eds): 166

Once the structure of a fieldwork enquiry has been planned and the objectives and strategies identified, attention can be given to the preparation of appropriate resources and equipment. Fieldwork usually involves collecting information for a specific purpose. Resource sheets may need to be prepared to provide instructions for pupils to follow or frameworks within which to record the data collected. This preparation needs to take into account the skills that you are intending the pupils to use and develop, as well as the degree of autonomy that you would like to see in the use of these skills. Highly structured sheets are often produced to support the collection, presentation and analysis of fieldwork data. There are numerous examples of such sheets and frameworks in the wide variety of fieldwork textbooks and resource packs. However, you may want your pupils to use *their* initiative and creativity to develop greater independence in their use of enquiry skills in fieldwork.

Figure 7.8 will provide you with an overview of the issues that need to be addressed in your planning of fieldwork.

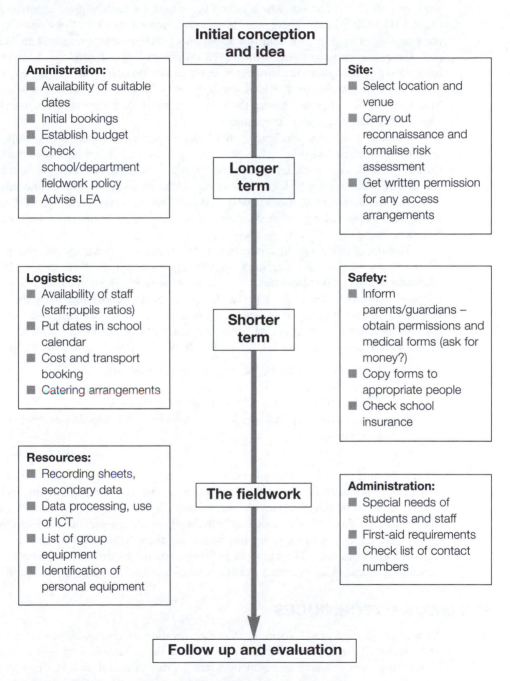

■ **Figure 7.8** Planning fieldwork – some important considerations
Source: Holmes and Walker, 2006, in Balderstone, D. (ed): 211

To be safe as well as successful, nothing must be left to chance in the organisation of fieldwork. Every school has a policy for the organisation and planning of visits and activities outside the school. This policy must be consulted and its requirements followed rigorously. The Geographical Association has also published guidelines for geographical work outside the classroom which have been based on current good practice in this country (GA/FSC, 2005). These provide us with an appropriate set of principles to guide our planning of high quality fieldwork experiences that are safe, successful and sustainable. Given the limited resources (financial and time) available for fieldwork, careful and imaginative planning should include thorough preparation of all stages of the experience from the initial development of ideas through the fieldwork itself to the post-fieldwork follow-up activities that will embed the learning gains made by the pupils in their longer term conceptual learing and development of skills.

Achieving safe, yet challenging fieldwork experiences means acting responsibly towards yourselves and others as well as recognising and following good practice in preparing for the fieldwork. Helpful checklists to guide the organisation, preparation and conduct of fieldwork can be found in May and Richardson (2005). There is no substitute for firsthand knowledge of the area where you will be undertaking the fieldwork so site-visits are an essential part of preparation, particularly when completing the obligatory 'risk assessments'.

The aim of risk assessment is to anticipate, minimise and manage possible risks for all those involved in the fieldwork activity (Holmes and Walker, 2006; May and Richardson, 2005). Site assessments and appraisals are carried out in advance to evaluate the potential risks to those taking part and to plan how to remove or control those risks. A 'hazard' is anything that could reasonably be expected to cause harm, while the 'risk' is the chance, however great or small, that someone participating in the fieldwork activity might be harmed by that hazard (DfES, 1998). Risk assessments need to take account of:

■ hazards specific to the location (i.e. rural or urban)
■ weather conditions likely to be experienced
■ the age and experience of the group and its leaders
■ students with special needs (e.g. mobility or visual impairment, medical conditions).

(Bland *et al.*, 1996)

When assessing the risk, you should consider how likely it is to occur, the likely severity of the outcome and on this basis, decide whether the risk is acceptable. Examples of risk assessments can be found in Holmes and Walker (2006: 214), in May and Richardson (2005) and in school policy guidelines. Fieldwork providers such as the Field Studies Council (FSC) also provide risk assessments for their fieldwork activities and these provide a good example of best practice to follow. You might also wish to consider taking a specialist course in safety management or first aid leading to a recognised qualification.

FIELDWORK TECHNIQUES

As well as giving careful attention to the preparation of risk assessments and to the organisation of the fieldwork, detailed planning of the fieldwork activities is needed to ensure that pupils' learning experiences are worthwhile and enable them to make progress in their learning through geography. The activities they engage in should reflect the purposes and frameworks you have identified for this fieldwork.

Three members of staff, one acting as a surrogate GCSE student, undertook the following assessment:

1. Using the route card for Area 1 shown below, the 'pupil' drew the route on to a map.

Area 1: Copthorne

This is the main route to follow but remember to survey adjacent aras. Walk along Racecourse Lane

➤ right along Welshpool Road to junction with the A5
➤ right along Shelton Road (A5) to the first roundabout
➤ right along Mytton Oak Road
➤ right along Wellmeadow Road
➤ left along Westlands Road
➤ left along Swiss Farm Road, cross Mytton Oak Road and down Crowmeole Lane
➤ left along Rad Valley Road
➤ left along Oakfield Drive
➤ left then right into Oakfield Road
➤ right then left into Kenwood Road/Kenwood Drive to Shelton Road (A5); turn right
➤ left into Woodfield Road
➤ left along Porthill Drive
➤ left along Copthorne Road
➤ right into Richmond Drive
➤ left into Barracks Lane
➤ right along The Mount (A458)
➤ right along Nealors Lane, across Copthorne Road then along Pengwern Road
➤ right along Woodfield Road
➤ left along Porthill Drive
➤ left along Porthill Road/New Street to the roundabout
➤ along Drinkwater Street
➤ right into St George's Street
➤ right into Mount Street and on to Frankwell Road
➤ go across the Welsh Bridge and follow Bridge Street to The Square.

2. The route was then followed on foot. Areas of concern/possible hazards and the whereabouts of phone boxes along the route were noted and listed. Two members of staff then completed the separate Urban site and instruction card below, listing areas of concern under 'specific things to be aware of in this section'.

Urban site and instruction card

Section: Copthorne to town centre (The Square, off the High Street)
Route: See the reverse of the card for a detailed route.
Time to meet in The Square:
Emergency telephone number:
Tell the person who answers:
1. your telephone number and location (if possible)
2. your name and group number
3. your centre tutor
4. the nature of your problem.

■ **Box 7.1** Example of a risk assessment for a fieldwork activity
Source: Holmes and Walker, 2006

Town Code:

1. Always stay in your group.
2. Be aware of traffic on all roads.
3. Keep to the given route at all times.
4. If there is an emergency, telephone the Centre.
5. Make sure that you are at the meeting place on time.

Specific things to be aware of in this section:

1. Racecourse Lane – narrow road and no footpath.
2. Welshpool Road and A5 junction – do not cross the road – stay on the verge you are already on i.e. the right-hand side.
3. Cross Shelton Road to Woodfield Road using the central island.
4. The left-hand entrance to Barracks Lane is only a footpath.
5. Take extreme care at Frankwell Roundabout as it is very busy and there is limited visibility.
6. Just over the Welsh Bridge, use the pedestrian crossing to cross into town.
7. Telephones can be found at: Mytton Oak Road; entrance to Woodfield Road from A5; junction of Woodfield Road and Porthill Drive; the Barracks entrance; junction of Copthorne Road and Richmond Drive; several in Frankwell and the Town Centre.

REMEMBER FIELD CENTRE RULES APPLY AT ALL TIMES

■ **Box 7.1** (continued)

Addressing relevant sampling issues is an important part of this planning (Holmes and Walker, 2006: 214). Pupils need to understand the role sampling plays in fieldwork and how it influences the reliability of the conclusions that can be drawn when analysing the data collected. Figure 7.9 summarises one way of approaching the selection of an appropriate sampling strategy. An effective way of introducing sampling techniques and their importance to pupils is to set up a fieldwork activity in which they use different sampling techniques to collect data within a defined area, for example within a grid square in an urban environment or within a ten metre square area of woodland. The pupils are organised in groups to collect the data with a larger group undertaking a total survey of the area while each of the smaller groups surveys the defined area using one of the sampling techniques. As well as collecting the data, the pupils should be encouraged to make a note of the strengths and weaknesses of the sampling technique they are using. The activity can then be debriefed comparing the relative accuracy of the different techniques as well as discussing their relative merits and limitations. Pupils can then make and justify a decision about which sampling technique is the most appropriate to use for collecting the data required. More detailed guidance on the selection of appropriate sampling techniques can be found in Holmes and Farbrother (2000: 74–79).

With all the detailed planning required to make fieldwork safe and successful, it would be easy to neglect the role of the teacher and the need to use strategies to engage pupils with the environments they are working in. Participation is the key, so get the pupils involved! Encourage them to use their imaginations ('close your eyes and imagine we are . . .') and give them some opportunities to 'explore' the areas being investigated,

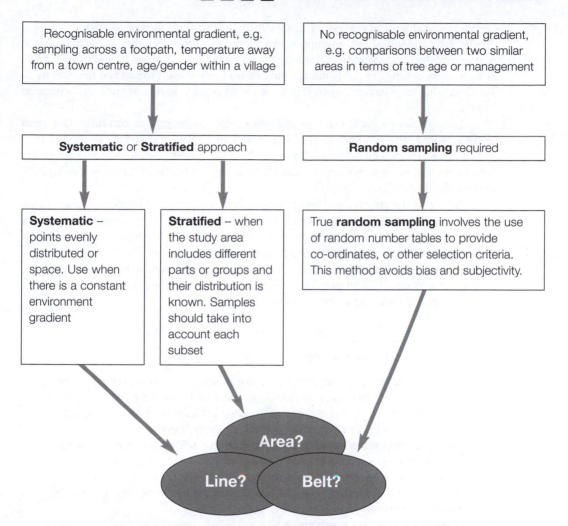

Recognisable environmental gradient, e.g. sampling across a footpath, temperature away from a town centre, age/gender within a village

No recognisable environmental gradient, e.g. comparisons between two similar areas in terms of tree age or management

Systematic or **Stratified** approach

Random sampling required

Systematic – points evenly distributed or space. Use when there is a constant environment gradient

Stratified – when the study area includes different parts or groups and their distribution is known. Samples should take into account each subset

True **random sampling** involves the use of random number tables to provide co-ordinates, or other selection criteria. This method avoids bias and subjectivity.

Area?

Line? Belt?

Sampling type	Advantages	Disadvantages
Stratified	✓ Reduces bias arising in an area of contrasts	✗ May be difficult to get background data to allow stratification, e.g. age structure of village
Systematic	✓ Straightforward to use, quick and provides good coverage	✗ Can miss variation, escpecially if a line, and result in bias, e.g. impact of road
Random	✓ No human bias in selection (if done correctly!)	✗ The points may not cover the whole study area/population or give a true representation, e.g. random samples using questonnaires

■ **Figure 7.9** Selecting an appropriate sampling strategy
Source: Holmes and Walker, 2006, in Balderstone, D. (ed): 211

within acceptable safety constraints. Get them to use their senses to describe how it smells, feels and looks. Use appropriate questioning to elicit what they know to reinforce and extend their understanding. Formative assessment (see Chapter 10 and Caton, 2006) is also important during fieldwork activity. Don't leave it until the end of the activity to find out what they haven't understood, check what they have learned and summarise regularly.

Manage the physical position and movement of the groups carefully. Use open body language, relax and smile! Use stories and anecdotes, particularly from your own experiences to hold their attention. Point to what you want them to look at and use drama techniques to bring in some fun and make the learning active (see Chapter 4, Caton, 2006 and Biddulph and Clarke, 2006).

Above all, be creative and imaginative when designing fieldwork enquiries. Think 'outside the box' and try out new ideas that will stimulate and engage pupils. Fieldwork does not always have to be driven by the need to achieve particular outcomes such as examination coursework or case studies, and even then it is possible to be imaginative and original to create more meaningful, motivating and open-ended fieldwork enquiries. Holmes and Walker (2006) provide a range of suggestions for some more imaginative and diverse fieldwork enquiries (see Box 7.2).

Ideas that are worth trying include:

- **Geographers as artisans:** Design a fieldwork activity which appeals to pupils who have strong artistic and visual tendencies. Take a physical geography theme and incorporate creative responses to the environmental processes. This might involve ideas using poetry, drama, sculpture, song or dance.
- **Making connections – linking local to global:** A fieldwork experience which explores interconnections between people and places at a range of scales. For instance, collect a series of images to illustrate how the area studied links with other parts of the world. What are the implications of such linkages and how do they influence other people's quality of life?
- **Web-designers:** Use a web storyboard as a mechanism for learning about a place. Encourage pupils to carry out Internet research to construct a virtual field course that could be used prior to the real excursion. How would they design navigation around their site? What would people like to know? This activity will engage and connect the pupils to the location while forming an important part of the pre-course preparation.
- **Tricky trails:** Ask the pupils to design two short trails around a local town. The first is a route which shows the best elements, high quality of life, best sights, etc. The other trail is an 'eyesore' route, which takes in the worst parts. Explore how the use of photographs and captions could illustrate these contrasts in such a small geographical area. This activity could be extended to introduce the more complex idea of bias and selectivity – how do these affect our views about both people and landscapes?

■ **Box 7.2** Creative approaches to geographical fieldwork
Source: Holmes and Walker, 2006, p. 218

FIELDWORK AND THE SUSTAINABILITY AGENDA

In his compelling critique of education in relation to the sustainability agenda, Stephen Sterling argues that education is behind other fields in developing new thinking and practice in response to the challenge of sustainability (Sterling, 2001). This critique has implications for those of us involved in fieldwork and, as Job asserts, should lead to a reappraisal of fieldwork restoring the emotional dimension and developing a deeper critique of the world:

> As soon as we venture outside the classroom and experience the real world we hopefully encounter beauty and harmony, but invariably we also find evidence of ecosystems which are falling apart, landscapes degraded by the junk of consumerism, and social structures in town and countryside which are losing cohesion. Having exposed the ecological and social wounds, do we also have responsibilities to guide our students into the healing process?
>
> (Job, 2002: 135)

The experiential approaches to fieldwork described earlier, based on Hawkins' (1987) model of outdoor experience, include activities that draw upon more individual experiences before conventional investigative activity and lead to a final more transformative phase of personal and societal change and commitment. Job provides examples of what he tentatively calls 'deeper' fieldwork based on this approach developed in the remoter parts of North Devon. They include sensory experiences to engage the emotions as well as the intellect in three woodland environments along the Tarka Trail. These are followed by more 'scientific' surveys of the woodland ecology and interviews with local users such as a woodsman, a charcoal burner and a herbalist. The 'concern and action' phase of the fieldwork includes coppicing and woodcraft activities providing creative and practical experience of what sustainable practice can involve, as well as developing new skills. It is certainly possible to envisage how this approach could be replicated in other areas of fieldwork experience in which pupils could gain insights into possible sustainable futures (Job, 2002).

PROGRESSION IN FIELDWORK

As in other areas of the geography curriculum, we should expect pupils to experience progression in their learning through geographical fieldwork between phases and age groups. They should make progress in relation to the skills and techniques used, the range of places and themes experienced, the degree of complexity and difficulty in conceptual learning and enquiry, and in the degree of independence required in undertaking fieldwork enquiry (see Table 7.3). Older pupils should be expected to use more sophisticated fieldwork techniques and where appropriate devise their own. They should appreciate the significance of sampling issues and demonstrate a greater range of skills in presenting, analysing and interpreting their findings. Careful planning is needed by a geography department to ensure that pupils continue to make progress in developing their skills and in extending their conceptual learning through geographical fieldwork.

■ Table 7.3 Progression in geographical fieldwork

Key Stage		1	2	3	4	5
Enquiry related skills		Other responses to questions. Some simple analysis of results.	Simple line of enquiry followed, teacher led/guided. Some will undertake additional independent investigations. Ask questions to help design enquiry, begin to hypothesise. Devise some fieldwork techniques. Decide how to record and present the data. Review fieldwork and the impact on their understanding.	Ask geographical questions, suggest an appropriate sequence of investigation and plan an enquiry. Collect record and display information. Analyse and reflect critically on their evidence and methodology, when presenting and justifying conclusions. Solve problems and make decisions, developing analytical skills and creative thinking.	Use of initiative in independently developing the enquiry process. Identify and collect a range of appropriate evidence and justify choices. Evaluate the whole enquiry process, including the limitations of their evidence and conclusions. Understand and apply the geographical principles and theory that underpin the enquiry.	Individual ownership of investigations. Understanding of piloting. Development of original data collection techniques. Systematic and robust enquiry process. Evaluate thoroughly and self-critically, including constructive proposals for further development. Wider geographical context fully explained and integrated throughout the enquiry.
Data orientated skills		Local walk making observations. Simple surveys and questionnaires (such as a traffic survey). Simple graphs. Simple maps and plans. Use of maps to record information.	Sketches including field sketches. Use of photographs. Measurements recorded using field equipment. Land-use survey using tally chart and colour coded key. Simple charts and graphs. Data used to answer question and interpret results.	Annotated field sketches. Maps interpreted (range of scales). Design surveys and interviews. Environmental assessments. Detailed, extended land-use mapping of multiple types of data. Range of data collected from a variety of sources including the internet, digital media and GIS. Sufficient data interpreted to substantiate conclusions. Data represented using a range of methods including ICT and GIS.	Precise data collection. Application of sampling. Data presentation using a wide variety of appropriate cartographical, graphic and numerical techniques including: choropleth and isoline maps, proportional symbols, annotated sketch maps. Quantative analysis. Detailed analysis cross referencing a range of data, establishing links, extrapolating and making inferences.	Rigorous data collection, high level of accuracy and detail. Full explanation of sampling strategy. Quantitative and qualitative data. Annotated data presentation; kite and vector diagrams, triangular graphs, and other complex graphical, diagrammatic and cartographic techniques. Statistical analysis of data. Explanation of anomalies. Analysis effective, coherent and independent. Conclusions fully justified and synoptic.
Example of fieldwork: 1 day River Study data collection		Possible use of stream in school grounds, or river in a village being visited, to make observations.	Short section of river visited, simple data collection at 3 sites. Predictions made Method devised using field equipment provided. Field sketch completed.	More detailed data collection at 3 sites, including use of hydroprops. Limitations discussed. Detailed annotated fieldsketches. Landscape features interpreted to support results analysis. Maps interpreted (range of scales).	Wider range of data collection – type and amount, completed with high level of accuracy. Discussion of sampling techniques. Methodology justified. Photographic evidence used to support observation.	Extensive data collection at 5/10 sites, detailed, thorough and precise. Hypothesis specific and individual. Additional sketches/notes to inform results and explain anomalies. Methodology and sampling techniques critically analysed and justified. Wider drainage basin features analysed. comparison with 'text book' river.
Examples of appropriate fieldwork equipment		Rulers, tape measures, stop watches, clinometer, thermometer, soil auger, digital cameras, video		Hydroprop/flow meter, ranging poles, anemometer, light meters, digital media, GIS, GPS, environmental sensors	Digital meters – decibels, pH, PDAs with spreadsheets.	

Source: Andrew Turney and Eve Jakeways, Field Studies Council, Brockhole.

Activity 7.2 **Progression in geographical fieldwork**

Working with a small group of other geography teachers, collect examples of field-work activities developed for pupils working in the following phases of education:

- Key stage 3 (11–14 year olds)
- GCSE (14–16 year olds)
- GCE AS and A2 Level (post-16)

For each age range, identify:

- the skills and techniques developed
- the range of places experienced
- the range of geographical themes covered
- the level of complexity and difficulty in the conceptual learning
- the degree of independence required
- the range of fieldwork approaches and purposes.

Compare your findings with the framework outlined in Table 7.3.

Where are the 'gaps' in pupils' experiences of geographical fieldwork?

Discuss possible reasons for these 'gaps' and suggest how they might be addressed.

SUMMARY AND KEY POINTS

Geographical fieldwork should not be seen as a 'one-off' and isolated learning experience. It needs to fit coherently within the wider curriculum experience through geography. This further emphasises the importance of careful and thorough planning and preparation. Pupils must be prepared in advance so that the learning gains from the fieldwork experience are maximised. Careful attention also needs to be given to how these learning gains will be built upon after the fieldwork in what Holmes and Walker (2006: 224) describe as 'closing the loop.' Evaluating all aspects of the fieldwork also makes an important contribution to your own professional development and to ensuring the success of future fieldwork (See Figure 7.10).

This chapter has explored many of the important issues involved in planning high quality, safe, successful and sustainable fieldwork. To conclude this discussion, we have chosen to draw your attention to David Job's challenge when thinking about the significant role geographical fieldwork can play in a young person's education:

> Engagement in real fieldwork, particularly of the deeper kind, addresses almost the full range of intelligences and learning styles. To promote and justify real fieldwork, it needs to be demonstrated that the experiences offered include not only the development of cognitive skills but also the nurturing of aesthetic sensibility, creativity, critique, co-operative endeavour, caring and healing. These attributes, rather than technical and rationalist aptitudes alone, form some of the foundations for the growth of ecologically and emotionally literate citizens.
>
> (Job, 2002: 144)

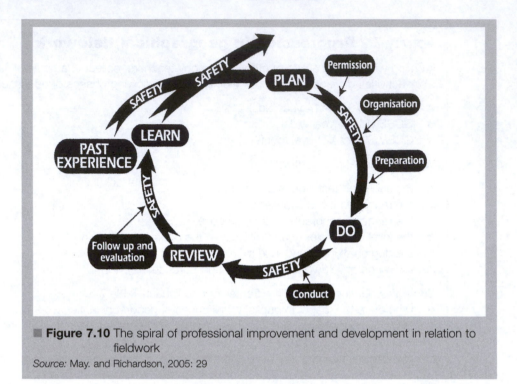

■ Figure 7.10 The spiral of professional improvement and development in relation to fieldwork

Source: May. and Richardson, 2005: 29

FURTHER READING

Caton, D. (2006) *'Real world learning through geographical fieldwork'*, Chapter 6 in Balderstone, D. (ed.) 'Secondary Geography Handbook', Sheffield: The Geographical Association.

This chapter provides a comprehensive overview of the different purposes of fieldwork and summarises a range of different strategies including some innovative approaches. David Caton explains how qualitative approaches can be used effectively to enhance fieldwork by involving emotions and developing pupils' sense of place through sensory activities.

Caton, D. (2006) *Theory into Practice: New Approaches to Fieldwork*, Sheffield: The Geographical Association.

This book explores experiential approaches to fieldwork and includes a variety of activities to illustrate these approaches. The author explains how such approaches can support the development of thinking skills and extended writing. The aim is to help pupils develop a more holistic appreciation of the environment.

Holmes, D. and Walker, M. (2006) *'Planning geographical fieldwork'*, Chapter 18 in Balderstone, D. (ed.) 'Secondary Geography Handbook', Sheffield: The Geographical Association.

This chapter provides very helpful advice about how to plan successful geographical fieldwork experiences. There is practical advice on planning fieldwork techniques and risk assessments as well as integrating fieldwork within schemes of work. It also presents creative ideas and approaches for improving the quality of geographical fieldwork.

Holmes, D. and Farbrother, D. (2000) *A–Z Advancing Geography: Fieldwork*, Sheffield: The Geographical Association.

Although this book was produced for use with post-16 students, it provides a wealth of useful advice and guidance about different fieldwork techniques and skills. It is a very useful resource to support the planning and preparation of geographical fieldwork and coursework.

May, S. and Richardson, P. (2005) *Managing Safe and Successful Fieldwork*, **Sheffield: The Geographical Association/Field Studies Council.**

A comprehensive overview of all aspects of fieldwork planning and conduct. There is clear guidance on essential aspects of health and safety for out-of-classroom activities.

http://www.geographyteachingtoday.org.uk/fieldwork/

The Action Plan for Geography is working with teachers to improve the breadth and quality of fieldwork in schools. The Geography Teaching Today website provides useful resources and advice for fieldwork including case studies of good practice, health and safety guidelines, field-work techniques, topics and themes. There are also suggestions about how to use ICT effectively to enhance geographical fieldwork.

http://www.teachernet.gov.uk/teachingandlearning/resourcematerials/outsideclassroom/

The DfES launched the 'Learning Outside the Classroom Manifesto' in November 2006 to promote the value of learning beyond the classroom, including fieldwork. This document shows how direct experience outside the classroom provides a powerful approach to learning that can raise achievement.

http://www.hse.gov.uk/schooltrips/index.htm

http://field-studies-council.org/parentsguide/

Both of these sites provide very helpful advice about health and safety issues on field trips and how to plan risk assessments.

In 2008 the 'one-stop-shop' Learning Outside the Classroom (LOtC) website was launched www.lotc.org.uk. This incorporates advice, guidance and examples for teachers, including CPD units, details on how assess risk and how to judge quality of commercial provision – note that LOtC encompasses far more than 'fieldwork' and educational visits, extending to adventure activities and expeditions.

TEACHING AND LEARNING GEOGRAPHY USING ICT

Globally connected electronic media are part of our daily lives, and twenty-first century geographical education must engage with the twenty-first century geography of people's lives. We interact with the wider world predominantly via electronic communication and information. Via the Internet, everyone can access a massive geographical database. The challenge for us as geography teachers (and a big responsibility it is) is to help our students use this communication and information in a constructive way.

Chris Durbin (Foreword in Martin F, 2006)

Geography teachers have an absolutely critical role to play in ensuring that the next generation understands the power and relevance of geographical information (GI) – and in equipping young people with the skills and enthusiasm needed to pursue future careers with confidence...Even those young people that have no interest in geography may well find themselves working in an environment that uses GI indirectly.

(Jeans, 2007)

The use of ICT in geography has grown with improvements in teachers' skills, better access to the internet and high quality software...In particular, the use of geographical information systems is revolutionising and extending pupils' experiences in geography.

(OFSTED, 2008: 22)

EDUCATION FOR A TECHNOLOGICAL WORLD

We need to help prepare young people for life in a complex and interconnected world experiencing rapid technological development, i.e. education in and for a technological world. This section examines your role in embracing Information and Communications Technology (ICT) as part of your remit, and the implications of doing so.

Two introductory points need to be emphasised. First, whilst we encourage a critical approach to using ICT (and certainly do not advocate using it simply for the sake of it – it needs to enhance the quality of the geography on offer), we are adamant that somehow 'ignoring' ICT is not an option. Technological illiteracy is not common in geography graduates in any case, but, even if a teacher is somewhat 'technophobic', to decide not to embrace ICT in the geography classroom is no more defensible than deciding that video images can be discarded or the data projector is a dispensable frill. Second, society is in a period of quickening and probably unending technological change; the scene is not 'set' and it is most unlikely that teachers will ever reach the point of finally 'getting to grips' with ICT, because the technology goes on changing. So, be prepared to jettison what does not work and to identify new opportunities as technology advances. But all the time, let yourself be guided by your aims – what you consider to be worthwhile geographical learning outcomes – in order to distinguish opportunities worth taking from those that can be left.

Sheila King and Liz Taylor (2006) also explore the role that ICT can play in your professional development as a geography teacher. You will develop your personal ICT skills in a variety of ways and use them to support your planning, teaching and assessment of learning. Younie and Moore (2005) provide a range of practical examples to show how you can develop your use of e-pedagogy including the development of e-mark books and e-portfolios.

OBJECTIVES

By the end of this chapter, you should be able to:

■ identify opportunities for developing pupils' ICT skills in geography
■ develop activities in which pupils can use ICT to enhance their skills of geographical enquiry
■ understand how geographical information systems can be used to enhance geographical enquiry
■ evaluate the use of ICT in learning geography.

Developing ICT capability

Information Technology is unusual in that it is both a cross-curricular skill, to be taught through curriculum subjects (including geography), and a National Curriculum subject with its own Programme of Study and Attainment Target (http://curriculum.qca.org.uk/key-stages-3–and-4/subjects/ict/keystage3/). The latter is useful, because it means that ICT has been defined. Technology and Media is one of the cross-curricular dimensions within the revised orders for the National Curriculum (QCA, 2008):

> To participate fully in a technology-driven society, young people must develop the practical skills to use technology confidently and productively. They need to develop the competencies to use technology safely and effectively to find things out, try things out, develop and present their ideas, and communicate and collaborate with others across the world.

(QCA, 2008)

The National Curriculum also requires pupils to be given specific opportunities to use ICT to learn in geography and to enhance their engagement with the subject's concepts, processes and content (QCA, 2008). This should include investigating 'important issues of relevance to the UK and globally using a range of skills, including ICT'.

It is worth noting that the Teacher Development Agency has now established the expectation that all new teachers, both primary and secondary, are functionally literate in ICT on becoming NQTs and must pass a professional skills' test in ICT. Without debating the pros and cons of such a move, it makes a highly significant point: though it is true that many young people have an open attitude to technology and are highly proficient at *some* operations – more so than their teachers – it is wrong to conclude that ICT therefore 'doesn't need teaching'. In addition to skills, there are knowledge and understanding components, as well as aspects of interpretation of information (involving a clear values component in that 'good' information needs to be distinguished from the 'bad', useless or irrelevant) into which pupils need induction and guidance by skilful and informed teachers. The key question is *how* teachers should do this (see below). But it is clear that teachers who lack meaningful knowledge and expertise themselves are not well placed to address such a question intelligently.

Before moving to the 'how' questions, we can briefly examine one way in which the *what* of ICT has been translated to the subject specific context of geography. For example, the GA produced a geography statement of pupil 'entitlement' – that is, those aspects of ICT use in which pupils may reasonably expect to gain experience and practice through their school geography course. Table 8.1 shows the five aspects identified. Geography provides meaningful and varied contexts in which new technologies can be used to enhance learning and reinforce ICT skills (OFSTED, 2004). Research shows that in geography, ICT can help pupils to:

- enhance geographical knowledge and improve geographical enquiry skills
- develop graphical, statistical and spatial skills
- develop mapping skills
- experience alternative images of people, places and environments and how environments change
- simulate or model geographical systems and environments
- communicate with other pupils in contrasting localities by email, webcams and video conferencing
- improve the appearance of work by enhancing presentation
- increase awareness of the impact of ICT in the changing world.

(Becta, 2004)

There is also the framework for developing ICT capability across the curriculum (ITAC) as part of the Key Stage 3 National Strategy (DfES, 2004). This framework provides examples of learning activities and guidance about how ICT capability can be developed through subjects. ICT capability involves more than just acquiring a range of technical competencies in using software. It also requires cognitive proficiency to access, use, develop, create and communicate information in appropriate ways using ICT tools (DfES, 2004: 7). ICT capability involves more than just acquiring technical competencies in using software. It also involves the appropriate selection, use and evaluation of ICT. Thus, pupils need to know *what* ICT is available, *when* to use it and *why* it is appropriate for the task. Using ICT in geography can provide pupils with opportunities to identify and select information to answer questions in geographical investigations. Computer-generated models can also help them to improve their decision-making skills. Their presentation of geographical ideas can also be improved using various presentation packages and through processes of reviewing, refining and redrafting.

■ **Table 8.1** A pupil's entitlement in ICT through geography

Pupils studying geography are entitled to use ICT:	When undertaking these activities in geography:	ICT can contribute by making possible:
• to enhance their skills of geographical enquiry	• collecting, investigating and questioning data from primary (fieldwork) and secondary sources • undertaking a broad enquiry approach to a topic	*The use of* • large amounts of data (e.g. data handling packages, Internet) and data otherwise difficult to obtain (e.g. data-logging); • a wide range of ICT techniques and approaches (e.g. creating and selecting maps, graphs for a report)
• to gain access to a wide range of geographical knowledge and information sources	• drawing on appropriate sources to obtain factual information, ideas and stimuli relating to place, physical, human and environmental topics	*Access to* • new sources about places and environments (e.g. newspaper on the Internet); different ways of viewing the world (e.g. remote sensing); moving images, sound, first-hand contact (e.g. Internet, E-mail); instantaneous images and information (e.g. remote sensing)
• to deepen their understanding of environmental and spatial relationships	• analysing change over time, locational decisions and people/environment inter-relationships	*Insight into* • relationships otherwise inaccessible to pupils (e.g. modelling) and monitoring change over time and (e.g. logging weather information)
• to experience alternative images of people, place and environment	• developing awareness and knowledge of other cultures, places and societies and creatively presenting one's own 'sense of place'	*Access to* • real images views, and first hand contact (e.g. E-mail, Internet, video); creative ways of mixing sound, text and images (e.g. multimedia, wordprocessing, graphics)
• to consider the wider impact of ICT on people, place and environment	• studying specific examples e.g. changes in lifestyle, environmental impacts and locational consequences	• knowledge and awareness of ICT use and applications in work and society

Source: The Geographical Association

The ITAC resources also provide further guidance about the ICT capability Key Stage 3 key concepts and suggest yearly teaching objectives for Years 7, 8 and 9 to support progression through Key Stage 3 (DfES, 2004).

ICT capability Key Stage 3 Key Concepts
- Communicating
- Using data and information sources
- Searching and selecting
- Organising and investigating
- Analysing and automating processes
- Models and modeling
- Control and monitoring
- Fitness for purpose
- Refining and presenting information

Activity 8.1 **ICT in geography in your school**

Examine Table 8.1 and the Key Stage 3 key concepts above.

1   How do they relate to each other?
2   Use the five entitlement opportunities in Table 8.1 and the key concepts and themes for ICT capability to 'audit' the Key Stage 3 scheme of work at your school.
    a)   Which aspects of ICT appear on the scheme of work already? Which do not?
    b)   Which aspects of ICT can be incorporated readily into the scheme of work?
    c)   In what ways might the scheme of work require more radical 'surgery'? For example, the redesign of a module or unit so that an aspect of ICT entitlement can be addressed sensibly.
3   After reviewing your scheme of work in relation to pupil ICT entitlement (question 2 above), prepare a list of practical considerations that now arise if such an entitlement is to be satisfactorily implemented.
4   Write a 'plan for entitlement'. This shows, on the basis that not everything can be achieved at once, a developmental agenda – your priorities, translated into targets with a note of how they are to be achieved.

Discussion: The exercise above asks you to think about ICT at the level of department within the context of the whole school – hence the identification of the scheme of work as the planning document in question. Therefore issues of classroom organisation and other lesson planning considerations are avoided for the time being. Instead, we are looking at the overall balance of the KS3 programme, giving us the opportunity to discover where scarce (ICT) resources may be directed for maximum benefit. (You may have noted for yourself in this exercise one of the drawbacks of an 'audit' approach to curriculum planning: simply ticking off bits of ICT in convenient locations in the scheme of work does not ensure progressive growth and development in knowledge, understanding and skill.)

In preparing a list of 'practical considerations' (question 3 in Activity 8.1), we can inadvertently focus only on reasons why ICT *cannot* be used in the geography classroom, for example, the physical constraints. We can overcome such obstacles in two ways. First, it is useful to interpret 'practical considerations' in a positive as well as a negative manner. For example, implementing aspects of ICT may be the catalyst to introduce some team teaching, or look into the possibility of shared teaching amongst colleagues; it may be the stimulus needed to upgrade display work in the geography department; it may be identified as the vehicle on which to pin a departmental policy on literacy and numeracy skills through geography (see for example, Table 8.2). You can think of many other examples of how to turn ICT *from a problem into an opportunity*.

Second, although resource and organisational constraints are often real and sometimes seem insurmountable, real progress can be made by developmental planning, which is a process based on the principle of identifying the targets that *can be achieved,* rather than being swallowed by the magnitude of what seems impossible. Table 8.3 presents a 'practical checklist' which may provide a useful basis for developmental planning for ICT: can you incorporate all eight types of ICT activity in a KS3 programme? If not how many could be included? And which will be next? What preparations do you now need to make? And most importantly, how is your ICT developmental target justified in terms of projected learning outcomes? You need to think both in terms of how the geography may be enhanced *and* relate the selected learning activity to the ICT National Curriculum.

Why ICT, and what are the implications?

In one sense, ICT needs no further justification: it is what drives the global economy; it is what has caused the coming of the global village; it has raised levels of global interconnectedness and may yet transform intercultural communication and contribute to a new dawn of 'international understanding'. On the other hand, the obvious significance of something to our lives does not in itself justify its inclusion on the formal curriculum – let alone part of every subject programme on the curriculum! The motor car has enormous social, economic and environmental significance, but the curriculum authorities have not seen fit to integrate motor vehicle studies into the subject curriculum.

Of course, many geography schemes of work *do* cover motor cars – from their manufacture, to the management of motor traffic and their environmental impact; but what such programmes do *not* cover are driving and engineering skills. Though not entirely fair (e.g. you cannot start to drive until you are 17 years old), this analogy is still instructive to our discussion of ICT in the curriculum. The crude point is that if ICT lessons in geography get bogged down in the whole-class-teaching of driving skills (the 'everybody now press Enter' syndrome), then this is arguably no more worthwhile than a geography lesson spent shading the sea blue or painstakingly constructing pastel coloured bar charts. 'Busy-work' with the computer is no better than 'busy-work' with the coloured pencil. It may be worse, in fact, because the product often *looks* so proficient; there is also a tendency to 'trust' the technology to do the job, rather than personally take full responsibility for the work.

■ **Table 8.2** Using ICT to develop numeracy development in geography in Year 7

Numeracy programme	Geography ICT examples
Numbers and the number system • Place, value, ordering and rounding • Properties and numbers • Fractions, decimals, percentages, ration and proportion	• Enter climatic data in a spreadsheet, using decimals for temperature • List data and rank in order, e.g. employment data in a table on a word processing package • Work out values for a map key to map data, e.g. in a spreadsheet, mapping or drawing package (e.g. Scamp Census data) • Use scale in a mapping package, e.g. Local Studies CD-Rom
Calculations • Number operations and the relationship between them • Mental methods and rapid recall of number facts • Written methods • Calculator methods • Checking results	• Calculations of population density either mentally or in a spreadsheet using a formula • Work out real distances from scale distances on maps, e.g. from a mapping package • Use the calculator (in accessories) to work out totals in a ranking exercise, e.g. to find the best site for a supermarket
Solving problems	• Predict best locations, e.g. modelling industrial location using a spreadsheet • Work out results of decisions (simulation), e.g. planning farm land use
Algebra • Equations and formulae • Sequences and functions • Graphs	• Use formulae in a spreadsheet to work out averages (means) from a weather data logger • Use of a spreadsheet/database to draw graphs, e.g. of a land use survey • Choice of appropriate types of graph from a spreadsheet to represent geographical data, e.g. to show population change over time or responses to questionnaires
Shape, space and measures • Lines and angles • Properties and shapes • Transformations • Co-ordinates • Construction • Measures	• Use a GIS package to measure distance and area • Use a mapping package to learn about co-ordinates (OS grids and latitude and longitude), e.g. Mastering Mapwork CD-Rom • Use a drawing package to present 3D images, e.g. contour patterns
Handling data • Specifying a problem • Planning and collecting data • Processing data • Representing data and interpreting and discussing results • Probability	• Enquiry work that collects raw data, e.g. of river flow and enters it in a spreadsheet or specialist data collecting package (CD-Rom) • Process and present raw data using statistics and graphing functions in a spreadsheet • Information research from a CD-Rom or the internet to interpret data • Presenting quantitative data on maps, e.g. in a spreadsheet using the mapping function

Source: Extract from 'Numeracy and ICT opportunities for year 7' from Geographical Association: www.geography.org.uk/download/RESECnumeracy.doc

■ **Table 8.3** An ICT practical checklist

Collect, keep and use their own or class collected data	• use a spreadsheet to present environmental impact scores derived from fieldwork (e.g. local housing issues) • use a data handling package to analyse information collected from a land use survey in an urban area
Explore and extract relevant information	• use UK Census data to extract information about population trends within the home region • use a newspaper website to explore the locations, causes and effects of oil spills on the coastline
Create and use appropriate maps	• use a mapping package to present comparative socioeconomic data about a European region • use a mapping package to present changing traffic flows on major roads in an urban area
Create and use appropriate graphs	• use a spreadsheet to present graphs of climatic data related to latitude • use a database with graphing facilities to display information about global economic development in graph/chart form
Present geographical ideas	• use a desktop publishing package to produce a leaflet promoting the case for or against a local bypass • use a word processing or DTP package to present a coursework report (using text, maps and graphics) about a third world country
Predict and solve problems	• use a simulation package to investigate the effects of migration on population change in a region • use a spreadsheet to calculate the costs of alternative development proposals for a derelict site
Monitor the environment	• use an automatic weather station to explore changes in weather conditions during the passage of a depression • use a weather satellite system to investigate the daily timing of equatorial rain cells
Pupils should also be able to explain the impact of ICT on geographical patterns, processes and events	• explain the influence of new technology on employment patterns in a particular area, as a result of increased home working • explain how remotely sensed information is used to monitor agricultural land use for EU subsidies.

Source: The Geographical Association

Activity 8.2 **Assessing the use of ICT**

Obtain two pieces of pupils' work produced using ICT in geography from activities you have either observed or taught. Alternatively, use two examples presented on the National Curriculum online website.

Imagine marking the two pieces of work. Two questions arise:

- on what basis should they be marked, and what should be fed back to the pupils?
- what can the teacher learn from marking this work?

Pupils' conceptions of learning geography, which according to research (e.g. Dowgill, 1998) are dominated by learning facts and remembering information, will need to change radically, as possibly will teachers' notions of what it means to teach. The knowledge base in Britain doubles every four years, and with the Internet, the availability of this information possibly expands faster even than this. Getting information, therefore, is not a problem, but handling it with discernment certainly is. In this way, we may teach discernment so that information is always treated as suspect, and, for example, is interrogated for its source, author and reliability. Box 8.1, shows one educationist thinking-out-loud about the kinds of adjustments teachers may need to make in their work in the face of new information and communications technologies.

There are many teachers in schools who have no idea what is barrelling down the road.

Take geography. Who needs a teacher to draw cross-sections of volcanoes on the blackboard, or even to push the button on a classroom video, when at a stroke you can access *Volcano World,* a vast database, with videos of any eruption you want to see and constantly updated data about worldwide volcanic activity? Ditto weather, Japan, rainforests, Africa, earthquakes, Antarctica, settlement patterns and anything else you can think of.

The teachers of tomorrow will have no choice but to become Web-wackers and Netsurfers, coaches and facilitators, there not to pass on knowledge but to encourage the development of higher-order skills such as source evaluation and data interpretation, not to mention the next century's most vital skill of all – time management . . . The well educated adults of tomorrow will be those who know how to cut straight to the core of any task, who will be able to sort necessary information from superfluous, husband their hours, divide up their lives, and set limits on how much time they intend to devote to each part.

■ **Box 8.1** What is 'teaching' in a technological future?
Source: Wilce, 1998: 44

The high-level skills mentioned in Box 8.1 – and there are others such as scanning and skim reading, estimation and guestimation, generalisation, synthesis and making judgements of merit – have always been in the sights of committed teachers. To develop such skills in pupils has always required teachers to employ a judicious mix of many teaching 'styles', including:

■ practical work and fieldwork
■ investigations/enquiry
■ exposition by the teacher
■ whole-class interactive teaching – questions of various kinds – probing, challenging
■ problem-solving and decision-making exercises
■ consolidation, revision and practice.

The advent of a 'wired society' changes none of this, though we do agree with the general tenor of the quote in Box 8.1, that the traditional notion of the teacher as main source and controller of information is fast disappearing. Over ten years on from when Hilary Wilce wrote this piece, you might consider whether her view of this technological future has been realised and what challenges it poses? The Internet has certainly become an important source of resources for geography teachers and a means of sharing such resources and ideas for learning activities. But as we have consistently argued in this book, this is an argument *for* the expert subject teacher, not against, as Wilce slightly implies. To help raise the pupils' powers of discernment requires expert knowledge as the basis for skilful intervention (or 'coaching' and 'facilitating' as Wilce describes it).

There is already a huge range of e-learning resources available to the geography teacher much of it free via the Internet. The British Library's recently launched National Life Stories collection (www.bl.uk/collections/sound-archive/history.html) is a stimulating interactive web resource reflecting current developments in the subject discipline. 'Food stories: From Source to Salespoint' draws upon research into cultures of consumption and enables pupils to find out more about recent changes in food and farming so that they can consider important issues about consumption and food safety (Jackson, 2008). Google Earth also has the potential to transform interactive learning in geography in creative ways.

Pulling together some threads: the impact of new technologies on schools of the future

Crystal ball gazing is hazardous. Nevertheless, the exercise shown in Activity 8.3, adapted from a pupil pack prepared by the EU to help prepare 11 and 12 year olds for a 'digital world', is worth exploring.

The discussion stimulated by the exercise in Activity 8.3 could form a springboard lesson for a sequence to consider the geography of the 'impact of technology' strand of the ICT attainment target (see http://curriculum.qca.org.uk/key-stages-3–and-4/subjects/ict/keystage3/).

To summarise the issues we have raised in this section, we should emphasise that we do not see the features of tomorrow's classroom in tomorrow's school in quite so clear cut a way as that implied in the exercise in Activity 8.3. One point we have made is that the role of the expert teacher is paramount, for without the teacher's questioning and debriefing of the pupils' learning, the learning is likely to remain at the surface level rather than at a deeper level employing those advanced practical and intellectual skills referred to in and around Box 8.1. Technology will not replace teachers. Neither will technology totally replace other familiar artefacts of the learning game, such as text-books. What will need to take place, however, is a rigorous appraisal of the role and purpose of these resources in the context of ICT: What is the teacher for? What is the textbook for?

Such questions require practical consideration. They also demand a response which has considered values dimensions, for the way we respond will say much about the kind of world we wish to live in (see later discussions about 'Geography and education for the future' in Chapter 9).

Activity 8.3 **New technologies in the schools of the future**

Read carefully the following lists.

List 1. Features of today's schools:

- large building complexes
- pupils travel to a central point for education
- pupils come from the same catchment area
- teachers interface with pupils
- schools help the intellectual development of pupils
- pupils are grouped in blocks
- pupils study predetermined courses
- books contain the subject matter to be learned
- course content is largely predetermined
- schools are run on a strict timetable
- social contact after class
- physical development catered for
- intellectual achievement is assessed
- schools give a sense of identity
- schools teach a clear sense of values.

List 2. Features of tomorrow's schools:

- no central buildings
- no travel to school
- classmates are from anywhere in the world
- contact with one another is by computer (Internet)
- no formal timetable; pupils organise their own
- infrequent physical contact with teachers
- no classrooms and no social contact
- mostly determined courses but lots of choice
- subjects are on interactive CDs, data bases and on line libraries
- study is the pupils responsibility
- no group support other than by electronic network
- intellectual achievement is assessed
- no sense of place identity
- value system is not so clear cut and pluralistic.

Questions

1   The second list is a projection. For each line in List 1, List 2 guesses what the
    future might be like. It projects what the school experience may be like for your
    pupils as a result of the continued development of ICT.
    For each line in List 2, explain why you think the projection could happen.

2   For each line of List 2, say whether you agree with the projection. Give your
    reason in each case.

3   Write a description of a day in the life of a twelve year old pupil in 'tomorrow's
    school'.

4   Write an evaluation of the technological future. That is, write two lists of your
    own: one including all the benefits of advanced forms of ICT (things you look
    forward to), and the other including all the problems you anticipate (the things
    you fear).

WHAT DO PUPILS LEARN AND NOT LEARN THROUGH THE USE OF ICT?

A fundamental assumption made in much of what is written about the use of ICT in
geography is that using ICT enhances children's learning. They may learn a little *about*
ICT, but the assumption may be that children will gain more knowledge, understanding
and skills of a more general nature *through* the medium of geography using ICT.

Is this true? Like most educational matters, the 'truth' is certainly complex –
depending on the topic, the setting, the pupils, the resources and the teacher. A familiar
comment is:

'The pupils clearly enjoyed using the computers and worked with enthusiasm.'

Such comments are common in evaluations of geography lessons using ICT, although
teachers making frequent use of ICT in their lessons have often observed that this
enthusiasm diminishes as the 'novelty value' wears off.

The impact of using ICT on motivation is clearly an important consideration.
Indeed, research into the views of pupils and teachers in thirteen secondary schools in
Birmingham showed that the general level of motivation among pupils increased
significantly when they used information technology (NCET, 1997). It also revealed that
using ICT enhanced boys' motivation even more than girls. Evidence from this research
has suggested that ICT can 'reach the parts of the population that schools have often
failed to reach in the past':

Two-thirds of those who say they find school 'completely boring' describe work
with ICT as 'interesting'. Half of those who claim they 'always behave badly at
school' get so interested in work with computers that they don't want to stop.

(Barber, 1995: 120)

It is argued that developments in ICT change our focus from thinking about teaching to
having more of a concern for learning. More specifically in relation to geography there
is a widely accepted view that ICT has the potential to enhance pupils' skills of

geographical enquiry. This requires geography teachers to improve their understanding of how ICT can help geographers to record, process, analyse and present information in words, tables, maps and diagrams from both primary and secondary sources.

But if pupils are to use ICT effectively to enhance their skills of geographical enquiry, they need to develop more than just their ICT skills in relation to data handling. We need to help pupils develop appropriate information skills as well as their understanding of geographical enquiry. These skills include the ability to select, evaluate, interpret and present appropriate information. Without these skills we are likely just to receive the outcomes of what we have described as 'busy work', that is, unnecessarily excessive amounts of data, sometimes from inappropriate sources, that have neither been processed nor interpreted. These skills need to be seen as part of a wider process contributing to the development of greater autonomy in learning:

> Having a range of analytical strategies to deploy and a critical approach to information and media is an essential requirement for an independent learner.
>
> (Leat and McAleavy, 1998: 114)

Information skills are central to geographical enquiry. Helping pupils to develop appropriate information skills enhances their learning generally as well as improving how they use ICT (Table 8.4). These skills should be identified with pupils and developed in a structured way using specific tasks. Once acquired, pupils are more likely to be able to apply these skills in an autonomous way. They need opportunities to select and evaluate appropriate sources of information and should be encouraged to consider the following questions when evaluating information as part of the process of geographical enquiry:

■   What information do I need to answer these questions, and why?
■   How much information do I need, and why?
■   Where do I get this information?
■   What does the information show? (and what does it not show?)
■   How useful is this source of information? (and how reliable is it?)

Pupils must learn how to search for and select appropriate information using ICT and how to apply these methods in different situations. This requires specific tasks and strategies designed to introduce them to particular data-handling skills. For example, how to use different search tools to find information from the Internet, or how to use a spreadsheet to record data about the weather and produce climate graphs. More open-ended enquiries can then be set up to provide opportunities for pupils to apply the skills they have acquired. The most significant learning gains are achieved when pupils are in control of the investigative decisions, search methods and what information should be used.

Geographical enquiries that require pupils to undertake research using ICT often reveal similar issues to more conventional research using printed sources. These can include problems with information overload, plagiarism, poor quality material and inappropriate data. Unlike more conventionally published print sources, the Internet is not subject to any strict editorial process. Information may be biased, so the reliability of data must be assessed and pupils need to develop skills of critical analysis to evaluate the accuracy and authenticity of data. The ease of 'copying and pasting' text and graphics from a source, though a useful skill, can mean that 'electronic plagiarism' is prevalent in pupils' work. Familiarity with pupils' normal writing styles will help you detect such problems.

■ **Table 8.4** How information-handling skills used in geography combine with data-handling skills in ICT for enquiry learning

Data collection

Information-handling skills

Posing a hypothesis; Developing a questioning attitude Identifying sources; Discriminating between sources. Organisation, observation, measuring. Map interpretation; Interviewing, questionnaire surveys; Record-keeping, collating

Data-handling skills

Structuring data; Designing data capture sheets Entering and checking data; Encoding data Storing data files Keyboard skills

Data retrieval and interrogation

Information-handling skills

Hypothesising; Accurate definition of a question; Modifying a question; Combining questions; Selecting and rejecting results

Data-handling skills

Browsing; Searching; Matching data; Framing a question in computer terminology; Sorting data

Data display and analysis

Information-handling skills

An understanding of the application of diagrammatic, statistical and cartographic techniques. Making a précis or report of the results of searches

Data-handling skills

An understanding of the methods for displaying data in graphs, tables , maps and statistics on computer

Data evaluation

Review of all methods of collection, retrieval and analysis
Criticism of the outcome
Discussion, self-assessment
Application of subject criteria to the enquiry: modification or acceptance of the hypothesis

Source: Freeman, 1997: 208

In an attempt to avoid some of these problems, Matthews (1998) developed an 'Internet research model' (Figure 8.1) by adapting more conventional research techniques. This model follows a similar sequence to the more common frameworks used to support pupils' writing.

Other areas of teaching and learning in geography where ICT has the potential to make a significant contribution to geographical enquiry include the measurement of environmental processes and conditions, and the modelling of real-world systems and situations. Automatic weather stations and environmental monitors can be used to collect and store data in a continuous and more reliable way. The use of data-logging devices in conjunction with portable computers (laptops and notebooks) also has the potential to enhance geographical fieldwork. Pupils can then use generic data-handling software and skills to process and analyse this data.

There are also animations and programs illustrating various dynamic systems and models such as the hydrological cycle, population change and industrial location. These provide opportunities to explore processes, patterns and relationships by modifying some aspects of the models in order to develop an understanding of their underlying principles. There is also the potential for pupils to create and use their own models.

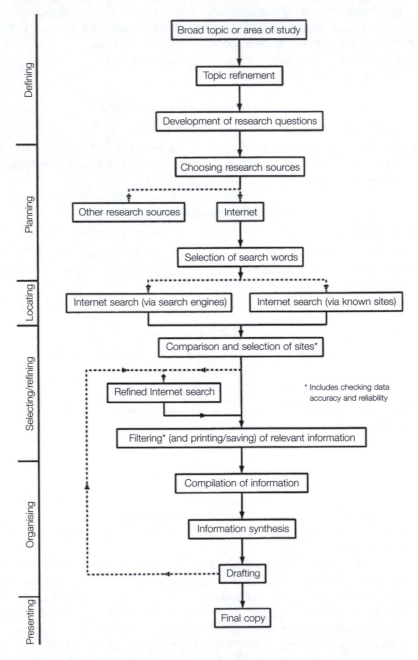

■ **Figure 8.1** An Internet research model

Source: Matthews, 1998: 15–19. Reproduced with permission.

Activity 8.4 **What do pupils learn and not learn through the use of ICT?**

1   Plan and teach a short sequence of lessons (two or three) which demonstrates the application of ICT in teaching and learning in one aspect of the geography curriculum at any level.

2   Write a report evaluating these lessons. Your report should contain a rationale and justification, the lesson plans and associated materials and, where appropriate, pupils' work.

3   Use the following approach to evaluate the resources and strategies used in terms of what the pupils did (and did not) learn.

   a)   Identify your learning objective(s).

   b)   Identify the criteria you value in order to evaluate the success of the project.

   c)   Translate the criteria into 'measurable' indicators (the source of your 'evidence').

   d)   Do the teaching and make your observations.

   e)   Make your judgement(s).

   f)   Report your evaluation.

Discuss the report with your tutor or class teacher.

Evaluating the use of ICT requires us to consider other aspects of learning as well as motivation. The effectiveness of particular ICT applications and software must be weighed up against alternative strategies. Using ICT is often time-consuming. Sometimes it takes more time to achieve the planned learning objectives using ICT than using other strategies. For example, a group of student teachers set up an investigation to compare the use of an electronic atlas with a more traditional printed atlas to study the geography of a country. They found that pupils working from the printed atlases took less time to produce work of a higher quality even though time had been spent in a previous lesson planning the task and deciding what information would be needed. They also found that information from the electronic atlas tended to be 'copied' without comment or integration of illustrative material.

On the other hand, another group of teachers investigating the use of ICT in processing fieldwork data found that using spreadsheets saved a considerable amount of time when analysing data about variations in housing and environmental quality in a town. Pupils designed their own questionnaires and environmental quality surveys, then used their ICT skills to construct spreadsheets to process and present the data collected. Different types of graphs and charts were produced quickly enabling the pupils to spend more time analysing the data, evaluating presentation techniques and exploring the geographical content of the enquiry.

However, developing ICT capability in geography is not just concerned with ICT skills such as using a database or spreadsheet. We must also develop pupils' knowledge and understanding of geography through the use of ICT. A common criticism of the way information technology is the lack of appropriate challenge with many activities requiring pupils to use only low-level skills:

Many lessons tend to develop low-level skills at the expense of knowledge and understanding. Few encourage the gradual development and improvement of interesting and substantial pieces of work in IT over a period, which enhance knowledge, understanding and critical judgement in using IT.

(Goldstein, 1997: 15)

These objectives are made explicit in statements about pupils' entitlement for ICT in geography (Table 8.1). For example, it is stated that pupils studying geography are 'entitled' to use ICT to 'deepen their understanding of environmental and spatial relationships' and to 'experience alternative images of people, place and environment'. These and the other statements about pupils' entitlement (Becta, 2004) can help you define more specific criteria for evaluating the use of ICT.

Your evaluations should also consider the needs of pupils of all abilities. To what extent did the use of ICT enrich able pupils' experience of geography? Did the use of ICT increase access to the geography curriculum for pupils with Special Educational Needs and address their individual needs? ICT can be successful in holding the attention of pupils with emotional and behavioural difficulties. It can help pupils with specific learning difficulties to develop their literacy and numeracy skills. ICT can also provide the means by which pupils with sensory or physical impairments gain access to the curriculum.

Finally, you may also be conscious of changes in learning styles when ICT is being used to facilitate learning in geography. Pupils sometimes appear to be in more control of the learning process and you may need to be more flexible in your expectations of the outcomes of this learning. Using ICT certainly encourages peer learning rather than only learning from teachers. You may need to respond to this in your organisation of the class-room and pupil groupings. It is not unusual, therefore, for learning relationships to be modified with pupils and teachers learning together or pupils teaching their teacher!

EVALUATING ICT RESOURCES

It is important to evaluate ICT resources critically as you would any other resources. There has been a tendency for teachers to be attracted by the presentation of new technological resources and what they appear to be able to do rather than any under-standing of their effectiveness in supporting teaching and learning. It is sometimes like a child being attracted to a new toy.

The quality and availability of appropriate electronic resources is an important issue. The 'content rich' nature of some resources usually means that pupils find it difficult to use them independently in their own geographical enquiries without careful guidance from and activities designed by their teachers. A key issue with the design of geographical software is how the user is able to search out information and 'navigate' around the content. Sometimes the way the content is organised can result in pupils passively browsing through material with limited learning gains. Geographical software that can be used flexibly and provides opportunities for a high degree of pupil interaction offers the greatest potential for enhancing the quality and depth of enquiry learning.

You should therefore evaluate the electronic resources available for you to use in the classroom to determine the reliability, accuracy and currency of the material and the benefits for pupils' learning. You should critically evaluate websites when selecting online resources for use in the classroom, and pupils should also be taught the value of this process as part of their core digital literacy skills development (Becta, 2005). Box 8.2 provides a helpful checklist for evaluating online resources. Pupils should be taught how to search for useful resources and how to evaluate the quality of the information and resources they find. The Internet for Education website (http://www.vts.intute.ac.uk/he/tutorial/education) has some useful guidance on how to search the Internet that can be adapted for use with pupils, particularly at GCSE and post-16. Some search engines like Ask for Kids (http://www.askkids.com/) are developed specifically to help young people find information, but most secondary pupils instinctively use Google or Yahoo search engines. Pupils benefit from being taught how to use such search engines effectively because entering broad terms such as 'environment' will return thousands of links, many of which have limited educational value (see also Martin, 2006 Chapter 3 for more guidance on using ICT resources to support pupils' research).

Accuracy and currency

When evaluating online resources you should consider the following:

- Does the information appear to be accurate?
- Is it based on opinion or fact?
- Are additional references given?
- Can the inforrnation be verified from other sources, whether online or hard copy?
- Is the spelling and grammar correct?
- Is the content dated?
- When was the content last updated?
- Are all links up-to-date and valid?
- Are any areas of the site 'under construction'?

Authority and coverage

You should also consider:

- Does the content have authority?
- Where does the content originate from?
- Is it clear who is the author and publisher of the site?
- Are they qualified to provide information on this topic?
- Is the material biased?
- Can the author be contacted?
- Where is the content published? What is the domain name of the website? Is it published by a large organisation, or on a personal website?
- Does the website cover the topic fully?
- Does the site provide information/advice/ideas/other choices?
- Does it provide links and references to other materials?
- If links to other materials are provided, are these evaluated or annotated to provide further information?
- Does the site contain any advertising?
- Does this influence the content?

■ **Box 8.2** Evaluating online resources
Source: Becta 2005 (Becta website)

Audience and relevance

You should/also consider:

- Who is the intended audience for this content?
- Is the content easy to read and understand?
- Is the site specifically aimed at children? If so, is the level and tone of the content appropriate?
- Is the site specifically aimed at adults? If so. beware of innapropriate material.
- Is the content relevant?
- Does the material provide everything that is needed?
- Could more relevant material be found elsewhere, for example in a book or magazine?

Educational focus

You should also consider:

- Is there an explicit educational focus to the content?
- Will it support learners with different learning styles? How does it use media to cater for people wvith auditory, visual, kinaesthetic or other learning preferences?
- Does it have links, or refer to, the appropriate stages of the National Curriculum or examination body?

Ease of use

In addition you should consider:

- Is the site easy to use?
- Is the site well structured?
- Is it easy to find relevant information?
- Is the content in an easy to use format?
- What facilities does the site provide to help locate information?
- Does it have a search facility? Is the menu navigation logical? Does it provide a site map or index?
- Does the site load quickly?
- Is the site attractive in design?
- Is the content copyright, or can it be used providing the source is acknowledged?
- Is the site technically stable?

■ **Box 8.2** Evaluating online resources (continued)

Source: Becta 2005 (Becta website)

There are also an increasing number of websites providing up-to-date information and resources to use when preparing materials and lessons. These often include opportunities for both pupils and teachers to communicate with experts asking questions and receiving answers. An increasing number of organisations are developing 'virtual teachers' centres that provide advice, resources and even lesson plans on topics related to their work.

Searching the Internet for resources to support teaching and learning, you will find material ranging from raw data to content-rich teaching and learning material. Some will provide excellent learning resources differentiating by task, resource and support. Evaluate the content and structure of such resources remembering that pupils' motivation is maintained when they are successful in achieving the learning objectives. Attractive and intuitive interfaces enable easy navigation and control the amount of information that is presented. The degree of interactivity also influences the level of pupil autonomy in learning.

Recent years have seen the growing use of 'virtual learning environments' (vle) in which learners and teachers interact online. The development of e-learning, particularly through the use of such 'virtual learning environments', varies between schools and even within schools where some subjects and e-learning enthusiasts have taken these developments forward at a greater pace than others. However, the government require-ment that all schools have learning platforms (or 'managed learning environments' within which 'virtual learning environments' are included) in place by 2010 will embed the use of such tools for e-learning. These learning platforms and their 'virtual learning environments' provide pupils with access to learning resources and activities from anywhere in a school, at home or elsewhere so that they are able to work collaboratively online as well as in a classroom. Learning platforms also provide pupils with e-Portfolios in which to store and access their own work. Many geography departments also have their own websites with a wide range of resources and activities to support teaching and learning including images, webcams, animations and links to other useful websites (Mitchell, 2007).

Activity 8.5 **Using the Internet with pupils**

(*Source:* Developed for use with student teachers on the Geography PGCE course at the Institute of Education, University of London)

A   Review at least one website that could be used with pupils.

Use the criteria in Box 8.2 to evaluate at least one online resource. Compare your findings with other teachers' evaluations.

1   Name the site and give its URL (address).
2   Describe the content of the site.
3   Which geographical topic(s) would it be useful for studying?
4   Which age group(s) would you use it with?
5   Would this site be suitable for all abilities within this age group?
6   What additional materials would you need to prepare to support the use of this site?
7   Are there any disadvantages with the site?

B   Plan a web enquiry in which pupils could use a selected website.

1   What are the aims of the enquiry?
2   Which aspects of geography (knowledge, understanding and skills) are developed in the enquiry?
3   Which specific ICT skills are developed in the lesson?
5   Is the written content of the site suitable for the ability of your class or does it need interpretation?

6   How will the enquiry be structured? Does the website have a clear path-
     way through it or do you need to provide a structure for the activities and
     other resources to support the enquiry?
7   What are the outcomes of the enquiry likely to be? How is what the pupils
     have learned (in geography and in ICT) assessed?

C   Use this web enquiry with a class or group of pupils that you teach.

D   Evaluate the outcomes of the enquiry.
     What did pupils learn and not learn? What geographical knowledge, under-
     standing and skills did they develop? What ICT concepts and skills did they
     develop?

Geographical Information Systems (GIS)

> The use of geographical information systems is revolutionizing and extending
> pupils' experiences in geography. Visual images from around the world bring
> immediacy to the learning. Satellite technology can bring landscapes to life. Data
> can be overlaid and used with interactive maps to interpret patterns and solve
> problems.
>
> (OFSTED, 2008: 22)

Although Geographical Information Systems (GIS) have been around for some years,
only now are they beginning to be used more widely in geography classrooms and fieldwork. As indicated in the OFSTED inspection findings quoted above, access to high
quality GIS software and digital resources via the Internet has been a significant factor
influencing this improvement (OFSTED, 2008: 22). There is also a clear statement in the
Key Stage 3 Programme of Study in the Geography National Curriculum that the
geography curriculum should provide pupils with opportunities to use GIS:

> GIS systems are valuable for mapping and visualizing information as well as
> linking and analysing spatial datasets. There should be opportunities to learn with
> GIS and about GIS.
>
> (QCA, 2007: Curriculum Opportunities)

GIS is one of the fastest growing applications of ICT in the world and is already part of
our everyday lives in satellite navigation systems used in cars, providing government
information online, supporting emergency services and enabling market research via
supermarket loyalty card schemes. Thus, GIS is an obvious way of illustrating the value
of geography in the current and future world of work enabling pupils to apply what they
learn in geography to real world situations (Balderstone, 2006: 24–5).

A Geographical Information System has three components: a digital map, digital
data to be displayed on the map and a piece of computer software (GIS) that links the two
together. More sophisticated commercial GIS also incorporate spatial modelling, spatial
query and analysis functions. GIS can enhance pupils' learning in geography by enabling
them to produce more professional maps and helping them to visualise landscapes
through 3–D imagery, aerial overlays on maps and 'fly-throughs' (Martin, 2006;

Freeman, 2005). It also enables them to experiment with cartographic techniques and significantly, leaves more time for higher level thinking and decision-making by replacing time-consuming and tedious mapping with interactive manipulation of digital mapping (Freeman, 2005). Table 8.5 shows how GIS can enhance geographical enquiry while Table 8.6 summarises some of the geographical skills developed using GIS.

Using free Internet GIS resources and activities is the best way to get started using GIS (Mitchell, 2007). The Geographical Association's 'Spatially speaking' project web pages (http://www.geography.org.uk/projects/spatiallyspeaking/) provide guidance and exemplars to help you getting started while the Ordnance Survey's GIS zone in its Mapzone for schools. (http://mapzone.ordnancesurvey.co.uk/mapzone/giszone.html) has resources and activities to support decision-making and problem-solving exercises using GIS. You don't need high level ICT skills to use these resources, just a geographical mind to think about the geographical relevance and application of these ICT tools and resources in e-learning.

■ **Table 8.5** How GIS can enhance geographical enquiry

Geography Programme of Study KS3	KS3 strategy	How GIS helps
Ask geographical questions to identify issues	Ask questions, predict and hypothesise	Enables spatial data to be collected, organised and investigated to show patterns and relationships
Suggest appropriate sequences of investigations	Find, organise and use information that is fit for the purpose	Provides a framework within which to collect data in tables linked to points, lines and areas on maps
Collect, record and present evidence	Seek patterns and relationships	Allows information to be selected and presented on maps quickly and easily to identify spatial patterns and relationships
Analyse and evaluate evidence and draw conclusions	Interpret results and evaluate evidence	
Communicate in ways appropriate to the task and audience	Present and communicate findings in a variety of ways	Resulting maps may be used in reports and presentations to different audiences
From: *Geography National Curriculum Programme of Study for England and Wales.* DfES 2000	From: *KS3 Strategy – Framework for teaching ICT capability - Using ICT across the curriculum.* DfES 2002	

Source: Freeman, 2005

■ **Table 8.6** Geographical skills developed using GIS

Geographical skills may be extended into the use of digital mapping and GIS. The list illustrates how skills gained using more traditional methods may be transferred to digital mapping and GIS.

Use an extended geographical vocabulary
- New vocabulary includes ICT keywords (such as raster and vector) and specific GIS terms

Select and use appropriate fieldwork techniques and instruments
- Small handheld computers (PDAs or palmtops) may be used to enter data directly in the field for transfer to GIS
- Handheld GPS systems are now accurate enough to collect location information for transfer to GIS
- Weather monitors and environmental data loggers may collect information for transfer to GIS.

Use maps and plans at a range of scales, including Ordnance Survey 1:25,000 and 1:50,000 maps
- Ordnance Survey digital map data provides the basis for vector and raster mapping.

Select and use secondary sources of evidence: aerial photographs, satellite images, ICT sources
- Aerial photographs and satellite images may be used in digital mapping and GIS
- Ground level digital photographs may be linked to 'hotspots' on a map.

Draw maps and plans at a variety of scales, using symbols, keys and scales...

GIS explores raster and vector maps:
- Draw and edit maps and plans in a GIS editor
- Import a variety of digital maps and plans in different formats
- Add information to maps and plans from a set of data
- Select separate vector map layers
- Zoom in and out at different scales and pan around an enlarged map
- Measure distances (in a straight line or along a feature), areas or perimeters accurately; Understand geo-referencing
- Select and use appropriate graphical techniques to present evidence on maps and diagrams including the use of ICT.

Present data at points, lines and areas (closed polygons) on maps using the functions of a GI.
- Areas: Choropleth and thematic maps.
- Lines: Flow lines of traffic or journeys by people.
- Points: Diagrams (bar charts, pie charts, divided pie charts, proportional circles and pie charts) at places on the maps
- Add pictures and notes at locations on the maps.

Source: Freeman, 2005

Google Earth is a good way to introduce pupils to GIS, not least because you can download a simple viewer for free (www.earth.google.com). Pupils can use a variety of digital map overlays to analyse spatial data and its relative simplicity of use enables you to create stimulating decision-making and problem-solving activities to develop pupils' geographical understanding and skills. Google Earth is an earth viewer which enables pupils to explore anywhere on the earth, with the high resolution enabling them to zoom in and out to view buildings and even individual cars.

Once pupils have been introduced to the basic principles and tools, they can practice using these tools to 'fly around' and view places from different angles. They can also develop a range of geographical skills using compass directions and latitude and longitude as well as planning and measuring routes. An attractive feature of Google Earth is the way pupils can use screen grabs to copy what they are viewing into another docu-ment so that they can annotate, describe and explain features. Aerial images from Google Earth can also be combined with maps (e.g. from www.multimap.com, www.google.com and www.ordnancesurvey.co.uk) to investigate land use patterns and transects.

Google Earth also makes it possible to create 'virtual fieldwork' using digital media (maps, photographic images and video) from real fieldwork or expeditions that you and others may have undertaken. Although virtual fieldwork is no substitute for the 'real thing', it can help pupils to develop a 'sense of place' and experience places it is not possible to visit in a typical school field trip. Virtual fieldwork can also be used to enhance and reinforce learning from fieldwork pupils have experienced. Images, video and digital data can be combined with fieldwork data the pupils have collected to support their analysis of geographical phenomena, patterns and issues.

As with other ICT applications, it is important to think about how the use of GIS will be integrated into the geography curriculum and how progression will be developed in pupils' understanding and use of GIS. You will need to consider how much pupils need to know about the theory about GIS to be able to use the technology effectively and how much time they need to become proficient in the use of GIS applications (O'Connor, 2007). Table 8.7 suggests three conceptual levels for developing progression in the use of GIS moving from the presentation of spatial data to the processing and analysing of spatial data. More advanced use of GIS involves the input and editing of spatial data (O'Connor, 2008: 148–9).

Using digital technology

ICT has great potential to nurture the development of the individual by encouraging pupils to take responsibility for their learning and by providing enjoyable opportunities for them to use their imagination and inquisitiveness for creative expression.

(DfES, 2002: 8)

Digital technology has dramatically changed the potential for teachers to develop more interactive learning activities that bring together a range of resources and skills and facilitate more active learning. Many of these resources (e.g. photographic images, maps and video) have been available before, but it is the ability to integrate their use in more efficient ways that ICT has improved so significantly. The potential for more pupil-centred learning has also increased as the availability and flexibility of such technologies has improved.

■ **Table 8.7** Progression in the use of GIS skills

Data processing and analysis skills level	Knowledge of GIS theory required	Knowledge of GIS software required	Teaching examples
Basic	Qualitative and quantative map classification techniques Map symbolisation and the use of size, shape, colour hue, colour intensity and texture Bivariate data display techniques Map layout and design issues Measurements of lengths, perimeters and areas	Students need to develop an understanding of the range of classification, symbolisation and mapping design techniques available within the software and how to access them. Students need to gain experience of how to output data using the software in the form of maps, images, graphs, tables and reports.	Year 9: Mapping the historical and future growth of Bishop's Stortford. Year 12: Mapping and symbolising global tectonic activity.
Intermediate	Data selection and queries Principles of basic logic (Boolean operations) Data aggregation techniques Statistical techniques 3D mapping and display	Students need to become familiar with the statistical and data processing capabilities of the software, the options available and their limitations and applications with various data types.	Year 10: Identifying areas of high and low levels of economic development on a global scale. Year 13: Hazard mapping, assessing the vulnerability of the USA to earthquake activity.
Advanced	Data reclassification Buffering and neighbourhood functions Map overlay Spatial interpolation and density mapping Analysis of surfaces		Year 13: Advanced GIS techniques most usually applied with experienced GIS users as part of A-level projects and fieldwork.

Source: O'Connor, 2008: 149

Digital resources, especially the growing number of animations available on the Internet, are very effective when teaching about geographical processes and what might be considered to be 'hard to teach' topics (OFSTED, 2008; Parkinson and Vannet, 2008). Animations can help pupils to visualise processes and abstract ideas that can be difficult to explain. This is because they can simplify processes and shrink spatial and temporal scales. Using digital images and video also help to develop pupils' skills of visual literacy and thus provide opportunities for them to use critical thinking skills (see Chapter 6). The Global Eye website (www.globaleye.org) has a wide range of resources and activities including photo trails that can provide ideas for using digital images in creative ways. Martin (2006) also provides an extensive variety of creative ideas for strategies, resources and activities using photographic images and video to develop pupils' visual literacy and their geographical understanding and skills.

The increasing availability of digital video cameras and digital editing software in schools means that pupils and teachers can use this technology creatively in their geographical enquiries (Raven-Ellison, 2005). Short video sequences can be used to introduce places and issues or as part of fieldwork data collection. This can help them to consolidate, revise and reinforce their experiences and 'sense of place' in the field once they get back to class. Pupils could identify, investigate and then produce TV news style reports on geographical issues. This might include interviews with individuals and representatives of different interest groups. Be imaginative and try to give them real and relevant audiences for this work, for example by getting them to produce 'Lonely Planet' or 'Holiday' style reports on places they (or you) have visited. Such approaches give them greater ownership and responsibility for their learning as well as promoting creativity. Parnell (2007) used the television programme 'Location, Location, Location' as part of a fieldwork enquiry in which pupils investigated places where people might live and changes in their local area.

Although filming captures the immediate, it does benefit from planning and preparation and using 'storyboards' can ensure that pupils make effective use of the time available. See also Burn, 2005 (Chapter 7 in Leask and Pachler, 2005) for more guidance on teaching and learning using digital video. Figure 8.2 shows the role of careful planning and preparation to support the use of digital video. This was part of an activity undertaken by student teachers using plasticine models digital technology (digital cameras and Windows Movie Maker 2) to create animations for use in teaching and learning to demonstrate geographical processes and landforms (Jones and Rycraft, 2007). With the growth of media courses and technology in schools, this could even be possible as a stimulating learning activity for pupils perhaps to assess their understanding of geographical processes.

Webcams are another useful digital technology that can help pupils to develop their sense of place and geographical imagination. They provide opportunities for virtual field-work and enquiries into a range of geographical processes, especially in relation to weather and climate. Live webcams (for example through the Meteorological office website) can be used in conjunction with weather maps to study weather processes, such as the passage of a weather system, and climatic variations. They can also be used creatively to explore what Massey (2007) describes as a 're-imagining of time and space' with a sense of connection between different people and places in both time and space. Student teachers we have worked with have used webcams to enable their pupils to communicate with pupils and others to explore issues and and environments in different parts of the world, exploring what Massey calls 'dynamic simultaneity'. The potential of

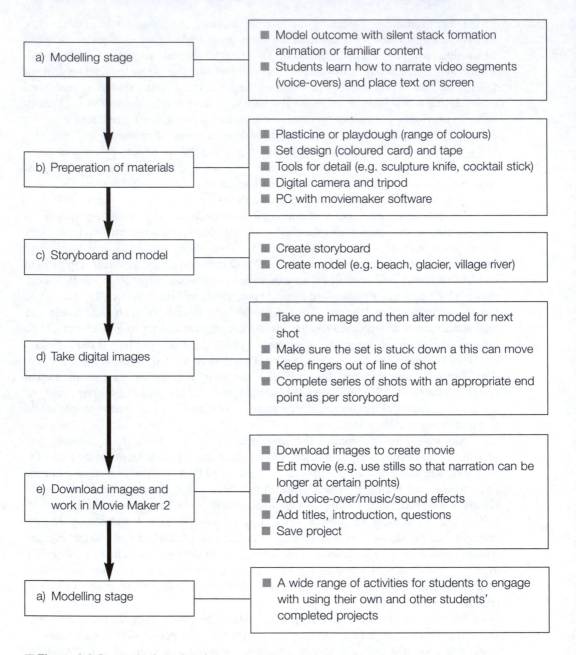

■ **Figure 8.2** Stages in the animation process
Source: James and Rycraft, 2007: 93–96

webcams to explore 'sense of place', connectedness and simultaneity has been developed in a Geographical Association project (http://www.geography.org.uk/projects/webcams/links). In one fascinating observation, one of the participating teachers describes what he called an 'Amelie moment' in his discussions with pupils:

He was referring to a scene in the film 'Amelie' (2001) in which a girl with a powerful imagination – a geographical imagination – imagines what many others are doing at that moment across space (all over Paris) and she feels a sense of connectedness with them. He went on to describe how he believed his pupils, by watching these people in a distant place, experienced a sense of 'I'm not alone'. He described the pupils' experience as a realisation that others were living their lives at that moment, and that space and time were being re-imagined by pupils through the use of the webcam. Their geographical imaginations were developing.

(Mitchell, 2008)

Communication and interaction

Communication is one of the key concepts in the ICT National Curriculum and the key processes in the programme of study includes the requirement that pupils should be able to 'communicate and exchange information (including digital communication' (QCA, 2008). The Internet now provides increasingly creative opportunities for teachers to communicate and collaborate about their learning. Although you should be aware of potential Internet safety issues (see Becta, 2005), there are clearly innovative ways of exploiting these technologies.

Wikis are collaborative authoring websites that allow visitors to the website to add, remove, edit or change content. Open source material such as photographic images and text can be added and the ease of interaction is one of the main attractions of wikis. Pupils often use the main Wikipedia site for their own research and enquiries so it is important to ensure that they are aware of factors influencing the reliability and accuracy of the information provided (see 'Evaluating ICT resources' earlier in this chapter). However, wikis can be used to develop collaborative enquiries with pupils working together to produce reports, analysis of data collected and evaluations of issues. They could also be used to support revision for examinations.

Blogs (short for 'weblog') are a now familiar feature of many websites supporting communication for a wide range of purposes. They are a form of 'instant messaging' to the web with participants contributing ideas, thoughts, questions and images. One of our own former students (and school tutors), contributed her travelogues and photographic images to a weblog while travelling the world so that her former pupils and colleagues could follow her travels. We also know many geography teachers who have established weblogs to enable pupils and colleagues to communicate and collaborate about their work in geography. These weblogs serve many purposes promoting collaboration and ownership of learning as well as a passion for the subject (Parkinson, 2004). Val Vannet's own blog provides a helpful introduction to the use of blogs to enhance teaching and learning in geography (http://ablogsnotjustforchristmas.blogspot.com/).

Improving presentation and exposition

The increasing range of multimedia resources and digital technology enables geography teachers to bring images and experiences of other places in the world into the classroom in ever more stimulating ways. It also helps us to demonstrate and explain geographical phenomena, patterns and processes using interactive presentations. Although electronic Interactive Whiteboards can be found in many of schools and classrooms, they are by no means available to every teacher and some recent research has questioned their benefits for learning and value-for-money. An increasing number of schools are investing in a 'mixed economy' concentrating on ensuring that most classrooms are equipped with digital projectors and interactive whiteboards are available in a few strategically placed classrooms or in subject departments who are able to make best use of their applications.

You should make sure you are aware of how to make effective use of this technology in the geography classroom. At the very least, digital projectors enable you to enhance the viewing environment for pupils by projecting larger images (photographic and video) and developing the use of more active watching strategies (see Chapter 6). This can help pupils to visualise the scale and complexity of some landscapes. You can use a variety of multi-sensory tools to explore landscapes and landscape change with them on large projections. Aerial photographs can be overlayed on to map projections, landscape features annotated and landscape sketching techniques demonstrated in interactive ways. Pupils can trace and annotate the main landscape features and the projector turned off to leave a sketch diagram. Weblinks can enable you to project animations and webcams to support explanations of geographical patterns and processes. A highly effective demonstration technique is to set up a video clip of a moving process (e.g. a river or waves reaching a coastline) in a 'loop'. Questioning can then be used to probe pupils' understanding of the processes with pupils coming up to label features and speculating about the impacts of these processes and possible changes to landforms. Completed diagrams can be saved and made available to pupils via department websites, school intranets or 'virtual learning environments'. Used in this way, technology can support more interactive whole class teaching (see Chapter 4 and Webb, 2005: 51–2).

You will find two main interactive whiteboard software products being used in schools – *Promethean* and *Smart*. The incompatibility between these two systems can be frustrating especially when moving between schools. However, you should be able to find some colleagues who are proficient in using your school's interactive whiteboard systems to show you how to make a start in using the main tools. Simple games based on multiple choice and 'hide and reveal' formats can provide some fun elements to debriefing sessions when you are seeking to check and reinforce knowledge and understanding (see Bayliss and Collins, 2006 and 2007). A range of simple game formats such as interactive 'drag and drop' games are readily available through the Internet (see for example www.contentgenerator.net which is widely used by a number of subject departments).

Presentation software such as Power Point is widely used by teachers to support whole class exposition. It can also provide a simple and effective way of promoting pupil autonomy and collaborative learning (Taylor, 2001). Digital images and video can be inserted into presentations and information progressively revealed to pupils to support differentiation. Pupils can produce presentations as the outcomes of collaborative research and decision-making, for example investigating suitable sites for new homes in their local area or evaluating different coastal or flood management schemes. As with all collaborative research assignments, pupils should be briefed about the objectives and constraints (time and number of slides, illustrations, etc.). It is worth devoting time to preparation and research so that technological aspects of the task do not dominate the time available. Storyboarding is a useful strategy to employ to structure this preparation.

PLANNING TO USE ICT

Journals such as *Teaching Geography* are an important source of ideas and advice, containing both reviews of software and suggestions about possible teaching and learning strategies. A number of websites that have developed to support geography teachers, including ones set up by innovative geography teachers willing to share their ideas and resources, also provide useful ideas and advice about using ICT in geography. Listening to the experiences of other geographer teachers will help you identify the opportunities and challenges, particularly when it comes to addressing the question 'what do pupils learn and what do they not learn using ICT in geography?' The school's ICT co-ordinator should be able to familiarise you with the ICT applications available on the school's network and pupils' experience with these applications and software. It would also be helpful to liaise with the ICT co-ordinator to ensure that the levels of expectation and challenge are appropriate for the pupils' experiences and levels of ICT capability. It is also wise to find out about the availability of technical support.

As well as planning the learning activities you will need to consider the implications for classroom organisation (see Webb, 2005). If only a few computers are available, the ICT activities could be organised as part of a circus of activities. If more computers or a dedicated computer room are available, then decisions will need to be made about whether pupils work in small groups or as individuals. Will they be undertaking common tasks following pre-defined learning pathways or will they be undertaking more independent geographical enquiries?

The key concepts for ICT capability across the curriculum (page 310) provide a useful starting point when planning to use ICT in geography. Remember that this framework provides objectives for what you can expect pupils to have been taught during the previous year (DfES, 2004). Although many of these ICT concepts could be applied and developed in geography, this framework identifies the following four concepts as being particularly significant for geography:

- Using data and information sources
- Searching and selecting
- Organising and investigating
- Refining and presenting information.

Use the framework to identify the ICT objectives pupils should have developed the previous year and the aspects they are learning during the current year so that you can ensure levels of expectation and challenge appropriate to their experiences and ICT capability. Consult with the ICT department about this. At the same time, identify your objectives for the geographical knowledge, understanding and skills pupils will develop and how this builds on their prior learning in geography. Consider whether these geographical learning outcomes could be achieved as or more efficiently without the use of ICT. You should also decide whether the ICT applications are the most appropriate to use. Although it may be appropriate for pupils to use low-level ICT skills for the planned activities, they should be given opportunities to use higher order skills whenever possible.

Start by identifying geographical topics, questions and issues in your school's schemes of work where there might be opportunities for using ICT to enhance learning activities. Search out useful resources from a range of sources to support the development of different geographical enquiry skills. For example, if you are investigating farming the 'Britain from Above' (BBC) website accompanying the TV series has some excellent short clips showing changes in farming and the impact of new technology in the East Anglia region (www.bbc.co.uk/britainfromabove). These could be used with a farm management decision-making activity using GIS in the GIS zone of the OS Mapzone mentioned earlier (http://mapzone.ordnancesurvey.co.uk/mapzone/giszone.html) to ensure that pupils use a range of geographical enquiry and ICT skills.

Pupils could also use the Internet to research relevant issues concerning food production, farming and the environment (see, for example, the Bioethics Education Project website www.beep.ac.uk for resources about farming and the environment and issues such as Genetically Modified crops). Pupils could use their geographical enquiry to produce a creative response, perhaps in the form of a report for a TV news or current affairs programme about the impact of new technology in farming.

Through this enquiry, pupils would develop their knowledge and understanding of patterns and processes in agriculture as an economic activity (including people-environment relationships) and explore environmental change and issues about sustainability. In the decision-making activity, they are using geographical skills (using maps and aerial images) and developing geographical enquiry kills by analysing and evaluating evidence, making and justifying decisions. They are also using ICT to support their decision-making skills, contributing to objectives in both geography and ICT. This enquiry also contributes to aspects of each of the areas of ICT capability listed above. Pupils are searching for and selecting appropriate information from different sources, developing ideas, exploring the impact of technology and evaluating the use of ICT tools (i.e. the use of GIS in decision-making and in economic activities).

Table 8.8 shows an example of how one school has made effective use of these resources to integrate GIS into a scheme of work. The use of energy is given personal relevance in an enquiry into ecological footprints and futures and a planning application to site a wind farm near a local village (Podington) in the school's catchment area enabled the teachers to connect a local issue to national contexts and global issues. The role of GIS in decision-making is explored. The enquiry also provides opportunities for pupils to explore controversial issues and 'think geographically' about the implications of sustainability for people, places and environments at different scales.

The Geographical Association's 'Spatially speaking' project (http://www.geography.org.uk/projects/spatiallyspeaking/) provides a variety of case studies illustrating how GIS is used in the world of work. There are creative ideas and weblinks for learning activities in which pupils can use GIS tools to question, analyse and explore issues through maps and 'think spatially' (Mitchell, 2008). In one, crime patterns can be analysed and related to socio-economic data. This could be used creatively with pupils taking on the role of the police and planning how resources (patrol cars, CCTV, etc.) might be deployed or even using digital video to produce a 'Crimewatch' programme about hypothetical crimes. Fieldwork could be used to explore fear of crime and environmental factors influencing crime patterns.

Flood risk can be investigated using a GIS based flood risk map on the Environment Agency website (www.environment-agency.gov.uk/subjects/flood/). This can be used with maps and images from mapping sites (www.multimap.com and www.ordnancesurvey.co.uk/oswebsite/getamap/) and Google Earth to assess areas at risk of flooding. There are also further resources to support enquiries into flooding on the Geographical Association website (http://www.geography.org.uk/resources/flooding/). Housing surveys undertaken in fieldwork can be given a different perspective by combining them with data about house prices (www.housepricemaps.co.uk) and the socio-economic characteristics of the areas (www.neighbourhoodstatistics.gov.uk). This could be part of a decision-making activity in which pupils have to find properties to purchase using information from estate agent's websites which use GIS to support property searches. The key here is to be creative to provide stimulating enquiries which engage the pupils and provide them with insights into the vocational applications of GIS.

■ **Table 8.8** Locating a wind farm: Extract from a scheme of work about Geographical Futures and Ecological Footprints

Sharnbrook Geography	Year: 9	Topic: Geographical Futures & Footprints

Learning Objectives	Resources	Learning Activities
8. Where is the best place to site a wind turbine/farm? (Assessment)		
What factors are important in siting a wind farm?	Ordnance Survey Mapzone: GIS zone Photographs of Wind Turbines Assessment Outline/Criteria	Photographs of wind turbines. Ask students what factors they would consider important in determining wind farm location? Could rank ideas most-least important. Assessment piece: students complete OS Mapzone GIS decision-making exercise, describing and explaining their choice of sites, using evidence from the layers provided
9. How many wind turbines would be needed to power the school's lights?		
How effective are wind turbines at generating power?	A3 sheet – 'What is the best site . . . ?' Map of school site Wind power data Electricity consumption – school data	Enquiry exercise: students establish the number of wind turbines needed to power the school's lights using the information provided (could be in groups with all necessary information between them). Introduce the local Podington issue
9. Why is the construction of windfarms so controversial?		
What is the proposal for Podington? Who are the stakeholders involved? Who will be the winners and losers from the proposed development?	Video 'Cover Story – Wind Farms in East Anglia' Airfield Wind Farm Proposal 'Answer is blowing in the wind' Newspaper Article 'The Podington Wind Farm'	Explore the local issue at Podington Read and discuss newspaper article about a possible wind farm at Podington, North Bedfordshire Divide students into groups and allocate each group a role – farmer, wind turbine company, local environmental group, local councillor, local Podington resident, etc, Students have a short time to discuss the stance of their group and devise appropriate arguments Class Role Play

■ **Table 8.8** (continued)

Year 9 Geographical Futures Assessment
What is the best site for a wind farm?

Aim
- The aim of the assessment is to make a decision about where to locate a wind farm selecting the best site from a number of possible locations.

Objectives
- To understand what locations make good sites for wind turbines.
- To make judgements about the quality of different sites.
- To decide upon the best site.
- To justify the reasons for your decisions.
- To learn how to use 'Geographical Information Systems'.

Task Instructions
In pairs:
- Log on to a computer.
- Open Internet Explorer and go to:
  http://mapzone.ordnancesurvey.co.uk/giszone/english/gismissions/Page2.htm
- Click on 'Accept Mission'.
- Read the mission 'briefing', pressing the '>' sign to move forward once you've read each.
- As shown by your teacher, score each of the possible wind farm locations by clicking on each one in turn. As you do this, complete the grid with any advantages (good points) and disadvantages (bad points) about each site.
- Once completed, click the 'next' column to see the overall scores for your proposal. Copy these scores onto the grid provided.
- To look back at your scores, click the 'Back to GIS' button.

On your own:
- Your task is to write a report for 'Green Energy Ltd' stating which of the 5 sites is best for a wind farm. You should use all the information on the map to help you. Follow the instructions in the box below.

The best site
  a) Describe the location of the best site.
  b) Explain your decision in as much detail as you can to help you explain why it was such a good site for a wind farm.

Rejecting the other sites (choose ONE only)
  a) Describe the location of **ONE** of the other sites
  b) Explain, in as much detail as you can, why you did **NOT** choose the site.

Extension task (OPTIONAL)
  a) Can you think of any other considerations that a wind farm should have? If so, explain why you think these considerations are important.

Use appropriate geographical vocabulary – the list below should help you.

contours	accessibility	settlements
environmental impact	local features	quality of life
protected areas	wind conditions	landuse
priority	requirement	wind speed
visual pollution	energy	landscape

Assessment
Remember that your work will be assessed using National Curriculum Levels. The assessment criteria for this task are given on the back of this sheet, giving you some clues about what to include in your discussion.

■ **Table 8.8** (continued)

What is each level looking for?

Level 3	• You simply describe the location of the best site and one of the sites you rejected. • You simply describe one thing about their positions.
Level 4	• You describe the location of the sites you have chosen. • You show simple understanding of why they are good and bad sites. • You begin to use geographical vocabulary in your answer.
Level 5	• You accurately describe the location of the sites you have chosen. • You show a clear understanding of why they are good and bad sites, including development of your explanations. • You use some evidence from the map, perhaps using examples to support. • You use geographical vocabulary in your answer and show that you understand it.
Level 6	• You accurately describe the location of the sites you have chosen in detail. • You show a very clear understanding of why they are good and bad sites, including well developed explanations. • You use a range of evidence from the map, perhaps using specific facts and figures to support your answer. • You make good use of geographical vocabulary to help in your explanation.
Level 7	• You very accurately describe the location of the sites you have chosen in detail. • You show a detailed understanding of why they are good and bad sites, including very well developed explanations. • You use a wide range of evidence from the map using specific facts and figures to support your answer. • You show very good use of geographical vocabulary in your answer. • You show some 'individuality' in carrying out the task in the way that you complete it, perhaps in how you discuss it, or you may perhaps use a figure or diagram to help you explain something.
Level 8	• You very accurately describe the location of the sites you have chosen in detail. • You show an excellent understanding of why they are good and bad sites, including very well developed explanations. • You use a wide range of evidence from the map using specific facts and figures to support your answer. • You make excellent use of geographical vocabulary and show that you understand it very clearly. • You reach very clear conclusions on the basis of the discussion. • You clearly demonstrate your own individuality in the way that you approach the task, including posing your own questions. (What sort of questions would you like to try and answer if you were investigating this idea further?)

Source: Geography Department, Sharnbrook Upper School

Activity 8.6 **Using GIS to enhance geographical enquiry**

This activity gives you experience of planning and using GIS in a geographical enquiry. It also provides an opportunity to evaluate the use of GIS in developing pupils' ICT capability and thus help to develop your understanding of the ICT National Curriculum and KS3 National Strategy framework for ICT capability.

Identify an area of the geography curriculum in your teaching experience school where there are opportunities to develop a geographical enquiry that makes relevant and effective use of GIS. Consider the issues, questions and problems where GIS plays an important role in making decisions that affect people such as the location of public facilities and provision of public services, urban planning, transport logistics, the management of natural resources, responding to natural hazards and disasters. All of these can find a place in the school geography curriculum.

Follow these steps:

1 Identify your learning objective(s) for geography and the use of GIS.
2 Identify the criteria you value in order to evaluate the success of the project.
3 Translate the criteria into 'measurable' indicators (the source of your 'evidence').
4 Plan the unit of work (2–3 lessons including follow-up work) and deliver it making your observations about the teaching and learning.
5 Evaluate the resources and teaching strategies used, and the resulting pupil learning.
6 Make a judgement(s) about the question: 'What did pupils learn using ICT in geography?'

What is reported here is a sequence of lesson plans (2–3) which demonstrate the application of GIS in the teaching of an aspect of the geography curriculum at any level.

The key to a successful task will be its evaluation, based around the question: What have pupils learned, and not learned, using ICT?

In writing up your report for this task, you should provide important information about the rationale and educational contexts for this GIS development including:

■ School/department, Age/ability range, Level (KS3/GSCE/A-Level)
■ Geographical content (NC/Syllabus) and Subject Knowledge
■ GIS applications and relevant aspects of the ICT NC covered, ICT software and hardware

Your evaluation of this enquiry using GIS is a crucial part of the task revealing your understanding of *how to use ICT to develop a geographical enquiry* as well as your skills of critical reflection. It should *analyse the ICT skills developed by the pupils* (i.e. in relation to the ICT NC) and the geographical learning outcomes. Annotated examples of pupils' work could be included in this evaluation to illustrate these learning outcomes. Finally, your conclusions should include ideas and recommendations for ways of improving or developing this use of GIS in geography.

Present your report to your tutor.

ICT and fieldwork

ICT can make a valuable contribution to geographical fieldwork especially in supporting the collection and processing of accurate and reliable data. Also, as discussed above, the use of GIS can support 'virtual fieldwork'. Digital and electronic monitoring equipment can be used to collect environmental data, for example to measure light, heat and humidity levels when investigating the microclimate of an area. There are also sensors for measuring noise levels and soil pH levels.

Spreadsheets can be used to process data and facilitate effective presentation and analysis of this data. Another benefit of using spreadsheets is that they can facilitate multiple access for entering and sharing data (Holmes and Walker, 2006: 223). Digital cameras (photographic and video) are increasingly being used as part of data collection (see above) with images edited digitally, presented to whole classes using digital projectors and shared with others via the Internet. The Internet can also be used to research additional secondary data sources to support enquiries. The use of ICT can also promote creativity and give pupils more autonomy in designing and developing geographical fieldwork enquiries.

As new technology develops, there are even more creative ways in which ICT can be used to enhance fieldwork. Mobile technologies have an increasing range of applications that can be utilised in fieldwork. Most mobile phones have cameras for taking digital images and video that can be downloaded for use in data analysis and presentation. Some schools have access to small hand-held computers to support data collection with environmental sensors, process digital images and provide access to other data. Global Positioning Systems (GPS) can be used to enhance fieldwork providing pupils with insights into 'real world' applications of technology (Martin, 2006: 141–142). Fieldwork data can be recorded along a transect or at sample points with the GPS used to record the position where this data was collected. Data can then be presented and analysed spatially using Google Earth or another mapping program:

> Knowledge of a six-figure grid reference system is no longer enough. Students now need to know how to work with a ten-figure reference grid. GPS located data can then be fed seamlessly into a GIS program, bringing data recording and mapping together.
>
> (Martin, 2006: 141)

SUMMARY AND KEY POINTS

This chapter has introduced you to the opportunities for developing pupils' ICT skills and capability in geography. It has provided practical suggestions for strategies and activities in which pupils can use ICT to enhance their skills of geographical enquiry. It has explained how the use of Geographical Information Systems (GIS) can enhance pupils' learning in geography by enabling them to produce more professional maps, helping them to visualise landscapes as well as linking maps and analysing spatial datasets to interpret patterns and solve problems. There are practical ideas to show how GIS can be integrated creatively in geographical enquiries.

The need to evaluate online resources and develop pupils' information skills when using such resources is emphasised. The role of ICT in supporting communication and interaction and in improving both teachers' and pupils' presentation skills is explained.

The potential of digital technology (including images, video, animations and webcams) to help geography teachers develop more interactive learning activities bringing together a range of resources and skills and facilitate more active learning is also explored.

You are encouraged to keep this question in mind whenever using ICT: What have pupils learned, and not learned in geography, using ICT?

FURTHER READING

Bennett, R. and Leask, M. (2005) *Teaching and Learning with ICT: An Introduction*, Unit 1.4 in Capel S, Leask, M. and Turner, T. (eds) *Learning to Teach in the Secondary School: A companion to school experience*, Abingdon: Routledge.
This chapter explores ways in which teachers can use ICT to support and enhance their teaching and pupils' learning. It also explains how ICT is used for administration purposes and how it can contribute to teachers' professional development.

DfES (2004) *ICT across the curriculum: ICT in geography*, Key Stage 3 National Strategy, London: DfES.
This is a useful publication exploring how ICT capability can be developed in geography and help to raise standards in the subject. It explains how ICT themes and key concepts can be developed in geography and provides examples of five geography lessons (with resources, weblinks and plans on an accompanying CD-Rom) to show how this can be done.

King, S. and Taylor, E. (2006) *Using ICT to enhance learning in geography*, Chapter 17 in Balderstone, D. (ed.) *Secondary Geography Handbook*, Sheffield: The Geographical Association.
This chapter explores the contribution ICT can make to learning in geography and how geography provides opportunities for developing pupils' ICT skills. It also considers how ICT can contribute to geography teachers' professional learning.

Leask, M. and Pachler, N. (2005) *Learning to Teach using ICT in the Secondary School: A companion to school experience*, Abingdon: Routledge.
This text focuses on the role of new technologies in the classroom, in subject teaching and in teachers' professional development. It provides practical ideas and advice about a range of ICT applications and issues.

Martin, F. (2006) *e-geography: Using ICT in quality geography*, Sheffield: The Geographical Association.
This book presents an extensive range of ideas about how ICT can enhance the quality of learning in geography. It includes techniques, activities and resources using a wide variety of ICT applications. As well as providing practical ideas for use in the classroom, the author stimulates discussion about ICT pedagogy and its impacts on standards in geography.

Martin, F. (2006) *Using ICT to create better maps*, Chapter 10 in Balderstone, D. (ed.) *Secondary Geography Handbook*, Sheffield: The Geographical Association.
This chapter makes the case for using GIS to enhance geographical enquiry and provides practical ideas for developing pupils' map-drawing skills.

O'Connor, P. (2008) *GIS for A-level geography*, Sheffield: The Geographical Association.
This book describes how governments, organisations and individuals are using GIS to tackle increasingly complex social, economic and environmental problems. This is a complete guide to the theory and applications of GIS and it includes practical exercises for classroom use to develop pupils' GIS skills using sophisticated GIS software. Included with this book are GIS software (12 month licence) and a DVD of digital map data for England.

Some useful websites

Professional skills and support

www.geography.org.uk

The professional association for geography teachers in England and Wales. Provides resources, teaching ideas, guidance and support for professional development. For example, the free, down-loadable resource ICT in secondary schools: a short guide for teachers (edited by David Mitchell in 2008) draws on the work of geography teachers and what they find really works. Each short chapter takes a separate area of technology and explains, in simple terms, its meaning, why it is helpful for teaching and learning geography, and practical steps to get started.

www.geographyteachingtoday.org.uk

This website is the main outlet for the 2006–11 Action Plan for geography, jointly led by the GA and the RGS and funded by the government. It has both resources to use in a digital form and a suite of online curriculum making 'courses', including one on ICT.

www.rgs.org

Royal Geographical Society and Institute of British Geographers

www.geographyinthenews.rgs.org

RGS Geography in the News

www.sln.org.uk/geography

Staffordshire Learning Net. This local authority network has grown into one of the largest communities of geography teachers and educators. Provides resources, teaching ideas, advice and a popular discussion forum. A number of teachers have also established their own websites for sharing ideas and resources, for example:

www.juicygeography.co.uk

A range of creative ideas and resources, including helpful advice for getting started with GIS and Google Earth.

www.geographypages.co.uk

Advice about digital resources and a wide variety of creative ideas.

GEOGRAPHY AND EDUCATION FOR THE FUTURE

9

What is exciting about geography today is that it is the first curriculum subject in the UK to take seriously the need for...critical and creative thinking about the future

(Hicks, 2007: 187)

The 'future' – preparing young people for adult life – is arguably what all education is for, yet remarkably little attention is paid to it overtly through the curriculum in classrooms and schools.

(Morgan, 2006: 276)

INTRODUCTION

These opening quotes take us back to Chapter 1 when we examined the role and purpose of geography in the school curriculum. There are also links with Chapter 5 in which we addressed the goals of education as expressed in the 1988 Education Reform Act, which include the notion of preparing young people for adult life (i.e. their future). This chapter is dedicated to exploring – and demonstrating – the nature of geography's contribution to preparing children 'for life in a changing world'.

Before embarking on this discussion, it is perhaps worth pausing with some words of John Huckle. They make a bold claim for school geography which may readily link with the ideals with which you came into teaching. What were your motives? Have they changed in any way during your training? Huckle argues that being a geography teacher is worthwhile because geography is such a powerful medium of education. Specifically, in his own words:

School geography has the potential to develop young people's understanding of their 'place' in the world and so to help them form their identity. It can enable them to perceive the structures and processes which help and hinder their development, and can also foster their commitment to social justice and democracy, and the conserving, participatory and critical forms of citizenship...and thereby help to create a better world.

(Huckle, 1997: 241)

This chapter is concerned with mapping some of the implications of such a statement. There is now a strong feeling that many of the established 'adjectival' geographies, such as environmental education and development education, whilst expressing distinctive traditions in thinking, have now converged into a single, albeit complex, notion. Some prefer to call this 'sustainability' or 'sustainable development'. Others prefer the broader concept of 'global perspectives'. All are concerned with understanding current and future crises in the way humans live and relate to each other. There is no doubt that such concerns are challenging to us personally – and that is before we begin to think about how, in our capacities as teachers, we engage young people with potentially over-whelming issues such as global climate change and its impacts, poverty, food security and so on.

OBJECTIVES

By the end of this chapter, you should be able to:

■ identify the value and the potential pitfalls of offering a futures perspective in your teaching

■ identify ways of engaging young people in thinking about their future adult life

■ explain the meaning of the spiritual, moral, social and cultural dimensions in education and the potential for exploring these aspects with children in geography lessons

■ make a judgement about the value of critical thinking in geography teaching and learning.

A FUTURES-ORIENTED GEOGRAPHY CURRICULUM

If you think about it, most of the curriculum experience of pupils is about the past – past discoveries, achievements and products of human beings. This is not surprising. The curriculum is a selection of the society's science, art and culture which it chooses systematically to 'pass on' to the next generation.

And yet it is arguably the case that all education is *for* the future, and that a curriculum that does not overtly prepare young people for thinking about alternative futures is inappropriate to 'life in a changing world'. This thought encourages us to rethink the purposes of school subjects: rather than bodies of knowledge to be passed on to young people, they are better seen as resources which introduce students to productive and significant ways of thinking about the world.

For geography teachers, the concept of an interdependent world is familiar and powerful, one which has been bolstered over the last quarter century with innovative work in 'global education' (see, for example, Fisher and Hicks, 1985; Hicks and Steiner, 1989; Pike and Selby, 1988). A futures-oriented curriculum makes explicit the interdependence which exists across the time dimension as well as space (Hicks 1994; 2007; Morgan, 2006). Rex Walford, addressing the Geographical Association as President, expressed the need for a futures orientation to geography teaching:

> The sustained study of a number of possible geographies of the short-term and middle-term future will encourage the student to consider those aspects of the

future which are desirable and those which are not. Hopefully such geography teaching can vitalise school students into an interest in their own futures... In urging that we teach a geography of the future, I do not mean to say that we should give up teaching the geography of the past: but we should make the past the servant of the future. If the future is unavoidable, let us at least not walk backwards into it.

(Walford, 1984: 207)

Of course, to suggest that young people do not think about the future would be absurd. They do, as Figure 9.1 shows. They have concerns and anxieties about the future and the majority of pupils surveyed think that school should teach more about the environment, for example. For the geography teacher, the task is to identify approaches and resources which enable us to structure ways for pupils to investigate and imagine alternative futures. This needs to be done within a theoretical framework, so that bolt on 'discussions' about the future, which can be repetitive and frustrating, can be avoided. Ill-prepared 'discussions' with the class may not help pupils understand the links between their personal lives and wider issues of change. For how do we seriously consider the future? Are there techniques to help us help pupils realise that we cannot opt out of the future? – and that 'all actions and choices, including the choice not to act or choose, have future consequences' (Hicks, 1994: 2).

Children's environmental concerns

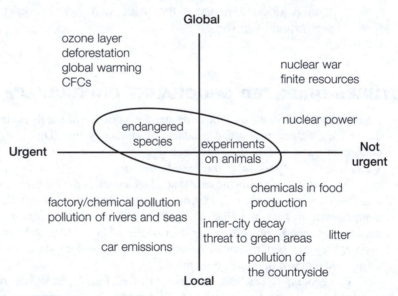

■ **Figure 9.1** Children's environmental concerns
Source: Young Eyes, Henley Centre for Forecasting, 1991, in Hicks, 1994: 2

Table 9.1 provides a summary of a more complete educational rationale for a futures-oriented curriculum. Before looking at some possibilities for translating such intentions into practical strategies, it is necessary to emphasise one broad feature of the rationale. If we agree that a futures dimension is a legitimate, indeed essential, component of geographic enquiry (it is worth recording that 'geographical enquiry', as a mandatory component of the National Curriculum geography Programme of Study, has established a sequence of 'enquiry questions' something like this: What is this place like? Why is it like this? How did it come to be like this? How ought it to be? The final question in this enquiry sequence is futures oriented and political. See also the discussion

---

■ **Table 9.1** Educational rationale for a futures dimension in the curriculum

---

1 Pupil motivation

Pupil expectation about the future can affect behaviour in the present, e.g. that something is, or is not, worth working for. Clear images of desired personal goals can help stimulate motivation and achievement.

2 Anticipating change

Anticipatory skills and flexibility of mind are important in times of rapid change. Such skills enable pupils to deal more effectively with uncertainty and to initiate, rather than merely respond to, change.

3 Critical thinking

In weighing up information, considering trends and imagining alternatives, pupils will need to exercise reflective and critical thinking. This is often triggered by realising the contradictions between how the world is now and how one would like it to be.

4 Clarifying values

All images of the future are underpinned by differing value assumptions about human nature and society. In a democratic society pupils need to be able to begin to identify such value judgements before they can themselves make appropriate choices between alternatives.

5 Decision-making

Becoming more aware of trends and events which are likely to influence one's future and investigating the possible consequences of one's actions on others in the future, leads to more thoughtful decision-making in the present.

6 Creative imagination

One faculty that can contribute to, and which is particularly enhanced by, designing alternative futures is that of the creative imagination. Both this and critical thinking are needed to envision a range of preferable futures from the personal to the global.

7 A better world

It is important in a democratic society that young people develop their sense of vision particularly in relation to more just and sustainable futures. Such forward looking thinking is an essential ingredient in both the preserving and improving of society.

8 Responsible citizenship

Critical participation in democratic life leads to the development of political skills and thus more active and responsible citizenship. Future generations are then more likely to benefit, rather than lose, from decisions made today.

9 Stewardship

Understanding the short and long-term consequences of current local and global trends, as well as the action needed to change these, can lead to a sense of stewardship both for the planet now and for those yet to come.

Source: Hicks, 1994: 12

of enquiry in Chapter 4 of this volume), we must be prepared to endorse its consequences. Asking questions of the future, about the future and for the future takes us into the realms of choice, priorities, and therefore, politics. A futures-oriented curriculum could provide, therefore, a useful contribution to political education requiring of pupils wider 'literacies', in the form of knowledge of political and economic structures, in order to engage seriously with questions of alternatives. In this way geography can contribute significantly to citizenship education.

We believe that geography teachers, because of the nature of their subject involving analysis and synthesis across a wide spectrum of contents, from the physical and human worlds, are particularly well suited to the kinds of pedagogic demands of a futures-oriented curriculum. The remainder of this section suggests a broad framework as a way forward, taken mainly from the *Global Futures Project* (Hicks, 1994; Hicks and Holden, 1996; Hicks, 2001; Hicks, 2007).

What you may find is under represented in the list in Table 9.1 is a sense of the more 'hard-nosed' knowledge and understanding educational outcomes. The scheme of work (Table 9.2), in contrast, shows a heavy emphasis on such elements of learning, and we would certainly agree that an educational rationale for a futures dimension in the curriculum is arguably incomplete without reference to knowledge and understanding – it *matters* that processes such as the greenhouse effect are understood, and that they do not just become slogans or icons designed to elicit only certain kinds of emotional response.

Activity 9.1 **Finding the future (individuals or groups)**

1   Examine the text in Table 9.1 (note that it was not compiled solely for geography teachers). For each item in the list, try to give a concrete example of what the skill, faculty or ability described could look like in a geography classroom. Perhaps you have an example from your own practice, or the observed classroom practice of another teacher, to draw from.

2   Now examine Table 9.2. This is a scheme of work designed for an A-level geography module on global futures.

   a)   Use the educational rationale in Table 9.1 to evaluate the module; i.e. identify where and how effectively aspects of the educational rationale are being tackled.

   b)   Using the scheme of work as your prompt, are there aspects of an 'educational rationale' that you feel are absent from the list in Table 9.1?

Discussion: The advantage of undertaking the activity in groups is that you will reveal a range of ways in which educational goals can be interpreted. It is worth checking that you have a clear concept of what aspects like 'critical thinking' really mean (see page 363 in this chapter), but, as is often the case when discussing curriculum innovation, a surprising amount of what you want to introduce may already be there! The issue is not that you have magically to find yet more space in a busy programme for this 'important and urgent new concern', but articulate more clearly what you are trying to do: merely having at your disposal terms such as 'anticipatory skills', 'stewardship' or 'values clarification' can be of enormous help when planning with colleagues and working with pupils.

Aim: To encourage and support pupils' individual and group research into understanding the processes involved in political decisions and their effect upon the environment.

A broad framework for a futures orientation

It is useful to take David Hicks' advice and to structure our thinking about how to plan a serious futures orientation to our work, by adopting the following progressive headings.

Thinking about the future

This takes pupils into asking questions about the future, exploring images of the future (e.g. in film, adverts, etc.) and refining concepts such as continuity, change and consequences. A powerful idea Hicks develops is that of the '200 year present' which is a fine way to link spatial interdependence with interdependence through time.

An idea that can be used in relation to virtually any thematic and/or place-based topic in geography is ask pupils to project 'the probable future'. With the help of a *time-line,* what pupils have learned about recent and current change (in population, or agriculture, or industry, etc.) can be projected into the future, say, at ten year intervals. As with most activities, the pupils need to get accustomed to this way of working (that is, they may not handle the exercise well first time around). The aim is to encourage critical thought about what pupils believe to be aspects of the expected future.

Envisioning the future

Imagining the future encourages critical thinking and creative imagination. It is important for pupils to practise such skills on entering an adult world, where change is constant and in which openness to unfamiliar ideas will be a prerequisite to progress and personal contentment. In contrast to the previous activity concerning probable futures, the core activity here, undertaken in the same manner, with a time line, is to imagine 'the preferable future'. Probable and preferable futures can be considered alongside each other, especially when a key event can be identified (or imagined) such as, for example, peace in Northern Ireland or international agreement on carbon emissions reductions. Another strategy can be to get pupils to follow through (probable and preferable) impacts arising from various 'what if?' scenarios: for example, *what if* the price of crude oil were to rise to $200 a barrel (i.e. about double the price at the beginning of 2008)?

Choosing the future

Activities under this heading are designed to emphasise the concept of choice, and the main technique is to create and compare *alternative* scenarios. Hicks identifies the dominant scenario types as:

- more of the same
- technological fix
- edge of disaster
- sustainable development.

■ **Table 9.2** Environments and political systems: scheme of work (extract showing the first four weeks from a 10-week course on Global futures

Key areas	Resources	Activities	Concepts	Assessment
The politics of conflict The broad context. The causes of conflict.	Gaia *Peace Atlas,* pp. 12, 14, 16 and 18. The roots of war pp. 38–9. Multiplying conflict points pp. 54–5. Third World War? pp. 56–7. Gaia *Atlas of Planet Management,* Crisis the threat of war 242–6. 'New wars for old' *(The Economist)*	Read the articles provided and: Plot on a map of the world some of the world's hot spots at the present moment in time. How many are there? How do these compare with those of the past? Choose a two month period between 1991 and 1993 and catalogue some of the major news events of the period. Plot them on a map, do they correspond with some of your chosen hotspots? Are there common threads? Choose 5 of the trouble spots and analyse by applying the roots of war tests to determine the main courses.	Conflicts between political groups take place in a spatial context at a variety of scales. The causes of political conflict may frequently be traced to disagreements over locations, distributions or use of environments.	Human beings create artificial boundaries in order to protect themselves from aggression – discuss.
Is there a need for boundaries? Where is the best place for a boundary?	*The Real World –* The value of boundaries The drawing of lines *Geography – A modern synthesis,* Haggett Partition problems pp. 372–8.	Find an example other than those given for boundaries 1–14 (with the exception of 12 which is the norm for states which are not landlocked). Where would you place a boundary on the island shown? Devise your own boundary and then discuss with others the issues that arise: Where is there general agreement? Where are likely sites of conflict? How could the conflict be best resolved? How might a change in conditions (population growth, new technology, mineral discoveries, etc.) put pressure on these boundaries? What is the best formula for creating fair political divisions?	Political (or other) groups tend, like animals to mark their boundaries as a sign to warn intruders to keep away, and to give a sense of unity to their own culture.	The best boundaries are those that were established early on in history – discuss

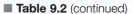

■ **Table 9.2** (continued)

Key areas	Resources	Activities	Concepts	Assessment
Geography and voting behaviour The example of voting patterns in Northumberland and Tynedale. Party politics in the UK – generalisations.	*Global futures –* option pack B. Environment and political systems unit 2.	Draw choropleth maps to illustrate the voting patterns in the area under consideration. Conduct a Spearmann Rank Correlation Coefficient to correlate the percentage of people voting Conservative in each ward with the percentage of households with no car. Describe your results. Do your findings support the conclusions of Dr Johnston's study? Can you predict the likely strength and direction of other possible correlations?	Political groups may be formed when people holding similar views or values group together to further common aims. Groups may reflect environmental, social and economic factors.	With reference to one political system you have studied: a) Briefly summarise the main features of the political system. b) Show how it has made a significant impact on the people and environment of chosen countries.
The geography of a topical political issue Our love affair with the motor car. The 'road to nowhere' Building a new bypass.	Heinemann *Global futures –* option pack B. Environment and political systems unit 3. *Problem-solving Geography* Law and Smith pp. 82–3. *Save the Earth –* J. Porritt pp. 106–8.	Match the statements on transport policy to the parties which you think they come from. Challenge each of the assertions made by the parties – can you find evidence to both support and refute these claims? What conclusions can you draw from your findings? Put forward your suggested solution to the problems identified by the bypass. Take on a role and debate the bypass issue with someone with a different viewpoint. Is there any common ground from within the roles, or is there hostility and distrust? How can a reasoned debate be promoted?	In some cases, decisions about the use of space and management of environments are party political in nature since they are part of government policy.	For a chosen issue, describe the potential conflicts in economic, environmental and social terms.

Source: Bob Grinham, Nobel School, Stevenage

Scenarios are like hypothetical sketches which show the impact of overdevelopment, resource depletion or (conversely) conservation and planning on people and environment; word sketches are also possible. Pupils can produce them or they can be prepared by the teacher for analysis by the pupils; either way, pupils need certain concepts and knowledge to facilitate an intelligent response. Analysis should focus on both the features and the processes. Pupils can be given the task of sketching the 'edge of disaster' and what 'sustainable development' may look like. The idea can be adapted in a number of ways: alternative scenarios for the High Street would be a worthwhile exercise which could readily include some fieldwork (e.g. land use mapping supplemented with an enquiry of people's views and perceptions (of shoppers, shop keepers, teenagers, chamber of commerce, etc.).

In geography lessons, we might emphasise specific matters such as transport options, energy choices, food production and supply – in other words, standard 'topics' but given a fresh dynamism and relevance with a futures orientation and subject to geographical thought, using concepts such as interdependence, spatial interaction, or place.

Exploring sustainable futures

The thrust here is to synthesise much of the thinking that has taken place hitherto. The key technique is to use a 'case study' approach for the deeper consideration of how a 'sustainable' future can be created. By case study we include both place exemplar studies (in the traditional sense of case study in geography education) and thematic studies. With reference to sustainable futures, there are two thematic studies of overriding importance: investigating *energy* options and examining *transport* choices. Both require ongoing research for up-to-date information and accurate portrayal; they are both subject to rapid changes in technology, are complex, controversial and go to the heart of any serious consideration of 'sustainability'.

Themes can, and should, be examined on a number of scales (local, regional, national, international). One of the learning outcomes is to see how the scale of analysis influences the kinds of questions investigated, and the kinds of information used to respond to those questions. For example, a local study may centre on the question of best route for a proposed bypass; in this context concepts such as 'not in my back yard' (nimby) are enormously useful. From a national perspective the more appropriate question may be whether new roads should be built at all.

For older pupils in particular, the whole concept of 'sustainable development' can and should be made problematic, and the following section discusses this further.

EDUCATION FOR SUSTAINABLE DEVELOPMENT

This is a large and challenging aspect of educating for the future. Whilst it is clearly the case that teachers of all subjects should take some responsibility for teaching 'sustainability', it is geographers who are often perceived to have the greatest contribution to make, at least in terms of the formal, subject curriculum of the school. It is noteworthy that sustainable development is one of seven 'key concepts' for the 2008 Key Stage 3 (KS3) Programme of Study (PoS) for geography (http://curriculum.qca.org.uk/key-stages-3–and-4/subjects/geography/index.aspx).

The first point to emphasise is the need to acknowledge the contested nature of the concept of sustainability. Following the gist of the previous section, just as the future is not 'given' it is probably inappropriate to teach sustainability as if it were simply a matter of identifying the 'right answer' to problems and then implementing the policies which subsequently flow. Activity 9.2 invites you into a serious debate which inevitably considers the form that education for sustainability should take.

And yet we should try not to avoid or side-step the tricky issues raised in the discussion. If you believe the present is unsustainable then you have to teach in such a manner that the present is rejected in favour of an alternative (don't you?). You certainly cannot teach in such a way that the *status quo* is accepted. This, perhaps, is what the authors of the quote in Activity 9.2 mean by 'commitment to action'.

But what does living sustainably mean? The term seems to imply 'stability', but such a condition has never been a part of the natural or human world, and it never will be. The passage in Activity 9.2 seems to take for granted that we know what a 'more sustainable society' is – and that the mission of teachers is to guide the new generation to the same wisdom – the 'answer', so to speak. Such an answer is not possible to identify and it serves nobody well to pretend that it is. For these reasons, pupils need educating in and for a 'culture of argument' (Myerson and Rydin, 1996) in which they can take an active, participatory role in coming to individual and community responses to environmental and development questions. It is most unlikely that they can be taught at school what 'the answer' is to the question how to live more 'sustainably'.

Maybe this is what is meant by the authors in Activity 9.2 telling us that we 'must find ways to change hearts and minds', that pupils have to ask more questions and become more sceptical.

Activity 9.2 **A question of values (individuals or groups)**

1   Read the following passage, which deserves careful analysis:

> 'For the survival of the world and its people teachers must do far more than just teach about global issues. We must find ways to change hearts and minds. This can be a response to reasoned argument and evidence or to experience where empathy leads to commitment to action.
>
> Teachers hold the responsibility for educating their participants to work for future change that will help create a better world for all. Together we must work towards a more ecologically sustainable and socially just society locally, nationally and globally.'
>
> (Calder and Smith, 1993, 2.1; cited in Tilbury, 1997: 105)

2   As an aid to analysis, copy out each sentence of the passage onto a separate card or piece of paper. Re-read each sentence. Write down your reaction to it on the card:
   - Do you agree with it?
   - If necessary, write down what it says to you in your own words.
   - What does the sentence leave unsaid?
   - What does it seem to assume?
   - Identify a 'keyword'.

3   In the rationale for futures orientation in teaching (Table 9.1), values clarification was identified as needful. Fien and Slater (1985) distinguish this, together with values analysis which involves the learner in analysing where different 'players' are coming from (i.e. their value position), from values inculcation where the teacher attempts to proselytise a particular value position (see page 134).

In your analysis of the passage,
- Which of the three values approaches do the authors appear to be advocating?
- Discuss the pros and cons of each in relation to education for sustainability.

4   Discuss the key words you identified in question 1. For example:
- Is there significance in the use of the term 'participants' rather than 'students'?
- What is meant by 'empathy'?
- What is the implication of the use of the word 'action'?

Discussion: Present-day ways of living are probably unsustainable – ecologically, socially, economically and politically. If you believe this, then teaching geography for a sustainable world sounds like a sensible idea. Nobody could entertain the idea of doing the reverse (teaching for an unsustainable world). But the activity shows that identifying, let alone achieving, our teaching goals in this field is by no means a straightforward matter.

A distinction of enormous significance is that between 'education' and 'indoctrination', and in our view geography classrooms oriented only to inculcating certain 'sustainable' ways to live are deeply suspect. Far more useful (and legitimate educationally) are geography lessons that enable young people to think creatively and critically using ideas such as interdependence, differential impact, etc.

In this sense, geography teachers do have a great responsibility, to keep up to date and work in appropriate ways with young people. But to inflate this responsibility in the way that some readings of the quote at the start of activity 9.2 may imply is not all that helpful. Teachers have enough to do without taking on the responsibility of changing society or saving the human race. Their achievable aim is to change the individuals they teach, principally by enabling them to respond to issues, and each other, more intelligently. If success at this individual level also leads to more informed personal choices and behaviours, it could also contribute to the creation of a better world. But the main interest of the teacher is with the person. A good illustration of how this might be achieved can be seen in Daniel Raven-Ellison's scheme of work on 'Ecological Footprints' developed to explore the concept of sustainable development (http://www.rgs.org/OurWork/Schools/Resources/ESD/EcologicalFootprints/). Pupils actively investigate how sustainable their lifestyle might be. They research, map, plan, take action on and evaluate their ability to reduce their individual footprints. Through this enquiry, pupils explore the links between social, economic, environmental and political dimensions of changing consumption habits.

Locating 'education for sustainable development'

The government (www.teachernet.gov.uk/sustainableschools/) has declared its commitment to education for sustainable development, declaring that 'All learners will develop the skills, knowledge and value base to be active citizens in creating a more sustainable society.'

It refers to a useful and enduring definition – from the Bruntland Report. Sustainable Development, according to this report is:

> Development that meets the needs of the present without compromising the ability of future generations to meet their own needs.
>
> (Bruntland, 1987)

This needs unpacking in more detail. 'Sustainable development', as Figure 9.2 shows, refers to the intersection of processes leading to environmental quality, social equity and economic security. Some would include additional aspects, including governance and cultural processes, but the three main pillars, the environmental, social and economic, are fundamental. Thus, the implications for the school curriculum are very interesting. Although aspects of sustainable development may be addressed through traditional subjects – arguably geography in particular as it promotes a holistic, 'synthesis' of physical and human knowledge – education for sustainable development implies the development of multidisciplinary understandings. There is a good case for geographers, scientists and historians, and indeed other subject specialist communities, to work in partnership when it comes to education for sustainable development.

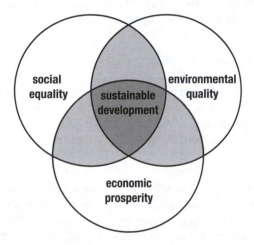

■ **Figure 9.2** Sustainable development

Sustainable development is, self evidently, a good cause, although a really difficult idea to bring to practical reality. Whilst most would agree with the idea in principle, a classic 'tragedy of the commons' is predictable when individuals are faced with leading their lives. For example, we may all agree that car usage in the UK is a problem causing congestion, poor air quality and contributing to CO_2 emissions and global warming, but far fewer of us choose to walk, cycle, share or take public transport. This is a typical knowledge-behaviour discontinuity that provides the context for policy makers to focus on education to make a difference. But we need to clear about the role education can adopt, and prior to this, it is advisable to explore a little further the nature of sustainable development. What is it that education can hope to achieve in relation to sustainable development?

When push comes to shove, politicians may find it difficult to persuade voters that restoring environmental resources, or protecting the environment, can be done at no expense to social and economic advantage. This may be the case even though in the long term we may come to accept that social and economic progress depends on the '*bottom bottom line*', the environment. Amongst other things, a key idea to flow from this is that the creation of an 'environmentally learning society', to which all citizens can contribute, is perhaps the long term goal of education. This is certainly a 'conversation' to which school geography can contribute.

Analysing a 'supercomplex world' in a holistic way

There is a view held by many which at its mildest seems to accept that something is seriously wrong and that the generation coming through may be the first in modern times who have not had a firm belief in progress and society's ability to 'sort out its problems'. It is in helping pupils make sense of, and to operate effectively in, such a world that geography teachers have a potentially powerful and important role to play. This is because of the subject's breadth and its well-known openness to change and development as a discipline. Geography can help young people to find ways of analysing a super-complex world in a holistic way. This keeps the problems whole, connected and in perspective though it does *not* necessarily present 'solutions' to the world's problems. Read, with these thoughts in mind, how Fritjof Capra introduces one of his books:

> The more we study the major problems of our time, the more we come to realise that they cannot be understood in isolation. They are systemic problems, which means that they are interconnected and interdependent [in time and space]. For example, stabilising world population will only be possible when poverty is reduced world-wide. The extinction of animal and plant species on a massive scale will continue as long as the Southern Hemisphere is burdened by massive debts. Scarcities of resources and environmental degradation combine with rapidly expanding popula-tions to lead to the breakdown of local communities, and to the ethnic and tribal violence that has become the main characteristic of the post-Cold War era.
>
> Ultimately, these problems must be seen as just different facets of one single crisis, which is largely a crisis of perception. It derives from the fact that most of us, and especially our large social institutions, subscribe to the concepts of an outdated worldview, a perception of reality inadequate for dealing with our over-populated, globally interconnected world.
>
> (Capra, 1996: 3–4)

Geography is a great subject through which to examine 'perceptions' and 'interconnect-edness'. Running a brainstorm with your pupils, carefully structured in the form of an 'effects wheel' (Box 9.1), is one way in which such thinking can be encouraged.

FUTURES? SUSTAINABILITY? IS THIS *MORAL* EDUCATION?

What is meant by the moral dimension?

> Geography can make a significant contribution to the moral education of young people. If ethics can be defined as the systematic reflection on moral questions or specific moral concerns, within geographical contexts, then all geography teachers are engaged in an ethical endeavour.
>
> (McPartland, 2006: 179)

- Choose a subject: e.g. increasing car ownership.
- Ask pairs or threes of pupils to consider the impact of this.
- From the list of *impacts*, pupils select one and brainstorm the effects of this.
- From the list of *effects*, pupils select one and repeat the brainstorm, i.e. consider the effects of this effect.
- Pairs or threes can then compare with others the results of their brainstorm. Similarities and differences can be identified and discussed.

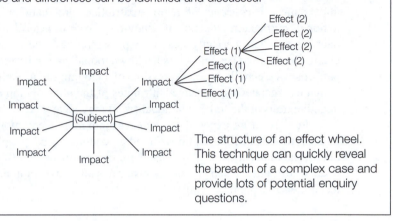

The structure of an effect wheel. This technique can quickly reveal the breadth of a complex case and provide lots of potential enquiry questions.

■ **Box 9.1** An 'effects wheel' brainstorm

A person's 'morality' combines their beliefs and values with those of the social, cultural and religious groups to which they belong, together with the customs and laws of the wider society. The combination is rarely a smooth one, nor without some tension and personal struggle when dealing with moral issues, for the latter are essentially to do with right and wrong.

Most schools have their rules and systems for supporting and developing an 'ethos' in which some values are encouraged (e.g. telling the truth) and others discouraged (e.g. bullying). In the geography classroom, as in any other, the behaviour of the pupils is perhaps the biggest indicator of moral development. Ill-disciplined groups are unlikely to learn much of value; at the same time, groups held with a rod of iron, or subdued by grinding boredom and routine, also are in a poor position to develop morally because they are not engaged in any meaningful negotiation, conversation or dialogue about moral issues.

As in spirituality, we should expect that pupils will *develop* morally, and that this progress can be assisted by a geography teacher who uses the contents and processes of the subject curriculum to:

■ help pupils recognise the moral dimensions to issues and to explore with pupils ways of distinguishing right from wrong

■ allow pupils to express their attitudes, values and feelings

■ encourage pupils to take responsibility for their actions, and the consequences for the choices they make

■ show pupils the value of developing a set of reasonable values and principles to guide their behaviour, and that these may change over time

■ encourage in pupils the formation of healthy attachments and allegiances on the one hand, and worthwhile distinctions on the other.

An excellent discussion can be had by identifying, with your tutor or a group of colleagues, where specifically geography teaching can link with a list as this. For example, with the final item on the list, geography is well placed to help pupils understand the concepts of nation, patriotism and nationalism, possibly within the national curriculum context of studying the European Union. What forces cause patriotism, where perfectly healthy expressions of 'love of country' can be made, to change its face and become a less healthy nationalism (and possibly xenophobia)? Whilst patriotism essentially is an expression of belonging, nationalism represents a process which exaggerates the perceived attributes of the home nation and distorts the supposed negative traits of the 'other': nationalism, it may be argued, fails, morally, to be justified.

Pupils can be exposed to such reasoning. It is common practice for geography lessons to examine perceptions of other countries and peoples; occasionally, and at opportune moments, issues such as these can be opened up (it may be useful to consult history colleagues when you do, as historians also have an interest in such matters – and teach the same pupils as you!).

Geography and citizenship education

What is where, why there and who cares?

(Gritzner, 2002)

We surely would not want to teach geography for a 'worse world' or the existing 'unjust and inequitable world'? If this is the case, it leaves us no choice but to teach for a 'better world', debatable though the meaning of that may be.

(Hicks, 2001)

From 2002, 'citizenship' became a statutory part of the school curriculum to be experienced by pupils in England and Wales. As well as having its own programme of study, citizenship is a cross-curricular dimension with a variety of subjects contributing to its delivery (see also Chapter 5). Citizenship and citizenship education are highly contested concepts. In the past they have been appropriated by politicians and educators of all persuasions to promote local, regional, national and global agendas as well as social, cultural, political or commercial interests. Different approaches to citizenship education place varying degrees of emphasis on civil rights and responsibilities, on compliance with and challenges to authority, and on participation in and critique of dominant practices in society (Lambert and Machon, 2001). In some schools, citizenship education is delivered across a variety of subjects while in others it may be taught as a discrete subject. Where it is productively integrated with other parts of the curriculum, it can enrich pupils' experience of both citizenship education and of those other subjects through its different perspectives and pedagogy.

There are several broad perspectives shared by geography and citizenship education. Table 9.3 shows a helpful framework for supporting the promotion of global citizenship education (Oxfam, 2006). There are direct and tangible links here with the

■ **Table 9.3** The Key Elements of Responsible Global Citizenship

Knowledge and Understanding	Skills	Value and Attitudes
Social justice and equity	Critical thinking	Sense of identity and self-esteem
Diversity	Ability to argue effectively	Empathy
Globalisation and interdependence	Ability to challenge injustice and inequalities	Commitment to social justice and equity
Sustainable development	Respect for people and things	Concern for the environment and commitment to sustainable development
Peace and conflict	Co-operation and conflict resolution	Belief that people can make a difference

Source: The Challenge of Globalisation: A Handbook for Teachers of 11–16 year-olds, Oxfam 2003: 5

geography education that pupils should experience in schools. These would include concepts and themes such as interdependence, sustainability, justice and equity; enquiry-based learning, simulation, active and participatory learning; and skills such as decision-making, argumentation and critical thinking.

Education for global citizenship aims to help pupils develop the knowledge, understanding, skills and values they need to 'participate fully in ensuring their own, and others', well-being and to make a positive contribution, both locally and globally' (Oxfam, 2006: 1). The goal is to stimulate thinking about the responsibilities of 'global citizens' so that young people can meet the challenges they face now and in the future. The global dimension in geography involves more than learning about places and themes at a global scale, more than just describing the world. It is concerned with developing pupils' 'geographical imaginations' and their understanding of the interconnections between people and places.

'Thinking geographically' involves exploring the spatial consequences of connections and interconnections between you, your place and other people's places (Jackson, 2006). Education for global citizenship should provide pupils with opportunities to develop their critical thinking skills exploring complex and often controversial global issues such as trading systems and globalisation, poverty and inequality, resource development and sustainability. Active and participatory approaches to teaching and learning enable pupils to develop decision-making skills and understand how decisions made by others affect our lives, as well as how our decisions affect the lives of others (see Action Aid, 2003). Figure 9.3 shows how the eight global dimension concepts can transform the geography curriculum and give pupils opportunities to 'think geographically'.

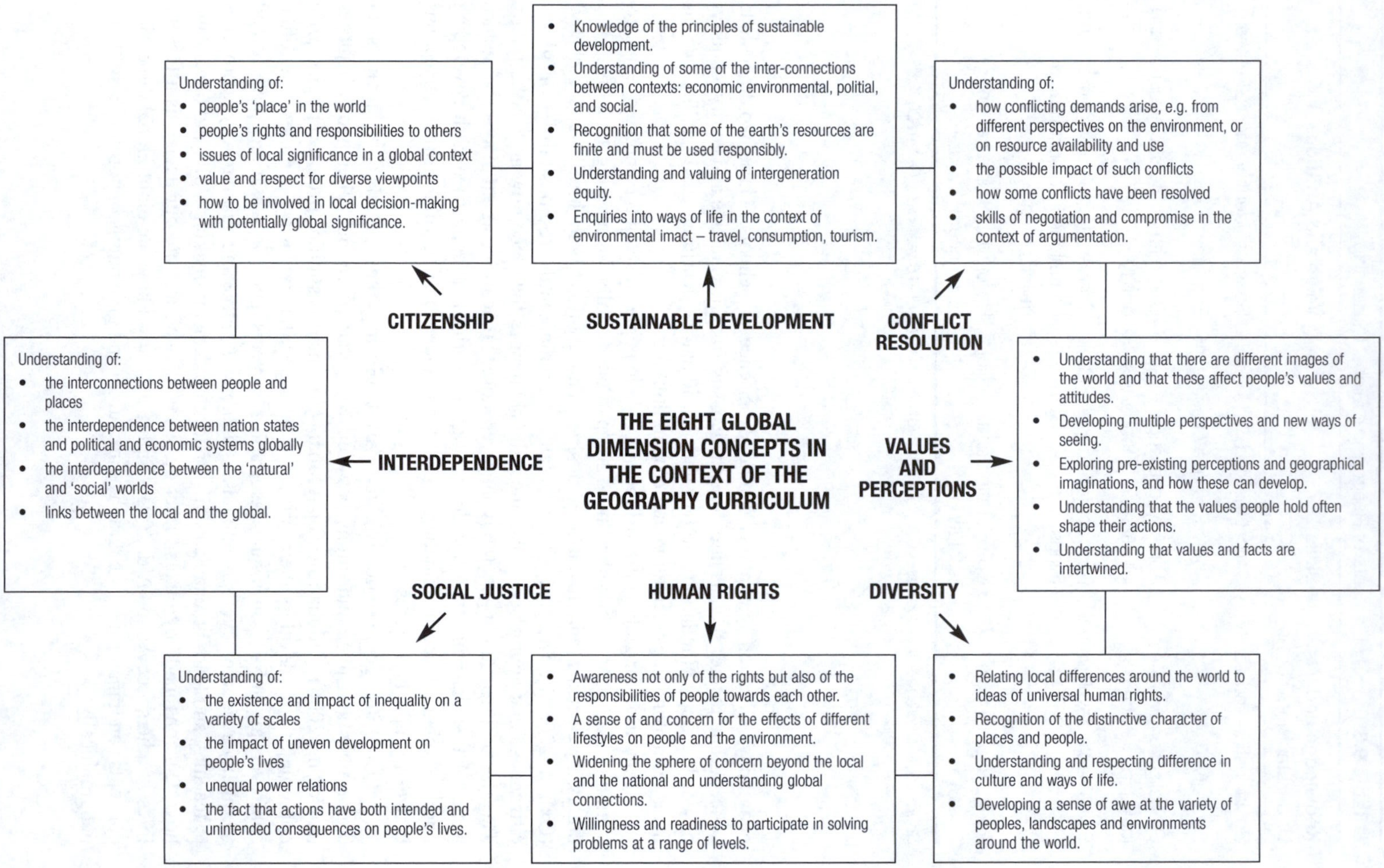

CONFLICT RESOLUTION

Understanding of:
- how conflicting demands arise, e.g. from different perspectives on the environment, or on resource availability and use
- the possible impact of such conflicts
- how some conflicts have been resolved
- skills of negotiation and compromise in the context of argumentation.

VALUES AND PERCEPTIONS

- Understanding that that there are different images of the world and that these affect people's values and attitudes.
- Developing multiple perspectives and new ways of seeing.
- Exploring pre-existing perceptions and geographical imaginations, and how these can develop.
- Understanding that the values people hold often shape their actions.
- Understanding that values and facts are intertwined.

DIVERSITY

- Relating local differences around the world to ideas of universal human rights.
- Recognition of the distinctive character of places and people.
- Understanding and respecting difference in culture and ways of life.
- Developing a sense of awe at the variety of peoples, landscapes and environments around the world.

SUSTAINABLE DEVELOPMENT

- Knowledge of the principles of sustainable development.
- Understanding of some of the inter-connections between contexts: economic environmental, political, and social.
- Recognition that some of the earth's resources are finite and must be used responsibly.
- Understanding and valuing of intergeneration equity.
- Enquiries into ways of life in the context of environmental imact – travel, consumption, tourism.

THE EIGHT GLOBAL DIMENSION CONCEPTS IN THE CONTEXT OF THE GEOGRAPHY CURRICULUM

HUMAN RIGHTS

- Awareness not only of the rights but also of the responsibilities of people towards each other.
- A sense of and concern for the effects of different lifestyles on people and the environment.
- Widening the sphere of concern beyond the local and the national and understanding global connections.
- Willingness and readiness to participate in solving problems at a range of levels.

CITIZENSHIP

Understanding of:
- people's 'place' in the world
- people's rights and responsibilities to others
- issues of local significance in a global context
- value and respect for diverse viewpoints
- how to be involved in local decision-making with potentially global significance.

INTERDEPENDENCE

Understanding of:
- the interconnections between people and places
- the interdependence between nation states and political and economic systems globally
- the interdependence between the 'natural' and 'social' worlds
- links between the local and the global.

SOCIAL JUSTICE

Understanding of:
- the existence and impact of inequality on a variety of scales
- the impact of uneven development on people's lives
- unequal power relations
- the fact that actions have both intended and unintended consequences on people's lives.

■ **Figure 9.3** The eight global dimension concepts
Source: Lambert, Morgan, Swift and Brownlie, 2004: 16–17

Activity 9.3 **Education for global citizenship in geography**

Identify a key stage 3 scheme of work in your school experience school which aims to develop global dimensions. Use Table 9.3 and Figure 9.3 to review this scheme of work.

■ Which concepts and themes are included and how are they developed in the scheme of work?
■ Which skills, values and attitudes are developed?
■ What teaching strategies and learning activities are used?
■ To what extent are enquiry-based, active and participatory approaches used?
■ To what extent do pupils have opportunities to develop critical thinking and decision-making skills?
■ In what ways could this scheme of work be developed further to promote more of the elements for responsible global citizenship?

Discuss your findings and reflections on this activity with your tutor or a small group of other student teachers.

Beware: Teaching for a 'Good Cause'

Bill Marsden (1995) has reminded us that moral dimensions to geography teaching have existed for a long time and have, not unexpectedly, stirred up argument. From the early part of the twentieth century, teachers have objected to the amount of 'imperialist' and, later, racist or eurocentric geography in school textbooks. Here Marsden quotes two Sudanese teachers writing seventy years ago:

> Teachers who have vivid imaginations, but little knowledge of the facts, find it easy to interest classes by telling exaggerated stories of the strange customs of savages ... They emphasise the strange things in other people's lives and ignore what is similar to our own.
>
> (Griffiths and Rahman ali Taha, 1939; cited in Marsden, 1995 :125)

There is contemporary research evidence to indicate that such a pattern is still a potential trap for geography teachers (Lambert, 1997c) and, though extreme imperialist and racist views, are for the most part avoided in textbooks (most publishers have clear policies and guidelines for authors); Hicks (1981) and Wright (1985) have shown that stereotyping people and places is a persistent problem.

Marsden (1989; 1997; see also Lambert 2008) has analysed such trends, most intriguingly, perhaps, identifying the substance of geography taught 'in a good cause' – that is, to serve some perceived worthwhile need in society. Marsden's analysis gives pause for thought, for he shows how the relationship between society and education is one which uses:

> the curriculum and informal channels of education to serve the ends of significant power groups, whether church, the state, or some other body, even the 'educational establishment', so that explicitly or implicitly employed techniques of inculcation,

indoctrination, and loaded selection of material, dictate the content, values, attitudes and beliefs to be transmitted.

(Marsden 1989; cited in Slater, 1996: 224)

Frances Slater picks up on Marsden's point with a telling question: if Mackinder (see Box 9.2 below) reveals the values of his time in describing the imperialist 'good cause' for teaching geography, then 'who is making equally loaded statements today, and what effect are they having?' (Slater, 1996: 224).

In 1911, the revered geographer Halford Mackinder wrote:

Let our teaching be from the British standpoint, so that finally we see the world as a theatre for British activity. This, no doubt, is to deviate from the cold and impartial ways of science. When we teach the millions, however, we are not training scientific investigators, but the practical striving citizens of an empire which has to hold its place through the universal law of survival through efficiency and effort.

■ **Box 9.2** Geography in a 'good cause'
Source: Mackinder, 1911: 79-80, in Slater, 1996: 225

The quote is fascinating, partly because it would not be too fanciful to imagine parts of this being written today: think of what our politicians say about globalisation, for instance, and the need for efficiency in the face of global economic threats. Equally interesting, and a different kind of response to Slater's question, is to imagine substituting 'environmental' for 'British': there are those who would say that geography's current 'good cause' should be environmental concern – to the extent that certain values should be inculcated. The damage this could do, ironically to environmental education, could be as great as that which Mackinder's good cause did for international understanding.

The following, turned, we hope helpfully, into questions, are those which we feel are particularly relevant to teachers of geography, linking relatively straightforwardly to the contents of the geography curriculum.

How can geography lessons help pupils:

■ understand and operate responsibly as citizens? (what is 'responsible' citizenship?)
■ understand how – and when – to refuse to support values or actions harmful to individuals or communities?
■ know about the law and legal process?
■ respect religious and cultural diversity?
■ understand and support concepts of equal opportunities?
■ participate in democratic processes?
■ understand more about the unequal distribution and consumption of resources?
■ respect, and chase, the truth?

Discussion of this list can reveal omissions – or at least societal issues which are well hidden. Of interest to many geographers in recent years have been the 'silent voices' of various components of society. Perhaps most notable, and with increasingly clear voices within geography that need to be listened to and reflected on, are women. Gillian Rose, for example, builds a case to demonstrate the masculinity of geography as a discipline (Rose, 1993). This is an interesting point, for it is not unusual to find a masculine geography in secondary schools, at least in terms of the numbers of boys and girls who opt for the full GCSE course at the end of KS3. In what ways may the subject, the selected contents and how they are presented (both of which reflect the values of the geography department to some extent) exclude women and girls and favour men and boys? Another group in society, strangely unheard and unseen in geography textbooks and curricula despite their large numbers and considerable economic significance, is older people (see Marsden, 1997). There may be other groups you can think of.

It is worth keeping the contents of the curriculum under review, therefore, from the point of view of their relevance to pupils' understanding the features and processes of contemporary society. Three illustrative questions may help you reflect on what we mean; their full scope may not be immediately self-evident and you are encouraged to discuss these with your tutor or other colleagues:

■ In studying the social world, especially through fieldwork, to what extent is there a grand unchallenged assumption about 'man's conquest of nature' – in the siting of settlements, for example, or the land use and structure of urban places?

■ In studying land use decision-making, to what extent do we accurately portray democracy at work – in role plays, for example, do we inadvertently give all players equal weight and influence, from the local Age Concern representative to the lawyers representing a major supermarket chain planning an expansion of services on an out-of-town site?

■ In studying the 'world of work', or 'industry', to what extent is this dominated by large-scale manufacturing industry (and to what extent is domestic or family work completely ignored)?

PRIORITIES FOR A CRITICAL SCHOOL GEOGRAPHY

This chapter has been concerned with how teachers and the geography curriculum can be interpreted, to help pupils face the challenges that lie ahead of them more confidently and more knowledgeably: education for the future. On a number of occasions the overlaps between the chosen headings have been evident. For example, there would be little to be gained in trying artificially to distinguish 'education for conversation', from a moral education. Though the emphasis and precise meanings are different, they are not divisible: they are both concerned and deal with human values.

One thread that runs through the whole chapter strongly is the notion of critical thinking. There are accounts of critical theory which are now fairly accessible (Huckle, 1997; Unwin, 1992; Morgan and Lambert, 2005), and space does not permit a full discussion here. But arising from the notion of a 'critical school geography', aspects of which we believe are helpful in envisioning a geography education for the future, Huckle presents us with a useful list of questions. We quote him at length:

> It would seem important to make more use of critical theory and pedagogy to help young people find their identity and place in the world – to find out how, why, with what, and where they belong, and to develop their sense of longing and belonging within a range of communities and collectivities. This requires us to develop curricula which help pupils answer the following types of questions:

- How are people and geography (places, spaces and people– environment relations) being constituted by society?
- What roles can people and geography play in constituting society?
- How should people understand and connect with history, the economy, the state, civil society, and the rest of nature as they affect their lives and local and distant geographies?
- What provides people with their identity, longings, sense of belonging and meaning in life?
- What social and cultural resources can people use to extend their imaginations, to construct places and communities where they can live sustainably with each other and the rest of nature, and to develop their identities and sense of belonging and meaning in life?
- What longings and belongings should I develop, and what kinds of society, geography, and community allow me to express my identity and desires?

Addressing such questions through socially critical pedagogy requires inputs of critical knowledge concerning the economy, the state and civil society, contemporary culture, and people-environment relations.

(Huckle, 1997: 248)

The questions Huckle raises are useful and may form an element of your self-evaluation of teaching strategies, content selection and the way you planned learning for your pupils. The contents of this chapter will help you interpret the questions and respond to them. But Huckle's final statement is, arguably, the most significant part of the whole passage. Huckle implies that the specialist knowledge you bring into secondary education from your degree studies is vital. Your degree took you close to the frontier, where new knowledge and understandings, of contemporary culture, people – environment relations and such like, are made.

But losing touch with the frontier quickly happens when you start teaching, and sometimes it seems that the way teaching is organised discourages you to even try to keep up with the subject; you often feel just too busy. Occasionally though, it is necessary to reforge your spirit of enquiry and enthusiasm to find out. What is happening on the frontier of the subject may not fit neatly into the programme of study or GCSE syllabus, but, suitably transformed, it may have enormous relevance in helping children 'travel with a different view' (see Chapter 1). Relying *solely* on school textbook writers (who themselves may not work near the 'frontier') to interpret the subject is not the best way to generate a lively and dynamic subject capable of responding to pupils' needs in a fast-changing world. As we have seen (Chapter 6), textbooks are powerful and valuable resources for teaching and learning, but they cannot be pupil centred in the sense that continually has informed this book, and which in this chapter we have argued is a prerequisite for educating for the future.

Teachers, therefore, should be prepared to inform themselves and to use their acquired techniques and creativity to enhance their teaching. Lectures, journals, books, newspapers, TV, travelling: they all count, but, we are arguing, only when subjected to a critical reading. It is one of your responsibilities as a teacher to do this.

SUMMARY AND KEY POINTS

Most people interpret 'back to basics' in terms of restricted literacies and fundamental skills, the absence of which makes continued learning next to impossible. Good teachers know about the importance of 'the basics' and pupils, too, respond well to teachers (any teachers, including those of geography) who make them into better spellers or better readers at the same time as enthusing them with interesting subject matter.

This chapter is concerned with an even more ambitious vision than making children into competent and confident processors of information. It is concerned with the real basics, by taking seriously the realisation that education has to prepare young people for the changes that will take place over their next seventy-five years or so. This realisation inevitably takes us into the realm of values. It takes into the consideration of wider educational goals and the need to clarify what is meant by (and what is possible by) a 'moral education'. The most difficult question of all is how to fuse aspects of moral education, those which acknowledge and respect personal autonomy and independence of mind, with an urgent and committed education for sustainability. This is, to coin a phrase, unfinished business.

FURTHER READING

Hicks, D. (2001) *Citizenship for the Future: A practical classroom guide*, Godalming: WWF.

> David Hicks' work on futures' education has been influential. He provides a range of ideas and activities for integrating futures' dimensions into the school curriculum including the use of scenarios to envision the future.

Lambert, D. and Machon, P. (eds) (2001) *Citizenship through Secondary Geography*, London: Routledge.

Lambert, D., Morgan, A. and Swift, D. (2004) 'Geography: The Global Dimension. Learning skills for a Global Society', London: DEA.

> This text explores the meaning of the global dimension in geography and how it can enrich the subject. It provides a variety of activities for developing the global dimension and helping pupils to 'think geographically' about global issues. There are also ideas about resources and support for developing the global dimension.

McPartland, M. (2001) *Theory into Practice: Moral Dilemmas*, Sheffield: The Geographical Association.

> This text explores ways of getting young people engaged in the process of moral reasoning through the medium of moral dilemmas. It shows how geography can contribute to a number of wider educational agendas relating to values education, citizenship education and pupils' spiritual, moral, social and cultural development.

McPartland, M. (2006) *Strategies for approaching values education*, Chapter 15 in Balderstone, D. (ed.) Secondary Geography Handbook, Sheffield: The Geographical Association.

> This chapter explores the significant contribution geography can make to the moral education of young people. It explains different approaches to values education and provides stimulating ideas for strategies that promote values' enquiry.

Morgan, A. (2006) *Teaching geography for a sustainable future*, Chapter 23 in Balderstone, D. (ed.) Secondary Geography Handbook, Sheffield: The Geographical Association.

> This chapter argues that not only is attention to the future in geography education desirable, it is positively essential with young people having an entitlement to explore their futures across a number of geographical and temporal scales. Alun Morgan suggests a range of inspiring ideas and approaches for integrating a futures dimension into geography education.

Price, J. (2003) *'Get Global!'*, London: ActionAid.

This is a useful teacher's guide on how to facilitate and assess active global citizenship in the classroom. It contains a wide variety of activities and resources to encourage pupils to move from thinking about issues that are important to them, to planning and participating in action, reflecting on their actions and assessing their learning.

www.globaldimension.org.uk

A useful website providing access to resources and activities for developing the global dimension in teaching and learning. There are resources on different countries and a wide range of global issues and themes such as water, population, energy, poverty, globalisation, sustainable development and fair trade.

The GA's leading journal Geography is a key source in helping stimulate and guide the continual development of school geography within wider moral, social, cultural, environmental – and academic geography – contexts. For example,

Butt, G. (2008) 'Is the future secure for Geography Education?' *Geography*, **93, 3, pp 158–165**

Lambert, D. (2008) 'Review article: The Corruption of the Curriculum', *Geography*, **93, 3, pp 183–185**

Members of the GA can access all journal articles electronically back to 2003.

10 VALUING PUPILS' LEARNING AND ACHIEVEMENTS

Assessment has always been an integral part of teaching and learning. We would all accept that the 'educational purpose' of teacher assessment is to help young people to progress in their learning in geography.

(Balderstone, 2000: 9)

The consideration of assessment opportunities and the types of assessment you will use with your pupils should form a key part of the planning process. It is important that assessment is not regarded as an inconvenient 'add on' to learning, but seen as a major component of curriculum and lesson planning. Without accurate assessment data how can you gain a full understanding of the achievements of your pupils and of the next educational steps to be taken?

(Butt, 2009)

The quality of assessment in primary and secondary schools is generally weak. Assessment focuses insufficiently on giving constructive feedback to pupils about their geographical knowledge, skills and understanding.

(OFSTED, 2008: 5)

INTRODUCTION

Much progress has been made in recent years concerning our understanding of assessment and (crucially) what it is for. It is vitally important to realise that assessment does not simply mean tests and examinations, important though these are. That is, the world of assessment goes far beyond the summative ritual of the education game, when pupils are given the final stamp of approval (or not) to indicate that they have satisfactorily completed the course (or not).

We are moving away from the system that relied simply on the 'gold standard' of GCE A-level to maintain rigid (and narrow) standards of excellence for the few, to one in which the goal is excellence and achievement for the majority. The results of examinations and tests, especially when reported in a comparative way as in, for example, examination league tables, often produce as many questions about the achievements of pupils as answers: for instance, why do some pupils do better than others? Are they just 'brighter'?

International comparisons of educational achievement help us develop this point further. Does the fact that Finland or Singapore (according to international tests) possess a greater proportion of 'bright pupils' than Britain mean that the British are born less clever? Probably not. But what it *does* mean is extremely difficult to say because international comparisons throw up complex issues to do with the culture of schooling, the contents of the curriculum and the expectations of pupils. It could be that *what* is valued as worthwhile achievement varies between countries and international tests do not sufficiently allow for this.

Returning to the national perspective, the question of what examinations tell us needs to be examined critically by teachers, as well as the issue of *how* achievement is best measured (and how pupils are best prepared for this). Under the gold standard, the system places trust in external examination procedures to maintain standards for the few. Now in Britain, policy makers seem increasingly aware that they must place their trust in teachers to raise standards for the many. This chapter explores the implications on practice of the evolving assessment system in England and Wales (Scotland has significantly different arrangements).

A thorough overview of the general principles and practice of assessment is provided in *Learning to Teach in the Secondary School* (Capel *et al.,* 2005: 300–338). Here, we briefly restate the fundamental principles of assessment by discussing the quality criteria of what we shall call 'educational assessment' (Gipps, 1994). In doing so we will discuss geography specific concerns of marking and using National Curriculum level descriptions.

In formal terms, we can define assessment in education as 'the process of gathering, interpreting, recording and using information about pupils' responses to an educational task' (Harlen, *et al.,* 1992: 217). This is an excellent definition and in this chapter we explore what it means in practice, particularly in terms of your developing the professional attitudes and skills needed to get to know your pupils and, through their geography, to help them improve. What all this requires, literally, is learning how to value pupils' work. The definition is wide enough to encompass external summative assessment, including public examinations, and the chapter begins with a brief consideration of these.

The Professional Standards for Teachers place considerable emphasis on you to develop an understanding of assessment which covers monitoring, assessment, recording, reporting and accountability. On the one hand, teachers feel judged by results and yet on the other, are encouraged to use techniques to promote Assessment for Learning (AfL). Terry Hadyn (2005: 302) outlines the main features of assessment you should have explored by the end of your professional training as a teacher.

OBJECTIVES

By the end of this chapter, you should be able to:

■ understand the role, purpose and some of the design principles of external assessment
■ identify the broad principles of educational assessment
■ identify the principles of 'assessment for learning'
■ understand the purposes of and practice of marking pupils' work in assessing pupils' progress
■ use appropriate recording and reporting systems
■ understand and use National Curriculum Level Descriptions.

Useful terms:

GCE AS level = General Certificate of Education Advanced Subsidiary
GCE A-level = General Certificate of Education Advanced level
GCE O-level = General Certificate of Education Ordinary level (abolished 1987)
CSE = Certificate of Secondary Education (abolished 1987)
GCSE = General Certificate of Secondary Education (first examination 1988)

EXAMINATIONS IN PERSPECTIVE

Though few people would deny that external examinations are necessary, and play an essential role in education, the current system is considered by many to be flawed. As a result, the field of external examinations is an uncertain one and dramatic changes can be expected in the coming years. It is not the purpose of a book such as this to second guess what those changes may be in any detail. But we can reaffirm that the pattern of examinations to which we have grown accustomed (outlined in Chapter 1 by Michael Naish (pp. 5–11) – that is, GCSE, followed by the 'gold standard' of A-levels, with 'vocational' routes grafted on (previously for 'less academic' pupils but now aiming to develop vocational skills for a broader group of pupils) – is expensive and may be inappropriate to the needs of a society in which it has become the norm, rather than the exception, to gain certification for educational achievement at 16 years old. Examination certificates are no longer the preserve of a select minority.

Therefore, this section does not attempt to describe in detail the external examinations available in geography. Such a list would quickly become dated. Instead we provide a short description of how the system is changing and has evolved in recent years. This is especially true for 14 to 19 year olds after the framework for national qualifications was revised in 2004 (see Youens, 2005: 320–332). This is followed with the identification of some principles that have helped shape the design of public examinations in geography. Our overall purpose is to help student teachers see how they may support pupils preparing for this major hurdle in their lives. We are mindful that preparing for public examinations is also a major hurdle for teachers as, rightly or wrongly, raw data on pupil attainment are used increasingly as an indicator of teacher effectiveness as well as pupil attainment.

Examinations at 16: what future?

When the majority of the population left school in their mid teens, it made sense to have a system of terminal examinations at 16. The main purpose of the exam was to inform the selection processes of employers and institutions of further education such as sixth forms and colleges. GCSE was introduced in 1986 to combine under one roof a two-track terminal examination system (of O-levels for the 'brightest' 20 per cent and CSEs for the next brightest 40 per cent) that had begun to emerge in the 1960s. It is still a terminal examination in the sense that it comes at the end of compulsory schooling and is now inclusive of nearly the entire age-cohort of pupils (i.e. very few 16 year olds in any one year do not acquire any GCSEs). But its role in selection is not quite so profound as in former years since the majority of 16 year olds now expect to continue in full-time education.

Furthermore, since the establishment of a national qualifications framework in 2004 (www.qca.org.uk/qualifications), the debate concerning the post-16 years is now more explicit than ever on the possibility of abolishing the academic stranglehold that some believe A-level to exert on the curriculum. The development of Vocational Diplomas corresponding to a range of occupational sectors and delivered by both schools and/or colleges (introduced in September 2008) adds fuel to this debate and broadens the range of courses and qualifications available to young people. Differences in pedagogy and assessment practice have posed some challenges to the development of vocational courses in schools. Such courses are assessed through an internally assessed portfolio of evidence and externally set tests and projects. Further discussion of vocational courses can be found in Brooks and Lucas (2004) and geography's contribution to vocational qualifications is outlined in Marvell, Holland and Shuff (2006). A Geographical Association survey in 2001 found that 23% of geography departments were contributing to the delivery of vocational courses.

Thus, the near future may see GCSE as an increasingly ambiguous legacy from a previous age, since parents and pupils will be encouraged to map out a 14–19 educational experience at the end of Key Stage 3, rather than a relatively short sprint to the GCSE. It may be that GCSE itself is radically reformed to reflect its 'interim' rather than 'terminal' status.

■ To what extent is the position of GCSE geography now a perilous one? Partly to make room for the vocational courses and partly to relieve the pressure of an over-crowded 'Key Stage 4' curriculum (when both geography and history were to be compulsory and full subject components of the National Curriculum, prior to the Dearing Review in 1995), geography appears to have been marginalised. In 1996, over 300,000 pupils entered GCSE geography; this healthy number may never be seen again. In 2008 203,862 pupils entered GCSE Geography. There has indeed been a steady decline in the numbers of pupils opting to study geography at GCSE in recent years leading to the establishment of the national Action Plan for Geography funded by government and led by the Geographical Association and Royal Geographical Society.

■ Should a school geography department encourage large numbers of pupils (possibly *all* pupils?) to do a short course GCSE or concentrate on a smaller more select group to do the full GCSE?

■ How is the full geography GCSE best marketed; what kinds of pupils choose geography and for what reasons?

■ What are the opportunity costs of concentrating creative energy on Leisure and Tourism as a principal outlet for geography's curriculum contribution, rather than developing GCSE short courses (see Rawling, 2001)? Or can the department develop both at the same time (in addition to ensuring a healthy take up of the full GCSE)?

How examinations have changed

Traditional public examinations were strongly criticised over many years for being dominated by the academic interests of subject specialists. 'If the "candidate" can't perform in the exam, too bad'...the examination seemed to say...'we just want to sort out the best'.

Indeed, this was the purpose of the GCE O-level, and to some large extent it remains the purpose of the A-level examination. Essentially, such norm referenced examinations (see Table 10.1) serve the interests of selection well. But because they guarantee failure for a substantial proportion of the candidature they are not appropriate if the candidature, consists of most of the year group: they stand little chance of motivating pupils who know they are likely to fail. Traditional examinations were also narrow in the range of skills and attributes they demanded of candidates and suited certain kinds of abilities (e.g. memory) far more than others (e.g. analysis). They tended to be opaque to many pupils, who found it difficult to 'crack the code' and therefore please the examiner. 'I can't do exams' was an often heard admission of pupils, who were resigned to their incompetence or at least lack of certain ill-defined capacities. But surely pupils should not have had to shoulder all the blame!

The introduction of the GCSE signalled an enormous effort to reform not only the structure of the system, but also the internal dynamics and design of the examinations themselves in the light of those well understood limitations outlined in the previous paragraph. In essence, the GCSE is built upon the ideal of finding out what candidates know, understand and can do – not what they do not know and cannot do. This became expressed by the phrase 'positive achievement' and the early rhetoric emphasised the role of criteria referencing (see Table 10.1) in devising an examination which could recognise positive achievement. It was recognised that the criteria would need to encompass a wider notion of achievement than perhaps most examiners and teachers were accustomed to, and thus issues concerning the validity of the examination assumed equal status to that more traditional (and still important) concern of examinations, reliability (see Table 10.1). From this basis emerged new examination paraphernalia, elements of what we might call an 'examinations technology' in which geography teachers require management and organisational skill as well as technical expertise. The main elements are:

■ assessment objectives and specification grids
■ grade descriptions and criteria mark schemes.

You will get to know the particular details of these in relation to the syllabuses your department has chosen to follow. The following brief comments are designed to help you place the particular detail into a general framework.

Assessment objectives and specification grids:
All GCSE syllabuses have to conform to the *National Criteria for Geography* which set out the broad aims of studying geography at this level and the content requirements (the *A-level Core* performs a similar function). In addition, the syllabuses set out what 'abilities' are to be tested by the examination. This is done by identifying assessment objectives. GCSE examinations test knowledge, understanding, application and skills, including inquiry each assessed at several levels (National Criteria for Geography).

The Criteria lay down weightings for the each objective in the 'scheme of assessment': giving broadly equal balance to knowledge, understanding and skills. Precisely how many marks are awarded for each can vary within the limits shown, but are stated in the syllabus specification grid.

One of the great achievements of the GCSE was the realisation that for the examination to be valid such skills cannot be tested via short answer questions under timed conditions. Thus, all GCSE geography examinations have historically had a coursework element which included 'a geographical investigation supported by fieldwork'. The wording of this is significant. It does not lay down that each GCSE pupil

■ **Table 10.1** A glossary of the principal features of educational assessment

Feature	Meaning	Feature	Meaning
Formative assessment	assessment to support future learning during a course of study	Summative assessment	assessment undertaken at the end of a course of study
Formal assessment	includes a degree of standardised procedure, as in tests	Informal assessment	based on observation and conversation with pupils
Formal records	often numerical, consisting of marks, grades, etc.	Informal records	qualitative information carried in teachers' heads
Marking pupils' work	one part of the overall knowledge building process; in practice can be little more than monitoring work done	Criteria referencing	pupils' work is judged in relation to explicit criteria which identify progress by describing levels of attainment
Norm referencing	pupils' work is judged in comparison with the performance of other pupils	Ipsative assessment	pupils' work is judged solely in the context of the individual pupil's previous performance and circumstances
Validity in educational	assessment usually refers to the content or strategy adopted: is this assessing what I think it is assessing?	Reliability of assessment	usually a reference to the influence of external factors on outcomes: how well standardised are the questions, procedures and marking?
Fitness for purpose	assessment information has several purposes to which it may be put; does the adopted assessment method provide data in the right form?	Achievement	a broader concept than attainment: includes non-academic goals such as motivation, social and personal skills
Attainment	usually described as a 'Level' in relation to specified 'Attainment Targets'	Teacher assessment (National Curriculum)	a summative judgement made near the end of the Key Stage based upon the pupil's overall performance and progress
Performance	a range of tasks, exercises, etc. provide the evidence on which judgements relating to attainment are based	'Ability'	a complex idea; over-hasty extrapolations about general 'ability' on the basis of limited evidence drawn from pupils' performances are best avoided

Source: Lambert, 1996, in Kent, Lambert, Naish and Slater (eds): 261

must undertake individually a piece of field research entirely independently; so long as some kind of field work investigation (undertaken in groups, for example) can be shown to support the pupil's individual coursework submission, then all is well. This considerably eased the management problem of supervising possibly hundreds of GCSE candidates annually, though the organisation and management challenge still should not be underestimated; it is fieldwork *enquiry* that is required, not merely 'experience' in the field. Coursework was set and marked by teachers; the mark scheme is provided by the Awarding Body and moderated by them.

Changes at GCSE and post-16

At the time of writing, new GCSE subject specifications are being developed as part of the wider changes taking place in the 14–19 curriculum including new restrictions on assessment, notably the loss of coursework and its replacement by controlled assessment. Teaching of the new GCSE specifications begins in September 2009 with Awarding Bodies allowed to offer two GCSE specifications as long as there is a clear distinction between the nature of these specifications. There is some evidence of attempts to modernise the geography curriculum in these revised specifications as the subject criteria developed by QCA highlighted the need for a geography fit for the twenty-first century as well as the development of new skills such as the use of GIS. Fieldwork is also included as an essential component of the geographical learning experience.

A detailed summary of the coverage of the new specifications can be found at www.geography.org.uk/download/GA_SECNewGCSEOverview.doc and by referring to the websites for each of the Awarding Bodies. Each Awarding Body appears to be offering one course based on a more 'traditional' specification and another alternative specification which, in some cases, represents a more radical change from what has been available previously.

External assessment will account for 75 per cent of the marks awarded and the remaining 25 per cent is for 'controlled assessment' (the balance for short courses is 50/50). External assessments will continue to be tiered (foundation level covering grades G-C and higher level from grades D-A*). Controlled assessments are a new form of assessment, but they will include the use of fieldwork. They will pose new challenges for school geography departments, particularly where Awarding Bodies require all of the work to be completed using ICT to facilitate the 'controlled' element of the assessment. Nevertheless, this form of assessment will at least ensure than fieldwork continues as an essential element of learning in geography.

Awarding Bodies

AQA	www.aqa.org.uk
CCEA (Northern Ireland)	www.rewardinglearning.org.uk
Edexcel	www.edexcel.org.uk
OCR	www.ocr.org.uk
WJEC	www.wjec.org.uk

Geography in the post-16 age group

Although the numbers of A-level candidates for geography have fallen over the last decade, the subject is still one of the most popular post-16 subjects with a high proportion of AS students progressing to A2 standard. Recent data shows that geography has the 12th highest numbers of candidates at AS and the 9th highest at A2 level (RGS-IB, 2007). It is also rated by OFSTED as the best taught age-range in the subject (OFSTED, 2003). However, OFSTED have also raised concerns about some of the dominant pedagogies used with this age group noting that 'limitations to the quality of teaching include a focus on content rather than learning' (OFSTED, 2008).

Recent changes in post-16 specifications have been significant and you should be aware of the implications of these changes for what you teach and how it will be assessed. In England and Wales, only one specification is allowed per Examination Awarding Body resulting in a reduction in choice from seven to four specifications. The examinations and assessment industry has become increasingly privatised in recent years with one Awarding Body now even owned by a large trans-national publisher. This means that they are far more concerned with maintaining or increasing their market share than other educational considerations.

The number of modules has been reduced from six to four in every A-level subject apart from Maths in order to reduce the assessment burden on students. These changes will affect course planning and decisions in schools about when to enter students for examinations and re-sitting modules. From 2009, the university application process will also require students to enter the results of all their module examinations, instead of just their best result in each module, placing additional emphasis on the timing of module criteria placed a requirement for 'stretch and challenge' in the new AS/A2 courses supported by the introduction of an A* grade at A2 (QCA, 2006).

The reduction in the number of modules and a general review of coursework assessment has resulted in the loss of coursework assessment in geography. This could have implications for fieldwork in post-16 geography. All Awarding Bodies have included a requirement for fieldwork to be assessed in written examinations; one at A2, the others at AS. However, this poses significant challenges for both geography teachers and examiners raising concerns about 'fitness for purpose', one of the key principles of assessment highlighted elsewhere in this chapter.

Alongside these changes in examination specifications there have also been significant developments in the subject discipline (highlighted in Chapter 1) in higher education. The gap between your experiences of the subject in higher education and what you observe and experience in school geography may be widening. Some university tutors have raised concerns about the theory levels of school pupils progressing into higher education. Learning in school geography is perceived to focus too much on facts and 'case studies' rather than promoting critical thinking about theoretical issues and questions.

Grade descriptions and criteria mark schemes:
The current GCSE is criterion referenced, that is a statement is made of what the pupil needs to do in order to attain a given grade, that is the level of achievement in a given skill. It proved difficult for Awarding Bodies to reference every grade and only Grade A, C and E are criterion referenced. These statements are the basis for the marking scheme, presented as a marking grid. Teachers soon become used to using such schemes. The marking is moderated by the Awarding Body and marks finalised in discussion between

teachers and the moderator, and not just statistical adjustment of marks, puts checks and balances in place to ensure the reliability (see Table 10.1) of marks.

The structure, procedures and design of GCSE examinations are sophisticated. In addition to the technical aspects discussed above, examiners have devised techniques to ensure fairness and maximum access to the questions. Take some past papers and examine for yourself how the *rubric* is designed to help the candidate, how the *layout* of

---

Unit 6471 Paper 1 Changing Landforms and their Management

General Comments

This paper was quite straightforward but the mean performance was relatively low. Sections a and b were completed with considerably more success than the short essays in the c sections where responses were disappointing overall. Questions varied in terms of popularity with 1, 3 and 4 being the most popular and question 2 the least popular.

There were signs of improvements in knowledge and understanding of some areas of the syllabus, particularly wetlands, river regimes, causes of long-term sea level changes and management issues relating to coastal protection, wetlands and flooding. However, there were also some worrying errors in basic knowledge of terminology such as 'sediment' which was frequently confused with discharge, and 'sustainable management', which was often understood as being hard engineering 'because it lasts a long time'. There were also very weak responses to the questions on wave refraction and river/valley profiles indicating fundamental errors in understanding and lack of knowledge of traditional physical geography.

Areas for centres to work on in order to improve candidate performance:

■ Interpretation of resources such as photographs, cartoons and diagrams: at the moment interpretation is inconsistent and whilst candidates may understand the general gist of the resource, they frequently lack the ability to interpret the resource thoroughly or to explain their ideas on paper, thus missing out on maximum marks.

■ Additionally it was quite clear that many candidates did not have a mental image of the place they were describing; performance can be enhanced by using photographs and maps as frequently as possible when teaching case studies.

■ Keep working on terminology – sediment, discharge, permeable, impermeable, long profile, cross profile, refraction...just some of the words that were used incorrectly, costing valuable marks.

■ Improve examination technique by using the marks available space as a guide as to how much to write. As a rule questions with 5 marks and over are level marked whereas questions with 4 marks are point marked and 2 or 3 of these marks may be gained by extending one point. Candidates who used extra sheets of paper to extend their answers do not often achieve more marks by doing so. Working with mark schemes and undertaking peer marking are often effective remedies to poor technique.

■ **Box 10.1** Advice and Guidance from the Chief Examiner. Extracts from a GCE AS/A2 Level Examiner's Report

Source: EdExcel GCE Geography B Examiner's Report, Summer 2008

the paper has been carefully considered and how the *wording* of questions is controlled and clear. Note also how the questions themselves usually have an internal structure designed to invite 'positive achievement', i.e. they have a built-in incline (or a number of clear steps) of difficulty. Even the best designed examination paper cannot, on its own, successfully examine the entire cohort of 16 year olds. Thus, the geography GCSE examination now consists of two 'tiered' papers: one for the higher attaining candidates and the other for more modest attainment. This requires teachers to make sensitive and informed decisions about the performance of their pupils so that they can be entered for the more appropriate papers.

Developing examination skills

To help prepare your pupils for public examinations you should become familiar with the specifications of your examination syllabus. Your school can provide that document together with past examination papers, which are also available from websites of the Awarding Bodies. Make sure you understand the marking scheme. Another important resource is the Chief Examiner's Annual Report, particularly the section dealing with candidate performance, see Box 10.1. You should teach your pupils how to develop study skills, how to revise and examination techniques to use in the examination (Balderstone and King, 2004; Chapman and Digby, 2006; Warn, 2006). Given the improved emphasis on study skills and greater focus on preparing pupils for examinations, it is not surprising that standards have risen in recent years.

One concern that has increasingly emerged in recent years is that creativity and other crucial intellectual aspects of learning have been sacrificed in the drive for higher standards of achievement through improvements in examination results. Pupils are increasingly taught how to meet examination criteria and to accumulate knowledge rather than develop conceptual understanding and higher-level cognitive skills (Bell, 2006:13).

ASSESSMENT MATTERS: WHY AND WHAT FOR?

Assessment is not an exact science and we must stop presenting it as such.

(Gipps, 1994: 167)

Assessment is for learning

International comparisons show the education system in England and Wales to be somewhat overloaded with external, state-controlled examinations of one sort or another, designed to sift and grade young people into fairly fixed categories of 'ability' or 'potential' at the beginning of their adult lives. But in recent years, there has been a growing realisation of the destructive impact of the assumptions that underpin such an assessment regime. If you assume that intelligence is general, inherited and pretty well fixed, then you will continue to 'prepare' pupils for their tests, knowing deep down that the results are more or less determined. You will make sure they cover the syllabus, practise answering questions, learn to avoid classic errors (for example, by using 'along the corridor and up the stairs' as a prompt for reading grid references) and boost confidence whenever you can.

If, however, you believe intelligence to be multifaceted, and that intelligences can be learned (see Perkins, 1996), you will do all the above but with important and potentially liberating differences; for example, you will not so readily adopt teachers' short-hand terms such as 'the less able' with their deterministic and, in fact, damning connotations about the general characteristics of groups of pupils. You might think of your class not as passive 'pupils', the sometimes reluctant recipients of what you have to give, but as active 'learners'. Part of your job in the latter regime is to 'tune in' to these learners as individuals, getting to know their work and its strengths and weaknesses; you may then use this knowledge to find ways of helping them meet new work more intelligently (and experience more success).

Figure 10.1 shows how the different purposes and functions of teaching, learning and assessment are interrelated. It highlights the important questions for both teachers and pupils during the assessment process. It also emphasises that the learner is at the centre of this assessment process with the information obtained being used to support learning through 'feedback' and 'feedforward' (Weeden and Hopkin, 2006).

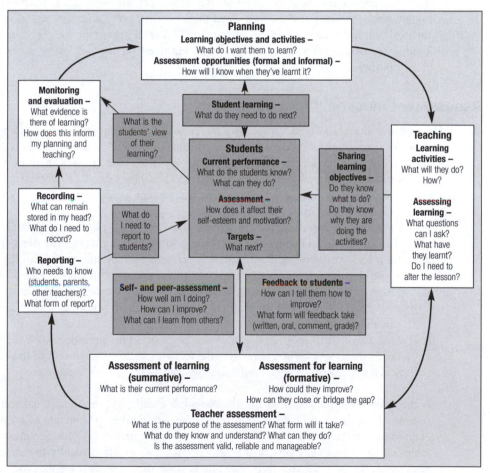

■ **Figure 10.1** Teaching, learning and assessment
Source: Weeden and Hopkin, 2006: 415

Assessment must have 'consequential validity'

This chapter explores how geography teachers can place value on, and respond to, children's work. It is driven by the concept of 'consequential validity' (Gipps, 1994). This concept identifies a basic touchstone of educational assessment: that its validity depends upon it having consequences for improving learning. This is a good test of worthwhileness; for example, how will marking this pile of books have consequences? Will not marking them have consequences? How do I mark these books to have the maximum positive impact on future learning?

The idea of consequential validity takes us to the heart of what Gipps meant when she reminds us that assessment is 'not an exact science' (Gipps, 1994: 167): that highly 'scientific' assessment (i.e. standardised testing under controlled conditions), with its emphasis on exactitude, does not serve well the educational purposes of teachers. Good assessment is altogether more messy – more 'art' than 'science' – and rests on teachers making dependable and fair judgements of value on pupils' work. By good assessment we mean assessment that is formative – literally, assessment for learning: this is different from summative assessment because the latter cannot feed back to pupils (it is undertaken at the end of the course) and therefore has very limited potential in feeding forward to inform future learning. This distinction is an important one (see Box 10.1 for a summary of others) and signals the persistent need for teachers using assessment to clarify purpose.

Assessment must be 'fit for purpose'

That assessment has to be 'fit for purpose' is another touchstone to be guided by. In the previous paragraph, 'good' assessment meant formative assessment, in which the educational purpose was to the fore. But the fact is that much assessment in education serves purposes other than educational ones and teachers need to be clear about this. Generally speaking, four broad purposes of assessment in education can be identified:

- Formative: recognising the positive achievement of the pupil, feeding back in terms that the pupil can understand and feeding forward in terms of next steps or targets.
- Summative: recording the overall achievement of the pupil, usually in the form of a useful summary that can be compared (i.e. ranked) with others, such as a grade.
- Diagnostic: designed to identify and measure particular learning difficulties which may be classified and scrutinised so that remedial action can be planned and implemented effectively.
- Evaluative: fulfilling the needs of the State or administration which legitimately needs some way of assessing the effectiveness (value for money) of the education service at various levels – individual teacher, school, LEA, sector, etc.

If the main purpose identified for assessment is evaluative, the occasional testing of a sample of pupils would suffice. In practice, the summative assessments of all pupils by examination are taken to be the appropriate data set: hence the introduction of league tables of examination results in the early 1990s. Examination results therefore have a high stake, not only for the individual pupils concerned, but also for the teachers: there is pressure to improve results year on year. This is fine so long as the distorting tendencies of high stakes assessment are understood and kept in check: primarily, the risk arises from pressure to 'teach to the test' and only to value achievement which 'scores' in examination terms. The way such pressure can (but need not) distort the geography curriculum is by reducing:

■ time for fieldwork
■ time in class devoted to open-ended, speculative or creative discussions or enquiry
■ class time devoted to topical issues or particular interests/experiences of pupils or teacher.

At the same time, there may be an increased:

■ reliance on classic case studies or examples, which can become stereotypical
■ tendency to teach (and learn) simple answers to complex questions, uncritically copying.

If the main purpose of assessment is formative, the stakes are lower and the priorities are quite different. Formative assessment may be combined with assessments designed for diagnostic purposes, but it is very difficult to see how, in practice, assessments may serve both formative and summative/evaluative purposes at the same time. Whereas, for example, high stakes summative assessment rewards people who can avoid mistakes, play safe and commit to memory the information and rules, low stakes formative assessment often centres on analysing mistakes and encourage risk taking. It exploits a range of assessment opportunities (see Table 10.2) from the more formal to the informal, from the written to the oral, from work done at home to work done at school, from work done individually to work done as a member of a group or team. And all the while, the purpose is not to compare and rank the pupil with others, but to get the pupil – and the teacher – to understand each other better and what it is they have to do next.

Another crucial distinction between summative and formative assessment is that the former, being designed mainly with the need to grade pupils in relation to each other (that is, essentially, to rank them for selection purposes), is likely to be *norm referenced* (Box 10.1). The latter, however, ought to be *criterion referenced,* as we shall see below.

It is interesting to make the historical note here that the influential TGAT Report upon which the National Curriculum assessment framework was based (see Lambert 1996; Marsden 1995), whilst recognising different assessment needs, tried to create a single, criteria-referenced system to meet all assessment purposes. To this day, it is still far from clear exactly how so-called National Curriculum 'Teacher Assessment' should operate in order to fulfill a formative role at the same time as providing a single, summative attainment level for reporting to parents or other schools and teachers. The final section of this chapter discusses this in more detail.

Educational assessment must be criterion referenced

There is a clear link between good teaching and accurate, helpful assessment. However, assessment continues to be a weakness in much geography teaching. Marking is an important part of such assessment and yet it is often poor, irregular, and not sufficiently formative or specific to geography. Targets, if they are included in the teacher's comments, are often too general to be helpful.

(OFSTED, 2008: 22)

▮ **Table 10.2** Learning activities which present opportunities to assess pupils' work

Oral evidence	Written evidence	Graphic evidence	Products
questioning	questionnaires	diagrams	models
listening	diaries	sketches	artefacts
discussing	reports	drawings	games
presentations	essays	graphs	photographs
interviews	notes	printouts	
debates	stories	overlays	
audio recording	newspaper articles		
video recording	scripts		
role play	short answers to questions		
simulation	lists		
	poems		
	descriptions		

Consider:
▨ Which of these are produced frequently in your classrooms?

Which are produced infrequently? Why?
▨ Are any of the above underused in your classrooms?
▨ Can you add to this list?

The principle here is simple. If we intend to engage pupils-as-learners in conversations about their progress, next steps or targets, we need a transparent common language. There are undoubtedly many readers of this book who have experienced for themselves the opaqueness of traditional assessments for which the *criteria on which the mark or grade were based* were not identified. The well-known cartoon about Billy (Figure 10.2) raises all the issues if you think hard enough, which is what Activity 10.1 is designed to make you do.

Activity 10.1 **Marking and educational assessment (individuals or groups)**

1 Examine Figure 10.2.
2 Identify and list the issues which Billy's story raises. Can you draw from your own assessment experience, as a student of geography, your own story which enables you to empathise with Billy?
3 What, in your view, is the assessment information that Billy needs?
4 In what ways could Billy's teacher improve the consequential validity of her marking?

Discussion: Were Billy's good marks for effort or for attainment? He does not know and it is possible that the teacher is not wholly clear about this either. Many teachers mark for 'effort', for understandable reasons, but it is a risky business: how does one person's effort compare with another's? How can you tell if a person is 'trying hard'? And how is a pupil to interpret consistently high 'effort' marks with low grades for 'attainment'? A few teachers may only mark for effort, often influenced heavily by the surface appearance of the work, in a vain (and we think irresponsible) attempt to encourage pupils. Only Billy knows his 'effort'. What the teacher can begin to show him is how to expend his effort, what aspects of his work to improve upon and what errors to avoid. The pupil expects the teacher to judge the value of the work; such a judgement is a necessary platform on which to base any formative advice.

But if Billy's marks were for attainment, he does not know what won the marks. He very significantly reveals his assumption that he dropped marks rather than gained them – betraying an attitude, that may be widespread and deep seated, that assessment is for punishing faults rather than rewarding virtues. Again, it is likely that the grounds for the eight out of ten may not be known with clarity even to the teacher – who may not have expectations of the work until she begins to look at it and establish norms on the basis of what the pupils give her. This is a natural and necessary process, especially for less experienced teachers, as is noted in Box 10.2.

It is perhaps clear that the final suggestion in Box 10.2, asking you to reflect consciously on the marking process, points you to the overwhelming justification for anchoring and explicating assessment with criteria. Billy and the teacher will find they understand each other better with explicit criteria which set out the basis for judging success: it will be possible to be able to say with some consistency (from pupil to pupil and from week to week) what 'eight out of ten' means.

Incidentally, the usefulness of assessment criteria reinforces the point made repeatedly in this book that effective planning for learning requires teachers to become fluent and adept at identifying 'lesson objectives'. It is difficult to see how, without a clear sense of the teacher's objectives, it would be possible to articulate very clearly the success criteria in learning.

So, we clearly need criteria on which to base assessment. What may not be quite so clear is the subtle interplay of norms with criteria. We do not want you to think norm referencing is 'bad' and criteria referencing is 'good'; they are not polar opposites. It has long been realised that 'behind every criterion lurks a norm'. To illustrate with an example: it is impossible to provide the exact, objective criterion for assessing success in explaining the location of the biotechnology industry in the Cambridge area, or outlining the arguments for and against eco-tourism in Costa Rica. It is not even possible to say *exactly* how to award marks for reading pie charts or Ordnance Survey maps. Any general guidance that criteria can provide has to be brought alive by the process of establishing norms – of skimming the work and setting expectations or standards. Without criteria at all, however, this process is without basis: teachers, even in the same department, will have different – and to pupils confusing – standards.

Assessment: A view from the receiving end

■ **Figure 10.2** 'Well-known cartoon about Billy'
Source: Capel, Leask and Turner, 2005

Assessment must be planned

All lessons should be planned with assessment in mind. Indeed, as we travel through the various 'scales' of planning – from individual lessons, to units of work, schemes of work, specifications, syllabuses and curricula – all these educational 'episodes' need to give a clear indication of the role of assessment within them. Therefore at the 'sharp end' – where the teacher is working day-to-day with pupils

Marking your first work

Before you set your first homework or classwork to be marked by you, you should have spent some time preparing in the following way:

1 Examine with the teacher a range of work from the class. You analyse it in terms of:

- presentation
- spelling, punctuation and grammar
- accuracy of the content (the geography)
- the style of work (how it has been structured; by the teacher or by the pupils?)
- how it has been marked – use some of the issues emerging in the present discussion to guide you: how is it graded?

what are the grades for?

does the teacher comment? How? With what tone;

is the pupil expected to respond?

2 With the teacher's help and advice, identify an individual, pair or threesome of pupils with whom you can have a discussion about their work. Your aim is to find out:

- what sense they make of the work,
- what they think it is for,
- why it is marked, and
- what sense they make of the marks.

(Use this as an opportunity to practise the art of engaging young people in a serious but unthreatening manner and finding out about their views, without interrogating them).

3 Nothing, however, can prepare you fully for that first pile of exercise books or file paper. It is useful to articulate, on paper, how you approach the task in detail. It is likely that you will take steps to skim the work in order for you to establish your expectations, norms or 'standards'; you may revise your judgement of earlier work in the light of later work. What were your feelings, your uncertainties or anxieties about the whole process? Discuss these with your mentor.

The purpose of records is to enable a fair and reasonable picture of the pupil to be communicated to others. This is the purpose of your *mark book*.

Note that the *day book* is an idea borrowed from primary teachers. It is not the same as the mark book and certainly different from the scheme of work or your lesson plans. It is also not a diary, though this is perhaps the closest analogy. It is simply a hard-backed exercise book with a number of blank pages allocated for each class you teach. You keep it with you all the time and it becomes the place to locate short notes to yourself, or *aide mémoires*, about significant events or insights concerning just those individuals who may particularly concern you, or for whom numbers in your mark book fail to build a meaningful picture.

■ **Box 10.2** Marking your first work

in classrooms – there should be a keen awareness on the teacher's part of the ways in which pupil achievement can be measured.

(Weeden and Butt, 2009)

Self-evidently, assessment is not something to be left to the end of a teaching episode, and nor is it something that can be applied without considerable forethought. In other words, assessment is a process which needs planning well before the children walk through the classroom door. As we have seen in Chapter 5, planning occurs at three levels. In assessment terms we can summarise these as:

Level 1 The General Level The assessment requirements and arrangements of the external agents: mainly QCA and examinations providers. These are published and updated annually and usually supplemented with materials designed to assist teachers. For example, make sure you read the Chief Examiner's annual report for the GCSE or A-level syllabus you teach; find and read the exemplification of standards of achievement at Key Stage 3 on the National Curriculum in Action website (http://curriculum.qca.org.uk/key-stages-3–and-4/assessment/nc-in-action/index.aspx?return=/key-stages-3–and-4/assessment/index.aspx). It may be useful to think of this level as being mainly concerned with summative assessment.

Level 2 The School Level Your department plans the geography for the pupils at your school by devising a Scheme of Work. This document sketches the 'big picture' or grand plan: it shows the overall organisation of topics, the deployment of resources, and aspects of balance such as the range of places studied and at what scales. It should show the overall scheme of assessment: when more formal assessments (tests) take place, but also the identification of variety and range in assessment *opportunities*. Analysing the scheme of work for assessment opportunities is a good discipline: what different kinds of writing do the pupils have the chance to try? What other forms of expression does the geography department value? Do we ever ask pupils to produce extended writing, perhaps based on extended reading? It may be useful to think of this level as being concerned with strategic matters, giving balance to the overall run of assessment. Table 10.3 shows one highly effective way of planning with assessment in mind. The teacher has indicated his 'expectations for learning' for a range of pupils and this will aid his monitoring of their progress in learning during the lesson as well as guiding his teaching to help them to achieve these expectations.

Level 3 The Classroom Level The day-to-day marking or on-going assessment of pupils. The evidence of your planning at this level is in your lesson plan, and it concerns what you do, to (or with) whom and why. Activity 10.1 invites you to think about planning your approach to marking: but beware!

Feedback – a vital process in assessment and learning

Marking takes up vast amounts of time outside the classroom, often eating into planning time; it is not enjoyed by teachers (some teachers even despise it) – and yet is highly valued by heads of department, head teachers, Inspectors, parents and pupils. Thus there are tensions in how marking is perceived. There are preconceptions concerning the way marking is understood, particularly in terms of what it is considered to be for. Whatever you decide are the priorities in marking guiding the approach which you would adopt, remember you work as a student teacher in a team setting in which, therefore, you must follow departmental and school policy (though you are free to state your point of view and exert influence if you can).

■ Table 10.3 Planning with assessment in mind

Date 2/10/08	Period 2	Teaching Group 7A	Subject Geography	Staff CLT

Context

The second in a series of lessons on geography – introduction to the subject. In the first lesson, students explored the three areas of geography developing literacy and group work skills. In groups, students evaluated a resource to pick out key words and feedback to rest of the class. Cross-curricular links and dimensions are identified with students.

Learning Objectives

To be able to identify key features of geographical writing
To write a report explaining the different themes within geography

Learning Outcomes

All students will:
Be able to give examples for each of the three areas of geography. They will draw on learning from lesson 1. They will know at least one feature of a good piece of geographical writing

Most students will:
Be able to pick out some good features different of geographical writing from level descriptors. They are able to access the support materials to produce a structured piece of writing

Some students will:
Identify the interaction between themes in geography. They will produce a detailed account of geographical themes drawing material from both lessons.

Students targeted:
Paul
Charlie
Rebecca
Fartun

Differentiation Strategies

Plan for less able/those on SEN code of practice/EMAS students.
Targeted questioning use random selection method at the beginning of lesson.
Images to support teacher exposition.
Less able seated next to more able to access peer support.
Writing frame to help students to structure their writing.

Plan for more able/those on Gifted & Talented register

Targeted questioning using random selection method at start of lesson
More able students seated together to develop ideas during pair work

Students targeted:
Egzon
Winnie
Mohammed

Resources:

Human, physical, environmental kinesthetic cards, flooding in York worksheet, writing plan learning mat, peer assessment sheet

Table 10.3 Planning with assessment in mind (continued)

Time	Learning Activities	Teaching strategies	Learning Outcomes
5	Outline learning objectives explicitly linking to prior and future learning		
	Starter activities		
7	Students to use words from lesson one to complete Venn diagram. Select students using random selection method or 'no hands'. Target questioning. More able to be asked to identify interactions.	Oral feedback from teacher questioning using lollipop sticks. Circulate during activity to monitor and support. Prompt more able to identify interactions.	All students to identify at least one human, physical and environmental feature Most successfully Venn diagram Some identify interactions
	Main activities		
10	Students to read through Flooding in York sheet. Model text marking technique. Students to mark, colour code examples of different types of geography. They are to circle examples of connectives.	Explicit model of activity to aid student understanding Circulate to monitor student understanding	All students to identify at least one human, physical and environmental feature Most interpret the Venn diagram successfully. Some identify interactions
2	Give students opportunity to share answers with partner in order to support other students.		
7	Randomly distribute A4 sheets with HUMAN, PHYSICAL, ENVIRONMENTAL marked on. Explain that as teacher reads out text, students are to hold up the relevant sheet. All students are to police this activity.	Model activity with students. Student understanding will be monitored through success in identifying themes. Opportunity for basketball discussion. Do you agree? Why?	All students to successfully identify features of text relevant to their theme.
10	Outline the writing activity through explanation of writing frame. Share success criteria and get students to pick out key points from each level. Students to bullet point main features of target level.	Circulate during activity to get a sample of student understanding, monitor and support	All students to know at least one feature of their target level Most to identify 3 things they must to do to be successful

■ **Table 10.3** Planning with assessment in mind (continued)

Time	Learning Activities	Teaching strategies	Learning Outcomes
10	Students to complete extended writing explaining different themes in geography	Monitor and support. Focus on weaker students. Guide more able to use dictionaries to develop independent learning	All students to write a description of geography that includes the three key areas
			Most describe geography and are able to give examples to support answer
5	Peer assessment – students to swap folders and assess each other. They are to underline good features of their partners work using level criteria and write targets	Randomly select pairs to feedback on their partner's work. Other students to note down good advice	Some describe complexity of geography and interactions between different themes.
5	**Plenary activities** Two stars and a wish	Teacher to review student understanding of features of good geographical writing using 'two stars and a wish'. Mark students' work to assess understanding and skills. Learning Outcomes	

Source: Sunil Collett (Haverstock School)

We need to make some choices – and realise that we do not have to:

■   assess every piece of work a pupil does
■   assess everything possible in the piece of work we are marking (what are the priorities? what is the focus this time?)
■   assess every pupil in the class every time work is handed in.

In other words, less frequent, but higher quality, pupil-teacher interactions may have beneficial effects on learning, and the pupils' understanding of their progress.

Providing feedback about learning is an essential part of assessment for learning. Effective feedback is one of the most helpful ways of supporting pupils' learning. Sadler (1989) describes the role of feedback in helping learners to make progress and turn potential into achievement:

'If improvement in work is to take place, learners must first know the purpose of the task, then how far this has been achieved and finally be given help to know how to close any gap there is between their current attainment and where they want to be.'

Marking and written comments are the most common way in which we have a dialogue with pupils and provide feedback. However, comments are often unhelpful or not used by pupils. A challenge for you is therefore to develop strategies that make comments more effective in developing pupils' learning and find ways of engaging them in dialogue about their learning (Weeden, 2005). Checking the completion of work or transfer of information is not going to bring about significant gains in learning for pupils. Feedback on tasks that are more challenging, requiring reasoning rather than simple recall, provide more evidence about learning. Such tasks often involve more extended writing.

Paul Weeden (2005) provides a helpful range of suggestions about ways of providing effective feedback comments. These include examples of prompts that can support students in making immediate improvements:

■   Reminder prompts – '*Say more about . . .*'
■   Scaffold prompts – '*Can you explain why . . . ?*' (questions)
■   '*Describe why . . .*' (directive)
■   Example prompt – '*Choose one of these statements or create your own.*'

Comments that prompt immediate action are better than those that refer to the 'next time' because they require pupils to think about their work and learning immediately. Questions encourage the learner to initiate improvement. This can help to ensure that the time you spend marking has consequences for pupils' learning:

At present, a teacher will typically spend more time marking a student's work than the student will spend following it up – which suggests that the teacher's work is less than valuable.

(Wiliam, 2002)

Black (2004) reminds us that concentrating solely on comments represents a decisive shift in the character of feedback – away from competitive and summative judgements towards supporting the process of learning. His fundamental point is that it is wrong to assume that the need to motivate pupils is best served by offering rewards through marks and grades. If pupils see learning as a competition, there will be losers as well as winners and those with a track record as losers will have little motivation to improve. Furthermore, research by Butler (1988) showed that learners who were only given comments see this as helping them to improve (task-involvement) whereas those given feedback as marks are more likely to see this as a way of comparing themselves with others (ego-involvement). Research by Carol Dweck (2000) has shown that the latter damages the self-esteem of low attainers while high attainers become reluctant to take risks as their 'ego-orientation' leads to a fear of failure.

So the security for teachers is in their planning. It can be decided at the beginning of the year how frequently pupils will receive in-depth feedback which may involve face-to-face contact for some minutes (three or four pupils a week?). The focus for the rolling programme of ongoing assessments is also decided and identified on the scheme of work. Lessons plans can then specify both focuses and individuals. It is unlikely that such planning translates into action without a hitch; in fact, the actual process is likely to be messy, and, as you get to know your pupils better, it will become obvious that some require more attention than others. The best-laid plans are adaptable.

Your experiment may, or may not, have worked smoothly. There are plenty of reasons why it should have been a little rough, especially if the pupils have not been used to working in such a way: it requires practice, self-confidence and trust, all attributes worth working for. Pupils may at first demand that the teacher 'ratifies' (or corrects) the peer marking. If so, there exists a splendid opportunity to get them to engage constructively and individually with their work, and to redraft it in the light of their feedback. You can then mark the redraft – their 'best shot'. It should be observed that the teacher's marks in any case may have to be added, if the marks (grades) require a sufficient level of reliability (see Table 10.1) for the purpose of making high stakes summative judgements. However, even in this case, the value of the peer-group marking should be plain to see:

- ■ pupils receive rapid feedback
- ■ pupils learn, through doing, the meaning of attainment according to the assessment criteria
- ■ the teacher is 'released' during the period when pupils are marking to focus on his or her own priorities (SEN; behaviour of some individuals, etc.)
- ■ assessment is focused and the teacher has to be clear in expressing this to the pupils
- ■ assessment is being used to improve performance.

Finally, the process of peer assessment takes time, including class time, especially in the early stages. This virtually precludes any possibility of it being *the* method of assessment, but it has to be used regularly for pupils to learn the skills. Parents may need convincing that it is worthwhile. It is therefore easy to find reasons for not introducing ways of working with pupils which can make their learning more effective. At the very least, you should be encouraged to implement some of the general messages from this discussion – about focus, targeting effort and so on.

But the experiment is worth trying and adapting for your own purposes: if you devote more *planning time* to assessment, and pupils spend more *lesson time* thinking and talking about assessment, it is at least a tangible and clear signal *that pupils' work is being valued.*

Assessment involves appropriate recording and reporting systems

Commenting on her marking, a teacher wrote that little of her dissatisfaction with marking:

> could have been deduced from my 'mark book', a large buff coloured commercially printed creation, containing hundreds of pink lines dividing large pages into thousands of little boxes, into which I carefully inserted the codes, grades and symbols derived from the rather cursory assessment process. At a glance everything appeared in order: there was something in every box, but what did it all mean? Not much actually.

> (Sutton, 1995:65)

The problem for her was that the records seem to have taken a life of their own – rather like the columns of figures which occupied the red-faced, fat man (an accountant) in St Exupéry's *The Little Prince,* (1947), who was always too busy with adding up neat columns of figures (his 'important matters of consequence') to talk to the little boy. Sutton's records were not part of a wider process with a distinct role to play. So, when she asks, 'What impact did this relentless effort have on my teaching or the pupils' learning?' she answers, honestly: 'Too hard to judge, and it never occurred to me to try.' (Sutton, 1995).

Our response to the familiar conundrum of how to handle recording both effectively and efficiently (i.e. in a manageable way) is a familiar one: the system we adopt should be determined by *its purpose* (i.e. by the information it needs to record) and not the other way around. What information do we need, for whom and for what purpose?

A useful way to think about the elements of a recording system is that shown in Figure 10.3. Records are not seen as a collection of discrete or finite assessments but as a profile of interim judgements that provide a basis for making composite, multifaceted or 'synoptic' assessments. The distinction being made here is similar to the distinction made between formative and summative assessment: the interim judgements are part of the formative process involving lots of interaction between the teacher and pupils, whilst the teacher's growing knowledge of pupils can, at intervals, be summated to provide a rounded, overall judgement (or synopsis) of each one.

Such assessments are required for a variety of purposes including writing reports and records of achievement, parents' evenings and case conferences. To have a rich knowledge of pupils based upon sources ranging from examination scripts to classroom observations, enables teachers to use their information flexibly, tailoring it for the particular purpose. It is for this reason that the central component of Box 10.4, 'making the assessment' is couched in tentative terms. All assessments are informed (by your records) but also contingent – not only in the light of further information which may force a change of view, but also in terms of the audience: other teachers, the Head, parents, the pupil each require different kinds of assessment information which your records, ideally, should enable you to supply. Note that *your* records (of what we have called interim judgements) should be serving your purposes.

The reminder that Figure 10.3 provides, therefore, that our assessments of pupils are always developing, serves to highlight once more that assessment is perhaps best conceptualised as an art form rather than a mechanical or primarily technical activity. For this reason also, it is worth emphasising that one further 'record' teachers have access to is the pupils' work itself. There is probably no more powerful and useful 'record' of achievement to pass on to the next teacher than the pupils' exercise books.

The obvious reason why we do *not* simply hoard pupils' work as the record on which to base assessment is the sheer inefficiency that this implies: we need summaries and interim judgements and we need to be able to avoid having to go back constantly to the 'raw data'. On the other hand, if teachers can develop ways to ground assessments in real work – the outcome of pupils' endeavours to get to grips with the learning we give them – then how much more useful and informative their assessments become. Such thinking is the origin, at least in part, of the notion of departmental or standards portfolios which are described in the following section.

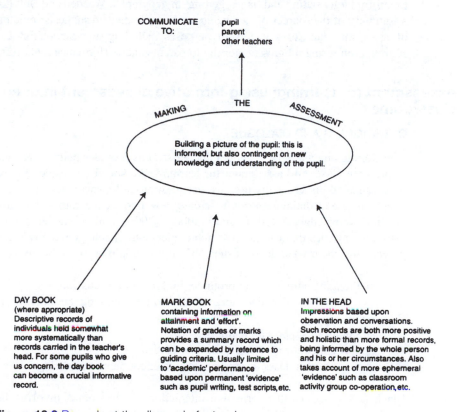

■ **Figure 10.3** Records at the disposal of a teacher

Using assessment data

Although many geography departments now have relevant data, they are used too rarely to plan schemes of work or sequences of lessons.

(OFSTED, 2008: 22)

You also need to be aware of the wealth of national, local and internal data that is available to schools and individual subject areas like geography, providing data on pupils' performance. This data is generated from external examinations, statutory end-of-key stage assessments and a range of school-based assessments. Your school mentors and senior staff responsible for assessment can help you to understand what this data shows you about the achievements and potential of the pupils in the classes you teach, as well as explaining the bigger picture for the subject and the school. Value-added data showing the progress made by pupils over a key stage is becoming increasingly important in evaluating the performance of schools and subjects in these schools. The standards for Qualified Teacher Status require you to demonstrate an understanding of how assessment data can be used to inform teaching and how to monitor and assess pupils' progress. Linda Thompson (2006) provides a very helpful overview of how assessment data can be used to inform target setting and 'target getting' in geography. Weeden and Butt (2009) provide a summary of the sources of data being used in schools and suggests some practical ways of using this data for a variety of purposes including assessment for learning, target setting, monitoring progress, reporting to parents and performance management.

Assessment *for* learning: using formative assessment in geography classrooms

QUESTIONING AND DIALOGUE

Questioning and dialogue in geography classrooms provides many opportunities for you to promote successful assessment for learning. We spend a considerable part of lesson time engaged in class discussions or question-and-answer sessions. However, this questioning and dialogue needs to create new knowledge rather than just rehearsing existing knowledge. Weeden and Lambert (2006) outline the essential features of learning activities that can provide rich evidence to enable geography teachers to make judgements about what the next steps in learning might be and how they can be made:

- challenging activities that promote thinking and discussion
- rich questions that encourage higher order thinking and the creation of new knowledge
- strategies to support all learners
- opportunities for peer discussion about ideas
- group or whole-class discussions which encourage open dialogue.

Black (2004) argues that formative interaction in classrooms involves far more than having good questions. He warns of the dangers of 'recitation' styles of questioning:

> What matters is both the question and the way in which the teacher handles the responses which it elicits. If a question is asked, but students given little time to think, with the inevitable one-word responses rewarded if correct or brushed aside if wrong, then there is no formative dialogue as the teacher continues along his/her predetermined path.

Since the research and development work on formative assessment entered the public domain (Black and Wiliam, 1998; Black *et al*, 2002), the ideas and practices advocated have been promoted widely and used in National Strategies at both primary and secondary level. However, Paul Black and Dylan Wiliam have raised concerns in recent years that practical implementation has often been based on limited understanding and superficial adoption of these ideas and strategies. They argue that 'doing assessment for learning' may fail to implement the crucial features of formative assessment if teachers are not supported by sustained commitment over several years (Black, 2004). Their research has shown that it takes at least two years before changes become embedded in teachers' classroom practices enabling pupils to become more confident and effective learners. So the message is clear, it will take longer than your initial training to feel confident in the application of these practices, but in the longer term, the benefits for pupils' learning will be significant.

Clarifying and sharing learning intentions and criteria

Low achievement often results from pupils failing to understand what is required of them (Black and Wiliam, 1998). This is not about posting the learning objective on the board at the start of a lesson. It means clarifying and sharing learning intentions that focus on what pupils will learn rather than what they will do in a lesson. These learning intentions should be measurable, achievable and realistic. The criteria for success should always be transparent to pupils and in language they can understand. Sharing examples of work completed by previous year's pupils can prompt discussion about quality; what's good about the good ones and what's lacking and needing improvement in the weaker ones?

A range of strategies can then be used to discover what pupils have actually learned. Perhaps select one pupil to summarise what the class has learned during the lesson or issue 'Exit tickets' on which pupils write an answser to a question posed towards the end of the lesson. These can then be used to review progress and prepare for the next lesson. A game of class football, basketball or tennis can add a fun element where pupils have to come up with questions about what has been learned in the lesson to be answered by pupils in the other half of the class. Alternatively, one pupil can state an idea or outcome from the lesson and pass a ball to another pupil who has to come up with a different idea, continuing until you feel all the main points have been covered.

Using peer- and self-assessment

Sadler (1989) argues that self-assessment is essential to learning because pupils can only achieve a learning goal if they understand that goal and can assess what they need to do to reach it. Helping pupils to develop peer- and self-assessment skills is one of the most challenging aspects of assessment for learning. Pupils often lack the understanding and skills to assess work and progress in learning against criteria for success and learning intentions. It also takes time to develop their skills in communicating their judgements about work and progress. Giving and receiving feedback are important skills in peer assessment. Peer work where pupils learn by trying to teach others and by being assessed by their peers will help them to develop these skills. A fear for some teachers is that one pupil's misunderstanding could be transferred to another, but choosing groups carefully and monitoring discussions can help to alleviate this problem.

Weeden and Lambert (2006: 18–19) suggest starting in a small way and then evolving pupils' practice gradually perhaps by getting them to exchange books once a week and check for specific items such as key words. This can be progressed to getting them to write a comment about at least one good point made and if possible, one thing to consider to improve in the future. Research shows that low achievers have most to gain from these approaches because repeated failure and a lack of clarity about what can be done to improve have been features of their learning.

WORKING WITH LEVEL DESCRIPTIONS

They (*Level Descriptions*) were designed to be used as 'best fit' descriptions to come to an overall judgement, drawing together evidence of what pupils know, understand and can do in relation to the taught curriculum, and not to require the assemblage of detailed evidence to prove every aspect has been attained. They provide general course-specific outcomes for the whole of KS3 (long-term).

(QCA, 2007)

'Teacher Assessment' (TA) is a term that became established after the introduction of the National Curriculum to distinguish externally set and marked, standardised tasks and tests from the judgements that teachers make of pupils. In geography, TA is the only source of assessment information on pupils; there are no plans to introduce geography tests at the end of KS3 though there are tests in the core subjects of English, mathematics and science. Level descriptions were designed to be used for these summative purposes, yet they are often used in a number of ways that were not intended, including as assessment objectives for homework and tests.

Officially, TA is the process by which summative assessments of pupils should be made in geography. It involves the principles and practices discussed in the previous section: that is, the range of ongoing assessments – what we called interim judgements – which, in combination, form the 'synoptic' view of a pupil's achievements and progress. The process is guided by a series of level descriptions (see http://curriculum.qca.org.uk/key-stages-3–and-4/subjects/geography/attainmenttarget/index.aspx?return=/key-stages-3–and-4/subjects/geography/) which purport to show progress through the learning of geography. Each level description is comprised of three parts (see Box 10.3):

■ The first sentence makes reference to the *geographical context* (what has been studied and the range of content and experience)
■ Reference to *key concepts* in geography and the intellectual skills pupils will apply in demonstrating understanding of these concepts
■ Reference to geographical enquiry and skills.

What these level descriptions attempt to do is establish a set of national criteria to help raise the dependability and public credibility of TA. After the National Curriculum order itself (containing the Programme of Study and the level descriptions for geography), the exemplification of standards in geography on QCA's National Curriculum Online web site (http://curriculum.qca.org.uk/key-stages-3–and-4/assessment/nc-in-action/) is a crucial source of guidance. It does this by:

■ highlighting 'key features of expectation and progression in the geography order'
■ showing 'the use of the level descriptions in coming to a judgement about... overall performance at the end of the key stage' (this is similar to the role of the standards portfolio which we discuss below)
■ providing examples of pupils' work from across the achievement range, together with a short introduction about each pupil and the context in which the work was done
■ providing detailed analysis of each piece of work, identifying significant aspects of performance and the reasoning behind overall judgements.

Geographical context
Concepts in geography and intellectual skills
Geographical enquiry and skills

Pupils use their knowledge and understanding of the geography of the UK and the wider world to describe and begin to analyse physical and human characteristics of places in a range of locations, contexts and scales. They describe and explain physical and human processes and recognise that these processes interact to produce the distinctive characteristics of places. They demonstrate understanding of the ways in which physical and human processes lead to diversity and change in places. They identify geographical patterns at a range of scales. They recognise how conflicting demands on the environment may arise and describe and compare sustainable and other approaches to managing environments. They appreciate that different values and attitudes, including their own, result in different approaches to environmental interaction and change. Drawing on their knowledge and understanding, they suggest relevant geographical questions and issues and appropriate sequences of investigation. They select a range of skills and sources of evidence and use them effectively in their investigations. They identify potential bias in sources. They present their findings in a coherent way using appropriate methods and vocabulary and reach conclusions that are consistent with the evidence.

■ **Box 10.3** The structure of a level description – Level 6
Source: adapted from QCA, 2008 and Rawling, 2007: 49

Box 10.4 provides a glimpse of the kind of 'common text' this exemplification contains in terms of how to approach pupils' work. As we shall see later in this chapter, the document is a useful starting point for each departmental team of geography teachers to establish their own version – what we go on to call 'standards portfolios'.

In principle, we can see how the level descriptions can be used to come to annual, or end of key stage, judgements about each pupil we teach. But, in terms of 'educational assessment' (i.e. that with a formative purpose), we cannot leave the process of 'teacher assessment' here. Using assessment educationally means that we want the process to feed-forward and help raise future levels of achievement. In other words, we need to find a way of using formatively a system devised for summative purposes. This is not easy because:

> Each level description is a cluster of interrelated elements, and, while boundaries between successive levels are not sharply defined, the image of progression which the levels present is more like a series of steps than gently sloping inclines.
>
> (Bennetts, 1995: 77)

This is because the level descriptions were designed for summative assessment purposes: each level description is a generalised pen picture of the type of overall attainment which qualifies for a particular level at the end of the key stage (Bennetts, 2005; Weeden and Butt, 2009).

Apart from being too 'generalised' and artificially 'stepped' in order to show grade differences, the level descriptions are not written in pupil-friendly language. It is, therefore, truly difficult to see how they could be used to support ongoing assessment with pupils. Although there are departments which claim to use 'level marking' successfully, we feel this is inappropriate – not least because an individual piece of work is unlikely to yield the range of information required to allow a generalised or 'synoptic' level judgement to be made confidently. Perhaps more useful in helping pupils to understand on a day-to-day basis what progress in geography looks like is for teachers to use a prompt such as shown in Box 10.5. Such a series of prompts breaks down aspects of progress and might help teachers formulate specific feedback to specific pupils.

But can the level descriptions be used formatively? For a fuller account of this see Rawling (2007) and Weeden and Butt (2009), Butt *et al.* (1995) and Lambert (1997a). In short, the answer to this question is 'indirectly': the level descriptions can help teachers as a group formulate in relation to pupils' work, ideas and arguments about standards.

Activity 10.2 **Understanding progression in aspects of achievement**

In order to acquaint yourself more thoroughly with the potential of using level descriptions in the manner suggested here, it repays the effort to analyse the aspects of performance identified by the levels.

Read the level descriptions in the Attainment target for geography (http://curriculum.qca.org.uk/key-stages-3–and-4/subjects/geography/attainment-target/). Complete a matrix along the lines of that suggested in Table 10.4. Table 10.5 shows a completed matrix to show pupils' ability to undertake enquiry and to use skills.

Figure 10.4 shows a teaching model drawn from the point of view of emphasising the role of assessment and recording. The diagram shows that the level descriptions are not to be taken as self-evident; as we have seen in our earlier discussion of criteria, the complex, multifaceted descriptions need to be 'brought alive' because they cannot, on their own, define standards. They can be used summatively (the purpose for which they were designed) but the resulting assessments can only be considered dependable if teachers' norms and expectations that lurk behind the criteria are shared among colleagues. So-called 'moderation' meetings therefore must take place where pupils' work is compared and argued about in order to come to a shared understanding of how to value it – how to judge it – in relation to level descriptions. Figure 10.5 shows an account of such a moderation meeting, based on the Activity 10.3, written by a student teacher participant.

New formulations of standards help teachers adjust their 'norms' and expectations. This process can feed-forward to planning future teaching and help teachers articulate to pupils their intentions and why they are doing what they are doing. For example, and arising directly out of a discussion of standards portfolios (see Box 10.5 on page 398), consideration of questions such as the following could have a dramatic effect on the attainment level of some pupils:

Summary and judgement about Julia's performance

In making a decision about Julia's performance, her teacher considered levels 5, 6 and 7. Level 6 was judged to be the 'best fit'.

The small amount of work presented here covers several aspects of geography, although environmental issues are not well represented. However, the piece of work on acid rain in the SCAA exemplification booklet (pages 28 and 29) was also completed by Julia and may be considered alongside this portfolio. Her teacher knows far more about Julia's work than can be included here; in particular she has evidence of Julia's work on other topics and knows that she is a capable participant in group activities and fieldwork.

The work presented shows Julia working at local, regional and national scales and, in particular, Should We Stay or Go and Household Spending reveal that she is capable of making connections across scales (village to larger town: village to nation).

In Should We Stay or Go, Julia has developed ideas from the textbook to draw a diagram which effectively summarises the reasons for rural-urban migration. In this she demonstrates characteristics of level 6 by describing how processes operating at different scales (family, village, town) create geographical patterns and contribute to change in places.

Julia's understanding of physical processes and the way in which they affect patterns and places is revealed in the Lynmouth Floods exercise in an interesting way. By using the views and opinions of local residents alongside the more factual explanation in the newspaper article, Julia shows that she has moved beyond making a simple link between cause and consequence in physical geography (level 5), and appreciates that different aspects of environmental change have different effects on people and places (level 6). The exercise did not give her opportunity to extend the work in this direction.

The work on Household Spending is competent. Julia has used the required technique (pie charts) accurately (characteristic of level 5) and has drawn conclusions consistent with the evidence. The question did not allow a choice of technique. Although her answer displays some confusion between absolute amounts and proportions, nevertheless the explanations are sound (emphasis on 'survival' in India; wider range of consumption in UK) and demonstrate understanding of the link between ways of life and patterns of spending (typical of level 6).

Overall these pieces of work reveal that Julia is competent in applying skills and understanding in structured enquiry work (typical of level 6) and, when given the opportunity, she is capable of some degree of independence in identifying questions and planning her own investigations (e.g. the structure of the newspaper article). Her teacher realises that she may be ready for greater challenge in this respect.

Although demonstrating the ability to explain human and physical processes and to make links between the features and character of places, Julia is not yet able to produce work with the depth of analysis and appreciation of interactions which would suggest performance at level 7. There has not been opportunity for Julia to show consideration of the global scale. On balance, **her teacher judges level 6 to be the best description of Julia's performance.**

■ **Box 10.4** A 'best-fit judgement' of a student's work using geography level descriptions
    Note: There is not enough space here to present Julia's work, but this figure shows the methodology of making the assessment

Source: Rawling and Westaway, 1996: 123–9

> ■ Increasing precision and sophistication in the vocabulary, language and grammar of geography
> ■ Increasing breadth and complexity of understanding at a range of scales
> ■ Increasing use of generalised knowledge, abstract ideas and linkage
> ■ More mature understanding of issues, values and attitudes
> ■ Greater independence in using the enquiry process and geographical skills (use of reasoning, explanations, linkages and judgements).

■ **Box 10.5** Aspects of progression in geography
Source: Bennetts, 2005

■ Do I allow pupils the freedom to pose questions for investigation? Unless I do, I may be placing a ceiling on their performance (at least in the terms described by the National Curriculum level descriptions).

■ Do I let pupils select how they will present information?

■ Do I give pupils opportunities to develop arguments and ideas? For pupils to perform convincingly at Level 7, they need to be able to show this.

■ **Table 10.4** A grid for analysing progression in levels 3–7

	Place and space	Scale	Interdependence	Physical and human processes	Environmental interaction and sustainable development	Cultural understanding and diversity
Level 3						
Level 4						
Level 5						
Level 6						
Level 7						

■ **Table 10.5** Analysing progression in geographical skills

	Questions for enquiry	Using skills	Communicating findings
Level 3	They use skills and sources of evidence to respond to a range of geographical questions.		
Level 4	Pupils draw on their knowledge and understanding to suggest suitable geographical questions for study.	The use a range of geographical skills and evidence to investigate places and themes.	They communicate their findings using appropriate vocabulary.
Level 5	Pupils identify relevant geographical questions.	Drawing on their knowledge and understanding, they select and use appropriate skills and evidence to help them investigate places and themes.	They reach plausible conclusions and present their findings both graphically and in writing.
Level 6	Drawing on their knowledge and understanding, pupils identify relevant geographical questions and suggest appropriate sequences of investigation.	They select and make effective use of a wide range of skills and evidence in carrying out investigations.	They present conclusions that are consistent with the evidence.
Level 7	With growing independence, pupils draw on their knowledge and understanding to identify geographical questions.	With growing independence, pupils establish a sequence of investigation, and select and use accurately a wide range of skills and evidence.	They are beginning to reach substantiated conclusions.

Activity 10.3 **Assembling and moderating 'standards portfolios' (groups)**

This activity should preferably be undertaken by a group of student teachers with their school tutors. You will need to refer to Boxes 10.6, 10.7 and 10.8 and draw upon the understanding of progress in learning in geography you developed from Activity 10.2.

1 Using pupils' work from the KS3 classes you teach, your aim is to create three portfolios of work which you believe exemplifies standards between two levels:

■ Level 3 – 5
■ Level 5 – 7
■ Level 7 – exceptional performance

(Note: if you tackle the job of assigning work to these levels, you will acquire a knowledge and understanding of the National Curriculum Levels and progression in learning in geography. Think about it.)

Analyse the level descriptions by identifying key words and phrases in the description. Think about what this will look like in pupils' work and learning. What evidence will you look for (from written and other sources)?

2 You need to consider the following practical points:

■ How is a portfolio presented? (a ring binder is suitable)
■ Do you select real work or photocopies of it for inclusion in the portfolio?
■ How much work needs to be selected – how voluminous is a portfolio?
■ What is a 'piece of work'? What kinds of work can a portfolio not show?
■ How many different pupils should be used?

3 There are further technical points to consider:

■ How do you show the context of the work? When it was done, what help was given, what resources were available (etc.) – because this affects the assessment of it (see Figure 10.5 and Box 10.6).
■ How do you show how the work was assessed? How you justify your valuation of it perhaps with annotation (see Box 10.7)?

4 The moderation meeting

■ Ideally you have representatives, with 'standards portfolios' for levels 3–5, 5–7 and 7–exceptional performance, from three or four schools.
■ Sit around a table and systematically read each others' – that is, the pupils' work, the context sheets and the annotations.
■ Then, discuss, argue and defend the standards applied by each of you in the work you have selected and the way you have interpreted (and annotated) it.
■ Finally, time permitting, the group may agree on a joint, or pooled, selection which should aim to select from the portfolios the minimum number of pieces of work which the group can agree exemplifies the level concerned.

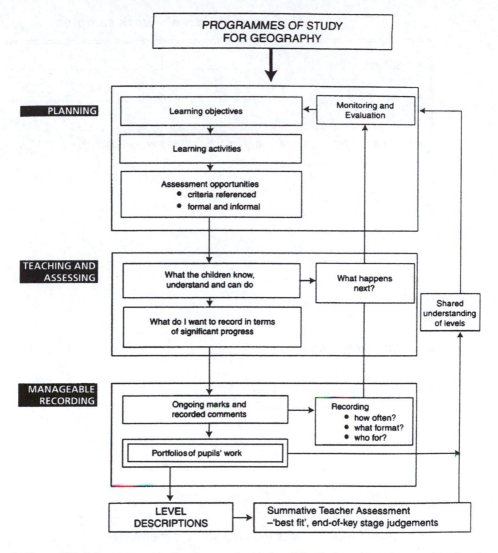

■ **Figure 10.4** Assessment in the Geography National Curriculum. Note the crucial role of the standard portfolios

Source: Butt, Lambert and Telfer (eds), 1995: 11

LEARNING FROM RESEARCH

This chapter has concentrated mainly on assessment that takes place within the geography classroom. This is not to undervalue external assessment such as GCSE and AS/A2 examinations: indeed you need to get to know the syllabuses, or 'subject specifications', well and you need to learn how best to prepare pupils for the examinations. The best way that practising teachers have of learning the expectations of the examination is to become an assistant examiner themselves – a goal for the future maybe?

But we also have consistently made the point in this chapter that external examinations, because they are summative, have little power to help pupils learn. True

Annotation of children's work samples

- Subject ....Date ....

- Topic/Unit ....PoS ref: ....

- Context (description of learning activity; degree of support)

- Who chose this piece of work? ....

- What does this piece show?
  (why has it been selected?)

- What (if anything) does this piece fail to demonstrate?

- Next steps:

■ **Figure 10.5** Context sheet
Source: adapted from Sutton, 1995: 94

The Standards Portfolio Exercise

A Report

The purpose of the 'standards portfolios' was to provide an insight into the level descriptions and how best to use them in order to analyse pupil performance, progression and attainment. Three portfolios, for levels 3-5, 5-7 and 7-exceptional performance, were created using a variety of work collected from partnership schools across London.

This is what we found and learned from undertaking this exercise.

■ The contents of portfolios should include a variety of work and tasks in an attempt to reflect the range of skills, knowledge and understanding described within each level. For example, Level 5 requires a pupil to demonstrate understanding of the sequence of investigation, to select and use appropriate skills, reach plausible conclusions, describe geographical processes and begin to offer explanations of geographical patterns and the way people affect the environment. A range of work requiring different approaches and skills is needed to illustrate these skills.

■ Taking into account the aforementioned characteristics, no one piece of work could display all of them. A pupil's piece of work can be examined for a particular skill or attribute, but it cannot be given a Level.

■ In order to produce reliable and useful portfolios (for both teacher and pupil) each piece of work needs to be annotated with references to characteristics of a particular level so that the reader can see how a piece of work may be attributed to a particular level.

■ Each selected piece of portfolio work needs to be described on a context sheet to provide background information about the piece and thus give a clearer indication of what the pupil was trying to achieve. Such information could include a description of the learning activity, whether it was a class/homework, etc., or how much support/information a pupil was given.

■ Standards portfolios are extremely useful as they remind people 'how' to analyse and interpret pupils' work – what was the pupil aiming to achieve?

A number of issues arose during the exercise:

■ Do tasks have a 'level ceiling'? e.g. can pupils select how they present information?

■ A piece of work may show different levels within it – what level, therefore, does it best illustrate? (This represents the skill of applying the 'best fit' technique.)

■ Finding agreement on a level was not easy but the arguing over its content is useful as it encourages a greater understanding of the Levels descriptions.

■ How do we present a task to pupils? Guidelines to help pupils achieve better and this sharing of knowledge is no longer considered as 'cheating'. If pupils know the criteria, and how levels are awarded, they can work towards a target level and achieve it.

■ Portfolios are extremely useful to parents, inspectors and colleagues as they provide a coherent way of explaining and identifying pupils' work at a particular level.

■ Portfolios can ensure equality of marking across a department as they highlight agreed marking criteria as a result of the moderating process.

■ Standards portfolios can have a major impact on day-to-day planning because they can be used as a tool when planning schemes of work. It has also been argued that Levels can be used to stress overall achievement rather than isolated goals.

■ **Box 10.6** The portfolio experiment

Source: Institute of Education, University of London

- A 'piece of work' is a completed task of some description; it may be a single homework or a more lengthy task representing several lessons' work.
- Work from three or four pupils may suffice; but it is the work, not the pupils, that the portfolio exhibits.
- Once pieces have been put into a portfolio, they are non-returnable to the pupils; photocopying can get over this problem – each portfolio must not become too voluminous, so the copying should not be prohibitive. To get pupils to complete a 'best draft' is also a possibility.
- The portfolio is meant to be indicative, not a document of 'proof'. It needs to be digestible and its contents easily accessed. It must not become too large therefore and experience indicates that about six to eight 'pieces of work' are appropriate.
- When selected, each piece of work needs detailed (but not copious) annotation in clear handwriting (green or red pen – whichever colour you choose, use it consistently) focused on *what the work shows* and *what it fails to show* in terms of elements of the level description.
- Each piece of work needs a completed context sheet (Figure 10.5). This helps other teachers 'read' the work and understand your assessment of it; increasing such transferability ultimately contributes to increasing dependability of assessments.

■ **Box 10.7** Compiling a standards portfolio: a checklist of key points

they can motivate pupils to some extent but fundamentally they are not part of learning. From this perspective it is amazing how external examinations have become reified in some quarters by the use of league tables, as if they were the be all and end all of education.

In an effort to redress the balance and raise the status of internal assessment, two researchers (Black and Wiliam, 1998a), both of them heavily involved in the initial design (Black) and the implementation (Wiliam) of National Curriculum assessment, undertook an exhaustive review of research into formative assessment over the last decade. Their quest was to answer the question: is there evidence that improving formative assessment raises standards? Their conclusion was that 'innovations including strengthening the practice of formative assessment produce significant, and often substantial, learning gains' (Black and Wiliam, 1998b: 2). Furthermore, the evidence they found showed that formative assessment helps the (so-called) low attainers more than the rest.

Thus, according to evidence from the several hundred research reports studied from around the world, the effect of good formative assessment is that attainment is raised overall and the spread of attainment is reduced. This suggests that any 'tail' of low achievement in a school (or whole-education system) is a portent of wasted talent, and produces young people who come to believe that they are 'no good' and unable to learn. These are bold claims. A lot hinges on exactly what the research counts as formative assessment. Clearly, what counts is not easy to achieve as:

- it must involve feedback which exhibits consequential validity
- validity is judged on whether the assessment evidence is used to influence teaching decisions

> ■ classroom practice changes significantly as a result of introducing effective feedback – which usually has to involve pupils directly; for example, in self-assessment.

Research also shows the hazards lying in wait to neutralise attempts to introduce innovative formative assessment, such as:

- ■ too much generous – but unfocused – praise is unhelpful to pupils
- ■ too many tests often encourage surface learning as opposed to deep learning (e.g. the 'facts' and not the processes)
- ■ classrooms are still too often like 'black boxes' – we do not share practice with colleagues, nor challenge each other about 'best practice'
- ■ quantity and presentation tend to be over-emphasised in marking
- ■ comparison of marks and grades tends to be over-emphasised, diverting focus away from self-improvement
- ■ feedback tends to be 'social and managerial' rather than about specific learning functions of pupils
- ■ although teachers can predict external examination results accurately, this shows only that they have a good understanding of the examination – not necessarily the individual learning needs of the pupils
- ■ the bureaucratic imperative (to collect a complete set of marks) can outweigh the educational (to analyse pupils' learning needs).

This is a long – but very useful – list. It forms the basis for identifying evaluation criteria for you to use in order to analyse your own practice and the practice you observe in your department.

Black and Wiliam's (1998) research review also offers signposts for the improvement of formative assessment practice. Teachers, the research suggests, should adopt the following goals:

- ■ use feedback that identifies particular qualities about the pupils' work and which offers precise advice for improvement. Comparisons with other pupils are best avoided
- ■ encourage a 'culture of success' in which pupils take risks and are not afraid of making mistakes. This requires that the comfortable but unchallenging 'contract of contentment' which often exists between pupils and teachers (lots of 'busy work' like colouring in the sea) needs renegotiating
- ■ begin to train pupils in self-assessment so that they come to understand for themselves the criteria for judging success in geography and gain a sense of longer term learning goals (see Activity 10.2, page 396)
- ■ work to break down the common pattern of passive learning and make the learning goals explicit (especially the 'big picture' – how each lesson relates to the longer term goals).

Try to establish the following pupil mentality:

- ■ what are the desired goals? – what's my present position? – how can I close the gap?
- ■ build opportunities into lessons for pupils to express their understanding orally. This enables the teacher to build-up knowledge of the learners

■ rigorously examine lesson plans to ensure that teaching strategies can be justified in terms of the learning aims they serve

■ in particular, critically examine questioning: do I only use 'closed' questions? do I fall into the trap of simply getting pupils to guess the right answer, rather than to think? how long can I tolerate silence? do I always fill the silence and answer my own questions? do I depend too much on only a few pupils to answer my questions? do I fall into the trap of dumbing down my questions to ensure a correct response?

■ ensure that tests and homeworks are stimulating in their own right, and relevant to the learning aims

■ go for frequent short tests, rather than occasional big ones. But avoid the trap of thinking that frequent assessment is truly formative – it is often nothing more than 'serial summative'!

Quality Criteria for teacher assessment (TA)

Curriculum fidelity: a similar idea to 'validity' (see Figure 9.2), but easier to specify as it relates strictly to the statutory National Curriculum (e.g. have the teaching and assessment programmes included opportunities for pupils to engage in active and independent enquiry?).

Comparability: a similar, though less rigid, idea to 'reliability' (see Figure 9.2) achieved through:

■ consistency of approach by teachers;
■ common understanding of assessment criteria.

Dependability and Public Credibility: terms which combine notions of validity and reliability (and recognises their relationship which is one of tension). Dependable assessment is that which can demonstrate that steps have been taken to:

■ maximise curriculum fidelity;
■ optimise comparability.

Assessment that is dependable gains public credibility. It can be maximised by training, using exemplars, moderation. Assembling *standards portfolios* can be instrumental.

Context description: authentic assessment, having maximum curriculum fidelity, is unlikely to yield scores which are generalisable. On the other hand, it is possible to judge the 'transferability' of an assessment if we have a detailed description of the context in which it took place. Those undertaking educational assessment should be prepared to offer such description.

Equity: this reflects the aim of good assessment to elicit quality performance from all pupils. This is achieved by providing multiple opportunities and various contexts and circumstances in which pupils can show what they can do.

■ **Box 10.8** An educational framework for teacher assessment
Source: adapted from Gipps, 1994

For many teachers, introducing formative assessment requires a huge leap of faith. Our advice is to keep ambitious aims but avoid trying to build Rome in a single day. You could start with three simple questions:

■ what do I know about the pupils I teach as learners?
■ is my classroom (and lesson plan) organised in such a way that my devotion to teacher-pupil interaction, the growth of pupils' confidence and my learning about them exploited to the maximum?
■ in what way do I gradually have to change my pupils' attitudes in order to achieve valid formative assessment?

Applying this research to geography classrooms, there are perhaps four key principles of learning which when used effectively can enable you to help pupils to make progress in their learning (Weeden and Lambert, 2006: 6–7). A *first* principle of learning is to start from where the learner is and recognise that learning occurs when pupils have opportunities to connect their personal experiences of the world around them to the subject geography and thus reconstruct their understanding. This can be achieved through classroom dialogue which is two way from pupil to teacher and teacher to pupil. If the teacher asks a question that enables pupils to identify their current thinking, these ideas can be used as a starting point for the subsequent dialogue about learning and assessment.

The *second* principle of learning is achieved when the pupils take an active part in the dialogue – when they are doing the learning. The teacher's role is to create a learning environment where pupils are prepared to give a range of responses, where either a right or wrong answer is acceptable and where pupils can be supported in clarifying inconsistencies so they can respond to challenges.

A *third* principle is that pupils must know the target they are trying to achieve. This means they need to know what a good quality answer might look like and how their work compares with this target. Having an understanding of quality criteria helps pupils understand better what they need to do to achieve the desired standard of work so they can take more responsibility for their own learning and make better judgements about whether the work does or does not meet the criteria. Peer and self-assessment are essential here, because the process of making judgements on both their own work and that of fellow pupils encourages active involvement and develops their understanding of expected standards.

Fourthly, when pupils are given opportunities to talk about geographical ideas, whether in a whole-class dialogue or in peer groups, they are learning to actively use the language of geography – the vocabulary *and* the grammar. This allows them to explore their understanding and 'scaffolds' their learning.

THE WAY FORWARD

Activity 10.4 **Developing assessment policy and practice (individuals or groups)**

1   Read the contents of Table 10.1. Compare and contrast the terminology and definitions with those on Box 10.8.
2   In practical terms, decide how your own assessment practice maximises 'curriculum fidelity' (rather like validity) and 'equity' (or fairness).
3   In practical terms, decide how the department in which you work could ensure 'comparability' and 'dependability' in assessment (together these terms are like the traditional, but rather rigid, notion of 'reliability').
4   Imagine a meeting with a number of colleagues from different schools called to help 'moderate' (or standardise) end of Key Stage 3 National Curriculum assessments. Design how you would present a Level 5 portfolio of pupils' work to maximise its 'transferability'; what would you include in your 'context description'?

As we stated in the introduction of this chapter, the principles and practice of assessment have developed considerably in recent years. There has been a consistent trajectory in these developments towards the goal of assessment being used to serve educational purposes. Without wishing to over-labour the point, this is why we spent some time earlier in this book discussing the significance of educational goals: if geography teachers are unclear about the educational goals of the subject they teach, it is unlikely that they can use assessment effectively, and avoid the traps which exist in unchallenged assumptions within the traditional, 'scientific' or psychometric model of assessment. The key questions are: What do we want pupils to achieve through learning geography? And how are we going to help them fulfill these aims? To put these questions in a modern and provocative idiom, how are we to 'grow their intelligence'?

Activity 10.4, above, is designed to help you discuss and clarify such ambitious notions. First, read this summary of what Caroline Gipps identified as the quality criteria for educational assessment, what we have 'translated' into the touchstones for effective teacher assessment (Box 10.8).

SUMMARY AND KEY POINTS

This chapter has explored the purposes of assessment, the principles and practice of both external and educational assessment. The overall message is that using useful information about pupils, acquired through the assessment of their work, can and should influence the teacher's planning of lessons and response to individual pupils. Can you show how your understanding of educational assessment has influenced your practice in these ways?

It is almost certainly the case that your level of effectiveness can be traced right back to your marking practice. If, within the necessary bounds of what can be achieved in the time you have at your disposal, your marking is analytical, focused and accompanied with precise, individualised feedback to inform the pupil of their next steps, it follows that your assessment practice is also effective and fully integrated into your curriculum planning and lesson design.

The summary of research findings (Black and Wiliam 1998), described in the previous section, should reassure you that it is worth the effort to work with your colleagues to put in place manageable and effective formative assessment practices to help pupils to make progress in their learning.

FURTHER READING

Balderstone, D. and King, S. (2004) **Preparing pupils for public examinations, Chapter 14 in Capel, S., Heilbronn, R., Leask, M. and Turner, T. (eds) '*Starting to teach in the Secondary School: A companion for the Newly Qualified Teacher'*, London: Routledge.**
This text examines the different types of assessment involved in external examinations at Key Stage 3, GCSE and GCE AS/A-level and provides practical advice about how you can prepare pupils effectively for these examinations. There are also suggestions about strategies for developing pupils' study skills.

Brooks, J. and Lucas, N. (2004) **'*The school sixth form and the growth of vocational qualifications*', Chapter 15 in Capel, S., Heilbronn, R., Leask, M. and Turner, T. (eds) '*Starting to teach in the Secondary School: A companion for the Newly Qualified Teacher'*, London: Routledge.**
This chapter provides an overview of the changes in the 14–19 curriculum and its impacts on schools. It explains the differences in teaching, learning and assessment between academic and vocational courses.

Chapman, R. and Digby, B. (2006) **'*Gotta get thru this' – GCSE examinations*, Chapter 37 in Balderstone, D. (ed.) *Secondary Geography Handbook*, Sheffield: The Geographical Association.**
This chapter explains the requirements of GCSE Geography examinations and provides practical guidance on how to prepare pupils for these examinations, including revision and specific examination skills.

Haydn, T. (2005) ***Assessment for Learning*, Unit 6.1 in Capel, S., Leask, M. and Turner, T. (eds) *Learning to Teach in the Secondary School: A companion to school experience*, Abingdon: Routledge.**
This text explains the different purposes, principles and mechanisms of assessment. The important role of assessment for learning in supporting pupils' progress is explored and tensions in assessment practice considered.

Howes, N. (2006) ***Teacher Assessment in Geography*, Chapter 34 in Balderstone, D. (ed.) *Secondary Geography Handbook*, Sheffield: The Geographical Association.**
This text explains the role of teacher assessment at Key Stage 3 in order to monitor pupils' progress and support end-of-key-stage judgements about their standards of achievement in geography. There is advice about designing teacher assessments, collecting evidence and making judgements about attainment.

Marvell, A., Holland, B. and Shuff, K. (2006) ***Geography's contribution to vocational courses*, Chapter 20 in Balderstone, D. (ed.) *Secondary Geography Handbook*, Sheffield: The Geographical Association.**
This chapter explores geography's contribution to vocational courses and provides practical advice on how to plan and assess learning in these courses. There is also advice about resources for investigations and activities.

Thompson, L. (2006) *Target setting and target getting in geography*, Chapter 33 in Balderstone, D. (ed.) *Secondary Geography Handbook*, Sheffield: The Geographical Association.

This text explains the process of target setting and its role in supporting pupils' progress in learning in Key Stages 3 and 4. The different sources of data used in schools to indicate achievement and progress are explained and the relationship between target setting and 'target getting' explored.

Warn, S. (2006) *Preparing for public examinations*, Chapter 36 in Balderstone, D. (ed.) *Secondary Geography Handbook*, Sheffield: The Geographical Association.

This chapter outlines the different levels of examining and associated expectations of pupils. There is practical guidance on how to prepare pupils effectively for GCE AS and A2 examinations including revision skills and developing specific skills required for success in these examinations.

Weeden, P. and Butt, G. (2009) *Assessing Progress in Geography at Key Stage 3*, Sheffield: The Geographical Association.

This is a practical guide to assessing the new Key Stage 3 National Curriculum. There is guidance on using assessment *for* learning effectively in geography.

Weeden, P. and Hopkin, J. (2006) *Assessment for learning in geography*, Chapter 32 in Balderstone, D. (ed.) *Secondary Geography Handbook*, Sheffield: The Geographical Association.

This chapter explores the different purposes of assessment and provides practical advice about how to use assessment for learning effectively in the geography classroom.

Weeden, P. and Lambert, D. (2006) *Geography inside the black box: Assessment for learning in the geography classroom*, Sheffield: The Geographical Association/London: nferNelson.

This text draws upon the widely acknowledged research into the power of formative assessment in supporting pupils' progress in learning. It explores the role of questioning and dialogue, effective feedback, peer and self-assessment in the geography classroom.

Youens, B. (2005) 'External Assessment and Examinations', in Capel, S., Leask, M. and Turner, T. (2005) *Learning to Teach in the Secondary School: A Companion to School Experience,* London: Routledge.

This text provides an overview of the framework for external assessment and examinations in secondary schools in England and Wales. It explores the purposes of external assessment and processes involved.

PROFESSIONAL DEVELOPMENT
The bridge to a career

Teachers have a difficult job. Faced with pressures from a variety of angles, teachers must struggle to maintain their motivation and their self-esteem. The fact that so many do is a miracle of sorts, testimony to their dedication and to their drive.

(Kincheloe and Steinberg, 1998: 1)

Even the best curriculum can't be effective without teachers who have the skills to motivate learners and the in depth knowledge to teach content in an interesting way
(QCA, 2006 www.qca.org.uk/futures)

INTRODUCTION

This book is aimed primarily at graduate student geography teachers. As we pointed out in the Introduction, the PGCE year is intensive and demanding. But it soon ends and successful 'student teachers' find themselves, perhaps a touch too soon, in the position of Newly Qualified Teachers (NQTs) – members of the teaching profession who are usually expected to take on 90% of a classroom teacher's normal timetable. A major challenge to all schools is how to maintain an appropriate response to the learning needs of such new teachers.

This chapter is written in an attempt to show new geography teachers what can be done to keep themselves professionally alive.

It needs to be said from the start that effective professional development is based on self-preservation and renewal. This needs to be understood clearly. Such are the complexities and stresses in teaching that there is sometimes a siege mentality in staffrooms whereby teachers only seem to be able to earn self respect and gratification if they push themselves, disastrously, into *self sacrifice*. This has very little to commend it. If teachers sacrifice themselves to the job, experiencing permanent tiredness and an inability to think effectively, then they are no use to the learner. Teachers need time and space away from the job during vacations, weekends and some evenings. This goes almost without saying. But what can we do as part of the job itself to help keep our teaching fresh and effective?

OBJECTIVES

By the end of this chapter, you should be able to:

■ identify ways to manage your personal and professional life
■ identify strategies and actions you can take to develop your knowledge and understanding of geography and geography classrooms
■ evaluate your progress as a teacher and explain the process of 'reflective practice'.

WHAT KIND OF GEOGRAPHY TEACHER DO I WANT TO BE?

We take it as read that most readers of this book would like to become 'good' teachers of geography. Furthermore, we also assume that readers will have their own criteria to judge 'good'. It is to be hoped that definitions of good include focus on the pupils, what they have learned and how they have responded, in addition to the teacher's performance.

There are dangers focusing only on the teacher's performance, understandable though it is to do so. For example, a teacher too concerned to keep his pupils quiet is not tempted to take risks, loosen the controls and see how far they can go. A teacher who is concerned mainly to keep on top of the paperwork is someone who might forget what and whose purpose the mark book is meant to serve in the first place.

The laying down of Professional Standards for Teaching, revised in 2007, has greatly helped teachers analyse and identify particular strengths and weaknesses. They are in some ways ambitious and form a useful code of proficiency. But can your professional development be framed entirely in terms of the official Standards?

It is to what the Standards, as laid down by the Training and Development Agency, do *not* say that we need to turn. Some teachers might argue that any attempt to define – or bureaucratise – the mysterious processes of teaching is bound to fail. We disagree. On the other hand the Standards are, unavoidably, written at a rather general level. They are strangely 'soulless'. To the enthusiastic geography teacher, they may resemble the worst kind of all-purpose guidebook, offering bland all-purpose recipes but taking the heart out of what makes the geography teacher sparkle. In making this statement, we are proposing that the geography teacher can sparkle (that is, do more than express mere competence or even proficiency), and in a different way from the history teacher, physics teacher or PE teacher.

For this reason we offer a list of additional Standards for Geography teachers (Box 11.1). Of course these have no official status. They do, however, form the basis of serious professional debate between you and colleagues, and may help identify what is special and particular about geography teaching.

My brilliant lesson

Another way of addressing the question about what kind of geography teacher you may wish to become is to examine teaching ideals. This was done with one group of student teachers by asking them each to share the planning and learning outcomes of one

---

Additional Standards for Geography PGCE Students

a)   In relation to subject knowledge, student teachers of geography will be able to:

■   articulate geography's contribution to the spiritual, moral, social and cultural development of young people

■   demonstrate geography's role in helping young people increase their understanding of the social, political, economic and environmental contexts in which they live

■   demonstrate geography's capacity to respond to the concerns of young people and engage them in informed and purposeful enquiry

■   participate actively in developing geography's contribution to education for 'citizenship' and 'sustainability'.

b)   In relation to the planning, organisation and management of teaching and learning, student teachers of geography will be able to:

■   translate their advocacy of geography in education (see (a) above) into appropriate and effective classroom content and strategy

■   appreciate and use critically a wide range of 'other learning resources' including GIS, newspapers, TV and film, Internet and less conventional resources such as NGOs, local communities and the pupils themselves and their families

■   develop their practice of active learning to encompass models of democratic participation and which foster autonomy and responsibility.

c)   In relation to assessment, monitoring and accountability, student teachers of geography will be able to:

■   recognise and value prior learning and prior experiences of all pupils

■   show pupils how achievement in geography can enhance their appreciation of the world and its people and introduce them to new interests and activities.

d)   In relation to other professional requirements, student teachers of geography will:

■   keep abreast of current affairs and topical interest at all scales from local (the school) to global

■   show the capacity to trace certain economic, environmental, social and political changes on the international stage

■   contribute to their institution's intellectual, social and cultural life in a way that helps it realise its potential as an intelligent, learning organisation.

■ **Box 11.1** Additional training standards

Source: Institute of Education, University of London, PGCE course

'brilliant lesson'. We can learn a lot from the way individuals interpret this task: what is 'brilliant'? Brilliant for whom?

Student teachers were asked to share their brilliant lessons in groups of four, taking it in turns to:

- *describe* the lesson
- *inform* the other three about content selection and decisions taken about strategies adopted.

The three listeners had to make notes – it can help formalise their thinking – and then offer:

- *challenge* to the person in the hot seat in the form of questions requiring answers with justification
- *reconstruction* or ideas about alternative approaches to the lesson or topic.

After each member of the group had had their turn in the hot seat, it then fell to the group to *generalise,* by asking the question 'what pedagogic practices or principles seem to be at work here – what grounds do we have to distinguish a successful (or brilliant!) lesson?'

As with most learning activities, it is in the debriefing of the discussion that the full learning potential can be realised: Who said what? How do we interpret what was said? Can we draw any general conclusions from the activity? Box 11.2 shows how the tutor facilitating the brilliant lesson discussion tried to summarise the plenary feedback session (when each group gave an account of their morning's work). Here the tutor was in the role of debriefing the group: trying to make connections; trying to make useful distinctions; expanding points only half made; simply recording and acknowledging the worthwhile outcomes of discussion.

REFLECTING ON PRACTICE

Reflection has become something of a dread word in teacher education and training. The 'R' word is overused and it is often used carelessly, as if it were the theoretical basis for becoming a teacher. Our position is that although 'reflection' can never become a theory for teacher development (let alone training), it is nevertheless a very important activity, especially if focused and undertaken within an enabling – and challenging – framework. The point is, few people can improve simply by reflection; indeed, we can cite cases of reflection taking on the characteristics of self-serving justification of all kinds of practice, some desirable, but some far less so. Reflection *per se* may be a dangerous thing therefore, and because it can give the illusion of intelligent action it is in some ways more dangerous than no thought at all!

So when we urge you to be a reflective professional, it is tough thinking we have in mind. But what kind of thinking? Some experts argue that the skilful teacher is one who can adapt and change through a process of reflection *in* action. That is to say, tough-minded thought leading to decisive action *during* a teaching episode. Presumably, this requires thought that occurs at an intuitive level, for classrooms are such busy places there is no time for leisurely pondering about what to do next. Good reflection-in-action results in a teacher's tactics being appropriate and effective. Presumably, reflection-in-action is therefore something that draws from experience: an experienced teacher just 'knows' that certain courses of action with Year 9 are ill-advised on a Thursday afternoon, for example.

But here again there are dangers. For example, 'Oh, you can't do that with the kids I teach' is a phrase often heard. It may be quite correct in the context of the teacher's relationship with the class and the pupils' expectations of the geography classroom – or

'My brilliant lesson': pedagogic principles and practices

Here are the results of one group of PGCE student teachers' reflections on what forms of 'pedagogy' make a 'brilliant lesson'. This is not an exhaustive list. It is not fully developed, but it may form the basis of a productive professional conversation with other geography teachers. Does a list like this help us identify what kind of geography teacher we would like to be?

Use a wide range of *technical devices* as teaching/learning aids:

■ show pupils how to use grids and organisers for *analysis*
■ encourage the use of *analogy* in explaining events and processes
■ provide a range of authentic *audiences* for pupils' writing tasks
■ use 'concrete' models – move from the concrete to *the abstract*
■ use *stories* of individuals' experiences to illustrate general processes
■ organise *resources* in accessible ways, e.g. book boxes.

Find the connection of the topic to pupils' *everyday lives;* 'start from where the kids are at'. This means practising *questioning* skills, using devices such as brainstorming, etc.

Help pupils to understand their own *agency:*

■ use overt *thinking strategies* with them
■ use *debriefing* and summarising to help them see what they have achieved
■ give the pupils *responsibilities* for their learning
■ encourage *intellectual skills* such as speculation, estimation, creativity, etc.
■ be clear *why* the work is arranged as it is – in groups, pairs, individual, class.

Make the learning as *active* as possible:

■ practising basic *skills,* including listening, reading, counting etc.
■ simulations, role *play* and game strategies
■ *fieldwork* (learning by doing) where possible and appropriate
■ building *models*
■ practising *advanced literacy* skills – skim reading, bias detection, etc.

Use the strength of *novelty:*

■ 'and now for something completely different', even mundane material can be dressed up in the form of a *mystery*.
■ Go for the 'full monty' – prepare lessons that are full and multifaceted, with pace which can be stepped up (or slowed down) at the teacher's discretion. Avoid long periods of busy work and refuse to accept that forty minutes shading in the graph is a reasonable way to spend Tuesday afternoon's geography lesson.

■ **Box 11.2** Brilliant lessons

classrooms in general! But it can often sound a life-sentence of predictable, undemanding work for the pupils leading to those very expectations which become so difficult to change once established. What the situation requires is something more than an immediate response dignified by the quasi-technical term 'reflection-in-action'. It requires a considered response resulting from rigorous and critical reflection *on* action. It probably also requires an attitude of mind not dissimilar to that revealed by the following piece of reflective writing from a student teacher, John. This person was a 'mature student' and former paratrooper:

REFLECTIVE WRITING

A fable: 'The student teacher who did not want to observe'

> Watching other people do things you want to do yourself can be frustrating. Quite rightly the beginner wishes to get stuck in and learn how to do it on the job.

I've never really been inclined towards the role of *voyeur;* I believe that there is far more to be gained from involving oneself in the act rather than observing the performance of others. Hence, I embarked upon my first period of classroom observation less than enthused about being cast in the non-contact role. I was to watch and take notes... Take photos if I liked, but under no circumstances was I to get mixed up in the action. To add insult to injury, there was the suggestion that my involvement was limited due to the 'impotence' implied by my position as *newly started student teacher*. Here I was at twenty-nine years of age being told I wasn't capable of doing that which I had the greatest urge to do!

I was to sit at the back of the classroom...'what, right in the corner?' Apparently, I wasn't being punished, which was a relief, although I still felt as though I should be wearing a large pointed hat marked with the letter 'D'. I was then introduced to the class, whose level of enthusiasm at my presence was on a par with the enthusiasm I had for my present position. The formalities over, the teacher commenced with the lesson, unfortunately, to what end I can't recall; by this time I was sulking: 'I should be up there... God, this guy is doing it all wrong, he's so out of touch... I ought to be taking this class and he should be at the Institute.' Then all of a sudden a silence fell over the classroom and all faces turned towards me, what the hell was going on? 'Mr Green, I thought perhaps that you'd like to add a few points.'

The tables had been turned! Now this wasn't fair at all; if he'd been reading my mind it was time for me to start eating large portions of humble pie. I felt like an actor who'd suddenly forgot his lines in front of a packed house at the Albert Hall.

'Nnnno, nnno, no, Mr Brown, I think you hit the nail on the head, spot on, that was fantastic, you covered everything'

After what seemed an age, the class turned back to face the *real* teacher; in the space of thirty seconds the view I had of myself had altered from *prodigy* to *pretender;* Perhaps this period of observation warranted slightly more attention than I had initially thought necessary!

The error I made was to have adopted a perception of teaching that naively ignored the complex nature of teacher and pupil interactions. Stupidly, I had accepted my introduction period at the Institute as a *complete picture* of teaching, when in fact it only provided the basic foundations. Up until the point of recognising this mistake, I was in danger of fast becoming, to use a expression from my military days, 'the proverbial pub paratrooper', i.e. the individual who talks a good game, but invariably struggles to put words into action – 'the tavern teacher!' Thankfully, I have since altered tack, and dropped the cynicism I previously aligned to certain aspects of teacher development. Ironically, I now find periods of observation to be extremely useful, and despite now having taken on a relatively substantial timetable, when the opportunity presents itself I welcome the chance to watch teachers at work.

If I was to look for a moral in this tale it might be 'don't think you can run before you can walk', or perhaps 'everything will come to he that waits'. Put into practice it is far better to learn from other people's mistakes than from your own; besides, when it's placed in the right light, and if you are looking at the right things, there's a lot to be said for watching.

It is noteworthy that this writer (who became an Advanced Skills Teacher) has shown himself capable not only of reconsidering his own assumptions and prejudices, but also of critically reflecting on practice of others as well as his own. He has turned classroom observation into an essential activity. One imagines this will remain the case for the duration of this person's career. You cannot stop learning about your job, if you take opportunities to stop and stare (and use this as a stimulus for reflection).

Another student teacher, Sophie, who was a recent graduate trainee, showed through her reflective writing (not reproduced here) how, in a rather different manner from John, concerted effort with a sophisticated classroom observation framework enabled her to engage in deep reflection on observed action: her brilliant, telling conclusion informed us that for her 'slowly classrooms became *less familiar*' as a result of observation. The framework used was based upon an ecosystem model of the classroom and, because this readily 'makes sense' to geographers. Models such as this are, as Sophie found, challenging but often productive aids to reflection. As you go forward into your NQT year, the picture of classrooms as ecosystems may simply help you resist the rush to blame the kids, yourself, the head of department, the Head or even the Secretary of State for when things go wrong: try analysing the whole dynamic first – which probably requires some careful prior observation.

REFLECTION AS EVALUATION

We can pursue the idea of reflection *on* action further with the help of some real overheard snatches of conversation during the PGCE year. What we wish to do with these examples is show that reflection involves mental processes not dissimilar to evaluation – the intent to assess something with a view of coming to a reasonable judgement of its worth.

Read the following, genuine short exchanges.

1. Student Teacher asking her tutor at the end of the lesson:
    ST: How did I do?
    T: Fine.

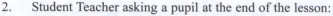

2. Student Teacher asking a pupil at the end of the lesson:
    ST: 'What did you do in geography today?'
    P: 'We did graphs.'

3. Student Teacher (early on during training):
    'I do not believe in group work.'

Each of these exchanges, in different ways, helps us identify why *evaluation* is a key component of reflection and professional development. In the case of the first quote it is the tutor who is failing to offer challenge. The person in the second quote, however, has at least begun to ask the kind of question that might enable an evaluation to be made of his or her teaching (and the pupil's response in this example may cause pause for thought). The third example is dogmatic and, for this reason alone, is unproductive – some would say the product of a closed mind! Before pursuing any of this in more detail, let us briefly specify what we mean by 'evaluation'.

Evaluation is 'the making of qualitative and quantitative judgements about the value of various curriculum processes' (Marsden, 1976: 3) Another view elaborates the purpose of evaluation, implying that it is almost bound to happen:

> In education, the ultimate purpose of evaluation is to improve the quality of... learning. Evaluation is to be anticipated, since there is a human tendency to reflect upon experience, to assess the value of one's actions and intentions, and to relate consequences to aims.

> (Kent, 1996: 133)

If we carry in our heads a simple objectives-led model of the curriculum process, then evaluation is something that is assumed to happen at or near the end of the process: you teach a series of lessons, and then you evaluate them. The fundamental flaw with this approach is that the 'judgement of value' that Marsden mentioned stands little chance of having any effect since all the curriculum decisions have already been made; the evaluation is, therefore, in terms of the current teaching and learning experiences, futile: any 'improvement in quality' is not possible – the curriculum horse has bolted!

It was the US educator Jerome Bruner who, as long ago as 1966, in his important, accessible book (still relevant and highly recommended, although written at a time when female teachers were apparently invisible), pointed out that:

> it would seem much more sensible to put evaluation into the picture before and during curriculum construction, as a form of intelligence operation to help the curriculum maker in his choice of material, in his approach, in his manner of setting tasks for the learner.

> (Bruner, 1966)

Bruner's view is also helpful in qualifying the implication in Kent's statement noted above; for although we may agree that reflection is to be expected in teachers, it does not always follow that it happens – it needs to be *put into* the frame, self-consciously and usually with some kind of procedure to ensure that it does indeed happen.

The quotes with which we began this section are all real. In different ways they help illustrate the importance of evaluation. Let us examine them, starting with the student teacher and her tutor.

Quote 1

The response 'fine' is of little use and is possibly even misleading, albeit, in a superficial way, reassuring. Nevertheless, it is a common response to the question asked. Why this should be so is explained in similar terms to the way in which the colloquial 'how are you?' or 'how are you doing?' also attracts (in England) the sometimes downright false response, 'fine'. In a way, the question is too big – some of us may be tempted to retort, 'well where would you like me to start?' or 'how long have you got?' Questions such as these are in fact not only too broad, but also wholly undefined; to give a meaningful answer requires some criteria to help the tutor and student teacher establish their common territory, to give focus to a conversation. It is precisely this that brings the Professional Teaching Standards to life: they provide a framework for the establishment of criteria on which to base judgement. It soon becomes apparent that in coming to a judgement, the evaluator (whether yourself or someone else, such as your tutor) has to have some kind of evidence. As in research (and evaluation is a form of research), data can be gathered effectively only after a focus has been agreed. Key questions include:

■ what is the purpose of the evaluation?
■ what is being evaluated?
■ what evaluative criteria should be used?
■ who is to do the evaluation?
■ what will be done with the evidence (data)?

(Kent, 1996: 135)

The mere posing of questions such as these reveals another possible deficiency in the student teacher's wholly understandable and natural question, 'how did I do?'. In addition to its need of specification (do *what* exactly?), the question also betrays a particular view of teaching which ignores its essential *relational ethic*. In other words, we not only require specification of 'the what?', but also the 'to whom?'.

So, 'how did I do?' is not only vague, it is not even the right question: a teacher may turn in a wonderful *performance,* but if the pupils fail to learn (or, more likely, we are not quite sure what they have learned), then the teaching may not have been wholly successful. One of the signs that a student teacher is moving beyond a basic level of competence (and beyond an initial focus exclusively on their own needs and their own performance, rather than the needs of their pupils and *their* performance) is a deep and textured knowledge of their pupils, and a willingness to respond to this knowledge. The appropriate question is not 'how did I do?' therefore, but possibly 'how did *they* (the pupils) do?'.

Assessment of pupils' work, therefore, becomes integral to teaching, which may be one reason why assessment and evaluation are often confused; assessment is a subset of evaluation, a source of evidence or data on which evaluative judgements are made. Pupils can also, occasionally, be asked directly to feed into a data set on which a teacher may be able to base a judgement on the effectiveness of a series of lessons or curriculum unit: Table 11.1 shows an example of how.

Quote 2

We can develop this line of thought further by thinking about the boy's response to the snap question at the classroom door, 'what did you do in geography today?'. 'We did graphs' may be wholly accurate and truthful, but disappointing to the teacher. Further probing may well result in a deeper more rounded answer, revealing a knowledge of the kind of graphs used and *what they were used for,* but without such evidence the thoughtful teacher may well conclude that the lesson had in some respects failed: geography is surely more than 'doing graphs'! On the other hand, there are not many geography teachers who have not experienced the beguiling manner in which 'busywork' (drawing the map; completing the table, using the Internet, constructing the graph) can stretch out to fill whole lessons. The problem of course is that such busy work is mentally undemanding and fails to engage the mind: it does not stretch the intellect; it does not motivate or involve. In fact, it does little to increase pupils' intelligences and is (if repeated too often) a symptom of low expectations: collusion rather than challenge; indulgence rather than guidance.

In making judgements in order to improve quality – that is, in making an evaluation – the teacher has to probe sources of data. But in addition, the teacher needs to apply imaginative insight to the data, for they do not always speak for themselves. This takes enormous practice, and the eyes and ears of another teacher, sometimes referred to as your 'critical friend' can be vital.

The following may offer food for thought. OFSTED has reported concern over the level of achievement of pupils in geography (OFSTED 2008). This concern has been a persistent message – for example:

> A weak feature of many schools is the insufficient emphasis put on practical and investigative work to stimulate students to higher standards. This contrasts with good standards, particularly in key stages 3 and 4, where skills of enquiring, through observing, recording and transforming data are acquired and practised (and) in lively classroom discussions where sharply focussed questions are posed... Where standards are low...unclear lesson objectives...lead to students being unsure of what they are doing and why, and as a consequence they are unable to build on previous work.
>
> (Smith, 1997: 125–126)

What we may conclude from all this is that 'the graphs' should not become an end in themselves: they should be seen as a means to an end. Perhaps geography teachers need to work harder than most to be clear about the purposes of their lessons – 'the graphs' being merely the chosen vehicle for 'observing, recording and transforming data' through 'focused questions' (Smith, 1997).

The teacher's capacity for self-evaluation is therefore paramount. Table 11.2 provides examples of self-evaluation schedules or checklists, devised by geography student teachers.

Quote 3

But what of the student teacher who 'does not believe in group work'? The statement reminds us of the old Guinness advert with the slogan 'I don't like Guinness because I've never tried it!' It represents an approach which may condemn this teacher to operate with a very limited repertoire of techniques.

Whilst it may be true that belief or intuition can play a significant role in motivating teachers – we need to believe in what we are doing in order to summon the relentless application that teaching requires – it is probably inappropriate when it comes to practical decisions such as which strategies to adopt in order to teach this or that. The value of evidence based evaluation is that it invites student teachers to face the question of

■ **Table 11.1** An example of pupil evaluation developed by a student teacher

Class:

1 How much did you enjoy the study of Kenya?

	Not at all	Very little	OK	Enjoyed it	Really enjoyed it
Topic as a whole					
Perceptions of Kenya					
Maasai people					
Kikuyu people					
Population distribution					
Nairobi					

2 How much do you think you learned about the following:

	Nothing	A little	Quite a lot	A great deal
Perceptions of Kenya?				
Maasai people?				
Kikuyu people?				
Population distribution?				
Nairobi?				

3 How much do you think you learnt from:

	Nothing	A little	Quite a lot	A great deal
Individual work?				
Pair work?				
Group work?				
Class discussion?				
Using textbooks?				
Using photographs?				
Using slides?				
Using a video?				
Using maps/atlases?				
Building clay huts?				
Using worksheets?				

4 Please make any general comments, favourable or unfavourable, on any part of the unit, if you wish.

Source: Karmjit Natt, PGCE student, 1994, in Kent *et al.*, 1996: 192. Reproduced with Permission

choosing the most apt teaching strategy (from a wide repertoire which they may not yet have acquired) for a given set of objectives. This may be done by trial and error, but what is not a satisfactory option is simply, always, to play safe – not if we have the interests of the pupils as our main focus. Effective evaluation helps us learn what works, in what situations, and with whom. If you 'believe' that group work (or whole-class teaching for that matter) does not work, then the challenge to you as a 'learner teacher' is to *dare* to test this 'belief' – and be willing to be surprised! OFSTED can again play the role of catalyst, the following based on literally thousands of lesson observations. It is worth checking whether this judgement still holds sway today (see OFSTED 2008).

> There is sometimes a narrowness in the range of teaching methods characterised by over-long expositions, over-directed styles inhibiting curiosity and initiative, and discussions mediated by and through the teacher, all of which reduce opportunities for developing thinking…Also some teachers intervene too quickly and then provide an answer in their own words.
>
> (Smith, 1997: 126)

■ **Table 11.2** An individual lesson self-evaluation checklist for teachers developed by a student teacher

Questions	1	2	3	4	5
How well have the lesson objectives been achieved?					
How varied are the resources?					
How up-to-date are the resources?					
How well is the work linked to the objectives?					
How easy will it be to measure pupil achievement from the class work completed?					
How well did I link this session to others?					
How well did I introduce this session?					
How well did I make the aims of the lesson clear?					
How well did I make the lesson progression clear?					
How well did I emphasise key points?					
How well did I summarise effectively?					
How well did I handle problems of inattention?					
How well did I cope with the ability range?					
How well did I handle student questions/responses?					
How well did I keep the material relevant?					
How well did I use my voice/body movements?					
How well did I convey my enthusiasm?					
How well did I maintain student interest?					
How well did I plan and prepare the lesson?					
How well did I produce good clear materials?					
How well did I handle control problems?					
How well did I make contact with individuals?					

Source: Joanne Clark, PGCE student, 1993, in Kent *et al.,* 1996: 189. Reproduced with permission

■ **Table 11.3** Teacher self assessment of a curriculum unit

How well did I...?	G	R	C
Link this session with others			
Introduce this session			
Make the aims of the lesson clear			
Make the lesson progression clear			
Emphasise key points			
Summarise effectively			
Pace the lesson appropriately			
Handle problems of inattention			
Cope with the ability range			
Handle student questions and responses			
Keep the material relevant			
Use my voice, body movements			
Convey my enthusiasm			
Maintain student interest			
Plan and prepare the lesson			
Produce good, clear materials			
Handle control problems			
Make contact with individual students			

G = good
R = reasonable
C = could do better

Source: Kent, in Kent *et al.,* 1996: 190. Reproduced with permission

Evaluation: a word about 'subject knowledge'

It is very easy, especially during the early stages of a teaching career, to pay so much attention to planning, pedagogy and classroom organisation that issues of subject knowledge become relatively submerged. Often, you can hear some teachers declare, perhaps a touch self-righteously, that they do not 'teach geography', they 'teach children', meaning that their main interest is people, rather than the furtherance of the subject. In the end, it is plain to see that this is not a question of either/or, for no matter how 'child-centred' teachers profess themselves to be, they have to be able to teach the children *something*. And that something cannot just be anything. It needs to be worthwhile, relevant and useful, as well as enjoyable, which is why excellent specialist teachers are highly sought after in schools.

We have seen how geographers have sought to justify the subject in Chapter 1, and the important role of the geography teacher in developing effective advocacy for the subject. What is at issue here is the *quality* of the subject knowledge being taught – not only its 'worthwhileness' and 'relevance' but also its accuracy, up-to-dateness and applicability. The process of evaluation at all levels of curriculum making should ensure that the question of content selection (that is, what we decide to teach, what the key questions are and how best to arrange the main ideas or concepts) is one that is returned to regularly and is properly influenced by developments in the discipline of geography. As recent graduates, many student teachers can exert a significant influence in this respect. Online materials on subject knowledge, including guidance on curriculum making, can be found at www.geographyteachingtoday.org.uk

As an individual, or as a member of a departmental team, you can find your favourite way to 'keep up'. The role of subject associations is increasingly important in this respect (see www.subjectassociation.org.uk). Without doubt, membership of the Geographical Association represents remarkable value through its journals and other publications and the annual conference (Easter time) at which the largest possible collection of published sources is exhibited and is available for your inspection. You can join online at www.geography.org.uk.

The role of research in supporting teaching and learning

Research has always had a role in play in supporting the professional development of student teachers during their initial teacher education courses. Margaret Roberts Research into geographical education can help us to see things differently and freshly, challenging assumptions and asking critical questions about purposes (Roberts, 2000: 293). It's role in supporting teaching and learning is greater than providing information about what works in the classroom. Roberts (2000: 293) argues that research can 'empower teachers to construct their own understandings, to clarify their own values and to have the professional confidence to make changes in classroom practices.' Through research geography teachers can learn more about pedagogy and ways of improving practice. Lofthouse and Leat (2006) argue that engaging with new ideas and frameworks, learning socially and getting feedback are fundamental conditions for successful professional development.

With most initial teacher education courses now incorporating elements of masters' level accreditation, student teachers not only need to engage with research but also undertake some small scale action research as part of coursework assignments. Guidance about undertaking practitioner research as a student teacher can be found in Bartlett and Leask (2005) and for research in geography education in Lofthouse and Leat (2006). Each initial teacher education course will have its own specific requirements for research-based assignments, but useful general advice about research approaches and techniques are readily available.

CREATING A PROFESSIONAL PORTFOLIO

Your 'Career Entry and Development Profile' or CEDP is a summary of your achievements and reflections as a student teacher, together with an account of your professional development targets for your NQT year. It is to be used by you and your first post school to underpin the next stage of your training and development. It should also be seen as beginnings of a professional portfolio.

The CEDP itself is a rather 'thin' document. A professional development portfolio, a somewhat thicker file (but not too thick: it has to be easily digestible). In essence, this is an expertly presented ring binder to 'evidence' your professional being. It shows what you can do: your approach to planning lessons, some examples of worksheets you have designed, one or two pieces of reflective writing which 'capture' your values, beliefs or simply your interpretation of slippery ideas such as progression or differentiation in geography education; it may even contain a photocopy of one or two pieces of pupils' work, marked by you, and which you happen to be proud of for some reason. Box 11.3 provides a list of suggestions of what may be included in your professional portfolio. It is potentially a very useful file.

It is probably best regarded as a document always 'in progress' and never the finished article. When you come to apply for your first post, an early prototype of your portfolio can be useful at interview (and should be mentioned in your letter of

---

The professional development portfolio

1　A personal statement of 'philosophy'.
2　Curriculum vitae.
3　A scheme of work and lesson plans(s), including evidence of your evaluation (which may include pupils' comments).
4　Example(s) of observation notes made on your lesson(s) and an example of observation notes made by you.
5　One or two pieces of reflective writing from your course (this could be an edited compilation).
6　List of professional development activities beyond your initial teacher education course, e.g. specific INSET sessions and courses (including school-based INSET activities) that you have participated in.
7　A report on school-based research undertaken as part of the course.
8　Examples of fieldwork and ICT in geography that you have been involved in developing and delivering.
9　One example of an 'educational' article that you have read within the last year, with a brief 'context statement' justifying your choice and your comments/thoughts about the article.
10　Evidence of your commitment to putting wider educational aims into practice (pastoral work, extra-curricular and 'out of school' work).

The personal statement of 'philosophy'

The 'Philosophical Statement' can be guided by the following questions:

■　What are the key characteristics of teaching geography?
■　What is the relevance/strength/potential of geographical education? (Why teach geography?)
■　What has influenced you in your thinking of this?
■　Can you identify key experiences in your development (critical incidents)?
■　What aspect of your training to become a teacher of geography have you found to be the most challenging?
■　In what aspects are you most confident or competent?
■　What particular strengths do you have to contribute to the profession, beyond your subject knowledge and subject application competences?

■ **Box 11.3** The elements of a professional development portfolio

Source: Institute of Education, University of London, Geography PGCE (Secondary) course material (2006)

application). You subsequently develop the portfolio as an instrument to support your Threshold application and further promotions – a supplement to you CV. But do not let it grow like topsy: keep it digestible, and do not be afraid to discard elements as new material takes its place.

CARRY ON LEARNING

How do we prepare to become a teacher? In our view, both *training* and *educational* opportunities and experiences are required. That is, *training* in specific techniques, approaches and even behaviours to give you the maximum level of teaching competence, but also *education* in order to broaden and deepen your understanding of geography, children and schools. The former without the latter can leave you professionally stunted, for what you make of teaching is not entirely for others to decide for you. What do *you* want to achieve as a geography teacher?

Here is R.S. Peters, an influential philosopher of education, writing over thirty years ago:

> Too often, it seems to me, reformers pass from the undeniable truth that the present 'subject centred' curriculum is often boring, to the conclusion that it should be abandoned and a topic-centred one substituted for it. They do not consider sufficiently seriously the less radical suggestion that the more traditional type of curriculum could be more imaginatively and more realistically interpreted. As with emphasis on 'discovery' methods, one can detect in all this a yearning for some overall recipe for teaching. My contention is that *no such overall recipe is possible. What is needed is a down-to-earth, clear headed, experimental approach* which takes due account not only of general criteria but the differences in what is taught and the children to whom it is taught.
>
> (Peters, 1965: 121)

He continues:

> For what is teaching? There is masses about learning... but almost nothing about teaching. Yet teaching can take the form of instruction, explanation, asking leading questions, demonstrating by example, metaphor, analogy, etc., correcting attempts at mastery, and so on. It can be done with a whole class, small groups and with individuals.
>
> (Peters, 1965: 121)

Now, we can never stop learning more about how children learn. But the skilled teacher is able to put such new knowledge and understanding to good use, by adapting teaching strategy, or tactic, or style in an appropriate manner – not by the application of some formula, but by the 'experimental approach' described by Peters. The teacher applies the principle of 'fitness for purpose' in order to decide not only what to teach but how to teach it. This is why the teacher needs to be clear about goals – that is, the purpose – which provides overall direction to the teacher's drive.

The following passage is frequently quoted because in it, Robin Richardson not only challenges us to think about goals, but also emphasises the autonomy of teachers which enables them (at least from time to time) to contribute their own vision in teaching geography. He writes that a geography teacher who is able to carry on learning, is likely to be able to say some or all of the following:

I am a teacher more than a geographer, and a person more than a teacher. I seek to widen the repertoire of techniques I use in the classroom to enable my pupils to grow as persons, talking thoughtfully and respectfully to each other, for I look to their growing commitment to social justice. I hope to extend not only my techniques of teaching but my skills, so that there is an optimum balance in my classroom of security and challenge. I aspire to deepen my tolerance and my commitment to justice, both in my immediate situation and in the wider world. I seek opportunities for such learning, and moral support, at inservice courses of various kinds. I reckon to improve my political skills, particularly within and around the school where I teach. I recognise that Brian [a disillusioned teacher who declines to attend an in-service training conference] speaks for me in some of my moods; but I have other moods also. In these I am a self-managing human being who dares – yes, who dares – to be a teacher.' Something like that. At least in a quiet murmur or whisper. Better still, out loud.

(Richardson, 1983: 130–131)

Rex Walford sums up the challenge in a similar way, emphasising the enthusiasm, skill and creativity on which a geography teacher can rely:

Looked at objectively, it is surely perverse for a geography teacher not to be able to stimulate students, given that the essence of the subject matter is of such variety, dynamic change and interest. In the last resort the survival of the subject will be dependent on the enthusiasm and expertise of those who represent it in the classroom.

(Walford, 1998:. 64)

Activity 11.1 **What is your quest? (for individual reflection)**

Read the following examples of various student teachers at work.

A *Sam was a science teacher*. He was teaching the periodic table. He was concerned about the final examination and he wanted to prepare students for it. His notes were prepared on Powerpoint. As he projected them, using the 'striptease' approach, he read them out to the class. He paused occasionally for questions. There were none. I noticed that the pupils also had the notes in front of them, which they were reading. This continued. At the end of the lesson he reminded them about the test on Friday.

B *Jan was an English teacher. Teaching Hamlet*, she wanted the pupils to see the interconnections between the themes of the play and learn skills of textual analysis (or as she put it, 'explication of text'). She also wanted the pupils to understand the power and beauty of the play's language. During the class, she led them through the play word by word focusing on the themes of linguistic reflexivity and the reflexivity of the play. Amongst other things, the pupils were asked to do a five-page assignment on a theme in the play, and a test with questions like: Write a well-developed paragraph on the importance of language in *Hamlet*. How does Shakespeare play with language? How are words juxtaposed with actions? How does Hamlet use words to act?

C   *Simon was a geography teacher.* Teaching about urban land use models, he wanted the pupils to see the connections between the general patterns and processes developed in the textbook and the knowledge they have of urban environments from their own lives. He wanted to maximise pupils' interest in the topic and geography lessons. He began without even mentioning 'urban land use'. He asked them to draw a map of their 'daily action spaces'. They were not sure, so they had to discuss what this could mean. He had the pupils comparing their maps: what did they show? what didn't they show? what did size of the action space seem to depend on? Then he asked them to analyse the maps – what kinds of spaces did they show? Did the different kinds of spaces form patterns? He then told the pupils that they were going to study the results of a number of similar analyses for whole cities in the next lesson.

Questions

Which of these teaching approaches 'typifies' secondary teaching, in your view?
Which, in your view, is most likely to engage pupils?
In what ways are the goals of the teachers different?
Is it possible to rank the three according to their effectiveness?

Discussion

The questions are, partly, trick questions. It is important to understand that one of the objects of your initial education and training is to enable you to move beyond these and other 'templates' and to develop your own ways and means of engaging young minds.

SUMMARY AND KEY POINTS

At the start of your first job the pressure is on to establish yourself. Quite right too. But you should note Norman Graves's warning as you move through your NQT year, that 'consolidation does not mean stagnation' (Graves, 1997: 30). Do not neglect your own professional practice, but continue the process of developing your pedagogic knowledge that you began during your initial teacher education. Professional growth requires attitude, a willingness to be flexible, imaginative and takes risks as much as knowledge, understanding and skills. We have therefore chosen to leave you with the following, timeless advice.

> Past successes pose a danger to person centred education in geography. Once something 'works' we tend to want to use the techniques over again in order to repeat the success...If an approach works, rejoice, but then approach the next situation freshly, on its own terms and seek a new perspective. Abandon 'techniques' that get to feel like formulas, and search for freshness as if you have had no past experience. Mistakes? Yes, mistakes must continue to be made if progress is to continue. Failure to make mistakes generally means failure to grow. Teachers must join their students in exploring all possible paths, including what may appear to be dead ends, if better paths into the future are to be found. It is amazing how often a 'safe' path becomes a blind alley and an unlikely, overgrown trail leads to a previously unknown highway.
>
> (Romey and Elberty Jnr, 1984: 315)

FURTHER READING

Balderstone, D. and Lambert, D. (2006) *Sustaining School Geography*, Chapter 42 in Balderstone, D. (ed.) Secondary Geography Handbook, Sheffield: The Geographical Association.

This chapter explores the idea of the scholarship of teaching and the important contribution that all teachers can make to subject leadership through curriculum making. It argues that we need to maintain a strong sense of direction in the subject when deciding what is worthwhile, relevant and motivating for young people to learn through geography and how we intend them to learn about these things.

Bartlett, S. and Leask, M. (2005) *Improving your teaching: An introduction to practitioner research and reflective practice*, unit 5.4 in Capel, S., Leask, M. and Turner, T. (eds) Learning to Teach in the Secondary School: A Companion to School Experience, London: Routledge.

The authors explore the role of practitioner research and critical reflection in improving classroom practice.

Burton, D. and Bartlett, S. (2004) *Practitioner Research for Teachers*, London: Paul Chapman Publishing.

This book explores the role of practitioner research in the professional development of teachers and provides practical guidance on designing research and collecting data.

Lofthouse, R. and Leat, D. (2006) *Research in geographical education*, Chapter 41 in Balderstone, D. (ed.) Secondary Geography Handbook, Sheffield: The Geographical Association.

The authors explore the role of research and collaborative learning in the professional development of geography teachers. Challenging oneself to learn more about pedagogy and ways of improving practice, engaging with new ideas and frameworks, learning socially and getting feedback are considered to be fundamental conditions for successful professional development.

Morgan, J. and Lambert, D. (2005) *Geography: Teaching school subjects 11–19*, London: Routledge.

The authors argue that geography teachers' professional development in their subject specialism turns on their growing appreciation of the complexities of learning. This requires a critical engagement with existing subject knowledge. Part 2 explores curriculum thinking, pedagogy and evaluation. Part 3 focuses on teachers themselves and how they view and work on professional development within their subject area.

http://www.geographyteachingtoday.org.uk/

Provides ideas and resources to support 'curriculum making' in geography, information about the national Action Plan for Geography and professional recognition for geography teachers (Chartered Geographer) and school geography departments (Geography Quality Mark).

http://www.geography.org.uk/

The website of the Geographical Association, the professional association for geography teachers, with an extensive range of resources and support for professional development.

www.geography.org.uk/projects/gtip

This site, funded by the TDA, has a wealth of material to support the professional development of geography teachers, especially new teachers. A suite of 'think pieces' help to introduce particular aspects of professional concern. It also has an up to date bibliography which overviews the current debates in research and professional literature. Finally, there is an on-line journal 'GeogEd' designed for geography educationists – this includes new teachers – who want to develop as writers and researchers. In particular, look out for the electronic 'new teacher network'.

REFERENCES

Abbott, J. (1994) *Learning Makes Sense: Re-creating Education for a Changing Future,* Letchworth: Education 2000.

ACAC (1997) 'A Local Issue: Oil Spill from the Sea Empress', Key Stage 3 Optional Test and Task Materials, Geography Unit 8. Curriculum and Assessment Authority for Wales.

Adey, P. and Shayer, M. (1994) *Really Raising Standards,* London: Routledge.

Ainscow, M. and Tweedle, D. (1998) *Encouraging Classroom Success,* London: Fulton.

Aldrich-Moodie, B. and Kwong, J. (1997) *Environmental Education,* London: Institute of Economic Affairs.

Ausubel, D. P. (1968) *Educational Psychology: A Cognitive View,* New York: Holt, Rinehart and Winston.

Bailey, P. (1991) *Securing the Place of Geography in the National Curriculum of English and Welsh Schools: a Study in the Politics and Practicalities of Curriculum Reform,* Sheffield: The Geographical Association.

Bailey, P. and Binns, T. (eds) (1987) *A Case for Geography,* Sheffield: The Geographical Association.

Bailey, P. and Fox, P. (1996) *Teaching and Learning with Maps,* in Bailey, P. and Fox, P. (eds), *Geography Teachers Handbook,* Sheffield: The Geographical Association.

Balderstone, D. (1994) 'An evaluation of the impact of a range of learning experiences on concept acquisition in physical geography', Unpublished MA dissertation, Institute of Education, University of London.

Balderstone, D. (2000) 'Beyond testing: some issues in teacher assessment in geography', in Hopkin, J., Telfer, S. and Butt, G. (eds), *Assessment Working,* Sheffield: The Geographical Association.

Balderstone, D. (ed.) (2006) *'Secondary Geography Handbook',* Sheffield: The Geographical Association.

Balderstone, D. (2006) *What's the point of learning geography?,* Chapter 1 in Balderstone, D. (ed.) *Secondary Geography Handbook,* Sheffield: The Geographical Association.

Balderstone, D., Dow, M. and Henn, V. (2006) *Geography and students with EAL,* Chapter 27 in Balderstone, D. (ed.) *Secondary Geography Handbook,* Sheffield: The Geographical Association.

Balderstone, D. and King, S. (2004) 'Preparing pupils for public examinations: developing study skills', in Capel, S., Heilbronn, R., Leask, M. and Turner, T. (eds), *Starting to Teach in the Secondary School,* London: Routledge.

Balderstone, D. and Lambert, D. (1992) *Assessment Matters,* Sheffield: The Geographical Association.

Balderstone, D. and Lambert, D. (2006) *Sustaining School Geography,* Chapter 42 in Balderstone, D. (ed.) Secondary Geography Handbook, Sheffield: The Geographical Association.

REFERENCES ■ ■ ■ ■

Balderstone, D. and Payne, G. (1992) *People and Cities,* Oxford: Heinemann.

Barnes, D. and Todd, F. (1977) *Communication and Learning in Small Groups,* London: Routledge.

Barnes, D., Johnson, G., Jordan, S., Layton, D., Medway, P. and Yeoman, D. (1987) *The TVEI Curriculum 14–16: An Interim Report Based on Case Studies in Twelve Schools,* University of Leeds.

Barnes, T. and Duncan, J. (1992) *Writing Worlds,* London: Routledge.

Barnett, M., Kent, A. and Milton, M. (eds) (1995) *Images of Earth: A Teacher's Guide to Remote Sensing in Geography,* Sheffield: The Geographical Association.

Barnett, M. and Milton, M. (1995) 'Satellite Images and IT capability', *Teaching Geography* 20(3), 142–143.

Bartlett, S. and Leask, M. (2005) *Improving your teaching: An introduction to practitioner research and reflective practice*, unit 5.4 in Capel, S., Leask, M. and Turner, T. (eds) Learning to Teach in the Secondary School: A companion to School Experience, London: Routledge.

Bates, B. and Wolton, M. (1993) *Guidelines for Secondary Schools for Effective Differentiation in the Classroom,* Essex County Council Education Department.

Battersby, J. (1995) *Teaching Geography at Key Stage 3,* Cambridge: Chris Kington Publishing.

Battersby, J. (1997) 'Differentiation in teaching and learning geography', in Tilbury, D. and Williams, M. (eds), *Teaching and Learning Geography,* London: Routledge.

Battersby, J. and Hornby, N. (2006) *Inspiring disaffected students*, Chapter 31 in Balderstone, D. (ed.) *Secondary Geography Handbook*, Sheffield: The Geographical Association.

Battersby, J., Webster, A. and Younger, M. (1995) *The Case Study in GCSE Geography: Experiences from the Avery Hill Project,* Cardiff: Welsh Joint Education Committee.

Bayliss, T. and Collins, L. (2006) 'Invigorating teaching with interactive whiteboards', in *Teaching Geography* 31(3), 133–5.

Bayliss, T. and Collins, L. (2007) 'Invigorating teaching with interactive whiteboards: case studies 3–6', in *Teaching Geography* 32(1).

Bayliss, T. and Collins, L. (2007) 'Invigorating teaching with interactive whiteboards: case studies 7–10', in *Teaching Geography* 32(2).

Beddis, R. (1983) 'Geographical education since 1960: a personal view', in Huckle, J. (ed.), *Geographical Education: Reflection and Action,* Oxford: Oxford University Press, pp. 10–19.

Bell, D. (2005) 'The value and importance of geography', in *Teaching Geography* 30(1), 12–13.

Bennett, N. (1995) 'Managing learning through group work', in Desforges, C. (ed.), *An Introduction to Teaching: Psychological Perspectives,* Oxford: Blackwell.

Bennett, N. and Dunne, E. (1992) *Managing Classroom Groups,* London: Simon and Schuster.

Bennett, R. and Leask, M. (2005) *Teaching and Learning with ICT: An Introduction*, Unit 1.4 in Capel, S., Leask, M. and Turner, T. (eds) *Learning to Teach in the Secondary School: A companion to school experience*, Abingdon: Routledge.

Bennetts, T. (1995) 'Continuity and progression', *Teaching Geography* 20(2), 75–79.

Bennetts, T. (1996) 'Progression and differentiation' in Bailey, P. and Fox, P. (eds), *Geography Teachers' Handbook,* Sheffield: The Geographical Association.

Bennetts, T. (2005) 'The links between Understanding, Progression and Assessment in the Secondary Geography Curriculum', in *Geography* 90(2), 152–170.

Biddulph, M. and Bright, G. (2003) *Theory into Practice: Dramatically Good Geography*, Sheffield: The Geographical Association.

Biddulph, M. and Clarke, J. (2006) *Theatrical geography*, Chapter 24 in Balderstone, D. (ed.) Secondary Geography Handbook, Sheffield: The Geographical Association.

Biggs, J. and Moore, P. (1993) *The Process of Learning,* Sydney: Prentice Hall.

Black, P. (2004) 'Formative assessment: Promises or problems?'

Black, P., Harrison, C., Lee, C., Marshall, B. and Wiliam, D. (2002) *Working Inside the Black Box: Assessment for Learning in the Classroom*, London: School of Education, Kings College.

Black, P. and Wiliam, D. (1998a) 'Assessment and Classroom Learning', *Assessment in Education* 5(1), 7–74.

Black, P. and Wiliam, D. (1998b) *Inside the Black Box: Raising Standards Through Classroom Assessment,* London: School of Education, Kings College.

Blyth, A., Cooper, H., Derricott, R., Elliot, G., Sumner, H. and Waplington, A. (1976) *Place, Time and Society 8–13: Curriculum Planning in History, Geography and Social Science,* Bristol: Collins-ESL.

Boardman, D. (1983) *Graphicacy and Geography Teaching,* London: Croom Helm.

Boardman, D. (1985) 'Spatial concept development and primary school mapwork', in Boardman, D. (ed.), *New Directions in Geographical Education* , London: Falmer Press.

Boardman, D. (ed.) (1985) *New Directions in Geographical Education,* Lewes: Falmer.

Boardman, D. (1989) 'The development of graphicacy: children's understanding of maps', *Geography* 74(4), 321–331.

Boardman, D. (1986) 'Planning, Teaching and Learning', in Boardman, D. (ed.), *Handbook for Geography Teachers* Sheffield: The Geographical Association.

Boardman, D. (1987) 'Maps and mapwork', in Boardman, D. (ed.) *Handbook for Geography Teachers,* Sheffield: The Geographical Association.

Boardman, D. (1988) *The Impact of a Curriculum Project: Geography for the Young School Leaver,* Birmingham: University of Birmingham *Educational Review,* Occasional Publications.

Boardman, D. (1996) 'Learning with Ordnance Survey maps', in Bailey, P. and Fox, P. (eds), *The Geography Teachers' Handbook,* Sheffield: The Geographical Association.

Boardman, D. and Towner, E. (1980) 'Problems of correlating air photographs with Ordnance Survey maps', *Teaching Geography,* 6(2), 76–79.

BFI (2000) *Moving images in the classroom: A secondary teacher's guide to using film and television*, London: British Film Institute.

Brooks, C. (2006) *Cracking the code – numeracy and geography*, Chapter 12 in Balderstone, D. (ed.) *Secondary Geography Handbook*, Sheffield: The Geographical Association.

Brooks, C. and Morgan, A. (2006) *Theory into Practice: Cases and Places*, Sheffield: The Geographical Association.

Brooks, J. and Lucas, N. (2004) 'The school sixth form and the growth of vocational qualifications', in Capel, S., Heilbronn, R., Leask, M. and Turner, T. (eds) *Starting to teach in the Secondary School: A companion for the Newly Qualified Teacher*, London: Routledge.

Brough, E. (1983) 'Geography through art', in Huckle, J. (ed.) *Geographical Education: Reflection and Action,* Oxford: Oxford University Press.

Bruner, J. (1966) *Towards a Theory of Instruction,* Boston: Harvard University Press.

Bruner, J. and Haste, H. (1987) *Making Sense,* London: Methuen.

Burn, A. (2005) 'Teaching and learning with digital video', in in Leask, M. and Pachler, N. (eds) *Learning to Teach using ICT in the Secondary School*, London: Routledge.

Burton, D. and Bartlett, S. (2004) *Practitioner Research for Teachers*, London: Paul Chapman Publishing.

Butler, R. (1988) 'Enhancing intrinsic motivation: The effects of task-involving and ego-involving evaluation on interest and performance', in *British Journal of Educational Psychology* 58, 1–14.

Butt, G. (1990) 'Political understanding through geography teaching', *Teaching Geography* 15(2), 62–65.

Butt, G. (1991) 'Have we got a video today?', *Teaching Geography* 16(2), 51–55.

Butt, G. (1997) 'Language and learning in geography', in Tilbury, D. and Williams, M. (eds) *Teaching and Learning in Geography,* London: Routledge.

Butt, G. (2001) *Theory into Practice: Extending writing skills*, Sheffield: The Geographical Association.

Butt, G. (2002) *Reflective Teaching of Geography 11–18*, London: Continuum.

Butt, G. and Lambert, D. (1996a) 'Geography assessment and Key Stage 3 textbooks', *Teaching Geography* 22(3), 146–147.

Butt, G. and Lambert, D. (1996b) 'The role of textbooks: an assessment issue?', *Teaching Geography* 21(4), 202–203.

Butt, G., Lambert, D. and Telfer, S. (1995) *Assessment Works*, Sheffield: The Geographical Association

Calder, M. and Smith, R. (1993) 'Introduction to development education', in Fien, J. (ed.), *Environmental Education: A Pathway to Sustainability,* Geelong: Deakin University Press.

Capel, S., Leask, M. and Turner, T. (2005) *Learning to Teach in the Secondary School: A Companion to School Experience,* London: Routledge.

Capra, F. (1996) *The Web of Life,* London: HarperCollins.

Carpenter, B., Ashdown, R. and Bovair, K. (1996) *Enabling Access: Effective Teaching and Learning for Pupils with Learning Difficulties,* London: David Fulton.

Carter, R. (ed.) (1991) *Talking about Geography: The Work of the Geography Teachers in the National Oracy Project,* Sheffield: The Geographical Association.

Castree, N., Fuller, D. and Lambert, D. (2007) 'Geography without borders', in *Transactions of the Institute of British Geographers* 32(2), 129–132.

Caton, D. (2006) *'Real world learning through geographical fieldwork',* Chapter 6 in Balderstone, D. (ed.) 'Secondary Geography Handbook', Sheffield: The Geographical Association.

Caton, D. (2006) *Theory into Practice: New Approaches to Fieldwork*, Sheffield: The Geographical Association.

Chambliss, M. and Calfree, R. (1998) *'Textbooks for learning: Nurturing children's minds',* Oxford: Blackwell.

Chapman, J. (1998) 'We can save the world!', *Primary Geographer,* 32 (January), 18–19.

Chapman, R. and Digby, B. (2006) *'Gotta get thru this'* – GCSE examinations, Chapter 37 in Balderstone, D. (ed.) *Secondary Geography Handbook*, Sheffield: The Geographical Association.

Chorley, R. J. and Haggett, P. (eds) (1965) *Frontiers in Geographical Teaching,* London: Methuen.

Chorley, R. J. and Haggett, P. (1967) *Models in Geography,* London: Methuen.

Christian Aid (1986) *The Trading Game,* London: Christian Aid.

Clark, C. M. and Peterson, P. L. (1986) *'Teachers' Thought Processes',* in Whittrock, M. (ed.), *Handbook of Research on Teaching,* New York: Macmillan, pp. 255–296.

Connolly, J. 1993, 'Gender balanced geography: have we got it right yet?', *Teaching Geography,* 16(2) 61–64.

Corney, G. (1985) *Geography, Schools and Industry,* Sheffield: The Geographical Association.

Corney, G. (1991) *Teaching Economic Understanding Through Geography,* Sheffield: The Geographical Association.

Corney, G. (1992) *Teaching Economic Understanding Through Geography,* Sheffield: The Geographical Association.

Cowie, H. and Ruddock, J. (1988) *Cooperative Group Work: An Overview,* London: BP Educational Service.

Davidson, G. (1996) 'Using Ofsted criteria to develop classroom practice', *Teaching Geography* 21(1), 11–14.

Davidson, G. (2006) 'Start at the beginning', in *Teaching Geography* 31(3) 105–108.

Davies, P. (1990) *Differentiation in the Classroom and in the Examination Room: Achieving the Impossible?,* Cardiff: Welsh Joint Education Committee.

Dearing, R. (1995) *Review of 16–19 Qualifications: Interim Report,* London: SCAA.

Dennison, B. and Kirk, R. (1990) *Do, Review, Learn, Apply. A Simple Guide to Experiential Learning,* Oxford: Basil Blackwell.

DES (1975) *Language Across the Curriculum* (the Bullock Report), London: HMSO.

DES (1990) *Geography for Ages 5–16: Final Report of the Geography Working Group,* London: HMSO.

DES (Department of Education and Science, now DfEE, Department for Education and Employment) (1991) *Geography in the National Curriculum (England),* London: HMSO.

DES/WO (1988) *Task Group on Assessment and Testing: A Report,* London: HMSO.

Desforges, C. (ed.) (1995) *An Introduction to Teaching: Psychological Perspectives,* Oxford: Blackwell.

DfEE (1995) *Geography in the National Curriculum,* London: HMSO.

DfEE (1998) *Health and safety of Pupils on Educational Visits*, London: DfEE.

DfEE (2000) *Research into Teacher Effectiveness: A model of Teacher Effectiveness*, London: Hay McBer/DfEE.

DfES (2001) *National Literacy Strategy*, London: DfES.

DfES (2002) *Transforming the way we learn: A vision for the future of ICT in schools*, London: DfES.

DfES (2002) *Literacy in Geography*, London: DfES.

DfES (2004) *ICT across the curriculum: ICT in geography*, Key Stage 3 National Strategy, London: DfES.

DfES (2005) *14–19 Education and Skills (White Paper)*, London: DfES.

Digby, B. (1997) *Global Futures,* London: Heinemann.

Dickenson, C. and Wright, J. (1993) *Differentiation: A Practical Handbook of Classroom Strategies,* Coventry: NCET.

Dilkes, J. and Nicholls, M. (eds) (1988) *Low Attainers and the Teaching of Geography,* The Geographical Association and the National Association for Remedial Education.

Dove, J. (1999), 'Immaculate Misconceptions', *Theory into Practice: Professional Development for Geography Teachers,* Sheffield: The Geographical Association.

Dove, J. and Owen, D. (1991) 'Teaching geography through music and sand', *Teaching Geography* 16(1), 3–6.

Dove, J. and Tinney, S. (1992) 'Using classroom display as a record of achievement', *Teaching Geography* 17(2), 57–60.

Dowgill, P. (1998) 'Pupils' conceptions of geography and learning in geography', unpublished Ph.D. thesis, University of London Institute of Education.

Dowgill, P. and Lambert, D. (1992) 'Cultural literacy and school geography', *Geography,* 77(2), 143–152.

Dowson, J. (1995) The School Curriculum', in Capel, S., Leask, M. and Turner, T. (eds), *Learning to Teach in the Secondary School,* London: Routledge.

Durbin, C. (1995) 'Using televisual resources in geography', *Teaching Geography* 20(3), 118–121.

Durbin, C. (1996) 'Teaching Geography with televisual resources', in Bailey, P. and Fox, P. (eds), *The Geography Teachers' Handbook,* Sheffield: The Geographical Association.

Durbin, C. (2006) *Media literacy and geographical imaginations*, Chapter 19 in Balderstone, D. (ed.) *Secondary Geography Handbook*, Sheffield: The Geographical Association.

Dweck, C. (2000) *Self-theories: Their role in motivation, personality and development*, London: Taylor-Francis.

Edwards, G. (1996) 'Alternative speculations on geographical futures: towards a postmodern perspective', *Geography* 81(3), 217–224.

Edwards, R. (1995) 'From the "box" to the classroom', *Teaching Geography* 20(4), 176–178.

Elliott, G. (1975) 'Evaluating Classroom Games and Simulations', *Classroom Geography* October, 3–5.

Enright, N., Flook, A. and Habgood, C. (2006) *Gifted young geographers*, Chapter 28 in Balderstone, D. (ed.) *Secondary Geography Handbook*, Sheffield: The Geographical Association.

Evans, L. and Smith, D. (2006) *Inclusive geography*, Chapter 26 in Balderstone, D. (ed.) *Secondary Geography Handbook*, Sheffield: The Geographical Association.

Everson, J. and Fitzgerald, B. (1969) *Settlement Patterns,* London: Longman.

EXEL (1995) *Writing Frames,* Exeter: University of Exeter School of Education.

Fairgrieve, J. (1926) *Geography in School,* London: University of London Press.

Fielding, M. (1992) 'Descriptions of learning styles', unpublished INSET resource.

Field Studies Council (2004) *A Review of Research on Outdoor Learning,* nfer/Kings College, London.

Fien, J. (1993) *Education for the Environment: Critical Curriculum Theorizing and Environmental Education,* Geelong: Deakin University Press.

Fien, J. (ed.) (1993) *Environmental Education: A Pathway to Sustainability,* Geelong: Deakin University Press.

Fien, J. and Gerber, R. (1988) *Teaching Geography for a Better World,* Harlow: Longman.

Fien, J., Gerber, R. and Wilson, P. (eds) (1984) *The Geography Teachers' Guide to the Classroom,* Melbourne: Macmillan.

Fien, J. and Slater, F. (1981) 'Four strategies for values education in geography', *Geographical Education* 4(1), 39–52.

Fein, J. and Slater, F. (1985) 'Four strategies for values in education in geography', in Boardman, D. (ed.) *New Directions in Geographical Education,* Lewes: Falmer.

Fisher, S. and Hicks, D. (1985) *World Studies 8–13: A Teacher's Handbook,* Harlow: Oliver and Boyd.

Fisher, T. (1998) *Developing as a Geography Teacher,* Cambridge: Chris Kington Publishing.

Freeman, D. (1997) 'Using information technology and new technologies in geography', in Tilbury, D. and Williams, M. (eds), *Teaching and Learning Geography,* London: Routledge, pp. 202–217.

Freeman, D. (2005) 'GIS in Geography Teaching and Learning', *GTIP Think pieces*, Sheffield: The Geographical Association. www.geography.org.uk/gtip

Freeman, D. and Hare, C. (2006) *Collaboration, collaboration, collaboration*, Chapter 25 in Balderstone, D. (ed.) *Secondary Geography Handbook*, Sheffield: The Geographical Association.

Fry, P. (1987) 'Dealing with political bias through geographical education', unpublished MA dissertation, Institute of Education: University of London.

GA/FSC (2005) *Setting the standards for safe, successful fieldwork for all*, Sheffield: The Geographical Association.

GA/NCET (1992) *Geography, IT and the National Curriculum,* Sheffield: The Geographical Association.

Gagne, R. (1965) *The Conditions of Learning,* New York: Holt, Rinehart and Winston.

George, D. (1997) *The Challenge of the Able Child,* 2nd edn, London: David Fulton Publishers.

Gerber, R. (1981) 'Young children's understanding of the elements of maps', *Teaching Geography* 6(3), 128–133.

Gerber, R. and Wilson, P. (1984) 'Maps in the geography classroom', in Fien, J., Gerber, R. and Wilson, P. (eds), *The Geography Teachers Guide to the Classroom,* Melbourne: Macmillan, pp. 146–157.

George, J., Clarke, J., Davies, P. and Durbin, C. (2002) 'Helping students to get better at geographical writing', in *Teaching Geography* 27(4), 156–160.

Ghaye, A. and Robinson, E. (1989) 'Concept maps and children's thinking: a constructivist approach', in Slater, F. (ed.), *Language and Learning in the Teaching of Geography,* London: Routledge.

Gibran, K. (1926) *The Prophet,* London: Heinemann.

Ginnis, P. (2002) *The Teacher's Toolkit: Raise achievement with strategies for every learner*, Carmarthen: Crown House Publishing.

Gipps, C. (1994) *Beyond Testing: Towards a Theory of Educational Assessment,* London: Falmer Press.

Goldstein, G. (1997) *Information Technology in English Schools: A Commentary on Inspection Findings 1995–6,* London: HMSO.

Good, T. L. and Brophy, J. E. (1991) *Looking in Classrooms,* New York: HarperCollins.

Graves, N. (1975) *Geography in Education,* London: Heinemann.

Graves, N. (1979) *Curriculum Planning in Geography,* London: Heinemann.

Graves, N. (1997) 'Geographical education in the 1990s', in Tilbury, D. and Williams, M. (eds), *Teaching and Learning Geography,* London: Routledge.

Graves, N. J. (ed.) (1982) *The New UNESCO Source Book for Geography Teaching,* London: UNESCO Press.

Grenyer, N. (1986) *Geography for Gifted Pupils,* London: School Curriculum Development Committee.

Hadyn, T. (2005) 'Assessment for Learning' in Capel, S., Leask, M. and Turner, T. (2005) *Learning to Teach in the Secondary School: A Companion to School Experience,* London: Routledge.

Haggett, P. (1965) *Locational Analysis in Human Geography,* London: Arnold.

Hall, D. (1991) 'Charney revisited', in Walford, R. (ed.) *Viewpoints on Geography Teaching,* London: Longman.

Hamilton-Wieler, S. (1989) 'A case study of language and learning in physical geography', in Slater, F. (ed.) *Language and Learning in the Teaching of Geography,* London: Routledge.

Harlen, W., Gipps, C., Broadfoot: and Nuttall, D. (1992) 'Assessment and the improvement of education', *The Curriculum Journal* 3(3), 215–230.

Harrison, C. M. (1986) 'Managing recreational areas; the effects of trampling on an ecosystem', in Slater, F. (ed.), *People and Environments: Issues and Enquiries,* London: Collins Educational.

Hart, C. and Thomas, T. (1986) 'Framework fieldwork', in Boardman, D. (ed.), *Handbook for Geography Teachers,* Sheffield: The Geographical Association.

Harvey, D. (1969) *Explanation in Geography,* London: Arnold.

Harvey, D. (1973) *Social Justice and the City,* London: Arnold.

Harvey, K. (1991) 'The role and value of A-level geography fieldwork: a case study', unpublished Ph.D. thesis, Department of Geography, Durham University of Geography.

Hawkins, G. (1987) 'From awareness to participation: new directions in the outdoor experience', *Geography,* 72(3), 217–222.

Hay, J. (1994) 'Justifying and applying oral presentations in geographical education',*Journal of Geography in Higher Education,* 18(1), 43–56.

Heilbronn, R. and Turner, T. (2005) *Moral Development and Values*, Unit 4.5 in Capel, S., Leask, M. and Turner, T. (eds) *Learning to Teach in the Secondary School: A companion to school experience*, London: Routledge.

Her Majesty's Inspectorate (HMI) (1980) *A View of a Curriculum,* London: HMSO.

Her Majesty's Inspectorate (HMI) (1985) *Education Observed: Good Teachers,* London: HMSO.

Her Majesty's Inspectorate (HMI) (1986) *Geography from 5–16, Curriculum Matters* 7, London: HMSO.

Her Majesty's Inspectorate (HMI) (1988) *The New Teacher in School,* London: HMSO.

Hewlett, N. (2006) *Using literacy productively*, Chapter 11 in Balderstone, D. (ed.) *Secondary Geography Handbook*, Sheffield: The Geographical Association.

Hicks, D. (1981) 'Images of the world: what do geography textbooks actually teach about development?', *Cambridge Journal of Education* 11, 15–35.

Hicks, D. (1993) 'Mapping the future: a geographical contribution', *Teaching Geography* 18(4), 146–9.

Hicks, D. (1994) *Educating for the Future: A Practical Classroom Guide,* Godalming: WWF.

Hicks, D. (2001) *Citizenship for the Future: A practical classroom guide*, Godalming: WWF.

Hicks, D. (2007) *Lessons for the Future: The missing dimension in education*, Oxford: Trafford Publishing

Hicks, D. and Holden, C. (1996) *Visions of the Future: Why We Need to Teach for Tomorrow,* Stoke on Trent: Trentham Books.

Hicks, D. and Steiner, M. (eds) (1989) *Making Global Connections: A World Studies Workbook,* Harlow: Oliver and Boyd.

Hirsch, E. D. (1987) *Cultural Literacy: what every American needs to know,* Boston: Houghton Mifflin Co.

Hirst, P. (1974) *Knowledge and the Curriculum,* London: RKP.

Hollingham, S. (1997) 'Using feature films in geography teaching', *Teaching Geography* 22(3), 111–133.

Holmes, D. and Farbrother, D. (2000) *A-Z Advancing Geography: Fieldwork,* Sheffield: The Geographical Association.

Holmes, D. and Walker, M. (2006) *'Planning geographical fieldwork',* Chapter 18 in Balderstone, D. (ed.) 'Secondary Geography Handbook', Sheffield: The Geographical Association.

Honey, P. and Mumford, A. (1986) *The Manual of Learning Styles,* Maidenhead: Honey.

Howes, N. (2006) *Teacher Assessment in Geography*, Chapter 34 in Balderstone, D. (ed.) *Secondary Geography Handbook*, Sheffield: The Geographical Association.

HSGP (American High School Geography Project) (1971) *Geography in an Urban Age,* CollierMacmillan.

Huckle, J. (1981) 'Geography and values education', in Walford, R. (ed.), *Signposts for Geography Teaching,* Harlow: Longman.

Huckle, J. (1983) *Geography Education: Reflection and Action,* Oxford: OUP.

Huckle, J. (1990) *Environment and Democracy,* Godalming: Richmond Publishing/WWF.

Huckle, J. (1993) 'Environmental education and sustainability: a view from critical theory', in Fien, J. (ed.) *Environmental Education: A Pathway to Sustainability,* Geelong: Deakin University Press.

Huckle, J. (1997) 'Towards a critical school geography', in Tilbury, D. and Williams, M. (eds), *Teaching and Learning Geography,* London: Routledge.

IAAM (1967) *The Teaching of Geography in Secondary Schools,* 5th edn, Cambridge: Cambridge University Press.

ILEA (1984) *Geography Bulktin* No. 19, London: Inner London Education Authority.

Inman, T. (2006) *Let's get physical*, Chapter 22 in Balderstone, D. (ed.) *Secondary Geography Handbook*, Sheffield: The Geographical Association.

Jackson, P. (1989) *Maps of Meaning,* London: Unwin Hyman.

Jackson, P. (2006) 'Thinking Geographically', in *Geography* 91(1), Sheffield: The Geographical Association.

Jacobson, D., Eggen, P. and Kauchak, D. (1981), *Methods for Teaching: A Skills Approach,* Columbus, OH: Merrill Publishing.

Jeans, R. (2006) 'Mapping for the future', Chapter 7 in Balderstone, D. (ed.) *Secondary Geography Handbook*, Sheffield: The Geographical Association.

Jenkins, S. (1990) 'Not just about maps', *Times,* 7 June.

Jenkins, S. (1994) 'Rotten to the Core', *Times,* 11 May.

Job, D. (1996) 'Geography and environmental education – an exploration of perspectives and strategies', in Kent, A., Lambert, D., Naish, M. and Slater, F. (eds), *Geography in Education: Viewpoints on Teaching and Learning,* Cambridge: Cambridge University Press.

Job, D. (1996) 'Geography and environmental education: an exploration of perspectives and strategies', in Kent, A., Lambert, D., Naish, M. and Slater, F. (eds), *Geography in Education: Viewpoints on Teaching and Learning,* Cambridge: Cambridge University Press, pp. 22–49.

Job, D. (1997) 'Geography and environmental education', in Powell, A. (ed.), *Handbook for Post16 Geography,* Sheffield: The Geographical Association.

Job, D. (1998) *New Directions in Geographical Fieldwork* (Geography UPDATE Series), Cambridge: CUP with Queen Mary and Westfield College, University of London.

Job, D. (2002) 'Towards Deeper Fieldwork' Chapter 10 in Smith, M. (ed.) *Aspects of Teaching Secondary Geography*, London: RoutledgeFalmer.

Job, D. and Buck, A. (1994) 'Learning through models in the laboratory', *Teaching Geography* 19(3), 106–110.

Jones, F. G. (1984) 'Using expository methods well in geography teaching', in Fien, J., Gerber, R. and Wilson, P. (eds), *The Geography Teachers' Guide to the Classroom,* Melbourne: Macmillan.

Jones, M. and Rycraft, J. (2007) 'Animated discussion in geography', in *Teaching Geography* 32(2), 93–6.

Joseph, K. (1985) 'Geography in the school curriculum', in *Geography* 70(4), 290–298.

Joyce, B. and Weil, M. (1980) *Models of Teaching,* New Jersey: Prentice Hall.

Kent, A. (1996) 'Evaluating the geography curriculum', in Kent, A., Lambert, D., Naish, M. and Slater, F. (eds), *Geography in Education: Viewpoints on Teaching and Learning,* Cambridge: Cambridge University Press.

Kent, A., Lambert, D., Naish, M. and Slater, F. (eds) (1996) *Geography in Education: Viewpoints on Teaching and Learning,* Cambridge: Cambridge University Press.

Kincheloe, J. and Steinberg, S. (1998) *Unauthorized Methods: Strategies for Critical Teaching,* London: Routledge.

Kinder, A. (2007) 'Planning a revised Key Stage 3 Curriculum' p.133 in *Teaching Geography* 32 (3)

King, S. and Taylor, E. (2006) *Using ICT to enhance learning in geography*, Chapter 17 in Balderstone, D. (ed.) *Secondary Geography Handbook*, Sheffield: The Geographical Association.

Kohlberg, L. (1976) *Recent Research in Moral Development,* New York: Holt, Reinhart and Winston.

Kolb, D. (1976) *Learning Style Inventory: Technical Manual,* Boston: McBer and Company.

Kyriacou, C. (1986) *Effective Teaching in Schools: Theory and Practice,* Oxford: Basil Blackwell.

Kyriacou, C. (1991) *Essential Teaching Skills,* Oxford: Basil Blackwell.

Kyriacou, C. (1997) *Essential Teaching Skills,* 2nd edn, Cheltenham: Stanley Thornes.

Lambert, D. (1996) 'Assessing pupil attainment', in Kent, A., Lambert, D., Naish, M. and Slater, F. (eds), *Geography in Education: Viewpoints on Teaching and Learning,* Cambridge: Cambridge University Press.

Lambert, D. (1997a) 'Teacher assessment in the National Curriculum', in Tilbury, D. and Williams, M. (eds), *Teaching and Learning Geography,* London: Routledge.

Lambert, D. (1997b) 'Geography education and citizenship: identity and intercultural communication', in Slater, F. and Bale, J. (eds), *Reporting Research in Geography Education,* no. 5, London: University of London Institute of Education, pp. 1–13.

Lambert, D. (1997c) 'Opening minds', in Slater, F, Lambert, D. and Lines, D. (eds), *Education Environment and Economy: Reporting Research in a New Academic Grouping,* London: Bedford Way Papers, University of London Institute of Education, pp. 9–36.

Lambert, D. (1999) 'Geography and moral education in a supercomplex world: the significance of values education and some remaining dilemmas', *Ethics, Place and Environment* 2(1) 5–18.

Lambert, D., Morgan, A., Swift, D. and Brownlie, A. (2004) *Geography: The Global Dimension: Key Stage 3*, London: Development Education Association

Lambert, D. (2004) 'Geography', in White, J. (ed.) *Rethinking the School Curriculum: Values, aims and purposes*, London: RoutledgeFalmer.

Lambert, D. (2005) 'An axis to grind', *Times Educational Supplement*, 4 March 2005.

Lambert, D. and Butt, G. (1996) 'The role of textbooks: an assessment issue?', *Teaching Geography* 21(4), 202–3.

Lambert, D. and Machon, P. (2001) *Citizenship through Secondary Geography*, London: RoutledgeFalmer.

Lambert, D. and Matthews, H. (1996) 'The contribution of geography to personal and social education', in Rawlings, E. and Daugherty, R. (eds), *Geography into the Twenty-first Century,* Chichester: John Wiley.

REFERENCES ■ ■ ■ ■

Lambert, D, Morgan, A. and Swift, D. (2004) *Geography: The Global Dimension. Learning skills for a Global Society*, London: DEA.

Laws, K. (1984) 'Teaching the gifted student in geography', in Fien, J., Gerber, R. and Wilson, P. (eds), *The Geography Teachers Guide to the Classroom,* Melbourne: Macmillan, pp. 226–234.

Leask, M. and Pachler, N. (2005) *Learning to Teach using ICT in the Secondary School: A companion to school experience*, London: Routledge.

Leat, D. (1996) 'Raising attainment in geography', in Williams, M. (ed.), *Understanding Geographical and Environmental Education: The Role of Research,* London: Cassell Education.

Leat, D. (1997) 'Cognitive acceleration in geographical education', in Tilbury, D. and Williams, M. (eds), *Teaching and Learning Geography,* London: Routledge.

Leat, D. (ed.) (1998) *Thinking Through Geography,* Cambridge: Chris Kington Publishing.

Leat, D. and Chandler, S. (1996) 'Using concept mapping in geography teaching', *Teaching Geography* 21(3), 108–112.

Leat, D. and McAleavy, T. (1998) 'Critical thinking in the humanities', *Teaching Geography* 23(3), 112–114.

Lofthouse, R. and Leat, D. (2006) 'Research in geographical education', Chapter 41 in Balderstone, D. (ed.) *Secondary Geography Handbook*, Sheffield: The Geographical Association.

Long, M. and Roberson, B. S. (1966) *Teaching Geography,* London: Heinemann Educational.

Lunnon, A. (1969) 'The understanding of certain geographical concepts by primary school children'. Unpublished M.Ed. thesis, University of Birmingham.

Lyle, S. and Sterling, S. (1992) *The Global Environment,* London: BBC/Longman/IBT.

Mackinder, H. J. (1911) 'The teaching of geography from an imperial point of view and the use which could and should be made of visual instruction', *Geographical Teacher* 6(30), 79–80.

Macleod, H. (1993) 'Teaching for ecologically sustainable development', in Fien, J. (ed.) *Teaching for a Sustainable World,* Brisbane: Australian Association for Environmental Education.

Marland, M. (1993) *The Craft of the Classroom,* London: Heinemann.

Marsden, B. (1997) 'On taking the geography out of geography education: some historical pointers', *Geography* 82(3) 241–252.

Marsden, W. (1992) 'Cartoon geography: the new stereotyping?', *Teaching Geography* 17(3), 128–130.

Marsden, W. E. (1989) '"All in a good cause": geography, history and the politicization of the curriculum in nineteenth and twentieth century England', *Journal of Curriculum Studies* 21(6), 509–526.

Marsden, W. E. (1995) *Geography 11–16: Rekindling Good Practice,* London: David Fulton.

Martin, F. (2006) *e-geography: Using ICT in quality geography*, Sheffield: The Geographical Association.

Martin, F. (2006) *Using ICT to create better maps*, Chapter 10 in Balderstone, D. (ed.) *Secondary Geography Handbook*, Sheffield: The Geographical Association.

Marton, F and Saljo, R. (1976) 'On qualitative differences in learning – 1: Outcome and process', *British Journal of Educational Psychology* 46,4–11.

Massey, D. (2007) 'For Space', London: SAGE publications.

Matthews, H. (1998) 'Using the Internet for meaningful research', *Journal of the Geography Teachers Association of Victoria* 26(1), 15–19.

Matthews, M. (1984) 'Environmental cognition of young children: images of journey to school and home area', *Transactions of the Institute of British Geographers,* 9, 89–105.

May, S. and Richardson, P. (2005) *Managing Safe and Successful Fieldwork*, Sheffield: The Geographical Association/ Field Studies Council.

Maye, B. (1984) 'Developing valuing and decision-making skills in the geography classroom', in Fien, J., Gerber, G. and Wilson, P. (eds), *The Geography Teacher's Guide to the Classroom,* Melbourne: Macmillan.

McCormick, J. and Leask, M. 'Teaching styles', in Capel, S., Leask, M. and Turner, T. (2005) *Learning to Teach in the Secondary School: A Companion to School Experience,* London: Routledge.

McDowell, L. (1994) 'The transformation of cultural geography' in Gregory D., Martin, R. and Smith, G. (eds), *Human Geography: Society, Space, and Social Science,* London: Macmillan.

McElroy, B. (1988) 'Learning geography: a route to political literacy', in Fien, J. and Gerber, R. (eds), *Teaching Geography for a Better World.,* Harlow: Longman.

McPartland, M. (2001) *Theory into Practice: Moral Dilemmas*, Sheffield: The Geographical Association.

McPartland, M. (2006) 'Strategies for approaching values education', Chapter 15 in Balderstone, D. (ed.) *Secondary Geography Handbook*, Sheffield: The Geographical Association.

Mitchell, D. (2008) *ICT in school geography: More than motivation*, Sheffield: The Geographical Association.

Mitchell, D. (2007) *Getting started with GIS ... on the internet ... for free*, Sheffield: The Geographical Association.

Mitchell, D. (2008) *Getting started with GIS ... online ... GIS in the world of work*, Sheffield: The Geographical Association.

Morgan, A. (2006) 'Teaching geography for a sustainable future', Chapter 23 in Balderstone, D. (ed.) *Secondary Geography Handbook*, Sheffield: The Geographical Association.

Morgan, J. (2003) *'Cultural Studies Goes to School'*, in *Geography* 88(3), 217–224.

Morgan, J. and Lambert, D. (2005) *'Teaching school subjects 11–19: Geography'*, London: Routledge.

Morris, J. (ed.) (1997) *Climate Change: Challenging the Conventional Wisdom,* London: Institute of Economic Affairs.

Myerson, G and Rydin, Y. (1996) *The Language of Environment: The New Rhetoric,* London: University of London Press.

Naish, M. (1988) 'Teaching styles in geographical education', in Gerber, R. and Lidstone, J. (eds), *Developing Skills in Geographical Education*, Brisbane: International Geographical Union Commission on Geographical Education and the Jacaranda Press, pp. 11–19.

Naish, M. (1997) 'The scope of school geography: a medium of education', in Tilbury, D. and Williams, M. (eds), *Teaching and Learning Geography,* London: Routledge.

Naish, M., Rawling, E. and Hart, C. (1987) *Geography 16–19. The Contribution of a Curriculum Project to 16–19 Education,* Harlow: Longman. National Oracy Project (1990).

Naish, M. C. (1982) 'Mental development and the learning of geography', in Graves, N.J. (ed.) *The New UNESCO Source Book for Geography Teaching,* London: UNESCO Press.

Nash, P. (1997) 'Card sorting activities in the geography classroom', *Teaching Geography* 22(1), 22–25.

National Oracy Project, Carter, R. (ed.) (1990) *Talking about Geography: the Work of Geography Teachers in the National Oracy Project,* Sheffield: The Geographical Association.

Natt, K. (1996) 'An example of pupil evaluation developed by a student teacher', in Kent, A. *et al.* (eds) *Geography in Education,* Cambridge: Cambridge University Press.

NCET/GA (1997) *Geography: A Pupil's Entitlement for IT,* Sheffield: The Geographical Association.

Nicholls, A. (1996) 'Who's to Blame for Sharpe Point Flats?' in *Northumberland 'Thinking Skills' in the Humanities Project: A Report on the First Year 1995–96,* Northumberland Advisory/Inspection Division.

Nicholls, A. (2006) 'Thinking skills and the role of debriefing', Chapter 16 in Balderstone, D. (ed.) *Secondary Geography Handbook*, Sheffield: The Geographical Association.

Nicholls, A. with Kinninment, D. (2001) *More Thinking Through Geography*, Cambridge: Chris Kington Publishing.

REFERENCES ■ ■ ■ ■

Northumberland 'Thinking Skills' in Humanities Group (1996) *Northumberland 'Thinking Skills' in the Humanities Project: A Report on the First Year 1995–96,* Northumberland Advisory/Inspection Division.

Novak, J. and Gowin, D. (1984) *Learning how to Learn,* Cambridge: Cambridge University Press.

O'Connor, P. (2008) *GIS for A-level geography,* Sheffield: The Geographical Association.

OFSTED (1993) *Geography. Key Stages 1, 2 and 3. First Year 1991–92. The Implementation of the Curricular Requirements of the Education Reform Act,* London: HMSO.

OFSTED (1994) *The Handbook for the Inspection of Schools,* London: The Stationery Office (TSO, formerly HMSO).

OFSTED (1995) *Geography. A Review of Inspection Findings 1993/4,* London: TSO.

OFSTED (2003) *Geography in secondary schools: Ofsted subject report series 2001/02,* London: Ofsted

OFSTED (2008) *Geography in Schools – Changing Practice,* London: Ofsted.

Orr, D. (1992) *Ecological Literacy: Education and the Transition to a Post-modern World,* Albany: State University of New York Press.

Oxfam (2003) *The Challenge of Globalisation: A handbook for teachers of 11–16 year olds,* Oxford: Oxfam.

Oxfam (2006) 'Teaching controversial issues', *Global Citizenship Guides,* Oxford: Oxfam.

Oxfam (2006) *Education for Global Citizenship: A Guide for Schools,* Oxford: Oxfam.

Palot, I. (1999) *Going Places: A Geography Careers Resource Pack,* Sheffield: The Geographical Association.

Parkinson, A. (2004) 'Have you met Geo Blogs?', in *Teaching Geography* 29(3).

Parkinson, A. and Vannet, V. (2008) 'Using digital learning resources in geography teaching', in *Teaching Geography* 33(1).

Parnell, E. (2007) 'Geography is all about location, location, location', in *Teaching Geography* 32(2), 91–2.

Payne, C. and Featherstone, R. (1983) 'Fieldwork in the classroom: How to make and use a stream table', *Teaching Geography* 8(4), 162–164.

Peacey (2005) *An introduction to Inclusion, Special Educational Needs and Disability,* in Capel, S., Leask, M. and Turner, T. (eds) *Learning to Teach in the Secondary School: A Companion to School Experience,* London: Routledge.

Perkins, D. (1996) *Outsmarting IQ: The Emerging Science of Learnable Intelligence,* Cambridge, MA: Harvard University Press.

Peters, R. S. (1965) *Education as Initiation,* Inaugural Lecture, London: ULIE.

Pike, G. and Selby, D. (1988) *Global Teacher Global Learner,* London: Hodder and Stoughton.

Pike, G. and Selby, D. (1995) *Reconnecting: From National to Global Curriculum,* Godalming: WWF.

Pomeroy, J. (1991) 'The press conference: a way of using visiting speakers effectively', *Teaching Geography* 16(2), 56–58.

Porter, A. (1986) 'Political bias and political education', *Teaching Politics,* September, 371–384.

Postman, N. and Weingartner, C. (1971) *Teaching as a Subversive Activity,* Harmondsworth: Penguin.

Powell, A. (ed.) *Handbook for Post-16 Geography,* Sheffield: The Geographical Association.

QCA (1997) *The Promotion of Pupils' Spiritual, Moral, Social and Cultural Development Draft Guidance for Pilot Work – November 1991,* London: Qualifications and Curriculum Authority.

Price, J. (2003) '*Get Global!*', London: Action Aid.

QCA (2001) *Citizenship: A scheme of work for key stage 3, Teachers' Guide,* London: QCA.

QCA (2007) *The National Curriculum for Geography,* London: QCA

QCA (2006) *GCE AS and A level subject criteria for geography,* London: QCA

QCA (2008) *The National Curriculum for Information and communication technology,* London: QCA.

Ranger, G. (1995) 'Choosing Places', *Teaching Geography* 20(2), 67–68.

Raths, J. (1967) 'Worthwhile Activities', in Raths, J., Pancella, J.R. and Van Ness, J.S. (eds), *Studying Teaching,* Hemel Hempstead: Prentice Hall.

Raven-Ellison, D. (2005) 'Using Digital Video in Geography', Geography PGCE workshop, Institute of Education, University of London.

Rawding, C. (2007) *Theory into Practice: Understanding Place as a process*, Sheffield: The Geographical Association.

Rawling, E. (1986) 'Approaches to teaching and learning in the classroom', in Boardman, D. (ed.) *Handbook for Geography Teachers,* Sheffield: The Geographical Association, pp. 56–67.

Rawling, E. (1987) 'Geography 11–16: criteria for geographical content in the secondary school curriculum', in Bailey P. and Binns, T. (eds), *A Case for Geography,* Sheffield: The Geographical Association.

Rawling, E. (1991) 'Making the most of the National Curriculum', *Teaching Geography* 16(3), 130–1.

Rawling, E. (1996) 'The impact of the National Curriculum on school based curriculum development in geography', in Kent, A., Lambert, D., Naish, M. and Slater, F. (eds), *Geography in Education: Viewpoints on Teaching and Learning,* Cambridge: Cambridge University Press, pp. 100–32.

Rawling, E. (1997) 'Geography and vocationalism: opportunity or threat?', *Geography* 82(2), 167–178.

Rawling, E. (2001) *Changing the subject: The impact of national policy on school geography 1980–2000*, Sheffield: The Geographical Association.

Rawling, E. (2007) *Planning your Key Stage 3 Geography Curriculum*, Sheffield: The Geographical Association.

Rawling, E. and Westaway, J. (1996) 'Progression and assessment in geography at Key Stage 3', *Teaching Geography* 21(3), 123–129.

Ray, A. and O'Brien, R. (1990) 'South American housing crisis: a role-playing exercise based on urban issues in developing countries', *Teaching Geography,* 15(1), 34–35.

Reid, A. (1996) 'Exploring values in sustainable development', *Teaching Geography* 21(4), 168–171.

RGS-IBG (2007) 'Analysis of the 2007 Examination Results and the Current Status of Geography in England and Wales, Northern Ireland and Scotland'

Rice, G. (1994) 'The global AIDS pandemic: a diffusion simulation', *Teaching Geography* 19(3), 124–125.

Rhodes, B. (1994) 'Learning curves…and map contours', *Teaching Geography* 19(3), 111–115.

Richardson, R. (1983) *Daring to be a Teacher: Essays, Stories and Memoranda,* Stoke on Trent: Trentham Books.

Roberts, M. (1986) 'Talking, reading and writing', in Boardman, D. (ed.), *Handbook for Geography Teachers,* Sheffield: The Geographical Association, pp. 68–78.

Roberts, M. (1996) 'Teaching styles and strategies', in Kent, A., Lambert, D., Naish, M. and Slater, F. (eds) *Geography in Education: Viewpoints on Teaching and Learning,* Cambridge: Cambridge University Press, pp. 231–259.

Roberts, M. (1997) 'Curriculum planning and course development: a matter of professional judgement', in Tilbury, D. and Williams, M. (eds), *Teaching and Learning Geography,* London: Routledge.

Roberts, M. (2003) *Learning through Enquiry: making sense of geography in the key stage 3 classroom*, Sheffield: The Geographical Association.

Roberts, M. (2006) 'Geographical Enquiry', Chapter 9 in Balderstone, D. (ed.) *Secondary Geography Handbook*, Sheffield: The Geographical Association.

Robinson, R. (1987) 'Discussing photographs' in Boardman, D. (ed.), *Handbook for Geography Teachers,* Sheffield: The Geographical Association.

Robinson, R. (1995) 'Enquiry and Connections' in *Teaching Geography* 20(2), 71–73.

Robinson, R. and Serf, J. (1997) *Global Geography: Learning Through Development Education at Key Stage 3,* The Geographical Association/Birmingham Development Education Centre.

Rokeach, M. (1973) *The Nature of Human Values,* London: Free Press.

Romey, W. and Elberty, Jr., W. (1984) 'On being a geography teacher in the 1980s and beyond', in Fien, J., Gerber, R. and Wilson, P. (eds), *The Geography Teachers Guide to the Classroom,* Melbourne: Macmillan of Australia, pp. 306–316.

Rose, G. (1993) *Feminism and Geography,* London: Polity.

Ross, S. (1991) 'Cartoons in the classroom', *Teaching Geography* 16(3), 116–117.

Rubins, L. (1985) *Artistry and Teaching,* New York: Random House.

Sadler, R. (1989) 'Formative assessment and the design of instructional systems', in *Instructional Science* 18, 119–144.

SCAA (1995) *Spiritual and Moral Development,* London: SCAA.

SCAA (1996b) *Consistency in Teacher Assessment: Exemplification of standards, London: SCAA.*

SCAA (1997) *Curriculum, Culture and Sodety, London:* SCAA.

Schaefer, F.W. (1953) 'Exceptionalism in geography: a methodological examination', *AAAG,* 43, 226–249.

Schools Council (1973) *Teachers' Guide; Starting from Rocks; Starting from Maps; Case Studies,* Environmental Studies 5–13 Project, Hart-Davies Educational.

Simon, F. and Wright, I. (1974) 'Moral education: problem solving and survival', *Journal of Moral Education,* 3(3), 241–248.

Slater, F. (1970) *The Relationship between Levels of Learning in Geography, Piaget's Theory of Intellectual Development and Bruner's Teaching Hypothesis,* Australia: Geographical Education AGTA.

Slater, F. (1982) *Learning through Geography,* London: Heinemann.

Slater, F. (1986) 'Steps in planning', in Boardman, D. (ed.), *Handbook for Geography Teachers,* Sheffield: The Geographical Association, pp. 41–55.

Slater, F. (1988) 'Teaching style? A case study of post graduate teaching students observed', in Gerber, R. and Lidstone, J. (ed.), *Developing Skills in Geography Education,* Brisbane: IGU Commission on Geographical Education/Jacaranda Press.

Slater, F. (1989) (ed.) *Language and Learning in the Teaching of Geography,* London: Routledge.

Slater, F. (1991) *Societies, Choices and Environments,* London: Collins Educational.

Slater, F. (1992) '…to travel with a different view', in Naish, M. (ed.), *Geography and Education: National and International Perspectives,* London: Kogan Page/ULIE.

Slater, F. (1993) *Learning through Geography,* The National Council for Geographic Education.

Slater, F. (1996) 'Values: mapping their locations in a geography education', Kent, A., Lambert, D., Naish, M. and Slater, F. (eds), *Geography in Education: Viewpoints on Teaching and Learning,* Cambridge: Cambridge University Press, pp. 200–230.

Smith, D. M. (1977) *Human Geography: A Welfare Approach,* London: Arnold.

Smith, P. (1997) 'Standards achieved: a review of geography in secondary schools in England, 1995–96' *Teaching Geography* 22(3), 123–124.

St Exupery, A. de (1945) *The Little Prince,* London: Heinemann.

Standish, A. (2009) *Global Perspectives in the Geography Curriculum: reviewing the moral case for geography*, London: Routledge.

Sterling, S. (2001) *Sustaining Education: Revisioning Learning and Change,* Shumacher Briefings 6, Dartington: Green Books.

Stevens, S. (2001) 'Fieldwork as commitment', in *The Geographical Review* 91, 66–73

Steiner, M. (ed.) (1996) *Developing the Global Teacher: Theory and Practice in Initial Teacher Education,* Stoke on Trent: Trentham Books.

Stimpson, P. (1994) 'Making the most of discussion', *Teaching Geography* 19(4), 154–157.

Stott, P. (1997) 'Teaching lies', lecture given at the Geographical Association Annual Conference, London: Institute of Education, April.

Stradling, R., Noctor, M. and Bains, B. (1984) *Teaching Controversial Issues,* London: Arnold.

Sutton, R. (1995) *Assessment for Learning,* Salford: RS Publications.

Swift, D. (2005) *Meeting SEN in the curriculum: Geography*, London: David Fulton/The Geographical Association.

Taylor, D. (1997) 'The role of inspection in initial teacher training', in Hudson, A. and Lambert, D. (eds), *Exploring Futures in Initial Teacher Education: Changing Key for Changing Times,* London: Institute of Education Bedford Way Papers.

Taylor, E. (2001) 'Using presentation packages for collaborative work', in *Teaching Geography*, 26(1), 43–5.

Taylor, E. (2004) *Re-presenting Geography*, Cambridge: Chris Kington Publishing.

Thomas, S. and McGahan, H. (1997) 'Geography – it makes you think', *Teaching Geography* 22(3), 114–118.

Thompson, L. (2006) *Target setting and target getting in geography*, Chapter 33 in Balderstone, D. (ed.) *Secondary Geography Handbook*, Sheffield: The Geographical Association.

Thompson, L., Roberts, D., Kinder, A. and Apicella, P. (2001) 'Raising literacy standards in geography lessons', in *Teaching Geography* 26(4), 169–174.

Tilbury, D. (1997) 'Cross-curricular concerns in geography: citizenship and economic and industrial understanding', in Tilbury, D. and Williams, M. (eds), *Teaching and Learning Geography,* London: Routledge.

Tilbury, D. and Williams, M. (1997) *Teaching and Learning Geography,* London: Routledge.

Times Educational Supplement (TES) (1996) 'Historians want to curb the growth of GCSE rival', 13 September.

Tolley, H., Biddulph, M. and Fisher, T. (1996) *Beginning Initial Teacher Training,* Cambridge: Chris Kington Publishing.

Tolley, H. and Reynolds, J. B. (1977) *Geography 14–18. A Handbook for School-based Curriculum Development,* Basingstoke: Macmillan Education.

Totterdell, M. and Lambert, D. (1997) 'Designing teachers' futures: the quest for a new professional climate', in Hudson, A. and Lambert, D. (eds), *Exploring Futures in Initial Teacher Education: Changing Key for Changing Times,* London: University of London Institute of Education Bedford Way Papers, pp. 178–202.

UNESCO (1965) *Source Book for Geography Teaching,* London: Longman.

University of Newcastle School of Education (1995) *Improving Students' Performance: Guide to Thinking Skills in Education and Training,* Newcastle-upon-Tyne: Tyneside TEC.

Unwin. T. (1992) *The Place of Geography,* Harlow: Longman.

Usher, R. and Edwards, R. (1994) *Postmodernism and Education,* London: Routledge.

Van Matre, S. (1979) 'Sunship Earth: An acclimatization programme for outdoor learning', Martinsville, IN: American Camping Association.

Vygotsky, L. S. (1978) *Mind in Society: The Development of Higher Psychological Processes,* Cambridge, MA: Harvard University Press.

Walford, R. (1969) *Games in Geography,* London: Longman.

Walford, R. (1984) Geography and the Future, *Geography,* 69(3), 193–208.

Walford, R. (1987) 'Games and simulations', in Boardman, D. (ed.), *Handbook for Geography Teachers,* Sheffield: The Geographical Association.

Walford, R. (1991) *Viewpoints on Geography Teaching,* London: Longman.

Walford, R. (1995a) 'Fieldwork on parade', *Teaching Geography* 20(3), 112–117.

Walford, R. (1995b) 'Geographical textbooks 1930–1990: the strange case of the disappearing text', *Paradigm* 18,1–11.

Walford, R. (1996) 'The simplicity of simulation', in Bailey, P. and Fox, P. (eds), *Geography Teachers' Handbook,* Sheffield: The Geographical Association.

Walford, R. (1998) 'Geography: the way ahead', *Teaching Geography* 23(2), 61–64.

Walford, R. and Haggett, P. (1995) 'Geography and geographical education: some speculations for the twenty-first century', *Geography* 80(1), 3–13.

Warn, S. (2006) *Preparing for public examinations*, Chapter 36 in Balderstone, D. (ed.) *Secondary Geography Handbook*, Sheffield: The Geographical Association.

REFERENCES ▪ ▪ ▪ ▪

Waterhouse, P. (1990) *Classroom Management,* Stafford: Network Educational Press.

Waters, A. (1995) 'Differentiation and classroom practice', *Teaching Geography* 20(2), 81–84 .

Watkins, C., Carnell, E., Lodge, C. and Whalley, C. (1996) *Effective Learning,* School Improvement Network, Research Matters: Institute of Education, University of London.

Waugh, D. and Bushell, T. (1992) *Key Geography Connections,* Cheltenham: Stanley Thornes.

Webb, M. (2005) 'ICT and classroom management', in Leask, M. and Pachler, N. (eds) *Learning to Teach using ICT in the Secondary School*, London: Routledge.

Webb, N. M. (1989) 'Peer interaction and learning in small groups', *International Journal of Educational Research* 13, 21–39.

Webb, N. M. and Kenderski, C. M. (1985) 'Gender differences in small group interaction and achievement in high and low achieving classes', in Wilkinson, L.C. and Marrett, C.B. (eds), *Gender Differences in Classroom Interaction,* New York: Academic Press.

Weeden, P. (1997) 'Learning through Maps', in Tilbury, D. and Williams, M. (eds) *Teaching and Learning Geography,* London: Routledge.

Weeden, P. (2005) 'Feedback in the classroom: Developing the use of assessment for learning' in *Teaching Geography* 30 (3), 161–3.

Weeden, P. and Butt, G. (2009) *Assessing progress in your key stage 3 geography curriculum*, Sheffield: The Geographical Association.

Weeden, P. and Hopkin, J. (2006) *Assessment for learning in geography*, Chapter 32 in Balderstone, D. (ed.) *Secondary Geography Handbook*, Sheffield: The Geographical Association.

Weeden, P. and Lambert, D. (2006) *Geography inside the black box: Assessment for learning in the geography classroom*, London: nferNelson.

Weeden, P., Winter, J. and Broadfoot, P. (2002) *Assessment: What's in it for schools?* London: RoutledgeFalmer

Wellsted, E. (2006) *Understanding 'distant places'*, Chapter 14 in Balderstone, D. (ed.) Secondary Geography Handbook, Sheffield: The Geographical Association.

Whitaker, M. (1995) *Managing to Learn: Aspects of Reflective and Experiential Learning in Schools,* London: Cassell.

White, J. (1997) 'Quest for new moral givens', *Times Educational Supplement,* 10 January.

Widdowson, J. and Lambert, D. (2006) *Using geography textbooks*, Chapter 13 in Balderstone, D. (ed.) *Secondary Geography Handbook*, Sheffield: The Geographical Association.

Wideen, M. and Grimmett, P. (1997) 'Exploring futures in initial teacher education: the landscape and the quest', in Hudson, A. and Lambert, D. (eds), *Exploring Futures in Initial Teacher Education: Changing Key for Changing Times,* London: University of London Institute of Education Bedford Way Papers, pp. 3–42.

Wiegand, P. (1996) 'Learning with atlases and globes', in Bailey, P. and Fox, P. (eds), *Geography Teachers' Handbook,* Sheffield: The Geographical Association.

Wilce, H. (1998) 'Timewasting is only a keystroke away', *Times Educational Supplment,* 30 January: 44.

Wilkinson, L. C. and Marrett, C. B. (eds) (1985) *Gender Differences in Classroom Interaction,* New York: Academic Press.

Williams, M. (1981) *Language Teaching and Learning in Geography,* London: Ward Lock.

Williams, M. (1997) *Progression and Transition,* in Tilbury, D. and Williams, M. (eds), *Teaching and Learning Geography,* London: Routledge.

Wilson, P. (1971) 'An investigation into the understanding of certain geomorphological concepts of first year college of education students', unpublished MA dissertation, London: University of London Institute of Education.

Winchester, H., Kong, L. and Dunn, K. (2003) *Landscapes: Ways of imagining the world*, Harlow: Pearson Education.

Winter, C. (1997) 'Ethnocentric bias in geography textbooks: a framework for reconstruction', in Tilbury, D. and Williams, M. (eds), *Teaching and Learning Geography,* London: Routledge.

Wright, D. (1985) 'In black and white: racist bias in textbooks', *Geographical Education* 5, 13–17.

WWF (1991) *The Decade of Destruction,* Godalming: WWF.

WWF (1995) *Reaching Out,* Surrey: Worldwide Fund for Nature UK.

Yorkshire Dales National Park Committee (1989) *Landscapes for Tomorrow,* Skipton: YDNPC.

Youens, B. (2005) 'External Assessment and Examinations', in Capel, S., Leask, M. and Turner, T. (2005) *Learning to Teach in the Secondary School: A Companion to School Experience,* London: Routledge.

Younie, S. and Moore, T. (2005) 'Using ICT for professional Purposes', Chapter 2 in Leask, M. and Pachler, N. (2005) *Learning to Teach using ICT in the Secondary School: A companion to school experience*, London: Routledge.

Yoxall, W. (1989) 'A regional laboratory for earth science instruction – a rationale for using regional laboratories for practical work in the earth science component of physical geography', *Teaching Geography* 14(4), 169–172.

INDEX

Studying PGCE Geography at M Level
Reflection, research and writing
for professional development

Edited by Clare Brooks

Studying PGCE Geography at M Level is for all students undertaking their PGCE, those working to gain Masters credits, and experienced teachers who wish to broaden their understanding of geography education.

Bridging the gap between theory and practice, it is designed to support and challenge teachers as they explore geography education research, consider how theory and research enhance practice, and develop critical reflection on practice.

Divided into three key sections, it:

• Investigates professional practice – what we understand about professionalism and quality in geography education, and how teachers can improve their practice.

• Introduces perspectives and debates on key themes – and ideas in geography education, including subject expertise, sustainable development, learning outside the classroom and assessment.

• Provides practical guidance on the skills involved in undertaking M level work – extended reading, engaging with theory, undertaking research and writing your dissertation.

Chapters include key readings and questions to encourage further research and reflection, and every chapter is illustrated with summaries of real students' dissertations, demonstrating the kind of research undertaken at M level.

Written by experts in geography education, *Studying PGCE Geography at M Level* offers invaluable support and inspiration for all those engaged in teaching, research and writing in geography education.

Studying
PGCE
Geography
at M Level

Reflection, research and
writing for professional
development

Edited by **Clare Brooks**

Contents:

Introduction Clare Brooks Part One: Reflecting on geography teaching in practice 1. Being a professional geography teacher David Lambert 2. What makes a 'good' geography teacher? John Morgan 3. Reflecting critically on practice Sheila King Part Two: Dimensions of teaching geography 4. Making sense of the global dimension Nicole Blume, Doug Bourn, Karen Edge 5. Developing and reflecting on subject expertise Clare Brooks 6. Education for sustainable development and geography education Alun Morgan 7. Being critical when teaching with technology David Mitchell 8. Assessment, teaching and learning Paul Weeden 9. Beyond a tokenistic multiculturalism Hakhee Kim 10. Approaches to learning outside the classroom Bob Digby Part Three: Writing and researching geography education 11. Engaging with theory Denise Freeman 12. Undertaking researching and writing dissertations Clare Brooks, Adrian Conradi, Alison Leonard 13. Writing at Masters level Clare Brooks

September 2009: 234x156: 192pp
Hb: 978-0-415-49074-0: **£75.00**
Pb: 978-0-415-49075-7: **£22.99**

www.routledge.com/education